Hero

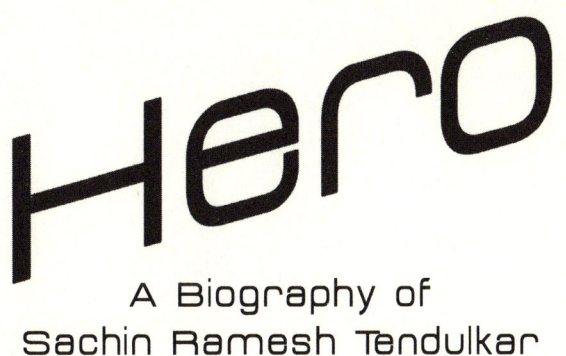

Hero
A Biography of Sachin Ramesh Tendulkar

DEVENDRA PRABHUDESAI

RUPA

Published by
Rupa Publications India Pvt. Ltd 2017
7/16, Ansari Road, Daryaganj
New Delhi 110002

Sales centres:
Allahabad Bengaluru Chennai
Hyderabad Jaipur Kathmandu
Kolkata Mumbai

Copyright © Devendra Prabhudesai 2017

First published in hardback in 2017

Photographs copyright © Prakash Parsekar, Pradeep Vijayakar Collection, markrayphotos.com, *The Sportstar* and *Afternoon Despatch and Courier*

The views and opinions expressed in this book are the author's own and the facts are as reported by him which have been verified to the extent possible, and the publishers are not in any way liable for the same.

All rights reserved.
No part of this publication may be reproduced, transmitted, or stored in a retrieval system, in any form or by any means, electronic, mechanical, photocopying, recording or otherwise, without the prior permission of the publisher.

ISBN: 978-81-291-4565-9

First impression 2017

10 9 8 7 6 5 4 3 2 1

The moral right of the author has been asserted.

Printed by Replika Press Pvt. Ltd, India

This book is sold subject to the condition that it shall not, by way of trade or otherwise, be lent, resold, hired out, or otherwise circulated, without the publisher's prior consent, in any form of binding or cover other than that in which it is published.

To Baba
and
My children, Abhimanyu and Ira

CONTENTS

Prologue   ix
Incarnations   xxiii

Section I: Prodigy (1984–91)

Early Days	3
The Nursery	12
Out of the Comfort Zone	24
Run-Machine	35
In the Big League	51
The Graduation	68
The Quintet	82
Icon	98
The Hero Cup and the Mumbai Reins	135

Section II: Peerless (1992–99)

Opening Aggressor	145
Crown Prince	163
The First Captaincy	179
Annus Mirabilis	207
'Brand'man	225
What Might Have Been	233
Tragedy	242
The Dark Age	249

Section III: Preceptor (2000–13)

A New Beginning	275
Generation Next	290
A Team Is Born	309
One Step Short	325
Out of Character	336

Speed Breakers	350
Trial by Fire	369
Resurgence	379
The Golden Age	389
International Cricketer of the Year	410
The Pinnacle	431
Jewel of India	443
Epilogue	453
Appendix 1: The Sachin Tendulkar Factfile	461
Appendix 2: Sachin Tendulkar's Longevity in Test Cricket	463
Appendix 3: Sachin Tendulkar's First-Class Centuries	465
Appendix 4: Sachin Tendulkar's Hundreds in List 'A' Matches	469
Bibliography	473
Acknowledgements	477
Index	479

PROLOGUE

November 1991....

> *I have seen a lot of video cassettes.... From that, I can make out that Australian wickets are very bouncy and fast, and the ball comes onto the bat. So, you can play your strokes, and my game is to play strokes, so I think I will do fairly well.*
>
> —Sachin Tendulkar, *Sunil Gavaskar Presents—India v Australia, Curtain-raiser*, PMG, 1991

There wasn't an iota of arrogance in the statement. In fact, the 18-and-a-half year-old Indian Test cricketer who said this during a TV interview, sounded almost apologetic.

Unlike him, some of his teammates displayed confidence that bordered on arrogance when they were interviewed for a programme on the eve of their tour of Australia.

One of them declared that he was enjoying his status as the 'premier batsman' of the side and was looking forward to what he called the 'tour of the decade'. Another player, a spinner, said that the Australian wickets would suit his brand of bowling. A member of the team management hailed the team's batting capabilities and said that the bowlers were capable of firing 'if it happened to be their day'. What he diplomatically did not state was that he had a lot more faith in the batsmen than the bowlers on a tour that was to comprise five Test matches and a 'triangular' One-Day International (ODI) series against Australia and the West Indies.

During those times, India's Test record on foreign soil was abysmal. Between 1932, the year of India's inaugural Test, and 1990, the national team had won only 12 Test matches overseas. Nevertheless, those who remembered the Indian team's performances on its last four visits 'Down Under' were hopeful of a good showing in 1991–92. The five-Test tussle in 1977–78 had gone down to the wire. Bishan Bedi's side had levelled the series after losing the first two Tests and fallen a mere 47 runs short of the target in the decider at Adelaide. Three years later, Sunil Gavaskar's team squared the series by winning the third and final Test at Melbourne after being beaten in the first Test and hanging on for a draw in the second. On India's next tour in 1985–86, Kapil Dev's outfit outplayed the hosts in every department in another three-Test battle, only to be forced to settle for a 0–0 stalemate, courtesy a combination of factors—the obduracy of Australian skipper Allan Border and his tail-enders, inclement weather and inconsistent umpiring. A season prior to that series, India under Sunil Gavaskar had triumphed on Australian soil in the 'World Championship of Cricket', a limited-overs tournament that involved all the then Test-playing teams.

The Indian team that flew to Australia in November 1991 comprised seven players who had experienced the joy of winning a Test match and series abroad. Dilip Vengsarkar, Ravi Shastri, K. Srikkanth, Mohammed Azharuddin, Kiran More and Chandrakant Pandit had been part of Kapil Dev's side that had conquered England 2–0 in 1986. Six of them had also been part of the side that had very nearly beaten Australia in 1985–86. It was this group that was expected to lead by example, six years later. Having said that, the optimism of Indian fans was laced with a bit of anxiety.

> Australia is the best place to play cricket if you get used to the conditions. The problem is that it takes you two months to get used to the conditions.
>
> —Sunil Gavaskar at the Wisden Indian Cricketer of the Century Awards Night, 2002

The 1991–92 Test series was to begin at the Woolloongabba in Brisbane, a venue known for its pace and bounce. It was to be preceded by two one-day games and just one three-day game. That gave the visitors hardly any time to acclimatize and adapt.

For Team India, the season had got off to a frenetic start. A tri-series at Sharjah against Pakistan and the West Indies was to have been followed by a bilateral ODI series at home against Pakistan. However, the Pakistan series was called off in the wake of political protests and replaced by a three-match ODI series against South Africa, the last game of which ended hours before the Indian team's departure for Australia. Two ODI series on flat wickets hardly constituted the ideal way in which to prepare for a tour on which most of the games, if not all, would be played on wickets that would have something in them for the bowlers.

Indian fans were also concerned about how the Australians themselves were viewing the upcoming engagement. A lot had changed since 1985–86, when they had been struggling to cope with the simultaneous retirements of the legendary troika of Greg Chappell, Dennis Lillee and Rodney Marsh, as well as the loss of more than a dozen top cricketers, who had undertaken a 'rebel' tour of apartheid-stricken South Africa and been slapped with a three-year ban from all 'official' cricket as a result.

From 1985 to 1987, Allan Border and Bob Simpson, the Australian captain and cricket manager, respectively, groomed a band of youngsters and steered their side through some turbulent times. The team's resurgence commenced with an unexpected triumph in the 1987 World Cup and culminated in the form of an Ashes victory in England in 1989.

Awaiting the Indians in the Australian summer of 1991–92 were pacemen Craig McDermott, Bruce Reid, Merv Hughes and Mike Whitney, and batters David Boon, Geoffrey Marsh, Dean Jones, Mark Waugh and Border himself. Ian Healy had done enough in three years of international cricket to be considered the best wicketkeeper in the world.

The Australians were expected to be assertive and aggressive. They lived up to the expectations.

February 1992....

> On that tour of Australia, I had the opportunity to bat in probably every condition and situation that a batsman can conceivably encounter in his career. By the grace of God, I was successful, and when you produce results of that kind at the age of 18 or nineteen, you start thinking differently. The assurance I gained on that trip has stayed with me till this day.
>
> —Sachin Tendulkar, *From Learners to Leaders, Platinum Jubilee Commemorative Volume*, BCCI, 2008

> I can still vividly remember the crack on the Perth wicket from where the ball was deviating dangerously off the track. The rest of the Indian batsmen struggled for survival at the centre and Sachin stood tall, not just negotiating the awkward bounce but belting the bowlers disdainfully. Under the shadow of Sachin, it looked as if the batsmen at the other end had been sent into oblivion. The common chorus that often rang in the dressing room was, 'why can't he give the strike to Sachin?'
>
> —Javagal Srinath, *India Today*, September 2010

Some Indians were upset that the scoreline was 3–0 in Australia's favour and not 2–2 by the time the fifth and final Test of the series commenced at Perth on 1 February 1992. India did come close to winning the third and fourth Tests, but then 'moral victories' hardly mattered at the highest level of the sport. What mattered was that Australia steamrolled India in the first two Tests, snatched a draw from the jaws of defeat in the third and then won the fourth by 38 runs, admittedly with critical umpiring decisions going in their favour. The hosts also beat India in the best-of-three finals of the tri-series.

Many a reputation had been dented by the time the fifth Test commenced. The batsman who had spoken about his 'looking forward to the tour of the decade' and 'enjoying his status as the team's premier batsman' before the tour, had failed to score a single 50 in the first four Tests. The much-vaunted batting line-up had flattered to deceive. It was the bowlers, the 'ugly ducklings', who had delivered with the ball and, ironically, with the bat as well.

The Indians also did not help themselves by taking some bizarre calls. After going 0–2 down in the series, they jettisoned a spinner and played four pacemen in the third Test that was to be played at Sydney, traditionally the most spin-friendly venue in Australia. On the other hand, Australia awarded a Test cap to a blonde leg-spinner who was taken to the cleaners by two Indian batsmen. Ravi Shastri batted splendidly to score 206. The teenager Sachin Tendulkar, who had 'watched videos of matches in Australia' before the tour, scored an unbeaten 148.

> Once we reached Australia, I realized that this was a different ball game altogether. I quickly got adjusted to the pace and bounce.
>
> —Sachin Tendulkar, *Thank You Sachin*, BCCI, 2013

Like his teammates, the teenager had looked out of sorts in the first Test at Brisbane. He then produced a couple of good innings in the first phase of the triangular ODI series, which was slotted between the first and second Tests. In the second innings of the second Test at Melbourne, the teenager gave a splendid account of himself in a knock of 40. It appeared that he was getting a hang of Australian conditions.

His unbeaten 148 in the third Test at Sydney made him the youngest batsman to score a Test century in Australia, but the cynics were quick to point out that for all his brilliance, the strip at the Sydney Cricket Ground resembled those of the subcontinent on which he had played all his early cricket. For all practical purposes, he had batted on familiar territory.

On the last day at Sydney, Australia commenced their second innings 170 runs behind. They were pushed onto the back foot by India's double centurion. Ravi Shastri, who had started his career as a 'left-arm spinner who could bat', bowled tirelessly to take four wickets. On the previous tour in 1985–86, he had teamed up with off-spinner Shivlal Yadav at the same venue to take India to the threshold of victory. The Australians had staved off defeat then, and their endeavour to do likewise in 1992 was boosted by the absence of a second spinner in the Indian line-up. Mohammed Azharuddin, India's captain, then tried to 'concoct' a spinner.

His batting gifts apart, the teenager had bowled his medium-pacers well enough in two seasons of international cricket to establish a reputation as a handy 'fifth bowler' in limited-overs cricket. He wasn't known to bowl spin, but one thing he could never be accused of was 'lack of effort'.

Much to the amazement of watchers, the teenager chose to bowl leg-spin, one of the toughest cricketing arts to practise, leave alone master. And he delivered! Merv Hughes, who had essayed a defiant innings in the company of Allan Border, his captain, was the recipient of a leg-break that turned sharply and flew off the outside-edge to Manoj Prabhakar at slip. Craig McDermott fell to Shastri next, but the Australians held on. At the close, they were eight wickets down and only three runs ahead.

India were unlucky to lose Shastri to a knee injury before the fourth Test at Adelaide. Australia were dismissed for 145 on the first day, but their bowlers retaliated strongly. India were an embarrassing 70–6 in response when Kapil Dev and Manoj Prabhakar came together to engineer a revival. India did take a first-innings lead of 80, but it was knocked down by the Australian top order. Mark Taylor and David Boon made the most of reprieves by the umpires and scored centuries. In the final innings, India needed 372 to win with a day-and-a-half left. With nothing to lose and everything to gain, the visitors decided to go for it.

The openers put on 52. Sanjay Manjrekar looked good in an innings of 45, before getting run out for the umpteenth time on the tour, this time in a mix-up with his captain. Azharuddin himself ended a string of failures with a spectacular century, but the innings nosedived as soon as he fell, and India lost by 38 runs. Prabhakar, who scored a fine 64, fell to a questionable leg-before decision, as did senior statesman Dilip Vengsarkar.

A significant feature of India's second innings was the reshuffling of their batting order. Vengsarkar had batted at number four in the first three Tests and in the first innings at Adelaide. In the second essay, he was pushed down to number five, and his slot was taken up by the centurion at Sydney. In his first outing as India's 'number four', the teenager fell for only 17.

It was an inglorious beginning to one of cricket's most glorious chapters.

The series already in the bag, Australia went for a fourth win in the last Test of the series, which was to be played on one of the fastest tracks in the world, at the WACA, Perth. Shane Warne, the blonde leg-spinner who had played at Sydney and Adelaide, was left out in favour of Paul Reiffel, a fourth paceman. India lost the toss and conceded a first-innings score of 346. The visitors were 69–2 in response when India's new number four arrived at the crease on the afternoon of 2 February 1992.

The teenager got going with a boundary off Reiffel. The ball took the outside edge of his defensive blade and neatly bisected the second and third slips. From the non-striker's end, he saw Dean Jones, one of his childhood heroes, take a screamer of a catch in the slips to dismiss Manjrekar. Merv Hughes got his third wicket in the innings when he induced Vengsarkar to nick him to the keeper. India were rapidly running out of wickets.

When Hughes dropped one short outside the off-stump, the teenager stood on his toes and smashed it through the covers for four. When he crossed over to the other end, he subjected Craig McDermott to a similar treatment, this time off the back foot. The spectators, most of them Australians, broke into applause when one of the teenager's drives passed Mike Whitney on the latter's follow-through and thudded into the boundary hoardings. This was an era wherein the stakeholders of the sport didn't deem it necessary to shorten the boundaries to ensure that more boundaries were scored. On most of the Australian grounds, there were no boundary lines, only fences.

Like many of his teammates, all of whom were senior to him not only in terms of age but also cricketing experience, the teenager was making an initial 'forward' movement just before the bowler released the ball. But unlike them, he seemed to have the time to fall back onto the back foot if required and play the ball on merit, even on that Perth track.

Azharuddin paid the price for nibbling at a McDermott delivery without moving his feet. Venkatapathy Raju came in as night watchman, and he helped the teenager take India through to the close on the second day. The night-watchman fell the next morning, and he was followed by Kapil Dev, who hooked Whitney down long-leg's throat. Manoj Prabhakar, who came in next, began his innings as if his individual score was 60 and not zero, and was duly snapped up in the slips.

What Kiran More, India's wicketkeeper, lacked in terms of batting technique, he more than made up for with grit. He hung on to give his young colleague the support he deserved.

When the teenager was on strike, it seemed as if he was batting not at Perth, but on the maidans of Mumbai* that he had dominated like a colossus in the latter half of the 1980s.

Sachin was occasionally beaten by deliveries that whizzed past the outside edge, but he was good enough to delete them from his memory bank and focus on the next ball. For him, it was the 'one-rupee coin' challenge, all over again. At the Shivaji Park nets just a few years previously, his coach Ramakant Achrekar would make him do five consecutive batting stints in the nets, the last of which would be the toughest. After batting in four different nets, the boy would be pitted against the best bowlers in the fifth. At stake would be a one-rupee coin, which the coach would place on the top of the middle stump. The bowler who would get the batsman out would bag the coin. Conversely, the batsman would get to keep the coin if he defied the bowlers and his own fatigue to remain unbeaten. The teenager had made it a habit to win those one-rupee coins; he had, in fact, preserved all of them, and he valued them more than any of the awards that he had won.

At the WACA in February 1992, there were no coins on offer; at stake was the reputation of his country, the team and his own self. He essayed a combination of drives, cuts and flicks and used the pace of the ball as well as the length and breadth of the crease quite brilliantly. When the bowlers, fed up with being spanked on the off-side, bowled a straighter line, the teenager was quite happy to target the leg-side. A delivery by Reiffel that was a fraction wide of off-stump and short was cut handsomely for four. A straight drive off McDermott gave the teenager four runs and a stunner of a century, his second of the series.

It was an innings that merited a Richie Benaud punchline, and the sage obliged: 'Wonderful to watch, and a splendid ovation. It's the sort of innings that deserved a crowd of a hundred thousand.'

In later years, Benaud would argue that while the Perth hundred was great, the one at Sydney earlier in the series, was better. For once, he was in a minority. Sunil Gavaskar, who was Benaud's colleague in the Channel 9 TV commentary team, disagreed, as did many others. John Woodcock, who had covered cricket across the globe since the early 1950s, wondered aloud in the press box whether it was the next Bradman they had just seen. Another individual who could not get over the knock was the teenager's roommate at that stage of the tour.

---

*Bombay was officially renamed Mumbai in 1995, Baroda was renamed Vadodara in 1974, Madras was renamed Chennai in 1996, Calcutta was renamed Kolkata in 2001 and Bangalore was renamed Bengaluru in 2014. To prevent confusion and ensure uniformity in the narrative, the new names of these cities have been used throughout the book.

Sourav Ganguly had been part of the squad for the Test series, but had been left out for the World Cup that was to start in a couple of weeks. His roomie had borrowed one of his bats for the Perth Test and used it to score a hundred against a four-pronged pace attack on a fiery strip.

It is easier for batsmen to adjust from high bounce to low bounce. To adjust from low to high is difficult. It was incredible that an 18-year-old (from the subcontinent) did it. I have seen Australian batsmen struggle at Perth in the Sheffield Shield. It usually took them a few innings to adjust to that wicket. But he scored a century, that too in a Test match.

—Ian Chappell, www.cricinfo.com, and *Sachin Sachin*, Star Sports, 2013

The teenager had moved to 114 when he did not commit himself fully onto the front foot to a Whitney delivery that pitched on a length. The ball took the outside edge and was snapped up by Tom Moody at second slip. The batsman's first mistake had cost him and his team dearly. The Indian innings ended soon after.

In Australia's second innings, the Indian players converged on Kapil Dev when he dismissed Mark Taylor leg-before to become only the second bowler in Test history to take 400 Test wickets. That was India's last moment of joy in the game and series. The visitors went on to lose by 300 runs, and with it, the series 0–4. Indian cricket lovers of the time were back to doing what they had been doing for decades—console themselves by basking in the glory of individual achievements. Kapil Dev had had a fabulous tour with 25 wickets from the five Tests. At the end of the series, he was 30 scalps short of Sir Richard Hadlee's record tally of 431 scalps. However, he was overshadowed by the teenager.

If he could play like this at 19, I shudder to think what he will be like, at 25.

—Allan Border, *The Sportstar*, 15 February 1992

Border himself was on the verge of surpassing Sunil Gavaskar's record for the highest number of runs in Tests. He eventually passed the mark a year later in the knowledge that his records would be broken by another 'little master' from India.

This little prick is going to get more runs than you, AB.

—Merv Hughes to Allan Border, as quoted on www.smh.com.au; 9 December 2007

By the end of the Australian tour and [subsequent] World Cup, I felt I was ready to play any team, on any kind of surface.

—Sachin Tendulkar, *Thank You Sachin*, BCCI, 2013

Three months after the Perth Test, Australian great Greg Chappell visited the MRF Pace Foundation in Chennai at the behest of Dennis Lillee, head coach of the academy and his former teammate. Among the objectives of the former Australian captain's visit was to provide a batsman's perspective on fast bowling and fast bowlers to the trainees. During his visit, Chappell had an extensive interaction with N. Ram, then editor of *The Sportstar*, India's premier sports magazine, on the sport and its exponents. When asked about the teenager, he was effusive in his praise of the teenager's technical and mental faculties.

One remark by him made N. Ram and his team sit up: 'If things were handled well and it went well, you will have Bradman [pointing to an unreachable level] and then you will have Tendulkar.'

> I am glad we resisted the temptation to publish all this in *The Sportstar* in 1992; our concern was that it might appear exaggerated and even go to the young man's head.

—N. Ram, *The Sportstar*, 20 May 1995

N. Ram and his colleagues were understandably wary. Over the years and decades, the country had witnessed the rise and fall of many a youngster who had possessed tons of talent, but not the temperament to sustain and handle success achieved at the highest level. However, this wariness was forgotten by the time the 1990s came to an end.

In April 1992, the age of Tendulkar was nigh.

> Greg Chappell in his interview with Ram had said: 'There is Bradman and then there will be Tendulkar.' That will happen only if Tendulkar can amalgamate his inherent genius and instinct with logic. And what a feast it will be when he gets it perfectly!

—Sunil Gavaskar, *The Sportstar*, 1 July 1995

November 1993....

> India...has to look to new sources of cricket revenue to keep the game alive.... India has never had a better opportunity than the present time to do so. Television is now more readily available to the masses, and by India's winning sequence in two successive World Series, there can be no question of the viability of the limited-overs product there.... My own experience

in India leaves me in no doubt that the Indian crowds will support the limited-overs format to the hilt. As it develops so, undoubtedly will night cricket develop with it. A few added attractions like...the Classic Catches competition so popular in Australia, will wrap up the packaging of the product... The Indian establishment should...ensure that in the packaging and marketing of an undeniably viable product, they hire, and if necessary, fire the best available expertise.... If they heed the lessons of experience, they will be laughing all the way to the bank, and what's more important, the future of Indian cricket will be assured.

—Tony Greig, 'The Packaging and Marketing of Limited-Overs Cricket', *Wills Tribute to Excellence: Champions of One-Day Cricket*

India proved Greig right within a decade of his penning these words.

After co-hosting the fourth edition of the Cricket World Cup in 1987, BCCI executed a six-nation limited-overs tournament titled the Nehru Cup, which commemorated the birth centenary of Jawaharlal Nehru, the country's first prime minister, in 1989.

The 1990s was a watershed decade. The Congress government, which emerged as the single-largest party in the general election of 1991, went in for 'liberalization', and the Indian economy was 'opened up'. The changes that came about—tangible and intangible, financial and psychological—were rapid and overwhelming. An early offshoot of liberalization was the advent of satellite TV. The monopoly enjoyed by Doordarshan (DD), the State-owned broadcaster, ended for good and the TV antennae that were an integral part of the skyline in urban and semi-urban India in the 1980s gradually gave way to 'dishes'.

India was no stranger to cricketing extravaganzas after 1987 and 1989, but the five-nation tournament that was organized in November 1993 to commemorate the diamond jubilee of the Cricket Association of Bengal (CAB) was different from its predecessors. It was a veritable microcosm of all the changes that had occurred in the country since 1991. For starters, the tournament was telecast 'live' on a channel other than DD. The tournament, played for the Hero Cup, was the first international cricket event in India to feature coloured clothing, white balls, black sightscreens and, of course, 'night' cricket. Floodlights were installed at the Eden Gardens, the CAB's home venue, which was slated to host the semi-finals and final.

The capacity crowd for the semi-final between India and South Africa was ecstatic when Mohammed Azharuddin won the toss and opted to bat. However, it soon fell silent. Ajay Jadeja was trapped leg-before, and both Vinod Kambli and Manoj Prabhakar committed suicide by taking on Daryll Cullinan's throwing arm. For the first time on Indian soil, the 'TV' umpire was called upon for assistance, twice in the same over, by umpire Steve Bucknor.

India's 20-year-old vice-captain came in three down and essayed a delightful cameo before he nicked Richard Snell to Dave Richardson, the keeper. The dismissal left India dangling on the precipice at 56–4, but then, the 'King of Kolkata' was still in there.

Mohammed Azharuddin essayed a captain's hand of 90 at his favourite venue, and he was well supported by Pravin Amre. The innings plummeted after the pair was separated and India were bowled out for 195, by no means an intimidating score.

India needed early wickets. It was only a handful of matches since the team management had entrusted new-ball duties to Javagal Srinath, thereby doing what it ought to have done at least a year previously. The Karnataka speedster ran in hard and bowled quick. He came close to dismissing Andrew Hudson, the South African opener, twice before winning a leg-before shout against Kepler Wessels, the other opener and South Africa's captain. A battle of attrition ensued. Hudson was solid, but his partners were not allowed to settle down. The Indian bowling and fielding was outstanding, and South Africa reached triple figures only in the 31st over. Ajay Jadeja, brought on for his brand of military seam-and-swing, complemented Anil Kumble's leg-spin with a tight spell.

In the next nine overs, the Indians tightened the screws, conceding only 30 runs and dismissing the dangerous Jonty Rhodes. The stadium erupted when Kumble uprooted Hudson's off-stump off the final delivery of the fortieth over. The score at that stage was 130–5, and the visitors now needed 66 from the last ten overs. When Pat Symcox and Richard Snell fell within four runs of each other a little later, all of India was convinced that it was all over. But of course, it was not. The return of Prabhakar and Srinath to the attack triggered a counterattack by the eighth-wicket pair of Dave Richardson, the keeper-batsman, and Brian McMillan, the all-rounder, both of whom discovered that the ball was coming onto the bat quite consistently and predictably. When Srinath went for 14 in the 46th over, one could have heard a pin drop inside the Eden. The South Africans had regained control.

With 7 needed from 10 balls, McMillan tapped Prabhakar on the leg-side and called Richardson for a single, only to freeze when he saw Ajay Jadeja swooping on the ball at short mid-wicket. Richardson, who by then was almost halfway down the wicket, was stranded as Jadeja ran to the bowler's end to dislodge the bails. It was a daft conclusion to what had been a fine partnership.

After one dot ball, McMillan took a single to long-on. The final delivery of the penultimate over was a yorker that missed Fanie De Villiers' stumps by very little. The equation was now down to six from the final six balls. Most critically from South Africa's point of view, they still had two wickets in hand and McMillan was on strike.

All eyes turned to Azharuddin. Ajit Wadekar, former India captain and now cricket manager of the side, sent out a message, advising his captain to fall back on experience. Kapil Dev had bowled eight economical overs for 31 runs and dismissed Cullinan. Srinath had one over left, but he had gone for far too many. Salil Ankola, the fourth paceman in the playing XI, had bowled well in the middle overs and had a couple of overs left in his kitty, but there was always the possibility of his being dealt with as harshly as Prabhakar and Srinath. It just had to be Kapil Dev.

Even as Kapil Dev walked towards Azharuddin, TV viewers saw him rolling up his right sleeve, as if to show his captain something. Did he have an injury? A discussion ensued between four players—the skipper, his deputy, Kapil Dev and Ajay Jadeja, who appeared to be doing most of the talking. The viewers then saw Kapil Dev walking away and Azhar handing over the ball to the juniormost member of the team—in terms of age, that is.

'It's going to be Sachin Tendulkar!' commentator Henry Blofeld all but yelled into the microphone. The Indian vice-captain hadn't bowled earlier in the match. 'This really is a decision on which Azharuddin's captaincy will be either hailed as being nothing short of genius or will be criticized mercilessly,' Sunil Gavaskar, seated next to Blofeld in the commentary box, remarked.

The initial reaction of the spectators and TV viewers was one of shock. But they then noticed the 20-year-old's body language as he marked out his run up, got the circulation in his bowling arm going, looked around the field and set out to do the job; there was something about his demeanour that was reassuring. The resolute expression on his face calmed an entire nation down. Even if India were to lose from that point, it would not be for want of trying.

The vice-captain aimed to take the pace off the ball. His first delivery was short of a length, and McMillan rocked back and cut it past cover. Even as Salil Ankola, fielding at sweeper, gathered the ball and hurled it flat and straight at Vijay Yadav, the Indian keeper, De Villiers, for reasons best known to himself, took off for a non-existent second run. McMillan did not reciprocate and both batsmen found themselves at the non-striker's end, giving Yadav all the time in the world to dislodge the bails. On the field, the Indian players started celebrating another 'gift' from the opposition and, in the stands, the spectators rediscovered their voice.

Allan Donald, South Africa's number 11, came in with a single-point agenda—to get McMillan back on strike. The vice-captain's second ball came onto Donald much slower than the batsman expected, made contact with his bat and fell dead in front. Five needed off four.

The pressure was back on the visitors and the spectators were getting noisier. Conversely, there was a pressure of a different sort on the home team. How would the crowd react if their side lost after the roller-coaster ride that they had had for the entire evening?

However, the person who mattered most—the bowler—wasn't thinking of victory or defeat. All he was thinking about was the next ball. It was pitched outside the off-stump, Donald played and missed, and Steve Bucknor, an umpire with whom the bowler and his teammates would enjoy a rather bumpy relationship in later years, decided against calling it a wide. Five needed from three.

A desperate Donald swung at the next ball, only to miss again. The bowler remained as impassive as ever, and the spectators cheered. With five needed from two, Donald just had to get off strike. He took a forward step and finally made contact. The ball landed in front of Anil Kumble at long-on. McMillan was finally on strike and South Africa needed four from one.

An animated discussion ensued between the bowler and keeper. Vijay Yadav, who had been standing up for the first five balls, moved back, the intent obviously being to prevent byes or an inside-edge racing to the boundary. The field was quickly examined, and the bowler set off, even as the spectators, millions of TV viewers and a mongoose that had strayed onto the playing arena, watched with bated breath.

The vice-captain's final delivery pitched on a length and hurried through. McMillan, whose concentration had been affected by the bizarre happenings in the last two overs, went for an almighty heave, but he only got an inside edge. Yadav, standing well back, collected the ball and raised his arms in triumph, allowing the batsmen to complete a meaningless single. Had he been standing up, the ball could well have gone through his legs for four!

The entire team made a beeline for the bowler. In the stands, thousands of newspapers were set ablaze, almost on cue. India, who had been in a hopeless situation just four minutes previously, had won the game by two runs. Four days later, they would win the competition, beating the West Indies in the final.

The last over of the Hero Cup semi-final would go on to become a rare 'happy' member of a club that is almost an exclusive preserve of natural disasters, terrorist attacks, riots and assassinations. Years later, thousands of Indians across the planet would vividly remember where they were and what they were doing, when that over was bowled.

I told Azhar that I was more than happy to bowl.

—Sachin Tendulkar, *Thank You Sachin*, BCCI, 2013

It was 24 November 1993, a year-and-a-half since that hundred at Perth. There, the 18-year-old had excelled with the bat. At Kolkata, the 20-year-old had volunteered to do the job for his team, this time with the ball, in another pressure situation, in another format of the game. And once again, he had delivered.

The Age of Tendulkar was upon us.

INCARNATIONS

To term cricket as a mere sport in the Indian context would be nothing short of a travesty. There is enough evidence at hand to prove that cricket, 'an Indian game accidentally invented by the British', as defined by sociologist Ashis Nandy, played a key role in the social and political transformation of a British colony into the largest parliamentary democracy in the world.

From Baloo Palwankar to Ravichandran Ashwin, India has produced some exceptional bowlers over the years and decades. They have won innumerable matches and series for the country. However, they have always—and a tad unfairly at times—been overshadowed by their batting counterparts.

The Indian obsession with batting has its genesis in events of the past. The history of India, especially that of the last thousand years or so, is nothing but a series of disasters and debacles, interspersed with phases of glory wherein one or two individuals challenged the prevalent order, held their own against adversity and inspired others to do likewise. In India's early days as a Test-playing nation, the spectacle of one or two batsmen delaying the inevitable by defying an opposing team of 11 that was on the rampage, probably reminded the Indians of their heroes from centuries gone by. The love for batsmen and batting continued even after the Indian team became a force to reckon with and started dictating terms to other sides. Test cricket's batting maestros gradually gave way to 'superstars' who called the shots, literally and figuratively, in the shorter versions of the sport. There have been times, especially in the recent past, when it has seemed that the shorter versions of cricket have been invented only to degrade the bowlers.

Any discussion on great Indian batsmen across eras generally begins with the Mumbai triumvirate of Vijay Merchant, Sunil Gavaskar and Sachin Tendulkar. Cricket, they say, is a religion in India. In this context, one can draw parallels between this trinity and one of the premier deities of Hinduism, the religion practised by more than 80 per cent of India's population.

Lord Vishnu, the 'preserver' of the universe, was said to have assumed 'dashavatars' (10 incarnations) in different ages or 'yugs' to annihilate the forces of darkness and resurrect virtue. Each of the dashavatars was an evolutionary stage ahead of its immediate predecessor. On the other hand, each of the four yugs—Satya, Treta, Dwapar and Kali—devolved from the preceding one in terms of virtue, lifespan, physical strength and wisdom. The righteousness of the Satya Yug gave way to the seven sins—Pride, Envy, Wrath, Gluttony, Lust, Sloth and Greed—all of which reign supreme in the ongoing Kali Yug.

The first four of Lord Vishnu's dashavatars appeared in the Satya Yug, the next three in the Treta Yug, the eighth in the Dwapar Yug and the ninth in the Kali Yug. The 10th and last incarnation, it is believed, will emerge at the end of the Kali Yug and usher in a new Satya Yug.

Lord Vishnu's first Satya Yug avatar was that of a Matsya (fish), who enlisted the help of Satyavrata, his devotee, to ensure the safe passage of not only mankind, flora and fauna, but also knowledge, from one yug to the next. The Matsya Avatar shared the sacred hymns and verses with the individuals, organisms and elements who were on board the boat that he guided through the stormy waters of the Prahlaya, or the Great Deluge, that had inundated the planet to mark the end of the Yug. His next avatar, the Kurma (tortoise), helped the virtuous devas acquire the nectar of immortality from the bottom of the ocean. The devas drank the nectar and avenged their military defeat against their cousins and sworn enemies, the vicious asurs.

The objective of his third avatar—that of the Varaha (boar)—was to slay a demon named Hiranyaksha, who had pushed the earth to the bottom of the cosmic ocean. Varaha slew the demon and restored the earth to its rightful place in the cosmos.

Lord Vishnu's next adversary was Hiranyakashipu, Hiranyaksha's brother, who had been bestowed with a boon that made him immune to death at the hands of man or beast, indoors or outdoors, during the day or night, on the earth or in the sky, and by objects animate or inanimate. To neutralize him, Lord Vishnu took on the form of Narsimha, who had a man's body and a lion's head. He was, therefore, neither a man, nor a beast. He emerged from a pillar and dragged Hiranyakashipu to the threshold of the latter's palace (neither indoors nor outdoors). It was the hour of twilight (neither day nor night). At the threshold, Narsimha placed Hiranyakashipu on his lap (neither on the earth nor in the sky) and tore him apart with his nails (used as a weapon that is neither animate nor inanimate).

The first four of Lord Vishnu's 10 incarnations thus evolved from aquatic (Matsya) to amphibian (Kurma) to animal (Varaha) to part-human (Narsimha).

Vijay Merchant could be considered the cricketing personification of the four Satya Yug avatars. In India's early years as a Test-playing nation, he was the link between the two ends of the spectrum—the princes, who had the money to run the game, and the commoners, who possessed the skills to play it. Merchant wasn't a prince by birth, but he was the scion of an affluent industrial family who had built his reputation as a cricketer by dint of performance. As a batsman, he possessed all the strokes, but he eschewed aggression and aerial strokes in favour of caution and 'carpet' shots, in a bid to lend solidity and stability to the national cricket team, which was then at the fledgling stage.

Merchant displayed impeccable defence, balance and courage in the face of adversity, on and off the field. Picked in the Indian team that toured England in 1932 to play its inaugural Test, he withdrew from the side to protest the British rule in India. He toured England four years later and made waves on and off the field. He took up the cause of the 'commoner' Lala Amarnath, who was being sent home on disciplinary grounds, and pleaded with the team management to revoke its decision, albeit unsuccessfully. He was bold enough to 'advise' the king of Vizianagaram, the captain of the team and a mediocre cricketer, to hand over charge to Col. C.K. Nayudu, the team's premier player and former captain, for the three Tests at least. A livid 'Vizzy' tried a bizarre stunt to get even. When Merchant and Syed Mushtaq Ali were putting together a record opening stand in the second Test at Manchester, Vizzy offered a gold watch to Ali on the condition that he run Merchant out. Ali refused, and in fact spilt the beans to Merchant. The openers proceeded to put on a record 203 for the first wicket.

Merchant's success in England in 1936 prompted C.B. Fry, veteran of many an Ashes battle, to suggest that England 'paint him white and take him to Australia for the Ashes series of 1936–37'.

World War II robbed several cricketers across the world of their best years. However, Merchant and his Indian contemporaries were fortunate as domestic cricket was not suspended in the country. After the War, Merchant returned to England in 1946, as vice-captain of an Indian team led by the Nawab of Pataudi (senior), and was almost as successful as in 1936. One of the bowlers who struggled against Merchant in that series was Alec Bedser, who held the world record for the highest number of Test wickets in the subsequent decade. At a function in Mumbai in the early 2000s, Raj Singh Dungarpur, an institution who served Indian cricket with distinction in several capacities, informed the gathering that Bedser had once told him that Merchant was the best batsman he had bowled to, bar Bradman. This was an extraordinary tribute.

From a political and cricketing perspective, the joy of independence in 1947 was offset by the trauma of Partition. India lost several outstanding cricketers, who opted to live on the Pakistani side of the Radcliffe Line. In those turbulent times, Merchant's presence in Indian cricket was comforting. He was appointed captain for independent India's first cricket series against Don Bradman's Australians, but was forced to withdraw from the tour due to injury. He did well against the touring 'Commonwealth' sides at the turn of the decade and retired from international cricket after an innings of 154 in the first Test against England in 1951–52. The man who started his career alongside stalwarts like Col. C.K. Nayudu, Mohammed Nissar and Amar Singh, ended it by spending time in the middle with the likes of Polly Umrigar and Pankaj Roy, both of whom excelled for India in the 1950s. He was thus the bridge between two generations of Indian cricketers.

In later years, Merchant had a memorable 'second innings' as industrialist, cricket analyst, commentator, selector and, most notably, philanthropist. Successive generations of Indian cricketers and, indeed, individuals in need of a helping hand from society cannot thank him enough.

His most critical contribution to Indian cricket in his 'second innings' was as chairman of selectors. The Nawab of Pataudi (junior) had led India through the 1960s with mixed results. India registered some notable wins, but also suffered heavy defeats. Merchant's first full season as chairman was the one of 1969–70, wherein India hosted Australia and New Zealand. The Australians won a five-Test series 3–1, and the three-Test tussle against New Zealand was tied at 1–1.

On the eve of India's tour of the West Indies a year later, there was speculation that Pataudi would be replaced as captain, but it wasn't the first time such stories had been circulated. The general impression was that despite the reverses of the previous season, Pataudi had the backing of not only the Board, but also the selectors, and would, therefore, retain the captaincy. However, Merchant had other ideas. Two of the four selectors who attended the meeting voted for Pataudi and two others, Merchant included, for Ajit Wadekar, who had led Mumbai to the Ranji Trophy title thrice in succession. The chairman then broke the 2–2 deadlock by exercising his prerogative of a casting vote, in favour of Wadekar.

Under Wadekar, India created history by winning the series in the West Indies and England back-to-back. His detractors branded the new captain as 'lucky' and accused him of reaping the fruits of all the hard work done by Pataudi in moulding the team in the 1960s, but the fact was luck alone could not have ensured two consecutive series wins against formidable sides on their turf, that too without the presence of a single specialist fast bowler in the playing XI. In fact, Wadekar's achievement as captain has no parallels in cricketing history.

As batsman and selector, Merchant laid the foundation for subsequent generations of India's batsmen to assert themselves.

Vaman (dwarf), Lord Vishnu's first Treta Yug incarnation, tackled Bali, the king of the asurs, whose successes against the devas had made him conceited. He was offering alms to the needy after a religious ceremony when Vaman appeared before him. The dwarf asked for a plot of land that he could span with three strides of his. Bali, visibly amused, offered him riches of all kinds, but Vaman reiterated his original request. When Bali finally acceded, the dwarf grew into a giant, large enough for one stride of his to cover the earth, and the second, the heavens. Since there was nothing left for him to cover with the third stride, he accused Bali of failing to keep his promise. The asur king then offered Vaman his head. Having brought Bali down to earth, literally and figuratively, Lord Vishnu bestowed immortality on him and conferred on him the ownership of the netherworld. The devas were thus restored to their kingdom in the heavens.

The next Treta Yug avatar was that of Parashuram, the Brahmin-warrior. He slew Kartavirya Arjun, the evil leader of the Kshatriyas, the warrior class, in battle. Kartavirya Arjun's sons retaliated by killing Jamadagni, his father. Parashuram avenged his father's death by eliminating the Kshatriya class 21 times over. Later, he became the guru of warriors such as Bheeshma, Drona and Karna, who were among those who shaped the great epic, the Mahabharata.

Ram, Lord Vishnu's seventh incarnation, was Maryada Purshottam—the 'Supreme Man'. He was born to eliminate Ravan, the 10-headed king of the demons. Ravan was an alter ego of Ram, being an accomplished warrior, ruler and scholar. But unlike Ram, he was arrogant and lustful. He abducted Sita, Ram's wife, and took her to his kingdom on the island of Lanka. Helped by an army of monkeys, led by their king Sugreev and talisman Hanuman, Ram tracked Ravan down, declared war and eventually killed his opponent.

Like Vaman, Sunil Gavaskar was a not-very-tall man but rose to conquer the cricketing universe. Like Parshuram, he took on the 'establishment', which was then represented by the likes of Australia and England. As an opening batsman, he confronted the fastest and fiercest bowlers the game had ever seen and emerged victorious. As a match-winner and record-breaker, he helped Indian cricket shed its inferiority complex and instilled self-belief in his team and Indian cricket lovers. He began his international career with a record 774 runs in the Test series that India won under Wadekar's captaincy in the Caribbean, and did not look back.

The landmarks Gavaskar achieved and the standards he set were Indian cricket's equivalent of Ram slaying the 10-headed genius Ravan. As a batsman, he was the epitome of technical perfection, born to excel in the game's traditional format. Just as the virtuous Ram found it difficult to defy convention, Gavaskar too took his time to come to terms with the 'shorter' variety of the game.

Apart from raising the bar with his extraordinary deeds, Sunil Gavaskar ensured that a generation of Indian cricketers who sought inspiration from him could just go out and express themselves. They did not have the additional burden of proving that Indian cricketers were as good, if not better, than anybody else; 'SMG' had done the job for them.

Vishnu's next, and only Dwapar Yug incarnation, was his most glorious.

Krishna was as much an epitome of virtue as Ram, but he was more worldly-wise. His was a lifelong mission to rid the world of villainy, vice and vanity.

The boy-wonder who slew a plethora of demons and eventually fulfilled the divine prophecy by killing Kansa, their ringleader and his maternal uncle, grew up to become the perfect friend, ally and diplomat. He was also an accomplished warrior and military strategist, a saviour of the righteous and the nemesis of evil-doers.

However, Krishna never boasted about his achievements and capabilities. Instead, he let his actions speak for themselves.

Throughout his existence, Krishna delighted, inspired, transformed and then moved on to his next mission and destination. It was his way of teaching his followers to stimulate the 'Krishna' that existed in their own selves and to enrich their own lives as well those of the people around them on their own, instead of relying on others, most commonly God, to bail them out.

Of course, he wasn't always successful. Even those close to him were not quite consistent in terms of taking the initiative to set things right. In the process, they allowed themselves and even their near and dear ones to be trampled upon by villains. Krishna, exasperated and infuriated, then had to step in. It was he who prevented the disrobing of Draupadi, the queen of the five Pandavas, by their cousins, the hundred Kauravas, after her own husbands had squandered away their kingdom, themselves and her in a game of dice. When a conflict between the cousins seemed inevitable, Krishna himself attempted to broker peace, but failed when the Kauravas refused to grant the Pandavas even five villages.

Even as kings from all over the land flocked with their respective armies to the battlefield of Kurukshetra to join either camp for the decisive confrontation, Krishna, who was related to both the camps, refused to take up arms. When Arjun, the third Pandava and his closest friend and brother-in-law, and Duryodhan, the eldest Kaurava and the father-in-law of his niece, approached him for help, Krishna offered them a choice between a 'non-violent' him and his army. Arjun chose Krishna while the vain Duryodhana was happy to avail the services of the redoubtable Yadava army that Krishna had raised and nurtured.

The start of the greatest of all battles was moments away when Arjun, archer extraordinaire and the supreme commander of the Pandava army, requested Krishna, his 'charioteer', to take him close to the Kaurava ranks. When Arjun saw Bheeshma, the grand-old patriarch of the family, Drona, his beloved guru, Kripa, another teacher of his, the Kauravas themselves, and several other near and dear ones in the opposition, his heart sank. He wondered aloud as to whether it made any sense to fight against individuals so close to his heart.

It was then that Krishna 'froze time'. Everything around him and Arjun became stationary, as the charioteer proceeded to propound the Bhagawad Gita to his close friend. Krishna entreated Arjun to fulfill his duties as a warrior and help re-establish Dharma (righteousness). He dwelt on the concepts of Dnyana (knowledge), Bhakti (devotion), Karma (deeds) and Moksha (salvation). The Gita is a document and way of life that has stood the test of time over centuries.

With Arjun's queries answered and apprehensions allayed, Krishna 'unlocked' time and the war began. Eighteen long days later, the Pandavas emerged victorious. Krishna's brain complemented their brawn and proficiency in warfare. For all their virtues and talents, the Pandavas might not have defeated their unscrupulous cousins had Krishna not been on their side. At the end of the war, Krishna was rebuked by Gandhari, the queen of Hastinapur who had lost all her hundred sons in the war, for not preventing the war despite being capable enough of doing so. She then cursed him that he would witness the destruction of his own clan, 36 years later. Krishna accepted her curse magnanimously. Starting from his childhood, Krishna was at his best in crises. The fundamental lesson he imparted was that when it came to the crunch, age did not matter as much as initiative and enterprise did. He inspired others to become 'leaders' themselves.

Sachin Ramesh Tendulkar led Indian cricket 'formally' for only 2 of the 24 years of his international career, and 'informally' for the other 22. He knew which side of the thin line that separated assurance from arrogance he had to stay on. He was aware that once a player donned his cricketing gear and crossed the boundary line, age did not matter, aptitude did. The bigger the challenge, the better was his response. He believed in discharging the duties that were assigned to him to the best of his abilities. Whenever criticized, he let his actions on the cricketing field do the talking and explaining. He never ever displayed feet of clay and was elevated to divinity in a land known to venerate its gods and goddesses. There were, of course, occasions when his followers were reminded of the fact that for all his gifts, their beloved Sachin was only human. While he did sometimes falter 'against the run of play' on the field, he steered clear of controversies and scandals off it. In the process, he united a nation. Sunil

Gavaskar and Kapil Dev had taken the lead in showing the world that Indian *cricketers* were capable of being world-beaters at the sport. Sachin was responsible for culminating what his predecessors had commenced. He made a *cricket team* and its followers believe that nothing was impossible.

Section I

Prodigy (1984-91)

EARLY DAYS

Sachin Tendulkar was born to Ramesh and Rajani Tendulkar at 1:00 p.m. on Tuesday, 24 April 1973, at the Nirmal Nursing Home on Ranade Road in Dadar, the cultural, educational, social, political and sporting hub of the bustling metropolis that is Mumbai. These diverse forces vied with each other for attention and space on an expanse of land called Shivaji Park, which lay a couple of lanes away from the Nirmal Nursing Home.

The infant weighed a healthy 2.850 kilos at birth.

Ramesh Tendulkar was a professor of Marathi (Language and Literature) at Dadar's Kirti College, a 15-minute walk from the Nirmal Nursing Home. A self-effacing individual who was committed to his students and profession, he was also a poet who expressed himself in simple and lucid language.

Rajani Tendulkar worked in the Foreign Department of the Life Insurance Corporation of India branch at Santacruz, a north-western suburb of Mumbai that was a 30-minute bus ride from Dadar. Sachin's elder siblings—brothers Nitin and Ajit and sister Savita—studied at the Balmohan Vidyamandir School, situated right next to Shivaji Park.

Dr Shraddhanand Thakur, who headed the Nirmal Nursing Home, ruled out a normal delivery and advised a C-section. While the procedure was on, Prof. Tendulkar waited at Dr Thakur's residence on the floor above the nursing room. Giving him company was his friend and Dr Thakur's brother-in-law. P.L. Deshpande, actor, singer, composer, musician, critic and connoisseur of classical music, playwright, writer and orator extraordinaire, was to Maharashtra what Gurudev Rabindranath Tagore was to Bengal. Considering what the infant went on to achieve in his chosen profession, it was significant that Deshpande was one of the first individuals to see and bless him.

P.L. Deshpande was one of many 'geniuses' the Tendulkars were used to rubbing shoulders with. Two years prior to Sachin's birth, Prof. Tendulkar and his family had shifted from a joint family set-up in the Tulsidas Tejpal Chawl on Padmabai Thakker Road, a five-minute walk from Shivaji Park, to a two-bedroom flat in the suburb of Bandra, which was six kilometres away. Their new home was one of 84 flats in a cluster of nine buildings, which together constituted a complex called Sahitya Sahawas (literally translated as 'literary coexistence').

This cooperative housing society housed luminaries from the field of arts and literature. Each of the nine buildings was named for a Marathi novel or poem. Among the neighbours of the Tendulkars were Gangadhar Gadgil, Y.D. Phadke, V.P. Kale and Vinda Karandikar, household names in Maharashtra, the Hindi writer and media personality Dharamvir Bharati, and the maverick theatre guru Satyadev Dubey.

Abutting Sahitya Sahawas was a creek of mangroves, which in later years would be transformed into a commercial hub called the Bandra-Kurla Complex.

The three older Tendulkar kids were delighted when their parents acceded to their request that their youngest sibling be named for Sachin Dev Burman, one of the leading music composers in Mumbai's Hindi film industry and their favourite.

Like all middle-class couples, the senior Tendulkars worked hard and did everything that they could to fulfil the needs and wants of their children. They inculcated in their kids, moral values and a sense of discipline.

The early 1970s were a time of transition. India had emerged victorious in the Bangladesh Liberation War in December 1971, but the subsequent months had been riddled with strife. The economy was struggling to keep up with the increasing population. Inflation and unemployment were on the rise. In the cities, the middle class felt the pinch.

Even after 25 years of independence, a mental and emotional insecurity lingered, as much the outcome of centuries of servitude that had preceded freedom, as of the three wars that India had fought between 1962 and 1971. The Green and White Revolutions were yet to make an impact. Just a few years previously, Lal Bahadur Shastri, the then prime minister, had appealed to the masses to skip one meal a day to tide over the scarcity of food grains.

Consequently, the public, and most of all, the middle class had got used to looking over its shoulder. Caution had gained precedence over enterprise. Jobs in the public sector, which insulated people from unemployment to a significant extent, were favoured, as were conventional professions like medicine, engineering and law, with accountancy catching up. The emphasis was on saving money, not spending it. This approach percolated into every aspect of life.

For instance, schoolboy cricketers in Mumbai, a sizeable number of whom belonged to middle-class families, were taught to go for victory only after every possibility of defeat had been eliminated. Risk-taking was discouraged.

Mumbai's middle class had always loved cricket more than any other sport. This was not surprising, considering the city's glorious association with the sport, and the number of cricketers it had gifted to the country over the decades.

However, for the majority, this love was conditional. It was all very well to follow the game, so long as it was being played by others.

Many middle-class cricketers of the time had to contend with parental opposition to virtually every form of sporting activity. The children were constantly reminded that to secure their future, it was paramount to utilize their brains—their only inheritance—to excel in academics. There was no way sports was to be allowed to supersede studies. For every middle-class cricketer who had gone the distance, thanks to his ability and the support of his family, there were at least 10 others, if not more, who were as talented, but were forced to sacrifice their cricketing ambitions at the academic altar. In all fairness to the parents, there was little or no money in sport in those days. This made a full-time career in sport unviable.

Prof. Tendulkar was happy to encourage Ajit, his second son, who loved to play cricket and was good enough to be picked in his school's cricket team. Savita, the lone girl among the Tendulkar siblings, was as interested in cricket as her brothers. She requested her parents that she be allowed to open an account with the State Bank of India because a mini-bat autographed by Ajit Wadekar, one of the bank's senior managers, was being offered as an incentive.

Wadekar was the man under whose leadership the Indian cricket team created history in the same year in which India liberated Bangladesh and the Tendulkars shifted to Sahitya Sahawas. A year later, all of Mumbai was thrilled when Doordarshan, the government-owned TV network, commenced operations in the city. England toured India in the winter of 1972–73, and the final Test of the series, played at Mumbai's Brabourne Stadium, just a couple of months prior to Sachin's birth, was telecast live.

Sachin enjoyed all the advantages of being the youngest in the family, and more. However, his parents and siblings ensured that while they did not deny him anything that he wanted, they did not go overboard. Most of the families in Sahitya Sahawas did likewise. Unlike the high-rise residential complexes of today, where people are sometimes unaware of even the names of their neighbours, the adults and children at Sahitya Sahawas mixed and mingled with each other regularly. It was as if the 84 households constituted one gigantic family.

> My earliest memories are of him as a very chubby and sweet child, with long, curly hair. As part of my medical studies, I had kept frogs at home, for dissection purposes. Sachin was aware of that. He once saw me eating cauliflower. When he asked what I was eating, I told him that I was eating 'bedkaachi bhaaji' [loosely translated as frog vegetable]. I was just trying

to pull his leg. I forgot all about it, until his mother told mine that Sachin had been insisting on her making 'bedkaachi bhaaji' for him.

—Dr Shrirang Purohit (Sahitya Sahawas neighbour), *Million Dollar Babies,* Star Cricket, 2008

Sachin's love for his mother's cooking outstripped all the passions that he acquired over the years. Among all the vegetarian and non-vegetarian delicacies that Mrs Tendulkar whipped up for the family, the one closest to Sachin's heart was *varan bhaat*, the staple food in Marathi households. Sachin relished the combination of cooked rice and boiled lentil, embellished with a dab of ghee and lemon.

Bandra IES, the school Sachin was admitted to, was a short walk from home. Most of his Sahitya Sahawas friends studied there. One of Sachin's first friends at school was Atul Ranade, who went on to represent Mumbai in the Ranji Trophy. Ranade initially thought that the kid with the flowing locks who was sitting in front of him in the junior kindergarten classroom was a girl. The duo got on like a house on fire. As the years passed, Ranade discovered that while his friend did not like to lose at anything, he also knew when to exercise discretion. In the second grade, Sachin hit a boy two years his senior, and the victim and his mates sought revenge. They camped themselves at the school gate, waiting for him to emerge, but Sachin managed to give them the slip.

Sachin assumed leadership of one of the children's gangs in Sahitya Sahawas, along with two boys of the same age—Avinash Gowariker and Sunil Harshe. Avinash and Sachin lived in the same building—Ushakal—on the third and fourth floors respectively, while Sunil lived in the building just opposite. Sachin was assertive, aggressive and street-smart, as younger siblings generally tend to be. If his gang had a new entrant, Sachin would 'test' him by determining how well he could 'hit' the others.

The word 'gang' is a bit of a misnomer in this context, as all that the kids did where they lived and in school was play a variety of games and pranks. The parents, elder siblings and teachers kept an eye on the kids, but they were wise enough to leave them to their own devices when it came to conflict resolution. Sure enough, friendships were made, broken and remade, day after day. There were exceptional circumstances, of course. When a girl classmate told him that 'his mother looked funny', the young Sachin was infuriated. He struck her so hard that she started crying. Sachin's mother was summoned to school, and she and the mother of the girl got the children to patch up.

Animals evoked the boy's curiosity. On a visit to the zoo, Sachin was so impressed by a tiger that he insisted on touching it, and was disappointed when he was told that he couldn't. One of his proudest moments was when he 'rescued' a black-coloured fish from a gutter, and gave it a new home in the form of a water bottle.

Complementing the parents, elder siblings and neighbours were other individuals. Sachin was born left-handed and wrote with his left, but he took to batting with a right-hander's grip.*

The first 'bowler' in his life was Laxmibai, his nanny, who watched over him in his toddlerhood, with his parents away at work and siblings in school. His first 'bat' was a bat-like piece of wood that was used as an accessory to wash clothes.† When he was five, Savita, his sister, got him a proper cricket bat from Kashmir. As Laxmibai visited her own children on weekends, Sachin's mother would take him to her workplace on Saturdays.

Also keeping an eye on the kids was Laxman Pardhe, security-in-charge at Sahitya Sahawas, who lived with his family just below Ushakal. Often exhorted by the adults to reprimand the children if required, Pardhe would eventually give in to the unbridled enthusiasm of the kids and indulge them. Ramesh, Laxman Pardhe's younger son, was part of Sachin's inner circle of friends.‡

Whether it was while playing hide-and-seek or performing stunts on a bicycle or teaming up with friends to bolt the doors of the residents' flats from the outside, Sachin wanted to be the best at everything. His adventurous streak resulted in quite a few injuries, from minor bruises to gashes that necessitated stitches. A daily ritual for Prof. Tendulkar was to examine his youngest son from head to toe for new wounds, if any.

Sachin would imitate his elder siblings, but not blindly. Even at a young age, he had a mind of his own. His seniors backed the icy Bjorn Borg in the 1981 Men's Singles Final at Wimbledon, which was telecast live on DD, but the eight-year-old Sachin was rooting for the fiery John McEnroe. Sachin was ecstatic when his hero ended Borg's five-year winning streak at the All-England

---

*More than three decades after Sachin started playing cricket, it was claimed in a study that natural left-handers would 'maximize' their potential in the game if they adopted a right-handed grip, and vice versa. Considering that the top hand on the grip was responsible for controlling and guiding the path of the bat to strike the ball, the batsman was at an advantage if his 'dominant' hand performed this role, the study contended. The study cited batsmen who had done things 'the other way around' and achieved extraordinary success, among them Christopher Gayle of the West Indies, who batted with a left-hander's grip despite being a natural right-hander and a certain S.R. Tendulkar who batted right-handed despite being left-handed.
†The Marathi term for the same is dhoka.
‡In later years, Ramesh became Sachin's personal assistant.

Club. Like McEnroe, Sachin then had a mop of curly hair. He sought to extend the resemblance, and asked for a tennis racquet, head-band and wrist-bands. His neighbours promptly nicknamed him 'Sachu McEnroe'.

Little did he know then that he would eventually become a regular visitor to Wimbledon.

With the older children monopolizing the 30-yards/30-yards patch of land that was the Sahitya Sahawas playground, Sachin and his friends played in any open space that they found.

Middle-class children in congested Mumbai have never allowed the paucity of space to stifle their sporting instincts. Like their elders, they are adept at adjusting and adapting.

Cricket has been their most preferred sport for decades. Over the years and decades, children have played either over-arm or under-arm, depending on availability of space. If stumps are not available, then stones, bricks or footwear are used to create a pyramid to serve the purpose. Alternately, chalks and bricks have been utilized to sketch stumps on a wall.

Like scores of youngsters before and after him, Sachin developed his flair for cricket and imbibed the basics of technique and temperament in an unstructured setting.

The year 1983 was a watershed year for Indian cricket and for all those who followed the sport. 'Kapil's Devils' confounded their critics as well as supporters by qualifying for the semi-finals of the World Cup. Cricket lovers were ecstatic when DD decided to telecast the semi-final to be played against England, the hosts, at Manchester on 22 June 1983. With television sets still a luxury in India, those who owned them had to make arrangements in their respective drawing rooms to accommodate friends, relatives and neighbours who didn't. The country erupted when India overhauled a target of 213 with five overs and six wickets in hand, to ensure a summit clash against the West Indies at Lord's, three days later.

In the final, the unthinkable happened. India stunned the West Indies and the world to bag the match and, with it, the title. Sachin, who had just turned 10, was among the thousands of star-struck Indian youngsters who celebrated the win.

There was another celebration six months later, when the nation came together again to salute a legend.

Sunil Gavaskar had displayed his propensity to rewrite the record books since his debut in the West Indies in 1971. He was the only pan-Indian sporting hero for most of the 1970s, until Kapil Dev Nikhanj, another cricketer, arrived on the scene at the end of the decade. As opening batsman, Gavaskar was pitted against the premier purveyors of what was cricket's 'Pace Age'. India apart, every Test-playing country of the time had at least two bowlers, who were either proficient at propelling the ball fast or making it swing or both. Gavaskar took them on and triumphed. The more formidable the opponent, the tougher it was to dislodge him.

Like Vijay Merchant four decades previously, Gavaskar cut down on aggression and risk-taking when he figured out that he needed to spend as much time in the middle as possible for his team to make an impression. He did his best during his stints as captain, mindful that the Indian bowling at the time was probably the weakest in the world. He had no option but to nullify every possibility of defeat before thinking of victory.

Gavaskar did not do anything notable as a batsman in the 1983 World Cup, but just as people were in the process of preparing his epitaphs, he regained his status as India's cricketing bulwark with his performances against the West Indies in the 1983–84 season. He equalled Sir Don Bradman's record tally of 29 Test centuries with a belligerent 121 in the second Test at Delhi and then overhauled the Don with an unbeaten 236 in the last Test of the series at Chennai. During the same series, he also became the highest scorer in Test cricket, surpassing Geoffrey Boycott's aggregate of 8,114.

To more than one generation of cricketers and followers, Sunil Gavaskar was a visionary, and not merely because of the runs he scored and the matches he either saved or won for India. Cricket apart, he tried his hand at journalism, television production, sponsorship and event management. He went on to demonstrate what a sportsperson could achieve even after his playing days came to an end.

Gavaskar ensured a marked difference in the way cricket was perceived by India's urban middle class. The game now seemed a viable career option. An equally critical role was played by the BCCI, which was running the sport better than other sporting bodies in the country, most of which personified callousness. A momentous event occurred in July 1984, at the Annual Conference of the International Cricket Conference (ICC). The BCCI and its Pakistani counterpart had been wondering aloud why England was being treated as the de-facto host of every World Cup. At the meeting, they put forth a joint bid to host the 1987 edition of the World Cup. Their endeavour was opposed, as was only to be expected, but eventually the Asians prevailed. No one knew it then, but a process had been initiated wherein India, which had been treated as a cricketing outpost for decades, would become its hub by the end of the first decade of the new millennium.

Would the BCCI have been emboldened to do what it did had India not won the World Cup in 1983? The answer is an obvious 'No'.

Given the gulf that existed in the cricketing standards in Mumbai and the rest of the country in the 1970s and 1980s, there is reason to believe that Ajit Tendulkar, who played school, college and club-level cricket with distinction, would have played first-class cricket as well had he been living elsewhere. A Mumbaikar had to be better than outstanding to succeed at cricket.

As was the norm in Mumbai's many housing complexes, the senior kids at Sahitya Sahawas were averse to allowing their juniors to play cricket with them, unless they were short of fielders, of course. However, some of them did keep a watch on the juniors, and inducted those who were deemed good enough into their fold. For a junior, being considered good enough to play with the seniors was the ultimate achievement. In the months following the World Cup win, Sachin graduated from the Sahitya Sahawas alleys to the main playground. Merit had played its part, but luck was also on his side.

Ajit discerned his kid brother's proficiency, not so much as an indulgent elder brother but as a competitive sportsperson who was aware of the skills one needed to possess to excel at sport. He tested his hypothesis by making his kid brother hit a ball with a tennis racquet. He also watched Sachin bat, bowl and field on the Sahitya Sahawas playground, and realized that his brother enjoyed cricket more than tennis. He also noted that while batting, Sachin would pick the line and length of the incoming ball earlier than boys his age. The kid displayed no discomfort while facing boys who were senior to him by several years. He would play every ball on merit and execute strokes fearlessly. When he bowled, he would give it everything. He also did not look down upon fielding as Indian boys of his time were known to do. As a cricketer, he was competitive but not petulant. The sportsperson within Ajit told him that his brother stood a good chance of doing well at cricket.

The rest of the family also felt that there ought to be some sort of 'structure' in Sachin's life, though for another reason. They had got more than a little perturbed with their darling's escapades. The final straw was when Sachin and his friends attempted to pluck mangoes off a tree in the Sahitya Sahawas complex on a Sunday evening. In the days when DD enjoyed a monopoly on Indian television, the Sunday evening Hindi film was considered sacrosanct. People would stay at home and watch it, irrespective of its quality. The triumvirate of Sachin, Sunil and Avinash was smart enough to plan a 'raid' of the mango tree on an evening when *Guide*, an all-time classic, was being screened. The prospect of plucking the mangoes at a time when all of Sahitya Sahawas would be glued to the TV excited Sachin a lot more than the fact that the music composer of *Guide* was none other than his illustrious namesake. Unfortunately for the boys, they were brought down to earth literally and figuratively, when the branch Sachin and Sunil had perched themselves on could not take their weight. The thud alerted the residents, and the boys' game was up.

> Sachin may endorse many products now, but when he was ten, he was not what many parents wanted their sons to be. He was part of an unholy trinity whom considerate elders used to point to and ask their fledgling wards to be exactly the opposite. He never let the fact that he was a Marathi professor's son draw him towards studies. To be precise, Mark Twain would have loved [the] ten-year-old Sachin.
>
> —Manu Joseph, *Outlook*, 4 January 1999

THE NURSERY

I never insisted on any particular stance or grip while batting. But I always insisted on two things: 1. While playing any shot, your feet should be near the pitch of the ball. 2. Each ball should be played with the sweet spot of the bat.

—Ramakant Achrekar, *Mumbai Mirror*, 11 December 2005

Ajit sought to structure his kid brother's life by linking it to an activity that the latter loved. Once he had spoken to his parents and made up his mind to channelize Sachin's cricketing skills, there was only one place he could have visited.

Shivaji Park, named after the great Maratha warrior-king, is situated on the western seafront of central Mumbai. Geographically, this arena that spans 112,937 square metres and has an inner circumference of 1.17 kilometres is a part of the area known as Dadar, but as usually happens with landmarks, the name of the park is used to denote the area that surrounds it. The park itself was formally inaugurated as a public place in 1927, the year that marked Shivaji's 300th birth anniversary.

Today, Shivaji Park is one of the few surviving open spaces in the concrete forest that the island of Mumbai has become. Over the years and decades, it has hosted political rallies, cultural programmes, religious festivities, public felicitations, exhibitions, open-air plays, the annual Republic Day and Maharashtra Day parades and investiture ceremonies, the swearing-in ceremony of a state government and even the funeral of Balasaheb Thackeray, the founder of the Shiv Sena, a political organization that was for all practical purposes born on the Shivaji Park.

A couple of kilometres to the east of Shivaji Park, on the other side of the Western and Central Railway lines that run parallel to each other through Dadar before breaking away and charting independent routes into the mainland, lies the Matunga Maidan. In the early 1990s, this arena was named after Major Ramesh Dadkar, who sacrificed his life in the 1971 war.

There was a construction boom around both the maidans in the two decades prior to independence. This was the phase when several middle-class families shifted from the congested chawls of southern Mumbai to self-contained flats in Dadar and Matunga which were then considered suburbs. The residential structures around Shivaji Park and the Matunga Maidan were similar. Most of them were two or three-storeyed buildings, with each floor comprising two to four flats. While the Marathi middle class was in a majority around Shivaji Park, the area around Matunga Maidan housed a combination of Marathi, South Indian, and later, Gujarati middle-class families.

Even as this migration from either southern Mumbai or the mainland was taking place, educational institutions were also coming up near the maidans. The Balmohan Vidyamandir School was a stone's throw from Shivaji Park. Not too far away were the D.G. Ruparel and Kirti M. Doongursee colleges. A two-minute walk from Matunga Maidan was King George School, and opposite the maidan were the Ramnarain Ruia College of Arts and Science and the R.A. Podar College of Commerce and Economics. While these educational institutions stand strong and tall even today, many of the residential buildings around the maidans have been 'redeveloped' into swanky high-rises, a process that seems set to continue until Dadar starts looking like another Nariman Point.

Both Shivaji Park and Matunga Maidan were also the nurseries of Mumbai cricket from the 1950s till the end of the 20th century. Dotting their respective peripheries were several cricket 'clubs'.

The inter-club matches at the maidans were known to attract crowds in thousands. The highlight for the cricketers—contemporary and aspiring—and cricket lovers of the area was the clash between the premier clubs of both arenas—Shivaji Park Gymkhana and Matunga Maidan's Dadar Union Sporting Club. These two clubs produced many outstanding batsmen, bowlers and fielders for Mumbai and India. The cricketers playing these games would be emulated by youngsters in soft-ball versions of the sport that they would play in the many lanes that abutted the maidans. When they grew older, these youngsters would 'graduate' to the maidans. The talented ones would invariably be spotted by an active cricketer, usually a neighbour or family elder. These boys would then be inducted into one of the many cricket coaching camps run by the clubs on the maidans. This was how bat and ball had been passed on from one generation to the other.

Complementing the talent-spotters were the educational institutions, all of whom went out of their way to encourage sportspersons.

In 1984, the year in which Ajit Tendulkar decided to 'structure' his brother's life, the ultimate yardstick for boys who played cricket at the two maidans and elsewhere in the city and country was Sunil Gavaskar, an 'alumnus' of Dadar Union. However, at Shivaji Park, Gavaskar was more worshipped and respected than loved. The object of Shivaji Park boys' affection was one of their own.

Sandeep Madhusudan Patil had played his early cricket in the lanes around Shivaji Park, before representing Balmohan Vidyamandir under the tutelage of Ankush 'Anna' Vaidya, the school coach. Patil had started his first-class career as a seamer and lower-order batsman, but soon acquired a reputation as a destroyer of bowling attacks.

Patil was the archetypal Shivaji Park batsman, prone to taking the bowling by the scruff of the neck and going aerial, unlike the Dadar Union and other Matunga batsmen, most of whom tended to be more orthodox in their methods. Their orthodoxy was a legacy of the British officers, who resided in the Police quarters at Dadar before independence and practised at Matunga Maidan. Their adherence to the basics was said to have rubbed off on the locals. On the other hand, Shivaji Park was home to the 'cowboys'.

However, these differences were anything but watertight; Dilip Vengsarkar, who was a Dadar Union alumnus like Gavaskar, was capable of being as belligerent as his contemporary Sandeep Patil if he so wished. The captaincy styles of Dadar Union's celebrated leaders Madhav Mantri and Vasu Paranjape were unorthodox and out-of-the-box. Shivaji Park's premier 'batting' alumnus was Vijay Manjrekar, who was considered Mumbai and India's most accomplished technician between Vijay Merchant and Sunil Gavaskar. In later years, Manjrekar's son Sanjay, another technician of repute, opted for Dadar Union over Shivaji Park Gymkhana because he wanted to follow the footsteps of Gavaskar and Vengsarkar.

Sandeep Patil became a national hero with his performances on India's tours of Australia and England in 1980–81 and 1982, respectively. In Australia, he was hit on the ear in the first Test at Sydney and hospitalized. He came back to smash 174 in the very next Test. In England, personal issues had driven him to the brink of retirement; he resurrected himself with an unbeaten 129 in the second Test at Manchester, inclusive of six boundaries in a Bob Willis over. The following year, he returned to England with Kapil Dev's team for the World Cup. His unbeaten 51 in the semi-final against England and 27 in a low-scoring final against the West Indies helped India conquer the world.

The seeds of that World Cup triumph had been sown on the tour of Australia in 1980–81. The Indian team, which had become notorious for its 'indifference' to limited-overs cricket in the 1970s, produced some fine performances in a triangular series involving the hosts and New Zealand. At the forefront was a new generation of cricketers that was at home in the shorter version of the sport. Kapil Dev, Yashpal Sharma, Dilip Vengsarkar and Patil himself were followed into the national side by the likes of Kirti Azad and K. Srikkanth. All these individuals were part of the Indian team that created history on the afternoon of 25 June 1983.

Like Sandeep Patil, Ajit Tendulkar was a student of Balmohan Vidyamandir and a disciple of Anna Vaidya's. He could have taken his kid brother to his own coach, who ran his own coaching camp at the Shivaji Park. However, he had other plans.

Ajit had reflected on his own stints in school and college cricket. Talent-wise, there was not much of a difference between him and most of the boys he had played with and against. However, some of them would stand out from the rest, for their temperament, fortitude and eagerness to seize the initiative. The one factor common to them was a guru answering to the name of Ramakant Achrekar.

The 1980s were a time when cricket coaching hadn't become the business it has today. Achrekar himself had got into it purely by accident. Apart from being a cricketer of repute in inter-club and office tournaments in his youth, Achrekar's was a name to reckon with, on the 'tennis-ball' circuit in Shivaji Park. Ajit Wadekar himself was one of those who had christened Achrekar the 'Don Bradman of tennis-ball cricket'. In the late 1960s, the New Hind Sports Club, whom Achrekar represented in local cricket, played a game against the Indian Gymkhana. Achrekar was dismissed in that game by a schoolboy off-spinner named Suresh Shastri. The 'Bradman of tennis-ball cricket' was impressed.

Around the same time, Achrekar happened to visit a prominent sports-gear outlet in his capacity as wicketkeeper–batsman of the State Bank of India team (which also included Wadekar) to pick up some equipment. He was at the shop when Suresh Shastri also showed up. The owner of the shop requested Achrekar to take the boy under his wing. Achrekar of course remembered the schoolboy who had bowled to him. He was initially hesitant to get into full-time coaching, but he then decided to take it up as a challenge. He offered his services to Dayanand Balak Vidyalaya, the school Shastri was representing. When told by the concerned authorities that the school was encountering financial issues, Achrekar made it clear that he was interested only in coaching, not money. All he wanted was ₹50 per month to cover his expenses. The school then took him on board. The authorities and students were delighted when the school team reached the final of the Giles Shield and Harris Shield, the two premier inter-school tournaments in Mumbai, in Achrekar's very first year as coach. That was only the beginning.

A few years later, Achrekar became the coach of Shardashram High School. Scores of Shardashram alumni who trained under Achrekar and went on to achieve national and first-class honours subsequently have reason to be grateful to Dushyant Mahale, who played for the school in the early 1970s and went on to represent the Railways in the Ranji Trophy.

Mahale, an admirer of Achrekar and his coaching methods, took it upon himself to convince the latter to become the coach of Shardashram. Achrekar was at that stage coaching two schools and managing some cricket clubs, and he also had a full-time job with the State Bank of India. He was, therefore, reluctant to take charge of another school, but Mahale persisted and set up a meeting between the coach and the Shardashram principal. Achrekar took up the assignment eventually, but ironically Mahale did not get the opportunity to play under him, as he had finished his schooling and moved on to college by then! In Achrekar's very first year as coach, Shardashram won the Matunga Shield. It was the very first tournament of any consequence that the school had won.

By this time, the trustees of the Kamat Memorial Club, impressed with Achrekar's commitment, had assigned him a plot for net practice at the northern end of Shivaji Park.

Achrekar was respected and feared in equal measure by his pupils. He emphasized the basics as much as he disciplined. He reciprocated the devotion of his pupils by supporting them through thick and thin. He nurtured children from economically disadvantaged families by drawing money from his own pocket. As a highly sought after coach, he could not have been blamed for his ambivalence when requested by Ajit Tendulkar to take his younger brother under his wing. It was by no means the first time a father or uncle or older sibling had approached him with a similar plea. He agreed to test Sachin out in the nets, but was not impressed with what he saw. He told Ajit to bring the boy back when he was older.

Ajit may not have represented Mumbai at the first-class level, but he had played enough competitive cricket to acquire the one attribute that characterized the city's cricketers. He was khadoos—a tough nut to crack and perseverance personified. He requested Achrekar that his brother be given another opportunity. He also suggested that the coach stand at a distance from the nets, so that Sachin would not be conscious of his presence.

Achrekar liked what he saw the second time around. Ajit's relief knew no bounds. Had it not been for his persuasive skills, the history of the sport may well have taken a different turn.

Ajit also had been pleased with what he had seen. Not only had Sachin adjusted to the gear, like gloves and leg-guards, all of which he had never worn before, but he had also played every delivery on merit. The hard cricket ball had not fazed him while batting or catching.

Sachin, who had been oblivious to the drama that preceded his admission, did not have any lofty cricketing ambitions then. The 11-year-old was simply delighted to emulate his elder brother by playing a 'structured' version of his favourite sport.

A few months earlier, Ajit had taken him to the Wankhede Stadium to watch a Test match between India and the West Indies. Like all cricket-crazy kids, Sachin savoured every single moment of his visit, from entering the stadium and beholding a massive expanse of green, surrounded by viewing galleries, which were packed with adoring fans.* Sachin's day was made when Isaac Vivian Alexander Richards, one of his heroes, scored a century. Both he and Sunil Gavaskar, Sachin's other inspiration, wore their respective hearts on their sleeves. Gavaskar demoralized bowlers by wearing them out, while Richards did likewise by tearing them apart. It was but natural that Richards' belligerence appealed more to the 10-year-old than Gavaskar's patience.

The emphasis on academics apart, many middle-class Marathi families of the time were known to have one peculiar characteristic. The slightest show of confidence from children would be met with a reprimand from the elders—family members as well as school teachers. The elders generally tended to overlook the fact that if a child who had a reasonable level of confidence in his/her own abilities happened to express that confidence, it did not necessarily mean that he/she was being arrogant. Most of the elders would not take the trouble of helping their children understand the difference between assurance and arrogance. Ironically, the same elders encouraged 'academic' arrogance. One of the middle-class' unwritten rules was that children who scored well in their examinations were entitled to be standoffish.

The Tendulkars thought differently.

Sachin's propensity to walk the talk was evident from a very early age. On his very first day at the nets, when he had done only fielding practice, he had told his brother about the mistakes he had observed the other boys make while batting. When they travelled to Shivaji Park the following morning, Sachin asked his brother whether he ought to attack or defend while batting. Any other

---

*Sachin invoked his memories of that game several times in subsequent years to underscore the impact that a visit to a cricket stadium to watch a big game was likely to have on young, impressionable minds.

elder brother would have chided the kid for being cocky. But Ajit Tendulkar was different. He belonged to a family that understood the difference between assurance and arrogance.

Sachin's elders had sown the seeds of discipline and dedication within him, and they were happy to assign him the responsibility of tending to those seeds.

Achrekar was quick to realize that his new pupil was a natural. He noticed that Sachin gripped the bat very low, close to its shoulder. This was a consequence of the boy's use of his elder brother's bat, which was obviously on the taller and heavier side for him. He, therefore, gripped it close to the shoulder to be able to control it better. Achrekar tried to get Sachin to adopt a more conventional grip, with the hands in the middle of the handle. However, Sachin's hands continued to slip downwards. When it dawned on the coach that his pupil was doing quite well despite his unorthodox grip, he relented.

> I started with that grip right from the beginning. It came naturally to me and I think it suited my style of batting. I like to attack the bowling to dominate and play shots and for that the grip is correct. In cricket, there are more shots with the right hand near the bottom of the handle. Initially, the coach tried to change this but he too realised that this grip was working for me and he let me play with my natural style. I think from the beginning, my batting, in terms of my technique or style, has not changed, except for some adjustments. I have always played the same way.
>
> —Sachin Tendulkar, *Outlook*, 4 January 1999

Two decades previously, another Shivaji Park coach had similarly decided not to tinker with a ward's technique. Sandeep Patil had been fond of playing lofted strokes in an era in which they were frowned upon. However, 'Anna' Vaidya had always encouraged his ward to play to his strengths.

What Achrekar worked on was the stance. He taught Sachin to balance his body weight evenly with his feet not too wide or too close to each other. The boy followed his coach's instructions and went through the paces till it became second nature to him. His stance remained the same for the better part of his career, as did the initial forward movement. There were of course situations wherein he made alterations in both, but his head stayed as still as always.

In the nets on the maidans of Mumbai, the general rule of thumb is that a batsman faces around 40 deliveries, with four or five bowlers operating one after the other. There is obviously no running between the wickets. Coaches generally tend to discourage attacking strokes, citing the possibility of the ball striking one of the many boys clustered around the net, awaiting their turn to pad up. A lofted shot, even if a delivery warrants one, can prompt an infuriated coach to terminate his ward's batting stint abruptly.

What tends to happen is that players who bat well in the nets struggle in the 'matches' that are played between teams drawn from the same coaching camp, or against a team being guided by another coach. Most of the players are simply not used to facing successive deliveries bowled by a single bowler and then running between wickets in the sweltering heat and humidity. Many of the bowlers also suffer because they are not used to delivering six balls at a stretch.

In these 'inter-net' matches, a batsman is supposed to 'retire' after his individual score crosses 50. The captains walk the tightrope between going for a win and ensuring that as many players get to bat and bowl as possible. Generally, matches are played between teams comprising 14 or 15 players, the understanding being that while everybody can bat, scorekeeping will stop at the fall of the 10th wicket. The game goes on till the allotted overs are completed. Nothing much has changed over the years.

What this writer observed during his existence as a mediocre cricketer at Shivaji Park and the Matunga Maidan in the 1980s and 1990s was that the 'inter-net' matches would end up being dominated by a mafia of sorts. With the coaches away at their respective workplaces when the matches were played, the 'stars' in the nets would rule the roost, and go out of their way to be obnoxious. While fielding, these 'stars' would station themselves in the infield, on the relatively well-maintained square around the pitches, with the 'lesser' players being banished to the uneven outfield. The lesser players would be summoned to the infield only to stand at potentially dangerous positions like silly point and short-leg, which the stars would always keep away from. The one fact that used to be conveniently overlooked during this charade was that the lesser players were lesser only because they did not have as much exposure to structured cricket as the stars did. The stars had become stars only because they had played a lot more 'structured' cricket than the others, thanks to their fathers or uncles or older siblings being cricketers themselves. However, mafias had no place in Achrekar's camp.

One factor that gave Achrekar's wards an edge over their peers was his conviction that 'match-practice' was as critical as net-practice. He insisted that they play as many matches as possible. It could have been a friendly match between boys playing in the same net, but a match was a match. There, the players were exposed to different situations, which in turn enhanced their ability to handle pressure. In many coaching camps, there was no net practice on match-days, but Achrekar did not grant his pupils that concession. Matches were played after the morning nets.

Sachin fell in love with Achrekar's regimen. Within a few days, he had shed the shy and reserved demeanour, and made new friends. Ajit soon realized that he did not need to escort his brother to the camp, which started at 7:30 in the morning. Sachin started travelling by bus alone. Practice ended at 10:00 a.m., after which he caught a bus home. The walk from the ground to the bus stop, post-practice, featured a fair amount of tomfoolery. Boys had to be boys, after all.

Sachin's siblings were thrilled when he informed them that Achrekar had slotted him at number four in the batting order for his first inter-net match. Number four had traditionally been to Indians what number three had been to Australians, with the best batsman in the side batting at that number. Vijay Merchant and Sunil Gavaskar, both openers, had been the exceptions to that rule. For Indian cricket lovers of the 1970s and 1980s, number four was synonymous with Gundappa Viswanath, one of the country's greatest match winners. Before him, the likes of Vijay Hazare, Vijay Manjrekar and Dilip Sardesai had excelled at that position.

Sachin invited his Sahitya Sahawas friends to watch him make his inter-net debut, only to be embarrassed when he fell for a duck. He met with a similar fate in his second inter-net match. However, Achrekar persisted with him at number four. Much to his relief, he got off the mark in his third game. In the subsequent games, he overcompensated for his initial failures.

There would be an encore to this chain of events, some years later.

An oddity of Sachin's batting, apart from his bottom-handed grip, was his propensity to play cross-batted strokes on the leg-side and hit the ball on the up. This was a consequence of the 'rubber-ball' cricket that he had played in Sahitya Sahawas. The red-coloured rubber ball, which was predominantly used in street and maidan cricket in Mumbai, was soft, but bouncy. Achrekar, mindful of Sachin's rubber-ball background, guided him accordingly.

The guru had his own way of testing the tenacity of his pupils. He made Sachin a member of his Kamat Memorial Club for an admission fee of ₹65 and a monthly fee of ₹10. A few days later, he came up with a question that took Sachin by surprise: 'What do you do in the afternoons?'

Summer vacation camps were generally run in two batches: early morning and late afternoon. Sachin was part of the morning batch, which the trainees favour, because it enables them to wind up before the heat and humidity reach their peak levels.

Sachin's reply to Achrekar's question was that he played with his Sahitya

Sahawas friends. Achrekar promptly instructed Sachin to attend nets in the afternoons as well. Sachin dithered initially, as any youngster would if encountered with the possibility of not getting to spend time with his friends during vacations. However, his love for cricket eventually overrode all other considerations. He cleared Achrekar's first challenge with flying colours.

Several years later, one of Sachin's contemporaries recalled an incident that underscored his transformation. Sachin and a few other boys had reported for practice earlier than usual, but the maalis (groundkeepers) had refused to erect the nets before the schedule time. Sachin took the initiative to request one of Achrekar's assistants to prevail upon the maalis to get working. He also provided an option: if the maalis were reluctant, then could he be allowed to erect the nets himself?

> What was a kind of a jhatka [jolt] for us, was his sudden alienation from us. Ajit had the great foresight and sensibility to see the talent in Sachin. So when he said, 'Enough. Start serious cricket', we could not understand what he meant. We were kids [after all]. And before we knew it, 'Sachu' was gone. The guy with whom I used to spend 20 of the 24 hours of the day was suddenly into cricket, full-time. He was out of my life.
>
> —Avinash Gowariker, *Million Dollar Baby*, Star Cricket, 2008

Sachin's induction in Achrekar's camp, at the start of his school vacation in April 1984, coincided with India's victory in the inaugural edition of the Asia Cup, played at Sharjah. The team was led by Sunil Gavaskar, one of Sachin's heroes. By the time the camp ended, another of Sachin's heroes had hit the headlines. On 31 May 1984, Vivian Richards hammered an unbeaten 189 in an ODI against England. In the month-and-a-half between India's Asia Cup win under Gavaskar's captaincy and King Richards' slaughter of England, their fan's life had changed forever.

Mumbai's heat and humidity helped Sachin tide over the difficulty of possessing only one cricket shirt and a pair of trousers. Both would be washed after morning practice. As it was summer, they would dry (the pockets excepted) by the time he would have to leave for the afternoon session. The set would undergo another wash after the second session and readied for the next day's morning practice. This sequence was repeated daily till the conclusion of the camp.

Nothing could have prepared Sachin for the next challenge that his coach hurled at him, in the form of a telephone call to Prof. Tendulkar. Achrekar was convinced that the boy had it in him to excel at cricket. However, for that to happen, it was necessary that he played inter-school cricket. Bandra IES, the school where Sachin studied, did not have a cricket team. Achrekar therefore suggested that Sachin shift to the Shardashram English Medium School in Dadar whose English and Marathi medium teams were coached by him.

Achrekar's conversation with Prof. Tendulkar was by no means the first time a coach was discussing a middle-class pupil's talent with the latter's father, and neither was it the last. However, the father's response in this case made the exchange unique.

Prof. Ramesh Tendulkar of all people understood the importance of education. He could have taken the easier way out and 'played safe'. He could well have told his son to play cricket in the vacations and concentrate on studies for the rest of the year. He could have put his foot down on the change of schools. He did not.

> I love my children and look upon them as my friends. I am against giving advice and leave the choice of their careers to them. It must be their own experience. If they have a problem, they will come to me. My son's education is important but if the priority is cricket then that must be pursued. If he fails one has to accept it.
>
> Prof. Ramesh Tendulkar, as quoted in 'Sachin Tendulkar—A Genius in Residence', Rohit Brijnath, *Live Mint* and *The Wall Street Journal*, 8 November 2013

Sahitya Sahawas was a fair distance away from Shardashram. There was no bus that plied between the two locations directly, which meant that Sachin would have to change buses on the way, that too early in the morning, as the school opened at seven. And he was only 11. Boys were generally inducted into inter-school cricket when they were a year or even a couple of years older, and studying in seventh or eighth grade. Sachin, on the other hand, was to enter sixth grade. The commute to and from Shardashram would eat into his leisure and study time.

> Boys joined Shardashram for cricket. If they wanted to study, they could have gone somewhere else.
>
> —Amol Muzumdar, *Outlook*, 4 January 1999

While it is true that families tend to dote on and indulge their youngest member the most, there is a flipside; the younger you are, the less seriously you tend to be taken. In all fairness, this isn't something that a family does consciously.

The youngest member of a family remains the youngest, irrespective of whether he is 4 or 40. For all the affection and independence that his seniors showered on him, they viewed Sachin as a carefree child who was still a few years away from taking life seriously.

They were, therefore, taken aback when Sachin informed them that he was ready for the change. What mattered to him, more than anything else, was cricket. For his parents and siblings, it was a revelatory moment. They ought to have patted themselves on the back for having brought him up the way they did. But then, it wasn't in their nature to claim credit.

The Tendulkars did not know it then, but they would go on to complete what Sunil Gavaskar had commenced. Within a decade after Sachin changed schools, cricket specifically was being considered as a genuine career option by the middle class.

> The one person who has influenced my life the most was my father—Ramesh Tendulkar. My 'baba' was an exceptionally calm and collected person. He was the kind of man who never seemed to lose himself in any situation. A single rupee or a million simply made no difference to him. Observing his dignified lifestyle, his considerate interaction with people and his depth of thought was enough to tell me what I should and should not do in life. He was and remains my beacon. He always said, 'Never let success go to your head or failure to get you down'. If I can inculcate even 50 per cent of his way of living into the rest of my life, I will have achieved something in life!
>
> —Sachin Tendulkar, *Cricket Today*, May 2005

OUT OF THE COMFORT ZONE

It was the winter of 1986. In Lucknow's idyllic cantonment, my uncle Shyam Babu Saxena, a former cricketer in the Delhi University circuit and later a frequent visitor to the Mumbai maidans, was giving me throw-downs with a tennis ball on our terrace. In the middle of this practice session, he said that he was going to tell me something that I should write down, and never forget. He said it was the name of a boy who would one day be the greatest Indian batsman the world had ever known. I fetched a pencil and paper.... Two decades later, I found that forgotten piece of paper inside a Class III textbook. It bore the faded, misspelt legend: Sachin Tendolkar.

—Kunal Pradhan, *India Today*, 25 November 2013

A new phase in Sachin's life commenced with the start of the academic year in June 1984. He took his time to adjust to the new routine. If changing buses early in the morning was a pain for someone who was used to walking to school, the Mumbai monsoon, which stretched from June to September, was a major frustration. There was no cricket, and there was many an occasion when the boy yearned for his old friends and some breathing space. However, he persevered. Things started falling into place when the cricket season commenced in October.

Sachin would leave home at six in the morning, and attend school from 7:05 a.m. to 2:00 p.m. He would then walk to the old family residence at Shivaji Park, where his uncle and aunt resided. He would dump his school bag there, collect his cricket kit, and make his way to the Shardashram nets. He would bat, bowl, field, jog and stretch till seven in the evening. He would then return to his uncle's home, deposit his kit, pick up his bag and catch a bus home. It being rush hour, very rarely would he get a seat, and so would stand for the entire duration of the journey, as the bus snaked its way through the evening traffic. At home, he would study for a while, before having dinner and going to bed. At a time when urban India was savouring prime-time TV programmes like *Humlog* and the comedy *Yeh Jo Hain Zindagi* on DD, there was one youngster who did not have the time and energy to do so. But he had no regrets.

Ajit would have remembered the eight-year-old John McEnroe impersonator when he and Achrekar took Sachin to a sports equipment outlet to buy a bat. Sachin was captivated by a piece of willow and he insisted on buying it, the way he had demanded a tennis racquet and wristbands, a few years previously. Both Ajit and Achrekar were of the view that the bat was far too heavy for him, but Sachin did not budge. The two khadoos seniors had to give in eventually. This was no mean achievement.

> I am just used to a heavy bat. I feel comfortable. It helps while playing on the up and forcing the ball in front of the wicket. I use three grips. The thick handle gives me a better grip and feel. I feel comfortable and that is important because the feel is crucial.
>
> —Sachin Tendulkar, *Outlook*, 4 January 1999

The year 1985 was an exciting time to be a young cricketer in India. March witnessed the Indian team's victory in the World Championship of Cricket, a limited-overs tournament involving all the then Test-playing teams, which had been organized to commemorate the sesquicentennial of the Australian state of Victoria. It was a triumph that underscored the Indian team's proficiency in the shorter version, and silenced all those who had labelled the 1983 World Cup win as a fluke. The seniors—skipper Sunil Gavaskar, vice-captain Kapil Dev, Dilip Vengsarkar and Mohinder Amarnath—were complemented by a band of boys—Ravi Shastri, who was declared the Player of the Tournament, K. Srikkanth, Mohammed Azharuddin, L. Sivaramakrishnan and Sadanand Viswanath. They were brilliant with the bat, ball and in the field.

The performance of their team apart, a highlight of the World Championship of Cricket for the Indian cricket-loving public was the outstanding TV coverage by Australia's Channel Nine network. Never had Indians watched a series of matches played in coloured clothing and under lights. It was also the first time they got to watch slow-motion replays from different angles.

> I used to watch all those matches on TV and tell my brothers, 'One day, I will play for India.'
>
> —Sachin Tendulkar, *The Sportstar*, 25 April 1992

The future held out a lot of promise, not only for Indian cricket but also for the country itself. In December 1984, the 40-year-old Rajiv Gandhi became the country's Prime Minister after securing the biggest mandate in Indian electoral history. A lot was expected from him, but not everything went as per plan. A string of controversies resulted in his party losing power in the next elections. The hung Parliament that was constituted in 1989 did not last long and fresh elections were announced in 1991. Disaster struck just before the polls, when Rajiv Gandhi was assassinated by a suicide bomber on the outskirts of Chennai.

Something similar happened to the 'Class of 1984–85' on the cricket field. Quite a few of the players who had been marked out as legends in the making after their showing in domestic cricket and the World Championship of Cricket faded away, unable as they were to build on their initial successes and cope with the pulls and pressures of top-level cricket.

The boy who idolized the Class of 1984–85, like many kids his age, had stars in his eyes by the time he completed one year under Achrekar's guidance. Sachin's inter-school debut for Shardashram (English medium) against Khoja High School, in the Giles Shield, was eventful, not because he played some crisp strokes in a knock of 24, but because of a lesson on ethics administered to him by his coach. Since local newspapers only reported individual scores of 30 or more in their coverage of inter-school cricket, the scorer at the game offered to 'transfer' six 'extras' to Sachin's individual score. The boy agreed, tempted by the prospect of seeing his name in print for the first time. He was ecstatic when he checked out the paper the following morning, but his coach was livid. A chastened Sachin promised him that he would never take the shortcut again.

> My gurumantra [advice] to all my students was 'scoring runs is your responsibility, and getting out is a sin'. After each match, I never asked them how many runs they scored, but how they got out. If somebody had played an irresponsible shot, I would never spare that boy. I had told them that a batsman should never be satisfied with any amount of runs he may have scored.
>
> —Ramakant Achrekar, *Cricket Today*, May 2005

In a subsequent match against Don Bosco High School, Sachin stroked 10 boundaries on the way to a score of 50. While Achrekar was used to receiving calls from people expressing their admiration of his wards, he was shocked when Mr Gondhalekar, one of the umpires in the game, called him and declared that 'the boy would play for India'. Achrekar would have none of it. Sachin was in his first year of inter-school cricket, after all.

Gondhalekar was by no means the only umpire who was captivated by the boy.

> Twenty-nine years ago, my friend Dr Pratap Raut called me up to tell me that umpire Marketkar had given an 11-year-old not out so that he could tell everyone at Shivaji Park Gymkhana to come and watch the small boy bat. I rushed to Shivaji Park, which was the nursery of cricket then, to see this young, four-and-a-half feet, curly-haired boy bat.
>
> —Milind Rege, *Mid-Day*, 19 October 2013

The concerns that Ajit had harboured about his brother's low grip affecting his off-side play had vanished even before he realized it. Sachin had mastered the cover drive, and his leg-side play was getting better and better by the day.

His coach continued to challenge him. In the summer vacation of 1985, by which time Sachin had completed his first season in inter-school cricket, Achrekar asked Ajit to take his brother to the selection trials conducted by the Mumbai Cricket Association (MCA) for boys in the under-19 age-group. Those who would make the grade would undergo specialized coaching at one of many centres in the city. Sachin was only 12, and so it wasn't a surprise that the head coach of the Bandra centre turned him away. There were of course plenty of outstanding cricketers in the 17–19 age bracket, something that Achrekar was aware of. He would have also known that it was unlikely that a 12-year-old would be picked for an under-19 camp. The guru most probably just wanted to make his pupil learn to 'take a no'.

In his whites and on the field, Sachin was the epitome of application and dedication. Off the field, the cricketer would make way for the 12-year-old. In the school classroom, he would engage in impromptu arm-wrestling bouts with his new mates, most of which he would win. He would occasionally bring a golf ball to the class and challenge his friends to defend themselves from it, with a bat. He was too quick for the others, and would watch gleefully as the boys kept getting hit all over their bodies. From the benches at the back of the classroom, he would chuck paper balls at his classmates seated in front. He was also part of a group that played under-arm cricket outside the school early in the mornings, just before it opened. This exercise ended abruptly when the ball broke a window in an adjoining building and a complaint was made to the school principal.

Of course, not everything was hunky-dory. The time and energy spent in commuting from Bandra to Dadar and back, coupled with the rigorous cricket schedule, took a toll on the kid's health. He had a couple of bouts of illness and, most seriously, contracted jaundice. The family then suggested that he take his commuting out of the equation altogether. The final call was once again his.

In the summer vacation of 1985, Sachin shifted to the old family residence near Shivaji Park, where Suresh, his uncle, and Mangala, his aunt, lived. He attended nets from 7:00 a.m. to 9:30 a.m. If there was a match, he would stay back at the ground. On non-match days, he would return home at 10:00 a.m., and report back at the nets at 3:00 p.m. He would practice till the sun went down. On match days, he would bat in the nets till 7:00 p.m., after the game ended at around 4:30 p.m. He would be so exhausted at the end of the day that his aunt would feed him his dinner, even as he fell asleep on the table.

On non-match days, his aunt would indulge him by chucking a golf ball, which he had shaved into the shape of an oval, at him. Once chucked, the ball would change its course, and Sachin would attempt to block it with his bat. The deviations of the golf ball posed a twin challenge—apart from helping him fine-tune his anticipatory skills, he also had to ensure that the furniture and other items in the drawing room were not damaged.

> The support which my family gave me was absolutely marvellous. My parents, my brothers, my sister, my uncle and aunt.... I stayed with them for four years and the encouragement they gave me was fantastic. I would consider myself a lucky guy to have such family members. My aunt used to get lunch for me whenever there was a match at Shivaji Park. Aunts are affectionate, but I am not sure how many aunts would bring lunch boxes during a cricket match. Looking back at all these things, I feel I was the luckiest guy.
>
> —Sachin Tendulkar, *The Sportstar*, 6 May 1995

His aunt's food apart, Sachin would gorge on the spicy vada-pav and bhel-puri, Mumbai's street delicacies. After matches, Sachin would buy one bhel-puri each for himself and his teammate Ricky Couto, and get a couple packed for his uncle and aunt. Another favourite street speciality of the boys was chatpatta chana dal mixed with lime and onions.

Before shifting to Shivaji Park, Sachin had demanded that his parents and siblings visited him daily. The family was only too happy to acquiesce. Prof. Tendulkar would visit him after completing his lectures at Kirti College, and the three elder siblings would make their way from their respective colleges. For his mother, however, it was an arduous proposition. Every evening she would brave the chaotic evening traffic to travel from her workplace at Santacruz to Shivaji Park, only to meet her son. She would then undertake another journey in the opposite direction, to Sahitya Sahawas.

> At the time, I used to think that this was my birth right. Today, whatever little I can manage to do for my own children has made me realise what

an ordeal it must have been for my mother then. The sacrifice and pain she went through can never be understood by me in its entirety.

—Sachin Tendulkar, *Cricket Today,* May 2005

Sachin was ready for his coach's next challenge.

> Sir wanted him to bat as much as possible. I remember Sachin batting in four nets at Shivaji Park and after that Sir used to ask him to bat for a longer period on a pitch where a match used to be held earlier in the day. This pitch had the wear and tear so batting on them was a challenge. Sachin was tireless. Even after batting on five pitches, he used to request other players for throw-downs and they loved doing it for him simply because he was so enthusiastic.
>
> —Mayur Kadrekar (Sachin's first Shardashram captain), *Mid-Day,* 28 October 2013

A special addition to the fifth and final net was a one-rupee coin that Achrekar would place on the middle stump. After batting in four nets, Sachin would find himself pitted against the best bowlers from the stable. A bowler who would get Sachin out, would get the coin. If Sachin remained unbeaten, he would get to keep the coin.

> I think the most important memorabilia for me is the coins that I have got from my coach Achrekar Sir, those are the most important ones.
>
> —Sachin Tendulkar, *The Times of India,* 27 November 2013

Achrekar may well have been pleased with Sachin's responses to challenges, but that did not mean he was going to go soft on his pupil. He reacted by making him play more cricket. Shivaji Park apart, the guru conducted nets at the Sassanian Cricket Club at south Mumbai's Azad Maidan, the southern tip of which was home to the Bombay Gymkhana, India's first Test venue. If Sachin fell early in a match being played at the Shivaji Park, Achrekar would take him on his two-wheeler to Azad Maidan and send him in to bat in a game being played by his boys.

> Coach Ramakant Achrekar made him play matches almost every day at that young age. You can improve and imbibe the fundamentals at nets, but the cricketing sense can come only through match practice. For example, throwing to the right end and backing up can only be learnt in matches.
>
> —Dilip Vengsarkar, *The Sportstar,* 25 April 1992

In the 60 days of the summer vacation of 1985, Sachin played a mind-boggling 55 matches. His coach's involvement did not stop at making him bat in multiple matches and challenging him in the nets. There was the odd occasion when the teenager in Sachin would come to the fore and he would bunk practice to be with his Sahitya Sahawas friends. Not to be outdone, Achrekar would land up at his house and take him to the ground. Any other teenager might well have rebelled, but not Sachin.

> I was so much into cricket that I did not miss anything else. There were times when I felt like going for a movie with my friends, but I could not do that often, because I used the time for practice, even with a rubber ball, when it was raining. I used to be looking forward to 3 o' clock in the afternoon. I used to really enjoy playing cricket for three or four hours. I thought my energy was channelised in the right direction at the right time....
>
> I was playing three to four matches a week and that helped me develop my temperament. I grasped the importance of it because I played so many games. There were times when I used to play a match in the morning at no. 4 for a team, and on the same day, bat for another team at no. 4 in the afternoon. I was practising very hard in the nets as well, but my coach thought match practice was important for me.
>
> —Sachin Tendulkar, *The Sportstar*, 14 September 2002

It was in the monsoon of 1985 that Achrekar permitted Sachin to play in the Kanga League, Mumbai's annual monsoon inter-club tournament. He was convinced that his ward was now good enough to cope with the vagaries of an uneven, rain-battered wicket. Sachin made his Kanga League debut for the Young Parsee Cricket Club in the 'F' division of the competition.

Achrekar also included Sachin in the Hind Sewak Club side, which he managed, which was participating in the Gordhandas Shield limited-overs tournament. On the morning of the first game, the coach had another commitment and he accordingly told Ajit to drop Sachin at Shivaji Park, where the game was to be played. Much to the chagrin of the brothers, Sachin was not picked in the playing XI, as the captain said that he had not received any instructions from Achrekar to that effect. The skipper was subsequently rebuked by the coach and Sachin played the next game, that too as the team's number four batsman!

Against boys several years his senior, he essayed some fine innings in the tournament, including a brisk 43 in the semi-final. He was, therefore, brimming with confidence when he joined Mangesh Adhatrao, his captain, in the middle during the final against Prabhu Jolly that was being played at the Khar Gymkhana, not very far from Sahitya Sahawas. Hind Sewak were chasing a target. Sachin was devastated to be run out.

> For his age and height, he could hit the ball really hard and far. Achrekar Sir had great faith in his abilities. But that day, the match situation was such that we needed to score fast. The only thing on my mind was winning. I thought we had a better chance with a more senior player,' he says. Ask him if the run out was intentional and Adhatrao smiles. He then nods his head in a manner that could mean both yes and no.
>
> —Mangesh Adhatrao, as told to Amit Gupta, *Mumbai Mirror*, 17 March 2012

Adhatrao went on to score a match-winning double century, a singular achievement in a one-day game. However, he gifted his trophy to Sachin after seeing how disconsolate the youngster was. It was Adhatrao's turn to be disappointed when Achrekar overlooked the victory and the double hundred and instead chided him for running Sachin out.

In the 1985–86 season, Sachin played in both inter-school tournaments—the Giles Shield for the under-15s and the Harris Shield for the under-17s. It was in the latter tournament that he scored his first inter-school hundred, against Don Bosco High School. Unbeaten on 94 at the close, he was so nervous that he decided to spend the night at Sahitya Sahawas. Early in the morning, Prof. Tendulkar took him to a temple of Lord Ganesh, his favourite deity. Reassured by the visit to the temple, Sachin then went to the ground and proceeded to reach triple figures in the very first over. That evening, Achrekar kept his promise by visiting Sahitya Sahawas for dinner. Sachin had invited him home on several occasions, but the guru had insisted that he would do so only after his pupil scored a century.

His hectic schedule notwithstanding, Sachin would occasionally find the time to return and play cricket 'where it had all begun', but not merely for purposes of recreation or nostalgia, as it turned out. On the Sahitya Sahawas playground, he would get his friends to bowl 'wet' tennis balls to him. This exercise served two purposes. Not only would the balls skid off the surface faster, but the soil that would get stuck to them because of their wetness, would leave an imprint on the bat. Sachin would check the location of the imprint after every stroke. If it was in the middle of the blade, then there was no problem. If it wasn't, then he would psyche himself to concentrate harder and watch the ball more closely.

> I was not in Achrekar Sir's stable initially, but with coach Anna Vaidya. At Shivaji Park, this buzz was there. I remember once I was in a bus with my mother. Sachin was in the same bus. I didn't know him then. I told my mother when we saw Sachin get off, 'That's Sachin Tendulkar. He will play for India'.
>
> —Amol Muzumdar, *The Times of India*, 14 November 2009

By then, Mumbai's famed cricketing grapevine had got into action. On the maidans, in the clubs, restaurants and tea-stalls that surrounded them, and in the offices of the Mumbai Schools Sports Association and the MCA, Sachin was being discussed by current and former players, officials, umpires, members of the groundstaff and even onlookers.

He was included in Mumbai's under-15 squad for the Vijay Merchant Trophy, but this was a forgettable outing. He was run out for two against Maharashtra, and the subsequent matches were abandoned due to rain. He was devastated to miss out on a spot in the under-15 West Zone side.

> I remember Abdul Ismail, our Coach and Manager when I was captain of the Mumbai under-15 team, saying, 'Sachin will play a high level of cricket and score lots of runs.' He picked the length of the ball extremely well and was always in position to play an attacking stroke rather than a defensive one. He had a sharp brain and figured out adjustments and corrective steps before coaches could point them out.
>
> —Rajesh Sanghi, *Sachin Forever*, MCA, 2013

In the monsoon of 1986, Sachin represented John Bright Cricket Club in the 'F' division of the Kanga League, and averaged nearly 20, which was as good as averaging five times that figure in a tournament played in normal non-monsoon conditions.

He was raring to go when the 1986–87 season commenced. His 123 for Mumbai against Maharashtra in the Vijay Merchant Trophy helped obliterate memories of his failure in the previous edition of the tournament. The knock ensured his inclusion in the under-15 West Zone squad. He impressed one and all in the inter-zonal tourney, with a knock of 74 against South Zone.

Sachin began the inter-school segment of the season with an innings of 276 against BPM High School in a Harris Shield game. Despite being only 13, he had been elevated to the vice-captaincy of Shardashram English's Harris

Shield squad on merit. He justified the promotion with 596 runs from five innings in the tournament, inclusive of an innings of 150 in the final against Shardashram's Marathi medium side, which was also coached by Achrekar. As captain of Shardashram English's Giles Shield side, Sachin led from the front with 665 runs from six innings. Shardashram English completed the 'double' that season, winning both the inter-school tournaments.

It wasn't batting alone that caught Sachin's fancy. He was also his side's frontline new-ball bowler. Against St Xavier's in the Harris Shield, he complemented his innings of 123 with figures of 8–29. In the semi-final of the Giles Shield against St Mary's High School, he scored 197 and bagged 5–75.

Ajit was by his side when he was interviewed by Sunil Warrier, a journalist working for *Mid-Day*, the Mumbai tabloid, in March 1987. The interview was conducted in an Irani restaurant close to Shivaji Park. The piece, which was titled 'Sachin—A New Star on the Horizon', dwelt on his versatility as a cricketer. It highlighted his scores in inter-school cricket, his preference for one-day cricket over four-day cricket, and his innate belligerence. It also mentioned his hero-worship of Sunil Gavaskar and Vivian Richards and his fondness for Western music. Warrier ended the piece by comparing Sachin to Sandeep Patil. For a Shivaji Park cricketer, it was a compliment to cherish.

Patil, a big-match player in his heyday, would have been proud of what Sachin did at the end of the 1986–87 season. Shardashram English took on IES English in the final of the Matunga Gujarati Seva Mandal Shield, on the Dadar Parsee Zoroastrian club's pitch at the Matunga Maidan. IES English fancied their chances against Shardashram English, having achieved a shock win over them in the quarter-final of the Giles Shield, just a year previously. In that game, Sachin had scored 48 on a dicey strip before being leg-before.

On the 'DPZ' pitch, IES English won the toss and opted to bowl. While on the way back to the clubhouse with his Shardashram counterpart after the toss, the IES captain was startled to see Sachin running towards his captain and asking him excitedly whether they were going to be batting first. At that instant, the IES skipper wondered whether he had erred by electing to field. However, the uncertainty evaporated when his bowlers claimed a couple of early wickets. As he viewed it, only one hurdle remained—Sachin.

The pride of Shardashram proceeded to take the IES English bowling apart. On the ground where the likes of Sunil Gavaskar and Dilip Vengsarkar had played their early cricket, Sachin rekindled memories of them at their best, reaching his hundred with a six and going on to score 216. The opposition players were shell-shocked, as much at the mauling as the amount of running they had to do to retrieve the ball, from the farthest corners of the maidan and beyond. Not for the last time, one of Sachin's opponents broke down in the dressing room.

From umpires to teammates to watchers to opponents, Sachin had impressed them all. However, there was an exception—the individuals who decided the winner of the MCA's annual award for the Best Junior Cricketer of the Year.

Sachin was gutted to miss out. In the heat of the moment, he even considered quitting the game altogether. His disappointment evaporated when, in the monsoon of 1987, he realized that he was in august company.

> I dropped Sunil [Gavaskar] at the airport on his way to England [in mid-1987]. On our way, we talked about local cricket. I expressed my surprise at the fact that the 14-year-old Sachin Tendulkar had not received the annual Best Junior Cricketer Award given by the Mumbai Cricket Association. By this time, we had reached the airport. Sunil had heard of the boy earlier. He pulled out his letterhead, placed it on the bonnet of the vehicle, and penned a letter, exhorting Sachin to carry on in the same vein, and not neglect his studies. He also wrote: 'Don't be disappointed at not getting the Best Junior Cricketer Award from the MCA. If you look at the names of the award winners, you will find one name missing, and that person has not done badly in Test cricket!' I gave the letter to Sachin's elder brother Ajit.
>
> —Hemant Waingankar in *SMG—A Biography of Sunil Manohar Gavaskar*

RUN-MACHINE

Because of the talent shown by Sachin, I never allowed him to play practice matches in the same age group. Sachin and Vinod were always pushed in higher age groups. Senior players were first aghast, then furious and finally frustrated.

—Ramakant Achrekar, *Mumbai Mirror*, 11 December 2005

Vasu Paranjape, the former Dadar Union captain and one of the country's foremost cricketing gurus and thinkers, was put in charge of a camp for the top under-15 cricketers in the country, which was held in the central Indian city of Indore, just before the start of the 1987-88 season.

I was woken up late on the first night by the sentry. He complained that the boys were playing cricket on the terrace. 'That fair boy [Sachin] was batting, and the others were bowling,' he said. I told the sentry to field for them.

—Vasu Paranjape, *Perfect Ten*, PMG, 1995

Whether it was disregarding a toe injury just so that he could get to play a game against a team comprising senior first-class cricketers or plotting the inundation of his campmates' room with water, Sachin had a great time in Indore. He was upset when his ultra-light leg-guards were stolen during this camp, but not for long.

In early 1987, my mentor, Ramakant Achrekar, asked me to hand over my batting leg-guards (pads) to a promising young batsman, Sachin Tendulkar. 'Your playing days are almost over,' said Achrekar, 'the ultralite leg-guards that you have are the ones that Sachin uses and his pair was stolen during the national under-15 camp recently,' he explained. That pair of leg-guards were handed over to me by the maestro Sunil Gavaskar. When Sachin came to my home to collect the leg-guards, I had no clue that I would unwittingly be part of a pre-ordained ceremony of fate where I would be the 'vehicle' that would pass on the baton of Indian cricket batting from one genius to another. I being a mere repository of an article that would protect the legs of two masters that were, literally, on the opposite sides of the spectrum called the 'Mumbai school of batting'.

—Hemant Kenkre, *The Asian Age*, 7 November 2013

Later, Sachin visited Gavaskar's home and presented him a 'Thank You' card, both for the letter and the leg-guards. The legend requested the schoolboy to inscribe the card. Unimpressed with what Sachin came up with, Gavaskar advised him to make his autograph more legible. This was important, as that would help people to identify his signature, 50 years down the line, Gavaskar explained.

Not for nothing was he considered a visionary.

Sachin's father had gifted him a Parker pen. Sachin tested it in school by signing repeatedly on rough sheets of paper. He was probably practising his autograph.

—Marcus Couto, personal interview

Sachin got to watch his hero in action from just outside the boundary rope in the 1987–88 season. The Indian team played two matches of the 1987 World Cup in Mumbai—a league game against Zimbabwe, and the semi-final against England. Sachin, who was one of the 'ball-boys' for the Zimbabwe game, had a close look at his idol's knock of 43, the first nine scoring strokes of which were boundaries. He was ecstatic when 'Mr. Gavaskar' took him to the Indian dressing room and introduced him to his teammates. The defending champions won that game by eight wickets, but their return to the Wankhede Stadium, for the semi-final against England, was forgettable. Set 255 to win, they began poorly, with Gavaskar falling for only 4, and despite fighting knocks by Mohammed Azharuddin and Kapil Dev, lost by 39 runs.

Nine days after the semi-final, the MCA announced its 30 probables for the 1987–88 edition of the Ranji Trophy. Sachin and his near and dear ones were thrilled to see his name in the same list as Sunil Gavaskar's. On the same day, the media also reported Gavaskar's decision to quit international cricket. The Little Master's fans, who had at the back of their minds, an earlier statement by him that he would continue to play first-class cricket after quitting international cricket, were excited at the possibility of his and Sachin's playing for Mumbai together, in case the youngster made it to the final squad. However, they were in for a disappointment. Gavaskar went on to declare himself unavailable for first-class cricket as well.

Even as one glorious career ended, the Mumbai selectors initiated another. Sachin was picked in the Mumbai team that was announced on 9 December 1987, for the side's first Ranji Trophy game of the season, against Vadodara. He was the youngest-ever cricketer to figure in Mumbai's Ranji squad. His selection had the blessings of both the captain and manager.

Dilip Vengsarkar, the reigning Mumbai and India captain, would rather he had watched Sachin bat before taking a call on him, but then, he was far too busy representing his country, city and office. He therefore chose to trust Vasu Paranjape, who was convinced that the teenager deserved an apprenticeship at the first-class level. Sandeep Patil, the manager of the Mumbai team, had first seen Sachin in the mid-1980s. He had requested Anna Vaidya and Ramakant Achrekar to get some of their boys to participate in a film shoot at the RCF Ground in Chembur, a north-eastern suburb of Mumbai, and Sachin was among those who turned up. Patil watched the boy bowl tirelessly, and was surprised when the two gurus, both of whom were sticklers for perfection and not known to get carried away easily, waxed eloquent about the boy's batting abilities. In the years that followed, Patil kept track of Sachin's exploits and endorsed Sachin's selection in the Mumbai squad.

> He was in the reserves against Baroda at Baroda. The practice pitches are not always good for batsmen. They are sometimes underprepared, bouncy, turning and sometimes nasty. There were a few seniors who would come out after batting for five minutes, but Sachin would not have any difficulty. He simply loved batting, irrespective of the nature of the pitch. I penalised him for reporting ten minutes late at the Motibaug Palace Ground. I made him run two laps of the ground before commencing his routine practice. This happened again at the Wankhede Stadium.... I was a little embarrassed punishing a 15 year-old.
>
> —Sandeep Patil, *The Sportstar*, 25 April 1992

I did feel a few changes and some pressure when I played in this selection trial match before I was picked for Mumbai. I never used to wear a helmet in inter-school matches. It was a green-topped pitch at the Wankhede and the rival attack had Raju Kulkarni, Rajendra Lele, Pradeep Kasliwal and Satish Pawar, all four of them fast bowlers. And I had gone in without a helmet. I did not realise then that if you don't wear a helmet, the fast bowlers will bounce at you. Raju started bouncing the ball and those days it was something new to me.... It was a great experience playing fast bowlers without a helmet. I got 55 and [Sanjay] Manjrekar got a century. And that was the first big match when I realised that there was a lot of difference between school cricket and top-class cricket. Because when I used to off-drive Raju (Kulkarni), the shots would go to cover or point because of the speed.

—Sachin Tendulkar, *The Sportstar*, 6 May 1995

Sachin did not wear a helmet in the practice game because he did not possess one. He handled Kulkarni's bouncers deftly and even hit him for a couple of boundaries, before giving the bowler a return catch. He accompanied Mumbai for all its league matches, and spent some time on the field as a substitute. His stint ended on a memorable note, when Vengsarkar gifted him a Gunn and Moore bat.

I was practising with Vengsarkar, Manjrekar and Shastri. Raju Kulkarni used to bowl in the nets. I played with players like Chandrakant Pandit and many others who had played at the first-class level for a long time, like Shishir Hattangadi and Alan Sippy. I think Kiran Mokashi also helped me a lot, which I will never forget. After the net was over, he would say, 'Pad up Sachin, I will bowl at you again.' So all these factors contributed to my early rise in cricket.

—Sachin Tendulkar, *The Sportstar*, 14 September 2002

The teenager's initiation into first-class cricket, albeit as a reserve, and Gavaskar's retirement from cricket were preceded by the end of a life dedicated to cricket and humanity. On 20 October 1987, Vijay Merchant passed into the ages.

Sachin's age did not deter the selectors from making the 14-year-old the captain of Mumbai's under-17 squad for that season's edition of the inter-state Vijay Hazare Trophy. While many of his teammates were senior to him in terms of age and even experience, Sachin was by far the best in terms of performance. He went on to score heavily in not only the under-17 tournament but also in the under-15 Vijay Merchant Trophy. He was also in top form for West Zone in the under-15 and under-17 tournaments. His best performance in the latter was an innings of 175 against East Zone at Kanpur. He had a long session in the nets after playing that innings, an indication that he was far from satiated! He found a fan in the form of a member of the East Zone team, who had been at the receiving end of his pranks at the all-India camp at Indore, earlier in the season. His name was Sourav Ganguly.

Sachin's performances at the under-15 and under-17 levels ensured his promotion to under-19 cricket, only for the law of averages to catch up with him. In the under-19 inter-zonal tournament, his performances were below-par and he ended up missing out on a spot in the Indian team that toured Australia for the first-ever 'Youth' (under-19) World Cup in early 1988. The good thing was that he was far too focused on the game to view this as a setback. By then, he had also forgotten the MCA's rebuff of the previous season. It wasn't often that a schoolboy cricketer received a letter from a batsman who had scored 10,122 runs in Tests, after all.

On 23 February 1988, five days before the inaugural under-19 World Cup was to get underway in Australia, Shardashram English took on St Xavier's High School on the Sassanian Club pitch at the Azad Maidan, in the semi-final of the Harris Shield. It was a three-day game.

Sachin, who was leading Shardashram, won the toss and elected to bat. Rupak Mulye, his opener–wicketkeeper, fell at 29. The next 'boy' in was a left-hander called Vinod Kambli. He and Atul Ranade, Sachin's friend from his old school who had also shifted to Shardashram, added 55 before the latter fell. Kambli was then joined in the middle by his captain and chum.

Their respective family backgrounds could not have been more disparate. Vinod Kambli, the eldest of three sons of Ganpat Kambli, a mechanic by profession, spent his early childhood in a joint family comprising 18 people, all of whom lived in one room in the congested area of Bhendi Bazaar, not very far from the Azad Maidan. In 1985, Ganpat Kambli shifted to a chawl in the north-central Mumbai suburb of Kanjurmarg with his wife and three sons. Kambli senior was a club cricketer of repute, and Vinod, his eldest son, would accompany him for matches. It was on the maidans that Vinod fell in love with the game. Like Sachin, he changed schools and shifted to Shardashram after Achrekar sensed his potential. Unlike Sachin, he relied financially on his teachers and Achrekar himself for his fees, railway pass and cricket equipment. Every morning, Vinod would leave his Kanjurmarg home at the crack of dawn and board a train for Dadar. It was a 25-minute journey. Since he would have a cricket kit with him in addition to his school bag, travelling in the crowded general compartment was not an option. He would therefore board the baggage compartment and share space with fisherwomen who were on their way to the market to sell their catch. From Dadar station, he would tow his kit and schoolbag to Shardashram, which was a 15-minute walk away.

Keeping him company during his daily walk from school to Shivaji Park after 2:00 p.m. were his friends and teammates, Sachin and Ricky Couto. After practice ended at seven in the evening, Vinod would have dinner at a friend's place and then take a train home. He would reach home by midnight, go to bed and wake up at five the next morning to repeat the sequence.

Thousands of Mumbaikars, who live in the far-flung suburbs and work in the central and southern parts of the city, follow a similar schedule, day in and day out. But Vinod was a child, just a year older than Sachin, when he adopted this regimen to pursue his cricketing ambitions.

Most children in his place would have given up. However, Vinod did not. His response to adversity was exemplary. Desmond Haynes, the West Indies opener whom he idolized, was known to wear a locket that bore the three Ls—Live, Love and Laugh. Vinod strove to do likewise. As a batsman, he was as dedicated and run-hungry as Sachin. In fact, his left-handedness gave him a slight edge over his friend. There weren't too many of that breed around at any level in Indian cricket in the 1980s.

Achrekar demanded hard work from his wards, and the two boys would deliver precisely that and a lot more. In the nets, he would find it difficult to get them to end their batting stints and give the others a chance. He allowed them to grow and flourish as cricketers, but not at the expense of discipline and ethics. Vinod was once slapped for dropping his bat and flying a kite that had strayed onto the ground, during an inter-school game.

> One favourite story that Baba [father] always told us was about how he had slapped Sachin after he went to watch a match at the Wankhede, instead of playing in one [that had been specially arranged for him]. 'If you play, the public will clap for you,' he told Sachin.
>
> —Kalpana Achrekar (daughter of Ramakant Achrekar),
> *Sachin Forever*, MCA, 2013

On the Sassanian Club pitch on 23 February 1988, Sachin was put down in the slips and Vinod Kambli survived a confident appeal for leg-before. Shardashram's numbers three and four made the most of these reprieves. At stumps, Sachin was on 192 and Kambli on 182. Amol Muzumdar, who was slated to bat next, had a net at the end of the day's play, just to keep himself in the groove.

The Shardashram players had by then established a routine for inter-school matches on the maidans of south Mumbai. If they were chasing a target, they would bring the team within 30–40 runs of victory by stumps. That would mean that they would have to return the next morning to finish the game and, in the process, get another day off from school! They would wrap up the game in the morning and then troop to either a cinema or the beach to play 'unstructured' cricket.

Unfortunately for the St Xavier's cricket team, it appeared that the Shardashram duo was in the mood to have a blast on the pitch itself, when the Harris Shield semi-final resumed on the morning of 24 February 1988. The third-wicket partnership encompassed the whole of the second day. As the runs piled up, so did the spectators. Cricketers playing on the adjoining pitches halted and watched, as did the passers-by. As the news spread, the media rushed to the venue.

> Tendulkar and Kambli were known to us Test players even when they were playing school cricket. This was quite rare, but the Mumbai cricketing grapevine had taken care of that. Our grassroots cricket 'reporter' Kiran Mokashi ensured that we were adequately informed about this prodigious talent. Let's not forget that Kiran was himself a top-class Ranji player at the time, but it seemed he was more dedicated towards promoting the talent of others than his own.
>
> —Sanjay Manjrekar, *Sachin Forever*, MCA, 2013

Sachin and Vinod drove, cut, pulled, swept, ran and did pretty much what they pleased. Achrekar was engaged elsewhere, and he had advised Laxman Chavan, his assistant, to keep him posted on the scores. When the score passed 500, Chavan telephoned the coach. He was instructed to tell Sachin to declare. The coach wanted his team to bowl the opposition out on the same day, so that Sachin could play a Giles Shield game that was to start the next day. However, there was a catch—Chavan could not cross the boundary line when the match was in progress. When he started signalling to the boys in the middle, Sachin assumed that he was trying to pass on his own instructions and suggested to Vinod that they ignore him. Even as Chavan ran around the boundary line, gesticulating wildly to convey the message, the duo batted on, and on, and on. Both being music buffs, they spent their mid-pitch conversations humming Wham's 'Wake Me up before You Go Go,' one of their favourites. It was finally at lunch that an exasperated Chavan told them that their coach was not going to be thrilled at the turn of events.

As was only to be expected, Achrekar lashed out at the boys when they called him from a public telephone. Vinod, who was one short of 350, pleaded with the coach to be allowed to score just one run, but to no avail. Sachin was left with no doubt that Sir meant business.

The scoreboard read 748–2. Sachin (326*) and Vinod (349*) had added an undefeated 664. The opposition was demoralized, to say the least. One of the bowlers was 'cheered' derisively after the scorers announced that he had conceded more than 200 runs. Another bowler broke down and refused to complete an over after Vinod hit his first three balls for six. These were schoolboys, after all.

It wasn't only Sachin and Vinod who enhanced their respective reputations that afternoon. Sairaj Bahutule, the St Xavier's captain, may not have heard the term 'man-management' at that stage of his life, but he ended up learning it on the job, as it were. He had to prod, coax and goad his team to carry on, even as he struggled with the mental baggage of knowing that in a way, he was responsible for the carnage, having dropped Sachin in the slips the day before. A talented leg-spinner and left-handed batsman, Bahutule went on to play for India and Mumbai, much to the delight of many a cricket quizmaster.*

The 664-run partnership was monumental enough to be reported even by newspapers not based in Mumbai. Already a star on the local circuit, Sachin made an impact at the national level. Thanks to the perseverance of Marcus Couto, Ricky's elder brother and a member of the newly instituted Association of Cricket Statisticians and Scorers of India (ACSSI), it was conclusively established that the stand was the highest in any class of cricket. The record was previously held by T. Palton and N. Rippon, who had added 641 for Buffalo River against Whoroughly at Gapstead in the Australian state of Victoria, way back in 1913–14. 'Tendulkar and Kambli' went on to find mentions in the *Wisden Almanack*, the premier cricketing publication that had been brought out annually since 1864, and also in the Guinness Book of World Records. The boys were feted by the ACSSI and later by the Sports Journalists Association of Mumbai where the chief guest was a certain S.M. Gavaskar.

The boys also attracted the attention of Sungrace-Mafatlal, a corporate house that was one of the biggest promoters of cricket in the country and had a competitive cricket team. Hemant Waingankar, a former university-level cricketer of repute who happened to be the manager/secretary of Sungrace-Mafatlal, and Suresh Trivedi, vice-president of the organization, were spoken to by Sharad Kotnis, senior journalist, about the possibility of sponsoring talented schoolboy cricketers. Achrekar himself had had a separate discussion with Waingankar on the same. For the organization, it represented an opportunity to identify and

---

*One of the commonest questions asked in cricket quizzes is—'Name the future Test cricketer who was part of the team against whom Tendulkar and Kambli added a record 664 in an inter-school match.'

nurture talent, and eventually rope the beneficiaries into its own cricket team when they turned 18. The proposal was accepted by Atulya Mafatlal, its vice-chairman, and Sachin and Vinod were both awarded a scholarship. In addition to a monthly cheque for ₹200 each, Sungrace-Mafatlal also provided for their school fees, books and uniforms, cricketing equipment and any other assistance, if required. Anil Joshi, a member of the Sungrace-Mafatlal cricket team and a former pupil of Achrekar's, was one of their points of contact.

> After they got the scholarship, Sachin and Vinod would come over to watch Sungrace-Mafatlal's cricket matches in local inter-office tournaments, whenever they could. They were enthusiastic and street-smart. I remember them visiting the office once and making some desultory conversation. When I realized that the talk was going nowhere, I asked them if they needed anything from me, as I wanted to get back to work. It was then that Sachin prodded Vinod, 'You made me accompany you all the way to the office, and now you aren't saying anything. Why don't you tell him that you wanted some shirts?' Vinod responded by asking Sachin why he was silent about his wanting a new bat. So essentially, they would fire from each other's shoulders! Both were inducted into the Sungrace-Mafatlal side when they turned 18, as was the plan. They represented us whenever they were available, for nearly a decade. I would visit Shardashram every month with their cheques and give them to the principal. She would then summon Sachin and Vinod to her cabin and hand over the cheques to them. Those were their first earnings in cricket.
>
> —Anil Joshi, personal interview

Sachin and Vinod could think on their feet on and off the field. They had this habit of 'raiding' the tiffin-boxes of their teammates before the scheduled time for lunch. Once, they polished off stir-fried okras* (ladies' fingers) before going in to bat, not realising that the lunch-box they had 'hijacked' belonged to a teacher and not a teammate. Both were in the middle when the 12th man ran onto the field to tell them what they had done. They put together a partnership and were unbeaten at the tea interval. Back in the tent, they walked past the teammates who were clapping for them and went straight to the teacher in question. Both 'thanked' the lady for the 'delicious' okra 'that had inspired them to bat well'. They described it as 'magical',

---

*Known as 'bhendichi bhaaji' in Maharashtra.

among other things. The teacher was so touched that she brought along two lunch-boxes of the vegetable to the ground for the rest of the season.

—Marcus Couto, personal interview

A few days after Sachin and Kambli's heroics in the Harris Shield semi-final, Shardashram English took on Anjuman-E-Islam in the final at the Brabourne Stadium, home of the Cricket Club of India (CCI). Minutes before the start of play, one individual made a beeline for the balcony of the clubhouse.

To say that Raj Singh Dungarpur loved cricket was an understatement to beat all other understatements. After representing Rajasthan in the Ranji Trophy for several seasons, he had had stints as national selector and manager of the Indian team. He had also done cricket commentary on radio and presented cricket highlights packages on TV, and would go on to be appointed chairman of the National Selection Committee. Keeping him company on the balcony of the clubhouse was his father who was as passionate about the sport and had read about the 664-run stand.

Much to the delight of the Dungarpurs, Shardashram won the toss and elected to bat. Much to the delight of the Anjuman-E-Islam supporters, Kambli fell early. The previous day, the coach-manager of Anjuman-E-Islam had met Ajit Tendulkar and told him that 'the match would be theirs if they got Sachin early'.

> Such was his awe, that even before he took his guard, there was a deep mid-on, a deep mid-off, a deep extra-cover, and a deep mid-wicket. I could quite see what the schoolboys thought of his cricket. I think he was playing on a full-size cricket ground for the first time. He took four or five singles with sizzling drives. He was not mechanical. Soon after, he started playing the ball into the gaps, so that the fielders had to run, and converted ones into twos and twos into threes. It was amazing. Nobody could have grasped it as quickly as he did. I was left in no doubt that I was watching a future Test cricketer.

—Raj Singh Dungarpur, *Sachin Tendulkar—Mr. India*, PMG, 2002

Sachin scored an unbeaten 346 and was carried off the field by his teammates. As his innings progressed, the number of watchers increased, but one individual who missed out was Dilip Vengsarkar. He rushed to the CCI after getting a message that Sachin was going great guns, but he was late. Anjuman-E-Islam had started their innings by the time he reached. The Shield was eventually shared between the two teams.

I first saw him in the inter-school final at Brabourne Stadium, a few days after he had had that partnership with Vinod Kambli. From then on, we just kept following him and his performances till he played for Mumbai. We came to know him as someone who was being looked at as the future of Indian cricket.

—Prof. R.S. Shetty, personal interview

Sachin's second successive triple hundred marked the end of an extraordinary run in inter-school cricket. His average in the Harris Shield was a modest 1,025. He had scored that many runs in five outings, and had been dismissed only once. The figure was staggering enough to prompt a Kolkata-based journalist to report it in the Bengali daily he worked for. However, the sub-editor on the sports desk goofed up by thinking that his colleague had goofed up. After all, how could a schoolboy cricketer have a four-digit average? Surely it was '125!' He left out the zero in 1025.

Something similar had happened in the case of another teenage prodigy in the Montreal Olympics in 1976; the spectators were stunned when Nadia Comăneci's flawless performance in the Uneven Bars event (Gymnastics) was awarded a score of 1.00. She had, in fact, scored a perfect ten, but the electronic scoreboard at the venue wasn't equipped to flash the same; it had room for only three digits.

What prevented 1987–88 from being a perfect ten of a season for Sachin was Shardashram English's loss to St Mary's in the Giles Shield final. The game, played at the Shivaji Park Gymkhana in April 1988, witnessed scenes that were to be repeated across the cricketing world for the next two decades and more.

St Mary's batted first and scored 518. Shardashram lost two early wickets, but they weren't worried, as their talisman was in tremendous form. He got a life early in his innings and Kiran Asher, the St Mary's coach, had just about started fearing the worst when a delivery bowled by Khurram Darbar, a left-arm spinner, kept low and trapped Sachin plumb in front. The dismissal was followed by delirium in the St Mary's ranks. Some parents watching the game dashed off to find a phone to spread the news, and others brought a cake to the ground. Asher was furious with the premature celebrations, but his wards stayed focused and clinched the title.

I remember a headline in one of the newspapers the following morning: 'St Mary's in driver's seat as Tendulkar fails'. I thought to myself, 'Bloody hell, this guy makes the headlines even if he doesn't get runs.

—Amol Muzumdar, *Mid-Day*, 21 October 2013

If that headline reminded some cricket aficionados of a former Australian batsman who averaged 99.94 in Tests and whose rare failures had inspired similar headlines, no one dwelt on the same for too long. The fact was that Sachin was by no means the first schoolboy to light up the maidans of the metropolis with his feats in junior-level cricket. Among his many predecessors was the St Mary's coach himself. Asher had been a heavy scorer at the junior level, but had somehow failed to make it to the big league. While watchers had no doubt that Sachin looked a class apart, they were not going to jump the gun.

Sachin kept a similar newspaper clipping in his pocket. It would come in handy when there was an argument to be won.

> He always seemed to have it at hand when Vinod used to talk about his scores. He used to pull it out and say to Vinod, 'forget your fifties, see this…even when I scored a duck, I got a headline.'
>
> —Ricky Couto, *Mid-Day*, 1 November 2013

Sachin and Vinod were regular visitors to their teammate Ricky Couto's house. There, Sachin would insist on Ricky playing a short action clip of the former Australian batsman, whose rare failures used to make as much news as his many successes, on the video. This individual had retired from international cricket a quarter of a century before Sachin's birth, but he was no stranger to those who played or followed cricket in later decades.

> Luckily for Sachin, there is a calming influence over him, just so he doesn't get carried away by this acclaim. His coach Achrekar knows exactly what he is talking about. 'He is not perfect yet…. He still has a lot of faults, particularly while driving through the on, which is an indicator of a class batsman. He still has a long way to go, but what I like about him is his ability to work hard. I don't think we should get carried away by his scores. After all, one has to take into account the nature of the wicket and the quality of the bowlers. By his standards the quality of the bowling he faced was not good enough.' Achrekar, in fact, is quite upset about the publicity Sachin is getting. 'People don't realise that he is just 15. They keep calling him for some felicitation or the other. The other day he was asked to inaugurate a children's library. This is ridiculous. These things are bound to go to his head. He will start thinking he has achieved everything. I hope all this stops so he can concentrate and work hard…. I think he should be playing the Ranji Trophy next year…. ' Clearly the

curtain call is still a long way off for Sachin Tendulkar. He has a lot of things going for him.

—Harsha Bhogle, *Sportsworld*, 1988

Achrekar need not have worried. Among the many lessons he had imparted to his pupils was that no individual was bigger than the sport itself. It was a lesson Sachin would never forget.

Another milestone was around the corner. Sachin's commitments for Mumbai, West Zone and Shardashram in the 1987–88 season had forced him to miss out on games for Shivaji Park Youngsters, the club he was a part of at that point. Providentially, he was available for his club for a Purshottam Shield encounter against the Cricket Club of India. Before the match commenced, Ajit was informed by Hemant Kenkre, who was part of the CCI side, that the club wanted to engage Sachin for the next season. Ajit and Achrekar were also spoken to in his regard by Milind Rege, the former Mumbai captain, who was now a junior selector and the cricket secretary of the CCI.

It was a no-brainer. Sachin would have played in the elite 'A' division of the Kanga League anyway, with several clubs vying for him, but then, the CCI was a venerated institution. There was no way he would miss out on the opportunity to hone his skills at the Brabourne Stadium, an international arena.

Whatever doubts any member of the CCI side may have had about his abilities, Sachin quelled them with a knock of 76 for the Shivaji Park Youngsters on a wicket that was behaving unpredictably. Among those he impressed was a sexagenarian, who had been a witness to more than five decades of Indian cricket and cricketers, from Col. C.K. Nayudu to Kapil Dev. Madhav Apte, who had opened for India quite successfully in the early 1950s and led Mumbai to two Ranji Trophy titles in the late 1950s and early 1960s, advised Sachin to 'wait for the ball to come to him', instead of pushing at it. He discovered that the teenager was a quick learner.

> That was the first time I watched him bat.... Hemant Kenkre told me, 'Just watch him.' I asked, '*Kon aahe?*' (Who is he?). 'Sachin', was Hemant's reply. The name instantly rang a bell.... For a young boy, it was absolutely brilliant—his strokeplay, his placement of shots and the shot-selection. At the end of the day's play, my teammates asked me what I thought of him. I said, 'I have been playing and watching cricket for over 50 years in the city. I have seen a lot of talent. I hadn't seen Sunil Gavaskar when he was 14 and a half. So, I can't compare. But, otherwise, this is an outstanding

talent. If this boy should keep his head on his shoulder, he should play for India sooner than later.

—Madhav Apte, www.cricketcountry.com, 7 November 2013

Sachin was of course no stranger to the Brabourne Stadium. He had played inter-school matches there, including the Harris Shield semi-final against Anjuman-E-Islam in which he scored 346. He had also fielded at the venue as a substitute, that too for a Pakistan XI captained by Imran Khan, in a festival match against an India XI, which was played in February 1987 to commemorate the CCI's Golden Jubilee. However, at no point had he been allowed to enter the clubhouse, which was out of bounds for minors. Madhav Apte himself had not been allowed to enter the clubhouse when he had represented the club in his teens.

In 1988, Apte, who was now the president of the CCI, was determined not to let history repeat itself. He discussed the issue with another admirer of Sachin's—Raj Singh Dungarpur. The duo convened an Executive Committee Meeting where it was decided to 'make an exception'. That paved the way for Sachin's inclusion in the CCI squad—and into the clubhouse—despite his being only 15.

Sachin announced his presence in the 'A' division of the Kanga League with a bang. The first ball he faced for the CCI was bowled by Sharad Rao, a competent new-ball bowler who had represented Mumbai in the Ranji Trophy. Sachin hit him over mid-off for six.

For cricketers who swore by the Mumbai School of Batting and the values it prescribed, like 'playing in the V and along the ground till you got your eye in', this was new. But then, Sachin was a product of Shivaji Park, and he had grown up in the era of limited-overs cricket. Most importantly, he possessed the ability and assurance to pull these audacious acts off.

Hemant Kenkre was Sachin's first captain at the CCI. Sandeep Patil, the incumbent, was available for the club's next game, and it was decided that the Shivaji Park senior would bat just below the junior in the middle order, to bolster the chances of the duo batting together. The view was that Patil could then 'groom' Sachin. This was in keeping with the traditions of Mumbai cricket.

We at the CCI decided to give this boy a feel of the 'big' company.... In difficult conditions of the Kanga League, Sachin played like a grown-up man. On a drying track, Sachin was right on top of the ball. Even the seniors in the team fell by way of class.

—Milind Rege, *Sportsweek*, 25 December–31 December 1988

It wasn't that the Kanga League was not covered by the media, but the presence of photographers at games was uncommon, unless an international cricketer was playing. However, lensmen started making their presence felt at the matches, just to 'shoot' Sachin. While he wasn't the first teenage prodigy that the maidans had seen, he was certainly the first to be chased by members of the fourth estate in this fashion.

He made a habit of revelling in adverse conditions. During a 'home' Kanga League encounter against New Hind Sporting Club, the CCI side wore a depleted look with their leading lights engaged in fulfilling their league cricket commitments on foreign shores. On what was a tricky Brabourne pitch, the hosts lost a few early wickets and Sachin, the sole surviving specialist batsman, was instructed to play safe. He complied till it was time for lunch. At the interval, he approached his seniors and requested their permission to bat the way he wanted to, for a few overs. When the team management agreed, his happiness knew no bounds. He strode out and launched an offensive, belting the ball to the farthest corners of the venue.

Before joining the CCI, Sachin made his first foreign trip as a member of the under-19 'Star Cricket Club' side in mid-1988. Kailash Gattani, the former Rajasthan paceman, was the manager of the team. He had been associated with this annual visit to England since 1986, the objective of which was to give India's best under-19 cricketers, an opportunity to hone their skills in alien conditions. With most of the boys belonging to middle-class families, their trips had to be funded. Sachin's 1988 visit was 'sponsored' by the Kolkata-based Young Cricketers' Organization. The boys played nearly 25 matches at different venues in England, most of them 50-overs-a-side encounters.

> The cost of the airfare was ₹13,600. I remember Sachin's father and mother coming to the airport to drop him along with his brothers Ajit and Nitin. For a 15-year-old boy, he had such a mature head on his shoulders.... There came a time when I had to tell him that he would not play all the games. If he was not playing in a particular match, he would coax his teammates who were fielding, to come in for a break, so that he could field. And when he had no option but to stay away from the field, he would be a scorer. You could tell the difference between the others and him in this aspect too. His inscriptions were neatly written. Everything in his kitbag was neatly kept as well.
>
> —Kailash Gattani, *Mid-Day*, 18 October 2013

One of his best performances on this 'study tour' was an unbeaten 70 against a team from Pakistan, which comprised a battery of pace bowlers. A Ranji Trophy debut in the forthcoming season was imminent.

IN THE BIG LEAGUE

In early February of 1989, I flew from Kolkata to Mumbai to interview a boy—an encounter that would effectively alter my life. Cricket had yet to explode across the nation, money was tight and teenagers who hadn't played for India came to the office and pleaded for a paragraph—you did not go to them. But this kid, even then he demanded your attention. Of course, it was a disaster. Sachin was 15, squeaky, uncomfortable, and in the end, politely asked, 'Okay, can I get back to the cricket?' For the first and only time, I agreed.... The only story worth remembering was that he spoke cricket in his sleep, and surely still does....

—Rohit Brijnath, *Wisden Asia Cricket*, September 2002

Sachin began the 1988–89 season with another fruitful outing as leading batsman and captain of Mumbai's under-17 side in the Vijay Hazare Trophy. Technically and temperamentally, he was in the right form and frame of mind respectively, for a baptism in Ranji Trophy.

The selectors apart, there was another individual whose opinion mattered. Dilip Vengsarkar, the captain of India, was yet to see Sachin bat in a competitive game. In November 1988, on the eve of a Test match against the touring New Zealanders at Mumbai, Vengsarkar instructed Sachin to report to the India nets. Impressed by Sachin's handling of the best bowlers in the land, Vengsarkar then subjected him to the ultimate test. Abetted by Dungarpur, who was by then chairing the National Selection Committee, the Indian skipper requested his long-time teammate, and a man who had been the lynchpin of India's bowling attack for a decade, to test the youngster out.

While Sachin had played the best fast bowlers in Mumbai earlier, facing an individual he had grown up idolizing was going to be a different proposition altogether.

> I was in no mood to bowl because I did not want anything to happen to him and also since I had removed my spikes. Yet, out of respect for Rajbhai [Raj Singh Dungarpur], I must have bowled seven or eight deliveries.... I

let one go to test him. He flicked it off his hips and I realised that he had the time to play his shots.

—Kapil Dev, *Cricket Forever*, MCA, 2013

When the gloves and pads came off, Sachin became a star-struck teenager. He was so excited to have faced Kapil Dev that he could not sleep that night.

> The shy lad, only 15-and-a-half years old, walked into the Mumbai dressing room and found himself a corner seat. 'That is Sunil Gavaskar's seat,' I told him, and he sprang on his feet, wanting to move to the other side. 'Sorry,' he said. I put him at ease and said that he could have it. 'But remember, you have to make that seat permanently yours.' I remember there were two schools of thought when it came to selecting him in the playing XI against Gujarat. Our chief selector Ramakant Desai was of the opinion that we should not expose him to the rigours of first-class cricket but groom him with time.... His colleagues Milind Rege and Naren Tamhane were convinced that we could play him.

—Lalchand Rajput, *Sachin Forever*, MCA, 2013

The majority prevailed. History was created on 10 December 1988 when Sachin was included in Mumbai's playing XI for their first Ranji Trophy game of the season against Gujarat. He was only 15-and-a-half and the youngest-ever cricketer to represent Mumbai in the premier domestic competition.

Sachin's inclusion in the XI was preceded by a bizarre happening. He missed three days of practice and an upset Vengsarkar asked Vasu Paranjape to have a word with him. Sachin's explanation for his playing truant was that he had a drawing examination at school! Paranjape, a man endowed with the gift of the gab, was quick to 'advise' Sachin to tell his teachers to take his 'driving' exam instead.

On the eve of his debut game, Sachin requested Sairaj Bahutule, the former St Xavier's captain and a teammate of both Sachin and Vinod's in the Mumbai under-17 side, to lend him his bat. Sachin had used his bat earlier and liked its 'feel'. Bahutule was only too glad to oblige. Kedar Godbole, another talented cricketer of the time, delivered the bat to Sachin.

It wouldn't be the last time Sachin would score a significant century with a bat that belonged to someone else.

Lunch was nearing on day two of the Ranji game against Gujarat when Lalchand Rajput, a former disciple of Achrekar's and Mumbai's stand-in skipper in the absence of Vengsarkar, who was on national duty, was run out on 99. Mumbai at that stage were a healthy 206–2 in response to Gujarat's 140, and Sachin made his way to the middle. It wasn't very often that one came across a teenager batting in his favoured slot on his first-class debut for a team of which he was the youngest and most inexperienced member. It was just that he had not given the administrators, selectors and of course, the captains he had played under at different levels from 1984 to 1988, any reason to question Achrekar's decision to assign the 'two-down' slot to him.

As he walked to the middle, Sachin stuck to his time-and-tested technique of donning his gloves, to take his mind off the 'non-controllables'—comments made by the fielders or the claps of the spectators—and enclose himself into a cocoon, so that nothing would matter, save the incoming ball and the positioning of the fielders. Even at that stage of his career, Sachin was doing what the greatest of batsmen were known to do—live 'one ball' at a time.

The time he had spent on the cricket field since 1984 had left him with little energy to check up on the history of the sport and read about the cricketers who had represented Mumbai, by far the most successful domestic team in the history of the sport. His ignorance helped him to be oblivious to the presence of those who had flocked to the Wankhede Stadium that morning, just to see him in action. Raj Singh Dungarpur and Naren Tamhane, members of the National Selection Committee were both there as were Sudhir Naik and Milind Rege, former Mumbai captains and now selectors. Eknath Solkar, one of India and Mumbai's most popular cricketers, was in attendance, as were Vasu Paranjape and Sunil Gavaskar.

The teenager was far more conscious of the presence of his Sahitya Sahawas and school friends in the North Stand. Ajit was there, as well.

Sachin's first bowling opponent in first-class cricket was the off-spinner Nisarg Patel. After two defensive strokes, Sachin fluently drove the third ball he received, *against* the turn. The ball rocketed through the covers for four. It was an appropriate way in which to open his account in first-class cricket. Two more defensive shots later, he drove the bowler past mid-on—*with* the turn—for another four. To those watching, these were not the strokes of a newcomer.

> While there was a boyishness in his humour, his observational skills were quite awesome. He could impersonate some of the great cricketers he may have watched as he played in the by-lanes of Bandra east and Sahitya Sahawas. An eye for detail, be it the quality of his willow and the fitting of his gear or even the complete focus of the job on hand even when it

came to eating his lunch. The concentration was unflappably admirable.

—Shishir Hattangadi, *Mid-Day*, 30 October 2013

In the post-lunch session, Sachin exhibited his full repertoire of front and back-foot strokes. At tea, he was in his 80s, the second new ball having made no difference to his belligerence. In the dressing room, Rajput declared that he would not feel bad to have got out on 99 if the teenager got a hundred.

Sachin was not fazed by the loss of partners in quick succession after the resumption. He moved to 99 with an exquisite off-drive off left-arm spinner Bharat Mistry, meeting a flighted delivery by advancing down the wicket, and giving it the treatment despite the presence of two men in the deep. The moment that everybody was waiting for, came soon after. He glanced a quicker delivery to square-leg, and ran a single. The Sahitya Sahawas and Shardashram brigades in the North Stand, exploded. Bang opposite them, the experts, who were sitting in the Garware Pavilion right above the dressing rooms, looked at each other and nodded their heads in appreciation.

Sachin was only 15 years, 7 months and 17 days old, when he became the youngest centurion in the Ranji Trophy, that too on debut.

As he applauded his kid brother's feat, Ajit's thoughts must have gone back to his first meeting with Achrekar 'Sir'. He would have also remembered the scores of high scores that Sachin had notched up at different levels in different tournaments, over the next four years. With his kid brother having cemented his place in Mumbai's Ranji Trophy team, at least for the next few matches, with a century on debut, Ajit would have also recollected a conversation he had had with Sachin, prior to the start of the 1987–88 edition of the under-15 Vijay Merchant Trophy.

Sachin had asked him what would happen if he succeeded in the tournament. 'You may be considered for the Mumbai under-17 side,' Ajit had replied. Another question followed—'What if I do well at the under-17 level as well?' Ajit responded by saying that he might then be considered for the domestic and international under-19 tournaments. The elder brother in him knew that another question was on its way. 'If you do well at the under-19 level, then the selectors may include you in the Mumbai Ranji Trophy side,' he had told Sachin, even before the question was asked.

Sachin had achieved precisely that without playing at the under-19 level!

In the next Ranji game against Saurashtra, Sachin marked out his guard after Mumbai lost two wickets without a run on the board on a square turner at Rajkot. He went on to score 58, adding 133 with Shishir Hattangadi. Ashok

Patel, a seasoned off-spinner who had represented India in eight ODIs, was thwarted by deft footwork and hit against the turn several times. In the second innings, Sachin did even better, essaying crisp strokes on the way to 89, before being caught at point *against the run of play*.

This was to be an irritant throughout his career.

Sachin followed these performances with 17 against Vadodara, and a classy 81 against Maharashtra. Those who watched the 'Trans-Sahyadri' clash between traditional rivals Mumbai and Maharashtra were treated to a duel between two youngsters who had made memorable debuts earlier in the season—Sachin and Salil Ankola, the Maharashtra quickie who had taken a hat-trick in his first game. The speedster did his best to intimidate the batsman with pace and bounce, but the latter was equal to the task. The watchers could only applaud as the teenager kept piercing the gaps with shots off both feet and on either side of the wicket.

Sachin finished the West Zone league with an aggregate of 349 at an average of 87.25, the best by a Mumbai batsman in the season.

> Sachin, though 15, bats like a 26-year-old. It would be a great sight to watch Sachin bat with his captain Dilip Vengsarkar. It will be an object lesson to him to learn the tricks of the trade from the world's no. 1 player.
>
> —Milind Rege, *Sportsweek*, 25–31 December 1988

In December 1988, Dilip Balwant Vengsarkar was indeed the best batsman in the world, as per the parameters of a rating system whose inception had coincided with a golden run by the man who had spent most of his international career in the shadows, as it were.

Since his international debut in 1976, Vengsarkar had been more successful against the fast bowlers from the West Indies than any other Indian batsman save Sunil Gavaskar. If a batsman's worth was to be determined from his performances against the best opposition of his time, then Vengsarkar had earned the right to be considered one of the all-time greats by sheer dint of performance. However, the masses, the media and most damningly, even the selectors, had been rather reluctant to bestow on him the adulation, attention and acclaim that he deserved. Simply put, he had been taken for granted, and for the better part of his career, he had felt that despite all his outstanding performances, he was always on trial. On the other hand, many of his teammates had been granted superstardom within a year or two of their international debuts.

Everything changed on India's victorious visit to England in 1986. Vengsarkar scored two impeccable hundreds, the first one of which enabled India to win the first Test, and the second, the series itself. His unbeaten 126 in the first Test made him the first non-Englishman to score three tons at Lord's and set up India's first-ever Test win at Headquarters. He then scored 61 and an unbeaten 102 at Leeds, in a game in which no other batsman crossed 40. India won the Test by 283 runs to take an unassailable 2–0 lead in the series.

A year later, Vengsarkar was awarded the captaincy of the Indian team after the selectors decided not to retain Kapil Dev after the 1987 World Cup. His ascent to the helm was a triumph of merit over every other factor, considering that he had never been 'groomed' for the top job like some of his teammates. He made his captaincy debut in a four-Test series against the West Indies in the winter of 1987–88, and led from the front with two hundreds. The icing on the cake was the tag of the number one batsman in the world. Nothing could change the fact that he was the first-ever batsman to be deemed the best in the world by a rating system.

Of course, in keeping with the maxim that nothing was perfect, there had been hiccups. His arm was broken by West Indies paceman Courtney Walsh in the third Test at Kolkata, shortly after he had completed his second century of the series. Ravi Shastri took over for the fourth and final Test at Chennai and India registered a famous, series-levelling victory with Narendra Hirwani, the leg-spinner, taking a record 16 wickets on debut.

There was another setback for Vengsarkar in the form of a six-month ban from playing for Mumbai and India. The BCCI was not amused by his defiance of the players' contracts, which forbade the signatories from writing for newspapers.

> I was served a show cause notice by the BCCI and I told them that they should also ask the West Indian captain Vivian Richards not to write. He was putting pressure on the Indian umpires through his columns. I scored two centuries against them and I started writing only after I was injured in the course of the Calcutta Test.
>
> —Dilip Vengsarkar, *The Hindu*, 29 September 2005

The only international tournament that Vengsarkar missed because of the ban was a tri-series in Sharjah. He was reinstated as captain for the 1988 edition of the Asia Cup, which was to be played in Bangladesh. Under him, India won the title, and then beat New Zealand 2–1 in a thrilling Test series. The second Test of that tussle was his hundredth. He was only the second Indian after Sunil Gavaskar, his India, Mumbai and Dadar Union senior to achieve this milestone. The form he and his team were in at the time, there was every reason to believe that India would beat England in the five-Test series that was to follow. However, the tour was called off, with India refusing to admit members of the touring party who had 'South African links', and England in turn refusing to back down. The cancellation of the series ensured that the top cricketers were available for key Ranji Trophy matches.

Milind Rege's wish of having the colt bat alongside the craftsman was fulfilled in the Ranji pre-quarter final between Mumbai and Hyderabad, played at Secunderabad. The hosts batted first and scored 270, and the spin combine of Arshad Ayub and Venkatapathy Raju had Mumbai in some strife on the second afternoon. Sachin, awaiting his turn to bat, was peeved when Kiran Mokashi was sent in as night watchman ahead of him. As it turned out, Mokashi did not last long, and Sachin had to go in before the umpires drew the stumps. That evening, an upset Sachin asked P.K. Kamath, the Mumbai manager, why the management 'had no confidence in him'.

Kamath had no answer; so Sachin went ahead and provided a reply on his behalf on the following day. He added 118 with Vengsarkar and ensured a first-innings lead. The craftsman scored 64 and the colt 59.

> At Hyderabad, I eventually saw Sachin's real potential. It was an underprepared pitch. The way Sachin countered the spinners, it was evident that a star was born.
>
> —Dilip Vengsarkar, *The Sportstar*, 25 April 1992

> A small group of former Mumbai cricketers then started to gather to watch him play at various tournaments in Mumbai. We did that from the anonymity of our cars and would chuckle when the little fella hammered bowlers much older than him. In the tradition of Mumbai cricket, we gave him a nickname 'Tendlya' and kept each other informed about his progress and where he was playing. He was our little secret, or so we thought. Such were the tabs that we kept on him that just about every action of his was known to us. His off-field style of dressing in a white shirt, with sleeves folded to just below the elbows, used to bother us as we wanted him to dress like a young man—in coloured clothes. When he first sported a printed shirt at a function, we called each other up delightedly that the young man had started dressing as we thought he should dress.
>
> —Sunil Gavaskar, *Sachin Forever*, MCA, 2013

The Little Master did his best to be discreet when he visited the Mumbai nets prior to Sachin's debut game. The fast bowlers were prone to overstepping in the nets, and Raju Kulkarni, one of the quickest in the country, was not an exception to the rule. From where he stood, Gavaskar saw Sachin get onto the back foot to punch a good-length delivery by Kulkarni between what would have been mid-wicket and mid-on. The teenager, it appeared, had all the time in the world to essay that stroke. The master decided that he had seen enough.

> Ayaz Memon and I were listening to Gavaskar in one of his rare, priceless moods. The 'Little Master' was delving deep into his own experience, his own genius, and bringing forth pearls of wisdom.... Then Gavaskar came up with the following statement: 'The two best batsmen in Mumbai today are Vengsarkar and Sachin Tendulkar.' Full stop. End of statement.... Sachin was 15 at the time.... Yet Gavaskar was certain. And a few months later, when we were planning a sports-video for *Sportsweek*, Gavaskar's words still filled my mind. I wanted to interview Vengsarkar and Tendulkar, the two best batsmen in Mumbai.
>
> —Tom Alter, *Outlook*, 4 January 1999

Tom Alter and Ayaz Memon shot the interviews in January 1989 at a cricket ground that owed its existence to Lord Harris, the individual whose name graced the Shield that Sachin and Vinod Kambli had made famous with their stand of 664. In his capacity as governor of the erstwhile Mumbai province in the early 1890s, Lord Harris had earmarked land on south Mumbai's reclaimed western seafront for three communities—the Parsis, Hindus and Muslims—to construct gymkhanas and further their sporting and cricketing interests. The three gymkhanas had gone on to gift scores of cricketers to the city and country.

The colt reached the Islam Gymkhana ground on the seafront after finishing a practice session with the Mumbai team and waited. The craftsman was being interviewed first. Although Sachin was not very articulate in those days, he had acquired the habit of being a thorough professional. Given a choice, the media-shy teenager would have skipped the shoot, but now that he had made a commitment, he was not going to back off. What would have relaxed him was the 'informal' nature of the interaction, with both the interviewer and interviewee standing next to each other on the periphery of the ground. Like a Sachin innings, his interaction with Tom Alter got off to a flier.

'Sachin, you must be getting used to all this media attention,' Alter began. Pat came the reply, 'Well, this is just the start.'

It was the verbal equivalent of a batsman trusting his reflexes and hitting the ball uppishly, but quite deliberately, between two fielders, and watchers being tempted to conclude that he had been lucky to get away with the stroke.

Alter's subsequent thrusts were precise and Sachin's parries prompt.

> Q: Have you always wanted to be a cricketer?
> A: Yes. I always wanted to be a cricketer.
>
> Q: What form of the game do you like?
> A: I like all forms—one-day, three-day, five-day....
>
> Q: We heard that Raju Kulkarni bowled to you in the nets. Did you have any trouble facing him?
> A: No. I did not have any trouble.
>
> Q: We also heard that Kapil bowled to you. How was the experience?
> A: That was also very good.
>
> Q: Would you like to go to the West Indies with the Indian team?
> A: Yes, I would like to go.
>
> Q: They have Marshall, Ambrose and the others. Do you think you will be able to face them?
> A: I don't think I will have any trouble facing them.

Like a batsman who doesn't mind looking awkward against the bowlers till he gets his eye in, Sachin persisted and finally, prevailed. He was assured but not arrogant.

> After the interview, we had Sachin walk across to where he had left his bat and kit-bag, pick up his bat thoughtfully, look into the distance, and then pick up his kit-bag and walk out towards Marine Drive and into the future. It was a shot which any veteran actor would have rehearsed several times, and probably muffed just as often. Sachin did it—first take 'OK'. It was as natural as his batting.

—Tom Alter, *Outlook*, 4 January 1999

The Indian team was scheduled to undertake the toughest assignment in the sport—a tour of the West Indies—a few weeks later. The teenager may have been optimistic about making the squad after his performances in the Ranji Trophy, but the national selectors were not so keen.

> The media had started discussing whether I should be in the Indian team.

Rajbhai said, 'I want you to focus on Ranji Trophy right now. Let me tell you now that you will not go to West Indies, after you have finished with your Ranji Trophy, make sure that you appear for your SSC* exams.' That was my plan, whether I got selected for West Indies or not, I had to appear for my SSC exam.

—Sachin Tendulkar, Press Trust of India, 25 July 2014

As prophesized by the chairman of selectors, the Indian team that was picked for the tour of the Caribbean did not have Sachin in it. The decision to keep Sachin out wasn't as significant as the one to omit Mohinder Amarnath who had scored 598 runs on India's previous tour of the Caribbean. He had started the 1988–89 season on an electrifying note, albeit off the field. Left out of the Indian squad for the first Test of the New Zealand series, despite having been in good form, he had convened a press conference and branded the selectors as a 'bunch of jokers'.

Among those who made it into the national squad was Sanjay Manjrekar, son of former Test batsman Vijay Manjrekar and an alumnus of the Dadar Union Sporting Club. He had the backing of his captain.

Manjrekar Junior had scored heavily in inter-university tournaments and the Ranji Trophy since the mid-1980s. He was 'blooded' into international cricket, quite literally, against the West Indies at Delhi in November 1987. He was doing his best to lend Vengsarkar support in the second innings, when paceman Winston Benjamin hit him below the left eye and forced him to retire hurt. Manjrekar had not played in the series thereafter and he had also not appeared in the Tests against the New Zealanders in the next season. Hence, his selection for the tour of the West Indies came as a surprise to many.

Vengsarkar did not erupt with joy when Manjrekar scored 108 against a bowling attack comprising Malcolm Marshall, Curtly Ambrose, Ian Bishop and Courtney Walsh on a lively Bridgetown pitch, in the second Test of the series in the Caribbean. For the Indian captain and, indeed, the veterans of Mumbai cricket, a batsman clearing cricket's toughest examination with flying colours at the start of his career was no big deal. What mattered was his ability to do likewise on a consistent basis for the remainder of his career.

Be that as it may, cricket lovers in India's cricket capital, especially those who had watched Sanjay Manjrekar in his formative years at the Shivaji Park and

---

*Final school examinations conducted by the Secondary School Certificate Board in Maharashtra.

the Matunga Maidan, celebrated the advent of who they believed was Mumbai's next batting great.

The Bridgetown centurion had warmed up for the Caribbean tour with an innings of 131 in the Ranji quarter-final against Uttar Pradesh, just before the Indian team's departure. Mumbai were bowled out for 234 in the first innings, but they retaliated by dismissing the opposition for 134. In the second innings, against off-spinner Gopal Sharma at his best, Mumbai's batsmen knuckled down. Manjrekar apart, Sachin mixed caution with aggression and scored 75. Mumbai won by 224 runs.

Chandrakant Pandit led Mumbai in Vengsarkar's absence in the semi-final against Delhi, at the Wankhede. Sachin came in at 137–3, with Mumbai reasonably placed to overhaul Delhi's 409. He got off the blocks with a flurry of strokes. Madan Lal, the Delhi captain, shuffled his bowlers around, but to no avail. He then asked his men to target the other end. Maninder Singh, then the premier left-arm spinner in the country, had the batsmen in trouble, but he could not fluster the teenager. Sachin outdid his seniors in terms of proficiency and brilliance and was last out for 78, inclusive of five fours and a six. Mumbai conceded a first-innings lead of 88 and bowed out of the competition.

Sachin finished the season as Mumbai's highest run-getter, with 583 runs from seven matches, at an average of 64.7.

In between the Ranji games, the 15-year-old led Mumbai to victory in the under-19 Cooch Behar Trophy, contributing to the triumph with a double century and century. These performances made him a certainty for the Indian under-19 side that was to tour Pakistan, but he had already decided to skip that engagement with his SSC exams scheduled in March 1989. The chairman of selectors had also reiterated the importance of his giving the exams, earlier in the season. Playing Ranji Trophy matches was not an issue, as he could carry his books along and study in the evenings.

> [In my first full season], I was the highest run-getter for Mumbai. That was another special moment. My schoolmates would say, 'He is not a schoolboy anymore, he is playing for Mumbai.' Another special aspect was that the school teachers were willing to help me whenever I went to them for guidance. I used to go and attend those special classes. It was just that I had to miss classes in my last year in school. It was hard to cope with studies.
>
> —Sachin Tendulkar, *The Sportstar*, 6 May 1995

It was a classic case of life coming full circle. Prof. Ramesh Tendulkar was known to take 'extra' classes for students who would miss lectures owing to their sporting commitments. His own son was now receiving assistance of a similar sort.

Sachin's family, friends and teachers, rallied around him as the examinations approached. He had only a fortnight in which to prepare. At his examination centre, he underwent the curious experience of being accosted for autographs by his co-examinees. The autograph-seekers' refrain was that they were unlikely to get an opportunity to meet him *when* he would start playing for the country—it was always *when*, never *if*.

Sachin followed the exams with his last hurrah for Shardashram—a match-winning 103 against Anjuman-E-Islam in the Harris Shield final. He then made another trip to England with Kailash Gattani's Star Cricket Club side. This time, he had Vinod Kambli for company.

> Sungrace-Mafatlal sponsored their trip to the UK with Kailash Gattani's team in 1989. When I told them to come with me to the Raymonds outlet at Fountain in Mumbai to get their blazers for the tour stitched, both were hesitant. When prodded, they revealed that they wanted to get their blazers stitched by a tailor who was based at Shivaji Park. They had heard a lot about his tailoring skills, and were therefore keen to go to him.
>
> —Anil Joshi, personal interview

Sachin's best performance on the 1989 tour was a 77-ball century against Haywards Heath Cricket Club.

> In one of the matches, Sachin batted very well to score 60. He was all set for a big score but was caught at extra cover. He just stood at the crease in disbelief before sitting in one corner of the dressing room and brooding. After a while, he asked me where he had gone wrong and I told him that he had played a bit too soon on the rise. Mind you, he never got out in that fashion again on the tour. He loved batting against the bowling machine. If I remember correctly, once Vinod Kambli set the machine to deliver balls at 100 kmph at a school ground and Tendulkar hit a ball across the road, breaking a window pane of a cottage. The sound of glass breaking alerted everyone in the locality and the locals threatened to take the matter up with the principal. Being visitors, we were scared and I had to shell out 10 pounds to fix the broken window.
>
> —Kailash Gattani, *Mid-Day*, 18 October 2013

> It was the summer holidays in schools around the time we travelled to England and so we stayed at various school campuses. Believe me, staying in those schools at that point of our lives was so pleasing that it could not be compared to staying in the five-star facilities in the next part of our lives.... All these institutions had tuck shops where you would get a variety of goodies.... Sachin, myself and most of the others would get a Mars bar for 10 pence and a Coke for 15. That was our staple diet.... We went to Scotland and thought that the sun never sets there! We had to draw the curtains before retiring to bed at 11:30 pm because it was still light outside.... Sachin used to use a heavy bat even then! He loved to bat the whole day.
>
> —Sourav Ganguly, *Sports Illustrated*, May 2013

Sachin cleared his SSC exams and joined Kirti College where his father taught. However, academics were relegated to second place by the excitement that was building up as the 1989–90 season approached. While there was still a possibility of his age—he was only 16 then—getting in the way of his elevation to a higher level, there was no way he could be deemed unworthy on grounds of merit. He had been Mumbai's top scorer in the previous season, after all.

> Imagine that you are on an African safari. Your tour guide spots a pride of lions. He drops you from your car right in the middle of those beasts and says, 'Have a good time, I will pick you up two months later, good luck!' and drives away. Touring the West Indies in the 1980s was a bit like this.
>
> —Sanjay Manjrekar, *Special Feature, India v West Indies*, PMG, 2006

The year 1989 was a time of tumult in Indian cricket, both on and off the field. The tour of the West Indies was a catastrophe. India lost every completed ODI and Test. A century apiece by Manjrekar, Sidhu and Shastri and some incisive spells by Kapil Dev apart, there was nothing to show.

The onus was on Dilip Vengsarkar to lead from the front, but he failed to fire as a batsman. That only intensified the pressure on him. He then compounded the crisis with a fiery interview to a periodical in which he castigated some of his teammates. As if this wasn't enough, he along with some of the players flew to the US after the end of the series to play exhibition matches without taking the permission of the BCCI. The Board reacted by 'banning' six senior players—Vengsarkar, Ravi Shastri, Kapil Dev, Mohammed Azharuddin, Kiran More and Arun Lal—for a year. This triggered a national outcry. The players sued the Board, and their bans were revoked after the Supreme Court stepped in.

Before the start of the next season, Vengsarkar was replaced as captain by K. Srikkanth who had been his deputy in the West Indies but had missed the Tests after having had his arm broken by Ian Bishop in the preceding ODI series.

Around the same time, the Indian cricketers sought to air their grievances through the Association of Indian Cricketers (AIC), a successor of the Players' Association that had been active for a couple of seasons in the 1970s before being put into cold storage. The AIC had Kapil Dev as its president, Arun Lal as secretary and Mohinder Amarnath as spokesperson. Unfortunately for the cricketers, they were not as proactive on the field of play as they were off it. They flopped in two successive limited-overs tournaments at the start of the 1989–90 season: a tri-series at Sharjah and the Nehru Cup, a six-nation tournament organized to commemorate the birth centenary of India's first prime minister.

The Nehru Cup was followed by the Irani Cup encounter between Delhi, the 1988–89 Ranji champions and the Rest of India, at the Wankhede Stadium. It was for all practical purposes a selection trial with the National Selection Committee comprising Raj Singh Dungarpur (chairman), Akash Lal, Ramesh Saxena, Gundappa Viswanath and Naren Tamhane scheduled to pick the Indian team for its next assignment—a tour of Pakistan—on the third afternoon of the game.

The Rest of India commenced its reply to Delhi's 461 on the second afternoon. The top order wobbled, and the scoreboard read 119–4 when Sachin went in. With nearly 2,000 spectators egging him on, he batted confidently to score 39, before inside-edging Maninder Singh onto his stumps. While there were some who were disappointed that he had not gone on to get a big one, there were others, including three of the five national selectors, who felt that he had done enough to merit a place in the Indian team.

> We completed one round of the discussion. There were a couple of selectors who were apprehensive of what would happen to him, if he 'failed'. It was then that Naren Tamhane said, 'Mr. Chairman, I want to tell you one thing. Sachin Tendulkar does not fail!
>
> —Raj Singh Dungarpur, *Sachin Tendulkar—Mr. India*, PMG, 2002

Another selector said that Sachin deserved to be picked as he was far superior in terms of ability to Ian Craig, the Australian, and Hanif Mohammed, the Pakistani, who had made their international debuts in the 1950s at 17 and 18 respectively. On the other hand, two of the selectors were reluctant to baptize the teenager in an away series, against a quality bowling attack and in front of crowds expected to be hostile.

Sachin had been kept out of the team that went to the Caribbean earlier that year. Would the National Selection Committee have been criticized had it chosen to exercise caution again? Yes, there would have been some disgruntled mumbles, but these would have been rendered inaudible by voices declaring that Indian cricketers were known to mature late. These voices would have cited instances of 'prodigies' who had either withered away after a promising start, or had simply drowned after being thrown in at the deep end. To top it all, 1989 was a time when Pakistan was considered cricket's 'second-deepest' end after the West Indies. The concerns of the conservative brigade were exacerbated by the fact that the previous Indian teams to have crossed the border had found the going tough against the Pakistani batsmen, fast bowlers, and even the umpires.

The team of 1989–90 did not of course have to worry about playing 13 men, with English umpires John Holder and John Hampshire requisitioned for the Tests by Imran Khan, Pakistan's captain and a staunch proponent of the concept of 'neutral' umpires. He was also someone who believed in walking the talk.

Refreshingly, pragmatism prevailed over conservatism. The selectors refused to let age get in the way of merit. Five-and-a-half years after he had worn cricketing whites for the first time, Sachin Ramesh Tendulkar was picked to represent his nation at the highest level. Picked along with him were two other rookies—Salil Ankola, the Maharashtra speedster, and Vivek Razdan, who had trained under Dennis Lillee at the MRF Pace Academy in Chennai. On the flipside, fans were miffed with the omission of Mohinder Amarnath and the decision of Vengsarkar to declare himself unavailable for the tour. They reckoned that the Indian side needed experience in the middle order to thwart the Pakistani fast bowlers.

Sachin, his family and friends congregated at the old family home at Shivaji Park after the news came through. It was appropriate that Sachin cut a celebratory cake in the house where he had spent the better part of his formative cricketing years.

There was every possibility of the fifth day's play of the Irani Cup game being rendered meaningless, with Delhi declaring their second innings on the fourth evening, and setting the Rest an impossible 555 to win. However, Sachin's arrival at 76–2 prevented the descent of the proceedings into farce.

Sachin went for his strokes. As his individual score increased, so did the number of spectators at the Wankhede. Taken aback, the Delhi bowlers upped the ante.

The reigning Ranji champions had a quality bowling attack. Atul Wassan was a fiery India hopeful. Sanjeev Sharma, his new-ball partner, had already worn national colours with a five-wicket haul against the West Indies at Sharjah to boast of. They were complemented by the veteran Madan Lal and senior spinners Kirti Azad and Maninder Singh. So fierce was the West–North rivalry at the time that the Delhi players had not paid much heed to all the talk about Sachin until he scored 78 against them in the Ranji semi-final of the previous season. The fair, short and stout youngster, endowed with strong forearms and legs, not to mention an insatiable appetite for runs, had dictated terms to them back then, and he was now doing an encore.

> What was clearly evident even at that time was the strength he possessed at that age, and though being vertically challenged, the poise and balance was evident in ample.
>
> —Atul Wassan, *Cricket Today*, May 2005

In the Irani Cup game, the Delhi bowlers repeated their tactic of targeting the other end when they failed to make an impression on Sachin. The wickets fell, but the spectators watched on, hoping that their blue-eyed boy would go the distance. Vivek Razdan contributed just two to a seventh-wicket stand of 35. He fell at 167 and was followed by Rajiv Seth at 180. Venkatapathy Raju, the incoming batsman, was effectively the last man as Gursharan Singh, the middle-order batsman, had broken his right arm and was not even padded up.

Enter Sachin's guardian angel. Raj Singh Dungarpur made his way to the dressing room and had a word with Gursharan Singh. Raju's dismissal at 209, with Sachin still 11 short of a hundred, was followed by a stirring sight.

Gursharan Singh had been a consistent performer at the domestic level since the early 1980s. He had had a brief stint at the international level, during the India–West Indies series of 1983–84, wherein he had substituted in a couple of Tests and held some sharp catches. However, he had never come even remotely close to being as popular in Punjab, his home state, as he was at the Wankhede on the afternoon of 7 November 1989, shortly after Raju's dismissal. The spectators rose when he emerged from the dressing room padded up, his bat in his left arm and his right arm in a sling. He assured his partner that he would do his best. Sachin was moved.

Sachin went for the runs, even as Gursharan thwarted the bowling with one arm at the other end. There was delight and relief for all parties in equal measure, when Sachin drove Maninder for four to bring up his century.

> He got 39 off 92 balls in the first innings and then came up to me to ask if I had found anything wrong in his batting. 'Are you a defensive or an

attacking batsman?' I asked him. 'Attacking,' he replied. I told him: 'Sachin, there is no bowler in India who can stop you from scoring a hundred if you face 92 balls.' In the second innings, the improvement was dramatic: 103* in 145 balls.

—Vasu Paranjape, *Wisden Asia Cricket*, September 2002

That Irani Cup game was played at a time when my father was critically ill. I remember coming out of the ICU devastated, after being told that he did not have much time. In the lobby of the hospital, I met Mrs Meenal Gavaskar, Sunil Gavaskar's mother. She had come to visit another patient. She told me that she had watched Sachin score a century in the Irani Cup game and had advised Rohan, her grandson, to make Sachin his role model. It was a statement that made me forget the impending tragedy for a moment—the lady who had given birth to Sunil Gavaskar was urging his son to follow Sachin's footsteps.

—Dwarkanath Sanzgiri, *Ashtapailu*, Diwali edition (Marathi), 2013

THE GRADUATION

> *Not since the emergence of Sunil Gavaskar in 1971 has India found a batsman of the class and calibre of Sachin Tendulkar. Just 16 years old, Tendulkar...is already being hailed as another Gavaskar in the making.... Unlike Gavaskar, Tendulkar is aggressive in his approach. He does not seem to have much belief in such accepted principles of batsmanship like getting the eye in, judging the behavioural patterns of the track, playing in the 'V' in the initial stages before opening out. Tendulkar likes to get on top of the bowling almost from the word go. Despite this approach, he cannot be faulted for indiscretion.... The other day, Colin Cowdrey, here for the Nehru Cup tournament, was curious to know from one of our selectors about the 'new Gavaskar'. The scenes at the fall of Tendulkar's wicket resemble the scenes when Gavaskar got out—a clear index of the value of the wicket. Tendulkar should not, and cannot expect any mercy from his rivals on the field, nor from the public—that is the price he has to pay for setting such high standards. He has to remember what Boris Becker once said: 'I win Wimbledon twice and people think I am 35. Maybe, I am a little different, because you cannot be average and win Wimbledon at 17.' Tendulkar is different. And how different!*
>
> —H. Natarajan, *The Indian Express*, 11 November 1989

The frosty relationship between the BCCI and the cricketers reached its nadir on 6 November 1989, 24 hours before Sachin celebrated his selection in the Indian team and 72 hours before the Indian team's departure for Pakistan.

It was the day on which the AIC went public with a 'charter of demands' that it claimed it had been discussing with Board officials since the start of the season. Mohinder Amarnath, the AIC spokesperson, declared that the players would sign a common, joint contract and not the individual ones that the Board wanted them to sign. The AIC also demanded a 70 per cent hike in the tour fee as 'compensation for being away from home' and a graded system of payment that would be computed on the basis of the number of Tests played by each player, along with a payment of 50 per cent of the tour fee to those named as 'stand-bys' for the tour. Further, the AIC questioned the tour itinerary, as per which the four Tests were to be played back-to-back, and demanded that the three-day game that the tour was scheduled to begin with, be played between the Tests instead. The Board was given two days to respond. With the team scheduled to report to Delhi on 8 November, there was very little time. To the layman, it appeared that the AIC wanted to push the Board into a corner, giving it no option but to accede to the demands.

The Board refused to revise its offer of ₹50,000 (plus allowances) per player and went for the jugular by announcing that in case the players selected for the tour did not fall in line, an alternate team would be sent. On 7 November 1989, *The Times of India* carried an assurance from Pakistan that even a 'second-string' side would be welcome.

Eventually, the original squad decided to tour 'for free'. Srikkanth was quoted by the media as saying that representing the country was paramount. Kapil Dev and Amarnath informed the media on behalf of the AIC that the players had signed the contract, which was in the form of a letter, under protest. The letter was signed by 13 of the 16 members of the team, all of whom declined to accept drafts of ₹25,000 as half-payment of the tour money. The three newcomers—Sachin, Ankola and Razdan—were sensibly left out of the fracas, and 'exempted' from signing the letter. The Board countered the AIC representatives' comments by claiming that some of the players had in fact signed individual contracts.

> Mohinder [Amarnath] clarified that he had never served any ultimatum to the Board. All he had said was that if the demands were not accepted, the team may not go, and 'there is a lot of difference between not going and may not go.' Reacting to the Board's plea that time was too short for them to negotiate on the charter of demands, Mohinder quipped: 'They had the time to pick another team, but not to negotiate with us.
>
> —*The Times of India*, 9 November 1989

The Indians started the tour as the overwhelming underdogs. The ability—or the lack of it—of the Indian batsmen to handle pace had been questioned in the Caribbean earlier in the year, and Pakistan was expected to be no different. Imran Khan, India's nemesis in the 1982–83 series between the two teams, had entered the twilight zone of his illustrious career and was concentrating more on his captaincy and batting. He could afford to do so as he had under him young men who could let it seam, swing and rip. The left-handed Wasim Akram was well on his way to being recognized as the best left-arm paceman ever. Also ready to explode at the highest level was a teenager answering to the name of Waqar Younis.

Managing the Indian team on the tour was Chandrakant (Chandu) Borde, a former national captain and one of the best players of the 1960s. Later, he had managed junior Indian sides and been part of the selection panels that picked the teams that won the World Cup in 1983 and the World Championship of Cricket in 1985.

> I first saw Sachin at the pre-tour camp in Delhi. He looked so young. The way he was practising, I was amazed. You could see that there was something in the boy.
>
> —Chandu Borde, *Sachin Tendulkar—Mr. India*, PMG, 2002

Sachin scored 47 in the three-day game against the Board of Control for Cricket in Pakistan (BCCP)* Patron's XI. The knock made him a certainty for the first Test at Karachi. The teenager's joy knew no bounds when K. Srikkanth, his captain, assured him that he would play all four Tests. The manager and captain apart, the 'senior statesman' of the team, who had bowled to Sachin in the nets a year previously, was also a fan of the teenager. In 1988–89, he had advised his India teammates against reading too much into Sachin's century on his Ranji debut. However, he had seen enough of the 'boy wonder' since then to change his mind.

> We heard Kapil Dev rave about him. In Asia, usually it is the fast bowlers who come to the fore in their teens. We were surprised that a batsman had been picked at 16.
>
> —Rameez Raja, *Sachin Sachin*, Star, 2013

> We were like, 'What can he do?' When we first saw him, he looked 14, not 16.
>
> —Wasim Akram, *Thank You Sachin*, BCCI, 2013

Imran's decision to bat after winning the toss in the first Test gave the teenager the opportunity to calm the butterflies in his stomach by expending energy in the field before getting his turn to bat. The date was 15 November 1989. At 16

---

*The BCCP was renamed the PCB (Pakistan Cricket Board) in 1995.

years and 205 days, Sachin Tendulkar was India's 187th Test cricketer and the youngest ever.

His first day in Test cricket came perilously close to being the Indian team's last day of the tour. A spectator breached security, ran onto the field and roughed up the Indian captain before being overpowered. Thankfully, the intruder was unarmed and the damage he did was limited to a couple of buttons on Srikkanth's shirt. Quite a few teams would have called the tour off there and then, but the Indians decided to trust the authorities who assured them of better security arrangements for the remainder of the series. Sachin was so drained out at the close of play that he fell asleep when the team returned to the hotel and woke up only for dinner. It wasn't the first time he had fielded for an entire day, but he had never been as excited.

The Pakistan team was all out for 409 on day two. Manoj Prabhakar and Kapil Dev, the latter was playing in his hundredth Test, took five and four wickets, respectively. Mohammed Azharuddin snapped up five catches, some of which were brilliant.

The visitors got off to a disastrous start. The Pakistani pacers reduced India to 13–3 and then 41–4. It was Sachin's turn to go in.

> When he came in to bat, we wondered whether it was right to put such a young kid in this position. He was quiet and probably nervous, and may have felt lost.
>
> —Waqar Younis, *Sachin Sachin*, Star, 2013

Sachin was wearing a white helmet but without a visor. This meant that while his head and ears had some sort of protection, his face was very much in the line of fire. But then, helmets with visors were not in vogue those days.

The stage was set for a battle between two debutants. Steaming in at Sachin was Waqar Younis. Sachin negotiated the first few deliveries. Waqar gave nothing away, but when he overpitched one, Sachin was quick to seize on it. He advanced his front foot, then his bat and met the ball with the sweet spot. The ball sped between the umpire and Mohammed Azharuddin, the non-striker, to the boundary. He had thus opened his account in Test cricket in much the same way as he had in first-class cricket.

> When I see a youngster beginning a Test career, I tell him that nervousness is normal. It will pass after a while…. Of course, everybody is nervous before a match and before going in. It's a good thing because it charges you, gets you more focused and helps in concentration. But the nervousness is

there only till you go in; once in the middle, I just think about the bowler and the bowling, nothing else.

—Sachin Tendulkar, *Outlook*, 4 January 1999

A little later, Sachin steered Waqar past point for another boundary. The bowler responded with a bouncer, which the batsman left alone with the composure of a veteran. The teenager, who was used to dictating the proceedings in first-class and junior-level cricket, then suddenly came to the fore. When Waqar pitched one in the 'corridor of uncertainty' outside the off-stump, Sachin went for an expansive drive. He missed, and the ball went through to the keeper. To those watching, he seemed in a hurry.

Sachin collected a few more runs off Waqar, but the paceman had the last laugh. He followed three outswingers with an express inswinger. Sachin could make nothing of it, and was bowled 'through the gate'. 'I was in a hurry,' he conceded to Ravi Shastri in the dressing room.

It was a tough situation. I was 16, totally nervous and did not know what was happening. My feet were not moving, my mind was almost blank, I thought the whole thing was too competitive…butterflies were flying around in formations in my stomach! I thought I was not going to ever play Test cricket again. At times I was beaten by pace, the ball going past my bat before I had completed my shot.

—Sachin Tendulkar, *Outlook*, 4 January 1999

Sachin may have been a bundle of nerves during that innings of 15, and he may have admitted the same to his teammates after his dismissal, but there was a silver lining. At no point during his brief stay in the middle had he looked out of sorts. He may have panicked internally, but he had displayed equanimity externally.

Among those who witnessed Sachin's straight drive that got him off the mark in Test cricket was an individual who was as adept at reading batsmen's minds as he was prolific in the game's most specialized art. To the world at large, there seemed nothing more to Sachin's straight drive off Waqar than the fact that it had been played in accordance with what was mentioned in the coaching manual—the advance of the front foot to the pitch of the ball and the red cherry being struck with the middle of the bat. However, Abdul Qadir, leg-spinner extraordinaire, had sensed something 'special' about Sachin's poise and body language.

At 73–5, things looked bleak for India. The lower order then fought back, with Ravi Shastri scoring 45 and Kapil Dev and Kiran More getting 50s. India finished with 262. Imran expectedly went for the kill and declared at 305–5, giving his bowlers a day and a bit in which to take 10 Indian wickets. With poor light always threatening to truncate play, every minute mattered for the hosts. That India needed 453 to win was purely academic. Their first-innings performance suggested that there was no way the visitors would go for the target. Sachin watched admiringly as Navjot Sidhu (85) and Sanjay Manjrekar (113*) ensured a draw.

Manjrekar's second Test century in four Tests ensured his anointment as India's newest batting bulwark. In the absence of stalwarts like Vengsarkar and Amarnath, India needed one of its younger batsmen to stand up to be counted, and Manjrekar had done just that. Sachin was very much the understudy. His teammates watched in admiration as he slogged it out in the nets prior to the second Test at Faisalabad, eager to make up for what he had perceived as a failure. He was also a source of unintentional amusement for them.

A couple of years previously, Achrekar had discovered Sachin's habit of talking in his sleep on a cricketing trip to Pune. In Pakistan, Sachin's teammates found him talking and walking in his sleep, late in the night. He emerged from his room and asked them whether the bats that he had ordered had been delivered. He was escorted back to his room. His desire and determination to succeed had taken over to the point that he was thinking about his batting even in his sleep.

Asked to bat at Faisalabad, India began with an opening stand of 68, but the hosts then bagged four quick wickets. Sachin came in at 101–4 and dropped anchor, mindful of not being as 'hasty' as he had been at Karachi. Manjrekar's presence at the other end was reassuring. The Mumbai batsmen proceeded to do what their predecessors had done for India several times over—fill the breach. They added 143 for the fifth wicket and Sachin became the youngest batsman to score a 50 in a Test. No longer did he feel out of place.

> I was tense [after the first Test]. Whatever I had expected to happen didn't happen.... I was hoping for another opportunity. I made up my mind not to lose my wicket. I got 59. When I got back, I remember saying I don't know any reason why I can't do that again.
>
> —Sachin Tendulkar, *Sachin at 25*, World Tel, 1998

Manjrekar scored 76, and India totalled 288. Pakistan replied with 423. In the second essay, Srikkanth fell to Wasim Akram for the fourth time in four Test innings, but Sidhu battled hard. He was third out at 91, and Manjrekar was joined in the middle by Mohammed Azharuddin.

The silken touch artiste from Hyderabad had failed to maintain the standards that he had set in his debut series in 1984–85, with a century in each of his first three Tests. He had not scored a Test hundred since the 1986–87 season, and more and more people were coming around to believe that he had kept his place in the Indian team only because of his exceptional fielding skills. One of the last players to be picked for the Pakistan tour, he had made it to the playing XI for the first Test at Karachi only because of a last-minute injury to Raman Lamba. Scores of 35 in both innings at Karachi and five catches had enabled him to retain his place for the second Test. However, a first-ball duck in the first innings had brought him back to square one. In the second innings, he was playing for his career.

In the lead-up to the Test, he had been shown a different batting grip by a former legend. Zaheer Abbas, the former Pakistan captain, had noticed that Azharuddin's right hand tended to come off the bat when he essayed strokes on the leg-side, thereby making him lose control.

Azharuddin had intended to try out the new grip in the nets before adopting it in a game, which was the prudent thing to do, of course. However, with nothing to lose, he decided to employ it in the second innings. The results were astounding. After a while, his right thumb started throbbing, but his timing was spot on. A partnership developed between him and Manjrekar. By the time the Mumbai batsman fell for 83, the match was safe and the pressure was off. At 274–5, Sachin had a great opportunity to consolidate on his first-innings' score of 59. He did impress one and all, but in another department.

Azharuddin batted with elegance and maturity until he entered the 90s in a Test for the first time in three years. The strain resulted in communication issues and a mix-up while running between the wickets, but Sachin sacrificed himself by running to the danger end. A grateful Azharuddin went on to complete his century, and the teams proceeded to Lahore for the third Test with the scoreline still reading 0–0 instead of the expected 2–0 in Pakistan's favour.

On the field, Sachin carried himself with the aplomb of a senior professional, but off the field, he was very much a teenager. When Manjrekar beat him in a game of tennis, he went into a major sulk, convinced that his opponent had not played fair. The culinary delights of Pakistan delighted him, especially the non-vegetarian variety. He relished a breakfast that comprised keema parathas, a local delicacy, and lassi. He also engaged in unofficial eating competitions with Salil Ankola, who had also made his debut at Karachi, but did not play another

Test thereafter. The fast bowler was much taller and heftier, but Sachin almost always came out on tops. Both were young enough to burn everything that they hogged. Whether it was a battle against an extraordinary bowling attack, a game of tennis or an 'eating competition', the teenager did not like to lose.

With the Lahore wicket as dead as a dodo, and poor light necessitating nearly finishes, the third Test witnessed batting marathons by both sides. India scored 509, and Pakistan replied with 699–7. The highlight of India's innings was another impeccable performance by Sanjay Manjrekar. It seemed that nothing could faze him, as he went about compiling the highest individual score by an Indian against Pakistan. He looked invincible till he went for a non-existent run off Qadir, only to be sent back, and was run out. It was a bizarre way in which to fall at an individual score of 218. Little did his fans, or indeed, Manjrekar himself, know then that he would display a fatal penchant for that mode of dismissal for the rest of his career.

A rejuvenated Azharuddin scored 77. Sachin did not make much of an impression, scoring 15 before being bowled by Qadir.

The greentop at the Jinnah Stadium, Sialkot, the venue of the fourth and final Test, was an indication that the hosts meant business. Imran won the toss, and to no one's surprise, put India in. The visitors were however unfazed. Manjrekar and Azharuddin led the way with knocks of 72 and 52 respectively, and India scored a competitive 324. The highlight of the innings, from Pakistan's point of view, was Imran's 350th Test wicket. Wasim Akram and Waqar Younis bagged five and two scalps respectively.

Then came the turnaround. The spectators, and the Pakistani players themselves, were caught unawares by Dennis Lillee's pupil. Vivek Razdan outbowled his Pakistani counterparts to take five wickets. His seniors were no less effective. Kapil Dev took two wickets and Manoj Prabhakar, who had had a fine tour, took three. When K. Srikkanth and Navjot Sidhu opened India's second innings with a lead of 74, there was tension in the Pakistani ranks.

Imran Khan, peeved at the position his side found itself in, decided to take matters into his own hands, quite literally. He had entrusted new-ball duties to his protégés Wasim Akram and Waqar Younis in the first innings, but with the series on the line, he decided to lead from the front. The move worked. Srikkanth went first, hitting him straight into Wasim Akram's hands. This meant that Akram had a hand in each of the Indian captain's seven dismissals in the Test series, either as bowler or fielder. Manjrekar and Sidhu had just about brought the innings back on track when Imran struck again with the prized scalp of Manjrekar. When Wasim Akram dismissed Azharuddin and Shastri in quick succession, the silence in the Indian dressing room was as overwhelming as the cheers emanating from the stands. Up against a team far superior to theirs, India had done well to share honours in the first three Tests and take the first-innings lead in the fourth. However, on the afternoon of 13 December 1989, it appeared that all the hard work would come to naught.

Sachin came in to join Sidhu. With the scoreboard reading 38–4, an overall lead of only 112 and more than a day left, the Indians had their backs to the wall.

In the middle, Sachin reminded himself of all the lessons that he had learnt during the series. His backlift had to be shorter and quicker and his foot movement precise. He was in the process of getting his eye in, when Waqar Younis unleashed a snorter that landed just short of a length and took off. Before Sachin could react, the ball struck him on the helmet and ricocheted off it onto his nose. The impact stung a lot more than all the previous occasions when he had been injured on a cricket field put together.

The teenager stepped back, taking care not to tread on the stumps, and felt the blood trickling down his chin. By this time, Sidhu had run across to him as had the Pakistani players. Salil Ankola, the 12th man, had also rushed onto the field. The Pakistani players, in what was a combination of concern and gamesmanship, suggested that he went off for repairs.

The final call obviously had to be Sachin's. He asked Ankola to apply ice on the wound. He then wiped the blood with a towel and decided to carry on.

> He got hit on the nose…I thought this was it. And then I heard him squeak, 'Main khelega' [I will play]. This was stunning. It was a situation where he had nothing to gain, actually.
>
> —Navjot Sidhu, *The Sportstar*, 7 December 2013

One individual who nodded in appreciation was Ajit Tendulkar who had travelled to Pakistan along with Avinash Gowariker, Sachin's childhood friend.

> We were in the stands when it happened. I froze, but Ajit said, 'Ok. Fine. This will only toughen him.'
>
> —Avinash Gowariker, *Sachin Sachin*, Star, 2013

Waqar returned to the top of his run-up and Sachin took strike on a pitch that had traces of his blood. Waqar, perhaps guessing that the batsman would expect another bouncer, served a fuller delivery. Sachin saw it all the way and drove it past cover for four.

> I got hit by Waqar Younis on my first tour. It was painful, but I told myself that that was the worst thing that could happen to me on a cricket field. Nothing could be worse. So, I was prepared to take it.
>
> —Sachin Tendulkar, *Perfect Ten*, PMG, 1995

It was an extraordinary display of leadership in a crisis. What it did was convince Imran Khan and his players that they need not 'feel sorry' for the boy, as some of them had, at the start of the series. He was as tough as they come.

> It was hard for the senior players to mix around with me in Pakistan. I was only 16 then. I don't think anyone was awestruck by my presence. Perhaps they were, when I did not come back after getting hit…. My teammates thought I would come back because my nose was bleeding…. When I got back [after the partnership], I could make out that everybody felt happy that I stayed there.
>
> —Sachin Tendulkar, *The Sportstar*, 6 May 1995

Sachin and Sidhu proceeded to add 101. Sidhu was unfortunate to fall just three runs short of a well-deserved hundred and Sachin got 57, his second 50 of the series. India were 234-7 at the end of the game, and the series thus ended with honours even.

> After the game, we all had a word with him. He was like a younger brother to everyone. All that he said was: 'Yes, I know I got hurt. But at that point of time, my team required me and that's what I have done. Why is everybody praising me? Anybody who plays for the team would have done the same.' That was incredible. He showed tremendous maturity for a 16-year-old.
>
> —Vivek Razdan, *Mid-Day*, 24 October 2013

> Only after we saw him bat a couple of times did we realize that he had the technique, the potential, the hunger and the focus.
>
> —Rameez Raja, *Thank You Sachin*, BCCI, 2013

The Test series was followed by four ODIs. The first game, scheduled to be played at Peshawar, was called off due to inclement weather, and a 20-overs-a-side 'exhibition' encounter was played instead.

India batted second, and their Sialkot saviour excelled in an innings of 53, scored off a mere 18 deliveries. The highlight was his attack on Abdul Qadir in the penultimate over of the innings. Shortly after he had belted leggie Mushtaq Ahmed for two sixes, Qadir challenged Sachin to attack him. Sachin's response was two-pronged; with his mouth, he flattered Qadir, telling him that he could not imagine hitting a legendary bowler like him. With his bat, he went berserk, hitting Qadir for as many as four sixes in the penultimate over of the innings. The first ball of the over flew over long-on, the fourth over the bowler's head and the fifth and sixth over long-off. The third six was the most remarkable of the lot. He realized after stepping out that he had not got to the pitch of the ball; he still carried on with the stroke, and his timing enabled him to clear the field.

It may have been an exhibition match, but Qadir was a bowler committed to his craft and the objective of dismissing his opponent. He had tied Srikkanth of all batsmen in knots. However, Sachin was different.

> Sachin hit him [Qadir] for one six, after which I teased Qadir that a schoolboy was launching into him. The wily leg-spinner gave me a wink to suggest it was a trap. Sachin went on to hit another one over the boundary and I gave Qadir the look. After the fourth six, the smile was gone from Qadir's face, and later that evening he told me that the boy was an extraordinary talent.
>
> —Imran Khan, *The Times of India*, 20 December 2010

It was 16 December 1989, just three days after his refusal to throw in the towel at Sialkot, and exactly 18 years since India's military victory over Pakistan in the Bangladesh liberation war. It was just the perfect day for cricket lovers in India to celebrate the advent of a new batting star.

> When Sachin Tendulkar travelled to Pakistan to face one of the finest bowling attacks ever assembled in cricket, Michael Schumacher was yet to race a F1 car, Lance Armstrong had never been to the Tour De France, Diego Maradona was still the captain of a world champion Argentina team, Pete Sampras had never won a Grand Slam. When Tendulkar embarked on a glorious career taming Imran and company, Roger Federer was a name unheard of, Usain Bolt was an unknown kid in the Jamaican backwaters. The Berlin Wall was still intact, USSR was one big, big country, Dr. Manmohan Singh was yet to 'open' the Nehruvian economy.
>
> —*TIME*, 2010

Sachin did not trouble the scorers on his ODI debut at Gujranwala, and was left out of the XI for the next two matches. The third ODI at Karachi was abandoned due to crowd trouble, and Pakistan won the two that went the distance. The two losses failed to dampen the spirits of the Indian fans of 1989. Plagued as they were by an inferiority complex when it came to the Pakistani team, 'not losing' a Test series in Pakistan was an extraordinary achievement.

> After his return from Pakistan, Kirti College wanted him to play against Jhunjhunwala College in the final of the Junior College Cricket Tournament. I was the Organising Secretary of the Junior College Cricket Committee at the time, and I received a call from the Kirti College Principal, requesting that Sachin be allowed to play despite his not being in the squad that had originally been picked. Jhunjhunwala College raised an objection, but the Committee ruled in Kirti College's favour. The game was played at the Parsi Gymkhana on Marine Drive. Sachin scored a double century.
>
> —Prof. R.S. Shetty, personal interview

The euphoria of the Indian fans ebbed a bit with media reports that some of the players were threatening to boycott the team's next international assignment—a tour of New Zealand—if the demands put forth on their behalf by the AIC were not accepted. However, this was denied by both Kapil Dev and Amarnath, both of whom said that there was no question of the players refusing to represent the country. Mr B. Dutta, the then BCCI president, was quoted as saying that the Board wasn't financially sound enough to meet the demands of the cricketers.

Like its predecessor, the AIC gradually withered away, even as relations between the players and the Board improved. The stated objectives of the AIC's office-bearers, which were 'to work towards bridging the financial divide between international cricket and first-class cricket, and ensure that cricketers who retired 'enjoyed a comfortable future', would be achieved in the new millennium, after discussions, presentations and deliberations between the Board and the players.

The selection of the Indian team for the tour of New Zealand was preceded by the Duleep Trophy final between South Zone and Central Zone at Secunderabad. Srikkanth, who had looked woefully out of sorts as a batsman in Pakistan, had been expected to lead South Zone and bat himself into some sort of form. However, he decided to skip the game. In his absence, Mohammed Azharuddin, a transformed cricketer after the Pakistan tour, was named captain.

In January 1971, Vijay Merchant, the chairman of the National Selection Committee, had changed the course of Indian cricket by changing the captain of the national side. Exactly 19 years later, a successor of Merchant's attempted an encore. Raj Singh Dungarpur accosted Azharuddin on the eve of the Duleep

Trophy final and offered him the captaincy of the Indian team. Azharuddin, who was warming up with his teammates, was distracted. He retorted by saying that he *was* the captain. It was only a few moments later that it dawned on him that the chairman of selectors was not referring to the South Zone captaincy.

> Let me disclose without any fear that when in England recently, Dungarpur had a long talk with the umpires [John Holder and John Hampshire] who supervised in Pakistan and learnt from them many things, but above all, their very poor opinion of Srikkanth's captainship.
>
> —A.F.S. Talyarkhan, *Mid-Day*, 5 January 1990

Clearly, Holder and Hampshire's views differed from those of Kapil Dev and Manoj Prabhakar, both of whom declared in later years that Srikkanth was the best captain they had played under.

> Azhar is an uncomplicated youngster, completely committed to the game. We hope for the first time, the Indian captain will be talking of cricket and not contracts.
>
> —Raj Singh Dungarpur, *The Times of India*, 5 January 1990

The chairman's statement pretty much summed up the distrust between the Board and the senior players at that point of time. Three India captains—Srikkanth, Shastri and Vengsarkar—were left out of what was christened 'The Team of the 1990s'. Bishan Bedi, former India captain and the greatest left-arm spinner in history, was named 'cricket manager', in what was clearly an attempt to replicate what the Australians had done with Bob Simpson. While Bedi's commitment and capabilities were never in doubt, there was a section that was unsure about whether an individual for whom diplomacy was an alien concept was the right man to manage a team as diverse as the Indian outfit.

From the old guard, only Kapil Dev remained, contrary to reports that he too had been on the selection committee's hit list. Kiran More, who had made his Test debut less than four years previously, was named vice-captain. There was a lot of talk about the average age of the squad, which was 24. It did increase slightly after the first Test when Vengsarkar was flown out at the team management's request.

The 33-year-old former India captain had experienced the winds of change well before he landed in New Zealand. On the afternoon of 19 November 1989, four days after Sachin became India's 187th Test cricketer, Vengsarkar was leading Mumbai in a Ranji Trophy game against Gujarat at Surat. He was at the non-striker's end when Vinod Kambli arrived at the crease to make his Ranji Trophy debut, coincidentally against the same side that Sachin had opposed on his Ranji debut in the previous season.

The veteran could not believe his eyes when Kambli drove the first ball he faced, bowled by left-arm spinner Bharat Mistry, for six. This was not what Mumbai batsmen of Vengsarkar's generation and those before his time were known to do at the start of an innings. 'I cannot help it. This is what my coach has taught me to do. He told us that if the ball was there to be hit, then it should be hit,' Kambli explained to his incredulous captain.

Times were changing, as were attitudes. Later that season, Bengal awarded a first-class cap to the 17-year-old Sourav Ganguly, Sachin's 1989 Star Cricket Club teammate. The following season, Karnataka picked a teenager named Rahul Dravid.

> I believe his [Sachin's] success was also beneficial to us in another way. After him, a lot more cricketers started getting fast-tracked into Ranji sides. Previously, you had to wait till you were 19 or 20 at least before you were considered.
>
> —Rahul Dravid, *Wisden Asia Cricket*, August 2004

THE QUINTET

> *Certain critical situations bring out the best in men, and they bring out the best men. Old Trafford 1990 was such a situation for Indian cricket. That was when Sachin Tendulkar came to the fore, and remember, he wasn't even a man then. He was seventeen.*
>
> —Sunil Gavaskar, *Sunil Gavaskar Presents—III*, PMG, 1995

Whether Sachin would have had a more successful start to his Test career had he begun it at home is a matter of conjecture. Two 50s in four Tests against a formidable attack, the second of which was a match-saving effort, was by no means a bad start. In fact, his debut series in Pakistan had allowed him to settle into international cricket without being unduly burdened by the expectations of his newly acquired fans. He was also fortunate to have the right people around him.

> In an interview, Tendulkar spoke of a moment early in his career when he said what had happened to him, just after pulling on the India cap and t-shirt, 'you start thinking that, oh, I am somebody special.' It was an unnamed friend who then passed on a message to him. 'Just tell Sachin that I have noticed he is probably starting to think differently; the sooner he realises it, the better it is. Tendulkar said, 'And I sat back and realised, yes, it was true….' It is not the most profound piece of wisdom, it was probably a mate saying, 'Hey, you, you are close to becoming a punk, you know.' But it came at the right time. For the particularly gifted and successful athlete, the penny more often drops all too late.
>
> —Sharda Ugra, *Outlook Special Commemorative Issue*, 2010

Sachin's fans would have to wait till October 1990 to see him play an international match on home turf. Before that, he was to get opportunities aplenty to further hone the technique that he had displayed to score a match-saving 57 on a Sialkot greentop. The tour of New Zealand was to be followed by a visit to England. It meant that form and fitness permitting, Sachin would begin his international career with three tours. Coincidentally, Sunil Gavaskar had also started his international career in similar fashion, touring the Caribbean and England with the Indian team in 1971, and then Australia, as a member of the World XI in the next season. The exposure to diverse conditions at the start of his career had stood him in good stead.

Sachin made the most of the opportunities that he got in the 18 months following the tour of Pakistan. Of all his performances during this phase, five stood out. Much like the dashavatars of Lord Vishnu, every component of this quintet was a stage ahead of its predecessor, in terms of assurance and quality.

The Indian team that landed in New Zealand may have sported a 'youthful' look, but there was nothing new in the way it started the Test series at Christchurch. For the umpteenth time, the first Test of a series on foreign soil was lost. Richard Hadlee, soon to be knighted, became the founder member of Test cricket's '400-wickets' club, when he castled Sanjay Manjrekar in the first innings. Sachin was one of the many Indian players who had a forgettable game. He fell first ball in the first innings and scored 24 in the second.

In the second Test at Napier, the New Zealanders got to see what they had heard. Sachin, who had spent a lot of time in the nets to come to terms with the juice and movement in the wickets, batted with panache. At stumps on the third day, he was unbeaten on 80. Twenty more runs the next morning, and he would displace Pakistan's Mushtaq Mohammed as Test cricket's youngest centurion.

He got going on day four with two imperious drives off the paceman Danny Morrison, both of which sped to the fence. To all those watching, it appeared that the opposition would need to produce something special to get the better of him. However, what they did not know was that even as he battled the opposition, he was engaged in another duel—with himself. The batsman within him had kept the teenager within him at bay in a bout that had lasted 265 balls and produced 88 runs. Suddenly, the teenager sprung out of nowhere and delivered a knockout blow to his adversary. After two boundaries, onlookers expected Sachin to work the ball around for runs, but he went for a third. Morrison held the ball back, and Sachin ended up driving early and uppishly. John Wright, the New Zealand captain, held a sitter at mid-off. Mushtaq Mohammed's record was safe.

> I was disappointed and in tears too. I cried while crossing the boundary line and cried for another five to ten minutes in the dressing room. I was upset that I missed a golden opportunity....
>
> —Sachin Tendulkar, *The Sportstar*, 14 September 2002

The second and third Tests were drawn, the highlight of the third being an innings of 192 by India's new captain. The hosts thus took the series 1–0.

> In Napier, he gave us a long good look at himself, and in terms of his skill, he was the real deal.... With Sachin, there were two things that caught your eye. He had great balance and the time to play his shots. You saw one shot of brilliance that for normal batsmen would not be their first shot of selection. His late cut comes to mind. It was like something rang in your head like being woken up by your alarm, and you knew you were watching someone special.
>
> —John Wright, *India Today*, September 2010

India then failed to qualify for the final of a limited-overs tri-series that featured the hosts and Australia. Bedi's alleged statement that he would not stop the players if they wanted to commit suicide by jumping into the Pacific, made more news than the cricket. India's sole victory came in their second league game against New Zealand, in what was Sachin's third ODI. Batting first, India were in a spot of bother at 93–4 when Sachin arrived at the wicket. He was yet to get off the mark in ODIs, having scored ducks in his first two outings. This was reminiscent of his first two 'inter-net' matches at Shivaji Park, all those years previously. In his third game, he infused the innings with muscle and momentum. His 36 off 39 balls comprised four boundaries, including a fluent straight drive and an audacious hit on the up off Hadlee. He then tore a thigh muscle while fielding, and missed what turned out to be a humdinger, with the hosts falling short of India's score of 221 by one run. He was ruled out of the subsequent league game against Australia.

Around the time India ended their tour, one of the legends of New Zealand cricket wrote in a newspaper column that a 'Test match was no place to learn how to play Test cricket'. It was clearly a dig at India's teenage wonder and his dismissal at Napier. There were those who agreed with the assessment, but not for long.

Just before the Indian team flew to Sharjah for the second edition of the Austral-Asia Cup in June 1990, the Mumbai crowd got an opportunity to view their new hero in flesh and blood, when he combined with Kapil Dev to win a double-wicket tournament at the Wankhede.

Mohammed Azharuddin's 108 against Sri Lanka and unbeaten 78 against Pakistan went in vain as India failed to qualify for the semi-finals of the Austral-Asia Cup, losing to both Sri Lanka and Pakistan. Sachin's first visit to the cricketing oasis ended in disappointment for him and his team.

For the England tour, Ravi Shastri gained the unenviable distinction of serving as deputy to as many as four captains. The Mumbai all-rounder's extensive experience of English conditions left the selectors in no doubt that he would be as competent an aide to Azharuddin as he had been to Kapil Dev, Vengsarkar and Srikkanth in the past. The 1990 visit to England would be Shastri's fifth as a member of an Indian team. He had captained the national under-19 side to England in 1981 and had toured with the senior team in 1982, 1983 (World Cup) and 1986. He had also been a regular for Glamorgan on the county circuit in the late 1980s, and so knew the conditions and wickets like the back of his hand. The selectors were also hopeful that Dilip Vengsarkar would rediscover his form on familiar territory.

A fortnight before the team left for England, Sachin contacted Balwinder Singh Sandhu, the former Mumbai and India paceman. The man who had made the initial breakthrough for India in the 1983 World Cup final had by then got into coaching. Aware that the strips at Sandhu's base—the RCF ground in Chembur, a north-eastern suburb of Mumbai—tended to assist seam and swing, Sachin sought the senior's help in preparing for the England tour. He would start his practice at the RCF ground at 3:00 p.m. sharp, and face a battery of pace and swing bowlers handpicked by Sandhu, for two hours. The line and length that the bowlers were expected to maintain, would be decided in advance. Sachin would intersperse orthodox strokes with the occasional lofted straight drive over the sightscreen. After practice, he would sit with Sandhu and the bowlers at a tea-stall to discuss everything that had transpired during practice and plan for the next day.

Sachin was only continuing what his predecessors had been known to do before touring a country where a cricketer could encounter as many as four different seasons during a single day's play. The pioneer was of course Vijay Merchant, who had prepared for the tour of England in 1936 by batting in the nets early in the morning, a time of the day when the Mumbai wickets would have a bit of dew on them. This was an attempt on his part to replicate the conditions that he would encounter in England with the pitches having a lot of moisture. Amar Singh Ladha, the then spearhead of India's bowling attack and Merchant's close friend, was only too glad to come over to Mumbai and bowl to him.

Sanjay Manjrekar, who had not scored significantly in New Zealand, got going at the start of the England tour, with an innings of 158 in the first three-day game against Yorkshire. His fellow batsmen also struck form, even as their bowling colleagues floundered. The bowlers' cause was not helped by the fact that the seams of the balls that were being used in England that season were not as pronounced as those on the red cherries that had been used on earlier tours. For bowlers who relied more on swing than pace, this was disastrous. To add to their woes, the wickets were more flat than green, which was the consequence of an unusually hot summer.

Sachin scored 19 in India's first game of the tour, a one-dayer against League Cricket Conference. He missed the three-dayer against Yorkshire and scored 32 against Hampshire, batting at number three. In the subsequent encounter against Kent, the management promoted Sachin to open the innings with Kiran More, with W.V. Raman and Navjot Sidhu, the 'specialist openers', having been rested. The new combination put on 75. Sachin, in what was his very first outing as opener, scored 92. He followed it with 65 against the Minor Counties, and an unbeaten 10 in a one-dayer against Scotland. The next one-day game, India's last before the start of the two-match ODI series, was against Derbyshire. The management decided to give Sachin, who had played several games on the trot, a break.

On the eve of the game, Madhav Mantri, former India Test cricketer, Mumbai and Dadar Union captain and now the administrative manager of the Indian team, was buttonholed by an upset teenager. Derbyshire had Ian Bishop, the West Indian speedster, in their ranks, and Sachin did not want to lose out on the opportunity to play against him. Mantri, a figure who valued discipline, dedication and determination over everything else, was as surprised as he was delighted. Most batsmen would have gladly avoided playing Bishop, one of the fastest bowlers in the world, in what was just a 'side' game. Sachin obviously thought differently. Mantri spoke to Azharuddin and Bedi and got the teenager inducted into the playing XI.

Sachin went in at number three, with his team 5–1 and in pursuit of 236 in a 55-overs-a-side game. He took control of the chase, even as his colleagues struggled. Kapil Dev (31) and Dilip Vengsarkar (28) apart, no other batsman got going but Sachin wasn't flustered.

Sachin kept finding the gaps and boundaries on a regular basis. The Derbyshire bowlers then opted to do what their Delhi counterparts had done in the previous seasons, and targeted the other end. Sachin's pyrotechnics got India to a stage, where 15 were needed from the last two overs. Ian Bishop had the option of bowling either over, but he chose to deliver the penultimate one, reckoning that he could keep things tight and leave the opposition more than 10 to get from the final six deliveries. He gave nothing away off his first few deliveries, but Sachin had reserved his best for the last. Bishop dug it in, only to be swung handsomely for six. India cruised to victory in the final over, with two balls to spare. Sachin was undefeated on 105.

At the start of the tour, the Indian cricket manager had been advised by many 'pundits' to alter Sachin's bottom-handed grip, which in their view was unsuitable for English conditions, but Bishan Bedi of course knew better. Despite a 'faulty' grip, Sachin was well on his way to win the approval of cricket's most discerning critics.

India outplayed England in both the 55-overs-a-side ODIs. The second win was more significant as the visitors overhauled a target of 283 in an era wherein anything over 250 was considered unreachable. Manjrekar, Vengsarkar and Azharuddin were among the runs, and Sachin starred with two cameos. His 19 in the first ODI featured a huge six off off-spinner Eddie Hemmings. In the second game at Nottingham, with India chasing 282, he came in at a crucial stage. India still needed 96, at nearly a run-a-ball. Azharuddin, who had just got his eye in at the other end, needed support. Sachin warmed up with a stunner of a cover drive 'on the up' off Chris Lewis. He hit two more boundaries off Philip DeFreitas, and ran superbly between the wickets to score 31. When he fell, India needed 34 more, but the required rate was below six, and the Indian captain took the team home.

Back in India, the fans had mixed emotions. They were delighted with the 2–0 win, but were also upset that they had been denied the pleasure of viewing the matches on TV. The British Broadcasting Corporation (BBC) and Doordarshan had failed to strike a deal, forcing cricket lovers to go back in time to their transistors.

India's last three-day game before the first Test at Lord's was against Gloucestershire. With Kapil Dev not bowling due to a stiff neck, Shardashram's former new-ball bowler was asked to take over. Sachin went flat out, bowling as many as 32 overs in the first innings and dismissing three specialist batsmen.

The Test series started on a bizarre note at Lord's. Azharuddin called correctly on what looked a batting beauty, but opted to bowl. England expressed their gratitude in the form of a modest 653-4. Graham Gooch, Azharuddin's opposite number, scored 333, and Allan Lamb and Robin Smith plundered hundreds. India's response was led by the seniors. Ravi Shastri, who had been promoted to the opening slot ahead of the in-form Raman, scored a round ton, and Vengsarkar got 54. Azharuddin, still feeling the heat after his call at the toss, drove, cut and flicked his way to a glorious 121. But even he was overshadowed by Kapil Dev. The entire Indian team emerged on the dressing room balcony to applaud when the great all-rounder hit off-spinner Eddie Hemmings for four consecutive sixes to avoid the follow-on. Narendra Hirwani, the number 11, was then dismissed off the first ball of the very next over.

With a lead of 199, England knew exactly what to do in the second innings. Openers Gooch and Mike Atherton put on 204, with the England captain getting his second ton of the game. Both perished in the scramble for quick runs. The score was 250-2, and a second declaration imminent, when Lamb came down the wicket to leg-spinner Hirwani, and was beaten in the flight. However, he went through with the shot, and swung straight and hard.

From his position at long-off, Sachin saw Lamb connect. Off he sprinted to his right, keeping his eyes on the ball as it descended to earth. The cherry had all but hit the deck, a few metres in front of the sightscreen, when Sachin bent and extended his right hand to take a remarkable catch, inches from the turf. For the regulars at Lord's, it was as incredible a piece of fielding as Kapil Dev's catch to dismiss Viv Richards in the 1983 World Cup final and Roger Harper's run out of Graham Gooch in the Bicentenary Test in 1987.

A target of 472 was beyond India's reach. The possibility of an honourable draw evaporated when Manjrekar and Vengsarkar, the accumulators in the line-up, fell cheaply. Sachin, who had been bowled through the gate for 10 in the first innings, scored 27 before being caught off Angus Fraser. India were bowled out for 224. Their bowling and batting being inconsistent throughout, the visitors were consistent in maintaining the ancient Indian 'tradition' of losing the first Test of an 'away' series.

In the second Test at Old Trafford, Manchester, England won the toss, took first strike and once again tore the Indian bowling to shreds. Gooch scored his third straight ton of the series, Atherton his first and Smith his second. The hosts totalled 519.

The cornerstone of India's response of 432 was a third-wicket stand of 189 between Manjrekar (93) and Azharuddin (179). Sachin came in at 246-4 and dropped anchor. After the Lord's Test, he had sought the advice of 'Mr. Gavaskar', the lone 'Indian voice' in the BBC TV commentary team. The legend had advised the learner to 'wait for the ball to come to him'. This was easier said than done, but the 17-year-old showed that he was a quick learner. He spent as many as 49 minutes in the middle, assessing the bowling, the wicket and the conditions, before getting off the mark by cutting Atherton for four.

For those who knew Sachin, and for Sachin himself, to spend that much time in the middle without scoring a run was unbelievable. He may not have troubled the scorers for 49 minutes, but in doing so, he had broken a mental barrier that was no less daunting than the one that he had smashed after being hit on the nose by Waqar Younis.

A little later, he ducked into a short delivery by Devon Malcolm, England's quickest bowler. He had done likewise in Pakistan and New Zealand, taking his eyes off the ball in the process. However, this time around, the ball struck him on the shoulder. It had kept lower than he had expected, and he had been decidedly lucky not to have been hit on the back of the head instead. Taking one's eyes off the ball was not advisable on a two-paced wicket like the one they were playing on, he learnt. He added 112 with his captain and was last out for 68.

The innings underscored the strides that he had made as batsman and cricketer since the Pakistan tour. In terms of technique and temperament, the batsman who scored 68 in the first innings at Manchester was a more rounded player than the one who had scored 88 at Napier and 105 against Derbyshire.

Another dismal bowling performance later, the visitors were thrown the challenge of batting out the last five hours on the last day to save the game. That they needed 408 to win was irrelevant. It was 1990 and not 2008.

As had been the case at Lord's, India got off to a disastrous start in their second innings. The openers fell early and Manjrekar and Vengsarkar added 74 before both perished at the same score. This brought in Sachin, into what one of the commentators called a 'white-hot' situation. He got his feet moving with a cover drive off Hemmings. The Indian supporters, delighted with the stroke, fell silent when Azharuddin was caught in the leg-trap a little later. India were 127–5 and in trouble.

India nearly lost a sixth when Sachin strode down the track to Hemmings and drove straight, but uppishly. The bowler got his palms to the ball but could not hold on. That was the cue for the teenager to put his head down. He made up his mind to eschew the drive until he had settled down and the team was in a more secure position. Ironically, it was a veteran who had a rush of blood next. Kapil Dev had added 56 with Sachin when he attempted a big hit off Hemmings 20 minutes before the tea interval, missed and was bowled.

Manoj Prabhakar, the next man in, had scored 95 as opener at Napier in the previous series, and so was more than capable of dropping anchor. He had for company, a batsman whose confidence was growing with every delivery he faced. Sachin leg-glanced Chris Lewis to fine-leg for four to bring up the 200 of the innings. When Lewis bowled one that rose from a good length, Sachin rose with alacrity and turned the face of his bat at the point of contact, to dispatch the cherry past gully for four. He was airborne when he essayed the stroke, a sign that he was on the top of his game in terms of confidence as well as timing.

The shot brought up his second 50 of the match.

The England bowlers gave it everything they had, but Sachin and his partner were firmly entrenched by the time the 20 mandatory overs commenced. Even as watchers went into raptures at Sachin's fluent strokeplay, impeccable defence and swift running between wickets, Prabhakar kept serving reminders of his existence every now and then, with some emphatic shots. When Sachin punched Fraser off the back foot, straight down the ground, for four, SMG would have smiled in approval from his seat in the commentary box. Two years previously, he had seen Sachin essay a similar stroke off Raju Kulkarni in the Mumbai nets and concluded that the boy was 'special'. He was being proved right.

Sachin entered the 90s, all the time urging himself to stay calm. After all, only four wickets separated England from a win. At 97, he had another slice of good fortune. He ducked into a short delivery by Fraser, but forgot to bring his bat down. Fortunately for him and India, the ball hit the inside-edge of his bat and went to fine-leg for a single. It could very easily have taken the outside-edge and been consumed by the slip cordon.

Sachin returned to the strike after Prabhakar took three runs to complete his 50. Fraser served another good-length ball, on the line of the off-stump. Sachin picked it early and drove it off the back foot. As the ball passed mid-off, the Indian players and supporters rose from their seats. By the time the ball was thrown back to the bowler, Sachin had completed three runs and, in the process, his first Test century. He was only 17 years and 112 days old.

> I remember when I scored my hundred, even to show my bat to the dressing room I was a little shy. If you go back and see my expressions, I was really shy to look up at all the people who were there and acknowledge them. I finally managed to do that. The pitch was two-paced and the odd ball kept low, but I wouldn't say it was a difficult wicket to bat on. It was just the pressure created by them that I had to deal with. The wicket hadn't deteriorated. If at all the odd ball kept low, it wasn't taking off as such…. It was somewhere at the back of my mind that I was out in New Zealand… But on that day, I was extremely determined… I was not going to stop with an 80 or 100 because it was important that we played out the whole day.
>
> —Sachin Tendulkar, *The Times of India*, 20 December 2010

'An innings of temperament, skill and delightful strokeplay,' declared Richie Benaud in the commentary box. Sachin celebrated the hundred with a punch off the back foot off Devon Malcolm, England's fastest bowler, and a square cut off Lewis. The match was called off with two mandatory overs left. An Indian journalist who was covering the series spotted one of the doorkeepers at the ground sobbing copiously. When asked what had happened, the affable old man replied that the teenaged centurion had reminded him of Denis Compton, his boyhood hero and the charismatic and cavalier cricketer of the 1940s and 1950s.

> His driving on the up, off the back foot, was a delight. To see a 17-year-old bat with such remarkable authority was something else. The confidence with which he went out, that made a deep impression on me. And then, when he spoke, he had that squeaky voice. In effect, when he spoke, he was a boy but when he batted, he was a man.... You got the feeling that he would not get out, that was the confidence he generated within his teammates even at that early stage of his career. He was extremely compact, he knew the situation and he knew that he had to bat till the end. For a 17-year-old to understand all that, go about his innings in the manner in which he did, and to end up saving the Test, it was quite an experience.... He just looked like he wasn't nervous at all. Now, that's total control. And when he came back unbeaten with the draw secured, he had a satisfied look on his face.... The general mood was that he was a 17-year-old who had saved the Test match, we must also stand up and do something for the team.
>
> —Anil Kumble, *The Sachin Sunset*, Wisden India, 2013

The century yielded the 17-year-old his first Man of the Match Award at the international level. His reaction on being gifted a bottle of champagne was to tell the presenter that he did not drink. The bottle was left uncorked.

> Long ago after the Old Trafford Test match becomes just another page in Wisden, the memory of a charming, almost embarrassed young man receiving the Man of the Match award will linger. Sachin Tendulkar will score many more hundreds for India, but the freshness of this one will never fade.
>
> —Harsha Bhogle, *Mid-Day*, 14 August 1990

The impasse between BBC and Doordarshan ensured that Sachin's innings wasn't watched on TV in India, neither live nor in the form of a highlights package. It turned out to be a classic illustration of the darkest hour preceding the dawn.

> I was sitting in the lounge, after breakfast (on the morning after the Test ended). He came over. There was space on the sofa on which I was sitting,

but he did not sit there. He sat on the ground, at my feet, and asked, 'Sir, how did I play? Did I commit any mistakes?' A teenager who scored his first Test century against England in England should have been flying high, but he wasn't. I told him that any cricketer would have been proud to have played an innings like that. What was important was his urge to learn.

—Madhav Mantri, *Million Dollar Babies*, Star Cricket, 2008

India batted first in the third Test at the Oval and ran up a score of 606, their highest on English soil at that point. Ravi Shastri's 187 gave him a Test series aggregate of 336 at an average of 67.2, inclusive of two tons. It had not been intended at the start of the tour that the Indian vice-captain open the innings, but he had now made the slot his own. It spoke volumes of his perseverance and adaptability that he was one of the few cricketers to have batted at every number from number 10 to 1. From starting his career in 1980–81 as 'a spinner who could bat a bit', he was now 'an opener who could bowl'. Indian cricket, it appeared, had found an answer to its post-Gavaskar opening blues by unearthing one who could fill the legend's shoes, especially in alien conditions, 'not wholly or in full measure, but substantially'.

India's second centurion at the Oval was Kapil Dev who scored 110. India scored 606, of which Sachin's share was 21. The Indian bowlers then bowled England out for 340 and prompted Azharuddin to enforce the follow-on, but England batted out the final day with ease. David Gower, that most elegant of left-handers, cruised to an unbeaten 157.

Sachin had a close look at another extraordinary left-handed batsman later in the year, when he turned up for a World XI in an exhibition game against a West Indies XI at Toronto, Canada. Interestingly, it was his second game under the 'captaincy' of Imran Khan, after his brief stint as a substitute in the CCI Golden Jubilee game in early 1987. Put in to bat, the World XI scored 309-6, with Sachin contributing 54. The West Indies XI comprised a left-handed batsman called Brian Lara. He scored only 14, but Sachin liked what he saw. The two youngsters got along very well.

Even as he went about rubbing shoulders with the illustrious present and promising future of cricket, Sachin was having issues with his home state's educational authorities. They were reluctant to promote him from the 11th standard to the 12th because he did not fulfil the basic criterion of 75 per cent attendance in junior college. Even first-class cricketers, they argued, were not exempt from this rule. But then, Sachin had missed classes only because he had been representing his country. The efforts of the Kirti College management to convince the authorities ultimately paid off. Like the CCI in the late 1980s, the Maharashtra State Higher Secondary Board amended its rules to allow Sachin to appear for the final exams. He gained a promotion to the 12th standard, but thereafter cricket took over his life completely.

Cricket lovers in India, aleady upset with the TV blackout of the England tour, were looking forward to the home season of 1990–91, the highlight of which was to be a five-Test series against Pakistan. But they were in for another disappointment. In what was a monumental irony, Pakistan of all countries cited 'internal disturbances' in India and declined to tour. In the wake of the cancellation of the England series two years previously, this was a massive blow. It meant that India's only international assignment of the season was a one-off Test and three ODIs against Sri Lanka, plus an Asia Cup that was for all practical purposes a 'South Asia' Cup after Pakistan's withdrawal. In the fray were India, Sri Lanka and Bangladesh, which at the time was an associate member of the ICC.

The one-off Test, played at Chandigarh, was memorable for quite a few Indian players. It was Sachin's first at home after 10 games overseas, and Sanjay Manjrekar's first on home turf since his debut at Delhi in 1987–88. Ravi Shastri continued his purple patch as an opener with an innings of 82. Venkatapathy Raju, the left-arm spinner who had returned home midway through the England tour after breaking a finger, spun Sri Lanka out with figures of 6–12 in the first innings. 'Local boy' Kapil Dev's four scalps in the second innings enabled him to draw level with Ian Botham's tally of 376 Test scalps and become the second-highest wicket-taker in Tests. India's win by an innings and eight runs was Azharuddin's first as captain.

India took the three-match ODI series against Sri Lanka with wins in the first two games. Sachin won his first-ever individual award in ODIs for his 53 in the second game at Pune, which India won by six wickets. He was presented the prize by Prof. D.B. Deodhar, centenarian and former Maharashtra captain, in whose name the BCCI had instituted its first-ever limited-overs tournament in the early 1970s. In the 'South Asia' Cup that followed, India lost their league match to Sri Lanka, but beat the same team in the final, played at Kolkata. Sachin contributed 53 to India's chase of a target of 205.

As had been the case a couple of seasons previously, the cancellation of an international series ensured that the 'stars' were available for domestic matches. Sachin scored 159 for West Zone against East Zone at Guwahati, in what was his first Duleep Trophy game. The century made him the first batsman to score a century on debut in all three of India's domestic first-class competitions—the Ranji Trophy, the Irani Cup and the Duleep Trophy. West Zone took the decisive first-innings lead and took on South Zone in the semi-final at Rourkela. In another high-scoring affair in which West Zone again took the first-innings lead, Sachin scored 131, his second hundred in succession. He fell early for 25 in the final against North Zone, a game that witnessed some deplorable behaviour by members of both sides, particularly West Zone's Rashid Patel and North Zone's Raman Lamba, who went at each other with a stump and bat respectively.

The Duleep Trophy was followed by the knockout stage of the Ranji Trophy. Sachin scored 69 in the pre-quarter final against Madhya Pradesh, who were led by Sandeep Patil. After his retirement from first-class cricket in 1986–87 and a brief stint as Manager of the Mumbai team, Patil was persuaded to make a comeback by Madhavrao Scindia, the erstwhile Maharajah of the erstwhile princely state of Gwalior in central India, a prominent political figure and senior functionary in the BCCI. Patil's brief was to lead and restructure the team of the Madhya Pradesh Cricket Association, which Scindia headed. Patil's old team beat his new team by 10 wickets.

Legal wrangles resulted in the postponement of the last three stages of the Ranji knockout, to April–May 1991. Sanjay Manjrekar was named Mumbai captain in the absence of Shastri, who was unavailable due to prior commitments. The quarter-final between arch-rivals Mumbai and Delhi was a cliffhanger. Mumbai batted first and scored 390, with Sachin contributing 82. Delhi came within a run of drawing level. Buoyed by the first-innings lead, the Mumbai batsmen made merry in the second innings with four batsmen, Sachin included, scoring centuries.

Before taking on Hyderabad in the semi-final at the Wankhede, Sachin achieved a significant milestone off the field. On 24 April 1991, the day he turned 18 and attained adulthood, he was inducted as a full-time employee by Sungrace-Mafatlal. Accompanying him on his drive from Sahitya Sahawas to the Sungrace-Mafatlal HQ at Nariman Point in his red Maruti 800 was Anil Joshi, who had spent a lot of time with both Sachin and Kambli during their Shardashram years.

> Arrangements had been made in the office to welcome Sachin into the fold. I was assigned the job of ensuring that Sachin entered the auspices during the auspicious time-period [muhurta] that had been identified. I reached his Sahitya Sahawas residence as per schedule. Sachin insisted that we meet Achrekar Sir before going to the office. A new chapter of his life was to start and he understandably wanted to seek the blessings of his Guru before it began. In those days, Achrekar Sir lived at Bhoiwada near Parel

in central Mumbai, which was a little out of the way. Achrekar Sir blessed Sachin, and his wife and daughters performed a puja for him. When we finally left for the office, I was a little jittery and worried that we would not make it to the Sungrace-Mafatlal office in time, but Sachin put me at ease. I realized that day that his driving was as splendid as his batting. We reached well in time. He was given a hero's welcome and ushered into an impressive cabin.

—Anil Joshi, personal interview

The semi-final against Hyderabad, on a Wankhede pitch baked in the April heat, was another 'batathon'. Manjrekar's 377 was the highest individual score by a Mumbai batsman; Vinod Kambli scored 126 and Sachin got 70, as Mumbai amassed 855–6.

The final, which began at the Wankhede Stadium on 3 May 1991, featured Mumbai and Haryana. Mumbai had won the title 30 times and had as many as seven Test cricketers in their playing XI.* On the other hand, Haryana were playing a Ranji Trophy final for only the second time. They had been runners-up to Delhi in 1985–86. Only two members of the side had played international cricket at the highest level—Chetan Sharma and Kapil Dev Nikhanj, the captain. On paper, it was a mismatch.

However, the man who had inspired India to lift the World Cup on 25 June 1983 provided yet another spectacular demonstration of his ability to inspire a group of underdogs to overcome a set of heavyweights. Haryana batted first and scored 522, and then bowled Mumbai out for 410 on the fourth morning. Having conceded a first-innings lead, Mumbai's only option was to go for an outright win. For that, they needed to terminate the Haryana second innings as quickly as possible. Paceman Salil Ankola and left-arm spinner Sanjay Patil took three wickets each, as Haryana were dismissed for 242 on the fifth morning. This meant that Mumbai needed 355 to win, with two sessions and a bit left.

The start of their chase could not have been more calamitous; openers Lalchand Rajput and Shishir Hattangadi, and skipper Sanjay Manjrekar, fell in quick succession. The score was 34–3 at the lunch interval.

During the break, Madhav Mantri, then the president of the MCA, was interviewed by the TV commentators. When asked what the strategy would

---

*The seven Test cricketers in question were (in batting order): Lalchand Rajput, Sanjay Manjrekar, Dilip Vengsarkar, Sachin Tendulkar, Chandrakant Pandit, Raju Kulkarni and Salil Ankola. Two other members of the XI—Vinod Kambli and Abey Kuruvilla—played Tests subsequently.

be, given that they were three down with over 300 to score, Mantri's reply was typical of the man: 'This is the Mumbai team. We won't give up.' There was another thing he said; 'We still have Sachin Tendulkar.'

Shortly after the resumption, the players who had partnered each other to win a double-wicket tournament at the Wankhede just a year previously, found themselves opposing each other. As he ran in to bowl, Kapil Dev decided to try and deceive his erstwhile partner with a slower ball. The veteran executed the delivery perfectly, but Sachin picked it early. He met it with the full face of the bat, and drove it straight and high, into the stands. November 1988, when the same batsman had faced the same bowler in the India nets on the same plot of land, seemed a century away. It wasn't very often that people had seen India's greatest all-rounder and an international icon being treated so contemptuously. With that one stroke, Sachin had conveyed his team's intentions. The chase was on.

Thereafter, it was carnage. Sachin tore into Pradeep Jain, the left-arm spinner, hitting him for three sixes. Kapil, who was doing everything he could to prevent his teammates from getting rattled, brought back Chetan Sharma from the Tata End. The bowler and his teammates were left gaping as Sachin thumped a good-length delivery into the North Stand, with a flat-batted swipe often seen in the 'rubber-ball' cricket matches played on the maidans and in the by-lanes of Mumbai. Applauding the stroke were several Mumbaikars, who had left the ground in disgust at lunch, only to rush back after hearing about the counterattack. By the time the last ball was bowled, there were close to 18,000 people in the stands.

An improbable win seemed imminent when, not for the last time, Sachin fell *against the run of play*. After hitting off-spinner Yogendra Bhandari for three boundaries, Sachin went for a fourth, off a full-toss, but found Ajay Jadeja at cover. He had scored 96 off only 75 deliveries, which wasn't something Indians were used to witnessing in first-class cricket, least of all on the last day of a game in 1991.

The target was still 187 runs away, but Sachin had created an opening for the hosts with his assault, and Kapil Dev knew that this in turn presented an opportunity for Haryana to win outright. Having shared dressing rooms and played with and against Mumbai cricketers for nearly 15 years, the legend knew very well that there was no way Mumbai would down the shutters after sniffing an opportunity. Sachin's innings had changed the complexion of the game.

Kapil Dev accordingly implored his boys not to relax and make every half-chance count. A spectacular climax unfolded, with Vengsarkar taking over from his junior colleague and bringing his team to the cusp of victory, even as wickets went down at the other end. Tragically for Vengsarkar and Mumbai, Abey Kuruvilla, the number 11, was run out with only three needed for a win. Vengsarkar, stranded on 136, cried unabashedly, as did Mumbai's supporters.

Sachin's 96 in the Ranji final, two weeks after he attained adulthood in legal terms, was the fifth decisive innings that he essayed in the year-and-a-half since his international debut. From March 1990 to May 1991, from the 88 at Napier to the 96 at the Wankhede, he had performed and delivered in varied situations and conditions, in different forms of the game.

At 18, Sachin's ascent to cricketing immortality seemed inevitable. What remained to be seen was *when* he would achieve it. Not *how*.

ICON

For a generation of Indians who were in their teens around the time Tendulkar was mounting a counterattack in Perth, he became more than a sportsman. He became a symbol of the aspirations of a new generation of Indians. A few years earlier, I had been on my maiden tour of India, and while the main cities were comparable to anywhere in the world, we also stayed at hotels where there was one telephone line and unreliable ISD services. This was the India in which Tendulkar made his debut. I don't write this out of disrespect for the India that was, but with complete admiration for the India that is. In the quarter century that was Tendulkar's career, India has progressed amazingly from one-telephone hotels to being a country with 900 million-plus mobile phone connections. This journey, with its peaks and troughs, has inextricably woven itself into the career of Tendulkar with its heroic highs and crashing lows.

—Steve Waugh, *The Week*, 1 December 2013

The year 1991 was seminal for India. The generation that was born in the 1970s and grew up in the 1980s was still at an impressionable age when the newly elected government, headed by Narsimha Rao, initiated the process of liberalization. The move set into motion, a series of transformations—physical, social, financial, political, technological and resultantly mental—all of which continued through the decade. This writer considers himself fortunate to be part of a group that can delineate as well as relate to the eras both before and after liberalization.

The year also marked the start of a new era of sorts for cricket lovers. The 1991–92 season was to feature quite a lot of the sport, after a veritable drought in 1990–91. The Indian team was to start the season with a tri-series at Sharjah and ODI series at home against Pakistan, to be followed by a full tour of Australia and then the fifth edition of the World Cup.

Not surprisingly, cricket lovers in India reacted to the tri-series in the cricketing oasis in October 1991, India's first international assignment in nine

The teenage prodigy

Hind Sewak Club, winners of the Gordhandas Shield Limited-overs Tournament, 1985. Sachin is squatting at the extreme left.

The Invincibles: Sachin with his Shardashram teammates in an inter-school game, mid-1980s.

Sachin and Vinod Kambli with Hanumant Singh, former India Test cricketer, at a function organized by the Sports Journalists Association of Mumbai to felicitate them for their record stand of 664 in an inter-school game in the 1987–88 season.

Early days in international cricket and autograph signing

Winning a double-wicket tournament in partnership with Kapil Dev (extreme left) at the Wankhede Stadium in June 1990.

Returning from the tour of England in 1990 with a bottle of champagne presented to him for scoring his maiden Test hundred.

Sachin with members of Sahitya Sahawas' generation-next, early 1990s.

24 April 1991: Cutting the cake to celebrate his adulthood and induction into Sungrace-Mafatlal. Also in the picture are Atulya Mafatlal, Vice-Chairman, Sungrace-Mafatlal Group of Companies (first from right); Sandeep Patil (second from right); Hemant Waingankar (third from right) and Anil Joshi (fourth from right).

Sachin's insignia on the tour of Australia in 1991-92

The young brand ambassador

The young brand ambassador

Early 1990s: Sachin with his parents, Rajani and Ramesh Tendulkar, and Vinod Kambli.

Early 1990s: Ramakant Achrekar (fourth from right) with seven of his many disciples who represented the country. From left, Vinod Kambli, Chandrakant Pandit, Lalchand Rajput, Pravin Amre, Sachin, Balwinder Singh Sandhu and Ramnath Parkar.

From Shivaji Park to the Wankhede Stadium: Sachin and Vinod Kambli with the Ranji Trophy in 1994-95.

24 May 1995: Wedding bells: Sachin with Anjali, his better half.

months, like a thirsty wanderer in a desert would after spotting an oasis. India's first game, against Pakistan, coincided with the final paper of this writer's first semester examination in his first year of junior college, and it was quite a task to resist the temptation to hurry up with the answers and rush home to watch the action on the television.

For Indian cricket fans of the time, Pakistan was a bogey team. It evoked mixed feelings, in that they hated it in public but admired it in private. Indians had always been envious of the abundance of genuine fast bowlers across the border. In the limited-overs era of the late 1980s and early 1990s, Pakistan's batsmen also elicited 'closet' awe. Leading the way was of course Javed Miandad, whose match-winning hundred and last-ball six in the Austral-Asia Cup final at Sharjah in April 1986 had scarred many an Indian psyche. There were many Indian fans who wished that their heroes imbibed the impudence that their Pakistani counterparts displayed in matches between the traditional rivals.

All of India was therefore ecstatic when Azharuddin's side prevailed over Pakistan in the opening game of the tri-series and then beat the West Indies twice. Sachin was in the thick of things in these wins with bat and ball. When he arrived at the wicket in the opening game against Pakistan, India were 149–3 at less than four an over. Great sports personalities can transform a game within minutes, and Sachin did precisely that with his ability and audacity.

The Pakistani bowlers, who had contained the batsmen till then, found themselves bowling the way he wanted them to. His signature strokes were a flick off Waqar Younis that sped to the mid-wicket boundary, and a straight-driven four off Imran that he executed by dancing down the wicket. The Pakistani captain was flustered enough to bowl full-tosses that were promptly given the treatment. Sachin completed his 50 off the penultimate ball of the innings with an incredible cross-batted swip—a 'rubber-ball' stroke—off Waqar Younis that found the point boundary. He returned undefeated on 52, scored off only 40 balls, and India finished with 238–4. Fifty-six of those runs had come from the last five overs of the innings, of which Sachin's share was 37.

Pakistan, who were 124–2 at one stage, were thwarted by some good bowling. The middle and lower order caved in and victory was India's by 60 runs. In the second of the two wins over the Windies, Azharuddin called upon Sachin to play the third seamer's role. The teenager responded with figures of 4–34. Among his victims were Richie Richardson, the opposition captain who had taken two hundreds off Pakistan in the tournament, and a certain Brian Lara. The West Indies were bowled out for 145, and India's seven-wicket win was their first over the West Indies while chasing.

All the pressure was on Pakistan on the eve of their second round-robin clash against India. With a solitary win against the West Indies, and a loss apiece to the Windies and India, Imran's side had a battle on its hands to stay in contention for a place in the final. India on the other hand had already qualified with three wins out of three.

Only a combination of poor planning and atrocious luck could have undone the Indians at that stage, and they ended up suffering on both counts on 23 October 1991, the day of the second round-robin game against Pakistan. The start was delayed by an hour, but surprisingly, the overs were not curtailed. That was a surprise, considering that both teams were Asian and hence aware of how quickly it got dark in their part of the world once the sun went down.

Pakistan won the toss and batted first. Needing to score at least 198 to qualify for the final, they ended up making 257–5. India began the chase well, with Ravi Shastri putting on 124 for the first wicket with Vinod Kambli. In only his fourth game for India, that too an encounter against Pakistan, the left-hander was asked to play an unfamiliar role in the absence of the indisposed Sidhu. The youngster displayed his professionalism with an innings of 40.

Pakistan came back into the game with the wickets of Kambli, Shastri and Azharuddin in quick succession. At 134–3, Sachin came in and went on the attack straightaway. Wasim Akram was hit for three boundaries, an imperious straight drive and magnificent short-arm pull being followed by a stunner that went over mid-on's head. Sachin's wet gloves, a result of the humidity at the ground, caused the bat to fly out of his hands when he went for a drive off Aamir Sohail, the Pakistani opener who doubled up as a left-arm spinner. Sachin compensated for the miss with a six over long-off, which brought up the 200 of the innings.

By this time, the sun had vanished and the lights on the streets lining the ground had been switched on. There were none at the ground, however, and India's best bet was for Sachin to take them through along with Sanjay Manjrekar, who was firmly entrenched at the other end. The red cherry, over 40 overs old, was barely visible, but both batsmen were 'in the zone'. The Indian sections in the stands went delirious when Sachin came down the wicket to Salim Malik and deposited him on the roof of the stadium. Ironically, the extra seconds spent in requisitioning a replacement ball worked against him and his team in the rapidly increasing darkness.

Sachin was one short of 50 when he came down the wicket to Malik again, eager to finish it off before the cherry became invisible. He was in the process of making the stroke when he realized that the ball was directed at his pads and he had no room in which to flex his arms. He still went through and hit it high, but not far enough. Mushtaq Ahmed, substituting on the mid-wicket boundary, ran in to take a tumbling catch. Manjrekar and he had added 85 for the fourth wicket.

Kapil Dev was then dismissed first ball. Manjrekar and the new man Prabhakar did try to raise the issue of the light with the umpires, but it was a pointless exercise as both sides had agreed to the Playing Conditions before the match got underway. The Indians needed 12 from the last over and they finished four runs short. Sachin's wicket had divested the Indian innings of its momentum and swung the match in Pakistan's favour.

The win was just the revitalizer that Pakistan needed at their happy hunting ground after the reverse in their first game against India. Ever since Miandad's last-ball six of 1986, the Pakistanis had felt invincible whenever they played their traditional rivals at Sharjah, and they resumed normal service in the final. The Indians did themselves no favours by opting to field after winning the toss, despite having beaten Pakistan while defending and lost while chasing at the round-robin stage. Pakistan scored 262–6, and then their bowlers took over. Paceman Aaqib Javed completed an all-lbw hattrick when Sachin followed Shastri and Azharuddin to the pavilion. All the hard work of the league stage came undone, with India losing by 72 runs.

Manjrekar (52) apart, India's best batsman in the game was Vinod Kambli, who scored 30. It was his second substantial innings of the tournament after the 40 in the league game against Pakistan. Hence, the decision of the selectors to exclude him from the squad after the tournament was shocking, to say the very least. Even as one disciple of Achrekar's went out, another came in.

The much-anticipated five-match ODI series against Pakistan was aborted after the pitch at the Wankhede Stadium in Mumbai, venue of the first game, was desecrated. The BCCI then did something unexpected.

Just a few months previously, the Board had sought the government's approval to propose the re-induction of South Africa into the ICC. The government had given the go-ahead, the outcome of which was the end of South Africa's 21-year cricketing isolation. Nelson Mandela's release from prison in early 1990 had marked the start of the dissolution of South Africa's policy of apartheid that had forced international bodies to impose a sporting embargo on the country in the late 1960s.

The BCCI invited the 'new' South Africa for a short, three-match ODI series, which would mark their return to international cricket. The residents of Kolkata lined the streets of the city to welcome the South African cricket team on its way from the airport to the hotel, and more than a hundred thousand spectators thronged Eden Gardens on the day of the match.

The galleries were abuzz when South Africa were restricted to 177–8 on a slow and low pitch. They fell silent when the home team was reduced to 3–2. Shastri and Manjrekar fell to the pace of Allan Donald, who had earned the appellation 'White Lightning' with his exploits in county cricket in England and in domestic matches in his own country. Sachin went in at number four, ahead of Azharuddin, who had manned that spot in Sharjah. From the non-striker's end, he saw Sidhu become Donald's third victim. At 20–3, an upset seemed a possibility.

> I like to go in at 10–2 when bowlers are on top. If it's 170–2, it means you have been padded for long, the bowling isn't strong. It's too easy.
>
> —Sachin Tendulkar, *Outlook*, 4 January 1999

Azharuddin and Sachin started rebuilding the innings. Luck was on India's side, with Clive Rice, the South African captain, opting to give Donald a breather. The duo added 40 before the captain was dismissed by Tim Shaw, the left-arm spinner. Sachin was then joined by debutant Pravin Amre.

The third Achrekar disciple to play for India in the calendar year of 1991 was senior to the first two in terms of both age and first-class experience. Amre had worked his way up the ladder in the mid-1980s, scoring heavily for Shardashram and then Mithibai College in Mumbai. He came into national prominence with knocks of 206 and an unbeaten 157 for West Zone against the Rest of India in the under-19 M.A. Chidambaram Trophy game in 1986–87. At a time when getting into the Mumbai team was as difficult as getting into the Indian team, Amre failed on his Ranji debut for his hometown. He was a lot more successful for the Railways, whom he joined on the advice of his guru. His consistency at the domestic level in the late 1980s earned him a call from the national selectors.

Not very long ago, Pravin Amre had been the player Achrekar's pupils, Sachin and Vinod included, looked up to. He had once promised Sachin a pair of Adidas shoes if he were to score a century in a junior game. Sure enough, Sachin had delivered, and Amre had gifted him a pair.*

On 10 November 1991, the Eden Gardens witnessed a reversal of roles. Sachin, far more experienced at the international level, dominated a stand of 56 before Donald had him caught by Richard Snell in his second spell. He had

---

*Years later, Sachin was signed on by Adidas as their brand ambassador. He told the media that had assembled for the formal announcement that he would never forget Amre's gesture.

scored 62, inclusive of eight fours and a six. At 116–5, it was still anybody's game, but Amre displayed all the qualities that Ajit Tendulkar had noticed in Achrekar's disciples all those years ago. His pluck prompted senior cricketers like Kapil Dev and Prabhakar to play second fiddle. Amre was eventually out for 55 with the scores level, and India won by three wickets. The hosts then took the series with a 38-run win in the second game at Gwalior.

For the Indians, the third and final game of the series, played at New Delhi's magnificent Jawaharlal Nehru Stadium, was a novelty. It was only the second official 'day-night' ODI on Indian soil since 1984, and the first time an Indian team had worn coloured clothing and played under lights with a white ball and black sightscreens, since an unofficial 'drought relief' game against Pakistan at the same venue in 1987. The Jawaharlal Nehru Stadium was primarily an athletics venue, which necessitated the covering of portions of the racing track with Astroturf to prevent damage by cricket boots.

The visitors wore green shirts and the Indians light blue, but both sides retained their white trousers and leg-guards. Splendid hundreds by Shastri and Manjrekar enabled India to finish with 287–4, which in 1991 was akin to scoring 450 in 2017. What the Indian fans, who thought that a clean sweep of the series was imminent, did not consider was the fact that while the South Africans were new to international cricket (ex-Australia cricketer Kepler Wessels excepted), they had a lot more experience of night and limited-overs cricket than their opponents. They played their premier domestic limited-overs competition under floodlights.

That apart, it made little sense to compare the South African outfit to a team like Sri Lanka, which had played its first Test in 1981–82, but even a decade later, was a few years away from being considered world-class. Most of the South Africans had represented English County sides in first-class and limited-overs competitions with distinction during their years of isolation. They had also battled 'Rebel' sides from England, Australia, the West Indies and Sri Lanka, all of which had comprised successful international cricketers from those countries. It was therefore but natural that the South Africans would not take long to make a statement after testing and tasting the waters of 'official' international cricket in the first two ODIs. They overhauled the target for the loss of only two wickets, with more than three overs to spare.

Hours after the game ended, two cricket teams flew out of Delhi in different directions. While the South Africans returned home, the India team departed for Australia. It was at this point that the reality of what had just happened started sinking in. While the South Africa series had scored high on history and of course, goodwill, the fact of the matter was that the romantic aspect had been allowed to supersede the practical. Had three ODIs on flat and dry tracks, not to mention the tri-series in Sharjah, in any way enhanced the possibility of the Indian team succeeding on the bouncy and juicy wickets that awaited them in Australia?

India started the tour poorly, losing one-dayers against the ACB Chairman's XI and Western Australia, followed by an innings defeat against New South Wales. Sachin shone in the three-day game, with knocks of 82 and 59. He seemed to be comfortable in Australian conditions, and essayed quite a few back-foot strokes, especially through the off-side.

The claim made by a member of the Indian team management that 'the batting line-up could not be dismissed twice in the same game' was already on shaky ground by the time the first Test began at the Gabba, Brisbane. Australia took less than four days to win by 10 wickets. India scrambled 239 in the first innings and 156 in the second. The much-vaunted batting line-up looked totally at sea on wickets that were according generous assistance to the pacemen.

The saving grace for the visitors was the performance of its 'non-glamorous' wing. Kapil Dev bowled splendidly in the first innings, swinging the ball almost at will. The highlight was three consecutive deliveries that he served in the middle stages of Australia's first innings. The first was a late inswinger that beat and bowled Allan Border, the Australian captain and a legend of the game. The second left and beat Dean Jones, the new man in, all ends up. The third swung inwards and dislodged the timber.

In an age wherein the two formats of the sport were interspersed and pretty much the same set of players figured in both, the Australian and Indian teams switched from whites to coloured clothing after the Brisbane Test. The triangular limited-overs series, an annual feature in Australia at the time, was split into two legs, with the first being played between the first and second Tests, and the second scheduled between the third and fourth Tests.

The opening game of the tri-series, a day-nighter between India and the West Indies on the world's bounciest pitch at Perth, witnessed some insipid batting and extraordinary bowling. Dismissed for 126 by the Caribbean pace battery, India gave their opponents a taste of their own medicine. Leading the way was Kapil Dev, whose outswingers accounted for the experienced Desmond Haynes and skipper Richie Richardson. The other three pacemen in the Indian XI—Prabhakar, Srinath and debutant Subroto Banerjee—also played their parts to perfection, and at 76–8, the Windies were all but down and out. Curtly Ambrose and Anderson Cummins then engineered a revival, which ended with Ambrose's run out at 113. Cummins regained his composure in the company of Patrick Patterson, the last man. Time and deliveries were not an issue. At the end of the 40th over, the Windies needed five more to win. Azharuddin's gambit of bowling out his four speedsters had all but worked.

For the 41st over, he had no option but to toss the ball to the player who had done the extra seamer's job at Sharjah earlier in the season. Cummins took a single to short fine-leg and then Patterson drove to mid-wicket for three to level the scores. With nothing to lose, the fielders were brought in for the final delivery of the over. Sachin ran in, eager to delay the inevitable, if not deny it altogether. An inswinger was what he decided to bowl. Much to his delight, the white ball did just a bit, and it took the outside edge of Cummins' bat and flew towards the slips. Azharuddin, who had stationed himself at second slip, dived to his left and came up with a stunner of a catch. The match was tied.

It was not the last time Sachin would excel as a bowler in the climactic stages of an ODI.

India played three more matches in the first leg of the tri-series, beating the West Indies once and splitting honours in two games against Australia. Sachin began well in almost every game but could not sustain. His best performance was an innings of 48 in the second game against the West Indies. He looked ominous till he gave a tame return catch to Keith Arthurton.

The return to whites was disastrous for India. Australia went 2–0 up in the series with another fourth-day win in the Boxing Day Test at Melbourne.

Interestingly, not all the Indian batsmen had looked out of sorts at Melbourne. Ravi Shastri scored 23 and 22, Sanjay Manjrekar 25 and 30, and Dilip Vengsarkar 23 and 54. Their scores indicated that they had got off to starts, before falling to a good ball or a poor stroke or a combination of both. The pace triumvirate of Craig McDermott, Merv Hughes and the left-handed Bruce Reid, who finished the Test with figures of 12–126, had bowled tight lines in helpful conditions. They were backed by their teammates in the field, and together the bowlers and fielders were ensuring that a batsman's first mistake was invariably his last. They had forced the Indian batsmen to go on the defensive, technically as well as mentally, so much so that the latter were finding it difficult to even capitalize on the rare loose delivery. A vicious circle was completed by the 'scoreboard pressure', which kept increasing because of the batsmen's failure to make the bad balls count, and forced them into making mistakes.

The 'dashers' in the batting line-up—Srikkanth and Azharuddin—had struggled at both Brisbane and Melbourne. In the second innings at Melbourne, with the match all but lost, another member of the batting line-up put up a fight. Sachin batted for two hours and hit five fours in a knock of 40, before lashing out at one that Peter Taylor, the off-spinner, held back. The ball gathered more height than distance and Border ran several yards to take a good catch. Sachin did not take too long to realize that he had got himself out. If he were to channelize his aggression constructively, there was no reason why he could not have a longer outing. As he viewed it, he had come to terms with Australia.

The 18-year-old had achieved what his senior teammates hadn't—he had won the battle between the ears. What was left was to win the battle on the ground.

> I was at the Cricket Academy in 1991-92.... We trained in the morning and I stayed back to watch the Indians train because I wanted to watch Sachin in the nets. I wanted to learn what he was doing in the nets and watch what he was doing.
>
> —Ricky Ponting, *Sachin Forever*, MCA, 2013

David Boon became the first centurion of 1992 when he scored 129 in the first innings of the third 'New Year' Test at Sydney. However, India had reason to be pleased. Three of their four pacemen—Kapil Dev, Prabhakar and debutant Subroto Banerjee—took three wickets each and restricted the hosts to 313. The Indians started their response disastrously. Navjot Sidhu, who had joined the side in Sydney as its 17th member after recovering from a finger injury, fell for a duck. Then, there was a lucky break for the visitors, in the form of an injury to Bruce Reid, the hero of Melbourne. He limped out of the attack after his fourth over and played no further part in the match. The loss of a specialist bowler forced Allan Border to introduce Shane Warne, the debutant leg-spinner, into the attack earlier than he would have wished.

Warne had elicited a fair amount of attention, with leg-spinners being a rare commodity in an age dominated by fast bowlers. Sanjay Manjrekar, who like his teammates had been 'bred on spin', welcomed the leggie to Test cricket with a cover-driven boundary. The one-drop batsman contributed 34 to a second-wicket stand of 79 before giving slip-catching practice to Mark Waugh off Merv Hughes. Once again, Manjrekar had looked relatively untroubled till he got out.

Most of the third day's play was lost to rain, and India's best bet was to amass a sizeable lead and attempt an innings win on the final day.

Vengsarkar batted well to score 54 before he fell on the fourth morning. India were a healthy 197–3 at that stage. McDermott greeted Azharuddin, the next man in, with a delivery on his pads. The Indian captain obliged by bringing his wrists into play and flicking the ball for four. The next delivery was a replica of its predecessor. Azharuddin, woefully out of form, sought to express his gratitude with another flick. However, the cherry did not quite make it to the fence this time around. The outstretched left palm of David Boon, the best short-leg in the world, played spoilsport. The ball ricocheted off his palm and dropped to his right, shorn of all its pace, and he dived to complete the catch. The Indian captain could only curse his luck as he walked off.

By then, Ravi Shastri had completed his century, India's first in the Test series. He now had for company, a batsman who was so charged up that he had been unable to sleep the previous night. After shadow-practising in his room through the night, Sachin had dozed off in the dressing room while awaiting his turn to bat. When the captain fell, he was woken up by Sourav Ganguly, his roommate.

His words to Shastri, when he overheard the latter's exchange with the Australian fielders, reflected his assurance. Shastri, never one to take a backward step, was speechless when Sachin told him that 'he would also give it back to the Aussies, after completing his own hundred'. Shastri, like Ajit Tendulkar, knew that the youngster was displaying assurance, not arrogance, but he exhorted Sachin to get his eye in first and think about landmarks later.

A splendid partnership ensued. Sachin punched McDermott past extra-cover for four and drove Hughes down the ground. Channel Nine's celebrated commentary panel, comprising as it did, a galaxy of former international captains, could not stop waxing eloquent on the batsmen's footwork, as also their running between the wickets.

Both Mumbai batsmen were severe on Warne. Shastri hit him for two huge sixes, one of which brought up his 150. Warne however did not lose heart, and his perseverance paid off shortly after Shastri became the first Indian to score a double hundred in Australia. The leggie held one back, and the Indian vice-captain holed out to Dean Jones in the deep.

Sachin carried on, eager to keep the promise he had made to himself. As he batted on, the fundamental difference between him and his teammates came to light. Like them, he was doing his best to treat each delivery on merit, but unlike them, he was quick to take full toll of anything that was loose.

> There is a cricket brain in him which ticks away with an amazing speed. He has been improving match by match and it was on the cards that he would get the big innings soon. It was no surprise when it came, though the sheer beauty of its execution made this the real highlight of the Test. Neither heredity nor environment could have made him what he is. Tendulkar's talent is a gift which would make a heretic think of God.

—R. Mohan, *The Sportstar*, 18 January 1992

A straight-driven boundary off Hughes elicited gasps from the spectators, as did a late cut off Warne. At 98, he leg-glanced McDermott down to fine-leg, and Prabhakar, his partner at Manchester 18 months previously, was quick to respond. The two runs made Sachin the youngest batsman to score a Test century in Australia. There was jubilation and acknowledgement of his proficiency all around, with even the Australian cricketers joining in the applause.

By then, the Test had entered its final day, and India were going for a declaration. The 'maidan cricketer' in Sachin came to the fore in the form of some improvised strokes, like an uppish drive off McDermott that just cleared mid-off. The dismissals of Prabhakar and Kapil brought to the crease Chandrakant Pandit, the Mumbai stumper who had replaced the injured Kiran More in the XI.

The fourth Achrekar disciple to represent India in the 1991-92 season, Pandit was recognized as the quintessential Mumbai cricketer—khadoos and street-smart—at the domestic level. Those attributes were on show, as the duo went for broke. They were quick to convert a wild throw from the outfield, which Australian keeper Ian Healy had to run backwards to intercept, into an overthrow. Pandit was eventually run out in a dash to the non-striker's end, despite his best attempts to come between the bowler Merv Hughes, who had collected the ball, and the wickets. The final wicket fell at 483, with Sachin unbeaten on 148. The Australian bowling hadn't 'conquered' him, but he had conquered the hearts of all of Australia. In what was a warm gesture, Dean Jones and Merv Hughes ran across to shake his hand. Among those who clapped him off the field was Warne, whose Test baptism had yielded him unflattering figures of 1–150.

> Their bowlers were quick and bouncing us but his positivity stood out. Ravi got a double hundred but Sachin's innings was an eye-opener. It told us that if you are a big-hearted player, have high ambitions then circumstances can never have a limitation. That innings really inspired all of us.
>
> —Subroto Banerjee, *The Sachin Sunset*, Wisden India, November 2013

The stage was set for an absorbing climax to the game. Shastri followed his double century with some splendid bowling. Even as his teammates floundered, Allan Border held his ground and found an ally in Merv Hughes, Australia's number eight. The decision to omit both specialist spinners—Raju and Hirwani on the most spin-friendly track in Australia, which had started turning square in the final session of the game, had come back to bite India hard. Azharuddin asked Sachin to try his hand at spin, and the teenager did get Hughes out, but the Indians could not close out the game.

The first time I saw Sachin was in 1991–92. My first impression of him was that he was incredibly small; he was tiny for his reputation which was building at that stage.... It wasn't really full-fledged, but it was certainly building. His bat seemed wider than Sachin himself. He treated Australia with a fantastic summer of cricket. Most times as well, India was a meek and mild-natured sort of a team...it didn't really have that kind of punch required to win in Australia. Sachin was just that—he just had this look; that stature and aura that came with his presence that brought confidence into the side.

—Matthew Hayden, *The Sachin Sunset*, Wisden India, November 2013

India would rather the fourth Test have started immediately as Sydney had given them a shot in the arm, but they had to don the 'blues' for the second leg of the tri-series. They lost three consecutive games—two to Australia and one to the Windies—and put their prospects of qualifying for the best-of-three finals in jeopardy. Sachin's 77 against the West Indies at Brisbane, his best effort of the series, went in vain. He batted quite magnificently, even as his teammates floundered. He did not find the pace of Ambrose, Patterson and Marshall, and the bounce they were extracting from the lively wicket, intimidating enough to stay on the back foot. On the contrary, he continued to transfer his body-weight onto the front foot just prior to the release of the ball, as he had done throughout the tour. He backed himself to make the necessary adjustments once the ball was propelled at him, and the outcome was some gorgeous strokeplay, particularly a couple of short-arm pulls off Patterson that he essayed off the front foot.

The West Indies won that game by five wickets. Five days later, the two teams met at the Melbourne Cricket Ground for the last league game of the tri-series. It was effectively a semi-final, with Australia having qualified already.

The Indians bowled and fielded splendidly to restrict the West Indies to 175-8. Curtly Ambrose then led his team's fightback with an incisive opening spell that accounted for Shastri. Srikkanth, who had been in terrific nick in the first leg of the tri-series with two individual awards to his credit, struck a couple of boundaries to soothe Indian nerves, but the pressure was back when Manjrekar fell to Patterson. At 38-2, India's two most successful batsmen of the tri-series joined hands.

Srikkanth, for whom defence had been an alien concept for the better part of his career, displayed his professionalism by dropping anchor. He let himself go only after the score had crossed 80, hitting Carl Hooper for six and then smashing Ambrose for four. The paceman had his revenge when he had the opener caught behind shortly after the hundred of the innings had been posted. Azharuddin then essayed a daft stroke to be caught in the deep. However, Sachin was solid and Pravin Amre as unruffled as he had been on his debut at Kolkata earlier in the season. India won by five wickets and Sachin won the individual award.

India were outplayed in the first of the best-of-three finals, but they came close to winning the second. Chasing a gettable 209 at Sydney, the visitors started poorly with Srikkanth falling early and Manjrekar adding to his tally of run-outs. The heroes of the Test played at the same ground, then got together to bring their side back into the game. They took as much time to do so as Sachin and Srikkanth had against the West Indies at Melbourne, but the Australians were a lot better at drying up the runs than their West Indian counterparts. Shastri eventually fell for 61, but Sachin carried on with crisp strokeplay and brisk running. The Indian contingent erupted when he came down the wicket to hit seamer Tom Moody over the top for four.

The match provided one of the early glimpses to what was to be a recurring feature of Sachin's career through the 1990s. Simply put, he did not get the support he deserved. Azharuddin slammed Border over his head for four and tried to repeat the stroke off the very next ball, only to hole out in the deep. 'The Indian captain deserves a kick up the backside,' Ian Chappell was moved to comment.

Sachin did his best to catch up with the asking rate, which was rapidly climbing. He had his share of luck, being caught off a McDermott no-ball and dropped by Steve Waugh, a miss that prompted Allan Border to sink to the turf in exasperation. These 'lives' convinced many that it was to be Sachin's and India's day. However, he gave one chance too many, and Mike Whitney ran several yards to catch a lofted stroke at a stage when 19 were needed off 16 balls. Amre, who had helped Sachin add 36, kept going, but he then fell to a big hit that landed in long-on's hands, a few feet short of the fence. A decade later, in an age of shorter boundaries, the same stroke would have yielded six runs. India lost the game by precisely that margin.

On an Adelaide wicket that was more Indian in terms of texture and behaviour than Australian, the visitors were guilty of squandering the initiative after bowling the hosts out for a paltry 145 on the first day of the fourth Test. In the absence of Banerjee, who was left out for Raju, Sachin was called upon to operate as the fourth seamer. Once again, he delivered, with the wickets of Mark Taylor (bowled) and Border (caught behind). The umpires had a poor game, but the Indians did themselves no favours by accumulating a first-innings lead of just 80. Australia regained the initiative by scoring 451 in the second innings.

Sachin had a hand in the dismissal of Boon, one of Australia's two centurions in the second innings. He surprised the batsman with a delivery that took off from a good length. Boon fended it away into the vacant square-leg region and ambled for a single. As he passed Sachin, who was still standing at the top of his follow-through, Boon subjected him to the Australian 'glare', taking his eyes off from the ball in the process. What he missed seeing was that Pandit had run across to square-leg, gathered the ball and hurled it at the bowler's end. The throw found its mark, and Boon was caught short.

With nothing to lose and everything to gain, India went for the target of 372. Sidhu scored 35 and Manjrekar got 45 before he was run out once again. Azharuddin scored a breathtaking 106 before he was neutralized by a gem of an outswinger by Craig McDermott. Ironically, the Indian captain may well not have got anywhere close to the cherry had he been as diffident as he had been earlier in the series. However, he was in such good nick by the time he received the delivery that he ended up nicking it. Manoj Prabhakar kept the chase going before being adjudged leg-before. The umpire's decision was as questionable as the one that went against Vengsarkar earlier in the innings. Sachin too fell leg-before and Pandit was at the receiving end of another lethal McDermott outswinger. India lost by 38 runs, and with it, the series.

The final Test at Perth, on the world's fastest and fieriest surface, was expected to be one-sided, and it was, but not before Sachin stamped his genius on the proceedings, with an innings of 114.

> He played very well to get to 50, but his acceleration from 50 to 100 was extraordinary. He hit 16 boundaries in all and a lot of them came in his second 50. His body language never changed—when guys start going for their shots you can see them getting agitated and playing a little faster; but he wasn't trying to slog, it was just crispness and magnificent shots all around. His cut shots and driving off the front foot were phenomenal.... There was a lot of bounce and carry, the ball swung a little bit, and seamed a lot all through the game. So the main aim for bowlers like me and Paul Reiffel was to keep hitting the right line and length and wait for the edge.
>
> —Mike Whitney, *Wisden Asia Cricket*, December 2004

Sachin adopted the tactic of rising on his toes and playing with soft hands whenever the ball climbed onto him. Unlike his colleagues, who attempted to cut anything that was short and pitched outside off, he opted to 'punch' good-length deliveries off the back foot. While he retained his initial front-foot movement, he kept himself primed to get onto the back foot if required. While his colleagues allowed themselves to be enveloped by thoughts of Perth's reputation as a paceman's paradise, Sachin opted to take it 'one ball at a time'. He convinced himself that once he spent some time in the middle and got a hang of things, it was an excellent wicket to bat on, as the bounce was consistent and therefore easy to 'adjust' to.

> The difference between an ordinary and a class player is the time he has to make last-second adjustments to play his strokes. Tendulkar has it. He is all class. I enjoyed every moment of his [Perth] innings.
>
> —Norman O' Neill, *The Sportstar*, 15 February 1992

> I remember John Woodcock, the venerated cricket correspondent of the *Times*, marvelling at Tendulkar and saying, 'If we did not know that he was 19, we would be calling him the *best batsman* in the world, not the best young batsman.'
>
> —Harsha Bhogle, *Wisden Asia Cricket*, December 2004

Twelve of the Indian players who had been in Australia since November 1991 stayed back for the World Cup, which began a fortnight after the Perth Test. The year 1992 was a time wherein selectors the world over had not warmed up to the idea of picking 'specialists' for different formats of the game. One or two players apart, the Test and ODI teams would be virtually identical. A notable exception to this thought process was New Zealand's selection panel.

The fifth Cricket World Cup had several 'firsts' to its credit. It was the first World Cup to be jointly hosted by Australia and New Zealand, the first to feature night cricket, coloured clothing, black sightscreens and white balls. In fact, two white balls—one from each end—were used. It was the first World Cup to involve nine teams, with South Africa joining the eight sides that had participated in the 1983 and 1987 World Cups. The 1992 edition was also the first wherein each team was to play every other participant in a round-robin format, with the top four teams qualifying for the semi-finals.

Azharuddin's side wore a new look in its opening clash against England at Perth. India's designated colour in the tri-series earlier in the season, and indeed, on its three post-Packer visits to Australia, had been light blue. However, for the World Cup, the team was assigned dark blue, with light blue going to England. Technically, India had worn light blue in a tri-series in Australia (in 1980–81) two years before England did, but the authorities deemed it appropriate to assign light blue to the team with the 'greater box-office appeal'. In 1992, it was England.

Sachin made his World Cup debut against England at Perth. Graham Gooch's side batted first and set India a target of 237. Shastri and Srikkanth provided India with a good start, but the middle and lower order stuttered. Azharuddin, who had promoted himself to number three, fell first ball. Sachin, who came in at number four, batted brilliantly to reach 35, inclusive of five fours, before he was outfoxed by one of the immortals. It was more than half a decade since Ian Terence Botham had last taken the new ball for England; he was playing the World Cup as an opening batsman and change bowler. He compensated for a lack in pace with guile, serving a gem of a delivery that swung away late and kissed the outside-edge of Sachin's bat on the way to the keeper. India lost by nine runs.

After their second game against Sri Lanka was abandoned due to rain, India took on the Australians at Brisbane, and did well to restrict the hosts to 237-8. Chasing a revised target of 236, India began slowly, but were put on track by Azharuddin. Sachin and Kapil Dev fell cheaply, but the captain essayed an exceptional innings, as did Manjrekar. Azharuddin had reached 93 when he committed the mistake of taking on Allan Border's throwing arm. Despite that blow, Manjrekar could well have taken India home had he not added to his 'run-out' tally by taking on Craig McDermott's throwing arm. He had scored 47 off 42 deliveries when he fell. At the start of the final over, India needed 13 to win with three wickets in hand. The canny Kiran More scooped Tom Moody's first two deliveries to the long-leg boundary, but fell as he went for a third. Several dramatic moments later, the Indians found themselves needing four from the last ball. Javagal Srinath swung hard and was dropped in the outfield by Steve Waugh, but the fielder's throw was spot-on and Venkatapathy Raju, India's number 11, was run out as he desperately lunged to complete the third run that would have ensured a tie.

India's margins of defeat against England and Australia—nine runs and one run respectively—said it all. With a little bit of luck, they might well have won at least one game, if not both.

Their next fixture was against the 'old enemy' at Sydney. Head-to-head stats suggested that Pakistan were favourites on the eve of the first-ever World Cup face-off between the traditional rivals, but Indian supporters were heartened by the fact that the match was being played in Sydney and not in Sharjah. Shastri, who had been pilloried for his 'slow' batting against Australia, was left out, and both Vinod Kambli and Ajay Jadeja, who had been added to the World Cup squad, were picked. Jadeja opened the innings and scored 46. In contrast, the experienced Srikkanth struggled, and was dismissed after taking 39 balls to score 5. Azharuddin looked fluent until he fell to Mushtaq Ahmed, the leg-spinner, for 32. Kambli was sent in at number four on the captain's instructions, ostensibly to counter Mushtaq with his left-handedness. Jadeja's dismissal for a well-made 46 brought in Sachin.

Sachin warmed up with consecutive boundaries off Aamir Sohail. A pull to mid-wicket was followed by a rasping square-cut. The Shardashram buddies had added 46 when Kambli was deceived by one that Mushtaq held back. The left-hander was caught by Inzamam-ul-Haq in the deep, and he was followed to the pavilion by Manjrekar, who played on first ball. That brought Kapil Dev to the crease. With the Pakistanis having come back into the game with two wickets in an over, the situation was ripe for the legendary all-rounder to do what he almost always did in a crisis. He made his intentions clear with a drive off Mushtaq that cleared the long-off fence.

The erstwhile double-wicket partners batted and ran superbly. Television viewers in India and elsewhere witnessed a singular moment, shortly after Kapil had thumped an Aaqib Javed full-toss to the fence. As the veteran made to return to his end, Sachin patted him on the back. It wasn't very often that one came across a 'youngster' egging on one of his idols, in this fashion. Sachin had of course earned the right to do so, exemplifying as he was, the adage that 'age did not matter as much as ability did'.

Sachin remained unbeaten on 54 and India finished with 216–7 from the 49 overs that were bowled before the cut-off point. Pakistan started poorly, losing two wickets with only 16 on the board, but a recovery was initiated by Aamir Sohail and Javed Miandad. Sachin, who had been assigned the fifth bowler's job, came on in the 17th over, and was promptly driven by the left-handed Sohail past point for four. The Pakistani opener looked in fine nick, but all of India knew that Miandad held the key. For India, Kiran More took it upon himself to ensure that the bowlers kept things tight. Knowing that Miandad had a dodgy left foot, he kept reminding the bowlers to pitch it up to the veteran, and kept the pressure on with some smart keeping. Miandad, no mean exponent of gamesmanship himself, did not appreciate the taste of his own medicine, and matters came to a head in a Sachin over. Miandad stopped Sachin, just as he was about to start running in, and had an exchange with the Indian stumper. The umpires then got involved, along with the fielding captain, and the affair climaxed with Miandad's hilarious impersonation of an appealing More.

Indian supporters started to worry when the score crossed triple figures. They needed a breakthrough, and Sachin provided them with one, off a low full-toss. Sohail, who had completed a 50, came down the wicket and drove hard, but Srikkanth held a fine catch at short mid-wicket. Salim Malik came in and hit two boundaries, but he got a beauty from Prabhakar that took the outside edge. That triggered a collapse. Imran was run out for no score and Wasim Akram was stumped off Raju, with More ensuring that he ran past Miandad, the non-striker, while celebrating the wicket. The fate of the match was sealed when Srinath scalped Miandad with a splendid yorker. Moin Khan, the wicketkeeper, played a couple of belligerent strokes before being caught at sweeper. India won by 39 runs and Sachin was declared Player of the Match for his 'all-round' heroics.

The Indians then flew across the Tasman Sea for their next set of league matches. Rain reduced their encounter against Zimbabwe at Hamilton to a 32-overs-a-side affair. Batting first, the Indians initially found it difficult to get the better of the wet outfield, even as the Zimbabwean fielders struggled to keep their balance on it. However, the conditions could not deter India's Number Four. Sachin batted brilliantly, exhibiting his entire repertoire of carpet and aerial strokes. He completed his 50 in the 24th over with a straight six off Ali Shah. His most emphatic stroke was off a delivery that kept low after pitching outside off. Sachin picked it early and pulled it to the mid-wicket boundary, as his idol IVA Richards would have. He looked good for his maiden ODI hundred until he mistimed one in the closing overs. He had scored 81, which at that stage was his highest individual score in the shorter format. Zimbabwe began well and were 104–1 in 19.1 overs, when the rain returned and this time, did not relent. India were declared winners with Zimbabwe 55 short of the revised target and Sachin received his second successive individual award.

That victory was India's last moment of joy in the competition, followed as it was by defeats against West Indies, New Zealand and South Africa respectively. Sachin improved upon his 81 against Zimbabwe with a knock of 84 against the Kiwis. He was put down in the covers at the start of his innings, and he stayed in to make the opposition regret the lapse. An improvised cut off the parsimonious Gavin Larsen was a beauty. The ball pitched outside off and came in, and Sachin reacted by backing away to leg and guiding the ball past point for four. He marked out the off-side for special attention, driving Willie Watson uppishly and Chris Harris along the ground through the covers. Larsen was cut and later hit over the top. India were reasonably happy to score 230–6, but the Kiwis won in a canter, with Mark Greatbatch doing successfully what K. Srikkanth had done spectacularly for India in the 1980s. Andrew Jones, a classy middle-order bat, complemented Greatbatch to perfection. With only two wins from seven completed matches, India finished seventh in the tournament. Their consolation was the form displayed by their teenage star. With three 50s and two individual awards in the game's premier limited-overs event, he had displayed his 'big match temperament' in the shorter variety, after having done so in the Test series against Australia, earlier in the season.

> There have been rare occasions when the Mumbai teenager has seemed to have been overawed by a deadly combination of an opponent's status and skills, as we saw in the match against England...but overall, the Indian superstar has come out a clear winner, handling the pressures more successfully than most of us would have expected him to.... After all, the ball is meant to be hit. And when you can hit it with as much grace and felicity as Tendulkar, it hardly matters if the match is meant to end in a day or five! Such minor details would concern only ordinary mortals. And Sachin Ramesh Tendulkar is anything but ordinary.
>
> —Nirmal Shekar, *The Sportstar*, 21 March 1992

The seventh spot notwithstanding, the 1992 World Cup was memorable for the average Indian cricket fan, and not merely because his team had beaten Pakistan, the eventual champions, at the league stage, and Sachin had done well. The World Cup was the first major cricket series/competition that cricket lovers in India watched live on a channel other than Doordarshan. In what was an offshoot of liberalization, the Singapore-based Star TV network initiated operations in India in the second half of 1991, and established itself in thousands of urban Indian households in the weeks and months that followed. 'Prime Sports', as the name suggested, was the sports wing of the Star network. While Doordarshan was also telecasting the key matches live, what tilted the scales in favour of Prime Sports, as far as Indian fans were concerned, was the presence of Sunil Gavaskar in the latter's Singapore studio, as an 'expert'. His prediction in the closing stages of the league stage that Pakistan would go the distance elevated him to 'demi-god' status across the border. Imran Khan's 'cornered tigers' looked down and out at one stage, but they turned things around when it mattered. Sachin was among the millions of Indians who watched the World Cup final on television and dreamt of holding it himself one day. In March 1992, he was a month short of turning 19. He was confident that his time would come.

History was created a few days after the Indian team returned from Australia. Yorkshire, one of the 19 English counties, expressed its interest in signing Sachin as its 'overseas professional' for the summer of 1992. The county's first choice was Craig McDermott, but the Australian speedster was forced to pull out due to injury. A flurry of phone calls and discussions later, Sachin signed on the dotted line. Chris Hassell, the county's chief executive, flew over to India to finalize the deal. A delighted witness was Sunil Gavaskar, who had advised Sachin to insist on the same fee that had been earmarked for McDermott—£30,000.

> I felt that it was an honour [to represent Yorkshire] in the first place and that it was going to be a good experience for me. I spoke to Mr. Gavaskar on this. He was sure that I would benefit from the experience, and so did a few well-wishers. Mr. Gavaskar said that I would get to learn a lot of things that would help me later in my career.
>
> —Sachin Tendulkar, *The Sportstar*, 25 April 1992

The first minor to enter the clubhouse of the CCI in 1988 was to become not only the first-ever non-Englishman, but also the first cricketer born outside the borders of Yorkshire to represent the county. Yorkshire had been a powerhouse of domestic cricket, like Mumbai in India, New South Wales in Australia and Barbados in the Caribbean, for decades. However, a steady decline in their performances and consistency since the early 1970s had prompted them to revise their selection policies.

> It was vital that we had as our first overseas player someone who was no trouble. How awful it would have been if he had been seen out disco dancing on match days or drinking late at night in pubs...Sachin was a dream. A boyish smile, warm, friendly—nothing was too much trouble for him. Our members and the office staff loved him.
>
> —Geoffrey Boycott, *Outlook*, 4 January 1999

While he did not exactly set the County Championship alight, Sachin fared well, scoring 1,070 runs from 25 innings, including a match-winning century against Durham and seven 50s. He did well in the limited-overs games, his best performance being a belligerent 107 against Lancashire in the Sunday League, but more importantly, he endeared himself to his teammates and Yorkshire supporters—former cricketers included—with his professionalism.

> He went about his business in a way that showed a dedication to his profession, a desire for self-improvement and an even-handed approach to life. He reminded Yorkshire that success required diligence. He was

wary of celebrity even then and asked for his name to be removed from his sponsored car so he would not draw attention to himself.

—David Hopps, *Sachin Tendulkar: The Man Cricket Loved Back*,

Not surprisingly for someone who was used to having people around him since childhood, Sachin was initially uncomfortable with the idea of being all by himself, especially on non-match days. The county had allotted him a car and a house, and he took his time to get used to both. He went on to forge new friendships and strengthen existing ones. Dewsbury in West Yorkshire was where Solly Adams and his wife Mariam and Solly's brother Younus and his wife Ruksan—all of whom were supporters of Indian cricket—lived. They treated him to the choicest of delicacies and even helped him with his laundry, among other things. Sachin's spell of loneliness was reduced when Vinod Kambli and Jatin Paranjape,* both of whom were playing league cricket in England, spent some time with him.

> So high are the expectations that even the 80s and 90s he is scoring for Yorkshire are not enough, and remember, these scores have come in only seven first-class matches so far. Yet, the general impression is that he has been having a tough season…let us give him some time to achieve greater success on his first outing in County cricket. And even if he does not do so, it does not mean that his sojourn was a failure. For he would have picked up invaluable lessons on how the pros play the game and he is intelligent enough to pick what is good for his game.
>
> —Sunil Gavaskar, *The Sportstar*, 18 July 1992

Sachin could not see the season through with Yorkshire, as he was instructed by the BCCI to play in the Duleep Trophy, which had been advanced to August–September. The Board was keen to field full-strength sides in the tournament to test out upcoming talent on the eve of the 1992–93 season.

A star-studded West Zone side went down to Central Zone by 179 runs in the semi-final at Chennai. The prime architects of the win were off-spinners Pradeep Gandhe and Rajesh Chauhan.

> One look and it was clear that this was going to be a spinners' paradise. And as luck would have it, we did not have quite enough spinners in our team, especially a quality off-spinner. Ravi [Shastri] and I talked about the

---

*Vasu Paranjape's son.

matter.... At one point, a soft voice interrupted me and Ravi; 'I will bowl my off-spinners.' Both of us were astonished. We well knew that we had a cricketing genius in our midst.... But we had never seen Tendulkar bowl off-spinners.... This was a five-dayer where a spinner was expected to bowl at least 25 overs in an innings... In that match, Sachin Tendulkar ended up bowling almost 30 overs of off-spin, all with short-leg and silly point in close-in catching positions, and we never felt short of a quality spinner. I suspect this was the first time Tendulkar had ever bowled off-spin at any level. This, his first attempt, came in a vital first-class game and he bowled like a veteran.

—Sanjay Manjrekar, *Outlook Commemorative Issue*, 2010

Sachin bowled 21 overs of off-spin in the first innings, the same number as new-ball bowler Rashid Patel, and 11 in the second and took one wicket. Earlier in the year, he had tried his hand at wrist-spin in the closing stages of the Sydney Test. Simply put, once he would make up his mind to try something new, he would execute it brilliantly.

The adjective 'historic' was back in vogue on the eve of India's cricket tour of Africa in the 1992–93 season. The South Africa leg of the tour, comprising four Tests and seven ODIs, was to be the first official cricket series to be played in the country since 1969–70. The Zimbabwe leg, which preceded it, was no less historic. The country had just been granted Full Membership of the ICC and was to make its Test debut.

The last player to be picked in the Indian squad for the twin-tour was a bespectacled leg-spinner from Bangalore who had toured Sharjah and England with the Indian team in 1990 before being discarded. What Anil Kumble lacked in terms of sharp turn, he more than compensated with unerring accuracy. There was no way he could have been ignored for the twin-tour after a 13-wicket haul in the Irani Cup game between the Rest of India and Delhi, the 1991–92 Ranji champions.

Haryana's Ranji and Irani Cup wins in 1990–91 and 1991–92 respectively yielded rich dividends for the north Indian state, with four of its players making it to the national side. Kapil Dev apart, Chetan Sharma was recalled, Ajay Jadeja kept his place and Vijay Yadav was brought in as understudy to Kiran More. Woorkeri Raman, the languid left-handed opener from Tamil Nadu, was recalled after an outstanding domestic season. Among those unlucky to miss out was Vinod Kambli.

The one-off Test against Zimbabwe was drawn, but the hosts walked away with the honours. They won the toss, batted first and scored 456. To the exasperation of its supporters, India almost did what it generally did in the 'first' Test of an overseas series. Had Sanjay Manjrekar not dropped anchor for nearly nine hours to score 104, anything could have happened. Among those who had a poor game was Sachin, who was caught-and-bowled by John Traicos, the 46-year-old off-spinner, before opening his account. The statisticians wasted no time in pointing out that Traicos, who had represented South Africa in the country's last series in 1969–70 before its isolation, had played Test cricket before Sachin's birth.

The chastened visitors gave a better account of themselves in the lone ODI, winning by 70 runs.

The Indian team was accorded a rousing welcome in the country where a certain M.K. Gandhi had waged the first of his non-violent battles, eight decades previously. The newly instituted United Cricket Board of South Africa (UCBSA) went out of its way to make the Indians feel at home, as did the locals who were of Indian origin. The socializing commenced from the time the Indian team landed at Johannesburg, and carried on for the next few days and weeks, much to the chagrin of Ajit Wadekar, India's new cricket manager. That they were there to play cricket seemed almost incidental.

Sachin twisted his ankle while trying to practice 'sliding' on a wet turf, during the visitors' three-day game against the South African Board President's XI. That made him a doubtful starter for the first Test at Durban, but he and the team management worked their way around the problem by deciding that he would stand in the slips, so that he would not have to run too much while fielding.

He was in the thick of the action straightaway. India asked South Africa to take first strike in the 'historic' Test. Jimmy Cook, who had spent the better part of his career playing domestic cricket at home and County cricket in England, was snapped up by Sachin at third slip off Kapil Dev, first ball. This happened even as Suresh Saraiya, the senior member of All India Radio's commentary team, was trying to regain his composure after being overwhelmed with the realization that he was the first Indian to broadcast live from South Africa.

Skipper Kepler Wessels (118) apart, none of the batsmen got going and 254 was what the hosts finished with. The Indian batting then flattered to deceive. Sachin came in after the early dismissals of Test debutant Jadeja and Manjrekar. For the second time in the game, he made history. He played the ball in the point region and took off for a run, only to be sent back. The painful ankle did not allow him to turn back as quickly as he would have liked, and Jonathan Rhodes, fielder extraordinaire, did the rest. Andrew Hudson, running in from short-leg, intercepted the throw and dislodged the bails. Cyril Mitchley, the square-leg umpire, wasn't quite sure whether the batsman had made it in time. He extended his hands in front of his body, then the forefingers of both and drew a rectangle in the air, thus requesting the assistance of the TV umpire for the first time in cricket history. The evidence in the form of slow-motion replays was conclusive enough, and the TV umpire switched on the green bulb.* It was the first-ever instance of a batsman being declared out by the 'third' umpire.

Shastri's dismissal soon after reduced India to 38–4, but the visitors fought back. Leading the resurgence was Pravin Amre, who had been drafted into the playing XI ahead of the more experienced Raman.

Allan Donald and the left-handed Brett Schultz, the mainstays of South Africa's bowling attack, were nearly twice as quick as the 'fastest' bowlers that Amre had faced in domestic tournaments in India. Very rarely had he got to bat on a wicket as conducive to pace as the one at Durban. However, once he was entrenched, there was nothing that could fluster him. After successfully thwarting the speed of Donald and Schultz and the stealth of the marginally slower but craftier Craig Matthews and Brian MacMillan, Amre's eyes lit up when Omar Henry, the left-arm spinner, was introduced into the attack. A barrage of boundaries later, the right-hander became the ninth Indian to score a century on his Test debut. Thanks to his 103 and Kiran More's 50, India gained a lead of 23.

That evening, an ecstatic Amre called his guru in Mumbai. The first sentence that Achrekar uttered was typical of the man; 'First tell me how you got out.'

Rain on the fourth day washed away the possibility of a result in the first Test. South Africa started the second, played at Johannesburg, on a disastrous note. They were 26–4 before Jonty Rhodes and Brian MacMillan came to the rescue and ensured a total of 292. India had reason to be upset with Steve Bucknor, the 'neutral' umpire in the first two Tests.†

Rhodes had barely got his eye in when he was appeared to have been beaten by a direct throw by Javagal Srinath at the non-striker's end. The TV replays confirmed as much, but Bucknor negatived the appeal and turned down the entreaties of the Indians to consult the TV umpire, even as the Indian reserves signalled 'out' from the dressing room. Had Rhodes fallen at that stage, anything could have happened.

South Africa were down to three pacemen, with Meryick Pringle having been

---

*The bulbs were 'switched' a couple of seasons later, with red signifying 'out' and green signifying 'not out'.
†All four Tests in that series were supervised by a South African umpire and one from a third country. Steve Bucknor was the 'neutral' official in the first two Tests. David Shepherd, the Englishman, took over for the last two.

hospitalized after top-edging Srinath onto his left eye. The ball somehow found its way through the gap between the peak of the helmet and visor. However, the Indian batting wobbled all over again, with one exception.

Sachin came in at 20-2, both openers having fallen to the pacemen. He seemed intent on a counterattack. Allan Donald, sensing what was going on in his mind, served him a tempting good-length delivery just outside the off-stump. Sachin went for an expansive drive, and played it uppishly between third slip and gully for four. A few inches to the left or right, and it could well have been fatal. Donald retaliated with a snorter, again on the line of off-stump. Sachin took him on and flailed at the cherry. It took the outside edge of his bat and flew over the slips for four. He was living dangerously.

After Manjrekar played on to McMillan to reduce India to 44–3, Donald nearly gave his side a fourth wicket. Sachin dropped his wrists to one that he anticipated would rise from just short of a length. However, the ball did not rise as much as he had expected and flew off his bat to the slips. Craig Matthews, the third slip, dived to his left, but could not hold on. To add insult to injury, the ball beat the other fielders and went to the boundary.

Once again, the dictum that cricket was a one-ball sport, which Sachin had followed since his days at Shivaji Park, came to his rescue. He reminded himself to forget about the last ball and think of only the next.

At the other end of the spectrum was Manjrekar. This writer was one of the many teenaged cricketers who watched India's number three of the time having a special net session at the Matunga Maidan, a few weeks after the Indian team's return from Australia in early 1992. What made that session unique, at least as far as this writer and several others were concerned, was that it was filmed. One cameraperson was placed at the bowlers' end and another at square-leg. The exercise underscored Manjrekar's resolve to make up for his lean trot in Australia in the subsequent season. He ended up tinkering with his technique by introducing a slight shuffle across the wickets just before the bowler released the ball. It seemed to have worked for him in Zimbabwe, but it did not in the first two Tests in South Africa.

His junior partner on the other hand was unchanged, in terms of technique as well as temperament. Sachin cut McMillan twice for four, proof that he was settling down after the shaky start. When he drove Matthews down the ground for three, he became the youngest batsman to score 1,000 runs in Test history. He was only 19 years and 217 days old.

Sachin continued to lose partners. His follow-up to Azharuddin's dismissal was a stunner of a back-foot cover drive off Donald. He was airborne as he dispatched a good-length delivery pitched just outside the off-stump, for four. He brought up his 50 with a square-cut off the same bowler. At stumps, the visitors were 128–6. Sachin's contribution to the same was 75.

He had been in fine nick, but the ineptitude of his teammates had forced him to be circumspect. On the third day, he dropped anchor, even as the lower order did what it had made a habit of by this time—making up for the failures of the superstars who batted ahead of them. The South African bowlers were operating to a plan, intent on trying Sachin's patience by targeting the 'corridor of uncertainty' just outside the off-stump. He outsmarted them by being content to play a waiting game. After scoring only 11 runs in the first session, he opened out in the second, deploying the drive and cut to splendid effect. The stroke of the day was a back-foot smash off Donald that neatly bisected point and cover. A drive on the up off Matthews gave him the fourth hundred of his Test career. He had batted for exactly six hours. He was eventually out for 111, when he failed to clear Andrew Hudson at mid-on, off Hansie Cronje.

> A statement was made that Sachin spent 372 minutes at the crease. That was out of order. He scored 111 off 270 balls. That must be the criteria. Under incredible pressure, he batted superbly. If you ask me, I have only this to tell him. Keep playing young man, it is a pleasure to watch you.
>
> —Eddie Barlow (former South Africa stalwart), *The Sportstar*,
> 12 December 1992

The other highlight of the Test, from India's point of view, was a haul of 6–53 by India's 'unorthodox' leg-spinner in South Africa's second innings. Anil Kumble impressed his teammates and the South Africans, but not Keith Fletcher, England's newly appointed cricket manager, who had flown to South Africa to 'study' the Indian team, as part of his side's preparations for its tour of India later in the season. The England team management, it appeared, was of the view that Kumble would not pose a big threat because he wasn't a big turner of the ball.

India batted out the last two sessions in Johannesburg to ensure a draw, and the teams then donned coloured clothing for a seven-match ODI series. South Africa won 5–2, outplaying the Indians in every department of the sport, and they carried the form into the third Test at Port Elizabeth where they crushed the visitors.

Commencing their second innings 63 runs in arrears, India were reduced to 31–6, and may well have suffered an innings defeat, had the lower order not supported Kapil Dev. Prabhakar, More and Kumble scored 17 runs each, and played second fiddle to the veteran, who scored an outstanding 129. However, it wasn't enough, and South Africa overhauled the target of 153 for the loss of a solitary wicket. Sachin had a forgettable match, falling to catches behind the wicket for six and zero. The second dismissal rankled, as the ball had hit his pad and not his bat on its way to the keeper, leaving him utterly disconsolate when David Shepherd responded to the bowling side's appeal in the affirmative. The umpire subsequently realized his mistake and was gracious enough to apologize to Sachin in the dressing room. South Africa's hero of the game was 'White Lightning' Allan Donald, who finished the Test with figures of 12–139, including 7–84 in the second innings.

A draw in the fourth Test at Cape Town did nothing to assuage the Indian supporters, all of whom had expected their side to have the better of a series against a team that had just emerged from a 21-year embargo. South Africa batted first and scored 330, and India then conceded a lead of 74. Manoj Prabhakar, promoted to the opening slot, gave a good account of himself with an innings of 62. Manjrekar, whose place in the side was being questioned after another ordinary series, laboured for over four hours to score 46. Sachin was the top individual contributor with 73. The innings featured yet another duel with a quality quick. Donald, India's nemesis at Port Elizabeth, sought to gain the ascendancy over his foe by going around the wicket. The idea obviously was to land the ball just short of a length, with the bounce in the track making the ball rise awkwardly, and forcing the batsman to either take evasive action or fend it away. Sachin responded by increasing the gap between his feet to two-and-a-half feet from his usual 10 inches, thus, making it easier for himself to duck whenever the bowler dug it in. Sachin got the better of Donald, only to fall to Hansie Cronje, South Africa's fourth seamer.

Despite Sachin's mastery, the scoring rates of both sides had been atrocious throughout the series. There was some excitement in South Africa's second innings, when Javagal Srinath bowled with pace and fire to take four wickets and win the individual award. Wessels declared at 130–6, and India were 29–1 in their second innings when play was halted. It was Azharuddin's fourth straight series defeat as captain.

In what was a perverse coincidence, the Indian team, whose reputation was in tatters, landed in Mumbai at a time when the city's reputation as a cosmopolitan hub was being torn to shreds by communal riots. The players were met by Polly Umrigar, the former India captain and the then executive secretary of the BCCI, who was coordinating the players' travel to their respective hometowns from the airport.

The pessimism in India's cricketing ranks was palpable on the eve of the first full Test series to be hosted by India in more than four years. A senior cricket writer went so far as to suggest that Sunil Gavaskar be brought back from retirement to lead India in the three Tests against England and subsequent one-off Test against Zimbabwe to 'put Indian cricket back on track'.

A more realistic possibility was the reinstatement of another legend. A prominent Marathi eveninger even went to the extent of announcing the 'start of Kapil Dev's third stint as captain of India' on its front page, a few days after the team's return from South Africa. India's 1983 World Cup winning captain had scored a century in South Africa, but as a bowler he had looked a shadow of the maestro who had taken 25 wickets in five Tests against Australia just a year previously. Some people had even accused him of placing self before the team; at the end of the South Africa series, he was 19 short of Sir Richard Hadlee's record tally of 431 Test wickets.

What Kapil Dev did went against the run of play. He declared that he would not take up the captaincy if Azhar was sacked; he would accept the job only if the incumbent stepped down on his own volition. Azharuddin on his part was in no mood to resign and he had a supporter in Wadekar.

A compromise was worked out, with the selectors naming Azharuddin captain for only the first two (of six) ODIs and the first of the three Tests that were to be played against England. This unexpected development delighted all those who believed that Azharuddin deserved a shot at the captaincy on home soil. After all, he had led only once at home in 17 Tests at the helm, and India had won that Test (against Sri Lanka) convincingly. The selectors also declared that if at all, there was to be a change at the top, then the reins would be entrusted to a player who was three months shy of turning 20.

It was more a practical call than anything else. Once Kapil was out of the reckoning, there was no other contender for the vice-captaincy. Ravi Shastri, India's captain-in-waiting since 1985, was still nursing the right knee that had forced him to miss the last two Tests in South Africa. Manoj Prabhakar's reputation as a temperamental cricketer went against him, and the likes of Nayan Mongia and Vijay Yadav were breathing down Kiran More's neck. G.R. Viswanath, the chairman of the Selection Committee, was courteous enough to call Sanjay Manjrekar, who had been touted as a future captain before the Australia tour, to inform him about his omission for the England series on grounds of poor form.

The reactions to Sachin's elevation were on expected lines. The worriers felt that he ought to accumulate a few more years' experience before the inevitable happened. Others, Sachin himself included, felt that he was ready for any responsibility, no questions asked. The selectors named him captain of the Board President's XI that was to play a three-day game against the visitors before the first Test. Sachin had to pull out of that game due to injury, but he led the Rest of India in a three-dayer that was played between the first and second Tests.

The three-dayer between the Board President's XI and the visitors was preceded by two ODIs, played at Jaipur and Chandigarh, respectively. The highlight of the first game, from India's point of view, was Vinod Kambli's maiden international century. The obvious choice to replace Manjrekar in the squad after his heavy scoring in the domestic season of 1992–93, Kambli had welcomed the English visitors with a knock of 61 for the Board President's XI. The knock ended prematurely when he sustained an arm injury and was forced to retire hurt. Fortunately for him, his arm healed in time for the ODIs.

18 January 1993, when India took on England at Jaipur, was a red-letter day for Ramakant Achrekar and Shardashram Vidyamandir, and not merely because Vinod Kambli scored a century on his birthday. It wasn't very often that one witnessed an instance of players who had batted one-down and two-down for their school, turning out for their country in the same slots. Ajit Wadekar saw no reason to fiddle around with the numbers that the man he used to call 'the Bradman of tennis-ball cricket' had assigned to Vinod and Sachin respectively. At Jaipur's Sawai Man Singh Stadium, India's numbers three and four batted magnificently to add an unfinished 164 for the third wicket. Sachin scored 82 and Kambli remained unbeaten on 100. However, England chased down the target of 224 with four wickets in hand. India then drew level with a six-wicket win at Chandigarh. Sachin failed, scoring only one, while Azharuddin displayed glimpses of his wizardry in a knock of 36.

The first Test to be played on Indian soil since November 1990 commenced on 29 January 1993 at the Eden Gardens, Kolkata. Partnering Manoj Prabhakar as opener was Navjot Sidhu who had been recalled at the expense of Ajay Jadeja. There were two debutants in the side—Vinod Kambli and the off-spinner Rajesh Chauhan.

Other than briefing the selectors and Board about the events in Africa and backing Azharuddin as captain, Wadekar had suggested a solution to the crisis that Indian cricket found itself in. The former India captain, who had once commanded a quartet of extraordinary spinners, recommended the selection of an off-spinner to complement the leggie Anil Kumble and the left-armer Venkatapathy Raju. It was a given that the wickets would have some turn in them. In the lead-up to the series, Wadekar, an outstanding close-in catcher in his heyday, went about fine-tuning the close-in catching capabilities of his boys.

On day one at Kolkata, Azharuddin essayed the kind of innings that would prompt a journalist to write that 'bowling to him was like bowling to a revolving door'. His 182, scored off only 198 deliveries, was his third Test hundred in his fourth appearance at the Colosseum that was the Eden Gardens. The best stand of the innings, which ended at 371, was one of 123 for the fourth wicket between the captain and his designated successor. Not for the first or last time in his career, Sachin fell for 50 *against the run of play*, just when he was looking ominous.

India's spin triumvirate then got into action. All the training in supposedly spin-friendly conditions that the England batsmen had done before flying to India, came to naught in front of quality spinners and vocal crowds. The visitors, 88–5 at stumps on the second day, were bowled out for 163 on the third, and Azharuddin enforced the follow-on, the second consecutive time he had done so in a 'home' Test.

Sachin's observation skills contributed to England's failure to make their second innings count. At stumps on day three, the visitors were a healthy 128–2, with Graham Gooch looking solid. Early on the fourth day, the England captain went forward to Kumble and was beaten. Even as More collected the ball, Sachin noticed from his position at square-leg that Gooch's back foot was outside the popping crease. He yelled at More to dislodge the bails, and Gooch was gone. Mike Gatting delayed the inevitable with a valiant 81.

An hour into the final day, India overhauled the target of 79 with eight wickets in hand. The Shardashram duo took the hosts through.

Across India, the fans were delighted, yet nonplussed. In early 1993, they were not quite used to seeing their side win Test matches against quality opposition, leave alone series. India had last won a Test against a 'top-rung' team as many as five years previously, when Narendra Hirwani took 16 West Indies wickets at Chennai.

The Kolkata win ensured Azharuddin's retention as captain for the remainder of the series. The visitors' next game, a three-dayer against the Rest of India at Vishakhapatnam, was Sachin's first first-class match as captain. Among those playing under him was Sanjay Manjrekar who struck 96. However, the selectors were expectedly reluctant to change a winning combination.

By the time the second Test got underway in Chennai, the Indian players were swearing by the 'Code of Conduct' that Wadekar had drafted for them. An outcome of the cricket manager's observations in South Africa, where in his view, the team's cricket had suffered on account of 'too much 'socializing', the conduct comprised 12 instructions for the squad:

1. Must attend the practice/nets well on time with the team, as desired by the manager.
2. Must get to the ground on time as decided by the manager with the team only.
3. Must come to the ground properly dressed in whites and not in shorts and casuals. The 12th man will wear India's blazer while carrying the drinks.
4. Must behave well on the ground in view of the penalties now being imposed. However, in case any penalty is imposed on a member of the team, it will be shared by all the members of the team.
5. The players and reserves must be found in the dressing room or in the place reserved for the players only. Any player required to go out/meet someone must have the manager's permission.
6. No player will be allowed to go outside the hotel without the permission of the manager.
7. No private dinner/function except official ones will be permitted.
8. No promotional activities/private sponsorships will be allowed.
9. No woman/girl will be allowed in the hotel room of the player.
10. No player's wife will be allowed to stay overnight in the hotel room.
11. No player will participate in the matches other than those approved by the Board during the series.
12. No talking to the Press by any of the players unless permitted by the manager.

The England team would have benefited by following a code pertaining specifically to their dining habits. Gooch had to drop out of the second Test at Chennai. Alec Stewart, leading in his place, lost the toss, and Azharuddin elected to bat.

> For the dusty turners of India we prepared on the hard rock surfaces of Lilleshall. We knew we would be facing a phalanx of spinners, so we left out our best player of spin, David Gower. In Kolkata the pitch looked dry and cracked, so we played four seamers. We knew that the food could be dodgy so we ate prawns in Chennai and got food poisoning. It was that kind of trip.
>
> —Michael Atherton, *Opening Up: My Autobiography*

India got off to a sound start in the southern Indian metropolis. Sidhu, who had demoralized the England bowlers, most notably the spinners with an innings of 130 for the Board President's XI in a one-dayer at the start of the tour, now exhibited another facet of his batsmanship. Even as he dropped anchor at one end, the youngsters sparkled at the other. Kambli scored 59, before Graeme Hick, bowling his off-breaks, won a shout for leg-before. The left-hander was replaced in the middle by his Shardashram mate. The score at that stage was 149–2.

Sachin's arrival at the crease marked the formal beginning of a memorable association between a batsman and a cricket ground. His association with Chennai had commenced nearly six years previously, when he had made his way there to attend the selection trials of the MRF Pace Foundation, whose objective was to unearth and train fast bowlers for India. Having taken 27 wickets in inter-school cricket in the season gone by, Sachin fancied his quick-bowling skills. However, his ambitions were nipped in the bud by a certain Dennis Lillee, the head coach at the Foundation. He told Sachin that he did not have the height and build to be a fast bowler.

At the M.A. Chidambaram Stadium, on the afternoon of 11 February 1993, Sachin was welcomed to the crease by Ian Salisbury, the leg-spinner, with a full-toss. It got what it deserved. Sachin followed his punch to the mid-wicket boundary with another, this time on the off-side which bisected the fielders at cover and mid-off. That everything that could possibly go wrong for the visiting team was going wrong was proved when the square-leg umpire turned down a confident run-out appeal against Sachin. He drove to cover and called Sidhu for a single, only to be sent back. The throw was on target, but Sachin survived. Had the TV umpire been in place for the series, Sachin may have struggled.

Sachin regained his focus with two boundaries off Salisbury. A pull was followed by a drive past extra-cover. The 'follow-through' of his bat after executing the second boundary would have pleased Achrekar and several other coaches. It completed a splendid arc just over the batsman's left shoulder with the face facing the sky. The Chennai crowd, one of the most knowledgeable in the cricketing world, was ecstatic, as were the photographers stationed on the edge of the boundary line. It was as if Sachin was posing for them.

He carried on with his batting 'masterclass', twice late-cutting Graeme Hick for four. What was notable about both strokes was that the ball sped past the right of the fielder at point and not the left, as generally happened with late-cuts. Not only did the shots underscore Sachin's extraordinary 'bat-speed' and reflexes, but also his confidence. Sidhu completed his hundred just before stumps on day one, which India ended at a commanding 275–2.

The panache that Sachin displayed on the second morning gave the impression that he had been batting all night. Not for him the ritual of an overnight 'not-out' batsman 'getting his eye in'. He punched Yorkshire teammate Paul Jarvis off the back foot for four, the ball passing the latter on his follow-through. That was followed by two cuts, the second of which was slightly uppish, both of which went to the boundary.

Sachin then set his sights on Jarvis' colleague Devon Malcolm. As the crowd cheered in anticipation of a century, Sachin flicked Malcolm to the square-leg fence. When the bowler responded by pitching one up, Sachin drove him through Sidhu's legs, back to the boundary. The spectators exploded when Malcolm was hit for another fluent drive down the ground. That took Sachin to 101. It was his first Test century on Indian soil.

Sidhu and Azharuddin fell in quick succession soon after, but Sachin, it seemed, was in the mood for a big one. He continued to treat the fast bowlers and spinners with contempt, as did Amre, who looked in fine nick. Sachin had moved to 165 when Salisbury tossed one up, a courageous delivery, given the battering that he had been subjected to. Sachin went for a big hit, but mistimed and the ball ballooned into the air into the off-side. Salisbury ran to his left to take the catch.

Sachin was visibly upset to have been dismissed in so tame a fashion. He did not know it then, but it wasn't the last time he would mistime a flighted delivery by a spinner and hole out on the off-side in a Test at Chennai.

Kapil Dev hastened the sprint towards a declaration with an entertaining 66, completing 5,000 runs along the way. India declared at 560–6 and the spinners then bowled England out for 286 and 252. Sachin did his bit in the field, taking a splendid one-handed catch at leg-slip to dismiss Paul Jarvis off Kumble, in the second innings. Chris Lewis delayed the end with a defiant hundred.

The series sealed, India went for a clean sweep in the third Test at Mumbai. England won the toss for the first time in the series, and scored 347, with Graeme Hick contributing 178 of those. A banner in the stands when India commenced its first innings, encapsulated the emotions of a certain educational institution—'Shardashram v/s England!'

The three Shardashram players in the Indian XI took the banner very seriously. With their guru looking on from the stands, Amre scored 57 and Sachin 78. As had been the case at Kolkata, Sachin was dismissed when he was looking impenetrable, with left-arm spinner Phil Tufnell winning a shout for leg-before.

Vinod Kambli made the biggest impact. The flamboyant left-hander completed his ascent to stardom with an innings of 224, India's highest individual score against England. India totalled 591, leaving England with the task of batting out the last day-and-a-half to save the game. The visitors failed spectacularly. Prabhakar made the initial dents, and then the spinners took over. India completed their third and biggest win of the series—by an innings and

15 runs—on the fifth morning. The players with similar sounding surnames were the toast of the nation. Anil Kumble finished the series with 21 wickets and the tag of India's premier strike bowler. Off the field, Kambli proved that he could be as sharp as he had shown himself to be on it, with his statement, 'Sachin took the elevator and I took the stairs!'

The team, teetering on the brink at the end of the South Africa series, wore a settled look at the end of the England series. Senior players like Shastri and Manjrekar had not been missed. Azharuddin seemed to have come into his own as captain, and not merely because he had regained form himself. Ajit Wadekar was to him what Bob Simpson had been to Allan Border in the mid-1980s. Like Simpson, Wadekar took charge of the training sessions and off-the-field issues, leaving Azharuddin to focus on matters on the field.

England staged a comeback of sorts by winning the third and fourth ODIs, which followed the Mumbai Test. Trailing 1–3 with two to play, India could only hope to square the series. The last two games, both of which were played at Gwalior, witnessed some spectacular batting. England, put in to bat in both the games, scored 257 and 265–4 respectively, but lost. Sidhu anchored the chase in the fifth encounter with an innings of 134, and Azharuddin batted as he only he could. He scored 74 off 72 balls in the fifth game and an unbeaten 95 off only 63 balls in the sixth, an innings that won him the individual award and Geoffrey Boycott's hat, presented to him by the former England captain-turned-commentator himself.

The last international engagement of the home season—one Test and three ODIs against Zimbabwe—proceeded on expected lines. India were no longer the team that had produced some insipid cricket at Harare at the start of the season. The one-off Test at Delhi commenced a day after Mumbai, the hometown of the Shardashram trio, was rocked by serial blasts. Sachin scored 62 and Amre got 52, but Kambli took the honours for the second Test in succession, with an innings of 227. He was now part of an elite group of batsmen to have scored back-to-back double centuries in Tests. The Indian spin attack wore a slightly different look for the game, with Raju having been replaced by Maninder Singh. However, the end-result was no different, with India winning by an innings and 13 runs.

Vinod Kambli may have upstaged his Shardashram teammate statistically, but he could not dent Sachin's popularity, as was proved in the third ODI against Zimbabwe at Pune. The hosts, who had already pocketed the series with wins in the first two games, needed 214 to win. The wicket of W.V. Raman, the second of the Indian innings, elicited deafening cheers rather than stoic silence. The spectators expected their favourite to stride in, only to be shocked to see Ajay Sharma, who had warmed the benches for the better part of the previous two months, come in instead. When Sharma was dropped at fine-leg early in his innings, the fielder who was at fault was booed by the capacity crowd, not because he had spilt the catch, but because he had denied—or delayed—Sachin's entry. As it turned out, Sharma scored an unbeaten, match-winning 59, and Sachin did not even get to bat!

A lot was expected from the spin and Shardashram triumvirate on the tour of Sri Lanka in July-August 1993. The visit represented an opportunity for the Indians to mend their abysmal record on foreign soil. At the start of the series, *The Sportstar* had cited an extraordinarily appalling fact—India had won only a single Test series abroad since Sachin Tendulkar's birth 20 years previously. The squad that flew to Sri Lanka comprised three players who had featured in that momentous series against England in 1986—Azharuddin, Kapil Dev and Kiran More.

However, history suggested that the Sri Lankans could not be taken lightly on their own soil. Eight years previously, India had started their first tour of Sri Lanka as the overwhelming favourites, but they had lost 0–1.

The 1993 series got off to a wet start, with only 40 minutes of play possible in the first Test at Kandy. The second Test, played at Colombo's Sinhalese Sports Club, witnessed quality and acrimony in equal measure. Azharuddin maintained his golden run at the toss and India scored 366, with Kambli scoring 125 and Sidhu making 82. Sachin was on 28 when he was adjudged caught at short-leg despite the ball having ricocheted off his chest and not his bat. Kumble then led the charge with the ball, as Sri Lanka were restricted to 254. The Indian batsmen went on the attack in their second innings with the objective of giving their bowlers as much time as possible, to take 10 Sri Lankan wickets. Sidhu got a hundred, while Prabhakar, his partner, was unlucky to fall on 95. For the first time since the Chennai Test earlier in the year, Vinod Kambli was outscored by his childhood chum.

Sachin got a life when he mishooked new-ball bowler Pramodya Wickremansinghe and was dropped in the outfield. That aberration apart, he batted magnificently. Shortly after he completed the sixth Test hundred and second 'second-innings' ton of his career, Azharuddin declared, setting the opposition an unattainable target of 472. Sri Lanka were bowled out for 236, with Aravinda De Silva waging a lone battle with an innings of 93. Anil Kumble was India's best bowler, with eight wickets in the game.

The Indians were ecstatic because as they viewed it, they had beaten a team of 13, not 11 opponents. They had perceived the umpiring as inconsistent and biased in favour of the home team, and that in turn had led to a fair bit of gamesmanship by members of both sides. Peter Burge, the former Australian batsman and now ICC referee, had been kept busy.

Even as the fans expressed their delight at what promised to be just the first of many instances of Sachin and Kambli scoring hundreds in the same international game, they could not help but note the fundamental differences in the personalities of the Shardashram duo. While the fans were divided over who was more talented, there was never any doubt as to whose temperament was superior, especially after that Test match. Kambli, when declared out caught-behind in the second innings, had let his feelings be known by slamming his bat on the turf, and consequently incurred a reprimand from Burge. On the other hand, Sachin had walked off impassively when he was declared out caught when his bat had been nowhere near the ball, in the first innings. Like any other batsman who got a dodgy decision, he was upset, but he did not display his emotions in public and accepted it as being a part of the game.

The 'heir-apparent' had his first taste of international captaincy on the last two days of the third Test at the P. Saravanamutthu Stadium, also in Colombo. With Azharuddin down with flu, Sachin took charge of a team that comprised the likes of Kapil Dev, Prabhakar, Sidhu and More, all of whom he had dreamt of emulating during his days as a schoolboy cricketer.

A stodgy hundred by Roshan Mahanama ensured a draw, but even in the final, 'dying' stages of the game, India's acting captain refused to let his guard down. He persisted with his regular bowlers and made the batsmen earn their runs. He also handled a ball-tampering allegation levelled against his bowlers by the umpires, with aplomb, and sorted things out before the issue could escalate. On the flip side, some people felt that he was talking to his bowlers far too often than was necessary.

India had won the Test series, but the tour did not end on a happy note for the visitors. Leading 1–0 in the three-match ODI series, they played some daft cricket in the second game, at one stage losing six wickets for 10 runs. The hosts won the decider to take the series 2–1.

> I remember one incident from the early 1990s that underscored Sachin's commitment. Sungrace-Mafatlal were playing the inter-corporate Shaheed Smriti tournament in April–May. It had been a long season for him and we had told him that he would be needed to play only if we reached the final. As it turned out, we did. I think we won the semi-final on a Friday, and the final against Mohan Meakins was scheduled to be played on the Sunday, a couple of days later. I called Sachin and told him to rush to Agra,

where the final was to be played. He was about to leave Mumbai for Silchar in the eastern state of Assam, to play the benefit match of Sunil Valson, a member of the World Cup winning side of 1983. This game was to be played at a ground that was 30 kilometres away from the town and Sachin's presence was critical to assuage the sponsors. We then started working out how to get him to Agra in time for the final. Valson assured us that he would arrange for Sachin to leave the venue as soon as he was through with his innings. The initial plan was for Sachin to play an aggressive cameo in the benefit game and then throw his wicket away, but then, that wasn't as easy as it seemed. After all, he simply hated getting out, regardless of whether the match in question was official or unofficial! Much to the crowd's delight, he scored a century. He was then driven to Silchar, where we had organised a plane for him. The aircraft flew him to Kolkata, from where he caught a flight for Delhi. He eventually reached Agra by road at around midnight. The entire squad was waiting for him at the hotel. We had dinner only after he reached. After dinner, the team made its way to his room. Even as the players started cracking jokes and pulling each other's legs, Sachin displayed no signs of exhaustion despite his marathon journey. As the banter went on, he opened his kitbag and started putting his gear in place for the final, which was scheduled to begin at 7:00 a.m., just a few hours later. The tournament comprised 40-overs-a-side matches that were scheduled to end by 1:00 p.m. The idea was to finish before the heat got unbearable. The next morning, we reached the venue for breakfast. There was pandemonium at the ground, as was only to be expected when the locals got to know of Sachin's presence, and the stands were full. We were batting second, and the game reached a stage wherein we needed around 80 to win off the last eight overs. In the middle were Sachin and our skipper Sandeep Patil, two of the most destructive batsmen of all time. However, they were up against bowlers who were masters at bowling on the dustbowl that the wicket was. The umpires called for drinks and I went in with the reserve players to get a sense of how our stars were assessing the situation. Things looked bleak for us. This was in the early 1990s, when a required rate of ten an over was deemed as difficult to achieve and impossible to maintain. What followed was extraordinary. Sandeep took a gulp of water and said in Marathi, 'Tendlya, *aata suruwaat karuya*' [Tendlya, let's start]. Sachin nodded in agreement. They proceeded to knock the 80 runs off the next five overs. They simply stepped on the gas and finished it off.

—Anil Joshi, personal interview

THE HERO CUP AND THE MUMBAI REINS

It is very difficult to analyse why you fail in the one-day games. It is also difficult to know what you have to do when you go out to the middle. You go out to bat in the 40th over, or even in the 30th over, and you don't know whether you have to go after the bowlers or hang in there, give the strike to the set batsman and play your shots later. That is what has been happening to me in one-day internationals. I have tried playing shots and got out early, I have not been able to get too many runs. But then I am as serious about the one-dayers as I am about Test cricket and so the failures are not coming from lack of seriousness. So, maybe, things will change with a big innings or two.

—Sachin Tendulkar, *The Sportstar*, 26 March 1994

The Indian cricketers got a two-month break before the 1993–94 season began with the Duleep Trophy. Sachin led West Zone in the first two games before resuming national duty. In the first game, West Zone beat South Zone, who were led by Mohammed Azharuddin, by an innings and 55 runs at Rajkot. Vinod Kambli and Sanjay Manjrekar scored centuries, and Ravi Shastri took five wickets in the second innings after South Zone were asked to follow-on. The next game was a setback; West Zone lost to North Zone by an innings and 47 runs, at Vadodara. Bhupinder Singh, a paceman from the Punjab, was North Zone's best performer, with six wickets.

The joy that Indian aficionados of Test cricket had experienced after the series win in Sri Lanka was nullified when they went through their team's schedule for the next two seasons. India were slated to play only three Tests in the 1993–94 season, that too at home against Sri Lanka. A one-off Test in New Zealand was added subsequently, but even four Tests in a six-month season was hardly a number to rejoice over. India had been scheduled to tour England in mid-1994, but their invitation was rescinded and passed on to South Africa. The schedule for the 1994–95 season did not inspire confidence either. India were again scheduled to play only three Tests, at home against the West Indies.

The cancellation of the England tour and paucity of Test cricket meant that someone like Vinod Kambli who was at the peak of his confidence after the series in Sri Lanka was denied opportunities to hone his technique against different opponents and in unfamiliar conditions at a time when he was most likely to learn and imbibe quickly. Sachin had been quite fortunate in this regard, having started his career with series in three different continents before playing a Test at home.

The shortfall of Test cricket was to be compensated by a surfeit of limited-overs cricket. No one knew it then, but the plethora of limited-overs matches and tournaments in the 1990s did more harm than good. While they did produce some memorable cricket, the high percentage of meaningless encounters attracted the attention of unsavoury elements who were keen on making quick money, and did not mind cutting corners to do so.

The showpiece event of the 1993–94 season, as far as India was concerned, was the Hero Cup, a tournament organized to commemorate the diamond jubilee of the CAB, the home association of Jagmohan Dalmiya, the then secretary of the BCCI. The Hero Cup was part of the BCCI's endeavour to capitalize on the popularity of limited-overs cricket in the country and showcase India as a hub of the sport. It was the first limited-overs tournament in India to feature coloured clothing, white balls and black sightscreens. Five teams—Pakistan, South Africa, West Indies, Sri Lanka and Zimbabwe—had confirmed their participation, but Pakistan pulled out. It was the third time they had done so from a series/tournament on Indian soil, in four years.

The format was the same as the Nehru Cup that India had hosted in 1989 and the 1992 World Cup. The league stage, to be played at different venues across the country, was to be followed by the semi-finals and final at the Eden Gardens, which became India's first cricketing arena to be embellished with light-towers.

A few months before the tournament, the India–Pakistan–Sri Lanka combine bagged the rights to host the 1996 World Cup in one of the most acrimonious meetings in the history of the ICC. At the forefront of the subcontinent's successful campaign were I.S. Bindra, the then president of the BCCI, and Dalmiya himself. This triumph made the Hero Cup a key 'lead-up' event to the Big One. However, Bindra and Dalmiya had little or no time to savour their win, forced as they were to wage another tussle, this time on home turf.

For two decades, Doordarshan, India's government-owned broadcaster, had covered and telecast cricket matches played under the aegis of the BCCI without paying the latter anything. On the contrary, it was the BCCI who paid production costs to DD. What the nation got in return was drab and uninteresting TV coverage. Nothing much had changed over the years, apart from the transition from black-and-white to colour in 1982–83, and the installation of additional cameras for the coverage of the 1987 World Cup. A standing joke that would do the rounds in the cricket season was that DD believed in taking its name very seriously. If translated literally, its name meant 'a view from afar'.

It took the 'historic' ODI series against South Africa in November 1991 to jolt the BCCI out of its slumber. For the first time ever, a TV organization from abroad—the South African Broadcasting Corporation (SABC) in this case—sought to 'purchase' the live telecast rights of a series to be played in India. This prompted the Board to do some fact-finding, at the end of which, it discovered that it owned the rights. With no experience of negotiating for TV rights, the Board's representatives decided to quote a certain figure, only to be stunned when the SABC offered 10 times the amount. For the BCCI, it was the moment of truth; the officials realized that they were sitting on a goldmine.

Grappling as it was with a deficit of ₹81.6 lakhs in 1991–92, the BCCI was incredulous when DD quoted a fee of ₹5 lakhs to televise every game. This demand was made in 1992, by which time liberalization had become a way of life, and TV channels like Star, BBC and CNN had established themselves in urban and semi-urban Indian households. The BCCI then sold the TV rights of the Test series against England to Trans World International (TWI), a UK-based production house, for ₹18 lakhs (US$40,000), and made a profit of US$600,000 in the process. TWI in turn did a deal with Star's Prime Sports Channel. Doordarshan was told to pay US$1 million to TWI to be able to telecast the matches in India. It did so, and beamed TWI's live feed, albeit with its own commentary team.

The England series was a watershed in the history of Indian television. The coverage was sleek and engaging. For the very first time on Indian soil, cameras were placed over the sightscreens at both ends. There were cameras at mid-wicket and square-leg positions as well, and microphones were installed at the base of the stumps to pick the nicks. Every attempt was made to bring TV viewers as close to the action as possible. Anchoring the proceedings was a team of commentators whose credentials were second to none—Sunil Gavaskar, Geoffrey Boycott and David Gower—along with seasoned professionals like Henry Blofeld and Charles Colville.

After its talks with DD regarding the TV rights of the Hero Cup hit a bottleneck, the BCCI–CAB sold the rights to TWI. Peeved by the snub and shaken by the realization that its monopoly over Indian skies and cricket was over, the broadcaster cried foul. The Union Ministry of Information and Broadcasting got involved in the fracas and denied uplinking facilities to TWI, citing a clause from the Indian Telegraph Act of 1885 that apparently made it mandatory for the Telecom Department to clear every such telecast. This was done despite an approval issued by the Ministry of Home Affairs to an application by the TWI, requesting to be allowed satellite transmission. Another application by TWI, for it to be permitted to import its own broadcast equipment, had subsequently been approved by the Ministry of Finance. The Ministry had in fact even waived customs and other duties.

With the initial Hero Cup matches not being telecast as a result of the standoff, there was concern not only in the BCCI, but also overseas. WorldTel, a US-based company that had bought the TV rights of the 1996 World Cup for US$10 million, was understandably jittery. The issue was finally resolved late on the night of 15 November 1993, by which time half the tournament had been completed. A bench of the Supreme Court of India met at 11:30 p.m. and ruled in TWI's favour.

Indian cricket would never be the same again.

India began the tournament with a five-wicket win over Sri Lanka at Kanpur, but then collapsed against the West Indies at Ahmedabad. The game could not be completed due to crowd unrest, but the Windies were declared winners on run-rate. India's next game against Zimbabwe at Cuttack went down to the wire. The Zimbabweans batted excellently to draw level with India's 235, and they were helped along the way by some shoddy bowling and fielding. The home team took longer than usual to emerge from its dressing room for the presentation ceremony, the reason for which was revealed later. A livid Azharuddin had given his team a dressing down and virtually demanded a win over South Africa in the next game. The Indians obliged with a 40-run triumph at the new stadium at Mohali, on the outskirts of Chandigarh.

India's semi-final against South Africa, the first 'night' game to be played at the Eden Gardens, was a classic, which culminated with a memorable final over by Sachin. Needing six to win from the last six balls, the South Africans managed only three runs.

As a batsman, Sachin had always sought to master the art of being at the other end of the wicket 'mentally', even as he stood at his own end 'physically'. He prided himself on his ability to read the bowler's mind; as a bowler, he was no different, and in fact, his proficiency with the bat made it easier for him to put himself in the shoes of the batsmen he was bowling to.

> Killer instinct plus intelligence is the winning combination.... I said to myself, 'At any cost, we have to win this game.' I had decided to bowl

each and every delivery at the stumps.... MacMillan needed four runs off the last ball. I decided to bowl a Yorker. We did not want a wicket, we were more concerned about preventing runs at that stage. So the keeper [Vijay Yadav] and I had a small talk and I asked him to stand behind the 30-yard circle. And as McMillan played that shot, it took the inner edge and went to the keeper. If the keeper had been standing up, the ball might have gone to the boundary.

—Sachin Tendulkar, *The Sportstar*, November 1994

The final against the West Indies had all the makings of another humdinger. India batted first and scored 225–7. Prabhakar dismissed Phil Simmons early, but Brian Lara was in tremendous nick, hitting Ajay Jadeja out of the attack with five boundaries in a single over. Azharuddin then gave Sachin a go. On the eve of the game, Ajit Tendulkar had visualized a duel between the two young titans. He had advised his younger brother to bowl stump-to-stump, if at all such a situation were to arise. Sachin followed the instructions to the letter. He bowled one just outside the off-stump, which nipped back. Lara went for an expansive drive, missed and was bowled.

That was the turning point. Kapil Dev, who was by this time bowling first-change, took two wickets and as the capacity crowd at the Eden roared as only it could, Kumble swooped in for the kill. He began by having Carl Hooper leg-before, and did not stop. The West Indies were bowled out for 123, with Kumble taking 6–12, the best bowling performance by an Indian in ODIs.

Azharuddin and Kambli took the batting honours for India in the tournament. Sachin's top score of the competition was 28, but his bowling had more than made up for his batting. It was not that he was out of touch, but he was finding it difficult to convert his starts. A wrist injury that he had sustained during an unofficial game just prior to the Hero Cup was also bothering him. It had forced him to use bats that were lighter than the ones weighing three pounds and two ounces that he normally used. However, even his 'lighter' bats were a lot heavier than those used by his teammates. He would never get over the fascination for heavy sticks that had gripped him when he shifted to Shardashram in the mid-1980s.

Indeed, many things that Sachin does are delightful to admire but disastrous to emulate.

—Vasu Paranjape, *Wisden Asia Cricket*, September 2002

The Hero Cup ended on 27 November 1993. With the Sri Lankans scheduled to arrive only in the second half of January 1994, India's leading lights were available for the league stage of the Ranji Trophy.

Sachin commenced his stint as Mumbai captain by articulating his desire to end the 30-time champions' barren run in the Ranji Trophy that had lasted nearly a decade. While Mumbai's batting had never been a problem, the bowling had been a let-down since their last triumph in 1984–85. However, things had changed by 1993–94. In pacemen Salil Ankola, Abey Kuruvilla and Paras Mhambrey, Sachin had under him, a young and potent bowling attack. There was also Ravi Shastri, as well as Sairaj Bahutule, leg-spinner and Sachin's former inter-school opponent.

Raju Kulkarni, Shishir Hattangadi, Chandrakant Pandit and Lalchand Rajput, all four of whom had represented the city with distinction in the 1980s, had either retired or shifted to other states by then. In fact, Shastri and Manjrekar apart, most of the members of the 1993–94 side were either Sachin's contemporaries or juniors who had played with or against him at the junior levels and watched admiringly as he scaled the ladder from inter-school cricket to the national side in next to no time. But naturally, they all looked up to him. With Sachin in charge, the opposition could only be wary.

> His commitment was 1000 percent. And if he spotted a dip in intensity and commitment from his position at slip, mid-on or mid-off, you got it straight, then and there. He abused you. When I started off in the Mumbai team, he would tell me what ball to bowl.... At that stage, you are not in a position to analyse why he is saying that. But when I look back and go through the one, two, three, four, five and six sequence again, I realise that's the way to set up a batsman; that's the way you bowl; that's how you put pressure and get him out. It helped me.
>
> —Paras Mhambrey, *Mid-Day*, 19 November 1993

Mumbai won all four matches in the West Zone league outright. The margins of victory spoke for themselves—an innings and 118 runs against Vadodara, 9 wickets against Maharashtra, 10 wickets against Gujarat and 8 wickets against Saurashtra. The bowlers were magnificent and the batsmen murderous, Sachin included. His top score was 138 against Maharashtra. For generations of cricket lovers brought up on stories of Mumbai-bred batsmen taking their time to 'settle' and eschewing horizontal-bat strokes 'till they got their eye in', this was new. But then, Sachin and his colleagues belonged to the 'liberalization era', wherein people were encouraged to 'spend' and not just 'save'.

India and Mumbai's numbers three and four batsmen were honoured by their home state in the form of the Shiv Chhatrapati Awards for sporting excellence, later in the season. A greater honour was bestowed on their guru, who was conferred the Dronacharya Award for his proficiency as a coach by the Government of India. Achrekar was only the third cricket coach to be conferred the award, after Desh Prem Azad who gave Indian cricket its greatest all-rounder in Kapil Dev, and Gurcharan Singh, who had guided the likes of Kirti Azad, Maninder Singh and Ajay Jadeja in their formative years.

The Test series against Sri Lanka in early 1994 was hopelessly one-sided. India seized the initiative in the first Test at Lucknow, with Sachin scoring a chanceless 142. Unbeaten on 88 at stumps on the opening day, he completed his hundred with an on-drive, off-drive and cover drive at the start of day two. Another highlight of the Indian innings was a knock of 61 by Sanjay Manjrekar who had been recalled after scoring heavily at the domestic level. The spinners then did the rest. India won by an innings and 119 runs and the hosts proceeded to seal the series with another innings win in the second game at Bengaluru. The final wicket that fell in the game was one that enabled Kapil Dev to draw level with Sir Richard Hadlee's record tally of 431. History was then created on the first day of the third Test at Ahmedabad, when Manjrekar caught Hashan Tillekaratne off Kapil Dev. The great all-rounder's accession to the summit was celebrated with more fervour than India's clean sweep, which they completed with a third successive innings win. Among those most delighted at the clean sweep was India's new wicketkeeper-batsman Nayan Mongia, who had made his Test debut at Lucknow.

> I remember back then in the nineties when after beating some hapless visiting team, we would just pack our bags and look for the first flight home. There were no great celebrations after the game. Deep inside, all of us knew that the wins were cosmetic. We knew how good we really were when we toured.
>
> —Sanjay Manjrekar, *Wisden Asia Cricket*, December 2004

Manjrekar's contention is of course debatable, given the unwritten prerogative of home teams to dish out wickets that suited their strengths. Would the West Indies have even considered preparing turning tracks in the 'Pace Age?' A factor that was far more likely to affect Indian cricket adversely was the team's schedule till mid-1996. The team's next full tour—of England in mid-1996—was more than two years away.

Those who expected Kapil Dev to call it quits after he scaled the summit were surprised when he was named in the Indian team for the short tour of New Zealand. A heel injury to Prabhakar gave Javagal Srinath the opportunity to play a Test after more than a year. The one-off Test was drawn, and New Zealand beat India in the first of four ODIs, with paceman Danny Morrison taking a hat-trick. Among those who failed was Sachin who scored only 15. Bishan Bedi would have permitted himself a chuckle when Azharuddin carried forward the Indian tradition of providing quotable quotes at media conferences in New Zealand. The Indian captain used the post-match presser to remind his players that they were 'not on a holiday'.

Sachin's ODI statistics at the end of the first ODI against New Zealand did not make for flattering reading—1,758 runs from 69 ODIs at an average of 30.84. A few months previously, Brian Lara had opined that like him, Sachin ought to open the innings in ODIs, as that would enable him to set the pace of the innings and give him more deliveries to play. Sachin himself had said as much in an interview to *Sportsworld* in December 1993. When asked why he wasn't doing a Lara, Sachin had said that he would surely open if asked to. As vice-captain, he was part of the team management, but the idea of forcing his way did not appeal to him. With India having just won the Hero Cup, no one took note of his statements, the obvious reason being that there was no need to fix a problem that did not exist.

A stiff neck was to change all that.

SECTION II
Peerless (1992-99)

OPENING AGGRESSOR

Something inside me would always tell me that I was cut out to bat higher in the order to be able to give more and more to the team.

—Sachin Tendulkar, *The Sportstar*, 21 April 2001

2, 4, 4, 4, 4, 3, 4, 4, 4, 4, 6, 4, 4, 6, 4, 4, 4, 4, 2, 4, 2 and 1.

This was the incredible sequence of scoring strokes in an innings that transformed Indian cricket and a certain 'limited-overs' career. Eighty-two runs came off only 22 balls. The innings comprised 27 dot balls.

Navjot Sidhu awoke with a stiff neck on the morning of 27 March 1994, the day his team was to take on the Kiwis in the second of four ODIs at Auckland's hexagonal Eden Park. With Prabhakar having flown home already to tend to his injured heel, Sidhu's exit left the Indians with no choice but to elevate a middle-order batsman to the opening slot. Sachin sensed his opportunity. He had expressed his desire to go in first in ODIs earlier as well, but the team management hadn't been too keen. Wadekar, Azharuddin and Kapil Dev all felt that he was a lot more valuable in the middle order.

At Auckland, Sachin reminded the cricket manager of their discussions and requested that he be given a chance. He did not speak like the vice-captain that he was, but as just another member of the squad who wanted to take on an additional responsibility. He stated that he possessed the strokes and nous to capitalize on the fielding restrictions in the first 15 overs. He also assured Wadekar that if he were to fail, he would never request to be sent up again. The cricket manager then had a word with Azharuddin and Kapil Dev. They responded in the affirmative. As far as his senior colleagues and several others were concerned, it was a question of just one game. Sidhu would return for the next encounter and normal service would resume. Sachin on his part was delighted to get the go-ahead. The possibility of failing was of course never on his mind.

He had to await his turn to pad up. New Zealand won the toss and elected to bat, only to be blown away by some excellent bowling. Kapil Dev, Srinath and Ankola took two wickets each, and Chauhan snared three, as the hosts were bundled out for 142. India had all the time in the world.

Their team's ineptitude in the first ODI did not deter the 'cricketing die-hards' in India from waking up at 3:00 a.m. IST to watch the proceedings on Prime Sports. By the time the New Zealand innings folded up, it was early morning. It happened to be the second day of Holi, the Festival of Colours, and the fans were keen on watching some cricket before commencing the celebrations.

The fourth over of the Indian innings, bowled by Chris Pringle, was when any hopes that the hosts may have had of a comeback, dissipated for good. Sachin drove the bowler on the up, past mid-off that had been placed wider than usual, for four. Pringle then tried a slower delivery, only to be hit straight and high. The ball dropped just short of the long-on boundary and rolled over. After hitting through the off-side and following it up with an aerial stroke down the ground, Sachin now turned his attention to the leg-side. He rolled his wrists and essayed an exquisite on-drive, between mid-on and short mid-wicket. Gavin Larsen gave chase, but in vain. Crossing over to the other end in the next over, Sachin leg-glanced Morrison for another boundary.

India's new opener continued with his disdainful ways against the new-ball bowlers, the standout strokes being a front foot punch through the covers off Pringle and a straight drive off Morrison. Even those who wanted the home team to win, could not but help admire Sachin's poise, pluck and panache. Those rooting for India in the stands got more and more animated, with patriotic songs like 'Saare Jahaan Se Achcha' soon giving way to deafening roars. The onslaught left Ken Rutherford, the Kiwi skipper, with no option but to throw the ball to Larsen, a medium-pacer proficient in the art of bowling stump-to-stump and putting the brakes on the scoring.

Sachin played Larsen's first three balls, all of which were pitched up, off the front foot and straight to the fielders. Larsen then pitched the next two short, which Sachin again played off the front foot. Convinced that he was onto something, Larsen produced another short-pitched delivery, which was exactly what Sachin had wanted him to do. He transferred his weight onto the back foot and pulled the ball over mid-wicket for six. India were 61–0 at the end of the ninth over.

Larsen's next over was forgettable for the bowler and sensational for the Indians. Sachin danced down the wicket to smash him over the top for a boundary. He then sought to repeat the stroke, but the bowler saw him coming and held the ball back. Sachin swung his arms anyway, but hit the ball straight back to the bowler. On TV, one could see the bowler smile at his 'victory' as he returned to the top of his run-up. Sachin responded with a contemptuous pull off the front-foot to the mid-wicket boundary, a stroke that took his individual score to 51. He had faced only 34 deliveries and hit 10 fours and one six. An Indian supporter who 'raided' the playing arena expressed his delight by giving the batsman a tuck on the cheek. Sachin then went down the wicket again and swung hard. This time, the ball cleared the straight boundary and landed in the stands. He rounded off the over with another magnificent hit over the top, this time for four.

It was not just the bowlers Sachin was toying with. He leg-glanced Pringle for four past a hapless short fine-leg, shortly after the man at deep fine-leg had been brought in to enable the placement of a fielder in the long-on region. Later in the same over, he came down the wicket and biffed the bowler through the covers for four. Pringle then tried a yorker, which Sachin met on the full and flicked for another boundary.

It was the sort of innings that made one forget the trappings of international and conventional cricket—the honour of representing one's country, the need to adapt to the match-situation, conditions and opposition, the pulls and pressures involved, the financial stakes, etc. What all of India witnessed that Holi morning was a young man besotted with the game and enjoying every moment of it with an approach that was as elementary as one could imagine. In the lanes, playgrounds and apartment courtyards across India and elsewhere, the first lesson handed out to kids when they were introduced to cricket, was that the bat was meant to 'hit' the ball. Weightier concepts like 'technique' and 'defence' came in much later. It was an innings that millions of Indian viewers could identify with, as it took them back to the cricket that they had played in their respective childhoods, a time when life was less complicated. Jadeja's dismissal off a slower ball by Pringle, somewhere in the middle of the joyride, did not even register.

One of the grandest innings of all time ended when Sachin paid the ultimate, but inadvertent, tribute to scores of 'gully' cricketers, with a 'soft' dismissal, *against the run of play*. He had scored 82 off only 49 balls when he was early in closing the face of the bat to Matthew Hart, the left-arm spinner. The ball took the leading edge and the bowler completed a simple catch. The ovation was stirring. Joining the spectators in the applause were Vinod Kambli, the non-striker, Mohammed Azharuddin, the incoming batsman, the New Zealand players and even Brian Alridge and Chris King, the umpires. India were as much delighted with their seven-wicket win as they were by the realization that they had hit pay dirt.

> When I open, I can pace myself better and try to make sure I bat through the 50 overs.
>
> —Sachin Tendulkar, *Cricket Talk*, 4 November 2000

Another game of cricket got underway on the same day as the Auckland ODI, in Mumbai. Leading the metropolis in the Ranji Trophy final against Bengal was Ravi Shastri, who took over for the knockout stage of the tournament after Sachin went on national duty. Mumbai beat Haryana in the pre-quarter-final by an innings and 202 runs, with Amol Muzumdar, another Shardashram alumnus, scoring 260, the highest individual score by a debutant in first-class cricket. In the quarter-final against Karnataka, Mumbai were 174–6 at one stage, in response to the opposition's 406. Shastri and Sairaj Bahutule then added 259 for the seventh wicket and secured the critical first-innings lead. Mumbai went on to take the first-innings lead in the semi-final against Maharashtra as well.

Mumbai dominated the final from ball one and completed an eight-wicket win on the fourth evening. It was their 31st triumph and first since 1984–85. As the celebrations began at the Wankhede, Shastri requested that 'Tendlya' be informed that the team had completed what he had initiated.

After his innings at Auckland, there was no question of Sachin returning to the middle order in the shorter format. Sidhu, who was back for the next game, took Kambli's place at number three, and the left-hander dropped down to number five.

In the next game at Wellington, Sachin scored 63 off 75 balls before falling leg-before to Larsen. The signature stroke of the innings was a down-the-wicket smash off Dion Nash that had the bowler ducking for cover. India won that game to go 2–1 up in the series. In the final game at Christchurch, Sachin blasted 40 off 26 balls, inclusive of three fours in an over off Larsen, before inside-edging the same bowler onto his stumps. Larsen, relieved and thrilled in equal measure, was delighted enough to do something that was out-of-character for him; he gave Sachin a verbal 'send-off' of sorts. New Zealand won the game off the penultimate ball to square the series.

India's next assignment was the third edition of the Austral-Asia Cup at Sharjah, their first trip to the oasis since October 1991. The Union Government had taken a serious view of allegations of 'foul play', spectator hooliganism and biased ticket-distribution that had surfaced during the 1991 tri-series, and the Sports Ministry gave the green signal to the Indian team only after the BCCI was assured by the organizers and the Emirates Cricket Board that no 'unsavoury elements' would be entertained at the venue.

While the Indian batting was expected to hold its own, the bowling department wore an inexperienced look in the absence of both Prabhakar and Kapil Dev. Prabhakar's heel had not healed, and it wasn't clear whether Kapil Dev had been dropped or rested.

India beat UAE in their opening game, but went down to Pakistan in the 'Friday clash', losing their way after a Sachin sizzler. In the early stages of the game, he brought the Indian supporters to their feet with some stupendous strokeplay against the new-ball pair of Wasim Akram and Aaqib Javed. A leg-glance and pull off Aaqib in the fourth over were the prelude to a stunner in the next over. Watchers were left gaping when Sachin met a good-length delivery by Akram on the rise and the front foot, and flicked it for six. His timing was impeccable, his confidence in his craft palpable and his genius undeniable. He was looking unstoppable when he fell in the 22nd over, *against the run of play*. India were 111–3, off which his share was 73, scored off 64 balls. The Indian middle order then caved in and Pakistan cruised to a six-wicket victory.

The win against UAE was good enough to get India into the semi-finals, where they beat Australia by seven wickets. For once, Sachin failed, but Jadeja (87) and Sidhu (80) batted beautifully. They were overshadowed by Kambli, who settled the outcome with two sixes and two fours in a Shane Warne over. Since his forgettable debut against India at Sydney in 1991–92, the leg-spinner had bowled Australia to Test wins over Sri Lanka, West Indies, New Zealand and England, but Indian batsmen, as he discovered once again, were in a different class altogether when it came to playing spin. Overseeing the proceedings from the Indian dressing room was Sunil Gavaskar, who had taken over as 'Interim Manager' after Wadekar suffered a heart attack.

Much to the delight of the organizers, the summit clash featured the traditional Asian rivals. A lot was expected from the Indians after their clinical display against Australia, but the Sharjah jinx manifested itself yet again. Pakistan prevailed, this time by 39 runs. Sachin fell for 24, and while Kambli and the newcomer Atul Bedade did their best in the middle overs, the lower order caved in. On the other hand, the Pakistani supporters were ecstatic. So smug had they been about their team's prospects that they had actually backed India during the semi-final against Australia, their contention being that defeating the 'old enemy' in the final would be a lot more satisfying than beating any other side. The Indian cricketers were left to lick their wounds for the four months that preceded their next assignment.

The 1993–94 season was the third in a row at the end of which, Sachin found himself being compared to a contemporary. Two years previously, some people had chosen to overlook his performances in the Test series and World Cup in Australia in the light of Inzamam-ul-Haq's heroics in the semi-final and final of the 1992 World Cup. Imran Khan had declared that Inzamam was better against fast bowling, and the pundits, especially those not from India, were obviously not inclined to argue with someone who had led his country to a World Cup win. A year later, Sachin had been pitted against his own childhood mate, Vinod Kambli, who ended 1992–93 with consecutive double centuries. The year 1993–94 ended with the cricketing world celebrating Brian Lara's record-breaking 375 against England. Sachin reacted on all three occasions by not reacting at all, at least verbally. His own outlook, shaped in no small measure by his father, brother and coach, was that it was pointless to compete with others; his only competitor had to be himself. His best bet was to strive to improve upon his own performances and hope for the best.

The quadrangular Singer Cup, played in Sri Lanka in September 1994, featured some fine cricket, heavy rain and an alleged altercation between two senior members of the Indian team that would make headlines more than half a decade later for all the wrong reasons. The tournament was preceded by the retirement of a versatile cricketer.

Ravi Shastri, one of Sachin's mentors at the start of his international career, called it a day as a cricketer and stepped into the commentary box. At 32, he still had a lot of cricket left in him, but being a pragmatist, he knew that the chances of his making an international comeback were next to nil. The complexion and composition of the national team had changed beyond belief since his last series in South Africa. Perversely, the fact that India were to play only at home for the next couple of seasons had worked against him. Given his record overseas and penchant for excelling when the chips were down, he might well have been one of the first to be picked had India toured England in the summer of 1994 as originally scheduled, or if India had toured the West Indies instead of it being the other way around in the 1994–95 season. On Indian wickets, the team did not need him.

The Singer Cup commenced with a day–night clash between the hosts and India at Colombo's Khettarama Stadium, which had been rechristened the R. Premadasa Stadium in memory of the Sri Lankan president who had been assassinated by a suicide bomber the previous year. The game was only a few overs old when the heavens opened and resulted in its abandonment. The teams returned to the venue the next day to play a truncated encounter, which Sri Lanka won.

The rains stayed away during India's next game against Australia, which was played at the Premadasa Stadium on 9 September 1994, the day 'Ganesh Chaturthi' was being celebrated in Mumbai and other parts of India. One of the most devout worshippers of the elephant-headed deity got going against the new-ball pair of Craig McDermott and Glenn McGrath, shortly after Azharuddin won the toss and elected to bat.

Sachin got two boundaries in the second over, punching McGrath through the covers and then slashing him uppishly but quite deliberately past third man. In the fifth over of the innings, Sachin flicked an overpitched delivery by McDermott that would have sped to the boundary had Michael Bevan not got in the way at short mid-wicket. When the bowler served him a delivery on middle-and-leg that was just short of a length, Sachin held himself back for a fraction of a second and then flicked it delectably behind square, well to the right of Bevan as well as the square-leg fielder, for four.

With Prabhakar also looking good, Mark Taylor introduced Shane Warne in the seventh over itself and switched McDermott to the other end. The move made no difference; the paceman served another short delivery on middle-and-leg, which a lesser batsman may have considered playing on the leg-side off the back foot. However, Sachin went for it with his front foot. His timing was precise, and the ball flew over the mid-wicket boundary for six. It was a stroke every bit as breathtaking as the one that he had essayed off Wasim Akram at Sharjah.

A couple of short deliveries by Warne begged to be hit, and Sachin obliged by cutting them through the covers. The outfield was sluggish with all the pounding that it had taken from the rain, but it could not prevent the Indian vice-captain from finding the boundary whenever he wished. For the second successive time since the Austral-Asia Cup semi-final at Sharjah, the Australian leggie was found wanting against an Indian batsman who was not scared to use his feet.

Sachin came down the wicket to hit him *against the spin* over mid-on for four to complete his 50, and followed it with another lofted stroke, also against the spin, this time for six. Warne was flustered enough to stride down the wicket and give the batsman a mouthful. Not that the batsman cared. With as many as 37 overs left in the innings at that stage, a big score looked imminent. What also loomed large in people's thoughts was a century—Sachin's first in the shorter format.

He lost Prabhakar with the score at 87. Sidhu and Azharuddin essayed invaluable supporting hands, as did Kambli. Sachin batted fluently till he had an anxious moment at 94. He tapped Mark Waugh and took off for a non-existent run, only to be sent back by his Shardashram mate. Bevan's throw missed the stumps by a whisker.

Life came full circle when Sachin cut Warne for two to reach triple figures for the first time in ODIs, in what was his 79th game for India. When Kambli had done likewise in ODIs and Tests, Sachin had been at the other end; when Sachin broke the century barrier for the first time in the shorter variety, his childhood friend was at the other end. As the Indian players and supporters and even the Australians applauded what had been a magnificent innings, Kambli gave his friend a hug. Knowing Sachin as well as he did, the left-handed batsman may well have sensed that the floodgates had opened. Sachin was eventually dismissed for 110 and India finished with 246–8, a total that would not have pleased them after an opening stand of 87. However, the bowlers gave a splendid account of themselves and dismissed Australia for 215.

The encounter against Pakistan was rained off, as was the game between Australia and Pakistan, and this left India with the second-highest points after the hosts, who had won all three of their games. The decision of the organizers to shift the final from the Premadasa Stadium to the Sinhalese Sports Club, ostensibly because the latter drained better, was all but rendered pointless by the rain which was still coming down hard. Just when a washout seemed imminent the rain-gods turned the taps off. The umpires assessed the conditions and decided to play a 25-overs-a-side game despite the dampness of the outfield. Chasing 150, Sachin fell for a duck, but the middle order took India through. It was an auspicious start to another season that was to be dominated by limited-overs cricket.

The start of West Indies' tour of India in October 1994 was nightmarish for a legend. At Faridabad, where India took on the visitors in an ODI, Kapil Dev Nikhanj was hammered for 37 runs in five overs. He pulled out of the subsequent set of ODIs, citing knee trouble, and then announced his retirement from all forms of the sport. Among the many tributes paid to him, the one that stood out was Sunil Gavaskar's: 'The light has gone out of this Diwali.'

The jury was divided on the all-rounder. Many believed that he ought to have quit after the Australia tour of 1991–92, on which he bowled splendidly to take 25 wickets from five Tests, including his 400th. Their contention was that he ought to have quit on a high instead of huffing and puffing all the way to the world record. The facts were damning. At the end of the series against Australia, Kapil Dev's tally of Test wickets had stood at 401. He had subsequently taken 15 Tests to take 31 more wickets to surpass Hadlee.

The counterview was that Kapil Dev still had a lot to offer to Indian cricket, if not with the ball, then with the bat. There were those who felt that the Board had missed a trick. It was hardly a secret that the team's overdependence on his bowling abilities for the better part of his career had prevented Kapil Dev from doing justice to the batsman within him. His century against South Africa at Port Elizabeth in 1992–93 and 50s in subsequent series against England and Sri Lanka had indicated that he had lost none of his aggression with the bat, even as his bowling had lost its bite. Despite that happening, Kapil Dev could have continued to be a part of the team for at least two more seasons, batting at number five or number six and at the same time, compensating in terms of variations what he had lost in terms of pace, as a bowler. He had proved in the latter stages of the Hero Cup in 1993 that he could be an effective first-change bowler.

Had Kapil Dev been utilized the way his great contemporary and rival Ian Botham was by England in the 1992 World Cup, India would have had an extra batsman and bowler in the XI for a few more years, and the semi-finalists in the 1996 World Cup may well have gone on to win the tournament.

Life and Indian cricket moved on. The West Indies, a formidable outfit, arrived in October 1994, minus Antiguans Richie Richardson and Curtly Ambrose. In Richardson's absence, Courtney Walsh was in charge. The tour comprised a plethora of ODIs, including a five-match bilateral series that was oddly split into two segments by a tri-series that also featured New Zealand. While the tri-series was played in coloured clothing, the bilateral series was played in whites.

The ODIs were preceded by the Wills Trophy, which Mumbai won under Sachin's leadership. Mumbai beat Bengal in the quarter-final and qualified for the final at the expense of Azharuddin's Hyderabad on the spin of the coin, a move necessitated by relentless rain. In the final, played at Chennai, Kapil Dev's Haryana batted first and scored an impressive 263–7. Expectations of an exciting finish were belied by Sachin and Sanjay Manjrekar. Both were at their imperious best and Mumbai cruised to victory for the loss of only one wicket.

Sachin's fans, looking forward to his opening the innings in ODIs on home turf, were dejected when he fell for ducks in the first two fixtures against the West Indies, played at Faridabad and Mumbai respectively. The team management was rattled enough to drop him to number three in the next game, which was the first of the tri-series. This time around, he fared marginally better, scoring eight. He was restored to the opening spot for the next encounter of the tri-series, against New Zealand at Vadodara.

Sachin proceeded to essay an innings that would have reminded the Kiwis of his assault at Hamilton earlier in the year, replete as it was with stunning aerial strokes against the pacemen and spinners. Unlike his masterpiece at Auckland, he reached triple figures. He later scored a match-winning 66 against the West Indies in the final of the tri-series and an unbeaten 105 in the fifth game of the bilateral series against the same team.

The West Indies ran out of steam in both the tri-series as well as the bilateral ODI series after starting well. The Indians 'won' the critical moments and bagged both the trophies, making a case for themselves to be considered one of the leading contenders for the World Cup that was to be played on the subcontinent a year-and-a-half later.

However, not everything was hunky dory. Indian fans were yet to get over the bizarre happenings in the tri-series league encounter against the West Indies at Kanpur. When Nayan Mongia joined Manoj Prabhakar in the middle, India needed 63 to win from the last nine overs. In 1994, this was a tall order, but both players were competent bats and they were expected to take some calculated risks. Amazingly, they batted as if they were trying to save a Test match, and scored only 16 runs off the remaining deliveries. The Board penalized them with a two-match suspension. Replacing them in the squad for the last league game and the final were Vijay Yadav and a fine, young batsman from Bengaluru called Rahul Dravid.

The ODIs were followed by three Tests. On the opening day of the first, played on what *Wisden* described as an 'underprepared horror' at the Wankhede, Vinod Kambli batted like he had a train to catch, cutting, driving and flashing hard. He completed 1,000 Test runs in the process and fell for 40, scored off only 39 deliveries, when he took one chance too many. His teammates followed his example, with the exceptions of Mongia and Manjrekar, who scored 80 and 51, respectively. The Indians, clearly struggling to overcome the ODI 'hangover', were dismissed for 272. They then bowled and fielded well to gain a first-innings lead of 29 just before stumps on the second day.

The spectators were getting ready to leave the ground for the day when Kenneth Benjamin, who had taken the new ball with his captain in Ambrose's absence, left them and the Indian dressing room shellshocked with three quick strikes in the closing stages. Prabhakar fell early for the second time in the match, Mongia failed to make his promotion to number three count, and Kambli was undone by a delivery that took off viciously and ballooned off his bat for an easy catch. At the close on day two, India were 11–3 and the West Indies held the advantage.

Luck was on India's side on the third morning. The umpires delayed the start of play by 45 minutes after discovering the dampness in the bowlers' footholds at the Pavilion End of the pitch. The West Indies, who were eager to exploit whatever little moisture there would be in the track in the first hour of play before the heat took over, were understandably livid. When play did resume, they came up against a batsman who was determined to counterattack.

Sachin brought the crowd to its feet with his strokes, particularly his drives. As was his wont, he allowed the ball to come to him instead of going for it. The purists could not get enough of his still head, which enable him to judge the ball to perfection and get in line. That gave him the time to place his front foot in the right place. Those who continued to be rankled by his bottom-handed grip were assuaged by the fact that he used his top hand to control the stroke.

The West Indies bowlers gave it everything. With Sidhu and Azharuddin failing to make an impression and the scoreboard reading 88–5, the visitors were still in the game. At this stage, Sachin was joined by his Mumbai senior.

The 74-run association between Sachin and Manjrekar turned out to be the turning point of the game. Sachin was on 85 when he was caught behind off Carl Hooper *against the run of play*. Manjrekar went on to complete his second 50 of the game and was looking good for a big one when he mistimed a drive off Walsh and was caught at mid-on, for 66. The Karnataka duo took over from where the Mumbai duo left off. Anil Kumble scored 42 and Javagal Srinath, who was playing his first Test on home turf in November 1994 after making his Test debut in November 1991, scored 60, inclusive of a six that cleared the roof of the Wankhede. India set the West Indies 363 to win.

Not many cricketers have had to endure the ignominy of being left out of the playing XI of a Test after receiving the individual award for their performance in the previous Test. That was exactly what happened to the speedster from Mysore, on the eve of the Kolkata Test against England in January 1993. His fiery bowling in India's previous Test at Johannesburg was forgotten as the team management plotted to confront the English with three spinners and use Kapil Dev and Prabhakar more as 'shine-removers' than 'new-ball' bowlers. For the remainder of the 1992–93 season and the home series against Sri Lanka in 1993–94, the fastest bowler in a country that had been hankering for one for decades, had carried the drinks. His exile ended only when Kapil Dev called it quits.

On day four at the Wankhede, Javagal Srinath was eager to show Indian supporters what they had missed. After Prabhakar had made the initial breakthroughs, dismissing Simmons and Lara in the very first over, he took over and bagged four wickets. India won by 96 runs and Azharuddin became India's most successful captain in Tests with 10 triumphs, one more than M.A.K. Pataudi and Sunil Gavaskar.

The century that had eluded Sachin at Mumbai was his in the second Test at Nagpur. His quest for perfection prompted him to put the players' lunch room at the match venue to good use, on the eve of the game. He pitted himself against rubber balls dipped in water, which were flung at him from 20 yards. The practice paid off, in the form of a belligerent innings. He stroked his way into the 1970s and then stormed his way through the 1980s and 1990s. He was on 99 when he took strike to the fourth ball of a Walsh over. When he received a short delivery first up, something told him that the next delivery would be similar. Sure enough, Walsh dug it in. Sachin, who was waiting for it, rocked back and hooked it out of the ground. So elated was he at having out-thought his opponent that he did something quite uncharacteristic; he pumped his fist and screamed in delight.

Even as one Shardashram alumnus was going from strength to strength, another was going downhill. By the time the Nagpur Test ended, Vinod Kambli was under serious pressure. The Windies quicks appeared to have rattled him. He followed his second-innings duck at Mumbai with another in the first innings at Nagpur. In the second innings, he fell for 6. All those who had celebrated his success a year before were now demanding his head, censuring him for everything from the multiple grips on his bats to his 'faulty' technique against the short-pitched delivery. It was even suggested that he return to Achrekar's nets at Shivaji Park to sort himself out. It remained to be seen how Kambli would handle the crisis, easily the gravest of his career until that point.

India had the better of the Nagpur Test, but the hosts failed to deliver the knockout punch. What went against them was the reluctance of their batsmen to step on the accelerator in their second innings to hasten the declaration, as also the loss of an hour's play on the very first day. Miscreants in the crowd had targeted the West Indies fielders on the boundary with rubbish, which led to the visitors leaving the field in protest. The West Indies, set 327 to win, were 132–5 at the close.

On the eve of the final Test, the first to be played at Mohali in the north Indian state of Punjab, Courtney Walsh reminded his players that he had never ever experienced a series defeat since his international debut a decade previously. Trailing 0–1 with one to play, the visitors had nothing to lose. A series defeat was a series defeat, irrespective of whether it was by the margin of 0–1 or 0–2. So, it did not matter if the team ended up losing in pursuit of victory. His players got the drift.

They won the toss and batted first on a wicket that had some juice in it for the quickies. The West Indies scored 443, with Jimmy Adams scoring his second century of the series. India scored 387 in response, with Prabhakar scoring his maiden Test hundred. Sachin looked good in an innings of 40, before he fell, once again, *against the run of play*.

> I tend to get overconfident very easily. It is the biggest problem I am facing right now. Like in the first innings [at Mohali], I tried something more than I should have. Because I was striking the ball so well—in 40 I had scored nine boundaries—I tried for a stupid shot I shouldn't have. And that really scares me a lot.
>
> —Sachin Tendulkar, as quoted in an interview with Rohit Brijnath,
> *India Today*, 1995

The visitors threw their bats in the second innings and declared at 301–3. Brian Lara, who had looked out of sorts till then, came good with an innings of 91. India were set a target of 358 with a minimum of seven hours' play left. In his very first over, Walsh got one to rear from just short of a length, and somehow the ball snuck through the gap between the peak of Prabhakar's helmet and its visor, and struck the first-innings centurion on the nose. He had to be rushed to hospital, and those who followed him to the middle were blown away by the fast bowlers. India, 68–9 at one stage, were spared the ignominy of being dismissed for a sub-100 total by the last pair of Javagal Srinath and Venkatapathy Raju. The West Indies won by 243 runs and left India on a high, their 15-year old record of not having lost a Test series very much intact.

The indictment of the Indian batsmen for their ineptitude on a strip that resembled the ones they generally encountered overseas, was short-lived. Limited-overs cricket was clearly the priority, with the World Cup around the corner.

For the second season running, the big guns were available for key Ranji matches, the consequence of a three-month gap between the end of the Windies series and another short trip to New Zealand to participate in a quadrangular tournament. Back in the Land of the Long, White Cloud for the second year in succession, India lost to New Zealand and South Africa, but beat Australia for the third time in a row, after the wins at Sharjah and Colombo the previous year. Warne was treated with disdain again. Prabhakar and Sachin, who put on 97 for the first wicket, took 19 off his very first over. Although the leggie pulled things back subsequently, his overall figures of 0–61 from 10 were hardly flattering. India overhauled the target of 251 with five wickets in hand. Kambli scored an unbeaten 51.

Mumbai's captain was in tremendous nick in the knockout games of the

Ranji Trophy. Sachin scored 166 against Tamil Nadu in the quarters, and followed it with 109 against Uttar Pradesh in the semis. These knocks were merely a prelude to his pyrotechnics in the final against Navjot Sidhu's Punjab. In the summit clash at the Wankhede, Manjrekar scored a double hundred and keeper-opener Sameer Dighe and Vinod Kambli got centuries, but their knocks were overshadowed by the captain's 140. He declared at 690–6 and then watched his bowlers dismiss the opposition for 372. The match sealed, he spearheaded another offensive in the second innings to complete his second hundred of the game. Punjab, left to score a modest 832 to win, played out time. Sachin, who had missed the previous season's final, was delighted to lay his hands on the coveted trophy.

The confidence that Kambli had regained through his knocks in New Zealand and the Ranji Trophy, evaporated within moments of his arrival at the wicket in the all-important league game against Pakistan, in the 1995 edition of the Asia Cup. It was a Friday and the Sharjah Cricket Stadium was packed to the rafters. Aaqib Javed, who loved bowling to Indian batsmen at Sharjah, had dismissed Prabhakar, Sachin and Azharuddin in quick succession. India, chasing 267, were 37–3, and the Pakistani supporters, who of course expected a win over India at Sharjah as a matter of right, were wearing broad smiles.

A technical adjustment Kambli had made after the horrific West Indies series was to stand outside the leg-stump and then shuffle across to cover the sticks just before the bowler released the ball. Unfortunately for him and India, he allowed the 'Friday' pressure to get to him and 'strode' across instead of shuffling. He exposed his leg-stump in the process and that was what the ball hit. India were eventually dismissed for 169, with Aaqib taking 5–19. For the losers, insult was added to injury when their detractors accused them of having lost the match 'mentally' even before it had begun.

Sachin led an Indian resurgence in the next league game against Sri Lanka. He got India off to a rollicking start after the opposition had been restricted to 202–9. For once, he adopted a more orthodox approach, preferring vertical bat strokes to their horizontal counterparts. This did not hamper his scoring rate however, and he struck 15 boundaries and one six on his way to 112 off only 107 deliveries, finishing the game in the 34th over itself. Not only did the win, India's second of the tournament after a nine-wicket triumph against Bangladesh, take their tally of points to four, but it also gave them a very healthy net run-rate. Then came an unexpected twist in the tale. Sri Lanka upset Pakistan in their last league game and India's western neighbour fell behind in the net run-rate stakes. Sri Lanka and India thus made it to the final.

India dominated the summit clash from ball one. Set to chase 231, an unbroken stand of 185 between Sidhu and the captain himself ensured India's fourth Asia Cup title in four appearances. Unlike its three immediate predecessors, the 1994–95 season did not end with comparisons between Sachin and a contemporary. His performances had been far too overwhelming for that to happen. He agreed with the assessment that the season had been his best till date.

> Towards the start of the season, I failed in three matches, and that was a good wake-up call. I had a good hundred against Australia in the Singer Cup. Maybe I relaxed after that. But that was a good wake-up call at the right time. Because it was not very late and I could get back into form.
>
> —Sachin Tendulkar, *The Sportstar*, 6 May 1995

On 24 May 1995, a month after the Asia Cup final, Sachin tied the knot with Anjali Mehta.

They had their first sighting of each other at the Mumbai airport in 1990, on the day Sachin returned from the tour of England. Anjali, who was then studying paediatrics at one of Mumbai's most reputed medical institutions, took the initiative to track him down. They developed a liking for each other and started courting a few months later. Doing what courting couples normally did, like dating in public spaces, was out of the question for obvious reasons, but they gradually learned to work their way around the difficulties. India's four-month tour of Australia in 1991–92 was particularly arduous for the couple. Anjali would plan meticulously when it came to posting the voluminous letters that she wrote in a pre-internet age. Each letter would be addressed to a hotel where the Indian team was to be based at, a few days after the letter was posted! It was necessary to take cognizance of the time it took for a letter from India to reach a city in Australia, after all. In the pre-cellular age, Anjali would save money to make international calls to Sachin from a telephone booth opposite her college, the conversation being interspersed by glances at the meter, which would keep flashing the rapidly escalating cost of the call. They got engaged in 1994. It was after the short tour of New Zealand that year, a significant one for Sachin, that they decided to take the next step.

> Sachin has never hankered for publicity or money. He received scores of lucrative offers from TV channels to cover his wedding, but he turned all of them down. He wanted his wedding to be a private affair. The wedding was brilliantly organized. The Tendulkars took the lead and we at Sungrace-

Mafatlal were only too glad to assist. Sachin was personally involved in every aspect. He insisted that the marriage be performed as per Hindu rites. Everything went off as planned. As per custom, Anjali was brought to the altar by her maternal uncle, who was British, but was appropriately dressed for the occasion—in traditional Indian finery. He was guided by Nitin, Sachin's eldest brother. No photographer was allowed. The media had been informed that the couple would make an appearance in the area outside the venue at around 1:00 p.m. Two chairs had been arranged in the area. The couple kept its word and the photographers had a field day. Sachin then answered a couple of questions, and he and Anjali then went back in. I had the honour of accompanying the couple to the old family home at Shivaji Park. It was here that Anjali performed the ritual of tipping a bowl filled with rice with her right foot, to mark the bride's entry into her new home.

—Anil Joshi, personal interview

The wedding festivities spanned three days. The marriage itself was solemnized on the first day, with only family members and close friends of the couple in attendance. Day two featured a 'reception', to which members of the cricketing community, Sungrace-Mafatlal employees and other influential individuals from the field of politics and business were invited. A separate get-together was organized for the Sahitya Sahawas residents on the third day.

Always a big eater, Sachin allowed himself to gorge on delicacies a little more than he should have in the days after his wedding, and he ended up expanding his waistline. He immediately set out to set things straight, cutting down on the calories and combining cardio-vascular exercises with sessions in the gymnasium. In less than three weeks, he was back to his old self.

He commenced another association six months after his wedding. The US-based WorldTel, headed by Mark Mascarenhas, signed him up for an incredible US$7.5 million (₹31.5 crores), for a period of five years. What made the deal remarkable was that it was done at a time when Sachin's biggest endorsement deal was worth ₹16 lakhs. The tie-up made him the highest-earning Indian sportsperson.

Almost on a daily basis, one or the other sponsor would approach me for a sponsorship contract. In a way, this started getting in my way and became a distraction. At this stage, Ravi Shastri introduced me to Mark Mascarenhas.... He soon told me, 'Sachin, you go out and concentrate on getting the maximum amount of runs, leave the sponsorship, negotiations and monetary matters...to me.

—Sachin Tendulkar, *Mumbai Mirror*, 11 December 2005

Within a few months, Mascarenhas had got brands like Adidas, Madras Rubber Factory (MRF), Philips, and Visa on board. They were only too happy to have Sachin as their Ambassador. Pepsi and Boost, with whom Sachin had been associated since the early 1990s, also escalated the worth of their contracts.

I chose to promote Sachin Tendulkar because I have never seen [Donald] Bradman play; never saw [Garry] Sobers play; I saw Viv [Richards], but he couldn't figure out [Bhagwat] Chandrashekhar on his debut. And then I saw Sachin. I had never seen anyone like this.

—Mark Mascarenhas, as quoted in *The Indian Express*, 18 November 2013

Sachin's tie-up with WorldTel overshadowed other events. Fans of Test cricket, already upset with the scheduling since 1993, were exasperated when the three-Test series against New Zealand in late 1995 was almost completely ruined by rain. The decision to schedule all three games in peninsular India, including two on the east coast at a time of the year when the North-East monsoon was at its most active, backfired badly. India managed to thwart the rain to win the first Test at Bengaluru, but the second and third Tests, played at Chennai and Cuttack respectively, were badly affected. The hosts won the ODI series that followed, 3–2. The tour ended in the last week of November 1995, three months before the game's premier quadrennial event.

The Indian players regrouped in the city of Bengaluru in the first week of the new year to commence their preparations for the World Cup. Considering their form in limited-overs cricket at home since 1993, they believed that they had it in them to become the first 'hosts' in the history of the tournament to go the distance.

For those following his career, it seemed that the 22-year-old phenomenon had the world at his feet. However, Sachin himself valued the need to keep himself grounded and not rest on his laurels, a lot more than his 'superstardom'.

For his opponents, this was an ominous sign.

Fortuitously, he is the child of a sophisticated moving picture revolution. Every innings we saw in pristine colour, every shot was replayed into the memory, and it became the vehicle to his gospel. We were all fellow travellers on Tendulkar's journey. He sold televisions, and televisions sold him. When Mark Mascarenhas bought the rights to Tendulkar for $7.5 million it seemed excessive, but Mascarenhas was prescient. Money was pouring into Indian cricket, the game had spread, and it was embraced by an increasingly consumerist middle class. The market had found its man.

—Rohit Brijnath, *Wisden Asia Cricket*, July 2002

CROWN PRINCE

If, at the end of his career, he does not get a minimum of 15,000 runs and 40 Test hundreds, I shall personally go and strangle him. Twenty years down the road, my hands will not have the strength, so he may still survive, but I think I will deputize someone to do the job for me.

—Sunil Gavaskar on Sachin Tendulkar,
Sunil Gavaskar Presents–III, PMG, 1995

The last four years of the 20th century and the first of the new millennium were momentous for the game of cricket and one of its greatest exponents. During this phase, Sachin experienced some lows, and several highs. Ironically, his 'prime' coincided with a traumatic period for the team he represented and a tumultuous time for the sport he played.

For India's cricket-loving masses, the 1996 World Cup began and ended with disasters at Kolkata's Eden Gardens. The opening ceremony that was organized at the venue did not quite live up to expectations, and the Indian players capitulated against Sri Lanka, the eventual winners, in the semi-finals at the same arena. They did play some good cricket in between.

Five years after liberalization, India was unrecognizable from the country of the late 1980s. Indians were catalysts in the international IT boom, and their successes resulted in their viewing their chosen professions and life itself, in a new light. Conservatism had given way to enterprise. The purchasing power of the masses had grown by leaps and bounds, and no longer did people earn only to save like their parents and grandparents. The urge to savour the present had become as vital as the need to save for the future. No longer was the majority afraid to take calculated risks. The advent of the internet and cellular phones, as well as the ever-growing popularity of satellite television, had yielded a 'whole, new, bold and smaller' world for the average Indian. The changes were visible wherever one cared to look; in the late 1980s, the Government Broadcaster would routinely snip scenes from films that showed people consuming alcohol or a couple that appeared to be entertaining thoughts of kissing; in the mid-

1990s, the satellite TV channels thought nothing of beaming programmes that comprised lovemaking scenes, not to mention skimpily clad men and women, at prime time.

No longer were 'unconventional' careers being frowned upon. The year 1994 saw two Indian girls being crowned Miss Universe and Miss World respectively, and what was unthinkable even half a decade previously had become a reality across the country. Parents were encouraging their children to consider modelling and sports as career options. Sachin wasn't the only 'sporting' role model around; there was Vishwanathan Anand, the chess whiz, and a tennis player called Leander Paes, who would win a historic Bronze at the Atlanta Olympics in 1996.

Cricket, the most popular game in the country, was by no means immune to the metamorphosis. The 1996 World Cup was the culmination of the process that had commenced with the Hero Cup in 1993. It showcased the newfound expertise of the BCCI in the 'marketing and packaging' of the sport. It institutionalized 'night cricket', with virtually all the frontline cricket stadia in the country being equipped with floodlights in the lead-up to the tournament. The event marked India's formal coronation as the new hub of the sport, in terms of popularity as well as commerce. The country hoped that its cricketers would make it the Numero Uno in terms of performance as well.

The 1996 World Cup got off to a controversial start, with both Australia and the West Indies, who were drawn in the same group as co-hosts India and Sri Lanka, declining to visit Colombo to play the Lankans at the league stage, citing 'security reasons'. The island nation had been stricken by terrorism for a couple of decades, but quite a few international teams had travelled and played there in the 1990s, Australia and the West Indies included. The concerns of the two teams in early 1996 were justified to an extent, given the fact that a bomb had gone off in the Central Business District of the Sri Lankan capital just days before the World Cup was due to begin. However, they ought to have been assuaged by the assurances of the organizers, who guaranteed unprecedented security arrangements and even suggested that the matches would be played in empty stadia. However, the teams and their respective Boards did not budge and their matches were deemed as 'forfeited', with Sri Lanka receiving full points for both. Sachin was part of a combined India–Pakistan side that flew to Colombo to play a 'solidarity' one-dayer against the Sri Lankan team.

The player who epitomized the 'New Indian' on the cricket field began his team's campaign with a match-winning 127 against Kenya at Cuttack. The signature stroke of the innings was a straight 'push' off medium-pacer Martin Suji that came across as a defensive stroke when essayed, but was timed so well that it beat the diving mid-on fielder to race to the boundary.

Sachin played a far more critical innings in the next game, a 'day-nighter' against the West Indies at Gwalior. After India had bowled and fielded superbly to bowl the opposition out for 173, the redoubtable Curtly Ambrose dismissed Jadeja and Sidhu in quick succession to reduce India to 15–2. However, Indian supporters were not perturbed, as their hero was in fine nick. Against Ambrose and his comrade-in-arms Walsh, Sachin tried to keep things simple. He negotiated the good balls and capitalized on the slightest deviation, utilizing their pace by flicking them for boundaries.

Lady luck was on his side. He went for a hook off Ian Bishop, but got a top-edge instead. Nearly a billion people, watching either at the ground or on TV, groaned when they saw Courtney Browne, the wicketkeeper, running in to position himself underneath it. Unbelievably, he spilt it, despite his gauntlets! Sachin then added to the bowler's frustration with back-to-back boundaries. A stunner of a cover drive off the back foot to a good-length ball was followed by a front-foot 'whip' off a delivery just short of a length, which sped to the mid-wicket boundary. Both deliveries had landed in the corridor of uncertainty just outside the off-stump, but they had been dispatched on either side of the wicket. It was the handiwork of a genius.

Azharuddin fell after a 79-run stand with his deputy. Sachin scored 70 before getting run out in a mix-up with Kambli. The West Indies came in hard at the left-hander after what they had done to him in 1994–95, but he lived up to the challenge with a match-winning cameo, which featured a handsome pull off Ambrose for six. The left-hander had not looked troubled by the short-pitched delivery. He had turned the corner, or so it seemed. All that he needed now was consistency and a bit of luck.

India's next challenge was against Australia, another contender for the title, in Mumbai. The capacity crowd at the first Wankhede game to be played under lights was privileged to watch an encounter that lived up to the hype. Australia rode on the back of an exhilarating hundred by Mark Waugh, his second in succession in the competition, and set India a target of 258.

Sachin brought the house down with a straight drive off Damien Fleming in the second over, but the galleries fell silent when the same bowler dismissed Jadeja and Kambli, who had come in at one-down in Sidhu's absence. At the other end, Glenn McGrath had started his spell with three maiden overs. After eight overs, India were 17–2 and the required rate was increasing. Something had to give.

Watchers and McGrath himself were taken by surprise with what Sachin did with the first ball of the bowler's fifth over and the ninth of the innings. The delivery wasn't short enough to merit a pull, but Sachin used the extra split-second gifted to him by the Almighty to 'read and process' the incoming delivery. He moved across the crease and back, thereby 'converting' a delivery that had been pitched on a length into one that was short. He then pulled it over mid-on for four. It was cricket's equivalent of a cross-court lawn tennis forehand.

Mark Taylor, the Australian captain, then positioned himself at short mid-wicket, where he had caught Sachin on earlier occasions. However, the batsman had learnt from his previous errors. Taylor could only watch as Sachin essayed another pull past him, this time off the front foot. The ball thudded into the hoardings beyond the mid-wicket rope, even before the capacity crowd had the time to react. A lucky break followed. Sachin, who it seemed was going for broke, mistimed a drive and the ball landed just short of Warne at mid-on.

He then diverted his attention to the off-side, and caressed a rare McGrath full-toss through the covers. The bowler who had started with three maidens had been hit for three boundaries in his fifth over.

Fleming conceded 10 in the next, inclusive of a boundary to third man and a three. At the end of the 10th over, India were 40–2, of which Sachin's contribution was 31 off 30 balls. He then punched an attempted yorker by McGrath down the ground for four, and slammed the bowler disdainfully over long-on to bring up the 50 of the innings. The very next ball, he drove past cover for another boundary. After starting with three maidens, McGrath had conceded 27 off his fifth and sixth overs.

Don't worry about the lights; Sachin has set this place alight.

—Ian Chappell, live commentary

McGrath was replaced in the attack by another titan. The cheers of the capacity crowd reached a crescendo when Shane Warne marked out his run-up. Sachin, eager to seize the advantage, welcomed him with an audacious cross-batted swat, which flew over the umpire's head for four. Warne soon found his length and nearly had Sachin caught by Stuart Law at mid-off. The fielder got his fingertips to a mistimed drive, but could not hold on. It was Sachin's second life after McGrath had failed to catch him off his own bowling earlier. So focused was Sachin on winning the battle that he went for another expansive drive. This time, the ball took the outside edge and was declared a boundary after replays revealed that Shane Lee, the fielder, had touched the ball from across the rope. For the second time that evening, Mohammed Azharuddin walked down the pitch to calm his partner down.

Fleming then took his third wicket of the innings when Azharuddin played on. At 70–3, in came Manjrekar, who many believed should have batted at number three instead of Kambli in a match of this significance. In the lead-up to the game, one of the leading Indian newspapers had likened Manjrekar to Mark Waugh, and wrote as to how fortunate India were, to have both Sachin and a 'Mark Waugh-like' batsman in their ranks. Manjrekar certainly had the aptitude to bat like Mark Waugh, but for that to happen, it was critical that he sorted himself out, sooner than later. Watching him in action in the mid-1990s, one got the impression that his failures in Australia and South Africa at the start of the decade were still haunting him.

At the Wankhede, Manjrekar sensibly held himself back and let his 'junior' partner dictate the proceedings. The roars from the stands kept getting louder as Sachin pulled Shane Lee for four and then subjected the bowler to another 'rubber-ball' stroke that would have been perfected on the Sahitya Sahawas playground—a cross-batted swipe over the bowler's head—that brought up the hundred of the innings. At the end of the 24th over, India were 115–3 in response to Australia's corresponding 113–1. A pull off a rare long-hop by Warne gave Sachin his 13th boundary.

He had moved to 90 off only 84 balls when Mark Waugh, bowling his off-spinners, outsmarted him. Seeing Sachin advance down the wicket, Waugh beat him with one that was way outside the off-stump. Sachin was stranded and Ian Healy, the keeper, brought the curtains down on one of the greatest limited-overs innings ever played. The Mumbai duo had added 73 in 16 overs.

The multitudes whom Sachin left spellbound that night comprised an octogenarian based in Adelaide, Australia. This individual saw Sachin on the television and experienced a feeling of déjà vu.

The target was 115 runs away and there were plenty of overs left when Sachin fell.

Prabhakar could not make an impression, and Manjrekar and Mongia added 54 before both fell in quick succession. Warne came back with a bang. After conceding 10 in his opening over, he went for only 18 in his next nine. He gave away only six runs in his last three overs and dismissed Mongia. Manjrekar was caught behind off Steve Waugh for 62. The Indian lower order was assertive, but the Australians were in total control by then and won by 16 runs. The final wicket fell off the last ball of the 48th over, which meant that India had wasted at least 12 deliveries.

'You get Sachin and half the battle is won,' remarked Sri Lanka skipper Arjuna Ranatunga. The other captains share the Lankan's opinion. It would give the impression that India is a one-man team, even though it may not be true always.

—Vijay Lokapally, *The Sportstar*, 6 May 1995

His dismissal at a critical juncture at Mumbai appeared to be on Sachin's mind when he opened in the next game, against co-hosts Sri Lanka at Delhi. He started sedately and opened out as the innings progressed, providing every indication that he wished to bat right through. An assault in the final stages took India to 271–3, of which Sachin's contribution was 137, inclusive of eight boundaries and five sixes. Azharuddin scored an unbeaten 72 in a third-wicket stand of 175. For Indian supporters, victory was a foregone conclusion.

This writer will never forget the afternoon of that game. He watched the Indian innings at home and then left for a friend's place, reaching just after the start of the Sri Lankan innings. The TV in the friend's house would take its own time to 'warm up' after being switched on, with blurred images gradually becoming sharper. When it was switched on, 10 minutes or so after the start of the Sri Lankan innings, this writer's eyes instinctively went to the corner of the screen, to check the score. The blurred images that appeared on the screen initially seemed to indicate that the score was '42–0 off 8'. That was surprising. How had eight overs been bowled in so short a time? Had India opened with spinners? This writer's surprise turned to horror within seconds, as the blurred images became sharper. Sri Lanka were 42–0 off three overs, and not eight.

Had the Sri Lankans wanted to showcase their radical batting strategy, which involved both openers going for broke, secure in the knowledge that their middle order was proficient at either maintaining the momentum or putting down the shutters, depending upon what the situation warranted, they could not have put together a more spectacular exhibition than the one they displayed at the Ferozeshah Kotla Ground on the afternoon of 2 March 1996. Sanath Jayasuriya and Romesh Kaluwitharana, Sri Lanka's openers, were on a roll. Their aggression gave the middle order all the time and deliveries in the world to knock off the runs. Arjuna Ranatunga, the captain, and Hashan Tillakaratne, tapped the ball around and literally 'strolled' their way to victory.

Ranatunga's men were riding high with two wins and two 'forfeits' under their belt. They added to their kitty of points with a victory over Kenya at Kandy in their final league game. Put in to bat, they blasted 398–4, then the highest score in ODIs.

India had the better of Zimbabwe in their last league encounter at Kanpur, but not before getting a scare. The 'law of averages' caught up with Sachin and he was bowled by Heath Streak for just three. The dismissals of Manjrekar, who had been promoted to number three, and Azharuddin, reduced India to 32–3. They were bailed out by Sidhu, who scored 80, and Vinod Kambli, who handled the pressure with elan and batted with flair to score his second ODI hundred. India finished with 247–5 and then bowled Zimbabwe out for 207.

One of the four quarter-finals that followed the league stage was a final before the final, at least as far as the subcontinent was concerned. India took on Pakistan, the defending champions, in what promised to be a high-octane quarter-final clash, at Bengaluru on 9 March 1996. The pressure on both sides was tremendous, and for once, those who fantasized about being in the shoes of their favourite cricketers were relieved that they were not. The game got underway with both teams trying desperately hard to focus on the next eight hours rather than think about the repercussions of defeat. The Indian camp was in a relatively better frame of mind at the start of the game; Azharuddin won the toss and elected to bat, which in 1996 was considered a safer option in a knockout game (unless you were Sri Lankan). On the other hand, the Pakistanis were jolted by the withdrawal of Wasim Akram, their premier player and captain, due to a torn intercostal muscle.

Sidhu and Sachin got India off to a sound start, even as Aamir Sohail, Akram's deputy, took his time to settle into the captain's role. At least half the side under him had captained or vice-captained Pakistan before, and at least one of them—Javed Miandad, who was playing his sixth World Cup—was aggrieved that he hadn't been named skipper in the incumbent's absence. India were 10 short of the hundred mark when Sachin played on to Ata-ur-Rehman. He had scored 31. Sidhu carried on, but the middle-order batsmen kept falling after getting off to starts. With five overs left, it appeared that India would just about cross 250, but the innings was turned on its head by Ajay Jadeja, whose breathtaking 41 off 25 balls took India to 287–8. Waqar Younis' last two overs went for 40 runs.

Aamir Sohail and Saeed Anwar, the Pakistani openers, replied in kind. There was pin-drop silence in the M. Chinnaswamy Stadium as the duo thrashed the Indian bowlers in the opening overs. After what seemed an eternity, Anwar fell to a mistimed stroke, but Sohail carried on. The game changed in the 15th over of the innings. The Pakistani captain swatted local boy Venkatesh Prasad for four, immediately after being subjected to a glare by the bowler. Sohail then strode down the pitch and indicated to the bowler that he would hit him again in the same area. From his seat in the commentary box, a certain Imran Khan implored his 1992 World Cup teammate to put his head down and concentrate on his batting instead of indulging in verbal duels with the opposition. The legend had obviously sensed that something was amiss. He was spot-on.

Sohail swung wildly at the next delivery, aiming to outsmart the bowler by hitting him on the leg-side. But he had chosen the wrong delivery to do so. He missed, and the ball crashed into the stumps. As the stands exploded, it was Prasad's turn to do the talking.

Sohail's exit was the turning point. Inzamam-ul-Haq fell early, and the middle and lower order failed to break the shackles imposed by a rejuvenated bowling attack. The cheers of the Bengaluru crowd could well have been heard in Pakistan when Miandad, India's 'bogey-man' ever since he had hit that last-ball six in 1986, was run out. India won by 39 runs, and the country celebrated as if the World Cup had been won.

The Indians, it appeared, were peaking at just the right time. When both Jayasuriya and Kaluwitharana fell in the very first over of the semi-final at Kolkata, most of India started celebrating all over again. The Indian supporters and players themselves were then brought down to earth by a stunner of an innings by Aravinda de Silva. The experienced heads in the middle order supported him and Sri Lanka finished with 251-8 on a wicket where the ball 'was stopping and coming, and keeping low'.

Sidhu fell early, but Sachin got the chase going with boundaries off the new-ball duo of Chaminda Vaas and Pramodya Wickremasinghe. Sidhu fell early, but Manjrekar dropped anchor and played second fiddle to the hero. The galleries erupted when Sachin completed his 50. The Sri Lankans, it seemed, had their task cut out. The score was 98-1, with Sachin having contributed 65 of those, when he tried to play Jayasuriya down the leg-side. The ball struck his front thigh-pad instead. Sachin, unsighted for a couple of seconds, made the mistake of advancing a step down the pitch for a possible leg-bye, before realizing that the ball had not run off his pads into the infield, but had become stationary just outside the crease. Before he could make his way back, Kaluwitharana dislodged the bails and in the process, roused the demons in the pitch from their slumber.

> When I came out to bat, even Kumara Dharmasena got the ball to spin and jump in his first over. I will never forget the smile on his face after that over. The smile of conquest.
>
> —Sanjay Manjrekar, *India Today*, 2003 World Cup Special

It was as if the pitch, which Sachin had made to look pliable and playable, had suddenly turned into a wrestling pit. The spinners started making the ball turn at obtuse angles, and the Indian batting simply crumbled. Before anybody, least of all the Indians themselves, realized it, they were 120–8 and their tournament was over. Unruly behaviour by some spectators resulted in Clive Lloyd, the match referee, awarding the match to the Lankans. Vinod Kambli, who had been battling hard in the middle, broke down. It was an inglorious end not only to India's hopes of regaining the title that they had won in 1983, but also Ajit Wadekar's three-and-half year stint as cricket manager.

The Indian dressing room resembled the scene of a funeral. Javagal Srinath, who was as dejected as his teammates, could not bring himself to cry like some of his teammates. He then discovered that Sachin wasn't crying either. Sachin explained that there was no shame in losing if one had played with conviction.

For the second World Cup in succession, Sachin had emerged as his team's best player. In fact, he had been the most successful batsman of the 1996 edition, with a record 523 runs at a stupendous 87.1 from seven matches, inclusive of two centuries and three 50s. No other batsman had scored over 500 runs in a single edition of the World Cup. However, all this hardly mattered after the catastrophe at Kolkata. Sri Lanka went on to win the tournament, beating Australia in the final at Lahore, and Sanath Jayasuriya, the 17th-highest scorer in the competition, was declared the Most Valuable Player of the Tournament for the impact he had made at the top of the order. He had also taken seven wickets with his left-arm spinners.

Manoj Prabhakar, who had been left out of the playing XI after the Delhi game, would have expected the axe for India's next assignment—a tri-series at Singapore. The omission that startled one and all was Vinod Kambli's, whose century against Zimbabwe and cameos against the West Indies and Pakistan in the World Cup were surprisingly overlooked. While the debate between his supporters and detractors went on, no one questioned the selection of Rahul Dravid. The 23-year-old from Karnataka had been a consistent performer on the domestic circuit since the early 1990s and had also excelled for India 'A' in the 1995–96 season.

The Indians joined Pakistan and Sri Lanka, the newly crowned world champions, in Singapore, barely 10 days after the Kolkata semi-final. India beat Sri Lanka in a league game, but lost to Pakistan despite an innings of 100 by Sachin—his first century against the 'old enemy'—and missed out on a berth in the final. The Indian innings was terminated at 226–8 from 47.1 overs when it started raining, and Pakistan were set 187 to win in 33 overs as per the

Duckworth-Lewis method. They got there for the loss of only two wickets.

His first century against Pakistan apart, two significant things happened during the game from Sachin's point of view. He had his first look at a bowler with whom he would have some absorbing tussles at the turn of the millennium. Saqlain Mushtaq, the off-spinner, impressed watchers with figures of 3–38 in his allotted overs. Although Saqlain wasn't fluent in English at that stage, it appeared that he wasn't completely unfamiliar with the language either. To those watching the match on TV, the movement of his lips after he had Sachin stumped, suggested that he had hurled a certain four-letter word at his opponent.

It was also during this game that Sachin was summoned by the ICC referee to 'provide an explanation' for the MRF logo on his bat.

> There was one bat which I used for about two-and-a-half years. It lasted till the last [1996] World Cup. I used to clean it myself. It was badly taped and each time I removed the tape, the blade would come off. I would then carefully rearrange each piece, put a lot of superglue on the blade and stick back each piece one by one, then bind it up with tape again. It was a very good bat and I made a lot of runs with it.
>
> —Sachin Tendulkar, *Outlook*, 4 January 1999

Sachin had been approached by a sponsor for his bat on the day of the World Cup game against Australia, but he had refused to discuss the same in the middle of the quadrennial event. After playing the World Cup with a bare bat, he had pasted the MRF logo on his blade in Singapore. The sponsor of the pace academy in Chennai that had overlooked Sachin's fast-bowling aspirations a decade previously was one of the first brands that Mark Mascarenhas had brought on board. The referee's objections forced Sachin to revert to a bare bat till the matter was sorted before the Test series against England.

Unlike some of his teammates, the Indian vice-captain had always been reluctant to endorse brands that were primarily associated with tobacco and alcohol, never mind their subsequent diversifications into hospitality and other sectors.

> He has always been levelheaded. Professional Management Group [PMG] got him a contract with a credit card company for ₹40 lakhs, which was an unheard-of figure at the time, around the time of the 1996 World Cup. A few individuals we had worked with in the past had insisted on being paid partly in black, and we had obviously resisted doing so. When I told Sachin about this, he said that his father had taught him to be above board

in everything that he did. So, there was no question of his expecting or indulging in anything that was dubious.

—Sumedh Shah, former Director, PMG

After the Singapore trip, India and Pakistan flew to Sharjah for another tri-series, this time with South Africa as the third team. India lost its first two games, but created history in their second league encounter against Pakistan. A second-wicket stand of 231 between Sachin (118) and Sidhu (101) and an assault in the closing stages by Azharuddin, enabled India to break the '300-barrier' for the first time in ODIs. The Indian captain, who was in the middle of a lean trot, was not too inclined to bat in the slog overs. His deputy literally pushed him out of the dressing room with some encouraging words, and Azharuddin responded by banging 24 runs off the last over. Pakistan started well in response, but ran out of steam in the middle overs and eventually lost by 28 runs. It was Sachin who rounded up the Pakistan innings by having Saqlain leg-before, after which the TV cameras caught him returning the verbal compliment that the off-spinner had paid him in Singapore. It was not something he was known to do very often. What was irrefutable was that he had a long memory. The win was India's first over Pakistan at Sharjah since October 1991.

India finished with a net run-rate higher than Pakistan's and qualified for the final, where they lost to South Africa by 38 runs. The triumph was a consolation of sorts for the Proteans, who had won all five league games in the 1996 World Cup before being beaten by the West Indies in the quarter-final.

All hell broke loose in Mumbai when the team for the tour of England, India's first 'full' series overseas since their trip to South Africa in 1992–93, was announced. Vinod Kambli's omission prompted some of his fans to burn an effigy of Gundappa Viswanath, the chairman of selectors. While the selections of Rahul Dravid and all-rounder Sunil Joshi, the chief architects of Karnataka's Ranji Trophy win in 1995–96, were expected, that of Bengal's Sourav Ganguly, who had toured Australia with the Indian team in 1991–92, was not, at least by the majority. Sambaran Banerjee, East Zone's representative on the Selection Committee and incidentally Ganguly's first Ranji Trophy captain, and Jagmohan Dalmiya, then secretary of the BCCI, were hauled over the coals allegedly for favouring their fellow Kolkatan. One of the country's biggest cricketing names was infuriated enough to declare on national television that Ganguly was a failure and would remain one.

The outcry was not restricted to Ganguly's selection. The selectors were criticized for picking only three specialist pacemen for a tour that was to be played in the more 'bowler-friendly' first half of the English summer and feature quite a few first-class matches in addition to the internationals. Another call of theirs that raised eyebrows was the one to send only one specialist wicketkeeper in Nayan Mongia, with the likes of Manjrekar and Dravid, both of whom had worn the gloves at some point in their formative years, expected to chip in whenever required.

> It does hurt when the Indian cricket team is dismissed as Tendulkar and 10 others by even such shrewd judges as Sir Richard Hadlee. Still, it does make a point about how dependent the team is on the firepower of its youngest and most powerful weapon in its armoury. This is where Tendulkar's greatness will be under the most severe test for any slump in his personal form would drag down team performance in any cricket away from the protected home environment.
>
> —R. Mohan, *The Sportstar*, 6 May 1995

A lot was expected of Indian cricket's 'Crown Prince' in England. The tour started badly. After a string of three-day games, the first ODI was rained off and the hosts outplayed the visitors in the next two. History repeated itself just before the final ODI at Manchester. Exactly 60 years previously, Lala Amarnath, a cricketer from the Punjab, had been 'sacked' from the Indian squad that was touring England, on charges of 'indiscipline'. In 1996, Navjot Sidhu, also from the Punjab, announced his retirement and flew back home in a huff.

> I was not treated well. For a senior cricketer like me, it was very suffocating. I have pointed out the reasons in my letter to the Board and it is for the Board to give a thought to it. I wouldn't like to go into specifics of what the humiliation was.
>
> —Navjot Sidhu, *The Sportstar*, 8 June 1996

The team management did everything that it could to pacify the senior-most member of the squad, but in vain.

England had the better of the first Test at Birmingham until the 'Crown Prince' asserted himself in the second innings. India, trailing by 99 in the first innings, were 17–2 in their second essay when Sachin arrived at the wicket. The conditions were as English as English could be, with the seamers making the most of the moist wicket—the cracks on which were widening—and the cloud cover that was aiding their endeavour to make the ball talk. Chris Lewis greeted Sachin with a delivery that pitched on a length in the 'corridor of uncertainty'. It was just about the perfect delivery to bowl to a new batsman. Sachin responded with a still head, decisive footwork and patience. He watched the cherry all along, and having realized that it wasn't doing much, waited till the very last split-second to play it, turning the face of his bat towards off at the point of impact. The ball took the carpet route past the slips to the third-man boundary.

Against an attack that comprised pacemen Chris Lewis, Dominic Cork and the left-handed Alan Mullally, medium-pacer Ronnie Irani and left-arm spinner Min Patel, Sachin flourished, even as his teammates floundered. The third wicket fell at 55, the fourth at 36 and the fifth at 68, but Sachin was unruffled. His shot-selection was exemplary and watchers could not stop marvelling at his brilliance. Sanjay Manjrekar, who had sprained his ankle during the game, came in at number seven with a runner, and helped him take the score along. When Mike Atherton, the England captain, set a 'semi-defensive' field with three men patrolling the covers on the off-side and three manning the region from mid-wicket to square-leg, Sachin responded with a pull off Mullally that neatly bisected the two fielders at mid-wicket. He completed his 50 with a flicked boundary off Lewis. So well had he batted despite the fall of wickets at the other end that he had taken only 50 balls and hit 10 boundaries on his way to the landmark.

Mullally, who shifted to around the wicket, was then driven exquisitely past mid-off for four. Sachin followed that stroke with a back-foot stunner that pierced the covers. He then forced Atherton to do something that did not quite jell with the match situation. The England captain banished all his close-in fielders, save a solitary slip, into the outfield when Sachin was on strike. This defensive field-setting by a team that held all the aces was an inadvertent but unique tribute to a master. India were leading by less than 50 with only four wickets in hand at that stage.

> How old is a great batsman? Answer—very young. There is very little chance of altering a player after the age of 23, bar the odd technical shift. Sachin was a great player when he was in his early teenage, so was Denis Compton, so was Don Bradman. Talent can develop but once you have it—you have it. There is more to Sachin Tendulkar than that. He has a most competitive temperament. He has not needed special coaches to teach him how to compete. It is inbuilt. All it requires for a great player is to be exposed to sharp competition… Given England cricket to control, I would think Tendulkar. Catch 'em young. Stimulate their cricket from the cradle and let them fight to win from an early age.

—Tony Lewis, *Outlook*, 4 January 1999

Among those delighted with the innings was the senior management at MRF. After expressing its reservations on the dimensions of the logo during the tri-series in Singapore, the ICC had finally permitted Sachin to sport it. Even as he kept presenting the full face of the bat to the ball at Edgbaston, he gave his sponsors a lot more than what they had bargained for.

Sachin permitted himself a grin when he completed his ninth Test century with a straight six off Patel. He of all people knew how well he had batted. He was eventually the ninth man out at 208, when he mishit Lewis in the deep, while trying to stretch the lead as much as he could in the company of the tail-enders. His contribution was 122. England overhauled the target of 121 for the loss of only two wickets.

Sachin apart, the bowling of Srinath and his Karnataka colleague Venkatesh Prasad had been a consolation of sorts for the visitors. Srinath had in fact contributed with the bat as well, with a 50 in the first innings that helped steer his team past the 200-mark. The problem was that the new-ball bowlers had not been complemented by their colleagues. Paras Mhambrey, the third paceman, had not impressed and Sunil Joshi's tour had come to a premature end due to a broken finger. With Sidhu gone and Vikram Rathour, the other opener, failing in both innings, there were problems at the top as well. Jadeja, who had to open in Sidhu's absence, seemed to be at sea in the conditions. All in all, there was a strong possibility of England avenging their 0–3 rout of 1992–93.

As many as four Indian players had made their Test debuts at Birmingham— Rathour, Joshi, Prasad and Mhambrey. For the second Test at Lord's, India replaced the injured Manjrekar and Joshi with two more debutants. The Test also happened to be Harold 'Dickie' Bird's last as umpire. He was visibly moved when both teams gave him a guard of honour at the start of the game.

England batted first and scored 344. Sourav Ganguly, who had batted well in the third ODI, then took to Test cricket and the pivotal number three slot like a duck to water. He left watchers awestruck and his army of detractors stunned with a splendid 131. Sachin, who had used his bat at Perth in 1991–92, returned the favour by taping the handle of Ganguly's bat during one of the intervals.

Like Ganguly, his co-debutant Rahul Dravid also batted as if he was playing in his fiftieth Test and not his first. As obvious as their talent was their temperament. Their success was in many ways, a vindication of the Indian domestic cricket structure. Both had come up the ranks and played first-class cricket since the early 1990s. They had also represented India 'A' against their counterparts from other prominent cricketing nations. Not only had they been exposed to different match situations, but they had also encountered and handled the twin imposters of success and failure on several occasions.

Dravid was unlucky to be dismissed just five short of a hundred. The evening before the Test, he and his Karnataka teammate Venkatesh Prasad had looked at the wall of their dressing room that bore boards bearing the names of all the cricketers from overseas who had either scored a Test hundred or taken five wickets in a Test innings at cricket's HQ. They then 'struck a deal' that Prasad would get his name on the bowlers' board and Dravid would do likewise on the batsmen's board. Prasad kept his word, but Dravid fell short.

Followers of Indian cricket were a delighted lot, convinced as they were that they had witnessed the birth of a new 'middle order'. The bulwark of that middle order had sparkled in a knock of 31 before he got a peach of a delivery by Chris Lewis that pitched on a length and moved away just a bit, beating him and taking the off-stump. Thanks to the debutants, India scored 429 to England's 344. The match was drawn.

India got off to a poor start in the third Test at Nottingham, with Rathour and makeshift opener Mongia falling with only 33 on the board. Sachin was yet to open his account when he cut Cork hard, but uppishly and without fully committing himself to the stroke. The cherry flew to Atherton at gully, but the England captain dropped a sitter. Sachin did not offer the opposition another opportunity. At the other end, Ganguly seemed intent on carrying on from where he had left off at Lord's. The duo added 255 for the third wicket, playing all their strokes and rotating the strike superbly, much to the discomfiture of the bowlers who had to keep changing their line of attack with a left-hander and right-hander batting together. Ganguly scored 136 and Sachin got 177. Later in the innings, Dravid scored 84. India's 'new middle order' was rocking. The visitors totalled 521.

Like Sachin, Atherton got a life before he opened his account, when Dravid spilt a chance in the slips. The England captain had another reprieve at 34 when Azharuddin missed a catch. The Indian captain injured his ankle in the process and had to leave the field for repairs. For the 'Crown Prince', this was a great opportunity to make a statement.

> After India had scored over 500 in their first innings, it was expected of me to put pressure on England by placing an attacking field and making proper bowling changes. Contrary to this, it appeared that I was adopting tactics which had slowed down the pace of the game. Obviously, my moves were not appreciated by cricket-lovers. The fact was that things were not so easy. Centuries by Hussain and Atherton reduced chances of our possible

lead in the first innings considerably. At this stage, I thought it would be unwise if we got England out quickly. This would have made India bat in their second innings rather too early, which could have created problems for us. Rathour was unfit to bat; Manjrekar and Mongia were to open in the second innings and were not in good form; Ganguly and Dravid were playing only their second Test; Azharuddin was injured and not in good form. He was to bat only if needed. I thought one or two wickets could have changed the complexion of the game and the situation could have been reversed. These two days of experience made me realise the ordeal of captaincy that I would have to face if I was selected captain of the team.

—Sachin Tendulkar, *The Times of India* (PMG), 28 June 1997

England shut the door on India with a total of 564. For some people, Sachin's approach did come across as defensive, especially when compared to the dynamism that he exhibited whenever he led Mumbai. The way Ganguly and Dravid had batted since their debuts at Lord's certainly suggested that his concern about the pressure getting to them were misplaced.

There were others who complimented Sachin for being 'ahead of the game' and visualizing likely twists, some of which he reckoned could go against his team. Be that as it may, India could still have been in a tight spot despite his tactics, had he not scored 74 in the second innings. Mongia (45) and Ganguly (48) also batted well. The match was called off after the Indian innings ended at 211.

India's failure to level the Test series against England made a change at the top a foregone conclusion. After close to seven years in the saddle, Mohammed Azharuddin was replaced as captain by his deputy of three years.

THE FIRST CAPTAINCY

Of course, the usual fears will be aired over what the added responsibilities will do to his batting. This in his case is a minor factor because he has for some time now been accustomed to carrying the burden of the batting which has tended to sink or soar with him. To be captain and bear the same responsibility cannot be all that much harder. Not in his case anyway.... His first day at captaincy in the training camp at Chennai was also revealing. You would expect a new captain to be at the very hub of things. Tendulkar was more like a dynamo, batting first and then bowling on and on before taking his team through a post-net session.... And then there was the press conference and then maybe a number of social engagements to round off the day. For the sake of Indian cricket, it must be hoped that this dynamo is not going to run out.

—R. Mohan, *The Sportstar*, 24 August 1996

While Sachin may have 'realized the ordeal' that the captaincy of the Indian team might become, during his shot at the responsibility in the Nottingham Test, the experience had by no means rattled him.

Sitting alongside him in his car as he drove home from the Mumbai airport after the Indian team's return from England, was a journalist. When asked if he was 'ready for the captaincy', Sachin replied that he had led Mumbai for two-and-a-half years. He had also captained the West Zone. He would do whatever he was expected to do, he said.

His formal appointment as India's captain delighted the followers and pundits. The majority predicted that he would be as successful with India as he had been with Mumbai. There were a few similarities in the two sides, in that both outfits comprised players who looked up to Sachin. So quickly had one generation replaced another in Indian cricket that Azharuddin apart, the Indian team that Sachin led to Sri Lanka for a quadrangular series against the hosts, Australia and Zimbabwe, did not comprise any player who had made his international debut before the Karachi Test of November 1989. Manjrekar had been left out, Sidhu had retired and Prabhakar was not in contention. Anil Kumble was the new vice-captain and Vinod Kambli was recalled.

In his column for *The Sportstar*, Sunil Gavaskar opined that the fans would not mind if Sachin was less flamboyant and adventurous, and more consistent.

Sachin's first match in charge followed what had become predictable sequence of events by then. Against Sri Lanka, India won the toss, batted first and scored 226–5. On his captaincy debut, he scored 110, but his jubilation was short-lived as the reigning world champions underscored their supremacy in limited-overs cricket with a nine-wicket win. Sanath Jayasuriya blasted an unbeaten 120, and Kaluwitharana, his celebrated opening partner, scored 53 before he was bowled by the Indian captain. The hosts cruised to victory with over five overs left. India then beat Zimbabwe, but lost to Australia and thus missed out on a place in the final.

In India's next assignment, a five-match series against Pakistan at Toronto in Canada, Sachin once again led from the front. The conditions at cricket's newest international venue were more English than Asian, and that gave Pakistan the edge, as their bowling attack was clearly superior to India's. The onus was on the Indian batsmen to give it their best shot.

The Indian captain led from the front. Set to score 171 in the first, rain-hit 33 overs-a-side encounter, Sachin was fortunate to survive two leg-before shouts by Waqar Younis, both of which could have gone the bowler's way. But Lloyd Barker, the umpire, thought otherwise and the Indian captain stayed. He settled in to essay a skillful innings against the most rounded attack in international cricket at that point. Wasim Akram and Waqar Younis apart, Pakistan had the off-spinner Saqlain Mushtaq and the all-rounder Azhar Mahmood. Sachin added insult to injury with an assault off Waqar in the latter stages of the innings, flicking, lofting and cutting one of the most feared quickies in the history of the sport with impunity. He remained unbeaten with 89 as India completed a win by eight wickets. Pakistan drew level in the second game, despite a fine 90 by Rahul Dravid. The Karnataka batsman starred in the third game as well, with a knock of 46 on a surface that could be described as 'tricky'. India's total of 191 was good enough for Srinath, Prasad and Kumble, who bowled out Pakistan for 136.

Trailing 1-2 in the series with two to play, the Pakistanis proceeded to do what they generally did against their traditional rivals in those days. Not only did India lose the series 2-3, but the new captain also found himself in the eye of a storm. His decision to pick Kambli ahead of Ganguly for the third and fourth games created a furore in the latter's hometown Kolkata. In what was a typically

Indian overreaction, the captain was 'warned' of a hostile reception during the Test against South Africa later in the season. Ganguly did replace Kambli in the XI for the fifth game, but he too failed. A casualty of the series loss was Sandeep Patil, who was sacked as cricket manager after less than six months in the job. Madan Lal, his co-1983 World Cup winner, was named his successor.

After three consecutive seasons of very little international cricket, India went to the other extreme in 1996–97. They were to host a one-off Test against Australia, which was to be followed by a tri-series also featuring South Africa. The Proteas were to then stay on to play a three-Test series, after which, both the Indian and South African teams were to fly across the Indian Ocean for another three-Test series in the 'Rainbow Nation'. The South Africa tour was to end with a tri-series that would have Zimbabwe as the third team. After a two-week break, the Indians were to fly halfway across the globe for a five-Test series in the Caribbean.

The advent of Ganguly and Dravid and the success of the Srinath–Prasad combine had made fans hopeful of a decent showing by their team in the matches to come, especially on the tours of South Africa and the West Indies. They were also hopeful that four Tests and a tri-series on home turf would help Sachin settle in his new role before the team flew overseas.

His debut as Test captain was memorable, with India beating Australia in the one-off Test at Delhi by seven wickets. The visitors sorely missed Warne on a slow and low pitch that steadily deteriorated as the game went on. Nayan Mongia, opening the innings, scored 152 and Kumble took a total of nine wickets at his favourite venue. Sachin was the recipient of the first Border–Gavaskar Trophy, which would henceforth be presented to the winners of bilateral Test series between the two largest cricketing nations. The institution of a trophy and the presence of the legends themselves to award it, suggested that the two teams would now be playing each other a lot more often than in the past. The fact that the governments of both the countries had been actively involved in the planning of the one-off Test, apart from the Boards in question, was indicative of the 'new' India's reaching out to like-minded democracies across the world and tying up with them to further each other's interests across different spheres. The only discordant note was struck by the trophy itself. It looked a bit like a jester's cap, and was replaced by a more conventional trophy a couple of years later.

The league stage of the tri-series that followed was dominated by South Africa. Batting, bowling, fielding and application-wise, Hansie Cronje's team looked streets ahead of India and Australia. Sections of the Indian media were besotted with the side, with reams of newsprint being devoted to the laptop that

Bob Woolmer, the team's coach, was said to be utilizing to guide his team to perfection. It was politely suggested that the Indian team could improve a great deal if it also acquired one. The first league game between India and Australia, a day-nighter at Bengaluru, was eventful. Needing 216 to win, India lost four quick wickets after a steady start. Luck was not on the side of Azharuddin and Ganguly. The former India captain's reaction on being adjudged leg-before triggered off a fusillade of rubbish by the spectators. Play was held up for 20 minutes and Azharuddin, who by then had regained his composure, was persuaded to request the aggrieved spectators to cool down. Shortly after the resumption, a mix-up between Sachin and Ganguly accounted for the latter. Sachin, livid at himself, set his heart on taking his team through. He batted steadily but positively in the company of Jadeja and Joshi, who was one of the six Karnataka players in the playing XI (Kumble, Srinath, Prasad, Dravid and opener Sujith Somasunder being the others). However, the Australians hit back by dismissing both Joshi and Sachin at 164. Sachin had scored 88. A thrilling climax ensued, with local boys Kumble and Srinath taking India to victory, egged on by a home crowd that comprised the leg-spinner's mother and grandmother.

Two days later, India lost to South Africa at Jaipur. The home team's chase of a target of 250 was hampered by the fall of wickets at regular intervals, which undid the foundation laid by the new opening combination of Sourav Ganguly and Sachin Tendulkar. The failure of Karnataka opener Sujith Somasunder in the first two games of the tri-series prompted Sachin to do what the Indian team management had done at Auckland in March 1994. He promoted Sourav Ganguly, a middle-order batsman, to the opening slot. The pair put on 126 in its very first association at the top of the order.

India's second encounter against Australia at Cuttack was rained off. It was in the next league game, against South Africa at Rajkot, that Sachin made another change in the top-order. Javagal Srinath, who had batted at number five in an earlier game, was instructed to 'pinch-hit' at number three. He responded by taking 69 deliveries to score 53, but there was no way the team management could find fault with him, with his teammates batting shoddily to be dismissed for 185. The Proteas won by five wickets.

With South Africa having won all their matches, the final league game of the tri-series between India and Australia at Mohali was for all practical purposes, a semi-final. After being put in by Mark Taylor, Sachin took it upon himself to wrest the initiative for his side. He scored 62, and Azharuddin (94) and Dravid (56), excelled in the latter half of the innings, enabling India to finish with 289–6.

Australia's 'Marks' gave their side a good start, putting on 84 before a versatile cricketer, who was playing his first international game after seven-and-a-half years, broke through. Robin Singh, who had been born in Trinidad and played his early cricket in the island-nation with the likes of Brian Lara, had travelled to the country of his origin in the mid-1980s for higher studies and stayed back. His consistency as a belligerent left-handed batsman, an underrated right-handed seamer, and an outstanding fielder for Tamil Nadu in the Ranji Trophy had won him a place in the Indian team that toured the country of his birth and its neighbouring nations in early 1989. However, he was discarded after a solitary ODI and ignored for the next seven seasons. In the first half of the 1990s, Mohammed Azharuddin had tried his hardest on more than one occasion to convince the selectors to pick the all-rounder, who he was convinced would be an asset in the shorter variety. However, he had been overruled every single time. His successor was luckier.

At Mohali, Robin Singh bowled Mark Waugh and then had Stuart Law caught by a certain Mohammed Azharuddin for a duck. Both teams came hard at each other from that point. As the innings neared its closing stages, the Indians managed to get their noses in front, but only just. With one over left, the visitors needed six runs and the hosts needed one wicket. Sachin sought to do an encore of the Hero Cup semi-final by introducing himself into the attack. Unlike the Hero Cup game, he did not have to complete the over, with the Australians losing their final wicket to a run out off the very first ball.

Despite the hard-earned win, India started the final at the Wankhede as the overwhelming underdogs against a side that was yet to taste defeat in the series. Even die-hard Indian fans were in awe of the South Africans and on the eve of the final, it appeared that there was only one Indian who believed that Hansie Cronje's team was fallible. This individual was none other than the captain of India himself.

Sachin won the toss and contributed 67 to his team's 220–7. He then confounded the opposition by dispensing with a deep point, usually a mandatory fielding position in ODIs. The leg-side was fortified instead and the South African batsmen challenged to target the vacant region on the off. His bowlers responded magnificently. Kumble and Prasad took 4–25 and 3–28, respectively, and South Africa were dismissed for 185.

> From the moment he addressed the team in the huddle prior to taking the field to the very last ball when Allan Donald was bowled, Tendulkar was an absolutely active, even hyper-active, hands-on captain whether in advising bowlers, running the field placements with great thought or even taking

advice at committee meetings. This is one triumph which came with him wholly in charge at the controls.

—R. Mohan, *The Sportstar*, 16 November 1996

People were quick to draw comparisons between Sachin's 'hands-on' approach and that of his allegedly 'uncommunicative' predecessor. Sachin was of course far too seasoned by then to get carried away by the adulation that followed the triumph. Focussing on his first full Test series as captain was paramount.

After the tri-series final in Mumbai, Sachin's 'hands-on' captaincy was on show once again in the first Test against South Africa. At Ahmedabad's sprawling Sardar Patel Gujarat Stadium, the batsmen of both sides struggled on a 'slow and low' surface.

The arrival of Ganguly and Dravid, as well as the decision of the selectors to award a Test debut to a talented batsman from Hyderabad called V.V.S. Laxman, meant that there was little room in the 'new' middle order. Manjrekar, trying to reinvent himself as a batsman, made himself available as opener. His ability to tackle the new ball was never in doubt, and those who had followed his career were convinced that a reasonably long outing in the middle would benefit not only him, but also the team, with one of its perennial concerns being addressed on the eve of visits to South Africa and the Caribbean.

Ganguly, Dravid and Laxman had also inadvertently affected Kambli's chances of returning to the Test side. All the left-hander could now do was constantly remind the selectors of his presence by scoring heavily at the domestic level.

On the eve of the Ahmedabad Test, Sachin had tried to allay the concerns emanating from the absence of 'specialist' openers by reminding the media that Manjrekar had scored a double hundred in Pakistan and Mongia had recently scored 152 against Australia. Unfortunately for the Indian team and Manjrekar himself, he failed, scoring 34 in the first innings and 4 in the second. He was left out of the XI for the next Test and never represented India again.

India conceded a first-innings lead of 21. The hosts were 124–7 in their second innings when Kumble joined Laxman for a crucial stand that realized 56. Laxman, in only his second Test innings, scored 51 and India were all out for 190.

Javagal Srinath struck twice before the South Africans got off the mark in their pursuit of a target of 170. Hudson was trapped leg-before and Cullinan undone by a good-length delivery on the line of off-stump, to which he had no option but to play. The ball did just a bit and took the outside edge, and Mongia did the rest. At 40–3, Cronje was joined by Brian McMillan. Both batsmen were excellent players of spin. They added 25 before Kumble had McMillan caught. Still, the South Africans were not flustered. Their skipper had got his eye in and the likes of Dave Richardson and Jonty Rhodes, both competent players of spin, were to follow. They had all the time in the world to get the runs, and all they had to do was wear the spinners out.

What they did not know is that the fielding captain, a man who knew a thing or two about batting, had put himself in their shoes. Sachin had done what he as a batsman would not have liked to encounter in the prevalent circumstances. Not only was the surface uneven, but it also appeared to be favourably dispensed towards reverse-swing.

The Indian captain sprung a surprise on just about everybody, the opposition included, by bringing back Srinath, who despite his two early strikes, had reconciled to spending the remainder of the game in the outfield. As India's pace spearhead commenced a fresh spell, he had at the back of his mind, his captain's directive to 'stop targeting the batsmen's thigh pad and concentrate on bowling fuller on Indian wickets'. At the other end, Sachin deployed Joshi. The left-arm spinner's brief was to land the ball in the rough outside the left-handers' rough and prevent them from rotating the strike.

Srinath, bowling fuller and 'reversing', dismissed Richardson, Rhodes, Paul Adams and Donald, to finish with figures of 6–21. The visitors lost their last six wickets for nine runs. India won by 64 runs, and the first man to rush to the Karnataka speedster at the end of the game was the triumphant captain. Hansie Cronje, the South African captain, conceded that he and his team had been outsmarted. For the second international match in succession, Sachin had proved that the South Africans, for all their efficiency on the field of play, were one-dimensional as far as their strategizing was concerned. They simply did not have a Plan 'B' to fall back on if their opponent repulsed their Plan 'A'.

The visitors executed their plan 'A' splendidly in the second Test at Kolkata and this time did not give India even a whiff of an opportunity to come back into the game. Cronje won the toss and chose to bat. The visitors seemed on course for a total of 600 when openers Andrew Hudson and Gary Kirsten put on 236, but the Indian bowlers struck back to round up the innings for 428. In Manjrekar's absence, Rahul Dravid opened with Mongia and the pair put on 68. The visitors then snared three quick wickets and forced Mohammed Azharuddin to retire hurt.

Anil Kumble was waging a lone battle in the middle when the former India skipper resumed his innings, with the scoreboard reading 161–7. Azharuddin, who was apparently upset with something that someone had said in the dressing room, proceeded to treat the South African bowling like a punching bag. Yet again, the visitors appeared to struggle when countered, although Azharuddin admittedly enjoyed more than his share of good fortune. Backing him every inch of the way were the spectators at his favourite venue. His 74-ball hundred, the fastest by an Indian in Tests, was his fourth in five Tests at the Eden. Kumble scored 88 and India finished with 329.

The hosts' second innings was a disaster. They were bowled out for 137 after being set 467 to win. Their nemesis was the debutant Lance Klusener, a right-handed paceman and plucky left-handed bat. Among his eight victims was Azharuddin, who had brutalized him for 20 runs in an over in the first innings.

India prevailed over the visitors in the series decider at Kanpur, on a pitch that was spin-friendly, to say the very least. Azharuddin, who had rediscovered his form at Kolkata, was among the runs once again, with a knock of 163. Qualitatively, it was a far better innings than the one at Kolkata.

South Africa's tour ended with a one-off ODI at the Wankhede, the proceeds of which were handed over to former India stalwart Mohinder Amarnath. His battles with the BCCI were forgotten, with the Board awarding him a 'benefit' game in the form of an 'official' international match. He was the fourth cricketer to be honoured thus, after his contemporaries Gundappa Viswanath, Dilip Vengsarkar and Syed Kirmani.

Sachin scored a century, his first 'international' hundred at his home ground, but the crowd did not endear itself to him with its behaviour after he was dismissed. Like Azharuddin at Bengaluru during the tri-series, Sachin had to make his way to a section of the spectators and appeal for calm. India won by 50 runs.

The Indian team for the three-Test series in South Africa, scheduled to begin after a couple of weeks, had been picked by the time the one-off ODI was played. Among the seven Karnataka players who made it were pacemen David Johnson and Dodda Ganesh, both of whom had starred in their state's Ranji Trophy win in 1995–96. While there was no doubt that both were talented, the fact was that Mumbai's Salil Ankola and Abey Kuruvilla were a lot more successful and experienced. If performances in the Ranji Trophy were to be considered as a yardstick, then the Mumbai duo had set up two successive triumphs for their side in 1993–94 and 1994–95 respectively. Ankola had even joined the Indian team that toured England in 1996, in the latter half of the tour.

The squad for South Africa also comprised as many as three wicketkeepers in Mongia, Syed Saba Karim and Pankaj Dharmani, which seemed odd for a tour that comprised three Tests and just two three-day games. The team for the tri-series that was to follow the Tests was to be picked later.

Vikram Rathour was brought back as opener in the absence of any viable alternative. Another player to be recalled was W.V. Raman, who had scored a fine 67 in the Kanpur Test.

'There is no harm in playing to your strengths. We need not worry about what kind of pitches we might get in South Africa and the West Indies.' Sachin would have remembered these words of his, spoken after the victory over Australia at Delhi, when he saw the strip at Kingsmead, Durban, where the Test series was to begin. It was greenish, hard and juicy. The crammed international calendar had permitted the Indians only one warm-up game before the first Test. From dusty Kanpur to bouncy Durban was going to be one hell of a transition.

Sachin won the toss in his first overseas Test as captain, and opted to give Srinath and Prasad first use of the pitch. India's new-ball pair combined splendidly to dismiss South Africa for 235 in the first innings. Other than disconcerting the South Africans with their pace, accuracy and carry, the Indian quicks succeeded in reminding their 23-year-old captain of the 13-year-old fast-bowling hopeful who had travelled to Chennai for the MRF Pace Foundation Selection trials, a decade previously.

David Johnson was the third paceman in the XI, and Sachin decided to add a 'fourth' to the mix by becoming one himself. He marked out his full run-up and told Mongia to stay back. It had of course been a while since he had bowled the way he did at school, and what he did not account for was the unfamiliarity of his 'bowling muscles' with the demands he was about to make on them. In trying to surprise Andrew Hudson, the South African opener, with a bouncer in his third over, Sachin strained his back. The pain forced him to leave the field and take three cortisone injections. Kumble deputized in his absence.

> I firmly believe that if Sachin were over six feet tall and a little more athletic, he would have been the Garry Sobers of the modern era. In fact, it is safe to bet that he would have given Sobers a run for his money.... I am guessing that it is only when he found out in his teens that he won't grow significantly taller that he gave up the ambition of being a fast bowler and decided that it had to be batting that would take him to cricketing greatness. Even today, Tendulkar gets more excited when he sees a good fast bowling talent than when he sees a special batting talent.... When I used to captain Mumbai, I had to very tactfully separate Tendulkar from a young fast bowler.... Sachin just can't hold back from giving advice to

a young quickie; the problem is his advice is a bit too complex for most. Also, what he has in mind is often impossible for a rookie fast bowler to produce. I used to feel sorry for him in such situations. It was as if Tendulkar was trying to live his dream of being a great fast bowler through another, more physically gifted, athlete.

—Sanjay Manjrekar, *Outlook Special Commemorative Issue*, 2010

The South African pacemen paid the Indians back with interest. The visitors were blown away for 100 even before they realized it. A highlight of the innings was a duel between Sachin and South Africa's premier bowler that lasted three deliveries. Allan Donald, brought back into the attack just before the lunch interval, bowled two looseners outside the off-stump that Sachin capitalized on, cover-driving the first and square-driving the second to the fence. The Indian captain had hit three boundaries in an individual score of 15 and looked good for many more. Donald followed the two overpitched deliveries with a rocket that pitched on a length, moved inwards off the seam, and hurried through the tiniest of gaps between Sachin's bat and front foot to send the off-stump for a walk.

Under Hansie Cronje, we studied hard for a Tendulkar weakness. We thought that he might be vulnerable, especially early in his innings, to the ball that is bowled from wide of the crease, coming back in off a good length. He might then be bowled through the gate, or be lbw.... The ball I bowled to him at Durban in 1996 was the best ball I have bowled to any cricketer.... He hit the first two balls after lunch for four, then I came from wide of the crease and the ball really went a long way to bowl him. I don't think I have ever celebrated like that—you save those for the big ones. We had discussed how to bowl to him, and I knew what I was trying to do, but I never expected it to go so far off the seam to knock out the off-stump. It was a great sight.

—Allan Donald, *Wisden Asia Cricket*, September 2002

After Venkatesh Prasad's second 'five-for' of the Test restricted the South Africans to 259, the 'tigers at home and lambs overseas' were annihilated for 66 in the second innings. Defeat by 328 runs was hugely embarrassing and potentially demoralizing, but the Indian captain refused to think negatively. He looked for positives amidst the rubble, and other than Srinath and Prasad's bowling, he found one in Rahul Dravid, who had held his own against the rampaging quicks in the second innings with an unbeaten 27.

The Karnataka batsman was thrilled to be offered the pivotal number three slot in the batting order by his captain. He had batted one-down in the Ahmedabad Test a couple of months previously, but that had been a stopgap measure with Sourav Ganguly, who had held that slot since the Lord's Test earlier that year, absent due to injury. In South Africa, Dravid was assured of a longer run at the pivotal spot. While Ganguly was unquestionably a fine batsman, Sachin reckoned that Dravid, with his immaculate technique would make for a better 'number three', especially on strips that had something in them for the pacemen.

At Cape Town, venue of the 'New Year' second Test, South Africa declared their first innings at 529-7 on the second afternoon. Srinath and Prasad impressed again, but Dodda Ganesh, who was making his debut, was unable to back them up as effectively as the captain would have liked. Sachin therefore had no choice but to rotate his bowlers in such a way that one of Srinath and Prasad would be bowling at any given time. This affected the balance of his attack and the opposition benefited by not having to face the new-ball duo in tandem after the first few overs. Three South Africans scored centuries.

The Indian team management had requested Mongia to return to the opening slot after the disaster at Durban, but he was unable to oblige in the first innings at Capetown as he was tending to an injury that he had sustained while keeping. India started disastrously, with W.V. Raman, his makeshift opening partner Dravid and night watchman Venkatesh Prasad falling just before stumps on the second day. India's woes only multiplied on the third morning, with the dismissals of Ganguly and Laxman. At 58-5, even the most optimistic Indian supporter would have contended that the situation was so hopeless that things could only get better from that point. They did, in the form of a sensational counterattack by the captain and former captain.

While the results they achieved were identical, the methods adopted by the two batsmen could not have been more dissimilar. While Azharuddin lofted, lashed and rode his luck, Sachin stayed 'in character', his innate belligerence coming to the fore against a formidable bowling attack, an attacking field-setting and a perilous situation for his team. He was aggressive but conventional. He played the bowling on merit and concentrated on 'carpet' strokes like drives, flicks and cuts. The one stroke that underscored his approach during the partnership was a boundary off Donald with which the partnership itself commenced at 58-5; the cherry pitched on a good length and reared, and Sachin, who was already on the front foot, checked his backlift and turned the face of the bat at the point of impact to dispatch the ball past the slips for four. His penchant for playing the ball as late as possible was evident even when he essayed his signature punches off the back foot. His use of the depth of the crease to move back was spot-on, as was the way he stood on his toes to counter the extra bounce.

Ever since he had started playing competitive cricket, Sachin had preferred 'getting forward' to pacemen on pitches that had something in them. The idea was to look to get on to the front foot at the first opportunity to do so, so that he could play through the line and hit on the up. His reflexes were swift enough to enable him move backwards if the delivery were to be pitched short.

At Cape Town, he switched to the 'back-and-across' shuffle that the likes of Sunil Gavaskar and Rahul Dravid had perfected. He tried it while having throwdowns before the start of play on the second day and felt comfortable. It was the second time he had tried something different during a Test match at Cape Town, and executed it brilliantly. On the previous tour, four years earlier, he had widened the gap between his feet to be able to duck into short deliveries during his knock of 75.

> I had asked him, after his knock, that his feet were moving in a certain manner before the ball had been bowled, which I had not seen him do before. He admitted that he had done it for the first time in his life, when he took guard at the start. For me, that was the most amazing thing I have ever seen. There is a rule in cricket, what you do in the middle, you practise in the nets before. This great man went on to get a big Test 100 against a top bowling team with a technique not practiced before!
>
> —Sourav Ganguly, *Sports Illustrated*, May 2013

The assault on the South African bowling realized 222 runs in 40 overs before Azharuddin was run out for 115. Sachin did his best to monopolize the strike thereafter, even as the wickets went down. The Indian captain was last out at 359 to an incredible piece of athleticism. Much to the amazement of watchers, Sachin included, newcomer Adam Bacher leapt skywards to clasp a full-blooded pull off McMillan one-handed, on the mid-wicket boundary. In a way, it was an appropriate end to what had been a spectacular innings of 169.

> I...will never forget his sublime innings at Newlands on the same tour. Sachin's ability to play the correct shot to the correct ball is a gift only the great players have. Indeed, he was dismissed playing the fiercest of pulls to a short ball only to find the only man on the leg-side and even then it was a catch to match any that I have seen.
>
> —Bob Woolmer, *Wisden Asia Cricket*, September 2002

India did not have much joy in the second innings. The hosts muscled their way to 256–6 and then bowled the visitors out for 144. The target of 427 was never in the equation. India's only consolation was an unbeaten 35 by V.V.S. Laxman, who batted as brightly as Dravid had in the second innings at Durban.

The series loss did not erode Sachin's faith in his team. On the eve of the third Test at Johannesburg, he reminded his players that they had nothing to lose and absolutely everything to gain. A victory, Sachin felt, would convince doubters that his was a competent team that would have fared even better had it got a little more time to get attuned to the conditions before the start of the Test series.

His resolve was reflected in the way he batted after winning the toss. He came in at 46–2 and contributed 35 to a 54-run stand with Dravid before his opposite number Hansie Cronje, a bowler he was never particularly comfortable against, had him caught in the slips for 35.

> I don't know why, but I hate facing an irregular bowler. It affects my concentration. Otherwise I don't have any difficulty with any kind of bowling.
>
> —Sachin Tendulkar, *Outlook*, 4 January 1999

At 100–3, Dravid was joined in the middle by Ganguly. The duo proceeded to add 145 for the fourth wicket. Dravid kept going after Ganguly's dismissal for 73 and completed his maiden Test hundred. He was last out for 148, after Srinath swung his bat around to get a quick 41. India's total of 410 was their highest on South African soil.

Bowling second for the first time in the Test series and that too with runs behind them, Srinath and Prasad combined to dismiss the hosts for 321 by stumps on the third day. Srinath's 5–104 was his second 'five-for' in Tests, after his stupendous show at Ahmedabad earlier in the season. The grin that Sachin sported when the team returned to the pavilion after taking a first-innings lead of 89, spoke for itself.

The resolve in the Indian camp to make a statement of sorts in the last Test was reflected in the way the openers Mongia and Rathour, both of whom had struggled till then, knuckled down and increased the overall lead to 179 before being separated. Just when the South Africans appeared to have got back into the game with three quick strikes, including that of the Indian captain, the heroes of the first innings came to the rescue with another fruitful and brisk partnership. Dravid's 81 and Ganguly's 60 enabled Sachin to declare at 266–8, and Venkatesh Prasad capped a memorable day for his team by dismissing Gary Kirsten just before stumps.

In the dressing room, Sachin heard V.V.S. Laxman, whose tour had ended abruptly due to a broken finger, pour his heart out. The youngster was devastated at having to return to India and concerned about his future in international cricket. The captain consoled and counseled. Injuries were part and parcel of the game, he said. He assured Laxman that a day would come when the world would marvel at the latter's talent. Sachin was not one to talk through his hat; he meant every word that he uttered.

Under pressure for the first time in the series, South Africa came apart against some splendid bowling on the fifth day. They were 77-5 when the heavens opened. The Indians, frustrated by the hold-up, snared two more wickets after the resumption. All that was left was the killer blow, but not for the first or last time, the Indian bowlers ran out of steam just when the destination was sighted. Daryll Cullinan and Lance Klusener added 127. Klusener fell in the sixth over of the last hour, but by then, it was too late for the visitors. When play was called off with four mandatory overs left, South Africa were 228-8. Sachin was gutted. While the hosts celebrated their escape, the Indian captain locked himself up in the bathroom of the dressing room and broke down. For him, being denied something that he had left no stone unturned to achieve was something he was not used to.

He may have been his side's premier batsman and captain, but at the end of the day, he was only 23.

For the tri-series that followed, reinforcements for the Indians arrived in the form of Robin Singh, Ajay Jadeja, Sunil Joshi and Salil Ankola. India's performances at the league stage were uninspiring, with South Africa beating them in three games out of three and Zimbabwe winning one and tying the other. Even as the batting kept flattering to deceive, Sachin tried to tinker with the batting order, even dropping down to number four and sending Dravid to open with Ganguly. However, nothing worked. In India's sixth and last league encounter of the series, against Zimbabwe at Benoni, he won the toss and opted to bowl. It was an obvious call to take. India were at the bottom of the table and batting second would enable them to know how many runs they would need to score in less than the allotted 50 overs, to edge ahead of Zimbabwe and qualify for the final.

Zimbabwe finished with 240-8, and the calculations revealed that India needed to knock down the runs in 40.5 overs. The Indian supporters at the venue and TV viewers back in India were delighted to see the captain accompanying

Ganguly to the wicket. He had abandoned his experiments with the opening slot in a must-win game.

He proceeded to bat brilliantly. He was severe on Heath Streak, coming down the wicket and hitting him through the covers and over the top for boundaries before punching him over the infield on both sides of the wicket. He used his feet quite brilliantly. Eddo Brandes, brought back for a second spell after going for runs in his first, was hit for 18 in an over. The bowler tried to counter Sachin's premeditated advances down the wicket by varying his line and length accordingly, but to no avail. When Sachin moved away to the leg-side to make room for himself, Brandes followed him, only to bowl a long-hop that Sachin drove high and handsomely over the sightscreen. He also flicked brilliantly and ran hard between the wickets. When he was fourth out at 158, Sachin had scored 104 off only 97. Jadeja and Robin Singh took the team through.

The final, played at Durban, did not go India's way. The game that got underway on the designated day was cut short due to rain and the teams had to reconvene the next day. On 'day two', South Africa scored 278–8, after which there was another downpour. Unlike the previous day however, it abated and India's target was revised to 251 from 40 overs. Dravid joined Sachin after Ganguly's dismissal at 18 and the duo put India on course with some exhilarating batting. One moment stood out. When Dravid lofted Allan Donald for six over long-on, the paceman strode down the wicket hurling a series of expletives and finished within handshaking distance of the batsman. While Sachin immediately had a word with the umpire, what was noticeable on TV was Dravid's body language. He stood his ground, looking Donald straight in the eye and not taking a backward step, even as the paceman continued to disgrace himself. Strangely, Donald did not subject the Indian captain to the same treatment, not even when Sachin whipped him for boundaries on the leg-side, utilizing the bowler's extra pace to perfection.

Sachin batted like a man on a mission until Cronje had him caught at short fine-leg by Rudi Bryson. The Indian captain had slammed seven boundaries and one six in a knock of 45 off only 33 balls. It was one of his most poignant dismissals *against the run of play*, as he had looked invincible till he made that one, fatal mistake. Azharuddin, the next man in, also scored 45 at more than a run-a-ball before falling to Pollock. Jadeja did not last long and India's hopes ebbed when Dravid was fifth out at 210. The visitors lost by only 17 runs, an indication that the outcome might well have been different had Sachin not fallen at the wrong time. For the Indians, insult was added to injury when the match referee let Donald get away.

The Indians stopped over in Zimbabwe to play a couple of ODIs, before returning home. They had hardly any time to recharge the batteries, with a five-Test series in the Caribbean coming up.

> I think we should have a third seamer who has a lot of experience. His job will be to give rest to Srinath and Prasad. Both of them were prepared to bowl whenever I wanted them to (in South Africa). They have bowled a lot this season. If any of them breaks down in the West Indies—I hope it doesn't happen—it's going to be very tough.
>
> —Sachin Tendulkar, *The Sportstar*, 1 March 1997

Sachin's worst fears came true within hours of the Indian team's arrival in the Caribbean. Javagal Srinath was ruled out of the series after being diagnosed with a rotator cuff injury to his bowling shoulder. It was a blow to India's prospects, considering the way he had been bowling since 1994. It was now left to Prasad and Mumbai's Abey Kuruvilla, who had finally been rewarded for his consistency. Salil Ankola, who had bowled well in the tri-series in South Africa, was unlucky to miss out, with Dodda Ganesh getting another chance to prove himself. Noel David, a little-known off-spinning all-rounder from Hyderabad, was named Srinath's replacement.

The selectors also ruled that India would have a new opening combination for the series. Raman and Rathour were discarded and V.V.S. Laxman, who had recovered from his finger injury, was assigned the job of facing the new ball. The youngster had never opened at any level before, but intent as he was on returning to the national squad, he took up the challenge. Navjot Sidhu was brought in as his partner, his dramatic 'retirement' in England having been forgotten. A player who was certainly not complaining with this new combination was Nayan Mongia, who could look forward to concentrating on his primary job without the additional responsibility of opening the batting.

The first Test at Kingston was drawn. The Indians acquitted themselves quite well, with Laxman scoring 64 in his first outing as opener and Kuruvilla snaring three wickets on a track that did not have much in it for the quickies. Both sides batted cautiously. The second Test at Port of Spain, India's favourite venue in the Caribbean, followed a similar pattern, the highlights being a double hundred by Sidhu and an innings of 88 by the captain, which ended in a run out.

Previous Indian teams touring the West Indies would have been wary of a Test at the Kensington Oval at Bridgetown, Barbados, given the venue's reputation and the home team's record there. Of the 33 Tests played on what had traditionally been the most pace-friendly track in the Caribbean, the West Indies had won 18 and lost only three. However, Sachin and his side had at least three reasons to think differently. Unlike their predecessors, they had not been trailing in the series prior to their arrival in Barbados. Secondly, most of their batsmen had struck form against a formidable bowling line-up that comprised Curtly Ambrose, Ian Bishop and Courtney Walsh, the skipper. Also, Prasad and Kuruvilla, their new-ball bowlers, were more than capable of exploiting a wicket that had something in it for the pacers.

On 27 March 1997, the first day of the Test, cricket lovers at the Kensington Oval and millions of TV viewers were treated to the sight of two contemporary giants walking out for the toss. Brian Lara, who was leading for the first time in a Test in the absence of the injured Walsh, tossed the coin, and Sachin called correctly. He elected to bowl.

Venkatesh Prasad took 5–82 as the Windies were dismissed for 298. When India batted, Sachin and Dravid joined forces at 42–2. Franklyn Rose welcomed the Indian captain with a delivery that rose awkwardly from just short of a length. Sachin picked it early and played it with loose hands. When Rose served another short ball that swung inwards, Sachin pulled him for four to open his account. Mervin Dillon, bowling from the other end, was dealt with harshly; Sachin square-cut a short delivery for four, and when the bowler overcompensated for the lapse by overpitching, the Indian captain essayed a copybook drive to get another boundary. This was followed by the pièce de résistance—Dillon landed one on a length and the ball entered the 'corridor of uncertainty' just outside the off-stump. Any other batsman would have either defended it or let it go, but Sachin, who was in sublime nick, rocked backwards and punched it through the covers for another boundary. He hit nine boundaries in all on his way to a 50. The Indian dressing room and supporters in the stadium continued to applaud as he hooked Rose for six and then got onto his toes to drive the bowler on the up, off the back foot, between mid-off and extra cover, for four. None of the bowlers could make an impression on him.

Sachin had moved to eight short of a richly deserved century when he played Ian Bishop away from his body and was caught at gully. The replays indicated that Bishop had overstepped the popping crease but the umpire had failed to call a no-ball. Errors were of course an integral part of the game, like the one committed by Courtney Browne the previous year, when he had dropped Sachin off Bishop in the World Cup game at Gwalior.

The Sachin–Dravid stand of 170 helped India take a slender first-innings lead of 21.

India's pace bowlers then went for the jugular. The wickets fell fast and quick, with only Lara offering resistance. When he was sixth out at 86, the innings was as good as over. However, the Indians were left tearing their hair in frustration. While the 'first Test' jinx had not manifested on this tour, the other one—the inability to deliver the knockout punch—did just when the Indians could have done without it. The last-wicket pair of Ambrose and Franklyn Rose joined forces at 107-9 and added 33 crucial runs, even as Sachin persisted with his pacers. Observers were left wondering whether Anil Kumble ought to have been tried out. Nevertheless, the Indians had two whole days and a bit in which to score 120.

The visitors were 2-0 at stumps on day three. That evening, they left the ground on a high. Sachin would never have won a quiz on the history of cricket, but then, he did not need to be an encyclopaedia of the sport to be aware of the fact that India had not come even remotely close to winning a Test at Bridgetown on six previous visits to the Caribbean.

What happened the following morning left him and supporters of Indian cricket dumbfounded. Rose made the initial inroads and his seniors Bishop and Ambrose did the rest, bowling India out for 81. While the bowling was exceptional and the wicket not the best for batting, the failure of an international team to score 120 runs was inexplicable. Laxman was the only batsman to reach double figures. While Sachin had triumphed in his and Lara's first face-off as batsmen in the 1994-95 series, the Trinidadian had triumphed comprehensively in their first clash as captains. He used only three bowlers—his pacemen—to do all the damage. The Indian innings was over in precisely 35.5 overs.

Particularly disheartening for the young captain of a young team was the charge levelled by some critics that the Indian team, for all its 'talents', simply lacked the will to succeed overseas. Sachin was seasoned enough to know that the real world did not have the time and inclination to recognize 'moral victories' like those at Johannesburg in January 1997. So disconsolate was he after the Bridgetown defeat that he did not venture out of his hotel room for two whole days.

The remainder of the tour was an anti-climax. Three days of the fourth Test and two of the fifth were lost to rain, and the hosts took the series 1-0.

As a batsman, Sachin had reason to be satisfied with himself for the way he had batted on wickets that were not exactly conducive to his style. He had come within striking distance of a hundred thrice.

I like the ball to come on to the bat. Since I became captain, it is only in South Africa that I have played on wickets where the ball was coming on.... If you look at it, we have basically played on slow tracks and not on pitches where I can play on the rise and play the cut. On slow tracks where you have two players in catching positions and a deep point, I have to curb myself. I just can't go and slam the ball because runs in international cricket are not easy to come by. I would rather wait than try to prove that I am not bothered by pressure and play my natural game. I would prefer getting slow 70s and 80s than a quick 20 or 30.

—Sachin Tendulkar, *The Sportstar*, 3 May 1997

Those who were surprised to see him elect to bat on a damp Port of Spain wicket in the first of four ODIs were stunned by the quality of his strokeplay. When Sidhu, his opening partner, complained to him about the ball 'misbehaving' off the pitch, Sachin responded by taking Bishop on the full and hitting him for four. He proceeded to stroke 10 boundaries in all, out of a score of 44, before he was declared out caught behind despite the ball going off his sleeve. If he expected his team to seek inspiration from his knock, he was in for a disappointment, as the innings ended at a paltry 179 and the West Indies romped home with eight wickets in hand.

Sachin then brought his team's campaign back on track with an unbeaten 65 in the second ODI played at the same venue. A spell of rain necessitated the invocation of the D/L method for the second consecutive time in the series. This time around, the Indians prevailed and the series was squared. Set 250 to win the third ODI at St Vincent, the captain fell early, but Ganguly and Dravid flourished in each other's company, yet again. The duo added 130 for the second wicket before disaster struck. Daft batting and running between wickets resulted in the last eight wickets falling for 46 runs. India were all out for 231 with 10 deliveries to spare.

In the dressing room, a livid captain gave his team a dressing down, unable as he was to comprehend his team's expertise at losing from winning positions. None of the players was brave enough to sit next to him while having dinner that evening. Ironically, it was at Bridgetown of all places that India's tour ended on a disastrous note, with a 10-wicket win for the home team in the fourth and final ODI.

Indian journalists covering the tour were concerned by what they perceived as the 'indifference' of some Indian players to the debacles. In contrast, their captain seemed to be unduly harsh on himself.

While he made no secret of his displeasure in the dressing room, Sachin continued to display exemplary composure in public. Earlier in the tour, he had offered a straight bat to a shocker of a revelation by an Indian journalist during an interview. The journalist had been befriended by someone who claimed to be a 'bookmaker' placing bets on cricket matches. This 'bookmaker' had sought the journalist's help to approach no less a person than Sachin himself to help him 'fix' matches. The journalist, having smelt a story, played along. When asked by the journalist if he had ever received such an offer, Sachin replied in the negative and emphasized that he felt privileged to represent his country. He also told the journalist that anybody who would make such an offer to him would find himself behind bars.

The journalist did a story on his encounter with the 'bookie', which made the headlines back in India for a few days.

There was little or no time for anyone associated with Indian cricket to reflect on what was or was not happening, what with one of the longest seasons in the history of Indian cricket simply refusing to end. Within hours of their return from the Caribbean, the Indian players took the field against New Zealand at Bengaluru in a league game of the Independence Cup, a quadrangular tournament organized to commemorate the Golden Jubilee of India's freedom. It was the first-ever cricket tournament to be held on Indian soil in May, a time of the year when the heat and humidity across the country were known to rise to unbearable levels. To circumvent the elements as much as possible, all matches were scheduled to be played under lights and start as late as 5:00 p.m.

Sachin did not display any fatigue while scoring a match-winning century against the Kiwis. However, India's quest to qualify for the best-of-three finals was derailed by successive defeats against its neighbours. Sri Lanka outplayed them at Mumbai and Pakistan won a high-scoring affair at Chennai. The Chennai game was notable in that Saeed Anwar established a world record for the highest individual score in ODIs. He scored 194, with Shahid Afridi running for him for nearly two-thirds of the innings. As fielding captain, Sachin had the option of turning down Anwar's request for a runner when he complained of cramps, but he chose to be magnanimous.

There was to be an ironic postscript to this episode, seven years later.

Sachin fancied his team's chances of chasing down the target of 324, but his early dismissal to a brilliant catch by Inzamam-ul-Haq proved to be a dampener. Rahul Dravid batted superbly to register his maiden ODI hundred, and Vinod Kambli, who had returned to the side after missing the tours of South Africa and the West Indies, scored 65. However, the lower order could not sustain the momentum and India fell 35 runs short. Sachin's involvement in the best-of-three finals was limited to being one of the Indian captains who was felicitated by the CAB and BCCI during the mid-innings break of the second final at Kolkata. Sri Lanka beat Pakistan in both finals to take the trophy.

Much to Sachin's consternation, the new season, which commenced a couple of months after the Independence Cup, got off to a bizarre start. Kambli was discarded for the ODI leg of the Sri Lanka tour despite his 65 in India's last ODI against Pakistan at Chennai. Replacing him in the squad was Mohammed Azharuddin.

> I should be expecting from the players. If I am going to fight for the player then I have a right to expect from the player. I will try and support my players all the time but in return they too have to perform for me.
>
> —Sachin Tendulkar, *The Sportstar*, 3 May 1997

Those were bizarre times. Azharuddin had been left out of the squad for the Independence Cup and the selectors had even been quoted as saying that the former India captain had paid the price for his reckless batting in the Caribbean. However, the same selection panel had recalled Azharuddin just a couple of months later, that too at the expense of a batsman who had scored a fine 65 in India's last game of the Independence Cup.

The selectors also replaced Mongia with Saba Karim. There were reports that Sachin and Ramakant Desai, the chairman of selectors, had fought tooth-and-nail for both Kambli and Mongia, but were overruled by the four other members of the committee.

Sachin had no option but to make do with what had been given to him, but he made no secret of his displeasure in an interview to a prominent Bengali publication, wherein he was quoted as saying that he had not been given the best team. Ironically, Desai was among those who reprimanded him—albeit gently—by saying that 'Sachin ought to know the futility of crying over spilt milk in public'. It was even reported that the selectors had seriously considered replacing him as captain and the matter had been put to vote. Apparently, he had scraped through with a 3–2 margin. He had also been quoted by the newspaper as saying that he was not enamoured of the captaincy.

If he was looking forward to some fruitful training sessions at the start of India's second visit to Sri Lanka in two years, then he was in for a disappointment.

Hours after the team's arrival, news broke out that a prominent Indian periodical had published an interview with Rashid Latif, the Pakistani wicketkeeper, wherein he had claimed that four Indian players who were on the

Sri Lanka tour were on the payroll of bookies. The claim created a furore and all four players denied the allegations. One of them claimed to have received a fax from Latif denying the interview. Subsequent events would prove that Latif wasn't the only individual who was in a state of 'denial'. Most cricket lovers, cricketers and cricket administrators opted to look the other way till the proverbial s**t hit the fan in 2000.

The Asia Cup followed an all-too-familiar narrative, with the invincible Sri Lankan side of the mid-1990s steamrolling its opponents to clinch the title. In yet another tournament played in Sri Lanka that featured rain as one of the protagonists, the consolation for Indian fans was that their team made it to the final at the expense of Pakistan and Bangladesh. The India–Pakistan face-off lasted only three overs.

The two-Test series that followed was nightmarish for the bowlers. Centuries by Sachin and Azharuddin in the first Test at Colombo took India to a score of 537-8, their highest on Sri Lankan soil. Nilesh Kulkarni, the left-arm spinner and one of the chief architects of Mumbai's Ranji Trophy triumph in 1996–97, became the first Indian bowler to take a wicket with his first ball in Test cricket when he had Marvan Atapattu, the Sri Lankan opener, caught behind. What happened next was sensational. Sanath Jayasuriya and Roshan Mahanama rewrote the record-books with a partnership of 576, then the highest-ever in Test history. Sri Lanka closed at 952-7, the highest-ever total in Test history. Jayasuriya, who had made quite a habit of feasting on the Indian bowling, was only 35 short of Brian Lara's 375 when he was caught at bat-pad off Rajesh Chauhan. Mahanama scored 235.

The second Test at Kandy also ended in a stalemate. India's centurions were Sachin and Ganguly in the first innings, and Azharuddin in the second. Normal service was on view in the three-match bilateral ODI series that followed, with the Sri Lankans making a clean sweep. The first match was a humdinger. Chasing 303, India were staring at an ignominious defeat at 64-4 when Azharuddin and Jadeja turned it around with a stand that realized 263. However, the visitors faltered at the final hurdle and finished at 300-7. They were outplayed in the next two games.

India's next assignment—the second edition of the annual bilateral series against Pakistan at Toronto—was preceded by speculation that some of the selectors were keen to hand the captaincy back to Azharuddin, who had batted well in both the Tests and ODIs in Sri Lanka. Like the former captain, Sachin had scored two centuries in the Tests in Sri Lanka. Yet, some quarters were trying to create an impression that Sachin's batting was falling apart due to the 'pressures of captaincy'.

> I got to spend a lot of time with Sachin on the tour of Sri Lanka in 1997, on which he was captain and I was the manager. As the captain, he was totally involved in everything on and off the field. I remember him being very upset on the first day of the Asia Cup when he discovered that the Indian tricolour had been hoisted upside down. He told me to speak to the liaison officer and get it sorted. It was a long tour of 43 days, which comprised the Asia Cup, a Test series and a bilateral ODI series. As it went on, I found him disturbed. A captain is only as good as his team. He felt that the team wasn't contributing as much as he wanted it to. Then, there was that article in the *Outlook* magazine in which some players were named. We ended up losing some close games on that tour, and there was a lot of loose talk on whether everything was right in the dressing room. That hurt him deeply.
>
> —Prof. R.S. Shetty, personal interview

The lacklustre showing in Sri Lanka ensured that India were the underdogs at the start of the second edition of the bilateral series against Pakistan at Toronto. Ramiz Raja was in charge and Aaqib Javed was the pace-bowling spearhead. Waqar Younis was injured, as was Wasim Akram, who was roped in for commentary by the official broadcaster. He held his own in the company of stalwarts like Sunil Gavaskar, Geoffrey Boycott and Harsha Bhogle and turned out to be Pakistan's only noteworthy performer in the series.

At the forefront of India's 4–1 triumph was Sourav Ganguly, who finished the series with 222 runs, 15 wickets and an appellation bestowed by Geoffrey Boycott—The Prince of Kolkata. The same people who had criticized Sachin's captaincy after the reverses in South Africa and the Caribbean were now praising him for his man-management and bowling changes.

After a warm welcome in India, the players took off to Pakistan for a three-match ODI series. The hosts won the first game at Hyderabad, and the second, played at Karachi, was a thriller. Batting first, Pakistan were going strong at 265–4 in the 48th over when the Indian outfielders, not for the first time, complained about rubbish being hurled at them from the stands. The Pakistan innings was declared closed at that point and India were asked to chase 266 in 47 overs.

Sachin, who had scored a solitary 50 in Toronto, fell cheaply. Ganguly batted well in the company of Kambli, who had returned to the side after missing the Asia Cup. The left-handers added 98 before falling in quick succession.

Pakistan regained control when both Azharuddin and Jadeja perished without making an impression. The workmanlike duo of Robin Singh and Saba Karim then joined hands and brought India to the brink of victory with a run-a-ball stand of 62 before Karim was bowled by Waqar in the penultimate over. When Rajesh Chauhan, the new man in, took a single off Waqar's last ball, a nervous Geoffrey Boycott quipped, 'That is good, and bad!' What he thought was 'bad' was that Chauhan had retained the strike when India would have rather Robin Singh had it.

With eight needed from six balls, Chauhan found himself facing fellow off-spinner Saqlain Mushtaq, who was not thrilled at having to operate with a newish white ball, after the original one lost its colour and had to be replaced. A newish ball was not quite as conducive to a good 'grip' as an older one. However, the job had to be done. The offie attempted a quick yorker, but the delivery that flew from his grip was full and its height a lot more than what he intended. In other words, it was hittable, and Chauhan obliged. The ball flew off the 'sweet spot' of his bat over long-on. Two singles later, India were celebrating a famous victory. Both teams were expected to come hard at each other in the series decider at Lahore, but Ijaz Ahmed's blistering hundred made it a no-contest.

If the scorelines of the two ODI series against Pakistan were to be combined, then India had won five matches to Pakistan's three. It was therefore surprising to come across reports that some of the selectors were determined to make Sachin 'pay' for his comments after the selection of the side for the Asia Cup earlier in the year, and remove him as captain.

The victory at Toronto had led Sachin to believe that his team had turned the corner. With Javagal Srinath back in action, Sachin expected his outfit to dominate the upcoming home series against Sri Lanka. However, things did not proceed as per plan. While Sri Lanka were an exceptional limited-overs side, they were still some years away from becoming an outstanding Test side. Arjuna Ranatunga, the Sri Lankan captain, probably had his team's 0–3 rout in 1993–94 at the back of his mind, when he decided to go on the defensive. As he viewed it, the series was India's to win, and so it was up to the home team to do what it could. The first Test at Mohali ended in a tame draw and the second at Nagpur was affected by rain. Sachin pulled out all stops in the third game at Mumbai.

He had not been among the runs since the Toronto series, and he found the going tough when he went in to bat late on the first day of the Test. He was unbeaten on eight at stumps. Unable to sleep that night, he called Atul Ranade, his friend, to the hotel, and the two drove to the temple of Lord Ganesh at Shivaji Park, where Sachin had been a 'regular' since his Shardashram days.

They then drove to Haji Ali in central Mumbai and sipped juice, all the while discussing everything but cricket. For Sachin, the time spent with his friend was far more therapeutic than a full night's sleep. The following morning, he added a fluent 140 to his overnight 8*. He dedicated his first Test hundred on his home ground to Sara, his newly born daughter.

The game was interestingly poised when Sachin declared India's second innings at 181–9 on the fourth evening and set Sri Lanka 333 to win in 94 overs. Sanath Jayasuriya and Marvan Atapattu put on 58 before Chauhan broke through, having Atapattu caught by Kumble. Jayasuriya fell 15 runs later and all of India was ecstatic when Aravinda de Silva, Sri Lanka's premier bat, fell shortly after the score had crossed 100.

Aravinda's dismissal was the outcome of street-smart cricket or gamesmanship, depending upon which way one looked at it. He pulled Srinath to what he had thought was an unmanned mid-wicket region, only to see Rajesh Chauhan emerge from nowhere to take the catch. It was claimed by some that Chauhan had darted from deep square-leg to deep mid-wicket *after* Srinath had started his run-up, and no one had noticed him doing so, not even Mahanama, the non-striker, who had brought an earlier attempt by an Indian fielder to move after the bowler had started running in, to the notice of the umpires.

Those who believed in 'poetic justice' would have smiled when the home team's prospects of victory were dampened, quite literally, by unseasonal rain. Sri Lanka were 166–7 when the match was called off.

A victory in the match and series would have given Sachin a shot in the arm just before he met the selectors next. Instead, what he got from them were explicit instructions that he should bat in the middle order in the ODI series against Sri Lanka and the tournament that had been slotted before it—a quadrangular tournament at Sharjah that also featured Pakistan, England and the West Indies. England turned out to be the surprise winners, in what was their first visit to Sharjah for over a decade. India on the other hand failed to even open their account. They came close to beating the eventual champions in their opening game, losing by seven runs despite Sachin's 91 off 87 balls. He seemed in control of the chase when, with 18 needed, he went down the track to Matthew Fleming, only to discover that the ball wasn't quite there to be hit over the top. The ball slipped under his bat and crashed into the stumps.

Pakistan had the better of the 'Friday' encounter as usual, despite Ganguly's 90, and the last and final league game against the West Indies was a disaster. Needing 230 to win, openers Ganguly and Sidhu put on 87, but the middle order could not sustain the momentum. Particularly galling was the fact that as many as eight Indian wickets were taken by slow bowlers, two of them being 'non-specialists'. While Rawl Lewis, the lone 'specialist' spinner in the Windies XI, took one wicket, specialist batsmen Carl Hooper and Shivnarine Chanderpaul bagged 4–37 and 3–18 respectively. A senior Indian player batted and ran as if he had a flight to catch, till his luck ran out, literally and figuratively. One of India's biggest cricketing names, who was doing commentary at the time, was enraged enough to say that 'there would be no tomorrow for the player'.

The selectors disagreed and retained the player for the three-match ODI series against Sri Lanka. Bafflingly, Rahul Dravid, who had scored 31 in his only outing at Sharjah against the West Indies, was left out. Here was a player who had scored 34, 92, 93 and 85 in the Test series against Sri Lanka, and 50 in the only ODI that he got to play on the short tour of Pakistan. Memories of his 107 against Pakistan in the Independence Cup and 80 against South Africa at Durban, both in the shorter versions of the game, were still fresh. It was difficult to comprehend how a player of his class could be branded as one suitable only for Test cricket.

One did not have to be an expert to deduce that the next World Cup, to be hosted by England in the first and traditionally 'wetter' half of its summer in 1999, would be played in conditions conducive to seam and swing, which would pose a challenge to the most impeccable of batting techniques; it was therefore critical that a batsman like Dravid, who possessed the technique and temperament to do battle in bowler-friendly conditions, was made to feel at home by the people who mattered. But that wasn't happening for the moment.

The captain did not disagree with the view that there was room for improvement, in that Dravid needed to rotate the strike more effectively in the shorter version. However, leaving the Karnataka batsman out of the side altogether made little sense. A batsman of his calibre deserved opportunities, not the axe. He was far too committed a cricketer and professional to not work on his shortcomings and rectify them sooner than later. However, there was nothing the captain could do to help, with diktats having been issued to him as well.

Those were indeed weird times.

India beat Sri Lanka in the first ODI, played at Guwahati, by seven wickets, largely thanks to Sachin's 82. The second game at Indore was abandoned after three overs of play, as the pitch was deemed 'dangerous', and an exhibition encounter played on an adjacent pitch to assuage the capacity crowd. Sri Lanka squared the series with a five-wicket win in the final game at Margao, which was India's last in the calendar year of 1997.

Many of us found it difficult to match his expectations. His demands and anticipation of his teammates' performances originated from his own talent. Lesser mortals found the going tough even to understand their roles, never mind the whole business of taking on the pressure of international cricket. Every time he was in charge, a curious pattern of a slump in form followed. To others, it may not have been a slump, but by his standards, it was. Sachin took some time to realize that it is not practical to expect others to emulate his feats. Basically, his talent was inborn and those skills cannot be acquired or transferred to anyone. The loss of any game under his captaincy worked him up so much that it preyed on his batting abilities.

—Javagal Srinath, *India Today*, September 2010

The statistics contradicted the claims that captaincy had affected Sachin's batting. He scored over 1,000 runs in both forms in the calendar year of 1997 and proved with his run-a-ball 91 against England at Sharjah that he had lost none of his belligerence. What was certainly concerning was his record as captain; he had led India in 54 ODIs, of which the team had lost 31 and won only 17. In the traditional form, Sachin had led in 17 Tests and won only thrice, and not one of those triumphs had been achieved in 1997.

This team needs two years of good exposure and there will be positive results.... I think we should have 15-day camps before such tours [to Australia, South Africa and West Indies]. The camp should be on hard wickets and should be run in a professional manner for not only those who are selected, but also for 25 probables. And the probables should be genuine India material.... It is important for the players to know each other.... And these probables should have a camp before the commencement of the season. They will then know that they may be called at any time as a replacement and they will know their role. And I think if a player is exceptionally talented, he should be included in the camp.... Another important need in India is indoor facilities. We don't have bowling machines. Well, during the off-season, I should be able to go to the indoor hall and practice for hours at any time...even at night.

—Sachin Tendulkar, *The Sportstar*, 1 March 1997

Sachin's stint as captain had started in much the same way as his career as a player, with a succession of challenging assignments. The tours he had undertaken in the late 1980s and early 1990s had only made him a better batsman. There was no doubt in the minds of his supporters, least of all in his own, that the various situations—most of them stressful—that he had encountered in his first year-and-a-half as captain had taught him and his side quite a bit. It had taken him a while to figure out that he could not lead India the way he did Mumbai. The Indian team wasn't half as potent a force at the international level as Mumbai was at the domestic level. He had realized the need to adjust and adapt. Under him, India had very nearly won the third Test in South Africa and they had produced better cricket than the West Indies over five Tests, save the last three hours of the Bridgetown game. There were still quite a few months left in the 'two years' that Sachin had requested his team be given to prove itself.

On 2 January 1998, news came through that Sachin had been removed from the captaincy. He was conveyed the news by the media.

The selectors entrusted the reins to someone who had been on the 'hit-list' just six months previously.

ANNUS MIRABILIS

The captain and the manager have no vote at all.... I am the one who handles the side and I must have the players I want.

—Sachin Tendulkar, *The Sportstar*, 3 May 1997

When the captaincy was taken away from him in the first week of 1998, Sachin had two options. He could either feel sorry for himself and sulk or he could move on and focus on doing what he did best—bat. Those who had followed his career since his inter-school days said that they were not surprised when he chose the latter, as that is what they had known him to do whenever he had been confronted by adversity and negativity.

For all his greatness as a cricketer, Sachin would not have been human had he not been rattled by the events of 1997. For all his greatness as a batsman, he was, at the end of the day, not even 25 years old, and he had spent the better part of the last 14 years on the cricket field. The impetuous young adult within him was bound to resurface every now and then, as the teenager had on several occasions in the years gone by. The near-misses and inexplicable defeats from winning positions, especially in the West Indies, had disturbed him to the extent that he had spoken to his wife about quitting cricket. She had, of course, heard him out and then calmed him down.

> Though he has a wonderful mind for captaincy and cricket, you don't like to bog your most talented player in that role. You need to put him loose. You need to tell him, 'Go on, take them tiger.'
>
> —Viv Richards, *Outlook*, 4 January 1999

An individual who was so used to having his way and dictating the proceedings on the field, would have found it difficult to come to terms with the setbacks as captain. The genius within him did figure out eventually that what came easily to him did not necessarily come easily to others. However, what he found difficult to accept was that the team comprised some individuals who did not seem to be as committed as he was.

I felt we were not all heading in the right direction and it was affecting me as a person. I couldn't switch off at all. Even 10 days after a match, I would be thinking about why this happened and why that happened, and it started affecting me as a person. Not as a player, as some people pointed out, because I scored over 1,000 runs in both forms of the game that last year [1997]. Also, I felt there was lack of support from every direction.... No, not the team, but from outside. I felt that if everyone had spent their energy in the right direction, we could have moved ahead.... I was not happy with the selectors at all. It just didn't work out. They had different ideas, I had different ideas. The only thing is, I had to go in there and play with their ideas.

—Sachin Tendulkar, *Wisden Asia Cricket*, 2004

Team India's first assignment of 1998 was a tri-series in Bangladesh, against the hosts and Pakistan. Sachin batted at number four in his first game 'back in the ranks', and contributed a sedate 54 to a four-wicket win over Bangladesh. The team management, comprising Mohammed Azharuddin, the 'new' skipper and Anshuman Gaekwad, who had taken over as coach from Madan Lal prior to the Sri Lanka series, restored the new 'former captain' to the opening slot for the next game against Pakistan. Sachin responded with a pugnacious 67 off only 44 balls, and then held a record four catches, including one off his own bowling, as India won by 18 runs.

He followed this innings with another stunner in the first of the best-of-three finals against the 'old enemy'. Sachin first excelled with the ball, taking 3–45 and helped restrict Pakistan to 212–8. The Indian openers then reduced the contest to a farce by putting on 159. Much to the disappointment of the spectators, Sachin fell five short of a hundred. His 95, which took him only 78 balls to score, was replete with drives—carpet and aerial, flicks both behind and in front of square on the leg-side, cuts both behind and in front of square on the off-side and sweeps that ranged from the traditional to the 'paddle'. The innings comprised six fours and five sixes. When his individual score reached 45, he became the first Indian to complete 6,000 runs in ODIs.

Pakistani supporters and the tournament organizers were ecstatic when Rashid Latif's side won the second final, thus setting up a grand finale on Sunday, 18 January 1998.

Latif may well have been surprised when Azharuddin won the toss and asked the opposition to bat at the start of the third final. While there was a bit of moisture in the track, one would have thought the side winning the toss in a final would want to put runs on the board rather than chase. Pakistan feasted on India's magnanimity to amass 314–5 from 48 overs, with Saeed Anwar and Ijaz Ahmed, two batters who loved the Indian bowling, scoring centuries. To win the game, and with it the tournament, India had to go where no team had gone before in ODIs. No side had ever scored that many to win a game.

India and Sachin started in sensational fashion. He attacked Aaqib Javed, but reserved his best for Azhar Mahmood, the other new-ball bowler. In the sixth over of the innings, Azhar was hit for four consecutive boundaries. Sachin began with a slightly mistimed loft off a no-ball, which had enough in it to cross the rope. The next ball, he lifted off his toes to find the long-on boundary. The one after that, he neatly bisected the two men in the covers. He then cleared the infield on the leg-side for the second time in the over. Back on strike for the first ball of Aaqib's next over, he deftly glanced past the keeper for another boundary, to bring up India's 50. Later in the over, he flicked the bowler to fine-leg for another four. By this stage, the fielding team was running ragged. Latif and his players could only watch as Sachin hit Saqlain's first ball of the innings out of the ground. However, the offensive was far too overwhelming for even Sachin to sustain. In going for a six off Shahid Afridi, Sachin holed out to long-off. India at that stage were 71–1 in 8.2 overs. The Pakistanis were delirious.

As he returned to the pavilion, Sachin would have noticed the player who passed him. Azharuddin had asked the left-handed Robin Singh to have a go at number three.

As the second-wicket partnership between the new batsman and Ganguly developed, Sachin would have reflected on the irony; a month previously, he had sent in the same batsman at number four to get a move on against Pakistan at Sharjah, but Singh had fallen third ball for a duck, and India had gone on to lose! At Dhaka, not only was Singh keeping the scoreboard ticking, but he was also matching Ganguly stroke for stroke.

The drama that followed befitted a contest between the traditional rivals, even when there was no cricket happening. The light was deteriorating rapidly as the Indian innings progressed. The floodlights that had been erected specifically for football matches were switched on, but they were obviously inadequate. At one point, the umpires decided to take the players off on grounds of poor light, but the Indians protested, and the match referee eventually ruled that the game be completed. Singh fell for a splendid 82 and Ganguly perished in the gloom for a magnificent 124. Visibility was next to nil by the time Saqlain was thrown the ball for the final over, from which India needed nine runs with three wickets in hand. On strike was the left-handed Hrishikesh Kanitkar, an all-rounder from

Maharashtra who was playing his third ODI. Saqlain's first ball was short and Kanitkar pulled it well, keeping the ball down, but it went so rapidly to the fielder at deep square-leg that the batsmen could take only one. Kanitkar was cross with himself for not placing the ball on either side of the fielder. He swore that if he received another delivery like that, he would hit it for four. Javagal Srinath swung at the second ball, connected and the batsmen completed a frantic two. The third ball, the Indian paceman went for an almighty heave. The ball ballooned into the air, but fortunately for India, it landed right in between as many as three Pakistani players. The batsmen collected another precious two in the process, and Srinath poked at the fourth delivery to get a single. Kanitkar had a quick conference with his partner and took a deep breath as he awaited Saqlain's fifth ball, with India needing three from two. The penultimate delivery of the game was slightly short and the left-hander kept the promise he had made to himself; he swung it hard and handsomely for four. Among those who celebrated the hardest after the win was Sachin, who shouted so much that he almost lost his voice.

That win in the Dhaka darkness put both the Indian cricket team as well as the average Indian cricket follower in the right frame of mind for the next contest.

A year-and-a-half after it was instituted, the Border–Gavaskar Trophy was up for grabs once again, this time in a full series of three Tests.

The Shane Keith Warne who landed in India as the bowling lynchpin of Mark Taylor's team was unrecognizable from the slightly overweight debutant who had taken a solitary wicket in the first two Tests of his career, both against India in 1991–92. The likes of Shastri, Sachin and Azharuddin had scored heavily against him back then, and the Sri Lankan batsmen had done likewise in what was his third Test, at Colombo in August 1992. It was in the second innings of that game that everything changed. Needing 181 to win, the hosts were cruising at 127-2, only to be bowled out for 164. Warne applied the finishing touches to one of the most remarkable Test wins of all time, with three wickets. He ended 1992 with a match-winning 7-52 against the West Indies in the Boxing Day Test, a performance that cemented his place in the side.

Warne then took a series-winning 17 wickets from three Tests against New Zealand, and was marked out as one of the players to watch out for in the 1993 Ashes. Allan Border, his first captain, deliberately 'underbowled' him in the three-day games and left him out of the ODIs that preceded the Tests. Warne's first ball in an Ashes Test was a leg-break that drifted towards leg, pitched just outside leg and turned right across Mike Gatting to hit the off-stump. From that point onwards, there was never any doubt that Australia would retain the Ashes.

Warne finished the Ashes with 34 wickets from six Tests, the highest-ever by a leg-spinner. In the years that followed, he only enhanced his reputation against the best of teams and batsmen.

However, there was some unfinished business. He was yet to bowl to the world's best players of spin in a Test series. The 1996 World Cup game at Mumbai excepted, the Indian batsmen had treated him with scant respect in his limited-overs tussles against them in the mid-1990s. The leg-spinner was keen to set the record straight.

In a way, Sachin's fans had reason to be grateful to Warne and the Australians. Had the world's number one team and number one spin bowler not toured India at that stage, he might have taken a little more time to recover from the hurts of 1997. The thought of pitting his strengths against those of arguably the greatest slow bowler of all time excited him. Paradoxically, that he was no longer the captain was a blessing in disguise. He could now concentrate on his own preparations for the series in general and Warne in particular without having to focus on the preparations of his teammates as well.

To combat the leg-spinner, Sachin eked out a strategy that was a combination of brawn and brain. In the weeks preceding the series, he studied Warne at length and concluded that the drift towards the right-hander's leg-side that Warne generated before pitching the ball, was dangerous and needed to be neutralized. To tackle the possibility of the ball landing in the 'blind' spot on the leg-stump, Sachin decided to adopt a slightly open stance and stand outside the leg-stump when the leggie was in operation. He also decided to stay within the crease as much as possible and play as late as possible. He also made up his mind to employ horizontal-bat strokes on either side of the wicket. Hitting a bowler of Warne's calibre on the leg-side, against the turn, was fraught with risk, but Sachin trusted his reflexes and ability to do so.

> I recall him getting ready to tackle Shane Warne on an Australian tour of India. Conventional wisdom would dictate that Indian batsmen get ready to counter Australian pace, given the state of things, but conventional wisdom would be wrong. What sense does it make to plan for pace when the pitches support spin? Sachin was perhaps the only member of the team who understood that. And he took the trouble of asking Laxman Sivaramakrishnan to bowl at him, around the wicket, into the bowlers' rough. The rest is history, clichés be damned. I remember that practice session largely because it impressed upon me Sachin's unorthodox intelligence. Here was a batsman who had spotted a potential loophole and was working on

it. He wasn't going through the motions as many do, no matter how hard they practise. Practice alone does not make your perfect. Only perfect practice makes you perfect.

—Geoffrey Boycott, *India Today*, 25 November 2013

Sivaramakrishnan apart, Sachin also faced other slow bowlers who were proficient in the art of turning the ball 'away' from the right-handers, in the nets. The leg-spinners and left-arm orthodox spinners were instructed to pitch the ball in a specially scuffed-up 'rough' outside the right-hander's leg-stump. Sairaj Bahutule and Nilesh Kulkarni were among those who enlisted. Sachin countered them with horizontal-bat strokes like sweeps, paddle-sweeps, slog-sweeps, pulls and cuts.

This 'customized' training before a series or tournament was something that he did throughout his career. He would assess the strengths and weaknesses of the opposition, the likely conditions and of course, the format, and train accordingly. His methods of preparing for a Test series, for instance, were thus entirely different from the way he trained for a limited-overs competition like the World Cup.

Years later, he did something unconventional at the MCA's academy ground, on the eve of a tour of Australia. Water was sprinkled on a plastic sheet laid on the batting half of a pitch. A group of bowlers, armed with rubber balls dipped in a bucket of water, was instructed to pitch every delivery short of a length. The rubber balls kept taking off after landing on the damp plastic sheet, and Sachin ducked, left, cut and pulled to his heart's content.

The Australians began their tour in early 1998 with a three-day game against Mumbai, the reigning Ranji champions, at Mumbai's Brabourne Stadium. The visitors won the toss and scored 305. Mumbai commenced their first innings, mindful of Sachin's exhortations to 'play the ball and not the bowler'. Sanjay Manjrekar, who went in at the fall of the first wicket, reminded the young opener in the middle of the skipper's words, when Warne was introduced into the attack.

Amit Pagnis, who had led India in the under-19 World Cup at the start of the year, took the advice to heart and attacked Warne from the outset. The opener scored 50 off only 60 deliveries before being dismissed. Sachin defended the first two balls he received. The third ball, he hit over mid-wicket for six.

The innings played by the Mumbai captain was reminiscent of his performances in inter-school cricket against hapless opponents. By the time he was dismissed, he had batted for four hours, in which he scored an unbelievable 204 off only 192 balls. It was his first-ever double century in first-class cricket. Warne went for 111 runs from 16 overs. Buoyed by their captain's innings,

Mumbai's bowlers bowled the Australians out for 135 in the second innings and the home team completed a sensational 10-wicket win on the third afternoon. It was a rare instance of a regional side outplaying the best international side in the world.

The euphoria was tinged with sadness; the three-day game signalled the end of a career that had started promisingly but faded out subsequently. Sanjay Manjrekar had earmarked the game as the last of his first-class career. He had in a way, gone the opposite way of Warne.

> Manjrekar's technique when he started out was almost faultless. But as happens to most batsmen when fast bowlers start to pound away, a little bit of experimentation to combat them leads to a slight change in technique. In Manjrekar's case, it has been the lowering of the bottom hand towards the shoulder of the bat. His bottom hand being more dominant than the left hand has resulted in him opening the face of the bat unconsciously and thus being consumed in the slips.... Some may point to Tendulkar and say he too has a low grip but in his case, it has been a natural one and so he has been comfortable playing off either foot with that grip. Manjrekar also has developed a slightly open-faced way of playing and his right foot, instead of remaining parallel to the crease, now points more towards covers than cover-point. This makes his right shoulder drop a bit and thus squared up, he has been encountering difficulties against the quicks. His temperament is still top-class and so long as he is batting with players other than Tendulkar, he is composed and unflappable. But when he is batting with Tendulkar, he gives the impression of wanting to match him.
>
> —Sunil Gavaskar, *The Sportstar*, 7 December 1996

At the start of his career, Sachin had looked up to Manjrekar. The two spent a lot of time with each other on the field, putting together crucial partnerships for Mumbai and India. They spent a lot more time with each other off the field. Although they were eight years apart in terms of age, they had started their respective international careers at around the same time and so had a lot in common. However, the expectations that cricket lovers had from them with regard of the 1990s were strikingly different—Manjrekar was supposed to take over the mantle of the Indian team's premier batsman and eventually the captaincy, and in the process, 'groom' Sachin to become a world-beater and hand over charge at some point, probably in the second half of the decade. But the tour of Australia in 1991–92 changed everything. Sachin superseded

Manjrekar and kept marching ahead in the seasons that followed. Manjrekar on the other hand seemed to have lost confidence in himself after unsuccessful tours of Australia and South Africa.

Although he returned to the national side in the 1993–94 season after missing a year of international cricket, he was never the same player again, despite some fine performances. Against the West Indies at Mumbai in 1994–95, Manjrekar successfully weathered storms in both innings to score 51 in the first and 66 in the second, and was one of the chief architects of India's 96-run victory. However, that he did not go the distance in at least one—if not both—innings, hurt him deeply. It was not in keeping with the traditions of Mumbai batsmanship that he had been brought up on. Once a batsman's individual score had crossed 30, it meant that he had got his eye in and he just had to get a hundred, unless he got an unplayable ball or fell to a brilliant catch. Manjrekar's dismissal in the second innings had therefore rankled both him and his fans. After doing all the hard work, he had given mid-on catching practice with an uppish drive. There is an unconfirmed account of something that happened when Manjrekar was making his way to the dressing room after his dismissal in the second innings. His eyes met those of a Mumbai and India all-time great on the edge of the boundary line. Words were superfluous as both men knew what the other was thinking; he ought to have made that innings count.

Cricket was, at the end of the day, a game played between the ears, after all. A match-winning century against a competitive West Indies attack might well have given Manjrekar a second wind. But that was not to be. He tried opening, but did not impress as one against South Africa at Ahmedabad in 1996–97 and he wasn't given another chance. In keeping with the maxim that there are some things that just don't change, he was run out even in his last first-class game.

Sachin had won Round One of his duel with Warne, as it were, but he was smart enough to have noted that most of Warne's deliveries to him had been leg-breaks. Not only had the genius not displayed his entire repertoire of variations, but he had also not pitched a single delivery in the 'rough' outside the right-hander's leg-stump.

Australia got off to a flying start in the first Test at Chennai. Despite losing the toss and the Indian openers putting on over a hundred, they bowled India out for 257 and then recovered from 137–6 to reach 328. In India's first innings, Warne took 4–85, one of his victims being Sachin. Eager to seize the initiative, Sachin drove the first ball that he faced from the leg-spinner for four. He went for another booming drive off the fifth, but the ball dipped quicker than he had anticipated and it went off the outside edge to Taylor at slip. Round Two had gone to Warne.

Kumble then emulated his Australian counterpart by taking four wickets. The bounce that he was extracting from the pitch, which bordered on the unpredictable, resulted in one of cricket's first instances of a wicketkeeper wearing a helmet with a visor while standing up to the spinners. Nayan Mongia did not know it then, but he was a trendsetter.

Anshuman Gaekwad, who like Mongia was a resident of Vadodara, was a worried man when India started their second innings, 71 runs in arrears. The Indian coach reckoned that only one man could dissipate the tension in the camp. Sachin assured him that he would do his best. He may not have been the official 'captain' anymore, but he remained his team's 'hero'.

Warne posed no problems to Navjot Sidhu, who repeatedly pasted him across and beyond the ground. Sachin came in when the Punjab opener fell after scoring his second 50 of the game. The score was 115–2. Already in the middle was Rahul Dravid, who had not allowed all the aspersions that were being cast on his capabilities as a 'limited-overs' batsman to affect his fluency in the traditional version. He had scored 52 in the first innings and seemed to be in fine nick in the second.

Sachin began by playing Warne *with* the turn, on the off-side. A short delivery was brutally smashed to the cover boundary. Sachin followed it up by outsmarting off-spinner Gavin Robertson. When Robertson pitched one up, Sachin plonked his front foot down the crease and slog-swept him over mid-wicket for six. Robertson then sought to compensate with a short one; Sachin, who was waiting, went onto the back foot and pulled him for four. A two off Reiffel took him to 50 and India to 200.

The moment everybody, Sachin included, had been waiting for since the arrival of the Australians, finally came in the second session of the third day. Warne came in for a fresh over and indicated to the umpire that he was going to bowl around the wicket. Sachin responded with an open stance.

Warne pitched a leg-break on middle. He was slog-swept to the mid-wicket boundary. The Australian then landed one in the rough outside the leg-stump. Sachin slog-swept him again, and this time, the ball landed in the stands. All the practice had made him perfect. The assault had only just begun.

Sachin was on song. One of his many strokes that left watchers gaping was a cross-batted thump *with* the turn, off a short delivery by Warne; the cherry flew through the covers for four. It wasn't too different a delivery from those that Sachin had played *against* the turn, earlier in his innings. One genius was outsmarting the other.

Sachin also demonstrated that he was as deft as he was daring. A leg-glance off Michael Kasprowicz gave him four runs and his 15th Test century. He then quite deliberately nicked Mark Waugh past Ian Healy, the wicketkeeper, for a couple of boundaries. The cascade of strokes ended when Azharuddin declared at 418-4, India 347 ahead. The visitors then came apart against the resurrected spin triumvirate of Kumble, Raju and Chauhan, to be dismissed for 168. Sachin had won Round Three of his duel with Warne with a knockout. He was the obvious choice for the individual award.

India completely dominated the next Test at Kolkata, handing the Australians one of their heaviest Test defeats—by an innings and 219 runs, and taking the series in the process. Sachin was among the runs again, but he was outscored by Laxman and Sidhu, who put on 191 as openers, Dravid, who scored 86, and Azharuddin, who reached triple figures for the fifth time in an Eden Test.

It wasn't as if Warne and Robertson had been bowling badly; it was just that the Indian batsmen, 'born and bred' on spin, were adept at reading their minds. In a way, it was the reverse of what the Australian quicks had done to Manjrekar and Co. in 1991–92. The Indians, Warne and Robertson were learning the hard way, were as capable of stroking the good balls as they were of punishing the bad ones.

The Australian spinners worked hard in the nets prior to the final Test at Bengaluru. Robertson did his best to follow the advice passed on to him by Erapalli Prasanna, the off-spinning legend, in terms of varying pace and dip to disconcert the batsmen and prevent them from using their feet.

The 'hard work' did not quite work against Sachin, who lorded over the bowling all over again, in a stupendous innings of 177. He was severe on everybody, but as was expected, his treatment of Warne was noticed and noted the most. Sweeps, cuts, drives, pulls and slog-sweeps; there was not one attacking stroke that he did not essay against the leg-spinner. The knock featured 29 hits to the fence and three sixes.

Australia replied to India's 424 with 400. In the second innings, the professionalism of the Australians came to the fore. Despite losing the series, they did not lose heart. Their perseverance was rewarded with success, as India were bowled out for 168. Michael Kasprowicz took five wickets and Warne bagged two, but the most-improved bowler was Robertson. His adherence to Prasanna's prescription yielded him figures of 3-28.

Australia overhauled the target of 194 for the loss of only two wickets, and the game ended with Azharuddin and Mark Taylor, the rival captains, returning to the pavilion with their arms around each other's shoulders. Even as the commentators and others waxed eloquent on the decorous behaviour of the captains that brought a memorable series to an end, Sachin wasn't quite swept away by sentiment. He did not like to lose and could not comprehend how his side had been defeated despite scoring 424 in the first innings.

The Tests were followed by a tri-series that also involved Zimbabwe. Sachin extended his golden run with a round ton against Australia at Kanpur. This was after he had added another feather to his cap by doing a Warne against Warne's team at Kochi. He tied the Australians in knots with his leg-spin and took 5–32, his best bowling figures in ODIs, narrowly missing a hat-trick when Mongia, who had affected two consecutive stumpings, could not hold onto a nick by Warne. What happened to South Africa in the Titan Cup in 1996–97 happened to India in 1997–98, in that they won all their league games but lost the final. Sachin fell early and India were restricted to 227. Australia, who had qualified ahead of Zimbabwe, went on to win by four wickets. The Indians were a disappointed lot when they flew to Sharjah for their next assignment—another tri-series, with Australia and New Zealand also in the fray.

As they say, the Almighty does not give everybody everything. Sachin was in the form of his life when he boarded the plane for Sharjah, but he was not as contented as he ought to have been. The dampeners had been the retirement of his old friend Manjrekar and a horrific injury to an individual whose friendship with him was even older and thicker.

Fate had been rather unkind to Vinod Kambli since his omission from the Indian team after the 1996 World Cup. While he had staged more than one comeback since, he had been let down by a combination of luck and his own inconsistency. He had then made a conscious effort to shed his alleged 'indisciplined' ways and weight, and emerged seven kilos lighter. His new-found resolve was reflected in his performances in domestic cricket in the 1997–98 season. Back in the Indian team for the tri-series against Australia and Zimbabwe, Kambli played the first three games with a reasonable degree of success and was then rested for the fourth and last game, against Zimbabwe at Cuttack. The story goes that when Azharuddin was forced to leave the field to tend to an injury, Harbhajan Singh, the 18-year-old off-spinner who had made his Test debut at Bengaluru, offered to go in as substitute, but Kambli reminded him that he was the senior player and went in himself. What in normal circumstances would have been a stint for a couple of overs ended up being a nightmare, when, in trying to stop a ball, his foot somehow did a 180-degree loop perpendicular to the ground and then bore the entire weight of his body, as he collapsed on top of it. The result was a dislocation, a fracture and two torn ligaments. As he saw his long-time friend being stretchered off the ground, Sachin sank to the ground.

Standing alongside Sachin was Ajit Agarkar, another Achrekar disciple, whose career had been turned on its head by Sachin himself. Agarkar had started off as a batsman and scored heavily for Shardashram. Like Sachin, he had also fancied himself as a quick bowler, but that department was never his priority. In his late teens, he was picked up by the CCI, for whom he bowled second or third-change in the Kanga League. Something stirred within Sachin when he saw Agarkar bowl in a club game; he proceeded to advise the team management to make him bowl more often. Agarkar's response was to pick wickets by the bagful and graduate to 'new-ball' duties. In 1996, Agarkar was representing Mumbai in the Buchi Babu tournament in Chennai when the Indian team was having a camp before Sachin's first assignment as captain—the quadrangular series in Sri Lanka. The Shardashram and CCI senior summoned his junior to the Chidambaram Stadium, where the camp was in progress, and instructed him to 'bounce' the Indian batsmen. The results were encouraging. Agarkar's incisive bowling for Mumbai in the 1996–97 and 1997–98 seasons earned him a call from the national selectors for the tri-series in India.

At Sharjah, Agarkar took a match-winning 4–35 and with it, the individual award, in India's first game of the tri-series, against the Kiwis. Two days later, Australia beat India by 58 runs. Sachin scored a splendid 80 at more than a run-a-ball, but in vain. India's chase of 265 folded up after he was sixth out. The very next day, India played New Zealand and lost. The Kiwis' four-wicket win brought them in contention for a place in the final. They were level with India in terms of points, but their net run-rate was superior. Australia had already qualified with three wins out of three.

India needed to either beat Australia outright or at least overhaul New Zealand's net run-rate in the sixth and last league game of the competition, which got underway at the Sharjah Cricket Ground on the afternoon of 22 April 1998.

Australia won the toss and batted first. Needing 285 to win and 254 to qualify, Sachin and Ganguly got the innings off to a quiet start. Nothing much happened till the fifth ball of the sixth over, when Sachin rushed at Kasprowicz and pulled him off the front foot over mid-wicket for six. The bowler, taken by surprise, sent down the next delivery without taking a few extra seconds to regain his composure. It was another short delivery, and Sachin this time pulled it off the back foot for another six. Game on. Ominously for the Australians, lady luck also appeared to be on Sachin's side. He escaped being run out and a miscued hit by him landed between the keeper and two fielders.

Fleming broke through by trapping Ganguly leg-before at 38. Mongia, promoted to number three, batted assertively. Sachin carried on with his harsh treatment of Kasprowicz. In the bowler's sixth over, Sachin glanced a delivery that had strayed down the leg-side, for four. When Kasprowicz attempted to adjust his line with his next delivery, he was driven off the back foot, through the covers, for four more. Mongia fell for an enterprising 35, shortly after Sachin had completed his individual 50. The pressure was back on India when Azharuddin and Jadeja fell within a few runs of each other. It did appear that India would fall short, but then, Sachin was still in there.

The score had moved to 143–4 at the end of the 31st over, when the game was interrupted. International matches had been known to be halted by rain, hail, poor light, spectator-invasions, bomb scares and even bee-invasions, but a sandstorm was something new, especially for those not living in the UAE. As the players took cover by either running into the dressing room or simply lying on the turf, heads down, Sachin was momentarily terrorized by the thought of being blown away by the sweeping winds. He even lay next to Adam Gilchrist, the Australian wicketkeeper, thinking that he would cling to him if the winds got stronger!

Fortunately, nothing of that sort happened, and Sachin eventually made it to the safety of the dressing room. The storm abated, but took with it 45 minutes of play. The target was revised and the Indians now found themselves needing 133 more from only 15 overs to win and 94 runs to qualify. In an age wherein 'Twenty20' was a term associated only with eyesight and not cricket, both were daunting propositions. Ian and Greg Chappell, both of whom were part of the TV Commentary team, alongside the likes of Sunil Gavaskar, Ravi Shastri, Tony Greig and the sagely Richie Benaud, were of the view that India would not make it. Mark Mascarenhas, who was managing the live telecast, told them that Sachin would 'get the job done'.

> I have not seen another batsman like Sachin in my entire career. I have bowled to many batsmen. Viv Richards was most outstanding and could demolish any bowler with his brutal strokeplay. If anyone can be better than Viv, it is Sachin.
>
> —Kapil Dev, *The Sportstar*, 9 May 1998

The 60 minutes that followed the resumption of play will live forever in the memories of all those who watched the action unfold, either in the flesh or on TV. A belligerent straight hit off Kasprowicz in the first over after the resumption earned Sachin six runs and an epithet from the bowler. After staying on the back foot for most of a Steve Waugh over, Sachin tempted the Australian captain to bowl fuller in his next; when he did that, Sachin came down the wicket, took the ball on the full and hit it over the bowler and umpire for four.

The running between the wickets was frantic, but purposeful. When V.V.S. Laxman, his partner, did not respond to a call for a single, Sachin was livid and let his feelings be known. A flick to square-leg gave Sachin two runs and one of his best-ever centuries.

When Waugh commenced the 42nd over of the innings, India needed 63 to win from 30 balls. But far more important for most Indian cricket lovers was the fact that they needed only 24 more to qualify. Surely, Sachin and Laxman could afford to take it easy now? What happened off the first two balls of the over blew their minds. Sachin slapped the first ball on the up, straight into the sightscreen. The next ball, he slammed in the deep, and not only did Damien Martyn miss a catch after getting his hands to the ball, but he also let it go for four runs. It was then that people realized what they had missed all along. Their hero was playing for a win, not to merely qualify!

During the break, many of Sachin's teammates had felt that they ought to focus on qualifying rather than winning. Sachin had disagreed, although he didn't do so openly. As captain, he had taken his time to come to terms with the fact that what came to him rather easily need not necessarily come to others that easily; as a batsman he now had an opportunity to prove that what others perceived as impossible was in fact achievable.

I don't think anything is impossible. Of course, I am not always right.

—Sachin Tendulkar, as quoted by Rohit Brijnath, *Wisden Asia Cricket*, September 2002

That Waugh over yielded as many as 15 runs, and Sachin kept the strike. The first ball of the next over, bowled by Damien Fleming, was a slower one that Sachin picked early, made room on the leg-side and deposited over the long-on boundary. It was his sixth six. By this time, qualifying had ceased to matter; what mattered was that India needed 42 from 23 balls *to win*.

A flicked two to deep square-leg in the same over took India through to the final, with 20 deliveries to spare. The two runs also took Sachin to his highest individual score in ODIs—139. Sachin, visibly tiring after the running yet finding the energy to play one audacious stroke after another, raised his bat to acknowledge the applause of his teammates. In his mind, the battle was far from over, of course.

The very next delivery, Sachin again made room on the leg-side and smashed to long-off for four. With 32 needed from 19 deliveries, a stunner of a victory seemed imminent, but the last ball of the over turned out to be the last of Sachin's innings. He went for a pull but the ball rose higher than he had anticipated, and it kissed his bat before lodging in Gilchrist's gloves. Sachin was upset because he reckoned that the delivery had gone over his shoulder and so should have been declared a no-ball. He strode back towards the dressing room, furious that an umpiring error had denied him a shot at victory. When he watched a replay of the game, he noted that he had 'walked like Viv Richards' after getting out. Indeed, not only had he walked like his idol, but he had also batted like him.

His dismissal took the wind out of India's sails and they finished at 250–5.

> Not only did he single-handedly get his team into the final, he then went on to try and win the game from an impossible situation. Allan Border was stand-in coach for that series, and I remember him saying that the knock was one of the best he had witnessed. He soothed our frayed nerves by adding that the good news was that Tendulkar had peaked early and that he would not make a big score in the final.
>
> —Steve Waugh, *Commemorative Volume*, CAB, 2013

As star-struck as the fans were the sponsors. Coke, the tournament sponsors, announced an award of £25,000 for Sachin, for his magnificent 143 that had enabled India to qualify for the final. The sponsors also declared that they would gift Sachin a Mercedes 500 if India went the distance.

Azharuddin won the toss and elected to field in the final, which was played on 24 April 1998, the day Sachin turned 25. Australia batted well to score 272–9. They were a confident lot as they began their defence, convinced as they were that lightning could not and would not strike twice. After all, it had been less than 48 hours since Sachin had scored 143 in the heat and humidity of Sharjah, and hence he was unlikely to be '100 per cent'. The fact was that he wasn't, but then, he had never allowed physical discomfiture to overrule his will.

Ganguly got India's chase off the blocks with two consecutive boundaries off Damien Fleming in the first over. Sachin drove Michael Kasprowicz through the covers and then got a life of sorts, when he attempted to leave a Fleming delivery after committing to it initially. He got an inside-edge and the ball just missed the stumps on the way to the boundary. In Fleming's next over, Sachin timed what was nothing more than a 'push' so impeccably that the ball nearly decapacitated Ganguly on the way to the boundary.

Ganguly's dismissal at 39 brought in Mongia, and the keeper once again did what was expected of him. The spinners—Warne and Mark Waugh—were not allowed to settle. Sachin completed his 50 and India reached 100 in the same over, the 20th of the innings. Warne switched an around-the-wicket line in his next over. Sachin showed what he thought of the bowler's change in approach by lofting his first ball over long-on for six. The bemused look on Warne's face said it all.

Mongia's fall at 89 brought in Azharuddin. Sachin's brilliance notwithstanding, the Australians ensured that the required rate did not fall below six in the middle overs. However, the Indians were not worried, with their seniors complementing each other in the middle. Tom Moody, bowling the 35th over, could not believe his eyes when Sachin tickled him down to the square-leg boundary, just wide of the short fine-leg fielder who had specifically been posted to prevent runs in that area. It was the handiwork of a genius. A single in Moody's next over took him to his second ODI century in three days.

The final burst commenced in the 42nd over, bowled by Warne. Sachin pretty much settled the issue of the required rate with two boundaries. The first was a straight smash that nearly took the umpire's head with it. The second was a scintillating cover drive to the right of sweeper. The result a foregone conclusion, Sachin then went on the rampage. In the next over, he hit the sightscreen on the full and the ball ricocheted back onto the field. A couple of overs later came the grandest stroke of all—another high and handsome drive onto the roof of the venue. Kasprowicz, the bowler at the receiving end, then achieved a pyrrhic victory when he won a shout for leg-before despite the ball having clearly pitched outside leg. Sachin had scored 134 off 131 balls, inclusive of 12 boundaries and 3 sixes. He returned to a stirring ovation, and it was left to his teammates to complete the formalities.

The presentation ceremony featured an unforgettable spectacle. An entire stadium—and across the Arabian Sea, an entire nation—sang 'Happy Birthday to you', as the birthday boy collected the keys of his Mercedes 500 and did a lap of honour, with virtually the entire Indian team perched in and on the vehicle.

We were beaten by one man.

—Steve Waugh, *The Sportstar*, 9 May 1998

The back-to-back hundreds had stirred a nation. Ajit, Sachin's elder brother, received a call from a friend, who told him that his mother had been so overwhelmed after watching both the innings that she had cried.

There is a story associated with those two innings that has done the rounds of social media for several years, but has not been confirmed or denied by the individuals involved.

As per the story, the coach of the Indian team received an anonymous phone call on the eve of the final, with the person at the other end informing him that India would lose the summit clash as some of their players had sold out to bookies. The coach mentioned the same to Sachin, who assured him that 'he would sort things out'. Sachin proceeded to score a match-winning century. The individuals who had 'sold out' were understandably crestfallen.

> Richie Benaud, that great modern sage, spoke recently of another rare facet to Tendulkar's life. A lot of exceptional players, he said, had the talent, even the temperament, to be the leaders of their generation. But nobody, he thought, brought quite the same passion to their game that Tendulkar did. The passion to be Number One.
>
> —Harsha Bhogle, *The Sportstar*, 9 May 1998

The Indian team continued its winning streak in the months that followed Indian cricket's equivalent of Operation Desert Storm. Victory in a tri-series that involved Kenya and Bangladesh was followed by success in another tri-series in Sri Lanka on what was India's fifth visit to the Emerald Isles in six years.

Sachin, who was rested for most of the league games of the tri-series in India, was at his best in the big games. He scored an unbeaten 100 against Kenya in the final of the first tri-series and 128 against Sri Lanka in the final of the second. More notable than his hundred against the world champions was his opening partnership of 252 with Sourav Ganguly, a world record at the time. India scored 307–6 and went on to win a humdinger by six runs. The century was the hero's 17th in ODIs, which meant that he now shared the record for the highest number of ODI hundreds with Desmond Haynes, the former West Indies opener and a hero of Vinod Kambli's. It had taken Sachin 79 ODIs to score his first century in the format; he had scored 16 more in his next 117. That the Indian team played that many ODIs from mid-1994 to mid-1998, besides a few more that Sachin missed, reflected the prevalent obsession with 50-over cricket.

This was also the time the BCCI attempted to get to the root of the aspersions that were being cast on the integrity of some individuals. The Board instituted a one-man commission in the form of Justice Chandrachud, a retired judge of the Supreme Court. He was assigned the job of interviewing players, administrators, journalists and others, and determine whether anything such as match-fixing existed in Indian cricket. Nothing emerged from the exercise.

Not even the most cynical cricket lover had unsavoury practices on his mind on 18 July 1998, the 150th birth anniversary of Dr W.G. Grace, England's first cricketing superstar. It was a day on which a capacity crowd at Lord's and a worldwide TV audience watched the MCC XI taking on the World XI in a one-day game, the proceeds of which were to go to the Princess Diana Memorial Fund. It was technically an 'exhibition' game, but there was no way the best cricketers on the planet, all of whom were among the 22 who played the game, were going to take the contest lightly.

The MCC XI, which included Mohammed Azharuddin, Anil Kumble and Sourav Ganguly, batted first and scored 261–4. The World XI were put on the road to victory by a stand of 177 between Aravinda De Silva and Sachin, his captain for the day. Against a bowling attack that comprised Glenn McGrath, Allan Donald, India's two strike bowlers and Brian McMillan, Sachin batted beautifully and breathtakingly to score 125 off 114 deliveries. Michael Atherton, the losing captain, commented after the game that even Dr Grace could not have been as good as Sachin.

> His hand-speed is so quick it gives tremendous acceleration to the ball. Normally he hits a single or a four. Very rarely a three.
>
> —Barry Richards, as quoted in *Outlook*, 24 August 1998

'BRAND'MAN

I saw him playing on the television and I was very, very struck by his technique. I asked my wife to come and have a look at him. Because, I said, I never saw myself play, but I feel that this fellow is playing much the same as I used to play. She had a look at him on the television and she said, 'Yes, there was a similarity between the two'. It was just his compactness, his stroke production, his technique, it all seemed to gel as far as I was concerned.

—Sir Donald Bradman on Sachin Tendulkar

On 27 August 1998, two arch-rivals made their way to Adelaide, for an audience with the greatest batsman of all time. On his 90th birthday, Sir Donald Bradman met the greatest leg-spinner in history, as well as the batsman who reminded him of himself. Shane Warne and Sachin were like starry kids as they went about savouring this experience of a lifetime. For both 'the Don' and Sachin, the interaction was a revelation. While Sachin was surprised to learn that the Don would attend office from 7:00 a.m. to 10:00 a.m. on match-days, the legend expressed his surprise at learning that Sachin had been coached. The reason Bradman felt that Sachin was a 'self-taught' batsman was because his left elbow did not point towards mid-off, as those of 'coached' batsmen generally did, in the stance. Sachin and his contemporary also noted that the legend was not someone who lived in the past. The Don was full of praise for modern-day cricket, particularly the improved fielding standards.

Another honour awaited Sachin at home. Two days after meeting the Don, Sachin became the first cricketer to be conferred the Rajiv Gandhi Khel Ratna, India's most prestigious award for excellence in sports.

Greatest living Indian today.

—Bishan Singh Bedi, *The Sportstar*, 9 May 1998

At 25, Sachin had the world at his feet. His performances against the best team of his time had ensured his anointment as the best batsman in the world, ahead of Brian Lara and other contenders for the title. What his performances in the first half of 1998 had also done was convince quite a few people that he was better off without the captaincy.

One of the appellations coined for him during this period was 'Brandman', a tongue-in-cheek reference to his connection with the Don as well as the fact that he was as successful as a brand ambassador as a cricketer. Just as he had evolved as a cricketer since 1989, he had also evolved as an 'actor', as could be seen from his steadily improving histrionics in television advertisements and photo shoots. The awkward teenager who appeared in a TVS commercial with Mohammed Azharuddin in the late 1980s had given way to a confident young man who implored TV viewers to 'go and get' a VISA credit card. The other prominent products he was endorsing in 1998 were Boost, an Energy supplement for children, Action Shoes, MRF Tyres and Pepsi, the soft-drink giant.

Observers, especially those from outside India, were wonderstruck by his humility, his ability to steer clear of controversies and his reverence for his roots. Sachin never hesitated to mention the support of his family and close friends, as also the lessons imparted to him by his inspirations—his elders and his coach. The superstar who had been accorded God-like status by his fans was the epitome of humility. The idea of being seen swatting cricket balls coming at him from different directions with a fly-flap in a Pepsi commercial did not appeal to him. He relented only when they replaced the fly-flap with a stump. He had not forgotten his guru's lesson that no matter how successful one might become as a cricketer, there was nothing bigger than the game itself.

> Winning matches for India is much easier for this man than taking his family to a restaurant. This explains why he loves those holidays in far-off places where none can reach him. Sometimes not even the Board. It also explains why he loves going on long drives because it helps him get away from the crowd.
>
> —Vijay Lokapally, *The Sportstar*, 28 November 1998

Those were heady days for Sachin, the Indian cricket team and the Board. The BCCI was on its way to becoming one of the richest sporting bodies on the planet by the end of the 1990s, a decade in which one Indian—Sachin—had been anointed as the best batsman in the world and another Indian—Jagmohan Dalmiya—had been elected president of the ICC. In 1992–93, the balance sheet of the BCCI indicated a deficit of ₹81.6 lakhs; in the year that followed, the Board wiped out the deficit and made a profit of ₹15.34 lakhs. That was only

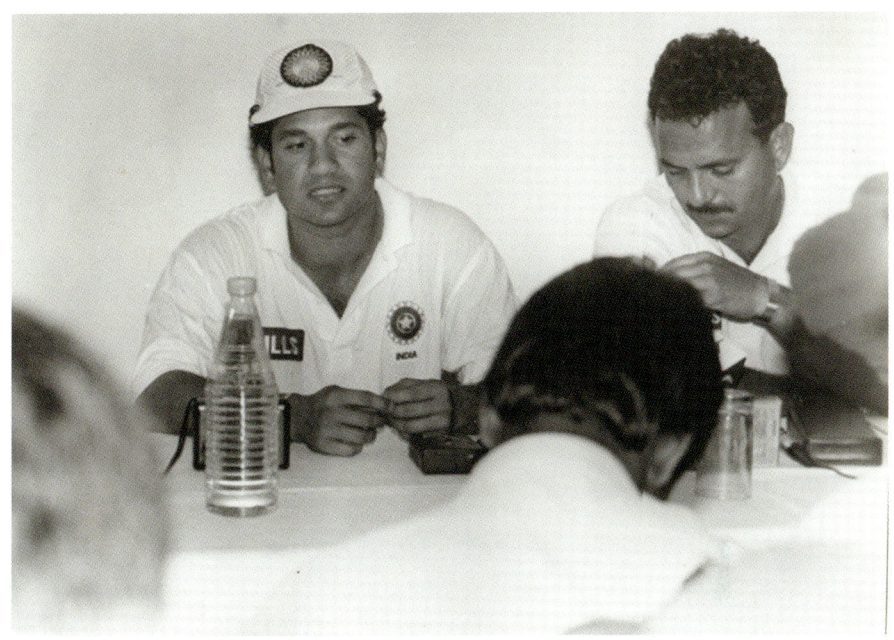

Addressing the media during his first stint as captain of India. Next to him is Madan Lal, then coach of the national team.

'Guardian Angel', admirer and BCCI boss during the first stint as the captain: Sachin with Raj Singh Dungarpur in the mid-1990s.

Nothing underscored the Indian team's overdependence on one player in the 1990s, as emphatically as this morphed image that appeared on the front page of the *Afternoon Despatch and Courier*, a Mumbai-based tabloid, on 16 May 1999.

Titans: With Shane Warne

Sachin speaks at a function after Mumbai's Ranji Trophy win in 1999-2000. Alongside him are (from left) his Mumbai and India teammates—Ajit Agarkar, Sameer Dighe and Sairaj Bahutule.

A straight bat, on and off the field

Essaying the cover drive, one of his signature strokes.

Cricket's best 'uppercut' exponent of all time.

Titans: With Sunil Gavaskar

Titans: With Viswanathan Anand, the chess whiz

Titans: With Brian Lara

Mr and Mrs Tendulkar with superstar Amitabh Bachchan.

Sachin has always been passionate about automobiles.

the beginning. The profits increased to ₹91.11 lakhs in 1994–95, and in the next year, of which the 1996 World Cup was a part, the Board crossed the ₹1 crore mark for the first time. The year 1996–97 yielded a profit of ₹13.4 crores, which increased to ₹16 crores in 1997–98. With overflowing coffers came power and stature.

One of the things the ICC did under Dalmiya was restore the four-year cycle of the World Cup that had gone asunder when the fifth edition of the tournament was held in 1992 instead of 1991. The seventh World Cup was accordingly scheduled in early 1999, a little over three years after the 1996 event. With the tournament a year away, all of India willed the 'dream runs' of its team and hero to continue for the remainder of 1998. However, an acrimonious debate played spoilsport.

With cricket having been included in the 1998 Commonwealth Games at Kuala Lumpur, there had been a lot of talk about whether the BCCI would send a team for the event or not. Over the years, people associated with the Olympic movement had often expressed their surprise at the fact that participation in multi-sporting events like the Olympics and Asian Games had never been a priority for the BCCI and its counterparts in other countries. These individuals would never lose an opportunity to talk about how cricketers were poorer for 'not experiencing the thrill of winning an Olympic medal', among other things.

They were conveniently missing the point. Cricket, due to the lengths of its two formats of the time, would have been a misfit in an event like the Olympics. This incongruence between the sport and multi-sporting events had ensured that the cricketers' priorities were different. For instance, the ultimate ambition of a Sachin or a Rahul Dravid was to win the World Cup and beat the strongest team of their time—Australia—in a Test series abroad. Winning an Olympic medal had never ever been on their radar. Why would cricketers feel bad about missing out on something that they had never aspired for in the first place?

There was also no doubt in the minds of the BCCI office-bearers and the fans that a bilateral series against Pakistan mattered a lot more than a multi-sporting event. The Pakistanis felt the same way. They accordingly picked their strongest team for the annual series at Toronto, and selected a second-string side for the Commonwealth Games. England—the founder of the Commonwealth and the birthplace of cricket—did not send a team to the Games at all. The nations that constituted the cricketing entity that was the West Indies competed in the Commonwealth Games as different entities, as in every edition. This meant that the ODIs that would be played in the Games would not get official status. On the other hand, the five ODIs to be played at Toronto were as official as official could be.

Despite these facts staring everybody in the face, the BCCI had to back down. The matter was magnified into a national controversy, with people who had always resented the success of the Board and the cricketers, hurling one bizarre charge after another at their pet peeves. Treason was among the milder ones. Under duress, the BCCI split the winning combination of 1998 into two teams. Sachin, the player the 'anti-cricket' brigade had fired away at with impunity, was named in the squad for the Commonwealth Games.

Not surprisingly, the Indian cricketers failed in both events. Pressure from the sponsors of the Toronto series resulted in Sachin being requested to fly all the way from Malaysia to Canada to play in the fifth game at Toronto, which did not make sense as the series had already been lost by then. He scored 77, but Pakistan, who had already sealed the series, won the game to take their margin to 4–1.

In a year during which it appeared that he could possibly do no wrong, the Commonwealth–Toronto fracas was a reminder of the fact that no matter what he did, he would not succeed in making everybody happy. Hence, it was better that he only concentrated on factors that were within his control. There was nothing he could do about those that were beyond his control.

A short tour of Zimbabwe seemed just the ideal platform for the Indian team to regroup after the split. India won the three-match ODI series, with Sachin surpassing Desmond Haynes' record tally of 17 ODI hundreds in the first game, but played poorly to lose the one-off Test. An exception was Rahul Dravid, who achieved three figures for the second time in Tests after a string of near-misses in the previous two seasons. He built on the gains that he had made after scoring 64 in the first ODI.

It had been more than a year since he had been branded a Test player and left out of Indian teams for quite a few ODI tournaments. The situation was compounded by his failure to impress the selectors in the latter stages of the tri-series against Kenya and Bangladesh, and later, the Toronto series. His lack of success notwithstanding, the selectors had given him a ticket for the one-dayers in Zimbabwe, and Dravid was reasonably happy to have made it count.

Sachin exasperated the Australians all over again in the quarter-final of what was the inaugural ICC Knockout (rechristened the ICC Champions Trophy in 2002) at Dhaka. The objective of the tournament, a biennial affair instituted by Jagmohan Dalmiya, the ICC president, was to involve all the Full Member Nations in a tournament to be played for a period of not more than two weeks at an 'outpost' of the game. The objectives were twofold: To promote and popularize the sport in non-traditional cricketing areas, and tempt sponsors to pour money into the ICC's coffers by associating with an event featuring the top cricketers on the planet.

Put in to bat, India were 8–2 and in trouble when Michael Kasprowicz commenced the fourth over of the innings. Facing him was the batsman who had been his nemesis earlier in the year. The first ball pitched just short of a length, just outside the off-stump. Most batsmen would have left it alone; Sachin went onto the back foot and cut it past third man for four. The very next ball, he played off the back foot, just to the left of Ricky Ponting, one of the best fielders in the world, who was patrolling the covers. The ball beat the fielder and went for another boundary. The slow-motion replay of the mid-wicket camera revealed that Sachin was totally indifferent to Ponting and his fielding abilities; he had got off the blocks and made to run as soon as he essayed the stroke, because he knew the very moment he had hit the ball that it would go to the boundary. This was a genius at the peak of his powers.

It was Sharjah all over again as Sachin annihilated the bowling as only he could. Insult was added to injury when Kasprowicz of all players missed a catch on the long-off boundary and the ball cleared the boundary. The spectators at Dhaka's Bangabandhu Stadium, where Sachin had begun the year with his pyrotechnics against Pakistan, accorded him a deafening ovation when he completed his 19th ODI hundred. It was his fifth against Australia, four of them having been scored in 1998. He was run out off the first ball of the 46th over for 141.

> 'I stand behind the wicket and visualise where the bowler will bowl and what shot I will play.' When he goes in, he tells himself, keep watching the ball. Then it all—the ego, the courage, the belief, the work at nets, the eyes, the hands, the strength—coalesces. And he makes magic.
>
> —Rohit Brijnath, *India Today*, 7 December 1998

He was far from done with the Australians. At 145–2, Steve Waugh's team was on course to overhaul India's 307–8. Azharuddin then tossed the ball to his hero for his by-now-routine 'right-arm over-everything'. Sachin's assortment of off-breaks, leg-breaks and seam-up yielded him figures of 4–38 and India won by 44 runs.

Of all his magnificent displays against Australia in 1998, Sachin rated his 141 at Dhaka as the best. He said in an interview that he remembered every stroke that he had essayed during the innings. What he was modest enough not to say was that he got out the only way he could have—run out.

It was reminiscent of Bradman's statement on his 254 against England at Leeds in 1930: 'Every ball went where it was intended to, including the one off which I was dismissed.'

The story goes that in his heyday, the Don had run into an off-spinner called Bill Black during a game at Blackheath. Bradman could not recall facing the bowler earlier, and so he asked the wicketkeeper what sort of a bowler Black was. The keeper then reminded him that Black had dismissed him in an exhibition game a few weeks previously, and had been boasting about it ever since. Bradman proceeded to take a modest 62 runs off the bowler's first two overs.

The Don would have been proud of what his 'successor' did on the evening of 13 November 1998 at his happy hunting ground in Sharjah. India were chasing 197 against Zimbabwe, in the final of a tri-series that also involved Sri Lanka. The Zimbabweans fancied their chances, after beating India in a league game by bowling them out for 192, just two days previously. Leading their attack in the final was speedster Henry Olonga, who had taken 4–46 in the league game. One of his victims that night was Sachin, who was taken by surprise by a delivery that reared up from just short of a length. The ball popped up into the air off the splice and Grant Flower held a simple catch. What followed was something that happened quite regularly in the Bradman era; a batsman's failure made as much news as his many successes.

Sachin's opening salvo on the night of the final was a smash through the covers in the fourth over. Among those delighted at the stroke was Ravi Shastri, who pulled out his trademark 'tracer bullet' line. Sachin made no secret of his desire to dominate when he slashed hard and missed off the very next delivery. He made the most of this near-miss. He pulled the bowler in front of square for two, and then slashed him hard for a six over third man.

Sachin was swinging his bat, deemed as 'too heavy' by others, like a rapier.

In Olonga's fourth over, the eighth of the innings, Sachin hit him 'on the up' for four and then deposited a slower ball in the stands over long-off. Olonga's first four overs cost him 41 and India went on to win by 10 wickets with 20 overs to spare. Sachin returned to the pavilion with an unbeaten 124, scored off only 91 balls with 12 boundaries and 6 sixes. He had proved a point, and how!

After winning yet another tournament for India and with it, his 32nd individual award that took him past childhood hero Viv Richards' tally, Sachin was asked by a journalist if he had 'set any target' for Sharjah. Sachin, by then a master in the art of offering a straight bat to questions thrown at him, replied that he normally did not talk about the targets that he would set for himself after every series, but would make an exception for this series as it was over and India had won it. 'I decided to win the tournament for India,' he said. He made it sound matter-of-fact.

This was assurance, not arrogance.

> He is not arrogant but his art is arrogant.
>
> —Ashok Mankad, as quoted in *India Today*, 7 December 1998

Sachin's consistency in 1997-98 made him the winner of the Castrol Indian Cricketer of the Year Award, in the first year of its inception. This award was unique at the time, as the winner would be 'elected', with every living Indian Test cricketer—former and current—voting for his favoured player. Sachin stood head and shoulders above the other 'nominees' for the award.

Indian cricket lovers exuded their customary optimism when their side boarded the plane for New Zealand in the last month of the year for a tour comprising three Tests and a seven-match ODI series. The tour did not get off to a great start, with the first Test at Hamilton being abandoned due to persistent rainfall.

The second Test at Wellington witnessed some fine cricket. Batting first, India were dismissed for 208 in the first innings and New Zealand then took a lead of 144. The visitors were 112-3 in their second innings when Sachin made his way to the middle. He announced his presence with an 'uppercut' off Nathan Astle that sent the ball over the slips' heads for four. Watchers were then treated to a masterclass of footwork and strokeplay, not to mention manipulation of the field placements. Sachin completed his half-century with a cover drive off Daniel Vettori, left-arm spinner and future New Zealand captain, for four. What was notable about the shot was that the ball had pitched on a length and turned a wee bit away from the right-hander; Sachin had picked it a fraction of a second earlier than others would have. He brought up his century, his 17th in Tests, with a straight six off Vettori. He was on 113 when he was caught by Stephen Fleming, the New Zealand captain, off Dion Nash, another seamer who like Hansie Cronje had troubled him more than many frontline fast bowlers.

India at that stage were 297-5, but not for the first or last time, the lower order caved in and the last five wickets fell for the addition of only 59 runs. Srinath and Kumble, seeking to atone for their failures with the bat, then reduced the hosts to 74-5. With 139 more to get, the visitors sensed victory, but not for the first or last time, an Indian bowling attack let the lower order get away after subjugating the specialist batsmen. Craig McMillan and Chris Cairns added a match-winning 137 and the hosts won by four wickets.

The third Test was a high-scoring draw and New Zealand thus took the series 1–0. The ODI series that followed ended in a 2–2 deadlock. The success of the tour was Rahul Dravid, who scored twin hundreds in the third Test and then a century, two 50s and a critical 38 in the ODIs. He had looked more comfortable than any other Indian batsman in the 'seam-and-swing' friendly conditions of New Zealand, which were like those in England. With the World Cup in England less than six months away, Dravid had settled the debate over his presence in the 'limited-overs' scheme of things, once and for all.

The defeat in the Test series gave some people an opportunity to have a go at Sachin. In declaring that his achievements had no substance until he 'won Tests abroad', his detractors were inadvertently echoing what many of Sachin's fans believed anyway—that India were a 'one-man' team. The tag was unfair, as it did not take note of the lionhearted contributions of Kumble, Srinath and Prasad with the ball. However, it did bring into focus the failure of Sachin's co-batsmen to deliver on a consistent basis in Tests, especially when the pressure was on and the conditions unfamiliar.

As the decade entered its last year, cricket lovers in India fervently hoped that the young men who had made their international debuts in the mid-1990s would emerge from their shells sooner than later; Indian cricket could not afford another wasted generation. The likes of Rahul Dravid, they hoped, would show the others the way.

As it turned out, the 1999 World Cup and the new millennium were preceded by the most damning indictment of India's Test side and its inability to complement its hero.

WHAT MIGHT HAVE BEEN

> *There is no omission of Tendulkar as such. He has not yet played an innings like Lara's 153 or Botham's 149. Tendulkar has a long career ahead of him and I am sure he'll get there in the end.*
>
> —Anthony Bouchier, Editor, *Wisden Online*, as quoted in *The Sportstar*, 11 August 2001 (On the issue of Sachin not figuring in the list of the 100 greatest Test innings)

Life and its many components, two of them being sport and religion, are replete with 'what-might-have-beens'. Cricket in India, which is a way of life, a sport and a religion put together, is no exception.

What if Tiger Pataudi had not lost his right eye in a car accident? He scored nearly 3,000 Test runs with one eye, so how would he have fared with two good eyes? What if L. Sivaramakrishnan and Maninder Singh had lived up to expectations and taken at least 200 Test wickets apiece, if not more? What if fast bowlers like Pandurang Salgaonkar, T.A. Sekhar and Raju Kulkarni had been given more chances to prove themselves in their heyday? What if the legendary spinners had not been thrashed the way they were by the Pakistanis in 1978–79? Had that happened, would Kapil Dev have managed to cement his place in the team, or would he have been treated the way Javagal Srinath was in home Tests in the early 1990s?

There was an addition to this list at the end of the first month of the last year of the twentieth century, and it was by far the most poignant 'what-might-have-been' of them all; *what if India had scored 13 more runs against Pakistan at Chennai?*

For starters, the confidence of the players would have soared and they might well have won not only the series in question, but also the World Cup later that year. The 'edge' that Pakistan had enjoyed since Javed Miandad's last-ball six in 1986 would have been blunted then and there. All that started happening to Indian cricket in March 2001, may well have started happening two full years in advance. Had that been the case, then the Indian team might well have held its own against Steve Waugh's Invincibles at the turn of the millennium, instead of been routed 0–3. Quite a few careers that were destroyed during that phase might well have blossomed. One can go on and on.

The long and short of it is that had India beat Pakistan at Chennai in January 1999, Sachin Tendulkar's 136 would have marched straight to the top of just about any top 100 innings list. Why heroic performances that may not result in victory for one's team are not credited, is a mystery. Cricket is after all a team sport, and however gifted a player might be, it is impossible for him to influence the outcome unless he is supported by his teammates. The obsession with individual performances that are supposedly *match-winning* is a contradiction that warrants a separate book altogether.

All roads in India led to Chennai in the last week of January 1999. After a lot of toing and froing, political protests and threats, the decks were cleared for Pakistan's first full tour of India since 1986–87. Initially planned as a three-Test series, it was subsequently decided that the arch-rivals would play two Tests in a bilateral series, to be followed by a third that would be the first game of a triangular Asian Test Championship, also involving Sri Lanka. The Championship was the brainchild of the Asian Cricket Council and intended to be a trial of sorts for the cricketing world to assess the feasibility of organizing a World Cup of Test cricket.

The 'action' started well before the Pakistani team landed in Delhi, when miscreants allegedly owing allegiance to a right-wing Indian outfit scuffed up the wicket at the Ferozeshah Kotla in the capital, where the first Test was to be played. At this stage, the Union Government came to the BCCI's rescue and assured additional security at the venues and for the teams. The Test venues were then switched and Chennai, which was to host the second Test, was allotted the first. The BCCI itself was in the line of fire when ruffians stormed into its Mumbai office, days before the series commenced. They manhandled some of the staff, smashed glass cabinets and even vandalized trophies that Indian cricketers had won with their sweat and blood. Photographs of the Mumbai Police examining the scars inflicted on Indian cricket's Holy Grail—the World Cup of 1983—infuriated cricket lovers across the world.

What the 'protestors' were not understanding was that by behaving the way they did, they were only providing the Pakistanis—their pet hates—with an opportunity to lash out at India. Through their mindless acts, they were only denting India's reputation as the land of love, peace, harmony and tolerance, which had already taken a beating after the communal riots of 1992–93.

The Union Government's firm stand and the average Indian's love for cricket triumphed over every other factor. On the morning of 28 January 1999, when Javagal Srinath ran in to bowl the first ball in the first Test between the traditional rivals since December 1989, the M.A. Chidambaram Stadium was threatening to burst at the seams, as much due to the sheer number of spectators as their deafening roars.

The Test lived up to the hype. Kumble, who had been troubled by neck spasms in New Zealand, displayed a welcome return to fitness by taking 6–70 and hastening Pakistan's demise for 238. India got off to a rollicking start, courtesy debutant Sadagoppan Ramesh and 'convert' V.V.S. Laxman, who still hadn't found a place in the middle order. India were 48–0 at stumps on day one and Indian fans had visions of a huge first-innings lead.

What they hadn't factored in was the genius of the Pakistani new-ball bowlers. Prior to the tour, Wasim Akram, who had commenced his third stint as Pakistani captain in seven years with this series, had requested his Board to request its Indian counterpart to send across boxes of the Sanspareils Greenlands (SG) balls that were to be used in the series, so that he and his team could use them in their preparatory camp. The Pakistani captain and his fast-bowling colleagues, all of whom were masters of the art of reverse swing, were delighted to discover that the SG balls started reversing earlier than those of other brands.

On day one, the Indian openers had played a lot of strokes and in the process, ensured that the SG ball assigned to the Pakistanis had rolled on the turf extensively and even crashed into the billboards on the boundary. The surface of the ball had been suitably coarsened, and all that was left was for the wizards, Wasim and Waqar, to weave their magic. Early on day two, Wasim dismissed both openers in quick succession. There was another blow to India when Sachin, eager to seize the initiative against off-spinner Saqlain Mushtaq, miscued a drive and was caught for no score. Dravid and later Ganguly dug in their heels and scored 50s, but no other batsman did anything substantial. India had to settle for a lead of 16.

In Pakistan's second innings, Shahid Afridi, who was opening with Saeed Anwar, curbed his impetuosity and did himself and his team proud with a fine innings. Inzamam-ul-Haq scored a 50 and Salim Malik scored 32 before he was fifth out, caught by Dravid off Sunil Joshi. The score at that stage was 275–5, and with Afridi still in and Wasim and Moin Khan to come, Pakistan looked to be running away with the game. Then came another twist, this time in the form of a sensational spell by Venkatesh Prasad. He took the last five Pakistani wickets in 18 balls without conceding a run, to finish with figures of 6–33. India needed 271 to win in two days and a bit. The stage was set for a grand finale to an absorbing game of cricket. A result was guaranteed. The team that would handle the pressure better would win.

Waqar Younis nearly gave Indian supporters a cardiac arrest by dismissing the Indian openers with only six on the board. Dravid, the half-centurion in the first innings, was then joined by Sachin. Waqar welcomed him with a couple of bouncers and a bit of lip. India's hero kept his mouth shut and his head still as he responded with a back-foot cover drive for four. A little later, he took an attempted yorker by Wasim on the full and dispatched the cherry past the bowler on his follow-through, for another boundary. A copybook cover drive off Wasim gave him his third boundary of the innings. Indian supporters found themselves breathing easier after this counterattack. The score had moved to 40-2 by the time stumps were drawn. Not many cricket lovers on the subcontinent, not to mention the cricketers in the thick of the action, would have slept well that night.

India's most dependable duo made their way to the middle on the fourth morning, aware that they needed to be on their guard all the time against a team whose fast bowlers were in fact waiting for the ball to get older! Also in the ranks was Saqlain Mushtaq, who had taken five wickets in the first innings and was mindful of the fact that not many batsmen knew how to pick his 'doosra', the one that went away. The slightest mistake by the bowlers needed to be capitalized on. When Wasim strayed down the leg-side, Sachin glanced him for four for the first runs of the day.

Wasim did not take too long to get his line back on track. He was unlucky not to have dismissed Dravid leg-before off the fourth ball of his second over of the morning. The delivery had curved inwards and struck the batsman on his front pad, but the umpire ruled that the ball had hit the bat first. The next ball was again aimed at the front pad, but this time, Dravid was better prepared, and the ball did hit his bat first. As he returned to his bowling mark, Wasim made up his mind to try and out-think the batsman, who he knew would be expecting a delivery that would go away after receiving two that came inwards.

The wizard served his pièce de résistance; a delivery that did exactly what Dravid expected it to and still got the better of him. The ball pitched on leg and swayed away and across the batsman who had done everything he could do to offer a straight bat and cover his stumps. But everything that he had done was not good enough and the ball whizzed past him and his bat to dislodge the off-bail. It was one of those moments that prompted even the most fanatical Indian supporter to marvel at the genius of the greatest left-arm paceman in history. Pakistan were only seven wickets away from a famous victory.

The last thing India needed in that situation was umpiring errors, but then, there were two. Saqlain won a marginal leg-before appeal against Azharuddin and Ganguly was declared out caught when umpire Steve Dunne failed to detect a catch on the half volley by keeper Moin Khan, after a cut by the batsman ricocheted off the silly-point fielder. Moments after Ganguly's reluctant return he dressing room, TV viewers watched pictures of him watching the slow-motion replay of his own dismissal on a TV set, wherein it could be seen quite clearly that the ball had bounced before the catch was claimed.

The loss of three wickets in the first session forced Sachin to go on the defensive. He scored only 24 runs before lunch, and survived an appeal for a catch at short-leg and a run out.

Ganguly, who was fifth out at 82, just before lunch, was replaced in the middle by Nayan Mongia, who had come in armed with explicit instructions from Anshuman Gaekwad—'You know you can bat, just stay in there with Sachin.'

The second session witnessed Test cricket at its most glorious. A tuck to the third-man fielder off Wasim gave Sachin, what Sunil Gavaskar described as 'one of his hardest-fought half-centuries'. The hundred of the innings soon came up, and a paddle-sweep off Saqlain took Sachin to 60, his highest individual Test score against Pakistan. It was the 75th Test of his career, but only his fifth against the traditional rivals, after the four with which he had begun his Test career. He then cut the off-spinner for another boundary.

It was Bengaluru 1987 all over again. Back then, someone called Sunil Gavaskar had waged a heroic battle against Pakistan on a minefield of a track, as India chased a target of 221. There, they had fallen 16 runs short. Would history repeat itself, or would Sachin go a step ahead of his illustrious predecessor?

The capacity crowd found its voice as the home team clawed its way back into the match. Sachin was delighted and relieved in equal measure to see Mongia applying himself to the task at hand. The introduction of Nadeem Khan and Shahid Afridi, Saqlain's spin sidekicks, into the attack, more to give the frontline bowlers a breather than anything else, also took the pressure off, and Sachin helped himself to a couple of searing cuts.

It was around this time that his lower back started throbbing and his body started cramping. While the latter was a common occurrence in the Chennai heat and humidity, the back pain was totally unexpected. Tea was not very far off and so Sachin eschewed aggression for accumulation, having decided to seek repairs during the interval. India were 145–5 at the break. Sachin assessed the situation of the game and the state of his body while lying in the dressing room, wrapped in cold towels to bring his temperature back to normal. The cramps had been brought under control, but the back pain was proving to be obstinate. Sachin figured that there was no way his back would hold up for two more hours. He just had to go for it.

At 150–5, Saqlain hit him on his front pad, and the ball flew to silly-point, who claimed the catch. Steve Dunne turned down the appeal as the bat had been nowhere near the ball. The reactions and gesticulations of the Pakistanis as they screamed their guts out in vain would have reminded V.K. Ramaswamy, Dunne's umpiring colleague and one of the two Indian officials[*] who had stood in the Bengaluru Test of 1987, of that acrimonious game. Thankfully, things had changed since then and the presence of a match referee meant that the Pakistanis could not behave the way their counterparts of 1987 had whenever an appeal did not go their way.

Two runs had been added to the score by the time Saqlain commenced his next over. His first delivery was just short of a length. Sachin spotted it early and pulled it over mid-wicket for four. The next ball, he paddled to the fine-leg boundary for another four. Just as it seemed that he had got the measure of Saqlain, he was beaten in the flight as he advanced down the wicket. The ball dipped and took the inside-edge of his bat. Amazingly, Moin Khan not only missed the catch, but also the stumping. Was it going to be Sachin and India's day?

All of India beckoned their hero to exercise restraint. Sachin complied, but only for one ball. The fifth ball of the over pitched on leg and Sachin paddled it for four.

The last ball of the over was slightly short, and Sachin smashed it to the deep square-leg boundary. The over had cost Pakistan 16 runs. The visitors were visibly upset at Moin's miss and their captain had to summon all his energies to calm them down in a brief conference between overs. Wasim kept reminding his troops that for all the application of Mongia and the batting capabilities of Mongia, Joshi, Kumble and Srinath, there was only one man who stood between them and victory.

The spectators went ballistic off the third ball of Saqlain's next over, which Sachin clipped to square-leg to take a single to complete his 18th Test century, one of the best ever scored by an Indian, given the conditions, the match-situation and of course, the quality of the opposition bowlers. India now needed exactly 100 more to win. Mongia, gaining in confidence, cut Saqlain for four in the same over. It was the 80th over of the innings, and Wasim immediately took the new ball.

The return of the two Ws made no difference to India's firmly entrenched

---

[*]Ram Babu Gupta was the other.

sixth-wicket pair. They fed off each other and the steadily growing exasperation of their opponents. The ones and twos came regularly, as did the boundaries, with even Mongia joining in. The keeper-batsman slapped Waqar for four past mid-on, and the bowler was reduced to kicking the turf in disgust when Sachin drove him past mid-off for another boundary. A roar went up when the 200 of the innings was posted, and Wasim responded by taking Waqar off after only two overs and bringing back Saqlain. Mongia greeted the off-spinner by plonking his front foot down the wicket and thumping him over mid-wicket for six, to bring up his individual 50. India were 215–5, and on song. The target was only 56 runs away, and the country relaxed.

And then something bizarre happened. Mongia heaved at the first ball of Wasim's next over. He hit it high, but not far enough, and Waqar held an easy catch at mid-off. An extraordinarily daft stroke had brought the pressure back on Sachin and India. He suddenly remembered his throbbing back, and the pain seemed a lot more intense than before.

Apart from battling the bowling and his back, Sachin now had another challenge to contend with—his temper. He was furious at Mongia for having surrendered his wicket. But it did not matter anymore and he had to somehow calm himself down. The pain made it just a little bit difficult.

Sunil Joshi, the new batsman and an outstanding all-rounder at the domestic level, negotiated the first few balls that he faced and opened his account with a six off Saqlain. That stroke reinvigorated the crowd.

Sachin was in acute pain by then and it was only sheer willpower that kept him going. A few ones and twos later, he drove Wasim to mid-off, but the fielder did not gather it cleanly and let it go for four precious runs. Another drive to mid-off in the same over was stopped, but Sachin felt a sharp twinge of pain in his back when he completed the stroke. At the end of the over, he walked up to Joshi and told him that he was perilously close to going through the pain-barrier. There was no option but to finish it off before the inevitable happened. Joshi wasn't so sure. He suggested to Sachin to take it easy and let him handle the bowling. But then, the hero had made up his mind.

Sachin started the over, bowled by Saqlain, with a two to fine-leg. The next ball, he came down the wicket to bang it over mid-on for four. The third ball was slightly short and Sachin swung it to the mid-wicket fence. The target was only 17 runs away.

Saqlain's fourth ball was a floater that Sachin picked early. However, the ball spent a longer time in the air than the batsman had anticipated, and instead of hitting it off the middle of the bat over long-off, Sachin mistimed and got a leading edge. Wasim ran backwards from his position to mid-off to complete the catch. The spectators and even TV viewers rose from their seats to acknowledge then maestro as he trudged back to the pavilion. It was a pity that he would be denied the privilege of taking India through, Indian supporters felt. They were not unduly worried. Joshi, Kumble and Srinath were capable enough of managing 17 runs.

What followed was heartbreaking for all of India. To put it as clinically as possible, the last three Indian wickets fell in the space of four runs and 23 balls. Kumble was leg-before to Wasim, Joshi gave a return catch to Saqlain, and Srinath inside-edged the off-spinner onto his stumps. India were all out for 258. Javed Miandad, the Pakistan coach, ran onto the field to hug his boys, who had literally snatched victory from the jaws of defeat.

A few metres away, the BCCI president, as gutted as the rest of the nation, made his way to the Indian dressing room to commiserate with the team.

> He was weeping like a schoolboy. I asked him why he was crying. I told him that he had made impossible possible by playing that great innings. But he said, 'No Sir. I have lost this match'.
>
> —Raj Singh Dungarpur, *Sachin Tendulkar—Mr. India*, PMG, 2002

It was gracious and decorous of Sachin to take responsibility for the defeat. The presentation ceremony witnessed a rare instance of a player winning the individual award despite being on the losing side. Azharuddin had to receive the award on behalf of his hero. Sachin simply did not have the heart to attend.

> [I]f Sachin was dismissed, it seemed to us if the match was over. It was his extraordinary brilliance which led to what I could think of as the diminishing value for the other performers around him. Sachin's dismissal often brought back the lost confidence of the opposing bowlers; there was a spring in their step, suddenly all the fielders perked up. Their attack looked more penetrative, the wicket looked more difficult to bat on. That's how it affected our own team.
>
> —Javagal Srinath, *India Today*, September 2010

Exactly two months after the Chennai Test, the West Indies beat Australia by one wicket in a cliff-hanger of a Test at Bridgetown. The chief architect of the win was Brian Lara who stroked an unbeaten 153.

For years to come, Sachin's detractors would cite Chennai 1999 and Bridgetown 1999 to justify their claim that the Indian wasn't as great a match-winning batsman as his contemporary from the Caribbean. What the detractors conveniently overlooked was Sachin's 155 against Australia in the same city, and a host of other match-winning contributions in both forms of the game. The 155, they argued, wasn't a *fourth-innings* knock, and a victory against Australia did not matter as much as a win over Pakistan. These were, of course, stupid arguments to make. How was it that a hundred in the first, second or third innings of a Test, not as invaluable as one scored in the fourth? Did centuries scored earlier in a Test not set up wins by giving the bowlers enough runs to bowl with?

Even as comparisons continued to be drawn between the match-winning abilities of Sachin and Lara, as also their record in high pressure situations in Tests, what was rarely mentioned was the support that the Trinidadian received during his unbeaten 153. He had arrived at the crease at 78–3, which was certainly a healthier position than the 6–2 at which Sachin had taken guard. In the latter stages of the Bridgetown chase, Jimmy Adams had helped his skipper add 133 for the sixth wicket and Curtly Ambrose had contributed 12 to a ninth-wicket stand of 54. Most importantly, both these players had held one end up as Lara went for the bowling at the other. At Chennai, Sachin was involved in 248 of the 258 runs that his team had scored, either as striker or non-striker. Mongia apart, no one had stayed in long enough, and two of the batsmen had been undone by umpiring decisions that could have gone the other way.

For Indian cricket lovers, the defeat served as a bitter reminder of what Geoffrey Boycott had said during the 1996 series in England: 'India need Sachin Tendulkar to bat at numbers one, two, three, four, five and six.'

Many of those who had followed Sachin's career from its beginning and had watched every ball of his Chennai innings, either at the stadium or on the TV, felt that something within them had died with that defeat.

Something had died within Sachin as well. He was never the same player again—not until December 2008 at least.

TRAGEDY

To be frank, when I suffered the injury, I did not know what it was. I played on disregarding the pain, which was not a sensible thing to do. Then I realised that there was a problem, so I went first to England and then to Australia for treatment. The point is I have to live with the fact that it might occur at any time, though I have to watch against dehydration in hot and humid conditions.... But once I was realistic enough to understand that I have a problem and have to live and play with it, I stopped worrying; I did not think at any time that I would have to cease playing.

—Sachin Tendulkar, *Cricket Talk*, 30 September 2000

The urge to get the better of Pakistan prompted Sachin not to withdraw from the next set of Tests, although his back was still acting up and the Board had left it to him to take a call. This was reminiscent of Imran Khan who disregarded his shin fracture to carry on bowling and led Pakistan to victory in the 1982–83 series against India.

India squared the series at Delhi, on a track that had been hurriedly re-prepared after its desecration prior to the series. The bounce was unpredictable and every run was therefore precious. Ramesh took the batting honours with scores of 60 and 96 in only his second Test, and Ganguly's 62 in the second innings enabled India to take an overall lead of 419. Adding 100 with him for the eighth wicket was Srinath, who had taken his inability to finish the Chennai Test with the bat to heart. The fourth day of the game belonged to Anil Kumble, who became only the second bowler in Test history to complete cricket's equivalent of the Perfect Ten. While Sachin had an unremarkable game with scores of 6 and 29, he did contribute to the proceedings after lunch on the fourth day, at which point Pakistan were a commanding 101–0.

> Invariably you have all these superstitions going in a match. And sometimes these superstitions work and you stick to them. After lunch, Sachin just said let me give your cap and sweater to the umpire. Let me change your luck. And in that particular over I got the wickets of Afridi and Ijaz Ahmed.

Two wickets in one over. And Sachin did not do this before every over. He would come and say let me take your cap and sweater. So it was happening and it went on till I picked up the 10th wicket.

—Anil Kumble, *The Times of India*, 16 May 2002

Incidentally, Kumble had stood for more than three hours in the dressing room along with other teammates to give Sachin luck on the last day of the Manchester Test in 1990. Sachin, then 17, had gone on to score an unbeaten 119.

After sharing honours in the bilateral series, India and Pakistan faced off in the first game of the Asian Test Championship at the Eden. It was in many ways a repeat of the Chennai game, in that Pakistan started shakily, but recovered to win all the critical moments and eventually, the Test match itself. The Indian tradition of letting the opposition off the hook resurfaced in the first innings. Pakistan were 26–6 and in complete disarray, but Moin Khan and Salim Malik staged a recovery and enabled them to reach 185. The Pakistani bowlers then restricted India to 223. The highlight of the innings was the bowling of Shoaib Akhtar, soon to be hailed as the fastest bowler in the world. Included in the XI at the expense of Waqar Younis, he silenced the doubters with two extraordinary yorkers that accounted for Dravid and Sachin. Dravid, who was undone by an express that made a mess of his stumps, had by then got used to Indian crowds cheering whenever he got out, in anticipation of the man who would replace him at the wicket. Never had a stadium gone from pandemonium to pin-drop silence so rapidly, as on the afternoon of 17 February 1999, when Sachin had his middle-stump knocked out of the ground, first ball.

Srinath took eight wickets in the second innings, in addition to his five in the first, but Pakistan still reached a competitive 316, thanks to Anwar, who carried his bat for an unbeaten 188. To win the Test, India needed to score eight runs more than what they had needed to do at Chennai.

Much to the delight of the capacity crowd, openers Ramesh and Laxman put on 108 before being separated. Sachin came in at 134–2 and got off the mark by driving Wasim past mid-on for two. He then drove the Pakistani captain uppishly for four. In Wasim's next over, disaster struck. Sachin clipped the bowler to mid-wicket. Dravid and he ran a comfortable two and then went for a third on one of the largest arenas in the country. In the outfield, Nadeem Khan intercepted the ball and threw it at the non-striker's end. Sachin had grounded his bat within the popping crease to complete the third run when he ran into Shoaib Akhtar, who had positioned himself to take the throw not behind the stumps as was usually done, but at the edge of the popping crease, literally in Sachin's path. Sachin had been watching the incoming throw and so had not seen the fast bowler standing in the way. The impact of the collision made Sachin raise his bat involuntarily, as he tried to regain his balance. Khan's throw hit the stumps at that precise moment.

Sachin's bat was raised and his feet were well outside the popping crease when the stumps were hit, and an appeal went up. The third umpire's assistance was sought, and going by the letter of the law, there was no doubt that Sachin was struggling.

Wasim Akram, veteran of many an India–Pakistan clash, would have had to be extraordinarily brave to withdraw his team's appeal and recall a batsman of Sachin's class to the crease. As it turned out, he wasn't. By the time he completed the over, the players had to leave the field, with the Eden crowd expressing its disapproval of the way Sachin had fallen. Tea was taken early and the crowd was placated only when Sachin himself responded to the local association's request and appealed for peace.

That freak dismissal was the turning point. Dravid fell just four runs later and the subsequent batsmen did not rise to the occasion. The crowd went berserk on the fifth morning after the dismissal of Ganguly, the local hero and the last recognized batsman. The police responded by driving most of the spectators out of the ground, and Pakistan completed a win by 46 runs in front of empty galleries. Those who had felt proud to see the Chennai spectators giving the Pakistani team a standing ovation after their 12-run win a couple of weeks previously were now embarrassed.

The Indian team then flew to Colombo to play Sri Lanka in the second game of the Test Championship. The encounter ended in a high-scoring draw, with the bowlers of both sides lacking bite and intensity, and poor light and rain truncating play on days three and four. Ramesh, who had impressed one and all since his debut at Chennai, and Dravid, scored centuries in India's first innings. The classy Mahela Jayawardene then scored a double hundred for Sri Lanka, and Sachin stroked his way to a hundred—his 19th in Tests—on the last day. The match saw the debut of the member of what was at the time, a rare commodity in Indian cricket—Ashish Nehra was the first left-arm paceman to represent the country since Rashid Patel in the late 1980s.

The Test Championship encounter between Pakistan and Sri Lanka at Lahore also ended in a draw. The highlight of the game was Wasim Akram's first hat-trick in Tests. Their win over India had assured Pakistan of a place in the final. Sri Lanka needed seven points to overtake India's tally and make it to the summit clash. In accordance with the points system devised for the tournament, Arjuna

Ranatunga's team got four points for taking nine Pakistani wickets inside 100 overs, in the first innings. To get three more points, they needed to cross 300 in less than 100 overs. They went past the mark in 77 overs. In the final, played at the neutral venue of Dhaka, Pakistan thrashed Sri Lanka by an innings and 175 runs. Inzamam-ul-Haq and Ijaz Ahmed scored double centuries and Wasim Akram performed the hat-trick for the second time in succession.

The Colombo Test was Sachin's last game of the season, as he opted to mend his back with the World Cup coming up. He thus missed out on two tri-series—one in India and another in Sharjah. India made it to the finals of both, only to be crushed by their traditional rivals.

Pakistan cricket had undertaken a roller-coaster ride in the 1990s. The World Cup win in 1992 was followed by a phase of uncertainty. The captaincy had changed hands almost every season, the team itself was said to have split into factions and accusations of match-fixing had made headlines and dented reputations. The tour of India could not have come at a better time for the country's leading cricketers. Not for the first time, they rediscovered their mojo while playing the old enemy. By the time they won the tri-series at Sharjah, they looked unrecognisable from the team that had lost to Australia at home at the start of the same season. Their performances in India and Sharjah made them frontrunners for the title of world champions.

Despite all the turmoil, India's western neighbour had an enormous cricketing riches in the 1990s. The generation that had been inspired to take to cricket in the previous decade after watching the likes of Imran Khan, Zaheer Abbas, Javed Miandad, Abdul Qadir and Wasim Akram himself, had yielded outstanding exponents of virtually every cricketing skill, from opening to wicketkeeping. The fact was that man-to-man, the Pakistani team of the 1990s was far superior to its Indian counterpart of the same phase in terms of talent and, in some cases, temperament as well. Sachin and Anil Kumble were the exceptions.

There is little doubt that Pakistan would have been the more successful team in an Asian equivalent of the Ashes, had the political heads of both countries made room for the same, in the 1990s. Given the proclivity of the players to forget their internal issues whenever they played India, there is every reason to believe that had the two nations played each other in both forms of the game on a regular basis in the 1990s, Pakistan with its abundance of talent would have become the dominant side in international cricket by the time the decade ended, ahead of even Australia. Regular victories against India would have infused self-belief and bestowed superstardom on the players and they would have never looked back.

An Indian player who certainly did not want to look back was Vinod Kambli. Eight months after sustaining that ghastly injury, the left-hander marked his return to top-level cricket with a blazing 90 off 61 balls for Mumbai in a Ranji Trophy one-day game against Gujarat. His consistency in the subsequent games earned him a recall to the national side for both the tri-series, but he did not set the scoreboard alight in any of the four matches that he played, and consequently missed out on a place in the squad for the World Cup. Amay Khurasiya, another left-hander who had been consistent for Madhya Pradesh for several seasons, was picked instead.

The hype in India on the eve of the first World Cup to be played in England since Kapil's Devils lifted the trophy at Lord's on 25 June 1983 was to be experienced to be believed. The logic doing the rounds was that India would win the 1999 tournament because it had won the previous edition to be played in England. For once, even the cynical sections of the media played along with this bizarre reasoning, totally disregarding the recent failures of the team. The obsession with the upcoming tournament was not restricted to the cricketing community. Almost every brand of note tweaked its advertising strategies to create a connect with cricket. The build-up culminated with an exhibition game between the Team of 1983 and the Team of 1999. Almost every brand sought to jump onto the cricketing bandwagon through its advertising campaigns, and every media outlet of note brought out a 'Special Issue' on the tournament.

One periodical listed '11 reasons why India would win the World Cup'. Reason number one was, not surprisingly, Sachin, who was 'fully fit', as per the writer.

The fact was that he wasn't. But then, missing the World Cup was out of the question. So Sachin did what he could in terms of training. To combat the stiffness of his back, he resorted to sleeping on the floor of his hotel room with a pillow below his knees, to ensure that his back stayed flat on the ground.

> The presence of Sachin Tendulkar should be an inspiration for everyone. The likes of Rahul Dravid and Sourav Ganguly should take over the mantle, and reduce the pressure on him.
>
> —Mohammed Azharuddin, *The Sportstar*, 15 May 1999

India did not start very well, losing their first match to South Africa at Hove. The team hoped to get things back on track in their second fixture against Zimbabwe at Leicester.

On the eve of the game, Sachin was with his friend Atul Ranade in his hotel room, when the bell rang. He opened the door to find Anjali standing in the corridor, flanked by Ajay Jadeja and Robin Singh. She had driven from London to Leicester late in the night to convey a terrible piece of news. Ramesh Tendulkar, the professor, philosopher and poet, was no more. The man who had penned the start of one of cricket's most glorious chapters in the summer of 1984 by allowing his 11-year-old son to change schools, had suffered a fatal heart attack.

Prof. Tendulkar had not been keeping well over the previous few months and had undergone an angioplasty. After the procedure, he had temporarily moved in with Sachin, who by this time had shifted from Sahitya Sahawas to an apartment on the western side of Bandra. With Anjali supervising her father-in-law's recuperation personally, things had started looking up. Sachin was relieved to see his father returning to normalcy, slowly and steadily. Hence, the news of the demise came as a shock.

The Tendulkars flew back to Mumbai early in the morning. At the funeral, which was attended by Prof. Tendulkar's friends, colleagues, associates, neighbours, students and scores of individuals whose lives he had enriched over the years, Sachin kept a gold coin bearing his image in the shirt pocket of the man who meant everything to him. Life for him would never be the same again.

Even as Sachin was grieving, his teammates did not do their World Cup prospects any good by losing to Zimbabwe by a mere three runs. This meant that they had lost two matches out of two. With three league matches to go, their only hope of qualifying for the Super Six, the stage before the semi-finals, was to win all three. The BCCI and team management were clear in their stand on Sachin; they had decided to respect his privacy and decision.

It was Sachin's mother, whose loss was bigger than Sachin's, who urged her youngest son to fly back to England. Convincing Sachin was not that difficult, as he too knew that that was exactly what his father would have liked him to do. For the fans, the news that Sachin was returning to England to try and resurrect his team's floundering campaign in the World Cup provided them with one of those hair-standing-on-end moments that make a lifetime of following the sport seem worthwhile.

He received a standing ovation on his arrival at the wicket during the next game against Kenya at Bristol, and he received another one on his dismissal after scoring 140 off only 101 deliveries, inclusive of 12 boundaries and three sixes. Coming in at number four, he batted exhilaratingly in the company of Dravid, who scored an unbeaten 104. A moment that left watchers with a lump in their throats was when Sachin completed three figures and looked up, towards the heavens; it was one of the most poignant moments they had ever witnessed on a cricket field. India finished with a mammoth 329–2 and won by 94 runs.

Sachin did not have do much in the next game against Sri Lanka at Taunton. He was once again designated to bat at number four, and he watched admiringly as Ganguly and Dravid annihilated the bowling. Both scored gigantic hundreds and added a record 318 for the second wicket. As Dravid had been designated wicketkeeper for the game, with Mongia missing due to injury, his 145 made him only the second wicketkeeper–batsman after Zimbabwe's Dave Houghton to score a hundred in the World Cup. Ganguly's 183 was the highest individual score by an Indian in ODIs, ahead of Kapil Dev's epic 175 against Zimbabwe in the 1983 World Cup. Chasing 374 was never going to be easy for the defending champions, and they were bowled out for 216.

Celebrations broke out all over the country when India beat England by 63 runs at Birmingham to qualify for the Super Six. Facing them in their first game of the second stage was another team that had started the tournament poorly and had no option but to treat every game they played as a knockout encounter.

At the Oval in London, Australia outplayed India by 77 runs. India were never in the game after losing their first four wickets for 17 in a chase of 282. The first to fall was Sachin, who had been restored to the opening slot, but failed to make any impression on the scorers. He nicked Glenn McGrath into Gilchrist's gloves, and the innings never recovered, despite a fifth-wicket stand of 141 between Jadeja and Robin Singh. Jadeja scored a round ton, but he and Singh (75) were the only two Indian batsmen to enter double figures. The defeat effectively ended India's campaign, even as Australia went all the way to the summit. India lost their final Super Six encounter to New Zealand, a game that meant little to them anyway as they were already out of it. Sachin's third shot at the World Cup had come a cropper.

> My gameplan would have been to try hard to get him out early with the one that comes back through the gate. Alternately, I would tempt him to drive and try to get the edge…. Pace bowling is all about tenacity, and when you are bowling to the likes of Sachin, you have got to be patient.
>
> —Sir Richard Hadlee, CAB, 2013

THE DARK AGE

Tendulkar and India are joined at the hip. The persistent counterpoint to his steady climb to this current mid-career apogee has been the disappointment attending the performances of his struggling teammates. Next to the English, the Indians are the greatest underachievers in cricket. Leading an Indian team in a sustained run of international one-day and Test success, home and away, seems to be most single-most glittering peak Tendulkar has yet to scale. The preconditions for his even attempting to reach that summit are his reappointment to the captaincy and a change of strategy on the part of the Indian cricket authorities.... Whatever else happens, the second half of Sachin's career is therefore likely to be even more challenging and unpredictable than the first.

—Mike Marqusee, *Outlook*, 4 January 1999

There was an unexpected development at the start of the next season. Ajit Wadekar, former India captain and cricket manager, who had taken over as chairman of the Selection Committee after the untimely demise of Ramakant Desai in May 1998, offered Sachin the captaincy of the Indian team. The panel had decided not to continue with Azharuddin after the World Cup fiasco. Earlier that year, Sachin had been offered the vice-captaincy after the Kolkata leg of the Asian Test Championship, and he had politely declined.

Sachin reacted like most Taureans do when taken by surprise; he was non-committal, reluctant even. His was a case of once bitten, twice shy. He expressed his reluctance to Wadekar, who had come all the way to his residence to make the offer. Sachin expected the chairman to communicate the same to his colleagues on the panel. However, what happened left him surprised.

On 28 July 1999, he was out of Mumbai with his family when the news came through that he had been reappointed captain. The selectors claimed that they had taken 'only a couple of minutes' to make the decision. That wasn't quite the case, as it turned out. The credentials of Kumble and Ganguly, both of whom were certainties in both forms of the game unlike Jadeja, were discussed at length, but both were ruled out. Ironically, the leg-spinner who had made India unbeatable at home in the 1990s was perceived as 'not being aggressive enough', and the left-handed batsman was apparently not a favourite of Raj Singh Dungarpur, the BCCI President. One of the selectors who was part of the panel that reinstated him as captain in 1999 was quoted as saying that 'Sachin would be making a mistake if he were to decline the post'.

After several unsuccessful attempts to contact the reinstated captain, Jaywant Lele, the secretary of the BCCI, left messages on Sachin's answering machine. The following day, Sachin called Raj Singh Dungarpur and accepted the job.

In a way, Sachin found himself trapped between the devil and the deep sea. If he accepted the job, then he ran the risk of revisiting the frustration that he had managed to put behind him. If he declined it, then there was the possibility of his being criticized by sections of the media and even the public. Eventually, his commitment to Indian cricket and the sport itself prevailed over the other factors. And then, there was the minor matter of his never having shirked a challenge.

> Captaining India was obviously an honour for me but it wasn't the ultimate thing for me. The ultimate thing was to play cricket for India and at that time, when I was removed from captaincy [1997], I said in my statement that you can stop me from leading India, but no one can stop me from playing cricket.... I felt that if you made somebody captain then he should be given a fair run, with the kind of support required.... I would not sit back after 20 years and think that I didn't try my best.... I am pretty sure that I did whatever I thought was best for Indian cricket.
>
> —Sachin Tendulkar, *Wisden Asia Cricket*, October 2004

There was reason to believe that Sachin's relationship with the selectors would be far better this time around. He had spent a lot of time with the individual who was now the chairman, in the first half of the decade. Wadekar had backed his candidature himself. The chairman had visions of Sachin having the same impact on Indian cricket as captain as Don Bradman had on Australian cricket in the 1930s and 1940s. The selection committee comprised Madan Lal, whom Sachin had worked closely with during his first stint as captain. Shivlal Yadav was the only 'survivor' of the selection panel that Sachin had interacted with during his first stint.

Sachin was assertive in his first Media Conference as India's new captain. He reiterated that he would open the batting in ODIs and he also said that he expected to have a greater say in selection matters.

> I believe he will succeed. He is two years older now, has a better coach and has a much better set of selectors. But the reason for my optimism comes from way beyond the cricket ground. His marriage has grown into a wonderful mature relationship and it is amazing how much a happy home can contribute to a successful man.... I have no doubt that is Sachin Tendulkar's biggest test. On this side of the peak is a great career. If he can conquer it, he can look down on the finest of all time.
>
> —Harsha Bhogle, *The Week*, 8 August 1999

Bhogle apart, many others were optimistic about Sachin's second stint as captain. These included S. Venkataraghvan and E.A.S. Prasanna, off-spinning rivals of the 1960s and 1970s, and Achrekar, his guru.

The start of his second stint was far from memorable. India did not qualify for the final of yet another limited-overs tournament in Sri Lanka, this time a triangular also featuring Australia. Sachin's back acted up on the eve of the second league game against Australia and Jadeja had to lead in his absence. The skipper played the final league game against Sri Lanka and endured tremendous pain to score a century, but although India won by 23 runs, their net run-rate was inferior to that of the other two sides.

The next engagement was another of those pointless tri-series that the 1990s had become famous (and later notorious) for. The venue this time was Singapore and the West Indies and Zimbabwe were the two other teams. Sachin's match-winning 85 against Zimbabwe got India through to the final, where his team lost to the Windies. The final was played twice, with the first having to be abandoned due to rain. Sachin scored 40 in the first game and fell for a duck in the second, completed fixture.

A greater priority than yet another limited-overs series, this one against the West Indies at Toronto, was his back, which was still troubling him. He flew to Australia for treatment. Dr Peter Barnes, a specialist at the Australian Cricket Academy in Adelaide, detected a bony defect on either side of the spine in the bottom half of the back. He pronounced the condition as Spondylosis. Sachin was also found to have an inflamed scar tissue in his lower back.

Years of relentless cricket had taken their toll. Sachin was relieved when the procedure was completed and the pain vanished.

With both him and limited-overs vice-captain Ajay Jadeja missing, Sourav Ganguly led India to a 2–1 win over the West Indies at the Toronto Cricket,

Skating and Curling Club. The Windies were invited when India refused to play Pakistan in what would have been the fourth edition of the annual series, in the wake of the battle between the two countries on the peaks of Kargil, earlier in the year.

Jadeja returned to lead India in a quadrangular series in Kenya, in which India was pitted against the three full members from Africa. India won all three league games, but lost to South Africa in the final.

The Indian team wore a new look at the start of New Zealand's full tour in October 1999. India fielded as many as three debutants in the first Test at Mohali—opener Devang Gandhi, Karnataka all-rounder Vijay Bharadwaj, who had impressed in the ODIs earlier in the season, and wicketkeeper–batsman M.S.K. Prasad. Nayan Mongia was displaced from the Test squad for the first time since his debut in 1993–94.

Another conspicuous absentee was Mohammed Azharuddin who had not played for India since the World Cup. There were reports of the new captain having opposed the inclusion of his predecessor, but Sachin had in fact stated in his very first media conference as captain that he had had no issues playing with his predecessor-turned-successor-turned-predecessor.

An altogether different view of his was to come to the fore one year later.

India started the first Test disastrously. They were bowled out for 83 and the bowlers then fought back, restricting the Kiwis to 215. The hosts' second innings featured a segment that underscored the virtuosity of Test cricket and the expertise of two of its greatest exponents. Sachin and Rahul Dravid were in the middle of a stand, but both were struggling against Chris Cairns, the New Zealand all-rounder, who was getting the ball to reverse.

Sachin then suggested to his partner that whoever was the non-striker among them ought to try to spot what Cairns was trying to do, as he ran in to bowl. If he had held the shiny side on the inside, it would mean that the ball would reverse into the striker, and if he were holding the shiny side outside, then the cherry would move away from the batsman. The non-striker would hold his bat in his right hand if he reckoned the ball would come in, and transfer it to his left hand if he felt it would move away. More than a decade ago, Javed Miandad had done something similar while standing at the non-striker's end to help his partner decipher the bowler's swing during a Test match against the West Indies.

At Mohali, the ploy worked and India's two most reliable bats settled in to add 229 for the third wicket. Rahul scored 144 and Sachin, in his first Test back at the helm, remained unbeaten on 126.

The next Test, played on a slow and low wicket at Kanpur, went India's way, with the hosts winning by eight wickets. Kumble took 10–134. India were also in with a chance to win the last Test at Ahmedabad, but the visitors salvaged a draw despite incurring a first-innings deficit of 275.

But before Sachin's decision to not enforce the follow-on at Ahmedabad made headlines, he made waves for creating history. A few weeks after his back had healed, he managed to shrug off the monkey that had perched itself on his back for several years. At Ahmedabad, he scored 217, his 21st Test century in all and his very first double century in Tests.

He had had enough of all the stuff that had been circulated to explain his inability to score a double hundred. Among the prominent reasons cited were the 'abnormal' weight of his bats, the excessive limited-overs cricket that had attuned him to taking too many risks even in the longer version and even a lack of stamina. In fact, there were not many interviews of Sachin's in the 1990s that did not feature a question about that elusive double ton.

> I have tried very hard, but somehow it hasn't happened. Maybe I haven't stayed long enough at the crease, maybe my concentration is not there after a stage. I should try and achieve this soon.
>
> —Sachin Tendulkar, *Outlook*, 4 January 1999

Sachin apart, Ramesh and Ganguly scored hundreds, and the declaration was made at 583–7. New Zealand were then bowled out for 308, but surprisingly, India batted for 32 overs in the second innings, scoring 148–5 at less than a-run-a-ball. New Zealand drew the game comfortably, and Stephen Fleming, the captain, said after the game that the Indians had given themselves lesser time to win the game by not enforcing the follow-on.

> It was extremely hot that day [42 degrees] and they had bowled about 140 overs. Asking them to bowl another 160 at that stage would have meant someone might have had a breakdown. We didn't want that kind of situation and that is why we gave the bowlers a break. They tried their best I would say.
>
> —Sachin Tendulkar, *The Sportstar*, 20 November 1999

Sachin had consulted his pacemen before taking the call. As captain, his concern for his bowlers was understandable, and he would have also had Javagal Srinath's injury prior to the tour of the West Indies in 1997 on his mind. He and the team could not have afforded losing either Srinath or Prasad on the eve of a tour of Australia. Whatever the reasons for not enforcing the follow-on may have been, the fact was that it was a defensive move. Wadekar may have wanted Sachin to do a Bradman, but the fact was that the Indian team of 1999–00 simply did not have the firepower or options as Bradman had as captain, several decades previously.

The five-match ODI series that followed was an eventful affair. The Kiwis batted first in the opening game at Rajkot and scored a mammoth 349–9, eventually winning by 43 runs. India drew level in the second ODI at Hyderabad. The captain biffed and blasted his way to 186, the highest individual score by an Indian in ODIs, ahead of Ganguly's 183 against Sri Lanka just a few months previously. Sachin faced 150 balls, hit 20 boundaries and three sixes, and added 331 for the second wicket with Dravid, who scored 153. After the first 20 overs or so, the Kiwis were reduced to going through the motions against two batsmen on song. Both did pretty much as they pleased, and their stand of 331 was at that stage, the highest-ever for any wicket in ODIs. India totalled 376–2 and won by 174 runs.

> Saeed Anwar's record was not in my mind. If I am destined to make it, it will happen.
>
> —Sachin Tendulkar at the post-match media conference

Ganguly, who had been unlucky to be run out at Hyderabad when a straight drive by Sachin ricocheted off the bowler's hand to hit the stumps at the non-striker's end with the left-hander out of his ground, dominated the third game at Gwalior with an innings of 153. India won by 14 runs to take the lead. The Kiwis then played excellently in the fourth ODI at Guwahati, bowling India out for 188 and winning by 46 runs. The defeat flustered India and prompted them to bring back Srinath, who along with Prasad had been rested for the series, for the decider at Delhi. India won by seven wickets after Srinath and his colleagues restricted New Zealand to 179.

Awaiting the Indians in Australia was a team that had won their last four Test matches in succession, not to mention the World Cup. Azharuddin and Mongia were left behind in India, although the latter was flown to Australia as a stand-by for M.S.K. Prasad, who injured his knee at the Kuala Lumpur airport on the way to Australia. However, Prasad played the first Test and was then declared fit for the second as well, at which point the team management sent Mongia back. Ajay Jadeja had to pull out due to his shoulder injury and he was replaced by Hrishikesh Kanitkar.

India lost their opening game of the tour to Queensland, but they beat

New South Wales, traditionally the most successful state side in Australia, in their next and last four-day encounter before the start of the tussle for the Border–Gavaskar Trophy. The frontline bowlers were among the wickets, with Kumble taking eight against New South Wales. The win buoyed the spirits of the visitors. Sachin had every reason to expect his bowlers to do as well in the Test series as their counterparts of 1991–92. Batting-wise, the onus was on him, his deputy Sourav Ganguly and Rahul Dravid, to deliver.

Australia won the toss and batted in the first Test at Adelaide. Indian fans at the venue and those watching on TV could not hide their glee when the hosts lost their fourth wicket with only 52 on the board. Prasad had struck twice and Srinath and Ganguly once each. India had the upper hand at lunch, but they let the initiative slip after the interval. That wasn't the smartest thing to do when batsmen of the calibre of Ricky Ponting and Steve Waugh were in the middle. Ponting, who led a charmed life, being reprieved at least twice by the umpires when he looked out, was eventually run out, but only after he had scored 125 and added 239 for the fifth wicket with his captain, who went on to score 150. The Australians finished with 441.

India surrendered their first wicket when Ramesh ran himself out at the non-striker's end while going for a fourth run. All-run fours and even fives were feasible on the vast Australian arenas, but there was clearly no need to take on a fielder's throwing arm at the start of an innings. Devang Gandhi fell a little later. Dravid and Laxman then staged a recovery with a stand of 81. Sachin, who came in three-down, survived a testing spell by Glenn McGrath in the final stages of day two. He had figured that the Australians were looking to frustrate him by bowling tight lines outside the off-stump; he decided to beat them at their own game by dropping anchor. He scored only 12 runs in an hour-and-a-half. When he resumed his innings the following morning, he discovered that he had forced his opponents to alter their tactics. He then commenced the proceedings with two boundaries in a McGrath over.

He felt good, and so did Ganguly. When Sachin took two consecutive boundaries off his old friend Michael Kasprowicz in the first over after the drinks interval in the first session, Indian fans sensed that they were in for something big. He followed an exquisite flick to square-leg with an imperious cover drive. The batsmen had added a fluent 108 when Sachin was declared caught at bat-pad off Warne for 61, *against the run of play*. The replays were inconclusive and the Indian captain was convinced that his bat had not touched the ball. But the umpire thought otherwise. Ganguly was stumped for 60 a little later, and although the lower order tried, the Australian bowlers tightened the screws. India were dismissed for 285 and rain was their only hope.

Australia declared their second innings at 239–8 and gave themselves four sessions in which to take 10 wickets. They closed out the game by stumps on the fourth day itself with five wickets, one of which was that of the Indian captain. Sachin had not even got off the mark when he ducked into a McGrath delivery that did not rise as much as he expected and struck him on his left shoulder. An appeal went up and the umpire ruled Sachin out shoulder before wicket, as Indian fans ruefully commented. Australia completed a 285-run victory on the fifth morning.

Sachin refused to back down and exuded confidence in a TV interview prior to the second Test. He praised his bowlers for their display at Adelaide and said that it was only a matter of 'getting the finer points right'. He also said that he was happy with the batting of his teammates in the four-day game against Tasmania that preceded the Test. His team would play to win, he declared.

Rain delayed the start of the Boxing Day Test at Melbourne and frequent interruptions forced the Australians to bat into the third day after Sachin had won the toss and elected to bowl in overcast conditions. Unfortunately, his pacemen failed to exploit them and the Australians scored 405. The captain barely had the time to relax in the dressing room, with Ramesh becoming debutant Brett Lee's first Test victim and makeshift opener V.V.S. Laxman falling to McGrath with only 11 on the board.

What followed was a contest for the ages. Glenn McGrath, well on the way to achieving cricketing immortality, kept pegging away just outside the off-stump, doing his best to test Sachin's patience. The Indian captain responded by respecting the good balls and either negotiating them or letting them go. He neatly evaded the bouncers that the bowler served from time to time. When McGrath pitched one just a little too short, Sachin cut it for four.

Against Warne, he adopted the same two-eyed stance that he had used to telling effect in the previous series in 1998. He played the leg-spinner on merit. A viciously spun leg-break went past him, even as he shouldered arms, and missed the top of off-stump by centimetres. It was exemplary judgement on Sachin's part. He had taken less than a fraction of a second to work out that the delivery was not going to hit the stumps, and had therefore let it go through; a lesser batsman would have played at it and most probably nicked it to the keeper.

By this time, Dravid had become Lee's second victim in Tests. Sachin carried on, thwarting the good balls and seizing upon every scoring opportunity. His running between the wickets, for himself and for his partner, was exceptional.

When Warne tried to beat him in flight, Sachin advanced down the wicket and lofted the bowler over the sightscreen for six. Warne very nearly had the last laugh when Sachin came down the wicket again and was this time beaten in the flight. He hit it a little too firmly, but luckily for him and India, the cherry fell just short of the mid-on fielder.

Sachin chided himself and put his head down. When Warne bowled him a delivery that was slightly fuller, the Indian captain's eyes lit up and he cover drove it for four. Damien Fleming was cut uppishly to the boundary and then pulled into the vacant mid-wicket region for an all-run four, which gave Sachin his second 50 of the series. McGrath, returning for a fresh spell, then had Ganguly caught in the slips. At the other end, Sachin brought the crowd and commentators on their feet with another splendidly timed cover drive off Warne, with the ball going further and further away from the chasing fielder, but close enough to keep him interested, and eventually beating him to the fence. When Warne pitched one short, Sachin was quick to transfer his weight onto the back foot and smash him to mid-wicket for another all-run four.

It was batting at its most glorious, that too against the most formidable bowling attack on the planet. Everything that Sachin was doing that afternoon was straight out of the coaching manual, be it his choice of the deliveries to either negotiate or score off, his timing and placement, his keeping his eyes on the ball even while taking evasive action and his footwork. Every movement of his—forward, backward and sideways—was precise. He completed 1,000 runs in the calendar year of 1999 when he punched a slower delivery by Lee down the ground for four.

The very least he deserved was a semblance of support from his lieutenants, but he did not get it. Kanitkar became Warne's 350th victim in Tests when he padded up to a delivery that in the view of the umpire would have hit the stumps. M.S.K. Prasad stuck around for a while before he, Agarkar and Srinath fell in the same over to Lee, giving the debutant his first 'five-for' in his first Test innings as a bowler. India were 169–8 and India still needed 37 to avoid the follow-on.

Anil Kumble held one end up as Sachin tried to farm the strike. Even as Kumble did everything he could to respond to his captain's calls and scamper his way to safety, the Australian fielders started targeting his end instead of Sachin's; the Indian captain was nearing a century, but the Australians clearly felt that it was pointless to try anything against him. A tap off Warne in the unmanned square-leg region gave Sachin two runs and his 22nd Test century. Joining the applause from the Indian sections of the crowd were their Australian counterparts and the Australian players themselves. Sachin then left watchers gaping with a disdainful off-drive off Fleming that beat the long-off fielder's dive and hit the advertising boards.

India were 212–8, 116 of those having come off Sachin's blade, when he pulled Fleming a little too soon and holed out to Justin Langer at mid-wicket. He received a warm ovation on his return, but he knew that it was not going to be enough. The last pair took the score to 238, and Australia declared their second innings at 208–5. India were then bowled out for 195, losing the match by 180 runs and with it, the Border–Gavaskar Trophy, for the first time since its inception. India's top scorer in the second innings was again their captain, who scored 52 before being trapped leg-before by Warne.

The fight had gone out of the Indians by that stage. In the final Test of the series and first of the new millennium, they were annihilated by an innings and 141 runs by an Australian team that had earned the right and record to be considered one of the best of all time. India's saving grace was V.V.S. Laxman, as reluctant an opener as Sachin had been captain in his second stint, who stroked a stunning 167, his maiden Test hundred. The innings would have reminded Sachin of the pep-talk he had given to the young man in South Africa, three seasons ago. The captain requested the BCCI to have Laxman stay back for the tri-series against the 1999 World Cup finalists.

> While the middle order is the right place for him [Laxman], I would say that the innings that turned his career came when he was opening. We all knew he could play some great strokes, but that day at the SCG, we saw him put it all together. It was mind-blowing batting, the kind of innings that breeds self-belief that makes you feel you can handle it at the international level.
>
> —Sachin Tendulkar, *Wisden Asia Cricket*, October 2004

India's failure to qualify for the best-of-three finals, with just one win from eight games, was not as disappointing as the impression that the Indian team did not seem to believe that it could get the better of the 1999 World Cup finalists. The first league game against Pakistan at Brisbane was a case in point. After being bowled out for 195, India reduced the opposition to 71–6. Wasim Akram and Yousuf Youhana engineered a recovery, but the captain fell at 120 and Youhana, the last recognized batsman, was eighth out at 153. All that was left was the mopping up operation, but somehow, Waqar Younis and Saqlain Mushtaq, two players known more for their bowling skills than their batting abilities, managed to take their side home off the last ball of the innings. India's 48-run win over Pakistan at Adelaide came a little too late.

He doesn't have the garrulous and warm marriage-host bearings of a Wasim Akram, the school headmaster severity of Steve Waugh or the ruthless pinstripe forbearance of Steve Waugh. He is not the strict dad that Gavaskar was or the believer in karma that Arjuna Ranatunga seemed to be. So what's captain Sachin like, apart from being 'God?'

—*Outlook*, 31 January 2000

Sachin had played international cricket long enough to expect brickbats, abuses and taunts after the rout. Those who chose to find fault with him took great pleasure in pointing out that this time around, he could not cite the non-cooperation of the selectors as an excuse. They referred specifically to the lacklustre performances of players from Mumbai, whom Sachin was alleged to have specifically asked for.

At a time when people were only drawing out the negatives, Ajit Agarkar was slammed for his five ducks from six Test innings; that he was primarily a bowler and had taken more wickets than any other Indian bowler in the Test series was overlooked. Wicketkeeper–batsman Sameer Dighe, who made his international debut in the tri-series, had had a tough time, but then, so had many others who toured Australia before and after him. Sachin did his best to keep a low profile, but as had been the case even during his first stint, he found it difficult to 'switch off' even when he was with his family. While the competitor within him recognized and respected the awesome ability of the Australians, he simply could not bring himself to digest his team's total failure.

He had expected Kapil Dev, a veteran of three Australian tours, to play a bigger role in the formulation of tactics, but that had not happened. The pressure on him had only increased. Unlike his first stint, wherein he had vented out his frustrations more than once, he pushed himself to the other extreme in his second.

> When he was captain of the team to Australia [1999–00], he had the media there looking for a comment or two about how to give the game a new direction. Owing to his phenomenal batting in the home series [1997–98], the Australian media was waiting to lap up every word of his, but he disappointed them by saying hardly anything of consequence. There were plenty of topics that were making news then, like the throwing issue, the sledging or mental disintegration aspect, use of technology for TV, to name just a few, but he did not venture an opinion and as one India-loving Australian mediaperson said, 'It was as if "no comment" was two words too many for him.' Perhaps Tendulkar was taking shelter under the ICC

Code of Conduct regarding comments, but there comes a time when the good of cricket counts before anything else and one has to stick one's neck out for the betterment of the game. For, when Tendulkar speaks, the world will stop and listen.

—Sunil Gavaskar, *The Sportstar*, 12 January 2002

For decades, Indian cricketers had been expected to compensate for their compatriots' failings on other fronts, namely corruption, inflation, unemployment and poverty. Whenever the cricketers did not cover themselves with glory and, therefore, *did not* compensate for their compatriots' failings, those who claimed to love them generally got apoplectic. A prominent Indian periodical rubbed it in by recommending 'remedial' measures for the cricketers. The list included a ban from playing international cricket for 18 months, banning all sponsorships and endorsements, making them play domestic tournaments, getting cricketers from overseas to play with them, instituting academies, professionalizing the BCCI, restoring the balance between Tests and ODIs, telecasting selection meetings and chucking the obsession with pace and encouraging spin instead.

The Indian cricket team had little or no breathing space after the disaster down under. Its next engagement was a two-Test series and five-match ODI series against another powerhouse—South Africa.

The first Test, which was to begin at Mumbai's Wankhede Stadium on 24 February 2000, was preceded by a three-day game between the visitors and the Board President's XI at the CCI. The Indian team for the first Test was to be picked on the second day of the game. The journalists who had turned up at the Brabourne Stadium to cover the three-dayer was surprised to see the Indian captain make his way towards them along with former India captain Chandu Borde, who had taken over as chairman of selectors. Sachin stunned the media by informing them that the Test series against South Africa would be his last as captain; he had decided to step down. He spoke about taking moral responsibility for the defeat in Australia and his regret at being unable to live up to the expectations of his compatriots. He said that the Tests against South Africa would give his successor enough time to prepare himself for the job.

> Any team would have met the same fate in Australia. So why should the captain alone take the blame? I could see from a distance that he was not happy with the job. There must have been valid reasons for him to take such a decision. I must say that he has been upright. I can't believe the man doesn't have cricket sense just because he doesn't want to lead the

side again. He should be left alone now at least to concentrate on what he deems best.

—Bishan Singh Bedi, *The Sportstar*, 4 March 2000

It would not have been easy for Sachin to take the decision that he did, as he wasn't someone to back off from adversity. However, for once, he felt that he had had enough. He discussed the issue with Ajit and Anjali and made up his mind.

> I wanted it the first time and I believed that I could make a success of it. But when I lost it, I did not think of it again. Let me make it clear that I did not want the job when it was thrust on me the second time. I had clearly communicated this to the then Chairman of the Selection Committee, Ajit Wadekar, who did not inform his colleagues on the committee. So when it became a fait accompli, I told myself that I would have another crack at it, though in hindsight, I would have been better off standing firm and refusing the offer. The tour of Australia convinced me that nothing I would do as captain would come right. So before the home rubber against South Africa last season, I made it clear to the powers that be, without exception, that I was doing the job in order to give my successor time to prepare himself mentally. Now, I do not think about the captaincy at all.... The second time around...I should have refused and spared myself unnecessary strain and hassles.... If I can't be me when I am the captain, then both the country and me are losing something. Other than this phase in my career, I have no regrets about any of my actions.

—Sachin Tendulkar, *Cricket Talk*, 30 September 2000

There was no doubt that Wadekar and his colleagues had the best interests of Indian cricket in their hearts and minds when they assigned the captaincy to the hero, but the fact was that they had inadvertently put him in a situation that was not too dissimilar to the one that Abhimanyu, another teenage prodigy, found himself in, on the 13th day of the Mahabharata War.

Dronacharya, teacher of the Kuru princes, who was commanding the Kaurav army, had been asked by Duryodhan, the eldest Kaurav, to capture Yudhisthir, the eldest Pandav. That would put an end to the war. Drona then planned meticulously. He arranged his army in the 'Chakravyuha' formation. Arjun, the third of the five Pandavas, the greatest archer on earth, Drona's favourite disciple and Abhimanyu's invincible father, was the only active warrior on the battlefield of Kurukshetra who knew how to breach and break out of the Chakravyuha.

He was cleverly drawn away to another part of the battlefield.

Abhimanyu knew how to breach the formation, but not how to get out of it. His uncles assured him that they would follow him into the Chakravyuha once he had made the breach. That did not happen. Abhimanyu breached the formation, but the enemy closed out the gap and prevented his uncles from flanking him. Abhimanyu saw the writing on the wall, but he was not going to give up without a fight. He fought warrior after accomplished warrior and beat them all. He was slain only after half a dozen of his adversaries flouted every rule of warfare and attacked him jointly.

Sachin had undergone a similar experience in Australia. He had tried to lead from the front, but at the end of the day, a General cannot fight all by himself, however brave he may be. He needs the individuals whom he is leading to fight equally fiercely and single-mindedly.

Coincidentally, his son, who was born in September 1999, was christened Arjun, which was the name of Abhimanyu's father.

Quite a few changes were expected in the Indian Test side after the 0–3 debacle, and the selectors did not disappoint. Wasim Jaffer, the Mumbai opener, was picked, as was Murali Kartik, a left-arm spinner who had done well for the Railways in the Ranji Trophy. Mohammed Kaif, who had recently led India to victory in the Under-19 World Cup, was promoted to the senior squad. Also picked were two players whose inclusion in the Board President's XI for the three-dayer prior to the Test had raised eyebrows. It was not often that senior cricketers like Mohammed Azharuddin and Nayan Mongia were picked to play in what was essentially a trial game to test out the so-called 'bench-strength'. Their inclusion in the Board President's XI indicated that they were certainties for the Test side as well, leading to insinuations that Sachin, who had allegedly not wanted them in the side that toured Australia, had decided to step down only because the selectors were recalling them for the South Africa series. Sachin of course refuted the claims. Azharuddin subsequently withdrew from the first Test due to a thumb injury that he sustained in the three-day game.

In his penultimate Test as captain of India, Sachin won the toss and elected to bat. Wasim Jaffer fell to Allan Donald for only four and a roar went up when V.V.S. Laxman was caught at gully off Jacques Kallis at 39. It was not that the spectators hated Laxman; they were thrilled because their favourite was the next man in. Laxman, of course, did not mind. It had been several years since those who batted over Sachin had got used to being 'cheered' off the field by even their own compatriots, in case theirs happened to be the second wicket to fall.

Cronje brought back Donald to have a crack at his opposite number. 'White

Lightning' tested Sachin, but even he broke into a smile when the Indian captain stood on his toes and brought his bat down to play a delivery that rose sharply; it was nothing more than a firm block, but the timing ensured that the ball sped past mid-on for four. At lunch, India were reasonably well-placed at 69–2, with Sachin looking good and Dravid seemingly intent on putting his poor tour of Australia behind him.

The next two sessions of India's first home Test of the new millennium encapsulated the second half of the decade that had just gone by. Against a formidable opponent, India's 'one-man army' waged a heroic battle with negligible assistance.

Dravid and Ganguly were outsmarted by Donald and Pollock respectively, but the captain kept the scoreboard ticking, being particularly severe on Lance Klusener and then left-arm spinner Eksteen, whom he pulled twice into the stands for six. The first of those sixes took him to another Test 50. Nicky Boje, the other left-arm spinner, was exquisitely late cut for four. It was not that Sachin's innings was flawless. He had been lucky early on in his innings, when Donald hit him on the gloves and the ball popped up in no man's land. Later, he was beaten by a Kallis delivery that missed the stumps by the proverbial coat of paint. Donald, returning for another spell, believed that he had Sachin caught behind when he was on 75, but umpire S. Venkataraghavan thought otherwise. India at that stage were 137–4, a score that underscored the team's dependence on Sachin.

The Indian captain began the post-tea session with a boundary off Cronje. The South African captain then packed off Jadeja and Mongia off consecutive deliveries. With the lower order exposed, Sachin had no option but to make every scoring opportunity count. When Pollock and Kallis gave him a little bit of width outside the off-stump, he punched them for fours.

It was the same old story of watchers getting the impression that the match was being played on two different pitches. One batsman was dictating terms to the bowlers on one hand, and on the other hand, the bowlers were dominating the rest. The South Africans were eventually rewarded for their persistence when Sachin tickled a Kallis delivery down the leg-side and walked without waiting for the umpire's decision. He was only three short of what would have been a splendid hundred. Across the fence, scores of spectators rose from their seats to walk out of the stadium. They mirrored the feelings of Indian fans across the world; they had no option but to treat the Indian team as a one-man outfit, given that the team itself did not seem too inclined to prove otherwise. Sachin apart, nothing mattered.

A last-wicket stand of 41 between Agarkar and Kartik enabled India to reach 225. The South African openers put on 90, after which they declined to 176 all out. India's most successful bowler was none other than the captain himself. He bowled only five overs, but dismissed openers Herschelle Gibbs and Gary Kirsten, and later Shaun Pollock as well, to finish with figures of 3–10, his best in Tests.

All India needed to seal the game was a good batting performance in the second innings. Instead, there was a catastrophe. Donald, Pollock and Cronje himself bowled India out for 113. Only Dravid and Ganguly reached double figures and Sachin fell to his South African counterpart and bogey bowler for the fifth time in 10 Tests. The Indians dismissed six South Africans in the final innings, but the visitors batted very deep, and Kallis and keeper–batsman Mark Boucher completed a victory on the third afternoon of the game. It was Sachin's fourth straight defeat as captain of India.

The selectors met the same day to pick the squad for the second Test and announce the captain for the subsequent ODI series. There was never any doubt in anybody's mind that Sourav Ganguly was the right man for the job. Sachin had wanted him to be his deputy in Australia, and he had been granted his wish. Ganguly was a certainty in both forms of the game, and he had led India to victory over the West Indies at Toronto earlier in the season. V.V.S. Laxman was surprisingly axed, despite having scored 167 against the best bowling attack in the world, just one game previously.

The second Test, played at Bengaluru, was another disaster for the home team, as Cronje's South Africans became the first team to win a Test series in India since 1986–87. The visitors won by an innings and 71 runs, one of the biggest defeats handed out to an Indian team on home turf. Ironically, the most spirited resistance from the home camp was put up by Mohammed Azharuddin, who scored 102 in the second innings of what was his 99th Test.

The ODI series that followed featured some high scores and close finishes, with India eventually prevailing 3–2. Sachin's best performance was an innings of 122 in the fourth game at Vadodara. Chasing 284, the new captain took the initiative in the opening overs and Sachin essayed a supporting hand. The openers put on 153 at more than a run-a-ball. Sachin took charge after Ganguly's dismissal and maintained the scoring rate. He completed his 25th ODI hundred, and with 27 needed from the last five overs with eight wickets in hand, India were strolling towards a series-winning victory. But Sachin fell *against the run of play*, when he hit a Kallis full-toss straight down the throat of Steve Elworthy at mid-on. The South Africans then nearly pulled off a miracle, choking the batsmen and silencing the spectators, before Robin Singh and Saba Karim took India through with one delivery to spare.

Prior to the ODI series, India's ex-captain endeared himself to another sporting legend. Sachin was chief guest at a function organized by Malayala Manorama, a media group headquartered in the south Indian state of Kerala, on the eve of the first game at Kochi. He felicitated the late Jimmy George, the volleyball star of yesteryear, and the 'Payyoli Express' P.T. Usha, both of whom had won a poll for the best Malayalee* sportspersons of the millennium gone by. The self-effacing sprint queen of the 1980s addressed him as 'her darling brother' and told the audience that 'while he was a multi-faceted genius, she was a village girl who only knew how to run when the gun went off'. Sachin struck a rapport with her young son, whom he proceeded to personally introduce to his colleagues in the Indian team.

Sachin would go on to establish an even closer bond with Kerala and its people in the years to come.

Ganguly's first overseas assignment as full-time skipper was a tri-series against Pakistan and South Africa at Sharjah. The Indians beat Pakistan in their first game, but failed to sustain the momentum and lost out on a place in the final.

For Sachin, a season that had been frustrating, to say the least, was to end with two domestic games. After failing to qualify for the knockout stage of the Ranji Trophy for only the second time since 1934–35 the previous season, Mumbai had played excellent cricket to reach the semi-finals of the 1999–00 edition. Standing between them and a spot in the final were Tamil Nadu. Both sides had reason to cheer as all their 'India' players were fit and available for selection.

Sameer Dighe, who was leading Mumbai 'on paper', won the toss and surprisingly elected to bowl, not the smartest call to take in the April heat and humidity, that too on a strip that was practically lifeless, at the end of a long season.

Tamil Nadu expressed their gratitude by amassing 485, courtesy centuries by left-handers Hemang Badani and Robin Singh, the skipper. Mumbai's quest for the critical first-innings lead was not helped by the fall of wickets at regular intervals. Sachin came in at 77–2, when Jatin Paranjape was caught by Aashish Kapoor off Thiru Kumaran. At stumps on day two, Mumbai were 141–4, with the Shardashram duo at the crease. The target of 486, which Mumbai had to achieve to take the crucial first-innings lead, seemed light years away. A pensive Paranjape was sitting all by himself in the Mumbai dressing room, when he felt

---

*Malayalam is the official language of the state of Kerala and the residents of the state are called Malayalees.

a hand on his shoulder. 'Don't worry, we will win this game,' Sachin reassured his teammate. Paranjape, who thought like all 'normal' people did, could not see how his side would score 350 more with only six wickets in hand, but he was polite enough not to mention that. He had played with Sachin long enough at the junior and senior levels to know that the latter did not think like 'normal' individuals did.

On the third morning, Sachin had moved to 42 when he nicked S. Mahesh to J. Madanagopal at second slip, and the fielder grassed a relatively easy chance. This reprieve was followed by lunch. During the interval, Paras Mhambrey exhorted Sachin to delete that moment from his memory bank and move on. Sachin retorted with two words; 'No more!'

The expression on Sachin's face when he uttered those words left Mhambrey with no doubt that Mumbai would go the distance.

Kambli outscored Sachin on the third morning, contributing 75 to a fifth-wicket stand of 139 before he miscued a pull and was caught-and-bowled by S. Mahesh for 75. He was replaced in the middle by another Shardashram alumnus.

Sachin stepped up a gear, with Amol Muzumdar lending support. The duo executed several sparkling shots in a stand of 125, before Muzumdar was caught by Robin Singh off S. Sriram. That gave the Tamil Nadu bowlers the opportunity to have a go at the Mumbai lower-order. Sachin did everything he could to bat from both ends.

His teammates did their bit in the dressing room, not budging from their seats when the game was in progress and doing exactly what they had been doing when he had commenced his innings. This practically meant that if a teammate had been under the shower when Sachin had gone in at the fall of the second wicket, he would have to return to the shower.

For Ashok Mankad, the Mumbai coach and a former Mumbai captain, the routine was to go up to Sachin at every interval and ask him if all was well. Sachin would always reply in the affirmative and Mankad would then turn around and walk away without asking him anything else!

At the close on day three, Mumbai were 16 short of the Tamil Nadu score, with two wickets in hand. Sachin had batted brilliantly to complete his first double century in the Ranji Trophy in the closing stages of the day's play, but that hardly mattered.

The tension in both dressing rooms was palpable at the start of the fourth day; it was all down to one man, like it had been at Chennai a year before. Abey Kuruvilla, Mumbai's number 10, had defended resolutely on the third evening, without opening his account. Sachin, who had retained the strike the previous evening, managed to take a single in the first over of the fourth day and cross over to the other end. In the second over, he drove Mahesh in the long-off region and called his partner for two; Kuruvilla, not exactly the fleetest between wickets, was run out even as he tried to complete the second. Mumbai were 472–9, 13 runs behind.

Tamil Nadu's obvious plan was to deny Sachin a single and then attack Santosh Saxena, the number 11, in the next over. Mahesh had containment on his mind, but what he did not anticipate was Sachin advancing down the wicket and lofting him, high, straight and out of the ground. Before the bowler and his team could regain its composure, Sachin secured another single to retain the strike for Kumaran's next over.

With all the fielders save the wicketkeeper in the deep, getting a boundary seemed difficult and getting a two almost impossible. But Sachin managed the impossible with a perfectly timed flick that ensured a comfortable two before the ball could be returned to the wicketkeeper. Kumaran's next ball was pitched short of a length and it gave the batsman some width. Sachin latched on to it and lashed hard. The cherry whizzed off the turf and went to the right of Robin Singh, who had stationed himself at sweeper. All that the Tamil Nadu captain and one of the best fielders in the world had to do was cover a mere 10 yards to stop it. But he couldn't. The ball was too fast for him. It beat his dive and thudded into the wooden plank across the rope. The scores were now level. Saxena then survived an entire Mahesh over, which included a confident shout for leg-before, before handing it back to Sachin. Kumaran began the next over with two dot-balls. The third ball was short. Sachin transferred his weight onto his back foot and swivelled as he met the ball with a horizontal bat. For the smattering of spectators at the venue that morning, Sachin's roar of delight when the ball crossed the mid-wicket boundary was more audible than the cheers emanating from the Mumbai dressing room.

Saxena fell at 490. Both he and Kuruvilla, the number 10, had not opened their accounts; Sachin had scored every single run that came off the bat, from 449–8 to 490 all out. He had batted for 565 minutes and scored an unbeaten 233, inclusive of 21 boundaries and five sixes.

Tamil Nadu may have conceded a slim first-innings lead, but with nearly two days' play left, they were by no means out of it. They could have tried to bat aggressively in their second innings and set Mumbai a target on the last day. After all, anything was possible in cricket. However, not for the first or last time did they show just why they had won the Ranji Trophy only twice in 67 seasons, despite having produced some fine cricketers over the decades. Sachin's 233 had taken the wind out of their sails. They were bowled out for 171 in their second innings and Mumbai completed an eight-wicket win on the final morning.

In the final, Mumbai faced off against another Ranji Trophy underachiever—Hyderabad. The game proceeded on expected lines, with the availability of Azharuddin and Laxman making no difference to Hyderabad's fortunes. Mumbai batted first this time around, and scored 376, with Kambli making 108 and Sachin getting 53. Three wickets by Agarkar hastened Hyderabad's demise for 195. Sachin scored 128 in the second innings, and Mumbai ended up winning by 297 runs. Much like Indian teams returning from tours, the Ranji runners-up of 1999–00 sought solace in the achievements of two of their players; the 62 wickets taken by Kanwaljeet Singh, their off-spinner, were the second-highest in a single Ranji Trophy season, and V.V.S. Laxman's aggregate of 1,415 was the highest-ever in a Ranji season. He delayed Mumbai's victory with a knock of 111 in the fourth innings.

However, these domestic feats were overshadowed by the skeletons that came tumbling and crashing out of many a cupboard. On 7 April 2000, two days before the start of the Ranji semi-final, officers of the Delhi Police force declared in a press conference that they possessed incriminating evidence of match-fixing. Their officers, who had been tapping phones while carrying out another investigation, had stumbled upon a chain of conversations between 'bookies' and no less a personality than Hansie Cronje, the captain of one of the best sides in the world. What followed ripped the fabric of the sport apart. Cronje refuted the accusations initially, but he eventually owned up to wrongdoing, and things just got progressively worse, not only in South Africa and India but internationally as well.

Among those who hit the headlines during this period was Manoj Prabhakar. He had earlier alleged that a teammate had offered him an astronomical amount of money to underperform against Pakistan in a league game of the quadrangular Singer Cup in Sri Lanka in 1994—a tournament that Indian fans remembered only for Sachin's maiden ODI hundred. The game against Pakistan was never played due to rain, as it turned out.

The Delhi all-rounder had also claimed that he had revealed the name of the player who had made the offer to a senior functionary in the then Union Government. A couple of weeks after the outbreak of what was called 'Hansiegate', I.S. Bindra, the former president of the BCCI, claimed in a TV interview that Kapil Dev was the individual whom Prabhakar had named in front of the government functionary.

The man who had led India to World Cup glory broke down while pleading his innocence in a TV interview. He was subsequently absolved of all match-fixing charges by the Central Bureau of Investigation (CBI).

This was also the time Prabhakar teamed up with a couple of journalists to conduct a 'sting operation' on the who's who of Indian cricket. The Delhi all-rounder's brief was to prod these members of the cricketing community to talk on topics that they would never discuss on record. A fair amount of the content was sordid, to say the least, and it reflected poorly on some big guns, whose names came up in the conversations.

The Union Home Ministry requested the CBI to 'probe the entire gamut of match-fixing and betting'. The objectives outlined by the Bureau when it began its work in May 2000 were as follows:

1. To identify the betting syndicates operating in India and examine their activities;
2. To unravel the linkages of cricket players or their intermediaries with these syndicates and their roles in the alleged malpractises; and
3. To examine the role and functions of the BCCI so as to evaluate whether it could have prevented the alleged malpractises.

The CBI began by clarifying that the term 'match-fixing' stood for instances of players being paid to underperform, players placing bets to undermine their own performance, players and ex-players being paid to pass on information on team composition and weather conditions, players and ex-players being used by bookies to gain access to other prominent cricketing figures and groundsmen being bribed to prepare the pitch in a certain way.

The CBI proceeded to examine all available evidence and unearth fresh evidence. Quite a few domestic and international matches played in the 1990s came under the scanner.

Individuals who had been accused of indulging in unsavoury practices and mingling with the 'wrong' people over the past few years were summoned and questioned by the CBI.

It was also necessary to get the perspective of people who did not have any aspersions cast on their integrity, but whose views and inputs mattered. Sachin belonged to this category.

> Sachin Tendulkar, former Indian captain, when asked about the India-New Zealand Test at Ahmedabad in 1999, stated that by the end of third

day's play when New Zealand had lost around 6 wickets, he had thought to himself that he would enforce the follow-on the next day. However, the New Zealand innings dragged on till after lunch the next day and by then he himself, coach Kapil Dev, Anil Kumble and Ajay Jadeja decided that the follow-on would not be enforced since the bowlers, especially Srinath had insisted that they were very tired. It was a collective decision not to enforce follow-on. On being asked whether anybody could have influenced this decision since the bookies in Delhi allegedly knew one day in advance that follow-on will not be enforced, he accepted that it was possible.... On being asked whether he suspected any Indian player of being involved in match-fixing, Sachin stated that during his tenure as Captain, he had felt that Mohd Azharuddin was not putting in 100 per cent effort and he suspected that he was involved with some bookies.

—Extract from the statement of Sachin Tendulkar that appeared in the 'Report on Cricket Match-fixing and Related Malpractises', CBI

The CBI's report, which was submitted on 1 November 2000 after a thorough investigation that comprised interviews and interrogations of players, former members of the national team's support staff, administrators and even bookies, scrutiny of telephone records and the tapping of informers, was as comprehensive as it was cataclysmic.

By early 1990s, betting on cricket had spread across India and had attained a measure of sophistication. Typically, all that a bookie needed to start his profession was a telephone connection, a television set, a notebook and a clientele who were basically known to the bookie through various contacts.... By the middle of the 1990s, with a surfeit of one day matches being shown live on television and also the onset of cable revolution in which international matches featuring countries other than India also began to be telecast live, betting had taken the shape of a massive organised racket. The introduction of mobile phones in the mid '90s also gave a major fillip to this racket, since bookies and punters were no longer solely dependent on P&T lines for communication and could therefore be more mobile. Bombay emerged as the main centre for betting, followed by Delhi and other metropolitan cities such as Calcutta, Chennai, Ahmedabad, and even smaller district towns. Bombay took the lead in this racket since the odds on which bets were played in any match throughout India were determined by the bookies based in Bombay.

—Extract from the 'Report on Cricket Match-fixing and Related Malpractises', CBI, New Delhi, October 2000

The report was not one-dimensional; it also featured some black comedy. One of the bookies who was interrogated during the investigation, admitted transferring a large sum of money to the bank account of Hansie Cronje, around the time of the third Test of South Africa's home series against India in 1996–97. Cronje had assured the bookie that South Africa would lose, but the game, which was played at Johannesburg, ended in a draw. The South African captain then promised the bookie that his team would lose some one-day matches,* but even that did not happen and the bookie ended up losing a lot of money. He confronted Cronje, only to be told that India had played so badly and missed so many chances that he could not do anything about the result.

The report will also go down in history for featuring the grandest tribute ever paid to a cricketer.

> In fact, in most of matches where fixing was taking place, the clue was that the game would 'be on' only when Tendulkar got out because he was one player who could single-handedly win the match and upset any calculation.
>
> —Extract from the 'Report on Cricket Match-fixing and Related Malpractises', CBI, New Delhi, October 2000

This inadvertent acknowledgement of Sachin's genius notwithstanding, Cricket's 'Age of Innocence' had ended for good. No longer were the fans prepared to trust their heroes blindly. Cynicism had crept in. Now every dropped catch, every misfield, every bad ball, every run out, was up for scrutiny—subject to the masses still caring for the sport, of course. The popularity of the sport had taken a thrashing.

A couple of weeks after the outbreak of Hansiegate, an Indian cricket fortnightly carried the results of a survey conducted by a prominent advertising agency, pertaining to cricket and its popularity. One thousand Indians across age-groups and categories were quizzed on their perception of cricket and cricketers, post the outbreak of the scandal. The good news was that 78.7 per cent of the respondents said that they still loved cricket, and 83 per cent declared that they would continue to watch matches. The bad news was that over 70 per

---

*Cronje was in all probability referring to the tri-series featuring South Africa, India and Zimbabwe that was played after the Test series between India and South Africa.

cent believed that Indian cricketers were involved in match-fixing, and over 98 per cent were convinced that match-fixing was to blame for India's below-par performances in the recent past.

They said that dawn was always preceded by the darkest hour. Would the same hold true in the case of Indian cricket?

> Expressing his views which have been awaited for long in an interview with a news weekly, Tendulkar dismissed attempts to drag his name into the controversy. 'I have always been out of this kind of thing. The nation knows I am clean. My whole career has been transparent. I don't have to go out and say anything in my defence', he said. 'The only reason I did not speak about it is that I didn't know anything about it. I would have given a statement if I knew something. So how can I say who is telling the truth and who is not?' Tendulkar asked. Tendulkar denied former Pakistan captain Rashid Latif's claim that he knew everything about match-fixing. 'It's not true. And it's not necessary that I have to react to any person's statements.' Tendulkar said: 'The players should have some freedom to speak about the game, not about things like match-fixing because that's a sensitive issue. Anybody who opens his mouth should also provide proof. It's important not to create controversies. It's the game that will suffer,' he said. On whether Indian cricket could recover from the scandal, Tendulkar said cricket was too great a game to be permanently affected by these scandals. 'It has given so much joy to people all over the world. This is just a passing phase. I am a positive person. I can only look at the positive side, he added. On the general impression that he was too diplomatic, Tendulkar said 'I don't think as an Indian cricketer I am a diplomatic person. Rather, I would say that I have always been soft-spoken. To me it's natural not to say much beyond the game'.
>
> —Sachin Tendulkar, as quoted on www.cricinfo.com, 18 July 2000

SECTION III

Preceptor (2000-13)

A NEW BEGINNING

But for me, having watched him grow and having known him even before he played his first match for Mumbai—and perhaps because of that, not completely blinded, as most are, by the aura that surrounds him—it's just that I somehow expect more from him. Not so much when he is on the field as when he is off it.... To stay non-committal has been his trusted method of handling matters.... Mind you, this formula has worked beautifully for him. You will not find a less controversial cult figure than Sachin anywhere. But then, the ability to do the right things, even if they are contrary to one's nature, is, I believe, the real test of an individual.... While the game was being ravaged by sordid revelations and allegations of wrong-doing, Steve Waugh, from one corner of the world, attempted to salvage whatever little he could by issuing non-controversial yet encouraging statements. Sachin's silence, on the other hand, almost gave the impression that he had washed his hands off the game when it was facing its worst-ever crisis. Cricket deserved more from one of its best products.... All over the world, there is nothing but goodwill, admiration and adoration for him. But it is not unreasonable that as his game matures and he grows in stature, the expectations people have of him will increase. Apart from continuing to pile up the runs, he will need to demonstrate a broad vision for Indian cricket and share his views with his adoring constituency. Mere good intentions are not always enough; sometimes you need to stand up for your beliefs. Sachin has represented the Indian cricket team with impeccable distinction.... It's time he also represented Indian cricket.

—Sanjay Manjrekar, *Wisden Asia Cricket*, September 2002

Sachin had always done things and responded to crises, his way. The crisis of 2000 was no exception.

After the CBI released its report, Sachin was part of a group of senior players who requested Board officials to ensure that besides the players who had been banned for their involvement in match-fixing, even those whose integrity had come under a cloud, ought to never represent India again. He was also part of a group that met Mr A.C. Muthiah, Mr Jaywant Lele and Mr Raj Singh Dungarpur, the president, secretary and former president of the BCCI, respectively, at Nairobi in October 2000, and emphasized the necessity of requisitioning a coach from overseas. The senior players reckoned that an individual from outside India's cricket system would provide a fresh perspective and a different approach. He would also be immune to charges of parochialism. The Board went ahead and shortlisted John Wright of New Zealand and Greg Chappell of Australia for the post. Wright, who had earlier coached Kent in the English County Championship, got the job.

There was a lot that happened before the appointment of the new coach. India crashed out of the Asia Cup, played in Bangladesh in mid-2000, with losses to Sri Lanka and Pakistan. The results of the poll conducted by the advertising agency notwithstanding, most fans were indifferent to the proceedings in Dhaka. In July, there were media reports of raids by the income-tax authorities on the homes of some cricketers.

The BCCI took some constructive calls during this phase.

In fact, the process that culminated with John Wright's appointment as coach in November 2000 began much earlier in the year, with the inception of the long-overdue National Cricket Academy, a finishing school-cum-rehabilitation centre for senior and junior cricketers, at the M. Chinnaswamy Stadium in Bengaluru.

One of Bengaluru's most famous residents also utilized the off-season optimally. After his fine performances in both forms of the game in the first 10 months of 1999, Rahul Dravid had been brought down to earth with his failures in Australia. A stickler for perfection and aware of the need to keep honing his skills, he signed up with Kent in the English County Championship and returned to India, a more rounded batsman. Another player who also took off for England was Sourav Ganguly, who represented Lancashire.

The Indian players regrouped in Nairobi at the end of September 2000 for the second edition of the ICC Knockout. Anshuman Gaekwad had been reinstated as coach after Kapil Dev resigned.

Those who watched India beat Kenya, the hosts, in the 'pre-quarters' of the competition, liked the look of a left-arm paceman from Shrirampur, Maharashtra, who had started his first-class career with Mumbai and then shifted to Vadodara. Ganguly was impressed enough to give him the new ball ahead of Venkatesh Prasad and Ajit Agarkar. The paceman's name was Zaheer Khan.

Four days after the game against Kenya, Ganguly's team took on the world champions in the quarter-final on 7 October 2000. It was a national holiday in

India on account of Dussehra, the festival that celebrated the triumph of good over evil.

The game commenced with a duel between contemporary legends. Steve Waugh had no hesitation putting India in after winning the toss on a Nairobi Gymkhana track that had some juice in it. The new ball was entrusted as always to Glenn McGrath, an interrogator par excellence and a bowler renowned not to let up after getting into a rhythm. On that strip, there was every possibility of his striking early and big.

The first ball of McGrath's second over was pitched on a length. Sachin met it on the up and swung hard. In fact, he swung a little too hard and the bat connected with the ball a fraction of a second earlier than it should have. The ball went a mile high, behind square. The initial reaction of watchers was that it would land in the hands of the fielder at the third man. However, it cleared him, as well as the boundary.

Sachin had made up his mind to test McGrath's patience instead of giving the bowler the opportunity to test his batting technique.

No fast bowler appreciates being hit over his head, and McGrath was no exception. He did not find it funny when Sachin met the third ball of his next over literally halfway down the pitch, and drove it straight into the sightscreen for six. The bowler looked up at the batsman to subject him to a mouthful, only to be outdone even in the verbal stakes; Sachin was anything but polite as he told the bowler to 'buzz off', albeit in more colourful language.

McGrath, so used to pitching the ball exactly where he wanted to, landed the next one just short of a length; it made no difference to what the batsman had in mind. Even before the ball had been released, Sachin had started advancing down the wicket. He flat-batted it past the bowler on his follow-through for four. This time, the bowler just nodded his head to indicate that he had been out-thought. Sachin's calculated assault had given the Indians momentum. A hook in McGrath's next over gave him his third six of the innings.

With Ganguly looking fluent at the other end, the openers scored at nearly a-run-a-ball. In the 11th over, Sachin bisected the two men patrolling the covers for four, and drove Brett Lee down the ground in the following over. But the bowler had the last laugh, as he induced Sachin to nick one to Damien Martyn at slip. India were 66–1 and Sachin had scored 38. Much to the dismay of Indian fans, Jason Gillespie then accounted for both Ganguly and Dravid in quick succession. At 90–3, the Australians were back in the game. Vinod Kambli, who had returned to the side, was fourth out at 130, but another southpaw and the star of India's victorious campaign in the ICC under-19 World Cup earlier that year, got going at the highest level. Like Zaheer Khan, Yuvraj Singh had made his international debut against Kenya, but he hadn't got to bat.

The left-hander from Chandigarh displayed flair and verve, holding the middle and latter stages of the innings together to score 84. A six by Venkatesh Prasad off the last ball of the innings took India to a competitive 265–9.

The underdogs then bowled well and caught and fielded magnificently to win by 20 runs. As they celebrated what was very much an upset, the Indian players were aware that they had won much more than a cricket match. If a comprehensive win over the world champions could not bring a smile to the faces of all those who had felt betrayed, then nothing would.

Sourav Ganguly took the opponent's attack by the scruff of the neck in India's next encounter, the semi-final against South Africa. He batted through the innings to score 141 and India finished just five short of 300. Sachin got off to another great start and fell for 39. Yuvraj's 84 against Australia earned him a promotion to number four, and the left-hander arrived at the wicket after Dravid's dismissal for 58. The score then was 211–2. Yuvraj, seemingly intent on carrying on from where he had left off, was lucky in the early stages of his innings, when a mishit of his landed in no-man's land. He was severely rebuked by his captain in the middle of the pitch for the stroke. This was new, as Indian captains were not known to be so demonstrative on the field of play. Yuvraj took the cue and did not do anything flashy, but still scored 41 off 35 balls.

The South Africans never recovered after losing opener Andrew Hall to a peach of a yorker by Zaheer Khan. Gary Kirsten, the other opener, was run out, and the fall of two more wickets reduced them to 50–4. Ganguly kept tightening the screws and the only blemishes were the two catches that the captain himself dropped in the slips off consecutive deliveries, in the latter stages. However, the game had already been sealed by then. India won by 95 runs and marched into the final as favourites. It had been an incredible turnaround and the traumatic events of the first half of 2000 seemed to belong to another universe.

In the summit clash against New Zealand, a side that had never made it to the final of a 'world' event, the Indian team got the better of all the opposition players, bar one. Chris Cairns put the brakes on the Indian scoring after the openers had put on 141. The all-rounder bowled his 10 overs on the trot to finish with 0–40, and the Indian middle-order failed to consolidate on the efforts of Sachin (69) and Ganguly (117). Still, 264–6 was a competitive score to make in a final, and New Zealand were 82–3 in response when Cairns came in. He proceeded to combine the roles of aggressor and anchor to perfection, and scored a match-winning century, taking his team home with two deliveries to spare.

The Indians could count themselves unlucky to have been at the receiving end of an exceptional all-round display.

India then failed to repeat their 1998–99 heroics against Sri Lanka and Zimbabwe in a tri-series at Sharjah. Sachin's 101 in the first league game against Sri Lanka went in vain as the island nation won by five wickets. India did make it to the final, where they found themselves confronting a tornado called Sanath Jayasuriya. Their old nemesis blasted his way to a record 189, and Sri Lanka set India 300 to win. India surrendered meekly, being bowled out for 54. It was a disappointing note on which to end a tri-series after just finishing an international tournament as the second-best team.

At an awards function in Mumbai a couple of days after the debacle, Sourav Ganguly, who won the International Cricketer of the Year Award for his performances in the 1999–2000 season, appealed to the fans to 'keep the faith' in the Indian team.

The post-Hansiegate phase, when the credibility of the sport and those who played it had come under a cloud, was a time when Indian cricket needed a leader who was forceful and did not hesitate to call a spade a spade in public. Ganguly was someone who fit the bill. He had also shown himself to be an effective man-manager. He began his stint as India's Test captain in Bangladesh's inaugural Test, which was played in Dhaka in November 2000. The newest full members of the ICC gave a good account of themselves in the first innings, but ran out of steam thereafter. India won by eight wickets.

John Wright's first assignment as the coach was a two-Test series against Zimbabwe. One of the first things he noted during his debut game was to avoid telling the batsmen how to bat, especially in Indian conditions. As was expected, the hosts had the better of the series, with Sachin in terrific form. He followed a match-winning century in the first Test at Delhi with a double hundred—his second in Tests—in the second Test at Nagpur.

The ODI series that followed the Tests turned out to be the last on Indian soil to be played in whites. The one discordant note struck by the hosts as they compiled a 4–1 win was the one-match suspension handed to Ganguly for 'excessive appealing' in the fourth encounter at Kanpur. In his absence, Rahul Dravid led India in the final game, played at Rajkot on 14 December 2000. The pecking order had been clearly defined; the Karnataka batsman was officially the second-in-command, the leader-in-waiting—on the field.

Nine days before Dravid first led India in an international game, the BCCI delivered an exemplary display of leadership *off the field*, on the day India and Zimbabwe played the second game of the ODI series at Ahmedabad.

The Board responded to the findings of the CBI report with alacrity. Those who had been found to have tarnished the sport were implicated. A couple of cricketers were banned for life and others embargoed for five years. The Rogues' Gallery included someone who had ironically tried to project himself as a whistle-blower. Other countries also initiated inquiries and investigations against their players who had been suspected of being on the payroll of bookies, but no other cricketing body was as proactive as the BCCI in flushing the toxins out.

The Board officials also sought to emphasize to one and all that the investigations had not yielded even a shred of evidence against the individuals who constituted the backbone of the Indian team—Sourav Ganguly, Rahul Dravid, Anil Kumble, Javagal Srinath, Venkatesh Prasad, and of course, Sachin Tendulkar.

It was upto this 'backbone' to lead by example in what promised to be the Indian team's toughest Test on home turf for a long time. Steve Waugh's 'Awesome Aussies' landed in India in February 2001 with a record 15 consecutive Test triumphs behind them. The Australian captain had hit the headlines well before the series, with his description of India as the 'Final Frontier'; Australia had not won a Test series on Indian soil since 1969–70.

The Indians readied themselves for the confrontation with an intensive 10-day camp at Chennai. Among the attendees was the 19-year-old Harbhajan Singh, who had undergone a horrid time on and off the field since his Test debut against the Australians at Bengaluru in 1998. First, the legality of his bowling action was questioned, and he was prescribed remedial treatment. He was then rusticated from the newly instituted National Cricket Academy on grounds of indiscipline. The expulsion from the 'finishing school' of Indian cricket put a question mark on his future as a cricketer. As if this was not all, he lost his father, who along with him was the breadwinner of the family. It was a situation that necessitated tough decisions. The youngster had all but made up his mind to fly to the US and drive trucks to support his family.

However, he found an unexpected supporter in Sourav Ganguly. The Indian captain had always admired the off-spinner since he had first seen him in action. During the Zimbabwe series, he had persuaded Wright to watch Harbhajan in the nets. The Indian coach was impressed by the prodigious turn he was getting, as well as the competitive spirit he was exuding. With Anil Kumble out of action after undergoing a shoulder operation, India needed a bowler who would combine the roles of 'stock' and 'shock' bowler. Sarandeep Singh, Harbhajan's Punjab teammate and a fine off-spinner himself, was very much a part of the group of players shortlisted for the Australia series, but the team management was sold on Harbhajan and insisted on his inclusion.

Harbhajan took five wickets for the Board President's XI against the visitors at Nagpur. Another player who did well in the tour-opener was V.V.S. Laxman, who led the home team and scored 94. Like Harbhajan, he too had found himself in a situation wherein he had to take tough calls before the start of the season. Thrust into the unfamiliar role of opener in his very first season of international cricket, he had responded manfully and essayed quite a few significant knocks in that role, but as far as he was concerned, he had had enough. Prior to the 2000–01 season, he had informed the Board that he was available only as a middle-order batsman. He was picked for the Australia series as one, on the strength of his extraordinary form in domestic cricket.

The Australians played another three-day game against Mumbai, the 1999–00 Ranji champions, at the Brabourne Stadium, before the first Test began at the Wankhede on 27 February 2001. Before the action got underway, the teams observed a minute's silence in memory of 'the Don', who had passed away just two days previously. Waugh won the toss and took a gut call in asking India to bat. His bowlers did not let him down. Ramesh fell to an attempted hook with only seven on the board and Dravid was second out at 25.

Dravid's dismissal triggered the usual wave of pandemonium. When Sachin emerged from the dressing room, many people who were at the Wankhede that morning, this writer included, could have sworn that they experienced aftershocks of the tremors that had rocked Mumbai exactly a month previously. The stands shook as the spectators accorded a rapturous ovation to their hero, whom they expected to do what he had done for most of the 11 years of his career—steer his team out of a crisis. The hero proceeded to play an innings that his spiritual predecessor, no doubt watching from the heavens, would have been very proud of. The only unfortunate aspect was that those who had watched his 97 against the South Africans in the previous Test at the Wankhede experienced a feeling of déjà vu. His batting was phenomenal but that of his teammates was pedestrian.

As in the Test played exactly a year previously, Sachin drove splendidly, pulled superbly, cut spectacularly and ran brilliantly. The highlight of his innings was three successive boundaries in a Damien Fleming over. Two stunning straight drives were followed by a cut. He had scored 76, inclusive of 13 boundaries, when he tried to drive a McGrath delivery pitched in the 'corridor of uncertainty' and got an outside-edge. Adam Gilchrist did the rest.

Laxman (20) and the recalled Nayan Mongia (26*) apart, no other Indian batsman did anything of note. India were all out for 176.

Harbhajan struck thrice on the second morning. Steve Waugh became the first Test victim of the debutant left-arm spinner Rahul Sanghvi, and with Australia 99–5, all India needed was one more wicket to attack the lower order. Ganguly then asked Sanghvi to take a break and threw the ball to Sachin. The captain probably reckoned that Matthew Hayden and Adam Gilchrist, the two left-handers at the crease, would find Sanghvi's left-arm spin easier to deal with. Sachin could not quite settle down, and he bowled a couple of loose deliveries that got the treatment.

By the time Sanghvi was brought back, the match had turned on its head. Both batsmen smashed their way all over the ground and occasionally beyond it, to help their team reach 349. India's cause was not helped by the absence of Javagal Srinath due to a finger injury, for a substantial part of the innings.

In the second innings, Sadagoppan Ramesh and newcomer Shiv Sunder Das, India's openers, put on 33 before being separated. Ramesh hit seven boundaries in an innings of 44 before he was caught in the slips. Mongia came in as the night watchman in the closing stages of the second day, but he sustained a finger injury and was unable to continue. Sachin replaced him in the middle and played out the remaining deliveries.

Day three witnessed a battle of attrition. The Australians gave nothing away, and Sachin and Dravid were content to play along. Sachin took on McGrath while Dravid tackled Gillespie. They did not set the scoreboard alight, but made sure that every loose delivery was accounted for. The closest Australia came to taking a wicket in the first session was when Michael Slater claimed a catch off Dravid, only for the appeal to be negatived as the ball had touched the turf despite the fielder getting his hands to it. This led to some unpleasant theatrics by Slater, who ought to have been reined in by his seniors well before he debated with the umpire and the batsman.

At lunch on day three, India were 116–2. Sachin brought the crowd to its feet with two drives to the boundary off Gillespie, the second of which took him to his second 50 of the game. A short delivery by Mark Waugh was contemptuously pulled to the mid-wicket fence. When Waugh dropped one short again, Sachin went for another pull, but this time, the left shoulder of Justin Langer, who was fielding at short-leg, came in the way. The ball ricocheted off his shoulder into the air, and Ricky Ponting, who was standing at mid-wicket, took an incredible one-handed catch. Not for the first time since 1989, the lights went out in the Indian camp after Sachin's freaky dismissal.

Ganguly fell cheaply and Laxman and Dravid fell at the same score. Dravid's was the most crucial wicket of the lot as he had battled hard in his knock of 39. All his perseverance was undone when he was beaten in the air by Warne and comprehensively bowled.

India's second innings ended at 219. Australia needed only seven overs to score 47 and record their 16th consecutive win.

To halt the Australian juggernaut, India needed every member of the side to produce his best cricket at the Eden Gardens. On the first three days of the Test, that did not happen. Australia won the toss and batted first. They declined from 193–1 at one stage to 252–7, with Harbhajan taking the first hat-trick by an Indian in Tests, but Steve Waugh essayed a captain's hand to take them to 445.

India's first innings was a disaster. Ramesh fell without a run on the board, Dravid played yet another attractive 'cameo' of 25 before being bowled by Warne yet again, and one could have heard a pin drop in the galleries when Sachin was trapped leg-before by McGrath for 10. At 97–7 and V.V.S. Laxman, the last recognized batsman still in single figures, a sub-100 score was a possibility. However, the tail-enders defied the bowlers and gave Laxman the confidence to go for his strokes. He had moved to 59, inclusive of 12 scintillating boundaries, when he was declared out caught at slip, although the ball appeared to have come off his forearm. With a first-innings lead of 274 under his belt, Steve Waugh enforced the follow-on. The fall of the 'Final Frontier' was only 10 wickets away, or so it seemed.

Back in the Indian dressing room, Laxman was told not to take his pads off. He had been promoted to one-down, with Dravid moving down to number six.

India's new number three returned to the middle after the openers had put on 52. Sachin came in at a relatively healthy 97–2, but did not last long, nicking a gem of a delivery by Gillespie that curled away, to Gilchrist. Ganguly, who had been struggling with the bat, knuckled down to contribute 48 to a fourth-wicket association of 117, before he was caught behind off McGrath. The Indian captain's dismissal brought Dravid to the crease.

It would not have been easy for the Indian vice-captain to give up the pivotal one-down position that he had manned with distinction for years. But the fact was that his own inconsistency with the bat had forced the team management to take that call. The only option for him was to shut himself off from all the negativity and bat as well as he could, not only to save the game, but also to silence those who had branded him a 'fairweather' batsman.

Just before stumps on day three, V.V.S. Laxman completed his second Test century. India were 20 runs shy of making Australia bat again at the close, and the nation was relieved that there would at least be no innings defeat.

The day 14 March 2001 was a red-letter day in the history of Indian cricket. Those privileged to view the game, either at the stadium or on TV, were treated to the spectacle of two talented cricketers whose temperament had been questioned in the recent past, metamorphosing into world-beaters. V.V.S. Laxman did not hit as much as caress the ball. Warne, whose ploy to bowl from around the wicket failed for the second consecutive time on a tour of India, and the pacemen could only watch as the artiste used his bat like an extension of his hands to pierce the gaps almost at will. He stroked a mind-boggling 44 boundaries, making sure that all the bad balls that he received—plus some good ones as well—crossed the ropes.

If Laxman was the sublime artist, Dravid was the silent assassin who had a point or two to prove. Both batsmen fed off each other and their colleagues and Andrew Leipus, the team physiotherapist, did their bit during the intervals.

At stumps on day four, watchers were struggling to come to terms with the events of the previous six hours; up against the best bowling line-up in the world that had scented a 17th win on the trot, Laxman and Dravid had batted through the day and scored 335 runs. On the fifth morning, Laxman was dismissed on 281, the highest individual score by an Indian in Tests, and Dravid was run out for 180. The duo had added a record 376 for the fifth wicket.

Ganguly's declaration left the visitors with 75 overs in which to score 384. Ironically, Australia's winning streak had ensured that most of the players were not used to being in a situation wherein all they could do was play for a draw or even confront the possibility of defeat.

The Australians were three down at the tea interval. A draw seemed imminent.

Five runs had been added to the score in the final session when Waugh tried to flick Harbhajan and was caught by Hemang Badani. Ponting, who came in next, negotiated three deliveries before being snapped up by Shiv Sunder Das at bat-pad, again off Harbhajan. The celebrations of the Indian players rekindled the memories of their predecessors jumping over each other at the fall of every West Indies wicket in the 1983 World Cup final.

Sachin's introduction into the attack had not worked against Hayden and Gilchrist at Mumbai. On the contrary, it had backfired. At Kolkata, with the same two batsmen at the crease, Ganguly decided to give the tactic another go. The situation of course was entirely different from the one at Mumbai, with the visitors on the defensive, an approach that did not come naturally to them. The Indian captain's probable ploy was to try Sachin for a couple of overs and see how he was shaping up, before reverting to his specialists.

With two left-handers at the crease, Sachin aimed to land his leg-breaks in the bowlers' rough. When he bowled a leg-break to Gilchrist that the batsman tried to sweep, but missed and was struck on the back leg, there was bedlam. The cricketer who had scored a breathtaking century in the first Test had got a king's pair in the very next game. Six runs had been added to the score when Hayden went for a sweep, missed and was hit on the front pad. The appeal was upheld. Sachin had now taken two.

At the same venue where he had bowled that memorable final over against South Africa in November 1993, Sachin was far from finished. The new man in was Warne. The two adversaries were in direct confrontation once again, but they had reversed roles. To the greatest leg-spinner of all time, Sachin bowled a leg-spinner's most potent variation—the googly. The delivery pitched in line and went the other way, completely befuddling Warne of all people. He was found plumb in front, and the scenes on the playing arena and the galleries were quite surreal, as no one could believe what was happening. Sachin may have failed as a batsman with scores of 10 in both innings, but he had made a mark on the proceedings with as many as three critical wickets.

When Warne fell, India were only two wickets away from completing the most extraordinary turnaround in the history of the sport.

Michael Kasprowicz, Jason Gillespie and Glenn McGrath displayed their professionalism as they defended stoutly but the momentum was with India. Gillespie was brilliantly caught by Das in the close-in cordon, and when McGrath padded up to Harbhajan without offering a shot, it was all over. India had won by 171 runs and dramatically levelled the series. It was only the third instance in 124 years of Test cricket of a team winning a Test after being asked to follow-on. As delighted as the winners was Peter Willey, the only witness to two of those three instances. He had played at Leeds in 1981[*] and umpired at Kolkata in 2001.

Matthew Hayden swept and slammed his way to a double hundred at the start of the decider at Chennai, but his team collapsed from 340-3 to 391 all out. Ramesh and Das put on 123, and with Laxman in imperious form, the score was a healthy 211-1 at stumps on day two. They started badly on day three, with Das, who had batted well to score 84, was leg-before to McGrath off the very first ball of the day's play.

Sachin had trained intensively for the game, especially working on his technique against reverse-swing. He made up his mind to keep looking at the ball, even between deliveries when it was being returned to the bowler. This exercise made it easier for him to reach a state wherein all he could see was the ball and the bowler's grip, and nothing else.

---

[*]England beat Australia by 18 runs.

Out in the middle, he got his feet moving with a cover-drive off Gillespie. Laxman, who looked good for another big one, then perished to a fine slip catch by Mark Waugh. The spectators rose to another Sachin drive that neatly pierced the gap between the covers and mid-off, this time off McGrath.

Tendulkar is beginning to stamp himself all over this match.

—Tony Greig, live commentary

Ganguly scored 22, adding 47 with his predecessor before McGrath again had him caught by Gilchrist. At 284–4, Sachin was joined in the middle by Dravid.

If there was one player who mirrored the transformation of the Indian team since the fourth day of the Kolkata Test better than anybody else, it was the technician from Bengaluru. The self-doubt a thing of the past, he matched Sachin stroke-for-stroke in a stand of 169. The batting from both ends was nothing short of delightful, with clinical efficiency as much on show as cheekiness. Sachin brought up his 50 with a 'paddle-pull' off a short delivery by Colin Miller, the off-spinner who had been picked ahead of Kasprowicz for the game; he simply helped it along to the fine-leg boundary with a vertical bat. This was shortly after he had punched the same bowler over mid-wicket for six.

A few more strokes later, India took the lead and Sachin got a life when Slater made a mess of a regulation catch at mid-wicket off Miller. A few minutes later, the M.A. Chidambaram Stadium was applauding the 25th Test century of a craftsman who had become a colossus. Sachin rubbed salt on Miller's wounds with a disdainful lofted drive for six, to reach the milestone. After Dravid's dismissal for a magnificent 84, Warne decided to test Sachin with a bouncer, of all deliveries. However, it rose a little higher than the bowler intended, but Sachin, who was by then 'seeing it like a football', raised his bat like a periscope to cut it over slip's head for four. Both adversaries broke into a smile; yet another duel of theirs had gone in the batsman's favour. Sachin had moved to 126 when he was caught behind off Gillespie. India finished with a first-innings lead of 110.

At the end-of-day media conference, Sachin was flummoxed when a journalist asked him how it felt to emerge from a 'bad patch'. Given that he had scored three centuries in his previous five Tests, plus two 50s at Mumbai, it was an odd assessment to make.

As many as eight Australians reached double figures in the second innings, but not one could settle in to play a long one, and the visitors were all out for 264 on the fifth morning. India's man of the moment was Harbhajan Singh, who had vindicated his captain's faith like very few players had before or after him; he had taken a record 32 wickets in the three Tests, inclusive of a match-winning 13–196 at Kolkata. What was now left to be done was for the Indian batsmen to score 155 in two sessions and a bit, so that Harbhajan's 15–217 at Chennai could be deemed a series-winning performance.

One of the greatest Test series ever played deserved a grand finish. Both teams obliged, with cricket that vacillated from the extraordinary to the mediocre and back. India were coasting at 76-1 when Ramesh was run out following a misunderstanding with Laxman. Sachin was confidence personified as he swivelled the upper half of his body to pull a short delivery by Warne for four. The score had moved to 101 when Gillespie, bowling from around the wicket, angled a bouncer across the first-innings centurion; Sachin was caught in two minds, by the time he sought to withdraw his bat, the ball flew off his gloves to Mark Waugh in the slips. The replays revealed that the umpire had failed to detect a no-ball. The Australians then clawed their way back into the game by dismissing Ganguly and Dravid in quick succession. At the tea interval, India were 20 short of the target with five wickets in hand, and the country hoped that V.V.S. Laxman, who was still finding the gaps at will, would take them through. Soon after the resumption, he thumped a long-hop by Miller with all his might, but Mark Waugh, standing at mid-wicket, flung himself to his right to clasp a blinder. The Australians were now cock-a-hoop and the Indians stunned. Sairaj Bahutule, Test debutant and Sachin's old opponent, was caught at slip before he opened his account. It was now all up to Sameer Dighe, another Mumbai player, friend of Sachin's and Test debutant, who had replaced the injured Mongia in the playing XI just half an hour before the start of the Test.

Dighe weathered the storm with a cool head and three boundaries. India were four short when McGrath, brought back for the kill, had Zaheer caught in the slips. With the tension getting unbearable and people starting to speculate about the possibility of a tie, the arrival of Harbhajan Singh, India's number 10 batsman and bowler of the series, was reassuring; he may have been a bundle of nerves, but he did not let that come in the way of his swagger.

Dighe and he concocted two runs, and then, with two more needed, the off-spinner jammed an attempted yorker by McGrath into the ground. The celebrations in the Indian dressing room and galleries began the moment the ball beat the fielder at gully. The batsmen ran a frantic two and minutes later, Ganguly collected the Border–Gavaskar Trophy. The 'Final Frontier', whose fall had looked a formality after the three-day rout in Mumbai, had proved to be impenetrable. Among the first to reach the middle to congratulate the pair that had taken the team home, was the former captain.

Sachin began the ODI series against the visitors with an assault like the one at Nairobi earlier that season. He flayed the Australian new-ball bowlers all over Bengaluru's M. Chinnaswamy Stadium and took 19 off a McGrath over, inclusive of a huge six. Then, just as suddenly, he was run out. He had scored 35 off 26 balls. Laxman and Dravid batted well, with the latter scoring 80. The thrust in the end overs was provided by two players from Delhi—wicketkeeper-batsman Vijay Dahiya and an all-rounder called Virender Sehwag. Both scored 50s and India reached 315. Sehwag then took three wickets with his off-breaks as Australia were bowled out for 255. The newcomer, playing for India for the first time since his debut against Pakistan at Jaipur two years previously, was named player of the match, but was forced to miss the remainder of the series due to injury.

After Australia levelled the series in the second game at Pune, India took a 2-1 lead in the third game at Indore. Sachin was circumspect to begin with. Waugh sought to test his patience by deploying a short cover and a silly mid-on in the batsman's line of vision, in the opening overs. Sachin broke the shackles with a square-cut off Fleming in the twelfth over. He followed it with a drive that beat both short cover and cover in the same over. A single to long-off off Warne in the 18th over made Sachin the first batsman to score 10,000 runs in ODIs.

> I am happy I have achieved this goal. It has taken a lot of hard work and I have sacrificed a lot of things, which every sportsman does. I love this game a lot. It is indeed a great feeling to know that history will have a place for you. It proves that I have done something for my country.
>
> —Sachin Tendulkar, *The Sportstar*, 21 April 2001

He went on to target every corner of the ground. Warne was cut in front of square on the off-side and paddle-swept behind square on the leg. Andrew Symonds, who was brought on to bowl off-breaks, was subjected to similar treatment. Damien Martyn was delectably dabbed past the wicketkeeper, through the vacant slips to the third-man boundary, first off the back foot and then off the front foot. In between, Sachin also placed him to the mid-wicket boundary and hit him straight down the ground, both along the carpet and over the top. A paddle-swept boundary off Bevan in the 35th over took him to his 28th ODI hundred and India to 200-1.

Sachin added 199 with Laxman (83) and got to 139 before he fell trying to force the pace. Needing 300 to win, Australia were dismissed for 181.

Sachin achieved another notable 'first' during the fifth game at Goa, which

Australia won to take the series 3–2. After Laxman had scored a century earlier in the day, the most versatile 'bowler' in the Indian squad was handed the ball in the middle stages of Australia's innings. Sachin decided to bowl off-spin this time around, but there was an issue—the index finger of his right hand, which takes the lead in finger-spin, was injured. But then, he had made up his mind to bowl off-spin, and off-spin it would be. So, he decided to use his middle finger to grip and spin the ball, and it did!

He finished with figures of 3–35. His second scalp—that of Steve Waugh—was his hundredth, making him the first to complete the 'double' of 10,000 runs and 100 wickets in the shorter form.

The loss of the ODI series did not dampen the euphoria of fans in the country. It was heartening to see that despite the proliferation and popularity of the shorter variety, those who followed cricket still regarded Test cricket as the apogee of the sport. The Indian cricket team had in fact won a lot more than just the Test series.

The manner in which the players responded to the crisis of 2000 and guided the team and in the process, the fans, out of the rut, was exemplary, to say the least. It was by far their greatest contribution to Indian cricket, far outweighing the runs they scored, the wickets they took, the catches they held and the matches they won.

> [The 2001 series win] was instrumental in bringing back the crowds to the stadia and we as a team really performed well…. The closed chapter, better to keep it closed.
>
> —Sachin Tendulkar, *Mumbai Mirror*, 14 November 2009

GENERATION NEXT

India hadn't won a Test outside the subcontinent for 15 years. I couldn't believe it. The way I looked at it, you'd have a better strike rate than that if you disregarded cricketing ability and just picked your fiercest, most dogged scrappers.

—John Wright (with Sharda Ugra and Paul Thomas), *Indian Summers*

Apart from witnessing a famous series win over Australia and two notable Test triumphs overseas, the year 2001 saw the cricketing rebirth of two individuals. Harbhajan Singh and Virender Sehwag, both of whom had made their international debuts in the 20th century, followed the footsteps of those who had steered Indian cricket out of the post-Hansiegate mess and went on to bring laurels to Indian cricket for the next decade and more. The year also witnessed the millennium's first instance of the BCCI indicating that it would not take things lying down, especially in matters that concerned its players.

The Indian team had a month's break after the Australia series. The tour of Zimbabwe, which was to commence at the end of May, was to be the first in a sequence of assignments that would give the players hardly any breathing space till the ICC Cricket World Cup, which was to be played in South Africa, Zimbabwe and Kenya in February–March 2003.

The preparatory camp for the Zimbabwe tour was preceded by a function at the Wankhede Stadium, where Sachin was felicitated by the MCA for completing 25 Test centuries. Sachin brought the house down when he darted back to the speaker's podium, seconds after finishing his speech. 'I have made a terrible mistake,' he informed the gathering. 'I forgot to mention my wife [her contribution] in my speech!' The audience was in splits as he mentioned in jest that he did not want to be denied entry to his house. The immediate priority of the Indian team and its coach was to open its account across the subcontinent. The first Test at Harare was an eventful affair in which India prevailed over what was then a very competitive side. All the specialist bowlers were among the wickets and Sachin was the most successful batsman, scoring 74 and an unbeaten 36 as India completed a win by eight wickets. Given the embarrassing past, everybody connected with Indian cricket, from the fans to the players themselves, was delighted. Wright, still relatively new to Indian cricket, couldn't quite get it; for him, a win over Zimbabwe was no big deal.

He and his team discovered during the second Test at Bulawayo that what the Zimbabweans lacked in terms of record and reputation, they compensated with resilience. India missed Ramesh due to injury, and Badani's elevation to the opening slot came a cropper. India lost their last six wickets for 37 in the second innings and left the hosts with only 157 to chase; they got there for the loss of six wickets. The series was thus squared.

India lost to the West Indies in the final of the tri-series that followed, after winning all four of its league encounters. Ganguly's side may well have overhauled the target of 291 had their openers extended their form of the league stage into the summit clash. The captain, who had scored two 50s at the league stage, fell for 28 and Sachin, who had scored a magnificent 122 against the same team in the last league game, repeatedly hitting the fast bowlers on the up and finding the gaps with clinical precision, did not trouble the scorers.

Compounding Sachin's agony, quite literally, was an injury to the great toe of his right leg. He first felt the pain during the knock of 122, and found even walking an ordeal. When the team physiotherapist took him to the hospital for an X-ray, Sachin made it clear that he did not want to know the findings, as he wanted to play in the final. In technical terms, there was a problem in the sesamoid bone in his great right toe. That ruled him out of India's tour of Sri Lanka and signalled the end of a run of 81 consecutive Test appearances from Karachi in 1989–90 to Bulawayo in 2001. It was two years since his back had acted up. Years of relentless cricket were taking its toll.

After initially considering surgery, Sachin was advised to seek another opinion and he eventually went to the Rosebank Clinic at Johannesburg in South Africa, where he was told to try walking with insoles. He gradually built up his endurance, progressing from walks to sprints.

In his absence, India lost yet another tri-series final and a Test series in Sri Lanka. There were, however, two silver linings—the 69-ball hundred of Virender Sehwag against New Zealand in the tri-series, and India's successful pursuit of a target of 264 in the second Test at Kandy, despite having to contend with Muttiah Muralitharan on a fourth-innings wicket. In the absence of Sachin and Laxman, who was also injured, the captain and vice-captain had to stand up to be counted, and they did precisely that. Dravid scored 75 and Ganguly ended a lean trot with an unbeaten 98.

The Kandy win and the innings essayed by the captain helped take the bite out of a bizarre event that had preceded the Test series; Raj Singh Dungarpur, the former BCCI president and a confidant of Mr A.C. Muthiah, his successor, had flown to Sri Lanka and told Rahul Dravid in front of the entire team 'to be ready to take over'. It was a phase when Ganguly's detractors were taking great delight in pointing out that he was as inconsistent with the bat as he was consistent at being pulled up by match referees for his alleged 'on-field misdemeanours'.

It seemed that there was another individual in the frame as well. In an interview to the Press Trust of India during the tri-series in Zimbabwe, Sachin had been quoted as saying that 'while he was not thinking about leading India at the moment, he hadn't ruled it out either'. The statement made news for a few days before his great right toe took over. Andrew Leipus, the team physiotherapist, summed it quite succinctly when he said, 'When Sachin gets injured, the whole of India gets an anatomy lesson.' The print and electronic media went into overdrive, devoting reams of newsprint and prime-time discussions respectively, on the injury, its causes and the expected time of recovery.

Much to the delight of the fans, Sachin, Laxman and Anil Kumble returned to the team for the tour of South Africa. All three were fit, and raring to make up for lost time. The selectors were not on the same wavelength as the former BCCI president and Ganguly was retained as captain.

The itinerary of the Indian team side made interesting reading when compared to that of their Australian counterparts who were to visit South Africa in the same season. While the 'box-office draws' from the southern hemisphere were to play their three Tests in the country's premier centres at Johannesburg, Cape Town and Durban respectively, the Indians were to play at Bloemfontein, Port Elizabeth and Centurion. It was in a way, reminiscent of the itineraries that the BCCI used to draw up for tours by Sri Lanka in the 1980s and 1990s, which had the islanders seeing more of India than the Indian cricketers themselves. In South Africa in the 2001–02 season, the Indian team was clearly the bridesmaid.

For the Indians, the league stage of the tri-series against South Africa and Kenya that preceded the Tests, began and ended with monumental partnerships by their top two limited-overs batsmen.

Sachin marked his return to international cricket with an innings of 101 against the hosts, in what was his first game for India since July 2001. Sourav Ganguly, with whom Sachin put on 193, also batted magnificently to score 127, inclusive of 14 fours and five massive sixes. However, their teammates could not sustain the momentum and they finished on 279–5, at least 20 runs short of what they ought to have scored. The bowling was not up to the mark, and

South Africa won by six wickets. Gary Kirsten anchored the chase with an unbeaten 133.

In the next set of games, India beat the South Africans once, primarily due to exceptional bowling by Kumble and Harbhajan, and lost to the hosts twice. Ganguly's side battered Kenya by 10 wickets and then lost to the same team by 70 runs.

The Indians atoned for the defeat with a 186-run win in their third and last league game against Kenya. The openers bettered themselves with a 258-run association against Kenya. It was the highest opening stand in ODIs, ahead of their own 252 against Sri Lanka three years previously. The captain scored 111 and Sachin batted splendidly for his 146. Earlier in the series, he had been forced to visit the Johannesburg clinic for a precautionary check, when his toe started troubling him all over again. His strokeplay in the last league game indicated that the issue had been addressed.

The final was a one-sided affair. Put in to bat, the Indians were dismissed for 183. The move to play an extra batsman by getting Rahul Dravid to keep wicket did not work. Ironically, Dravid was the only batsman who got runs—77 of them. South Africa won by six wickets. It was India's eighth straight defeat in a multi-nation final since the tri-series against Pakistan in March 1999.

In the first Test at Centurion, South Africa asked India to bat on a strip that had juice in it. Dravid, who had kept wicket in the tri-series final, was now asked to open the innings. He fell for just two and Das was the second to go, at 43. Just eight runs later, Laxman, who had batted as only he could to score 32, inclusive of four boundaries and a six, was caught behind, and Ganguly did not score many. At 68–4, Sachin was joined in the middle by his 'disciple' Virender Sehwag.

> Everyone has a different method, what works for one may not work for others. Also, you must be honest to yourself in terms of hard work and dedication, and honest to the game. Try sincerely. There is no magic formula for success in cricket—it depends on so many factors like skill, opportunity, destiny.
>
> —Sachin Tendulkar, *Outlook*, 4 January 1999

Virender Sehwag was far too talented a batsman in his own right to have to imitate someone else. It was just that he had watched so much of Sachin in his formative years that he could not help but unconsciously imbibe elements of what could be termed as the master's style. Coincidentally, he also bore a physical resemblance to his favourite cricketer.

The Delhi batsman had honed his skills under the tutelage of A.N. Sharma, one of the city's most respected coaches. Even as a youngster, Sehwag had revelled in taking the bowling by the horns. However, his belligerence would have amounted to nothing had he not possessed something that his idol had in abundance—balance. Like Sachin, he kept his feet evenly apart and his head still before the bowler released the ball, and did his best to be side-on at the time of playing the ball. He allied his adherence to the basics with his remarkable hand-eye coordination.

At Centurion, Sehwag was living his dream. Could it get any better than batting with his idol on his Test debut? The master put him at ease by reminding him that he would never be this tense again, and so, he ought to enjoy the moment. The disciple watched his hero take 16 off a Makhaya Ntini over. A cracking square-cut was followed by a square-drive past the slip-cordon, and then, an uppercut over the slips. Not many had seen this stroke being played before. Only the best could execute it effectively, given the risks involved. A mistimed uppercut would have looked like cricket's equivalent of a suicide, with the keeper and slips on the prowl, so the batsman had to have complete confidence in his own abilities before dealing with a short delivery in this fashion.

Sachin proceeded to take three boundaries off a Jacques Kallis over. He drove the bowler down the ground off the front foot, and then flicked him to the mid-wicket boundary. Then came the grandest stroke of the three—a back foot off-drive, on the up. He brought up his 50 with a cut off Nantie Hayward. Just before lunch, the maestro had to his credit, eight gorgeous boundaries in the space of 18 balls. The disciple too opened out after the interval, and imitated his role model by essaying an uppercut himself. Sachin kept targeting the region behind square on the off-side with cuts and glides. He was boosted by the reluctance of Shaun Pollock, the South African captain, to man that area. Apart from a top-edged pull off Pollock that just evaded Ntini at mid-off, the maestro hardly put a foot wrong. An on-drive off Pollock took him to 7,000 runs in Tests.

He was within striking distance of a hundred when he uppercut Kallis for six. A pull for two off Lance Klusener gave Sachin his 26th Test century. He had achieved the landmark off only 114 balls.

If you don't clap that innings, then you are a bit mean-spirited.

—Geoffrey Boycott, live commentary

After putting the pacemen to the sword, Sachin trained his guns on Nicky Boje's left-arm spin. He had moved to 155 and India to 288–4 when he was caught on the mid-wicket boundary.

His disciple took charge of the innings from that point. As had been the case with Sachin, all the attacking strokes that Sehwag essayed were conventional. Sourav Ganguly, the last Indian to score a century on Test debut, led the applause when Sehwag emulated him. The newcomer's baptism concluded when he was bowled by Pollock for 105.

For all those who had followed Indian cricket in the bad, old 1990s, the Delhi batsman appeared to be a dream-come-true. Exasperated by their team's over-reliance on one man, they would often wish that they acquired 'another player like Sachin', before coming back to reality and chiding themselves for harbouring fanciful thoughts.

At stumps on day one, India were a sensational 372–7. They had lost a few more wickets than they would have liked, but with Deep Dasgupta, Sehwag's co-debutant, middling the ball well, there was reason to believe that they would cross the 400-mark. That did not happen as the last three wickets fell for the addition of only seven runs on the second morning.

The visitors were then shut out of the match. Gary Kirsten and Herschelle Gibbs opened with a stand of 189 and their team went on to score 563. Virtually every batsman, from the specialists to the all-rounders, got runs. While veterans Srinath and Kumble took five and three wickets respectively, the Indians missed Harbhajan, who was out of action due to a groin infection. The South African bowlers maintained the momentum and bowled India out for 237 in the second innings, with only Das, Ganguly and Sehwag offering some resistance. Not even India's worst critics would have anticipated a nine-wicket loss for their team, that too on the fourth day of the game after the Sachin–Sehwag show on the first. On the eve of the second Test at Port Elizabeth, the mood in the Indian camp was grim, to say the least.

Far from improving, it deteriorated after four days of the game. On the field, India conceded a first-innings lead of 161 and the hosts then increased it by more than 200. Off the field, Mike Denness, the match referee, decided to impose himself on the proceedings after stumps on the fourth day. He booked as many as five Indian players for their 'misdemeanour' during South Africa's second innings. Shiv Sunder Das, wicketkeeper Deep Dasgupta and Harbhajan Singh were fined for 'excessive appealing, showing dissent and trying to intimidate the umpires', and Sehwag was banned for one Test for the same 'offence'. Ganguly was slapped with a suspended one-Test and two-ODI ban for 'not controlling his players' and Sachin was also handed out a suspended sentence for 'alleged interference with the ball, thus changing its condition', while bowling. What made the referee's intervention extraordinary was that at no point had the South African batsmen or even the umpires themselves reported or complained about anything.

The backlash was extraordinary. The Indian media got stuck into Denness with a vengeance, and it was only a matter of time before the entire nation got involved. Effigies of the referee were torched in demonstrations on the streets and the controversy was even discussed in Parliament. Indian news channels kept screening loops of slow-motion replays of what they claimed was Pollock's 'excessive appealing' that Denness had chosen to overlook while choosing to penalise the Indians. The subcontinental nations backed the Indian stand and it became an 'Us vs Them' situation.

Of course these protests would have amounted to nothing had the BCCI not backed its players. Jagmohan Dalmiya, who had been elected as president of the Board just a few weeks previously, took on the ICC, a body he had presided over not very long ago and made it clear that the Indians had lost confidence in Denness.

What hurt the fans the most was the punishment meted out to Sachin. Being a compulsive nail-biter, there was no way he could have tampered with the ball by picking its seam, as was being claimed. In the hearing, Sachin informed Denness that he had been using his thumb to clean the grass that had got stuck on the seam. While he apologized for not telling the umpires the same, he also reminded the referee that the umpires were examining the ball every 2–3 overs, and so would have noticed had anything been amiss. But Denness was not convinced.

> Somebody should have had the sagacity to stand up and say that if liberal, intelligent, moderate Indians were feeling outraged by what had happened, then maybe they should try to see why.... The punishment was extraordinary, not so much because of the fine and suspended sentence, but because of the opportunity it gave the world to call an honest man a cheat.
>
> —Harsha Bhogle, *Wisden Cricket Monthly*, January 2001

After four eventful days and several rain interruptions, India began the final day at 28-1, needing 367 more to win.

Buoyed no doubt by the support they had received from their Board and of course, their supporters, India achieved an honourable draw. Deep Dasgupta,

India's newest opener, batted resolutely in the company of Rahul Dravid, and the duo added 171 for the second wicket. Their defiance in the middle was the perfect foil to the aggression that was being displayed simultaneously by the Indian cricket administrators, fans and media off the field.

A back injury to Sameer Dighe just before the start of the first Test of the series had resulted in Deep Dasgupta, the designated deputy wicketkeeper in the side, getting an opportunity. Dasgupta's sound batting technique had prompted the team management to try him as opener, and he had delivered with a score of 63 against a quality attack in his second Test innings in that role. Dravid, who scored 87, was back at the number three position, with the team management getting him to re-swap slots with Laxman, who since his 65 and 66 against Australia at Chennai had begun well in nearly every innings, only to get out 'against the run of play'. The swap seemed to have worked for both players, with Laxman scoring 89 in the first innings.

The series ended on a sour note, with the ICC relegating the third Test to 'unofficial' status after refusing to endorse the bilateral decision of the South African and Indian boards to replace Denness with Denis Lindsay, a South African, for the game. India batted poorly in both innings and South Africa won by an innings and 73 runs.

By the time the tour ended, the England cricket team was already in India for its first series in the country since 1992–93. The first Test at Mohali began within days of the Indian team's return from South Africa and the hosts won by 10 wickets. Dasgupta scored a round ton and Sachin got 88. Kumble and Harbhajan took eight and seven wickets respectively. India's new-ball attack wore a new look in the game. Trivia hunters were delighted when Iqbal Siddiqui, who had taken the new ball with co-debutant Tinu Yohannan in both innings, was sent in to open the batting in the second innings, with India needing only five to win; it made him the only player in Test history to open the batting and bowling in the same game on debut.

India's refusal to go for a target of 374 on the last day of the second Test at Ahmedabad ensured an anti-climactic end to an absorbing contest. Batting first, the visitors scored 407 and then bowled India out for 291, with left-arm spinner Ashley Giles taking 5–67. India owed everything to Laxman and Sachin, who scored 75 and 103 respectively. Sachin batted quite brilliantly, making a mockery of the 7–2 and 8–1 off-side fields that Nasser Hussain, the England captain, had set for his fast bowlers. Earlier in the year, the Zimbabwe seamers had attempted something similar against Sachin, as they bowled wide outside the off-stump to test his patience.

The Zimbabweans' tactics had paid off on a couple of occasions, but against England at Ahmedabad, Sachin was six months older and wiser. He was content to play along, but when the opportunity presented itself, he made sure to either drive or flick deliveries pitched on or outside the off-stump through the leg-side with a flourish that would have done Viv Richards proud. After taking 128 balls to complete his first 50, he went on the offensive, reaching his second 50 off only 55 deliveries. He was looking good for many more when he drove Matthew Hoggard on the up a little too early and popped up a catch to Hussain at mid-on.

India's spin twins then took eight wickets between them to dismiss England for 257, and the hosts were 17–0 at stumps on day four. Openers Das and Dasgupta completed 50s on day five, but they took too many deliveries to do so and the fate of the game was sealed by the lunch interval. It would be safe to say that at least one member of the Indian team would have been bitterly disappointed with his team's defensive tactics on day five.

Virender Sehwag, who was back in the team after his one-match ban, batted at number seven in the first innings and did not get to bat in the second.

The third Test at Bengaluru was preceded by the fourth annual Castrol Awards ceremony, where Sachin polled the maximum votes from India's current and former Test cricketers for the second year in succession, to win the Indian Cricketer of the Year Award for the third time in four years.

At the M. Chinnaswamy Stadium, England batted first and scored 336, and then had India in trouble at 22–2. Any other bowling side, especially one that was 0–1 down in the series, would have gone for the kill in such a situation, but Sachin's arrival made the visitors go on the defensive. Ashley Giles, the left-arm spinner, bowled to him with a packed leg-side field, with James Foster, the wicketkeeper, crouching outside the leg-stump. The objective was to deny scoring opportunities and frustrate the batsman.

> On helpful tracks, you get more scoring opportunities because captains set attacking fields. On flat surfaces, the bowling sides try to dry up the runs, so it's a different kind of challenge. When we played Australia [in 2001], I remember Steve Waugh posting a deep point in Chennai when I had scored only two runs. Colin Miller was bowling to a seven-two field. Nasser Hussain did that too. Matthew Hoggard was bowling two feet outside the off-stump to a seven-two field and then Flintoff and Ashley Giles bowled to similar fields on the leg-side. On flat surfaces, bowlers have to find a way of making it difficult for you.
>
> —Sachin Tendulkar, *Wisden Asia Cricket*, October 2004

There was nothing in the rules to prevent England from employing leg-theory, just as there had been nothing that got in the way of Douglas Jardine, an India-born England captain like Hussain, from commanding Harold Larwood to bowl bodyline to try and derail the express train called Don Bradman, way back in 1932–33.

At Bengaluru, both the game and duel were drawn. Giles kept pegging away from over the wicket outside leg, and Sachin kept padding him away and occasionally, even letting the ball hit him on his backside. Giles could not prevent him from crossing 50 for the third time in the series. The battle commenced on the second day and extended into the third, with rain threatening to strike anytime. There was also some old-fashioned gamesmanship, with Sachin and Hussain as its protagonists, which was defused by the umpires; this wasn't something that Sachin was known to indulge in. As he neared a hundred, Sachin threw caution to the wind, taking inspiration from his 'disciple'.

Virender Sehwag made a mockery of Hussain's leg-side fields by using his feet and backing his instincts to essay some incredible strokes, including a reverse-sweep for four. His partner, who had been circumspect till then, reciprocated by taking 12 off a Giles over. By this time, the spectators, who had struggled to keep their eyes open for the better part of the Indian innings, had sprung to life. Sachin had moved to 90 when the left-arm spinner had him stranded down the wicket and stumped. It was the first time he had been dismissed in that fashion in Tests.

> I was stepping out and easily hitting my shots. He [Sachin] was mostly padding. I said there is no spin, you can charge and play. It took me 2–3 overs to convince him. The only ball that turned was the one on which he stepped out of crease and was stumped. I did not go back to the dressing room that day at the tea break. I sat in [the] umpires' room. Later I was called. Tendulkar said 'only once in my career I have got out stumped in Test cricket and that's because of you'.
>
> —Virender Sehwag, as quoted on www.rediff.com, 7 December 2016

Rain put an end to the game shortly after the start of England's second innings, giving India the series 1–0. While the England bowlers had certainly slowed Sachin down, they hadn't been able to outmanoeuvre him. He had scores of 88, 103 and 90 to his credit and was in fact declared the player of the series.

England did not win the six-match ODI series that was played in the New Year, but they were far happier than their opponents were at its conclusion. India dominated the first few games and led 3–1 after the first four games.

Sachin was in fine nick, striking 68 and 87 in the third and fourth encounters at Chennai and Kanpur respectively. In both games, he put on over a hundred with Sehwag, his new opening partner. Ganguly missed the Chennai encounter due to injury and so did Rahul Dravid, who had taken the entire series off to tend to his shoulder. In their absence, Anil Kumble got an opportunity to lead India. The Prince of Kolkata returned for the next game at Kanpur, but he chose not to disturb the new opening combination; the hero and the fan matched each other in terms of strokes and style, as they took 134 runs off the first 17.2 overs at Kanpur.

Put in to bat, England scored 271–5 in the fifth ODI at Delhi. The hosts were 211–3 at the end of the 40th over of their innings, which meant that they needed to score at a-run-a-ball with as many as seven wickets in hand. Unbelievably, they lost their way, and with it, the game, by two runs.

It was déjà vu, all over again in the final game at Mumbai. Needing 256 to win, India at one stage needed 75 from 80 balls with seven wickets in hand. And they lost again, this time by five runs! The series might have been tied 3–3, but England had reason to believe that had Marcus Trescothick—their best batsman of the series—not fallen to a questionable leg-before decision in the first game at Kolkata when they were cruising to victory, they would have won the ODI series instead of squaring it.

John Wright identified the failings of the team in a report addressed to the selectors that was supposed to be confidential, but ended up appearing verbatim in a leading national daily. India had scored more runs and hit more fours and sixes than their opponents, but had still not won the series. The coach had calculated that England had taken 590 singles and played 842 dot-balls in the ODI series, while India had taken 509 singles and played 884 dot-balls. In the second game at Cuttack for instance, which India had lost by 16 runs, the hosts had scored 234 off 292 deliveries. Ninety-two of those runs had come through boundaries (23). This implied that the team had scored only 131 runs off the remaining 269 balls, which was nothing short of sacrilege.

Wright did not hesitate to mention names. At Cuttack, Sachin had scored 45 off 60 balls, inclusive of six fours. This meant that he had scored only 21 off the remaining 54 deliveries. Sachin was also named as one of the fielders who did not deter opposition batsmen from going for quick singles within the circle, along with Sehwag and the captain himself.

For once, someone had criticized Sachin and been allowed to get away with it, presumably because that person had a point. There was no way Wright was going to refrain from doing his job just because he had a negative but constructive observation to make on India's premier batsman. It was not his fault that the report had found its way into a newspaper, in any case. In fact, it was his professionalism and ability to call a spade a spade that had won him the respect of not only the players but also Dalmiya. Contrary to the speculation that the new Board president would sack appointees of the dispensation that he had defeated in the September 2001 elections, Dalmiya had sought the players' feedback and then renewed the contracts of Wright and Leipus for a year. Wright was understandably peeved when his report was leaked, but he comforted himself with the conviction that Sachin would not take the criticism personally. He was right.

Tragedy struck Sachin right in the middle of the ODI series, when Mark Mascarenhas, his manager, died in a road accident near Nagpur. He was 44. It was a sad end to what had been an eventful and pathbreaking journey.

In seven eventful years, Mascarenhas had silenced all those who had questioned the wisdom of striking a five-year deal with Sachin, guaranteeing him ₹31.5 crores, in 1995. He had complemented Sachin's on-field brilliance with his penchant for spotting and exploiting endorsement opportunities, and had initiated a revolution of sorts in celebrity management, which until that point had been an unexplored territory in India. Not too many eyebrows were raised when he renewed his deal with Sachin for ₹100 crores for another five years, in May 2001. On the flipside, Mascarenhas' other projects, like a cricket fortnightly and website, had run into rough weather, and he had also lost the highly sought-after TV rights in markets like India and Sharjah, which he had controlled earlier.

Sachin, for whom Mascarenhas had become a family friend, flew to Bengaluru for the funeral service in between the ODIs, and before that, he convinced his teammates to wear black armbands during the Kanpur game, which was played a day after the fatal accident. That gesture did not go down very well with some people who believed that Mascarenhas had not been above board. They alluded to the income tax raids on his Bengaluru offices in July 2000. However, Sachin's faith in him had remained unshaken throughout and that ought to have settled the matter.

> It was a big moment for me when I signed WorldTel in 1995. Unfortunately, we lost Mark in 2002 when England were playing in India. That was a huge blow, not because I lost my manager, but because I lost my friend, who understood how I operated; how my family operated, and who never pressured me to do advertisements when a series was on.
>
> —Sachin Tendulkar, as quoted in *The Indian Express*, 18 November 2013

In an age wherein everybody associated with the administration of cricket in India was bemoaning the absence of crowds at domestic matches, a two-month hiatus from international cricket, between the end of the ODI series against England in early February and the start of the tour of the Caribbean in April, would have given at least some of the international stars the opportunity to represent their respective domestic teams at the knockout stage of the Ranji Trophy. Their presence would have drawn crowds to the venues. Instead, the players found themselves playing a bilateral series against Zimbabwe for the third time in 18 months.

The visitors failed to capitalize on their decision to bat in the first Test at Nagpur, scoring only 287. Das and Dasgupta opened with a stand of 79 and Dravid carried on with Das as the latter completed his second Test hundred. Only five balls were left for the end of play when the opener was caught in the slips. The score was 209–2. Sachin came in instead of a night watchman and played out the last four balls. He warmed up on day three with five brilliant boundaries. There was hardly any bounce in the wicket and the batsmen had to be wary of the odd ball keeping low. Zimbabwe had a left-arm spinner called Raymond Price, who was extracting turn, as well as a lot of dust by consistently pitching the ball on the bowlers' footmarks at the other end. His colleagues were doing their best at the other end and they were backed by their traditionally reliable fielders.

Sachin had seen enough of the Zimbabweans to know what they were upto. Barring a heave off Heath Streak that just missed the outside edge, he refused to play into their hands. He eschewed aggression and lofted strokes, playing as straight as possible and making every loose delivery and slice of luck count. Shortly after he had inside-edged Heath Streak past the stumps and the keeper for four, he essayed a straight drive off the same bowler that sped like a bullet; it was clearly the shot of the day. It was then overshadowed by a splendid piece of improvization in the last over before tea, bowled by Travis Friend; Sachin merely rolled his wrists over a short delivery pitched outside off-stump and 'guided' more than 'pulled' the ball to the mid-wicket boundary. That boundary took his individual score to 99, and the spectators got what they desired in the same over, when he flicked a two. It was his second consecutive hundred against Zimbabwe at the venue, after his unbeaten 201 in the previous season.

The visitors had bowled well enough to create roadblocks just when the hosts looked poised to launch an offensive. They had put the brakes on Dravid and got him to play onto the stumps for 65 and Ganguly had hit Price to long-on after batting quite fluently to score 38. Laxman was fifth out at 376, at which point India were 89 runs ahead.

The next man in was Sanjay Bangar, a versatile cricketer who had made his debut in the series against England earlier in the season.

Sachin and he went on the attack on the fourth morning. It was an eventful passage of play that saw Bangar drilling a hole in a spectator's chair with a six, Sachin hitting his partner on the chest when the latter failed to get out of the way of a booming drive, then essaying a stupendous reverse-sweep for four, and eventually getting caught off Price in the dash for a declaration. He had scored 176. Ganguly declared at 570–7 after Bangar completed his maiden Test century. Anil Kumble, who had taken 4–82 in the first innings, opened the bowling with Srinath and bowled India to victory by an innings and 101 runs, with figures of 5–63.

Although India also won the second Test on another 'slow and low' pitch at Delhi, the game wasn't entirely one-sided. Ganguly, who promoted himself to number three, scored 136, his first Test century since his 125 against New Zealand at Ahmedabad three seasons previously. Later in the innings, Sehwag, batting at number six, scored an attractive 74, but the cynics still preferred to focus on Sachin's 36, which had spanned 119 balls and ended with him being leg-before to Price. By no means was he fluency personified during the knock, but the contention that he was susceptible to 'left-arm spin' was preposterous to say the least.

Both Ashley Giles and Raymond Price, the left-armers who were supposed to 'have the wood' on Sachin, were representing their respective countries and were not exactly there to make up the numbers. They deserved all the credit for sticking to their plans and trying and trying till they succeeded. However, the fact was that for all their 'success', Sachin had still scored two centuries and two 50s in four Tests against them. Simply put, he had played enough cricket to have worked out that discretion sometimes served the interests of the team better than daredevilry. If Ganguly was having a better day than him, then the team stood to gain if Sachin batted *with* him instead of trying to bat *like* him.

It was not as if he had never played second fiddle earlier.

> Ambrose was bowling a good spell and I could not read him. I would just go forward in a predetermined manner and defend or let the ball hit my thigh-pad. So I told Rahul that I was unable to make much of Ambrose. We decided to rotate the strike so that the bowler could not attack one batsman and he had to adjust all the time, bowl a different line.... In this your body language is important, your bearing can convey everything to

the bowler so you should not show your fear to the bowler [on India's tour of the West Indies in 1996–97].

—Sachin Tendulkar, *Outlook*, 4 January 1999

In Delhi, India found themselves needing 122 to win in a day and a bit. With nothing to lose, the Zimbabweans gave it everything they had and snared three wickets by stumps on day four. Sachin, who came in on the fourth evening after night watchman Kumble's dismissal for a duck, counterattacked on the fifth morning. He stroked seven boundaries and a six before Price had him leg-before with one that skidded. It was the second time in the game and third instance in three Test innings of Sachin falling to the left-arm spinner. India were 93–4 at that stage. Das and Dravid then fell in quick succession, and with Sehwag unlikely to bat due to a shoulder injury that he had sustained while going for a catch in Zimbabwe's second innings, there was an outside chance of the Zimbabweans creating history. However, Harbhajan dissipated the tension with a couple of hefty blows and Bangar kept him company to complete the chase. Not surprisingly, the series win was overshadowed by talk of Sachin's 'repeated failures' to take India past the finishing line.

Ashley Giles had troubled Sachin in India on the previous tour and enjoyed a fair amount of success by bowling a negative line', he says. 'But I had made up my mind before the tour began that I won't go over-the-wicket to Tendulkar and aim for the rough. Why, you ask? Because cricket is all about being positive.... [The plan was] Simple. Stay around-the-wicket. Bowl it fuller because he's short. And on middle, so that if I can get turn it will head towards the top of off-stump. And if it skids, then I'll have him LBW.

—Ray Price, as quoted in *The Indian Express*, 14 July 2015

Sachin skipped the five-match ODI series against Zimbabwe to rest his knees. There was a lot of cricket coming up, and it made sense to acknowledge the niggles before they got out of hand. India won the series 3–2, but the team did not cover itself with glory. The hosts in fact trailed 1–2 after the third game, and looked set to lose the fourth ODI at Hyderabad as well before two youngsters turned things around with a stand of 94. Although India won the final ODI at Guwahati comfortably and took the series, the fact was that the lessons learnt after the reverses against England were yet to be put into practice.

It was difficult to envisage the Indian team of March 2002 impressing in the ICC Cricket World Cup 2003 that was to be played in South Africa, exactly a year later. Hearteningly, the fielding had improved significantly with the presence of Mohammed Kaif and Yuvraj Singh, the heroes of the Hyderabad ODI.

The limited-overs concerns were put on the backburner when the Test squad flew to the Caribbean for what turned out to be an encore of the 1996–97 tour. As had been the case six seasons earlier, the Indians lost a key player to a shoulder injury before the tour began and they undid a promising start with some daft cricket.

The rain reigned supreme in the first Test at the Bourda Oval in Georgetown and both sides acquitted themselves well whenever it relented. Batting first, the West Indies scored 501 and then had India 275–7, before Sarandeep Singh, who was playing in the absence of the injured Harbhajan, helped Rahul Dravid put down the shutters. The duo added an unbroken 120 and Dravid was on 144 when the last ball was bowled.

Sarandeep's defiance and Dravid's resilience despite a blow to his jaw, which resulted in his having to be on a liquid diet for two days, were preceded by a Sachin dazzler. He arrived at the wicket at 21–2 to perform the all-too-familiar role of saviour. He nearly nicked the first ball he faced to the keeper, but did not make another mistake till he got to 79, when he missed a pull and was leg-before to a skidder by leg-spinner Mahendra Nagamootoo. Among those watching his 'masterclass' was Sir Everton Weekes, one of the legends of West Indies cricket. He was captivated by Sachin's balance, among other things, and expressed regret over the fact that not many people would notice, leave alone appreciate, the batsman's technical refinement.

It wasn't the first or last time Sachin had elicited such a reaction from someone who had played and watched the sport at the highest level long enough to read between the lines and look beyond the obvious. The majority loved Sachin for his genius and big scores, but the minority revered him for the technical flourishes that he displayed, while attacking as well as defending. The game had not seen too many players before him who had managed to blend technical perfection with unbridled aggression so successfully and consistently, for over a decade.

Put in to bat in the second Test on a greenish strip at the Queen's Park Oval, Port of Spain, Trinidad, India experimented with a new set of openers— Shiv Sunder Das and Sanjay Bangar. While Deep Dasgupta had done well as an opener, he had failed to impress in his primary role of wicketkeeper, and that cost him his place in the side. A Test cap was awarded to Ajay Ratra, who along with Yuvraj and Kaif had been a key member of the under-19 World Cup winning team of 2000. The wicketkeeper from Haryana had made his ODI debut against England a couple of months earlier.

However, the change in the opening combination did not work, and Sachin arrived in the middle at 38–2.

> Once again, [Sachin] coming in with his side in trouble…. If you wake him up, he will ask, 'Is it 20–2 or 30–2?' It is never anything more than that.
>
> —Harsha Bhogle, live commentary

Lady luck was on Sachin's side that morning. He got his feet moving with his signature straight drive off Adam Sanford. Another comfortable two later, the same bowler pitched one just short of a length, outside the off-stump. Sachin went for the cut, but the ball reared off the pitch a little quicker than he had anticipated, and missed kissing the bat on its way to the wicketkeeper. Sachin, eager to dominate, then got one on middle-and-leg that he attempted to clip to mid-wicket, but this time around, the ball came a little slower than anticipated, and it flew off the leading edge. Sachin's groan gave way to a sigh of relief when the cherry dropped just short of Cameron Cuffy at mid-off. What happened next left Sanford with no doubt that it was not his day. Sachin played a short ball tentatively, and the ball deviated just a bit after pitching to take a faint outside-edge. However, umpire Ashoka de Silva was unconvinced.

India's numbers three and four exuded calm, as they always did in such situations, and started rebuilding the innings, but Sachin had two more reprieves, with leg-before appeals by Cuffy and Dillon not going the bowlers' way. The second one looked plumb, but the appeal appeared to have been turned down because the umpire reckoned that the batsman had got an inside-edge. The replays however did not suggest the same.

Sachin made the most of the reprieves. The Queen's Park Oval, which comprised a sizeable number of spectators of Indian descent, rose to him when he completed his 29th Test century and his first in the Caribbean. Only two batsmen had scored 29 or more Test tons previously—Sunil Gavaskar, his childhood hero, and Sir Don Bradman, his spiritual predecessor.

Sachin's 117 set up the game for his team, and it gave his colleagues to dictate terms to the opposition. After some fine bowling by the visitors and brilliant batting by Ganguly and Laxman in the second innings, the hosts found themselves needing 313 to win. The Indian bowlers then gave a splendid account of themselves for the second time in the game. They were backed by the fielders and the captain, whose bowling changes were timely and brilliant. India's 37-run win was their first in the Caribbean since their chase of a record 403 at the same venue in April 1976, exactly 26 years previously. India's most successful bowler of the game was Javagal Srinath, who had of course missed the previous tour of the West Indies due to a shoulder injury. What the outcome of the 1996–97 series would have been had he been available to Sachin, the then captain, is one of the many 'what-might-have-beens' of Indian cricket.

India's celebrations did not last long, as Carl Hooper's side struck back in the very next Test at Bridgetown, bowling India out for 102 in the first innings and going on to win by 10 wickets. The fourth Test at Antigua was a high-scoring draw and the first in history to feature hundreds by the rival wicketkeepers—in this case, Ridley Jacobs and Ajay Ratra. But this feat was eclipsed by Anil Kumble, who insisted on bowling despite having had his jaw broken while batting. He did not remember too many instances of his team scoring over 500 in the first innings of an overseas Test, and was therefore intent on trying to take his side closer to victory. He returned to the field with a plastered head and sent down 14 overs, during which, he dismissed Brian Lara.

For those who had known him since his early cricketing days, what Kumble did was not surprising. He was someone who as vice-captain and strike bowler of the Indian team in Sri Lanka in 1997 had offered to skip a game just to prevent the team management from dropping a player, who was talented but a little low on confidence, at the time. Kumble was apprehensive that if the player were to be treated harshly just when he needed to be made to feel valued, he might be lost to Indian cricket forever. Fortunately, that did not happen, and the player in question went on to become one of the all-time greats.

Sachin was not in the best of moods prior to the decider at Kingston, Jamaica. His sequence of scores since his match-winning hundred at Port of Spain read 0, 0, 8 and 0. The last two ducks were two-ball and one-ball affairs and inflicted by Pedro Collins, a left-arm paceman from Barbados.

Sachin had noted his use of the inswinger in a tour game and accordingly played for the inswing whenever he faced the left-armer, but on both occasions, the ball had gone the other way and taken the outside edge of the bat. Sachin prepared extensively for the final Test, even speaking to some West Indies players, who told him that Collins' stock delivery was the one that he angled away from the right-handers.

Ganguly won the toss and decided to bowl on a grassy strip, but his bowlers struggled with the swing and served up quite a few loose deliveries. The West Indies helped themselves to 422 and then bowled India out for 212. Sachin was among the runs with 41, but with Laxman going strong at one end and remaining unbeaten on 65, he and Ganguly (36) ought to have stayed in longer. The Indian bowlers did get it right in the second innings and dismissed the hosts for 197, with Zaheer Khan taking 4–79. The visitors were certainly not in the right frame of mind to go for a target of 408, but they certainly possessed the wherewithal to offer a straight bat to everything till the weather gods, who had been threatening to unleash their fury over the past couple of days, would do so. India were 25-2 when Sachin came in. He proceeded to bat as fluently as he had at the start of the tour. He drove, cut and pulled splendidly, dominating stands of 52 with Dravid and 93 with Ganguly before being bowled by 'bogeyman' Pedro Collins for 86. India at that stage were 170-4. For the umpteenth time, the Indian innings went downhill after the fall of the talisman. Some of those who followed him batted like they had a flight to catch instead of a Test to save, and at 237-7 at the close on the fourth day, a series win for the hosts was a formality.

Minutes after the end of the match and series on the final day, the skies opened and did not close for the next few days. Drawing the series 1-1 would not have been as great an achievement as winning, but it would not have been as traumatic as losing to a team whose premier batsman—Brian Lara—had not been among the runs, and whose bowling attack had been nowhere as potent as the one in 1996-97. For the umpteenth time, the Indian team had squandered a golden opportunity with some insipid cricket.

> Now you come to the Relataa
> And you questioned me about Gavaskaa,
> You even want the Relataa,
> To sing about Tendulkaa,
> But Mr Gentleman I will tell you plain,
> I'm not singing about Indian cricketers again,
> I don't want you to say that Relator pass,
> But Tendulkaa is not in Gavaskaa class....
>
> —Lord Relator, Port of Spain Test, 2002

A TEAM IS BORN

> *The grip should be such that you can manoeuvre the bat any which way you want.... The closer you get to the bottom of the handle, your control improves, but that also puts pressure on your right hand...you should be careful not to use too much of your right hand.... You have got to be comfortable in your stance...it eventually boils down to adjustment—before you face the ball, you have got to be comfortable...it is important to stay still...you got to be as still as possible and keep your mind as blank as possible.... Your initial movement depends on the track and what the bowlers are planning to do...if someone is bowling short, I will look to go back.... My head won't go back...you want the ball to stay down. 70% of your weight has to be on the left foot...the idea of shuffling is to prepare to play the ball, not committing to play off the back foot....*
>
> —Sachin Tendulkar, *Masterclass*, Channel 4, 2002

The Indian team wore a new look on the eve of the ODI series, with players like Yuvraj Singh, Mohammed Kaif, Ajit Agarkar and Dinesh Mongia expected to play key roles. The Indian skipper and coach were determined to end the tour on a high note. Those upset with the brainless cricket that had been on offer in the Test series were pleasantly surprised during the ODI series. Ever since the retirement of Kapil Dev and the exit of Manoj Prabhakar, the Indians had struggled to find someone who could provide them with an extra batting and bowling option in the shorter format. That in turn had affected the balance of the side. Then, there was also the hunt for a wicketkeeping all-rounder that hadn't yielded any positive result either. With no solution in sight, the team management 'manufactured' one.

A suggestion made by Jagmohan Dalmiya in 1999 was pulled out of cold storage. Rahul Dravid, who had chipped in as wicketkeeper in the odd game and session whenever required, was asked to don the gauntlets full time in the shorter format, and a decision made to play as many as seven specialist batsmen and four specialist bowlers, with the likes of Sachin, Sehwag and Ganguly expected to share among themselves the fifth bowler's 10 overs. The other significant call concerned Sachin and the slot that he had occupied since 1994. He was requested to inject experience into the middle order, while Sehwag was told to continue 'doing a Sachin' at the top of the order, with Ganguly for company. This meant that there would still be a left-right opening combination.

Dravid was the vice-captain and Sachin the seniormost member of the squad and the best batsman in the world. While Dravid had dabbled in wicketkeeping in his formative years, he was no longer used to it, and the additional responsibility would require him to work even harder. On the other hand, it was hardly a secret that Sachin enjoyed opening in ODIs.

Both players were senior and influential enough to refuse what was being asked of them. However, they did not. When two players of their stature put the team above self, the younger members in the squad learnt an invaluable lesson.

The strategizing of the team management was complemented by the foresightedness of the BCCI. Helping Dravid prepare for his new 'all-round' role was Adrian Le Roux, a South African who had joined the Indian team as its fitness trainer. Once Dalmiya was convinced of the need for a specialist to complement Andrew Leipus, the physiotherapist, Le Roux's appointment was a formality. Much like Wright and Leipus, the new joinee did not take too long to win the confidence of the players.

The trainer was on the same wavelength as Sachin, who by this time had worked out the workout regimen that suited him. For a batsman, running between the wickets was a critical area, and Sachin believed that if one could run hard and then recover quickly to face the next ball, then one was fit enough to spend the entire day in the middle. Le Roux concurred with Sachin's preference for sprints over long-distance running, to keep his body attuned to the challenge of running hard for himself, his partner and his team.

After the first two ODIs against the West Indies were washed out without a ball being bowled, India opened their account with a seven-wicket win at Bridgetown. Dravid held a catch and affected a stumping in his new role, and Sachin scored an unbeaten 34 as India overhauled a target of 187 with more than six overs to spare. He missed the next game at Port of Spain, a truncated 25-over game that the Windies won by seven wickets. The decider, also played at Port of Spain, was memorable for Sachin and India; he top-scored with 65 as India scored 260. Rain resulted in West Indies' target being revised to 248 from 44 overs. The Indian bowlers then complemented their batting counterparts with a splendid show, bowling the opposition out for 191. Sachin was declared the player of the series.

The joy of the ODI series win, India's first-ever in the Caribbean, was offset by the decision of Javagal Srinath to retire from the traditional version. Had it not been for his shoulder injury prior to the previous West Indies tour and the reluctance of the team management to play him in home Tests in the early 1990s, he would have take a lot more than the 232 wickets he finished with. He had toiled manfully for more than a decade and brought laurels to the country both at home and overseas. In the second half of his career, he had taken it upon himself to mentor the next generation of pacers—Ajit Agarkar, Zaheer Khan and Ashish Nehra, among them. Indian cricket would always remain indebted to him.

India's performance in the ODI series against England earlier in the year had fuelled a theory that they were poor chasers. Nasser Hussain, the England skipper, certainly thought so, while Ganguly strongly repudiated his opposite number's claims on the eve of the tri-series in Old Blighty. The Indian captain bagged the bragging rights, thanks to an unbroken stand of 131 for the fifth wicket between Yuvraj Singh and keeper–batsman Rahul Dravid that enabled India to overhaul 272 in the very first game against England at Lord's. But for a 64-run loss to England, India did everything right at the league stage, winning four games out of six with one game abandoned due to rain. The bowling was consistent and the batting impressive, with Sachin leading the way.

He scored two centuries at his new position in the middle order. The first of those, an unbeaten 105 against England at Chester-le-Street, encompassed 108 deliveries and comprised eight fours and a six. In the last league game against Sri Lanka, he blasted 113 off only 102 balls, with 12 fours and a six. In one of the games, he elicited gasps when he switched to a left-hander's grip and gave the ball the treatment; this was years before Kevin Pietersen came to be synonymous with what was christened the 'Switch Hit'. There was some concern when a strained hamstring prevented him from taking the field after his hundred against Sri Lanka, but there was no way he was not going to participate in the summit clash, scheduled to be played against the home team two days later.

At the halfway mark in the final against England at Lord's on 13 July 2002, it appeared that India would need to do something extraordinary to end their three-year run of defeats in the finals of multi-nation tournaments. Batting first, England scored 325–5 with Hussain and Trescothick scoring hundreds. Ganguly and Sehwag got India off to a flier, but once England separated them at 106, the wickets started tumbling. When Sachin was fifth out, bowled by Giles for 14, it seemed all over bar the shouting. The equation at that stage was 180 runs from 156 deliveries with all the biggies in the side back on the Lord's balcony.

Thousands of TV sets across India were switched off in disgust.

The two men who were in the middle had played a lot of cricket with each other. Yuvraj Singh and Mohammed Kaif belonged to the generation that had grown up in the 1990s, the decade when cricket from across the world started being beamed into Indian households. While kids of Sachin's generation had only one TV channel and matches involving India to rely on for visual inspiration in their formative years (apart from the images that appeared in newspapers and periodicals, of course), life was a lot easier for those who grew up in the 1990s. They had grown up watching the greatest cricketers from India and elsewhere at the peak of their respective powers. They picked up a lot from the excellent TV coverage and slow-motion replays from different angles, both in terms of technique and temperament. They got to observe how the world's leading batsmen, bowlers and even fielders, approached the game and reacted to pressure, among other things.

The kids of the 1990s had grown up in an era wherein limited-overs cricket reigned supreme and they therefore identified more with the shorter version and its requirements than the traditional version. While Sachin's generation had typically learnt to improvise while batting and slide/dive while fielding at a relatively later stage of their careers, the members of the under-19 World Cup winning team of 2000 had employed 'unconventional' methods ever since they could remember. Fielding for them had always been as important as batting and bowling, which wasn't something one could say about preceding generations. As batsmen, they were not the types to get bogged down by a stiff asking rate. They had tremendous faith in their ability to handle such situations by batting positively and running with alacrity.

At Lord's, on the afternoon of 13 July 2002, Yuvraj and Kaif batted on and on and on. Their running between the wickets was magnificent and their strokeplay incredible. As their partnership grew, so did the confidence of the Indian supporters and even the supposedly neutral commentators; after one thumping boundary, Harsha Bhogle was moved to question on air, 'Are we onto something here?'

Back in India, those who had switched off their TV sets switched them back on after hearing screams of delight from neighbouring households.

Yuvraj fell for 69, with 59 needed from 50 deliveries. Harbhajan helped Kaif keep India in the game. The Sardar and Kumble both fell in the 48th over, but Kaif continued to keep his cool and Zaheer Khan exuded assurance. When the duo capitalized on an overthrow to take India home with just three deliveries left, there was pandemonium. The hosts would have felt badly let down by the spectators; the Indian supporters had clearly outnumbered and outshouted their England counterparts. Kaif, 87 not out, was lucky to escape unhurt despite his captain and other teammates, most of them heavier than him, throwing themselves into his arms like men possessed. Minutes before leading his team's raid of the playing area by running down the pavilion stairs, Sourav Ganguly reacted to the win by taking off his jersey and doing a jig on the balcony, whirling the piece of clothing over his head. It was his riposte to a similar act by Andrew Flintoff shortly after England had squared the ODI series earlier in the year.

For the Indians who loved their film music as much as they did their cricket, Ganguly's half monty on the balcony of cricket's most venerated institution was their favourite sport's equivalent of Rahul Dev Burman, musical genius and the son of Sachin's namesake, adopting a 'gargling voice' to belt out 'Duniya mein logon ko dhoka kabhi ho jaata hain' (*Apna Desh*) exactly 30 years previously. Like the Indian captain, the composer, fondly known as Pancham, valued the ethos of the profession he had dedicated his life to. However, that did not mean that he reckoned time-and-tested traditions could not be challenged or turned on their head. Pancham was not afraid to push the envelope and boundaries, and loved doing what his heart beckoned him to do. If some timid old-timers were to be offended in the process, then it was their problem and not his. He believed that what mattered most was to be honest to one's passion and profession.

The Indian skipper belonged to the same breed. What the cricketing world saw after the final was a leader who wore his heart on his sleeve and had no qualms about displaying his passion and emotions in public; so what if he was in a place seeped in tradition and known for its stiff upper lip? In that sense, he was quite unlike the men who had preceded him as the captain of India, and the nation loved the change.

The first Test at Lord's was preceded by two momentous events. During the three-day game between the Indian visitors and Hampshire at the state-of-the-art Rose Bowl in Southampton, the wheel turned full circle when Ramakant Achrekar's star pupil delivered a batting masterclass for an adoring crowd that comprised fans, junior cricketers and former stalwarts like Richie Benaud, Barry Richards and Ravi Shastri. Sachin had the gathering spellbound as he dwelt at length on his interpretation of the basic tenets of batsmanship, like the grip, stance, backlift and feet movement. Benaud made it a point to mention the uncanny similarities not only in the batting styles of Bradman and Sachin, particularly the way they whipped deliveries through mid-wicket, but also in the way they gripped the bat. While Sachin rested the bat, face down, on the ground and simply picked it up with both hands to make it his grip, Bradman, Benaud said, would pick up the bat with his right (top) hand and then bring in his left hand to complete the grip.

> [Placing his hand on his temple].... It is important to concentrate with your eyes on what is happening at that height and just below.... Anything over that [the temple], you don't need to worry about.... Your eyes have got to be on the ball.... I would try and watch the whole run-up.... There might be a slight change in action.... You then make a note.... There are times when you have to play with your opponents' patience, there are times you can't allow them to get on with the game in that fashion.
>
> —Sachin Tendulkar, *Masterclass,* Channel 4, 2002

The masterclass was followed by a grand celebration of Indian cricket. India's greatest cricketers of the past, present and future congregated in London for the Wisden Indian Cricketer of the Century Awards. Awards were presented in different categories, but the premier award was obviously the one for whom the function was named. Quite a few eminent names were spoken of as contenders, but one did not have to be a genius to figure out that it was essentially a three-horse race between Sunil Gavaskar, Kapil Dev and Sachin Tendulkar. As was expected, the all-rounder triumphed. Kapil Dev, who had declared two years previously that 'he would never wear whites again' in the aftermath of the unsavoury allegations of 2000, marked his return to the cricketing mainstream with a bang.

The first Test that followed was a forgettable affair for the visitors for two reasons. They lost by 170 runs and Sachin, who was playing his third Test at HQ, was among those who disappointed with scores of 16 and 12. Needing 568 to win, India did well to reach 397 after being bowled out for 221 in the first innings. The show-stealer was Ajit Agarkar. The Shardashram alumnus who had started off as a run-hungry batsman before switching to bowling, got his name engraved on the honours' board in the visitors' dressing room with an unbeaten 109.

The other significant positive that the Indians drew from the game was Virender Sehwag. He was asked to open the batting in Tests as well, by default rather than design. With the middle order bursting at the seams, there was no other way he could be fitted into the XI. Sehwag had only opened in limited-overs cricket till that point. The team management's decision to offer the opening slot to him was followed by a lot of talk and theories about his technique being far too one-dimensional, which, the critics claimed, was certain to be exposed in conditions conducive to seam and swing. But then, Sehwag was the last person to allow himself to be shackled by negative thoughts. In the first innings of the Lord's Test, his first outing as opener in Tests, he scored 84 at nearly a-run-a-ball, inclusive of 10 fours and 1 six.

Sehwag went a step ahead on the first day of the second Test at Nottingham, with an innings of 106. His transformation as full-time opening batsman was complete. Those associated with the team could not help but think of what might have been had he not been forced to miss the West Indies tour due to a shoulder injury. He might just have provided an impetus at the top of the order by taking the attack to the inexperienced West Indian pacemen, who ended up dominating instead.

England replied to India's 357 with another outstanding batting performance. They got 617, and the pressure was back on India. To save the game, it was important that the big guns dropped anchor. They did exactly that as it turned out. Sachin was fluency personified in a knock of 92. After blunting the frontline bowlers for more than two-and-half hours, he was taken by surprise when an off-break bowled by part-timer Michael Vaughan turned a mile to bowl him all ends up. Ganguly was as unlucky, losing his wicket to Steve Harmison when only one short of a hundred. Dravid did better than both, scoring 115. India achieved an honourable draw with Zaheer Khan playing out time with the 17-year-old Parthiv Patel, the youngest cricketer to represent India since Sachin himself in November 1989. He had been inducted into the XI after Ajay Ratra was ruled out due to injury. Like an opener, India's search for a wicketkeeping all-rounder continued unabated.

India defied convention at the start of the third Test at Headingley, Leeds. At a venue known to favour the faster bowlers, they left out Nehra and picked two spinners in Kumble and Harbhajan. With the team management deciding to leave out the inconsistent Wasim Jaffer, Das and Bangar found themselves competing for the second opener's slot. Both opened in the three-day game against Essex that preceded the Test, and while Bangar scored 21 and 74, Das batted just once and scored 250, the second-highest individual first-class score made by an Indian on English soil. The Odisha opener would have fancied his chances of playing the third Test on the strength of that innings, but it was Bangar who got the nod. His sound technique and unflappable temperament apart, the Railways captain was also an underrated medium-pacer who could generate movement in helpful conditions.

True to its reputation, the wicket at Headingley was as English as English could be—it was green and had a lot of juice in it for the quickies. The sky was overcast as always. It was just about the perfect scenario for a captain to insert the opposition in after winning the toss. However, not for the first time, Ganguly stared history in the face and made it blink. He elected to bat after calling correctly.

Sehwag fell with only 15 on the board, and then Dravid joined Bangar to put up a phenomenal exhibition of grit and application. They added 170 before the makeshift opener fell for 69. Sachin came in to bat on his home ground of 1992 to discover that the wicket was still so damp that the ball was creating impressions on it every single time it pitched.

The senior statesman sought inspiration from his partner, who completed the transition from good to great with an innings of 148. Rahul Dravid had not looked back since his match-winning and career-altering 180 against Australia at Kolkata the year before, and he never would. The two batsmen fed off each other. Sachin completed a half-century with a classy pull off Alex Tudor, with his left leg airborne; it was his version of the Nataraja stroke made famous by Kapil Dev.

An imperious on-drive off Giles, against the spin, gave Sachin his 30th Test century in what was his 99th Test. He was now ahead of Bradman and behind only Sunil Gavaskar in the all-time list. Coincidentally, Gavaskar had also scored his 30th Test hundred in his 99th Test!

Among the many traits that the two little masters had in common was their fastidiousness in terms of their preparation, gear and the sightscreen. Both SMG and SRT were prone to losing their equanimity if bothered by movements around the sightscreen while batting, and rightly so.

However, the sightscreen hardly mattered on the second evening of the Leeds Test. Sachin and Ganguly declined the umpires' offer of going off for bad light in the closing stages and went for a declaration, lashing and bashing a hapless bowling attack with impunity. Off all the audacious strokes essayed by Sachin during this dash, two stood out as much for their assurance as their arrogance. The first was a scoop over mid-wicket off Andrew Caddick that Sachin dismissed from his presence by shuffling across the crease and twirling his heavyweight bat like a feather at the point of impact; the bowler's bewildered expression said it all. The second was a flat-batted swat for six off the same bowler; Sachin came down the wicket and deposited him deep into the stands, over long-on. At the other end, Ganguly accentuated the psychological damage to the home team with a succession of stupendous strokes, including one that unfortunately hit a spectator on the face.

> Right now, Tendulkar is a great batsman who doesn't scare the opposition. It's as if the fact that he sees the ball so early has begun to work against him: he has almost too much time to play the ball and he uses it to think and fret instead of using it to attack the bowling. There is a tense pre-meditation in his play these days, which is different from the calculated aggression we used to see earlier. Viv Richards said after Tendulkar's failures on the tour of the Caribbean that Tendulkar didn't seem to be enjoying his cricket. Perhaps he is right.... Perhaps Tendulkar could take a leaf out of Virender Sehwag's carefree book. He could stop being Atlas and just go with the flow.
>
> —Mukul Kesavan, *Wisden Asia Cricket*, September 2002

Sachin proved at Leeds that he was more than capable of batting in Tests as he had in ODIs in the previous decade, whenever he was required to do so. Whether the opposition was scared of him or not did not matter to him as much as playing in accordance with the situation and requirements of his team. That was precisely what he had done in the shorter variety in the tri-series in England, with his job description having changed from 'opening aggressor' to 'mid-innings stabilizer'.

> Time may have changed my game a little bit here and there. It's like one's health; it's not the same every morning. You don't get your backswing right everyday, not everyday are your feet moving well. Sometimes the wicket may not allow you to play the big shots. It's a team sport, not an individual sport.... I go out to do what the team wants me to do.... I think I am better at analysing the game now, having played for so many years. This happens only with experience.
>
> —Sachin Tendulkar, *The Sportstar*, 14 September 2002

Sachin was seven short of a double hundred when he was leg-before to Caddick. Remarkably, only seven of his 193 runs had been scored in the 'V' from mid-on to mid-off. In other words, he had turned one of the time-and-tested tenets of batsmanship—of starting a Test innings by playing in the 'V' with a straight bat—on its head. It wasn't something he could have managed had he eschewed his fundamental approach to batting. He had driven, cut, flicked, pulled and even slogged with audacity and abandon.

India declared on the third morning at 628–8, a score that not even the most ardent supporters of the side, leave alone those who had come down hard on Ganguly for his decision to bat first, could not have imagined 48 hours previously. The bowlers then got to work. Led by the spin twins, they worked their way through the England batting and dismissed the hosts for 273. After Ganguly enforced the follow-on, the man who had bowled India to many a famous victory in similar circumstances at home, did likewise on foreign soil; Anil Kumble's 4–66, in addition to his 3–93 in the first innings, took India to victory by an innings and 46 runs. In terms of the conditions, the quality of the opposition and of course, the quality of the cricket produced by the victors, it was easily India's greatest Test win away from home. Bangar, who had helped set up the win with his dour innings on day one, further vindicated the team management's faith with two key wickets in the second innings. An ecstatic Sourav Ganguly wanted to ensure that everybody savoured the triumph to the fullest; with the match sealed, Parthiv Patel wanted to go off to tend to an injury, but his captain vetoed his request, insisting that he be on the field when the win was completed.

What made the series-levelling win even more significant was the fact that it was achieved at a time when the players were on a collision course with the apex body of the sport as well as their parent body. The ICC had signed on several sponsors in the lead-up to the third edition of the Knockout, which had been reformatted and rechristened the 'Champions Trophy', and the 2003 World Cup, which was to be co-hosted by South Africa, Zimbabwe and Kenya. India was the main market of most of these sponsors and their products were direct competitors of brands that were being endorsed by Indian cricketers. The 'Ambush Marketing' clause in the ICC's Participating Nations Agreement prohibited players who were contracted to the signatory Boards from having endorsement tie-ups with rivals of the ICC's official sponsors for a period of 30 days before and after the tournament and during the tournament, of course. The Indian players, most of whom had signed lucrative deals with the rival brands long before the ICC signed its sponsors, were not amused.

Matters came to a head just before the Leeds Test, when the BCCI, which was also trying to get the players to sign the Player Terms, announced an alternative team for the Champions Trophy, which was to be played in Sri Lanka immediately after the England series. This team was to be sent to Sri Lanka in case the members of the team that had originally been picked refused to sign the contracts. Sachin may well have remembered November 1989.

The players of 2002 displayed a lot more pluck and spunk than their counterparts of 1989–90. They were aware that an excellent showing in the Test match would give them and their stand a shot in the arm. That they went on to outplay England in English conditions, that too by an innings, left no one in any doubt whatsoever that this was India's best Test team ever. As was only to be expected, considering the popularity of the Indian team, a compromise was worked out between the players and the ICC and the best Indian team went to Sri Lanka and later, Africa.

In the fourth Test at the Oval, Sachin became only the fourth Indian after Sunil Gavaskar, Dilip Vengsarkar and Kapil Dev Nikhanj to complete a century of Test appearances. Among those who commemorated the achievement was Gavaskar's PMG, with a 50-minute documentary titled *Sachin Tendulkar—Mr. India*, which took the viewers through the extraordinary story of the maestro, from his teens to the present day, with Salil Ankola, who had made his Test debut alongside Sachin at Karachi in November 1989, as the principal narrator. The documentary that this writer was privileged to script, featured soundbites by several of Sachin's teammates, mentors and members of the media.

The Test match itself was a 'batathon'. England scored 515 and India replied with 508. Two future captains—Michael Vaughan and Rahul Dravid—scored their third centuries of the series. The Indian vice-captain went on to get 217. He was only four short of Sunil Gavaskar's 221, the highest individual score by an Indian in a Test on English soil, when he was run out. Sachin contributed 54 to a third-wicket stand of 91 before he was leg-before to Caddick. He was cross with himself, because he had been batting well till he misread the swing and played for one that he thought would deviate away from the bat, only for it to go the other way and hit him plumb in front. England were 114–0 in their second innings at the close.

The Indian team's performances in England obliterated memories of the unsuccessful tours of the Caribbean and South Africa. Both the Test and ODI squads appeared to be settled, and with less than six months left for the World Cup, the consensus was that Ganguly's side could not have timed its resurgence better.

India took on Zimbabwe in a Pool 2 game of the ICC Champions Trophy in hot and humid Colombo, a mere five days after the end of the Test series in the English autumn. Dravid and Kaif enabled India to recover from 87–5 and post 288–6, and the runners-up of 2000 won by 14 runs. England were then thrashed by eight wickets, with openers Sehwag and Ganguly both scoring hundreds and ensuring that a chase of 270 was completed with more than 10 overs to spare. The Indians then excelled themselves in the semi-final against South Africa. Batting first, all seven specialist batsmen entered double figures with Sehwag and Yuvraj Singh getting 50s. India's 261–9 was a competitive score. In response, South Africa were 192–1 and in control, when Herschelle Gibbs retired hurt due to cramps. He could not have known it, but his exit was the turning point. Tight bowling and two incredible catches by Yuvraj Singh made the South Africans frantic and, not for the first or the last time, they choked. At the end of the 50th over, they were 251–6 and India were in the final. It was not often that the Indian team snatched victory from the jaws of defeat, and suddenly, the team had produced two such instances in the matter of three months.

The final, or 'finals', were two of the most bizarre games of cricket ever played. Sri Lanka batted first and scored 244–8, and India were 14–0 in response when heavy rain ended the proceedings. There was a provision for a reserve day, on which the organizers were naturally expected to take note of the propensity of the weather gods to keep the skies clear during the day and unleash showers in the evenings. However, the replay was scheduled in the same day–night slot. Sri Lanka batted first again and scored 222–7. India were 38–1 in the ninth over in response, when the skies opened all over again, almost at the same time as the previous evening. The finalists were forced to share the trophy.

While Sehwag was the highest scorer in the competition with 271 runs from five games, his idol had a quiet tournament, with only 39 runs. Sachin had failed against Zimbabwe and South Africa, and hadn't been required to bat against England.

The Test series against the West Indies, which began at the Wankhede a little over a week after the farcical end of the Champions Trophy, was significant, in that it was the first since the inaugural one between the two teams in 1948–49 that India began as favourites. The West Indies were no longer the force they had been, and the non-availability of Brian Lara for the series had weakened them further. Their victory over India earlier in the year had more to do with the lackadaisical cricket of Ganguly's side than any brilliance on their part.

India made amends for their poor showing in the Caribbean with thumping wins in the first two Tests, played at Mumbai and Chennai respectively. At Mumbai, Sehwag, by now established as an opener, blasted 147 and Dravid scored 100 to become the first Indian to score centuries in four successive Test innings.

Sachin played bit roles in both the wins, with scores of 35, 43 and an unbeaten 16. He had been overshadowed by his colleagues, which ought to have been interpreted as a sign that the Indian 'team' was playing like a team. However, the cynics opted to see things differently. They continued to harp on his 'conservative' approach, which they argued was out of character. That he no longer needed to be belligerent all the time, but was more than capable of stepping on the accelerator if required to, was conveniently overlooked.

> The younger Sachin may have been more fun to watch, but I know who I would want in my team.
>
> —Rahul Dravid, *Wisden Asia Cricket*, September 2002

Dravid of course had a point. In his first 61 Tests, from his debut game at Karachi till the end of the 1997–98 series against Australia, Sachin had scored 4,552 runs at an average of 54.84, inclusive of 16 centuries. From the end of that series against Australia till the end of the series in England in 2002, he played in 39 more Tests, in which he scored 3,853 runs and averaged an astounding 62.14, inclusive of 14 centuries.

The series winners were guilty of letting their guard down in the first innings of the third Test at Kolkata. With as many as six of the top seven batsmen, Sachin included, crossing 20, they ought to have scored a lot more than the 358 they finished with. Another player who was among the runs was Javagal Srinath, who had put his retirement plans on hold after missing the England series. He scored 46. The West Indies then batted well, with three batsmen—Wavell Hinds, Shivnarine Chanderpaul and Marlon Samuels—scoring hundreds. They took a first-innings lead of 139 and their bowlers then gave it everything. When Sehwag and Bangar were back in the pavilion with only 11 on the board, it seemed like the bad, old times all over again.

Sachin began his innings with deft nudges and glides and then focussed on playing in a slightly elongated 'V', from the covers on the off-side to mid-wicket on the on-side. Primarily, he sought to play everything with a a straight bat, but took full toll of anything that was loose. It was good, old, 'old-fashioned' Test match batting.

The visitors were ecstatic when Dravid fell leg-before to Darren Powell at 49. Ganguly, who received a tremendous ovation at his home ground, added a further 38 with Sachin before falling to Cameron Cuffy. India were 87-4 and Sachin was joined in the middle by V.V.S. Laxman, who had scored 281 in his previous second-innings outing at the Eden.

He did not take long to acclimatize to familiar surroundings, and the duo put together a match-saving stand. Sachin was in the zone, executing some stunning cuts and booming drives, especially a couple which went past the bowler and non-striker. The galleries erupted when he completed his 31st Test century in the closing stages of the fourth day. It was his first Test century at the colosseum. At stumps, India were 56 runs ahead and both batsmen were firmly entrenched. Sachin, not out on 114 overnight, continued to be assertive on the fifth morning. He had moved to 176 and India were a healthy 301–4 when he was caught at point off Cuffy.

> Tendulkar's innings deserves to be projected as an example for the sake of all those wanting to educate themselves in the intricacies of committed batsmanship. The determination in Tendulkar's knock was evident quite early when he curbed his desire to have a go.... For long, Sunil Gavaskar had been looking forward to a different—defensive to be precise—innings from Tendulkar. 'That would make him a complete batsman,' Gavaskar would say.
>
> —Vijay Lokapally, *The Sportstar*, November 2002

Sachin's out-of-character innings earned him encomiums from the pundits and masses alike. For once, no one was complaining about him not batting like the 'old Tendulkar'. The match-winner had proved that he could be an equally effective match-saver as well. Laxman was on 154 and India were 471–8 when the game was called off.

A hamstring strain ruled Sachin out of the seven-match ODI series against the visitors, which they won 4–3.

India's last international engagement before the World Cup was a tour of New Zealand that comprised two Tests and seven ODIs. It was New Zealand's last series before the tournament as well. With the wickets in South Africa expected to be batting friendly, the Indian team management assumed that the Kiwis would dish out similar strips. After all, it was critical that their own batsmen went into the World Cup with some confidence. That was not to be.

The tour began with a one-off Cricket Max International. Devised by Martin Crowe, the 'Max' format was an amalgamation of both forms of the game, with some radical innovations thrown in. It comprised four innings of 10 eight-ball overs each, with a batsman getting double the value of runs if he were to hit the ball in specially designated 'max' zones, the batting side getting a 'free hit' for a no-ball, and the bowlers not allowed to extend their run-ups beyond an 'inner grid', among other things. Laxman led India in the absence of both Ganguly and Dravid. After the Kiwis batted first and scored 123–5 in their first innings of 10 overs, India replied with 133–5. The top scorer was Sachin, who struck 72 off 27 balls. The Kiwis then scored 118–7 and restricted India to 87–6, thus winning by 10 runs. Sachin received the individual award for his innings. The merits of the 'Max' format notwithstanding, it wasn't quite lapped up by the cricketing world the way Twenty20 was, in the years to come.

The wicket at the Jade Stadium, Christchurch, where the Max International was played, turned out to be the most batting-friendly strip that the Indians encountered on the tour. The first Test at Wellington was over in three days, with the hosts winning by nine wickets. Put in to bat, India posted 161 only because of an exceptional 76 by Rahul Dravid. The hosts took a lead of 86 and then bowled India out for 121. This time around, Sachin waged a lone battle on a damp and green wicket, against a band of bowlers who were making the ball talk, with an innings of 51. The second Test at Hamilton entered the fourth day only because the first day was washed out due to rain. The two teams were dismissed for sub-100 scores in the first innings, the only such instance in Test history, and India scrambled to 154 in their second innings. The hosts were given a torrid time by the Indian bowlers, but they hung in to win by four wickets. The trivia hunters had reason to cheer when Ashish Nehra became the first player in Test history to bat and bowl in all four innings on the same day.

Nehra and his co-bowlers from both camps had plenty of reason to cheer, but the batsmen and most critically, even the spectators, were far from impressed. While there was nothing wrong in preparing pitches that would test the batsmen, the fact was that the local authorities had taken things to an extreme by making both teams play in 'gardens', as a member of the Indian team put it. India would have still won the series had Zaheer Khan's colleagues matched his efforts with the ball. He took 11 wickets, inclusive of two five-wicket hauls, but no other Indian bowler bagged more than five scalps. On the other hand, New Zealand's triumvirate of Daryl Tuffey, Jacob Oram and Shane Bond took 13, 12 and 11 scalps respectively.

Javagal Srinath's arrival for the seven-match ODI series did not change India's fortunes. The veteran took 4–23 in the very first game, but he and his colleagues had only 108 runs to defend, and the Kiwis scraped through by three wickets. India's scores in the remaining six games spoke for themselves—219, 108, 122, 169-8, 200-9, 122. The visitors tried everything, from shuffling the batting order to aiming for 180-190 instead of 250-plus when they batted first, but nothing worked, and they lost the series 2–5. One batsman who emerged from the series with some credit was Virender Sehwag, who struck two centuries when his colleagues were struggling to cross 20.

Sachin missed the first four games due to an ankle injury that he sustained when he accidentally stepped into a dent next to a practice pitch, while bowling in the nets. His return made no difference to the team's fortunes, as he fell for scores of 0, 1 and 1.

Even worse than the performances of the side in New Zealand was the concern that all the gains of mid-2002 had been undone, that too on the eve of the World Cup, of all events. The team management tried to put up a brave front despite the censure of the fans and even their own Board. While there was a point in their contention that the conditions in Africa were not likely to be as hostile to the batsmen, did the players at the top of the order possess the character to bounce back?

The world would know very soon.

ONE STEP SHORT

Basically, his talent was inborn and those skills cannot be acquired or transferred to anyone. The loss of any game under his captaincy worked him up so much that it preyed on his batting abilities. The genius then realized very soon that detaching from the top seat was the way forward in his career. Unlike many other captains who stand down, the fact that Sachin was not leading the team made no difference. Players knew very well who the true leader was in the dressing room and on the field.

—Javagal Srinath, *India Today*, September 2010

The buzz in the media conference hall when he entered gave way to pin-drop silence when he proceeded to make a statement that read thus: 'We ourselves are disappointed with the kind of performance we all have put up. I also understand the disappointment you have gone through. I am just here to assure you that we will be fighting till the last ball is bowled.'

The situation was such that it warranted a show of leadership. The most experienced member of the side knew that he just had to do it.

Barring the decision to leave Laxman out of the World Cup squad, which many people were justifiably unhappy with, the individuals associated with Indian cricket did not appear to have put a foot wrong in the period between the end of the New Zealand tour and the start of the quadrennial event. Durban, where the team set up camp before the start of the tournament, had a large population of Indian origin, which made the players feel at home. They trained with intent, with the 53-year-old Wright being particularly delighted to note that while he had beaten most of the players in a run on the Durban beach during the 2001–02 tour, he came second-last this time around. The optimist that he was, he credited Leipus and Le Roux for the transformation than his own physical decline.

The BCCI had requisitioned the services of Sandy Gordon, the noted sports psychologist, who prepared a 'vision document' for the side. Just before India's first game against Holland, he had individual and group sessions with the players and recommended that they adopt a theme for the competition: 'Now or Never' was what the team agreed on. Gordon also suggested that the players get together on the field whenever possible 'to communicate and keep the team vibe going'; the players took the thought to its logical conclusion by borrowing the concept of a team huddle from England's county circuit.

The players planned intensively. Ganguly apart, six captains were identified—Dravid and Sachin for batting, Yuvraj and Kaif for fielding, and Kumble and Srinath for bowling. Each player was designated a specific role even in the team meetings.

And yet, it all fell apart, or at least threatened to. After rain put a premature end to the team's first practice game against KwaZulu Natal, India lost the second game to what was not even a frontline XI, by 32 runs. The batting collapsed yet again for 158.

> Clearly uncomfortable at number four, or number three, Sachin would be justified in his desire to return to his slot as opener…. Given a choice, Sachin would like to open and this is now for the team management to solve. Sachin is the only complete batsman in the team when it comes to dealing with mean opponents and one would back him all the way. It will be in the interest of the team if Sachin is left alone to chart his tactics and the captain would do well to utilise Sachin's bowling too.
>
> —*The Sportstar*, 8 February 2003

A chat with Kumble and Srinath convinced Wright that the team needed leadership at the top of the order. And who better to provide it than the team's talisman? The coach accosted Sachin, who was his professional self and replied that he would bat wherever the team wanted him to. When asked by Wright to forget the team for a moment and think about himself, Sachin initially dithered. But the coach was persistent. It was then that Sachin confessed that if given the choice, he would like to open.

Sachin got what he desired, but only because that was what the team management also wanted him to do. He was not at his fittest, going into the tournament. The ankle that he had injured in New Zealand was still troubling him. Strapping it before every practice session and match was an ordeal, and the wound would sting when it would come in contact with seawater during the team's recovery sessions on the beach. A torn ligament and tendon in a finger were making it difficult for him to even hold a cup of tea properly. He also had a strained hamstring, due to which he could not jog or sprint with his teammates and was forced to cycle. Then was the issue of his back. However, these 'irritants' were never going to get in the away of his cricket, least of all in a World Cup. He was prepared to compromise.

> During the 2003 World Cup, I went to his room at Sandton Hotel at Johannesburg. It was a huge room, with a big double bed, but Tendulkar was sleeping on the floor carpet, with a thin pillow and a towel, because he was suffering from a backache. He was so eager to win the World Cup that he decided to make a few sacrifices along the way.
>
> —Debasish Datta, *Outlook Special Commemorative Issue*, 2010

The resurrection of the legendary Ganguly–Tendulkar association at the top of the order did not make any difference. In the opening game against Holland, the batting was as insipid as it had been in New Zealand, with the notable exception of Sachin, who scored 52. India struggled to post 200–9 and it was left to the bowlers to save the day; Kumble and Srinath delivered with four wickets apiece. The next game, against Australia, the reigning world champions, was a catastrophe; India were bowled out for 125 and lost by nine wickets. Sachin was India's top scorer with 36.

In Africa and across the Indian Ocean, former cricketers tore into the team on television and in print, and so-called fans took to their favourite activity of burning effigies of the players. Mohammed Kaif's house in Allahabad was attacked, Rahul Dravid's car was damaged and a mock 'funeral procession' of the team was organized in Kolkata. The Indian media contingent in South Africa was posing uncomfortable questions at media conferences. The players obviously did not appreciate the hostility. It was then that Sachin Tendulkar decided to take charge with a succinct statement.

He took charge on the field with a fluent 81 against Zimbabwe at Harare. The Indians had changed their batting order again, with Sehwag and Ganguly exchanging spots. India totalled 255–7 and the bowlers then took over. The Heath–Streak led side, which had fancied its chances against India particularly after its successes in the recent past, was outplayed comprehensively by 83 runs. The Indians then returned to South Africa to play Namibia at Pietermaritzburg, where the Mahatma had been famously evicted from the whites-only compartment of a train, 110 years previously.

Batting first, India amassed 311–2 with Sachin scoring 152 and Ganguly remaining unbeaten on 112. The only alarm during the innings was when Sachin nearly decapacitated Aleem Dar, the umpire, with a straight drive. Fortunately, no damage was done as Dar got out of the way just in time.

India needed to win at least one of their last two league games to assure themselves of a place in the Super Six, the next stage of the competition. The best-case scenario was for them to beat both England and Pakistan, so that they would not have to depend on the performances of other teams to determine their fate.

Against England at Durban, India won the toss and elected to bat. Opening the England bowling was Andy Caddick, who had been quoted as saying that he was happy to have Sachin open the batting, as that gave him a chance to dismiss him early. Sachin and Sehwag were assertive from ball one and the scoreboard ticked along at a fair clip. Both were severe on anything loose and their running was brilliant as always. Short-pitched deliveries were only to be expected on the Durban track, and when Caddick bowled one in the ninth over, Sachin was ready. He transferred his weight onto the back foot and went for the hook. The ball cleared the stands. In Caddick's next over, Sachin hit him for three boundaries, an off-drive on the up being the best stroke of the lot. The bowler had gone from being happy to hapless!

Sachin was on 50 when he essayed an uppish cut off Flintoff and was caught at point, *against the run of play*.

> Somewhere down the line, I think Tendulkar himself became fixated on the idea of batting through fifty overs. Having played with and against him, I know that the opposition fear the Tendulkar who gets 70 off 40 balls more than the one who looks to anchor the innings. The second Tendulkar scores at four or five runs an over and keeps the opposition in the game for longer. The first one just takes the game away.
>
> —Sanjay Manjrekar, *Wisden Asia Cricket*, April 2003

Simply put, Sachin was back to doing what he had done throughout the 1990s because he had been reassigned the role of the 'opening aggressor'. Following his dismissal, the middle order helped India reach 250–9. Thereafter, it was Ashish Nehra's show all the way. The left-arm paceman from Delhi ran through the England batting in one straight spell, finishing with figures of 6–23. India won by 80 runs.

The 'it-is-just-another-game' gibberish emanated from both camps on the eve of the first clash between India and Pakistan on a cricket field since June 2000. Of course, even those who made those statements knew that they were talking absolute nonsense, leave alone those who read and heard them. Streets all over the subcontinent wore a deserted look on the afternoon of 1 March 2003, when the teams faced off at Centurion. It was a day game and the Indians would have fielded first anyway, but the Pakistanis were delighted to win the toss and bat first, convinced as they were that they were better off without the additional pressure of chasing in a 'final before a final'.

Saeed Anwar, a batsman who had taken an enormous amount of runs off the Indian bowling in the 1990s, scored a hundred, and Pakistan set India a target of 274; at that stage, India's highest successful chase of a target in a World Cup game was 222.

Sachin, who like many of his teammates had not slept on the nights leading up to the game, cocooned himself from the rest of the world during the break. He gobbled a banana and a tub of ice cream, and focussed on the job at hand. During the tournament, he had opted for throwdowns over nets. He had batted for hours against deliveries chucked at him from a short distance. It was just that he felt more comfortable with this form of preparation.

The batsman who usually made his way to the non-striker's end at the start of an ODI innings then surprised one and all by taking strike. What followed was even more puzzling—he stood in such a way that all three stumps were exposed to the bowler. His reasoning was that an unblocked view of the stumps would make the bowlers attempt yorkers, which he could capitalize on by shuffling across the crease. His feet were slightly wider than usual and he was grounding his bat between them, as opposed to grounding it behind his right foot. It would not have struck him then, but this was how the Don himself stood.

It was by no means the first time Sachin had altered his stance in an international match. Earlier, he had taken middle-stump guard, a departure from his usual practice of asking the umpire to 'give him leg-stump', to make it easier to get inside the line of the ball against bowlers targeting his body on bouncy tracks.

At Centurion on the afternoon of 1 March 2003, he was for all practical purposes replicating what he had done in a Test against South Africa at Cape Town in January 1997. He was not used to standing wide of the stumps or ground his bat between his feet or shuffle. Any other batsman would have practised a change in approach for days in the nets before implementing it in a match, but then, Sachin was one of those who viewed things differently.

His face was as inexpressive as ever, the nod as firm as ever. There were the two trademark adjustments of the abdomen guard, just before he settled into his stance.

You have got to be comfortable in your stance.... It eventually boils down to adjustment.... It is important to be as still as possible and keep your mind as blank as possible....

—Sachin Tendulkar, *Masterclass*, Channel 4, 2002

The openers' plan was to get through the first 10 overs without losing a wicket. Sachin shuffled across the crease to cut the third ball of Wasim Akram's opening over for four. The ball neatly bisected the cover cordon. A single off the next ball took him to the non-striker's end and prompted David Shepherd, the umpire, to ask him why he had taken strike. Sachin's reply was as succinct as his statement to the media earlier in the tournament: 'I want to impose myself on this match.'

Sehwag took another boundary in the first over and Sachin then geared up to face the bowler who claimed to operate only in top gear. Waqar Younis, the captain, had held himself back and thrown the ball to Shoaib Akhtar for the second over. After three uneventful deliveries, the Rawalpindi Express hurtled in with all his might. Sachin sensed something different in the run-up and expected a short delivery. He was right.

Shoaib's fourth ball was way too short, and well outside the off-stump. In a Test match, Sachin may well have left it alone, but this was a high-octane limited-overs game against a high-profile opponent; it was vital to seize the initiative. He extended his bat horizontally and lashed, opening the face of the blade at the point of impact. The ball flew over backward point for six. Even as those who had spent an entire decade and more agonising over India's defeats against Pakistan came to terms with what their hero had just done, Sehwag was spotted on the TV screen, punching his colleague on the glove with a big grin on his face; this was something new. His body language, like that of his partner's, was unlike anything the generation of Indians who had grown up in the 1980s and 1990s had seen, particularly when their team played the old enemy.

Shoaib sought to compensate with his next ball, and bowled one on middle-and-leg; Sachin picked it early and shuffled across to flick it past square-leg for four. Convinced that he had done enough for the over, he offered a firm push to Shoaib's last ball, but his timing was such that the ball beat Waqar to the boundary. Sachin and India were rocketing along, and Shoaib was removed from the attack after only one over.

The carnage continued. Waqar brought himself on from Shoaib's end, only for Sehwag to scoop his first ball over point for six. It was the disciple's tribute to his idol's stroke a couple of overs earlier. Sehwag then took two boundaries off Akram. The drooping Pakistani shoulders became ramrod straight when their captain dealt a double blow; Sehwag was caught in the covers and Ganguly was leg-before, first ball. Mohammed Kaif, promoted to number four, kept the hat-trick ball out.

The two strikes did not stop the adrenalin from coursing through Sachin's veins. He went for an expansive drive off Akram, and was lucky to be put down by Abdul Razzaq at mid-off. Had the fielder been standing a couple of yards back, it would have been curtains. 'Do you know whose catch you have dropped?' A livid Akram asked the fielder. The Pakistani all-time great, who was only a couple of wickets away from completing 500 scalps in ODIs, had certainly sensed trouble for his team.

Sachin, chastened by the miss, eschewed the aerial route from that point. However, the carpet strokes kept flowing. The spectators kept shouting and the commentators kept searching for superlatives as India's talisman continued to find the gaps and boundaries. He had often said that he found it difficult to be in the zone. Maybe he could not articulate the same, but then, he did not need to. He was providing a live demonstration of being in the zone on 1 March 2003.

When he drove Akram off the back foot between cover and mid-off for four, he froze on his follow-through, almost as if he were admiring his own stroke; nobody would have faulted him if that had indeed been the case. Kaif also found the boundary on a regular basis and the Pakistani fielding, never the best at the best of times, was mediocre in a crisis. Sachin went past 50 and India were cruising. The score was 126–2 at the end of the 16th over when the TV cameras caught Sachin signalling to the dressing room. It appeared that his hamstring was acting up. Leipus did what he could and Sachin carried on in discomfort and pain. On the other side of the Indian Ocean, scores of cricket lovers admonished themselves for remembering Chennai 1999; surely, it wasn't going to happen again, or was it?

Sachin carried on stroking and running, as he had at Chennai in January 1999. Kaif was on 35 when he dragged Afridi onto his stumps. The wicket notwithstanding, India were 155–3 in 22 overs and in the driver's seat. The only concern was the condition of Sachin, who had become the first batsman to score 12,000 runs in ODIs.

He marched into the 90s with a straight drive off Razzaq. Those watching him reckoned that he ought to call for a runner. However, he had always been reluctant to use one, unless he found it impossible to run, and so he carried on. When he did ask for a runner, those watching the game in India on the SET network were stunned to hear Ramiz Raja, the former Pakistan captain-turned-commentator, say that 'he was unsure whether Pakistan would grant him a runner or not'. The mind went back to the Independence Cup game in May 1997, wherein a certain S.R. Tendulkar, as captain of India, had allowed a certain Saeed Anwar a runner when the batsman was in his 30s. He had gone on to score a record 194! Pakistan's captain in that game—who would certainly have made an issue had Sachin not permitted Anwar to have a runner—had been none other than Ramiz Raja himself!

Sachin was two short of a hundred when Shoaib, striving hard to forget his first over of the innings, bowled one that climbed awkwardly into the batsman. Sachin was caught between taking evasive action and fending it away, and Younis Khan took a fine catch at point. India were 177–4, needing 97 with more than 20 overs in hand, but the hero was gone. Would history repeat itself?

Across India, the atmosphere was tense. There were those who shed tears, even as they rose from their chairs and sofas to give their hero a standing ovation. The new man in was Yuvraj Singh, who was playing Pakistan for the first time after making his international debut in 2000. He negotiated the first ball he received, and clipped the second to the boundary. That one stroke settled Indian nerves.

Yuvraj had for company, one of the coolest heads in international cricket. Rahul Dravid was serene and splendid. They kept it simple, putting their heads down and finishing the job. Dravid pulled Waqar to the mid-wicket boundary in the 46th over to finish the game and give India her fourth win over Pakistan in a World Cup game on four occasions.

There was a reversal of roles at the presentation ceremony. While the usually blunt Ganguly took the diplomatic route by talking about how he and his team were happy to have done India proud, Sachin, who normally chose his words with caution, let himself go after collecting the individual award. 'This has always been a special game for us. This is the fourth World Cup we have beaten them in a row, and nothing means more than this to us.'

For several Indians, the World Cup ended there and then, as a fan explained to Wright in the hotel lobby. For them, it did not matter what the team did later in the competition. Beating Pakistan was paramount.

It wasn't the first time Sachin Tendulkar had essayed a remarkable innings against a formidable opponent, nor was it the last. However, those who had watched Javed Miandad's last-ball six off Chetan Sharma in April 1986 placed Sachin's 98 on a different pedestal. While Pakistan had been the dominant side since that Sharjah game, it wasn't as if India hadn't registered significant wins, especially in the World Cup. But the 2003 win was different. Much like an A.R. Rahman song, the win and Sachin's innings of 98 grew on Indian fans as the minutes, hours and days passed. They came to regard the second-over six off Shoaib Akhtar as an epiphany; the stroke, essayed off supposedly the world's fastest paceman, broke the spell that had been cast by Miandad's six of 1986. Sachin's lash over point was perceived as a representation of a *new* Indian team that was not carrying baggage of the past and was intent on achieving goals that were far more notable than merely beating its traditional rival.

> I think it was in 2003 that I told him he could score a hundred [international] hundreds. It was just a matter of simple arithmetic, looking at the number of runs he was scoring every year and the number of years he had left. I thought it was quite obvious. I have seen him closely for years.
>
> —John Wright, as quoted in *The Sachin Sunset*,
> Wisden India, November 2013

The six-wicket win enabled India to storm into the Super Six with eight points. There were some anxious moments in the encounters against Kenya and New Zealand, before one pair of batsmen settled in and took the team through. Sachin failed in both games, but excelled against Sri Lanka. Put in to bat on what looked a wicket tailormade for the batsmen, the Indians expressed their gratitude with a score of 292-6. The openers put on 153 at nearly a-run-a-ball, before Sehwag fell for 66. Sachin carried on, and he was three short of a century when he nicked Aravinda de Silva of all bowlers to the keeper.

India's batting heroics in the tournament would have amounted to nothing had the pace triumvirate of Srinath, Zaheer Khan and Ashish Nehra not complemented him. The pacers were at their best against the Lankans. They needed only 23 overs to dismiss the opposition for 109; Zaheer took two wickets and Srinath and Nehra snared four each. Ganguly did not need to introduce a fourth bowler.

India then ended Kenya's dream run in the tournament in the semi-final at Durban. Ganguly won the toss and did what everybody did in a day-nighter— bat first. The captain and his predecessor added 103 for the second wicket, and India reached 270-4. Sachin scored 83 and Ganguly scored an unbeaten 111, his third hundred of the competition. The pace triumvirate then struck early and Sachin chipped in with two wickets, to seal victory by 91 runs.

The way India were playing, it seemed that there was only one team that could prevent them from lifting the trophy. On 23 March 2003, Ganguly's team arrived at the Wanderers, Johannesburg, to take on that very side. Ricky Ponting's Australians had not put a foot wrong in the tournament; those who had expected them to be demoralized when Shane Warne, their star player, confessed to have consumed a banned diuretic and was handed a one-year ban, hours before their first game, were astounded at their response to the setback. Leave alone their frontline batsmen and bowlers, even their reserves were in form. Andy Bichel, who had come in for the injured Jason Gillespie for the Pool game against England, had done so well that he could not be left out in the subsequent games.

The Indian team management had decided to bat first if they won the toss in what was to be a day game. However, they changed their plans on the morning of the game. There were some damp patches on the strip that they reckoned their pacers could capitalize on. Ganguly won the toss and elected to bowl.

To say that everything went awry would be an understatement; Zaheer gave Matthew Hayden some lip in his first over, but he also conceded 15 runs. The Australians hammered the Indian bowlers to finish with 359–2, with Ricky Ponting and Damien Martyn unbeaten on 140 and 88, respectively. In the Indian dressing room, where one could have heard a pin drop, Anil Kumble sought to lighten the mood by suggesting that it wasn't an impossible task; all the batsmen had to do was strike at least one boundary in every over and then look to score 160 runs off the remaining 250 deliveries. In another day and age, a team might have been optimistic about scoring at seven an over for 50 overs, but then, this was 2003, and the introduction of the Twenty20 format in England was still a couple of months away.

Sachin took strike, as he had against Pakistan, and opened his account with a boundary off Glenn McGrath. He then went for a pull, only to get a top-edge, and the bowler held a simple catch. An offensive by Sehwag and a sudden shower gave the Indians some hope, but once both ended as dramatically as they had begun, it was all over. The batsmen went down fighting, with the final wicket falling at 234 off the second ball of the fortieth over.

Sachin put up a brave face when he received the Sir Garfield Sobers Trophy and a cheque of US$62,500 for being the player of the tournament from the great all-rounder himself. He had scored a record 673 runs, beating his own 1996 record of 523 runs. It was by far the highest aggregate ever achieved by any batsman in a World Cup. But all that amounted to nothing. The players were shattered, and they could only console themselves with the thought that they had beaten every team they had faced in the tournament, save the eventual champions, to whom they had lost twice. Reaching the final of the World Cup was by no means an insignificant achievement.

The time was ripe for the side to show that it was as competent and capable of delivering when confronted with stressful situations in the longer version, as it had in the shorter version. It was necessary that the seniors led by example, as they had in the World Cup.

Tendulkar deserved to be the player of the tournament but how sweeter would it have been with a World Cup final victory to his credit. Mother cricket was not to give him this accolade. Or maybe she still will.

—Daryll Cullinan, *India Today, World Cup 2003 Collector's Edition*

OUT OF CHARACTER

I think if there hadn't been a Sunny [Sunil Gavaskar] there would have been no Sachin. I would like to think that Sachin did see a lot of Sunny. There is no better person to learn from. In terms of being so technically sound and having a wide array of shots, I think Sachin had taken all of what Sunny had a step further. You see great players don't come in isolation. You have to have some kind of history.

—Viv Richards, *Outlook*, 4 January 1999

The World Cup was followed by a tri-series in Bangladesh, also involving South Africa, which was skipped by quite a few players, including Sachin and Dravid. The Indian team's longest layoff since 2000 lasted a good five months. Some of the players utilized the gap to hone their skills in England, while the others recharged their batteries. There was a lot of action coming up in the months to follow. A two-Test series against New Zealand was to be followed by a tri-series with Australia as the third team. Following that, the Indian team was to plunge into Test cricket's equivalent of the World Cup—a tour of Australia. The season was scheduled to end with a full tour of Pakistan—India's first since 1989–90—subject to clearance from the government, of course.

Prior to the start of the cricket season, Sachin found himself involved in a needless controversy. One of the car brands that he was endorsing in the early 2000s had presented him a Ferrari 360 Modena after he equalled Sir Don Bradman's tally of 29 Test centuries against the West Indies in April 2002. As the car had been gifted to him, as opposed to being won as a prize, it was not exempted from customs duty. Sachin applied to the government for a waiver of the duty and received a positive response. However, the exemption was questioned by the Delhi High Court. There was a fair bit of negative press with people demanding to know why Sachin was being given special treatment. The company that had gifted the car then stepped in to pay the duty, which is something it ought to have done before it made the presentation.

Sachin had always been fond of automobiles. With his superstardom coming in the way during normal hours of the day, he would take to the wheel late in the night. His first car was a Maruti. In later years, he acquired vehicles like a BMW and a custom-built Mercedes.

The year 2003 also saw Sachin teaming up with hotelier and friend Sanjay Narang to open Tendulkars, a restaurant near the Taj in Colaba in south Mumbai that had all his favourite dishes on the menu. Sachin was very much an active partner in the venture. He had a say in virtually everything—the décor, the menu, the colour of the aprons that the stewards would wear and even the cutlery. One of the attractions of the venue was Tendulkars' merchandise that bore his autograph. The cricketer was on his way to becoming an entrepreneur.

Exactly a decade after his initial appointment as captain of Mumbai, Sachin decided to take another shot at the job in the 2003–04 Irani Cup clash against the Rest of India, who were to be led by Sourav Ganguly. In what was the first star-studded Irani Cup game in years, both teams were at full strength. The Rest of India side was for all practical purposes the Indian team minus Sachin, with Ganguly in charge. Mumbai, winners of the Ranji Trophy in 2002–03, included the likes of Agarkar, Sairaj Bahutule, Nilesh Kulkarni and Vinod Kambli, who was on another comeback trail.

Kambli had not played for India since the tri-series in Sharjah in October 2000. After two decent domestic seasons in 2000–01 and 2001–02, he had flown to South Africa to represent the province of Boland in the 2002–03 season. There, the batsman who was supposed to be susceptible to short-pitched deliveries gave a good account of himself on lively tracks.

After returning to India, a confident Kambli declared that he wished to score as many runs as possible and 'place them in a plate' in front of the selectors.

Unfortunately, that wasn't to be, as he was dismissed for 2 and 0 in the Irani Cup game at Chennai. The left-hander ended up slipping off the radar for good. What he and his childhood friend could have achieved for the nation in tandem, is anybody's guess.

Put in to bat, Mumbai scored 297 with Sachin batting splendidly to score 94. The Mumbai bowlers then raised visions of a shock win by dismissing the Rest of India for 202. Mumbai had all the time in the world to bat their opponents out of the game, but they messed up and were bowled out for 244. Sachin once again scored the highest with a 50. The Rest of India were then put on the road to victory by the old firm of Dravid and Laxman. They added 168 for the fourth wicket and although both fell in quick succession, Ganguly finished off the game with the lower order. The Rest of India won by three wickets.

Sachin may not have been a successful captain of India as per the record books, but his track record for Mumbai was nothing short of outstanding. The Irani Cup defeat was his first outright loss as captain of Mumbai. He did not lead Mumbai in first-class cricket again—at least not officially.

Both the Tests of the 2003–04 series against New Zealand were drawn, but the Kiwis outbatted their opponents. Rahul Dravid scored a double century in the first Test at Ahmedabad and made his debut as captain in the second, with Ganguly absent due to an abscess in his left thigh. When India were reduced to 18–3 in the second innings with Sehwag, Dravid and Sachin back in the pavilion, there were some worried faces in the home dressing room, but opener Akash Chopra, who had made his debut in the first Test at Ahmedabad, displayed his temperament in a stand of 110 with Laxman. Sachin's best performance of the series was a 55 in the first innings at Mohali.

The hosts continued to underperform in the tri-series that followed. The bowling was uninspiring and the batting sparkled in patches. The two brightest spots were the games against Australia and New Zealand at Gwalior and Hyderabad respectively. At Gwalior, Sehwag fell with only one run on the board, but Sachin then commenced a fruitful association with Laxman. The duo added 190 and both ended up scoring hundreds. India finished with 283–5 and won by 37 runs. In the last league game, a must-win affair against the Kiwis, Sachin reminded watchers of his 186 against the same team at the same venue in 1999–00, with a knock of 102. He put on 182 with Sehwag, who went on to score 130. A whirlwind 22-ball 50 by Dravid helped India reach 353–5, a total that they defended easily and qualified for the final. In the summit clash, played at Kolkata just three days later, the same batting line-up minus Ganguly fell 37 runs short of a gettable target of 236.

The tri-series did nothing to dispel the sense of impending doom that loomed on the eve of the tour of Australia. Even the most fervent supporters of the Indian team were among those praying that their side avoided a 0–4 whitewash. Ganguly spoke for many people when he said, 'At the end of this series, we will know how good we really are.'

The Indian captain showed how good he was in the first Test at Brisbane, where India had lost all the five Tests that it had played in the past. The Australians scored 323 on what looked a spiteful pitch, after being put in by Ganguly. Sehwag and Chopra opened with a stand of 61 before the Australians pulled things back with three quick strikes, including that of Sachin, who could not believe his eyes when umpire Steve Bucknor upheld a shout for caught behind. India were 62–3 and Ganguly made his way to the middle.

The southpaw had utilized the long off-season in 2003 to focus on his batting and had even flown to Australia to consult Greg Chappell, the former Australian captain. The gains of that trip were visible at the Gabba, Brisbane. The Indian captain handled everything that was thrown at him, from the ball to expletives, with aplomb, to score 144. V.V.S. Laxman scored 75 against his favourite opponent and India gained a first-innings lead of 86. The game was drawn and the Indians left Brisbane on a high, their only concerns being the injuries to Zaheer Khan and Harbhajan Singh, two of their key bowlers.

The second Test at Adelaide was a remarkable game of cricket. Australia won the toss and went on the attack, scoring as many as 400 runs on day one, but the Indians did not wilt. India were 85–4 in response to the hosts' final score of 556, and the match was in the balance, when Laxman joined his Kolkata comrade. It was déjà vu again as the pair put together another triple century stand. Laxman's 148 and Dravid's 233 took India to 523 on the fourth morning.

What followed was one of the greatest days in the history of Indian cricket. Matthew Hayden, first-innings double centurion Ricky Ponting and Damien Martyn fell to outstanding catches and the bowlers then took over. The feeling of déjà vu returned when Ganguly handed over the ball to Sachin. India's captain on the previous tour of Australia, who had scored a solitary run in the Test series at that stage, obliged with the key wickets of Martyn and Steve Waugh, both caught at slip by Dravid. The bowling honours went to Ajit Agarkar, who finished with figures of 6–41.

India had the whole of the fifth day and a bit to score 230. Sachin contributed 37 to a third-wicket stand of 70, during which, he displayed his disdain for Stuart MacGill, the leg-spinner, by essaying what could be termed as a 'reverse drive', wherein the ball was hit like a proper drive, excepting that the batsman was facing the wicketkeeper and not the bowler when he did so.

The moment of triumph came when Dravid, who had been on the field for practically the entire match, cut a MacGill long-hop for four. It was India's first Test win on Australian soil since February 1981. For most of the players, particularly Sachin and Ajit Agarkar, captain and 'Bombay Duck' on the previous tour, respectively, the win took a while to sink in. That night Rahul Dravid, who had followed his double hundred in the first innings with an unbeaten 72 in the second, slept in his whites. The Indian vice-captain, who had excelled at Kolkata, Kandy and, of course, Leeds, in the past, had mastered the art of bettering his own performances.

Indian cricket fans could not wait for the next Test and the prospect of seeing the two legends in the line-up guide the side to bigger things. Ganguly and Laxman were also in their prime, and then there was Virender Sehwag, who blasted an impudent hundred in the first two sessions of the Boxing Day Test in Melbourne. The openers weathered a fiery opening burst by Brett Lee and put on 141, and then Dravid came in to add a further 137 with the Delhi marauder. At 278–2, the stage was set for a Sachin special. However, he nicked Lee into Gilchrist's gloves for his second duck of the series. Sehwag himself fell a few runs later and India squandered the start to be all out for 366. The home team then totalled 558. Ricky Ponting scored his second consecutive double century of the series and Matthew Hayden got 136. As in the previous Test, they scored at a fair clip. About 45 minutes were left on the third day when the Indians began their second innings.

The Australians, who now held all the aces, dismissed the Indian openers with only 19 on the board. The Indian captain joined Dravid at the fall of the second wicket and saw his team through to the close. It so happened that before the innings commenced, Sachin indicated to Ganguly that he would rather not bat that evening.

Was Sachin's reluctance to go in at his customary spot at a time when the bowlers were on top a sign of cowardice? Far from it. Wasn't he the same player who had bowled the last over in the Hero Cup semi-final? Wasn't he the same player who had scored back-to-back hundreds, two days apart, in the heat and humidity of Sharjah? Wasn't he the same player who had defied crippling back pain to take India to the threshold of victory against Pakistan at Chennai?

Sachin had been a celebrity for 15 of the 30 years of his existence. Everything he did outside the walls of his house was scrutinized, dissected and commented upon by millions of people the world over. He had the world at his feet ever since he could remember, but he had chosen to walk with it, not tread on it. He was as human as anybody else, and his lean patch in the series was obviously on his mind when he spoke to Ganguly. Like any other professional, he had his share of insecurities and apprehensions and was perfectly entitled to think that there were times when discretion was a better option than valour. For the captain, who believed that great players needed looking after because they were special, going in at number four was no big deal. The matter ought to have ended there and then, but it didn't.

Despite some fine batting by the captain and vice-captain, India could not last beyond the fourth day. Sachin came in when Ganguly had to go off for repairs after being hit on the head by Brad Williams. He scored 44, his highest of the series, before being caught behind off Williams. Ganguly resumed after Laxman's dismissal and added 93 with Dravid, but both then fell within a few runs of each other and the tail did not wag. Australia needed only 95 to square the series.

The last Test of the series, played at Sydney in the first week of 2004, marked the end of Steve Waugh's career. The entire series had been labelled as the 'swansong' of the Australian captain, and he had been cheered on and off the field at all the venues. Things had not gone as per the plan for him and his team, with the defeat at Adelaide, but the win at Melbourne had re-energized the side and raised expectations of a triumphant farewell at the Sydney Cricket Ground, his home turf. Even as Waugh prepared for the last act of what had been an unforgettable career, the man whom everybody expected to overhaul his record for playing the maximum number of Tests, introspected and planned.

> On the eve of the Test, we went out for a cup of tea and we talked about how the tour had gone for the team. He made his decision to not play the cover drive and showed remarkable discipline in executing his plans, even though the Australians often attacked him outside the off-stump. Some said it was a different Tendulkar. I said it was the same Tendulkar who understood that it was important for him to get runs in a critical Test.
>
> —John Wright, *Sachin Forever*, MCA, 2013

It wasn't the first time Sachin had had this sort of a discussion with Wright. On the eve of his very first Test as coach, in fact, Sachin had told him that he would avoid taking the aerial route. Wright had watched admiringly as the hero had kept his word in an innings of 201. Since that Delhi Test that was played in November 2000, Wright had spent enough time with and watched enough of Sachin to know that he was a determined man.

> One need not be protective of Tendulkar. He may not have finished a few matches, but then please spare a thought for the man and the pressure that he endures every time he bats for the team. Remember those occasions when he would have made batting easy for his partners by taking on the demon bowlers all by himself. The occasions when he would have sprinted like a hare to take runs for his partner. The current famine of runs is a minor concern for this accomplished batsman with no technical flaws. He is one batsman who can read the bowler's mind faster than anyone and take batting to a different level. He has a role to play and he has performed it impeccably thus far.
>
> —Vijay Lokapally, *The Sportstar*, 3 January 2004

Waugh lost the toss in his last Test. Ganguly had no hesitation opting to bat, and his team's objective was to not repeat the Melbourne madness and shut their opponents out of the match. For that to happen, they needed a solid start, and their openers provided them with just that. Sehwag and Chopra fell soon after posting a century stand. The score was 128–2 when Sachin came in to a generous ovation from a capacity crowd, many of whom had witnessed the unbeaten 148 in the New Year Test of 1992 that had put him on the road to superstardom.

The Australian bowlers, led by Brett Lee and Jason Gillespie, tried to entice him by pitching the ball just outside the off-stump. The fielders were placed accordingly. However, Sachin waited. He waited for deliveries pitched on middle- and-leg, and worked them away for runs. He drove and flicked his way to 9,000 runs in Tests. He was only the second Indian to achieve the milestone. An on- drive for three off Steve Waugh gave him his first 50 of the series. He swept MacGill against the spin and played Simon Katich, the chinaman bowler, with the turn on the leg-side. When given room outside the off-stump, he cut. When served a gift in the form of a long-hop on middle and leg, he pulled mightily.

Unbeaten on 73 at stumps on the first day, he got off the blocks on day two with back-to-back stunners off Brett Lee. He first executed his trademark 'punch-masquerading-as-a-push' between the umpire and non-striker, and then cut the bowler past point.

The Australians kept tempting him to go for his trademark cover-drive, but Sachin would have none of it. It was as if one of the greatest cover-drivers of all time had forgotten how to play the stroke. Two hundred and ninety-three minutes after he had started his innings, he glanced Katich to square-leg and took off for his hundredth run. As the spectators rose, Sachin shifted his bat to his left arm and punched the air with his right arm, before reaching the non- striker's end and taking off his helmet to acknowledge the crowd and thank the Almighty. His resolve had paid off.

By that time, the score was a monstrous 365–3 and India had all but achieved their objective of eliminating the possibility of an Australian victory. With V.V.S. Laxman, Sachin added a record 353 for the fourth wicket, before the artiste from Hyderabad fell for a superlative 178.

For once, Laxman's elegance was matched by his partner. Watchers were enraptured by Sachin's deft placements of deliveries pitched on or outside the off-stump on the leg-side, a fair number of which crossed the boundary. He got a life soon after tea when MacGill put down an uppish drive off Nathan Bracken at mid-on. The resultant single took Sachin to 150. He then added insult to injury by timing Bracken down the ground for four, with MacGill forced to give chase. Ganguly, who had dropped himself down to number six to accommodate Laxman at 5, fell early, but Parthiv Patel went on the attack and further exasperated the already exhausted opposition.

Another clip off his legs off Lee took Sachin to 199. The bowler switched to around the wicket, to try and angle the ball across the right-hander. A single to mid-on gave Sachin the third double hundred of his career. A pull off Katich took him past Ravi Shastri's 206, previously the highest individual score by an Indian at Sydney. India batted on into the third day and touched 700 for the first time ever. At 705–7, Ganguly declared. Sachin returned undefeated on 241. He had batted for 613 minutes and faced 436 deliveries. He had stroked 33 boundaries, most of them straight down the ground and on the leg-side. Incredibly, he had scored only 54 of his 241 runs on the off-side!

It was like Bradman was back, only playing for the wrong side.... There is certainly a romanticism in his batting that amazes the purist in me. Today, batsmanship is vigorous, aggressive and sometimes ugly and violent: but not from this little genius.

—David Frith, as told to Vijay Tagore, *DNA*, 13 November 2009

Sachin's unbeaten 241 was in many ways like Sunil Gavaskar's stunning 121 against the West Indies at Delhi in October 1983. For starters, both innings were essayed against the most formidable bowling attack of the time. Secondly, both knocks had been out of character. Gavaskar, who by 1983 had acquired a reputation as a defensive batsman (rather unfairly), took only 94 balls to complete his hundred; Sachin on the other hand took nearly five hours to complete his first hundred and batted for more than 10 hours in all. The third similarity concerned a stroke. Gavaskar possessed every stroke in the book when he started off in the West Indies in 1971, but the over-reliance of his team on him had forced him to eschew the riskier ones, like the hook. However, at Delhi in October 1983, he surprised everybody by essaying it to perfection, not once but time and again. His co-Mumbaikar went the other way, putting the cover-drive, a stroke he could have played in his sleep, in cold storage, for the entire duration of his double century.

The lead-up to both innings was identical, with both batsmen having had their respective capabilities questioned by the Doubting Thomases. Gavaskar had fallen for zero and seven in the Kanpur Test that preceded the one at Delhi and been branded a 'spent force' by his detractors. Two decades later, Ganguly's coming in at number four on the third evening of the Melbourne Test had prompted some to question Sachin's courage and commitment.

Both Gavaskar in October 1983 and Tendulkar in January 2004 had something to prove.

The highlight of Australia's first innings at Sydney was Anil Kumble's 8–141. The performance silenced all those who felt that the leg-spinner should not have been on the plane to Australia in the first place. After being India's premier spinner in the 1990s, he had been superseded by Harbhajan Singh in the new millennium. Both played in most of India's home Tests of the early 2000s whenever available, but Ganguly preferred the off-spinner as the lone specialist slow bowler in Tests abroad.

Like all resilient professionals, Kumble bounced back at the first opportunity.

Australia were all out for 474, but Ganguly did not enforce the follow-on. Dravid and Sachin added 138 for the third wicket before the declaration was made in the closing stages of day four. Australia were set a target of 443. But for a couple of leg-before decisions that did not go in India's favour, a couple of catches that were put down and a fighting innings by Waugh on his last day as a Test cricketer, India might well have pulled off what had been imaginable at the start of the series. Australia were 357–6 at the close.

The first person to rush to shake Waugh's hand after his dismissal for 80 was the player expected to surpass the record for the maximum number of Test matches, which stood in the Australian captain's name. Sachin had a role to play in the dismissal as well, having caught a mistimed slog-sweep off Kumble in the deep. With the series tied 1–1, India retained the Border–Gavaskar Trophy.

Coming as it did on the heels of the epic series in 2000–01, the 2003–04 face-off established the rivalry between India and Australia as the foremost of the new millennium, ahead of even the Ashes, in which the Australians had for all practical purposes been enjoying a walkover of sorts since 1989.

In the tri-series that followed, India were good, but the world champions were better. Zimbabwe, the third team, lagged behind.

A month after the conclusion of the tri-series, Sachin completed a cricketing circle by returning to the place where it had all begun for him.

The Indian team was assured unprecedented security on its first full tour of Pakistan since 1989–90. The BCCI, backed by the Indian Government, ensured that the one-day series was scheduled before the Test series and visits to cities like Karachi and Peshawar that had unfortunately come to be known more for violence than anything else, were truncated.

The five-match ODI series commenced on 13 March 2004 at Karachi's National Stadium, where Sachin had become India's youngest Test cricketer, 14 seasons previously. On his first day of Test cricket, Sachin had seen K. Srikkanth, his captain, being assaulted by a spectator. On his second visit in 1997, by which time he was the captain of India, he had seen some of his fielders being pelted with stones from the crowd. He had also experienced the pin-drop silence that had ensued after Rajesh Chauhan's six off Saqlain Mushtaq in the final over. That Indian team had comprised the likes of Ganguly and Dravid, both of whom were captain and vice-captain respectively on the 2003–04 tour. Their experience may well have prompted them to anticipate some form of hostility. However, they were in for a surprise.

Most of the spectators had Indian and Pakistani flags painted on either cheek, and they did not hesitate to appreciate quality cricket, regardless of which team played it. Enjoying the game from the stands were Priyanka and Rahul Gandhi, members of India's first political family, and Arun Jaitley, a senior figure in the National Democratic Alliance (NDA) that was running the country.

Inzamam-ul-Haq, the captain of Pakistan, did not endear himself to his compatriots by putting India in after winning the toss. The visitors amassed 349-7, and were in the driver's seat when the second Pakistani wicket fell with only 34 on the board. At that stage, in came Inzamam. He proceeded to atone for his decision earlier in the day with a stupendous innings. His teammates batted around him, and with 72 needed from 48 deliveries with the captain going strong, the hosts looked poised to win. It was then that Murali Kartik struck with the scalp of Inzamam, who fell to a reflex catch that would have done a specialist wicketkeeper proud. Rahul Dravid, who could have refused to continue keeping wicket after the 2003 World Cup, still had the gauntlets on. For him and Ganguly, ensuring a balanced team overrode every other consideration.

As in the tradition of most India–Pakistan contests, the match went down to the wire and India could feel reasonably safe only when Mohammed Kaif pulled off a remarkable diving catch to dismiss Shoaib Malik off the penultimate ball of the penultimate over. With six needed from the final ball, Nehra bowled a low full toss to Moin Khan. The batsman heaved hard, but the ball did not clear Zaheer Khan at mid-off.

The hosts drew level in the second game, a day-nighter at Rawalpindi. Inzamam chose to bat this time around, and his side scored 329-6. Sehwag got India off to a flier, but the innings stuttered after Shoaib sent his off-stump for a walk. The batting line-up struggled to get going, with one exception. Sachin, who had scored 28 at Karachi, warmed up with consecutive boundaries off Shoaib in the fifth over. He followed a searing cut off the front foot with a delectable flick off his feet. Laxman fell early, Ganguly was anything but fluent, and although Dravid tried his hardest to replicate his 99 in the first game, he wasn't quite successful. Sachin batted like a dream. He cut sensationally, drove spectacularly and essayed some scintillating drives on the up off the pacemen.

A single to third-man off Shoaib made him the first Indian to score an ODI hundred on Pakistani soil. He celebrated the feat by thumping Shahid Afridi over mid-wicket for six.

The heat and humidity were rising to intolerable levels, but Sachin was not flustered. The job was far from over, and he ensured that the required rate did not rise beyond eight. He was on 141 when he lashed hard at Shoaib Malik. Unfortunately for him and his team, the ball gathered more height than distance, and Abdul Razzaq held a fine running catch on the mid-wicket boundary. The Indians did not give up though, with off-spinner Ramesh Powar and paceman Laxmipathy Balaji going down all guns blazing. Pakistan won by 12 runs.

Pakistan took a 2–1 lead in the series with a four-wicket win in a day game at Peshawar. Sachin failed to trouble the scorers, nicking Shabbir Ahmed to the keeper. The hosts were fancied to seal the series in the fourth game, which was the first of two day–night double-headers at Lahore. They had every reason to be satisfied with their score of 293–9, but the Indians of 2004 displayed the sort of resilience that their counterparts of the 1990s were not known for. Dravid and Kaif came together at 162–5 and guided their team to victory with a good five overs to spare.

Asked to bat first in the decider, India achieved a score identical to Pakistan's in the earlier encounter, for the loss of seven wickets. The star of the innings was V.V.S. Laxman, who during a knock of 107 that encompassed 104 balls, essayed the kind of strokes that kept reminding watchers of the adjective 'gorgeous'. The Indian bowlers then reduced Pakistan to 58–4, but they knew that they could not relax until the Pakistani captain was in there. The score had moved to 87–4 when Inzamam stepped down the wicket and biffed Murali Kartik over the infield. Standing on the long-on boundary was Sachin, who had done little of note in the series since his hundred at Rawalpindi. The ball would have soared over his head, had he not timed his jump to perfection, at the same time ensuring that his feet did not touch the rope. He could not have chosen a better player or juncture to complete a century of catches in the shorter version.

Inzamam's exit proved to be the turning point of the game. History was created when Balaji breached Moin's defences off the fifth ball of the 48th over. Pakistan were all out for 253 and India had registered its first-ever ODI series win across the Radcliffe Line.

> Between my first stint as manager of the Indian team in 1997 and second in 2004, a lot had changed. John Wright's appointment had been a turning point, of course. The team was more united and its approach was more

positive. The Board had taken some important decisions after 1997, all of which had been put into operation by the time we went to Pakistan. The team had a qualified physiotherapist, trainer and even a video analyst. The team meetings of 2004 were also different from those in 1997. The players would watch videos and strategize during the meetings.

—Prof. R.S. Shetty, personal interview

The victory in the ODI series naturally made Indian fans optimistic about the Test series to follow. While Pakistan had beaten India in India four times and even won a Test series in 1986–87, India had not come even remotely close to winning a Test in Pakistan. Could the team of 2003–04 do what their predecessors couldn't?

As it turned out, India completed a win by an innings and 52 runs within minutes of the start of the final day's play of the first Test at Multan, but the question mentioned above had been answered at stumps on day three itself. The answer was reflected in the way Sachin celebrated after bowling Moin Khan around his legs off the last ball of the day. Just 24 hours previously, he had been one of the protagonists in an episode that could well have split the side. The way the potential crisis was handled and defused underscored the fact that the Indian team of 2003–04 was unlike many of its predecessors.

Batting first, India were dictating terms at 675-4 when Yuvraj Singh, who was playing because Ganguly had suffered a back injury during the final ODI, was caught-and-bowled by part-time bowler Imran Farhat. At the non-striker's end was Sachin, who had batted superbly to score 194. He was thus yet to be dismissed in a Test in the calendar year of 2004, following his unbeaten 241 and 60 at Sydney. He had at the back of his mind, a message that Ramesh Powar, the substitute had brought out a little earlier: Dravid, who was leading in Ganguly's absence, wanted to give the Pakistanis 15 overs of batting that evening. Sachin had done his math and calculated that he still had one full over in which to get six more runs to complete his second double hundred in consecutive Tests. Earlier in the innings, Virender Sehwag had scored the first triple century by an Indian in Tests.

Much to Sachin's surprise, Dravid declared moments after Yuvraj started his walk back to the pavilion. That the declaration would be raised ahead of Sehwag's 309 at the post-match media conference was a foregone conclusion. When asked if he was disappointed, Sachin replied in the affirmative.

In India, the reactions ranged from the pragmatic to the melodramatic. Some hailed Dravid's move as a 'declaration of independence' and a watershed in the history of Indian cricket; the team had finally triumphed over the individual, they claimed. Others wondered what the hurry was all about; giving Sachin an over or two to score six runs would not have made a difference.

India's captain for the game did not hesitate to approach the aggrieved player the following morning. During their discussion, both Sachin and Dravid reiterated their respective viewpoints. In any relationship, be it personal or professional, there were bound to be disagreements, which needed to be forgotten for the greater good; this was one such. The discussion ended with Sachin clarifying that his commitment to his side would in no way be affected by what had happened. His jubilation when he deceived Moin Khan off the final delivery of the third day with a leg-break (that would have made Shane Warne proud) said it all.

Pakistan were dismissed for 407 and Dravid enforced the follow-on. The possibility of the hosts saving the game vanished when Yuvraj ran Inzamam out for a duck in the second innings. It was one of India's greatest Test wins, and not merely because it was the first in Pakistan; to take 20 opposition wickets on a strip that had nothing in it for the bowlers was no mean feat. In the second innings, Dravid had only three specialist bowlers at his disposal, with Zaheer Khan unable to bowl due to injury. Leading the attack was Anil Kumble, who took 6–72 in the second innings.

> Sachin was furious when the declaration was made. However, the team management handled the situation very well and got things back on track. After the game, we travelled from Multan to Lahore, where we arranged a dinner for the team to get the players to have a good time and forget what had happened.
>
> —Prof. R.S. Shetty, personal interview

Pakistan squared the series at Lahore. Ganguly's return for the decider at Rawalpindi forced the team management to leave out Akash Chopra, the only member of the batting line-up who hadn't fired at least once in the series, with Yuvraj Singh, Ganguly's replacement in the first two Tests, scoring his maiden Test century at Lahore.

It was always going to be uphill for the hosts after they were dismissed for 224 in the first innings, with India's new pace triumvirate of Irfan Pathan, Balaji and Nehra bowling brilliantly. Sehwag fell first ball, but then, Rahul Dravid came in and batted for 740 minutes to score 270. India were all out for 600 and the bowlers came in hard at the hosts in the second innings, led once again by the indefagitable Kumble.

The leggie took four wickets, Balaji bagged three and Pathan and Nehra chipped in with one each. The romantics could not help but smile when Sachin, brought on for the first time in the game, dismissed Danish Kaneria, the number 11, with the last ball of his first over. Kaneria's ungainly swipe was pouched by Sourav Ganguly. It seemed appropriate that India's greatest series win on foreign soil was completed through a collaboration between its leader and hero. The victory, by an innings and 131 runs, was also India's biggest on foreign soil.

On 15 April 2004, the day the Test series ended, Sachin had every reason to look back on his 15 years of international cricket with satisfaction. It had taken a wee bit longer than imagined, but the outfit he had first represented with distinction in Pakistan in 1989–90 had evolved as a 'team', as capable of producing excellent cricket on foreign soil as in familiar surroundings. The accusations hurled at him at the start of the new millennium—that *he* had made no difference to India's fortunes abroad—were no longer valid. Not that they had been any valid earlier. Cricket to him had been a 'team' game ever since he could remember.

> In the first half of my career, we didn't have as much success away from India, but then we started, from 2000 onwards I felt we started touring well.... Wherever we went, we were able to win Test matches and that is something that helps the teams progress because if you are doing well in Test matches, the standard of playing naturally gets better and we were able to do that.... So that changed the approach and because of that, the youngsters getting in the side, in the early stages of their career, got the taste of victory away from India and how big and how important it is, so we all understood the importance of that and we started believing that away from India you can go and have the opposition in trouble.
>
> —Sachin Tendulkar, *Bradman Museum and International Cricket Hall of Fame Interview*, 2010

SPEED BREAKERS

The injury to my elbow has created an instability of sorts over the last 3–4 months. A kind of concern and worry has been gnawing. Doctors keep on telling me that a broken elbow would have been far easier to treat and mend. But torn tendons is a far more complex injury. When such an injury heals, it is very difficult and unpredictable. Being a doctor, Anjali has always helped me understand the nuances, and has put me at ease. Her advice has been simple—follow the doctors' orders to the 'T'. She has encouraged and helped to stop speculating and prevented my mind from playing games…my daughter Sara went to the Mount Mary Church and placed a wax model of a hand in front of God and prayed for my injury to heal! My little boy, Arjun often would ask me, 'Baba, is your hand hurt? Can I apply some magic potion to cure it?'…. Anjali always said to me—'With so many people's good wishes and prayers behind you, your injury is bound to heal quickly.'

—Sachin Tendulkar, *Cricket Today*, May 2005

The year 2004–05 ought to have been the season when Indian cricket capitalized on the gains made in the previous 12 months. The team was to play at home, and face the same sides whom they had outplayed and out-thought on their own turf in the previous season. But not for the first or last time in the history of Indian cricket, the cricketers flattered to deceive. They came crashing down to earth with a lacklustre performance in the Asia Cup in Sri Lanka. They beat the UAE and Bangladesh, but lost a critical game to Pakistan. Needing 301 to win, India lost Sehwag early, but Sachin and Ganguly steadied the boat with a stand of 62 before the captain was bowled by Mohammed Sami. Rahul Dravid, still standing behind the wicket, fell to a single-digit score, as did Kaif. Yuvraj gave Shoaib Malik a return catch at 28. At 151–5, Sachin decided to change tactics and gave up the chase, targeting the mark of 241 that India needed to achieve to deny Pakistan a bonus point, instead. He added 63 with Irfan Pathan before falling for 78. The lower order managed to deny Pakistan the bonus point, and India qualified for the final for a four-run win over Sri Lanka in their last league encounter. The hosts avenged the loss in the summit clash, winning by 25 runs.

Although he scored two 50s, Sachin's batting in the tournament had been anything but fluent. Interestingly, he had seemed more assured while bowling. His 12 wickets were the second-highest in the competition.

His fans viewed it as an auspicious sign. It certainly suited him and India to get an off-key phase out of the way before taking on the Australians for the next edition of the Border–Gavaskar Trophy.

Sachin was batting in the nets on the eve of a tri-series against Pakistan and Australia in Amsterdam when he sensed something amiss with his left elbow. The pain only worsened and the problem was diagnosed as tennis elbow. It forced him to pull out of not only the tri-series, but also a three-match ODI series against England that was to precede the 2004 edition of the ICC Champions Trophy. Most critically from India's point of view, Sachin also missed the first two Tests of the Border–Gavaskar Trophy. He did whatever the doctors advised him to do, even as an anxious nation was administered another 'anatomy lesson' by the print and electronic media.

By the time the pain ebbed and Sachin was back for the third of four Tests against Australia, the team was in tatters. In his absence, the side had floundered in the tri-series and ODIs against England, failed to qualify for the semi-finals of the Champions Trophy, and was trailing 0–1 in the Test series against Australia. Australia's 'un-Australian' tactic of targeting the strengths of the Indian batsmen instead of their weaknesses had worked wonders. No longer were the men from 'down under' on the attack from ball one. Instead, they spread the field and blocked the boundaries that the Indians loved to stroke. The visitors won the first Test at Bengaluru by a whopping 217 runs. Virender Sehwag with the bat and Anil Kumble with the ball led an Indian resurgence in the second Test at Chennai, a game that showcased the twists and turns of Test match cricket in all their splendour. At stumps on day four, the game was interestingly poised with India needing 210 more to win and Australia requiring 10 wickets. Unfortunately for the teams but fortunately for a parched part of India, the last day's play was washed out.

Even as Sachin came in, Ganguly and Harbhajan Singh both withdrew from the third Test at Nagpur due to injuries. The visitors made the most of a wicket that looked more Australian than Indian, to hand the hosts a resounding defeat by 342 runs. Among those who had a forgettable game was Sachin, who scored two and eight. The Final Frontier had finally fallen, for the first time since 1969–70.

The last Test at Mumbai was a remarkable game of cricket, although the Australians thought otherwise. Ganguly was still unavailable and Dravid, leading for the second time in the series, won the toss and elected to bat on a wicket straight out of a spinner's dream. The Indians had left no one in any doubt as to how they expected the strip to behave by picking just one specialist fast bowler in Zaheer Khan. India were knocked over for a paltry 104, and they retaliated by dismissing Australia for 203. Despite the challenges being posed by the wicket, nobody could have predicted that the third day would be the last of the series. The fall of debutant Gautam Gambhir, who had replaced his Delhi teammate Akash Chopra in the side, brought V.V.S. Laxman to the crease. This prompted watchers to wonder why Dravid had sacrificed his one-drop slot in a 'dead' Test, that too after top-scoring with 31 in the first innings. Sehwag fell nine runs later.

India's batting heroes of the Sydney Test earlier in the year then commenced a partnership that was nothing short of delightful. They dug in initially, scoring only 15 runs over 10 overs. Once they had come to terms with the vagaries of the wicket, they attacked. The next four overs yielded 40. Sachin was alarmed by a recurrence of the pain in his elbow, which he countered by taking two painkilling tablets instead of the recommended one. The spectators rose to their feet when he cover-drove Nathan Hauritz, the off-spinner, for four and then struck him for six. He completed his 50 off 62 balls and looked good for many more, but Hauritz had the last laugh, having him caught by Michael Clarke with his individual score at 55. After Laxman became the off-spinner's second victim for an exquisite 69, Clarke took over the proceedings with his brand of left-arm spin. His incredible 6–9 left his team with 107 to win. They had all the time (and days) to do it. But they didn't.

Murali Kartik took three wickets to add to his four in the first innings, and Harbhajan, who opened the bowling with Zaheer Khan in both innings, took five, as the visitors were dismissed for 93. Sachin starred in the dismissal of Gilchrist, who could have turned the match around with his belligerence. He caught the Australian keeper on the mid-wicket boundary off Murali Kartik. More than being outbowled, the Australians had been 'outbatted' by Sachin and Laxman.

The win at Mumbai did a lot to resurrect the self-confidence of the Indian players. They proceeded to beat South Africa 1–0 in a two-match series. Virender Sehwag was in prime form with the bat and Kumble and Harbhajan were devastating with the ball. Sachin did not have a particularly productive time, scoring only 55 runs from three innings.

The victory over South Africa did not inspire an improvement in the shorter version. The Indian team's failure to defend a score of 292–9 against Pakistan in front of a packed house at the Eden Gardens in November 2004 underscored its stagnation since its ODI series win across the border in the previous season. Pakistan extended their winning streak over India that had commenced in the Asia Cup earlier that year, losing only four wickets before overhauling the target in a one-off ODI that had been organized to commemorate the Platinum Jubilee of the BCCI.

Sachin made amends for his inconsistency against South Africa, in the first of two Tests against Bangladesh. He was not at his best when he got underway, getting as many as three lives before he completed his half-century. However, he brought all his experience into play and watched the bowlers until they lost their spark and energy, and were then forced to watch him. His century was his 34th in Tests, which brought him on par with the individual who had been the batting consultant of the Indian team during the series against Australia and South Africa.

Sunil Gavaskar, who had been specially requested by Ganguly to come on board, did what was expected of him in his usual meticulous and methodical manner, but he would have missed the batsman whom he had seen evolve from a prodigy to a legend, at the start of his stint. What the Little Master and the player he had christened the 'Little Champion' would have achieved, in terms of discussing different approaches to batsmanship and devising counter-strategies to those employed by the opposition bowlers, if only the latter had been available for the entire series against Australia, is a matter of conjecture.

Coincidentally, both had scored their 34th Test centuries in their 119th Test. Gavaskar ran down from the commentary box to shake Sachin's hand as he came in at an interval after completing his hundred. The senior later gifted the junior 34 bottles of champagne.

Sachin went all the way to 248, his highest individual score in first-class cricket. India won the Test, played at Dhaka, by an innings and 140 runs, and took the second game at Chittagong by an innings and 83 runs. At Chittagong, Rahul Dravid became the first batsman in Test history to score a century *in* every Test-playing nation. Unlike him, Sachin had not reached triple figures in a Test in Zimbabwe, and he never would.

Not just the Chittagong Test, but even the ODI series that followed was significant for Dravid. The three-match tussle, which India won 2–1, marked the end of an experiment that had served India well for two years. It was evident that the vice-captain would not keep wicket in ODIs anymore, unless there was an emergency. The epitome of selflessness was free to focus on his batting.

The selectors had been scouting for specialist keepers for quite a while. Unfortunately, Parthiv Patel had not lived up to the promise he had displayed in his first few games for India in 2002. The selectors and team management had given him a long rope till they lost patience and dropped him after the Nagpur Test against Australia. He was replaced by Tamil Nadu's Dinesh Kartik for the final Test at Mumbai. Up against three quality spinners on a turner, Kartik emerged from his baptism with flying colours and played in the subsequent Tests against South Africa and Bangladesh. He had made his ODI debut a few months previously, in a three-match ODI series against England that had preceded the Champions Trophy. For the limited-overs games in Bangladesh, the selectors drafted in another wicketkeeper–batsman who had started off as a goalkeeper in his hometown Ranchi, before he was persuaded to play cricket. He had taken to the game like a fish to water and displayed his proficiency on both sides of the wickets at the domestic level and later, for India 'A'. His name was Mahendra Singh Dhoni.

Dhoni's first international series was an eventful one. India won the first game by 11 runs and then lost the second by 15 runs. The batsmen delivered in the decider and took their side to 348–5. Sachin, who had missed the second game, scored 47. Bangladesh fell short by 91 runs.

The elephant in the room, as far as Sachin was concerned, was the prospect of going under the knife for his tennis elbow. While he was aware that it would take him closer to a near-permanent solution to the affliction, it would also mean a forced sabbatical from the game for at least a couple of months. In early 2005, he continued to follow his doctors' diktats and took it one cricket day at a time.

His commitments for India ensured that Sachin missed out on a lot of domestic cricket in the early years of the new millennium. He could not figure in the Mumbai sides that won the Ranji Trophy in both the 2002–03 and 2003–04 seasons, the Irani Cup game at the start of the 2003–04 season being his only notable domestic appearance of the phase. However, his non-availability for Mumbai did not prevent him from following the exploits of his team in the Ranji Trophy.

He and I would keep track of Mumbai's performances when we were touring Pakistan in early 2004 [Mumbai went on to win the Ranji Trophy that season]. In fact, Yuvraj Singh once interrupted a discussion of ours during one of the Test matches and asked us whether we could tell him what the score was in the ongoing Test at that stage! 2005 was a difficult year for Mumbai, with some top players shifting to other teams. I was surprised to

Going through the paces in a 'customized' session at the MIG Club, Bandra, Mumbai.

Sachin with the gold coin that was brought out to mark his 200th (and last) Test.

A and B: Practice makes perfect: Spreading a plastic sheet on a pitch and wetting it, and the bowlers digging it in, at the MCA Recreation Centre, BKC, Mumbai.

Self-effacing, inspirational and exceptional: A hero for generations

With his Madame Tussauds likeness

Before the start of his last Test: An expression of appreciation from the Little Master.

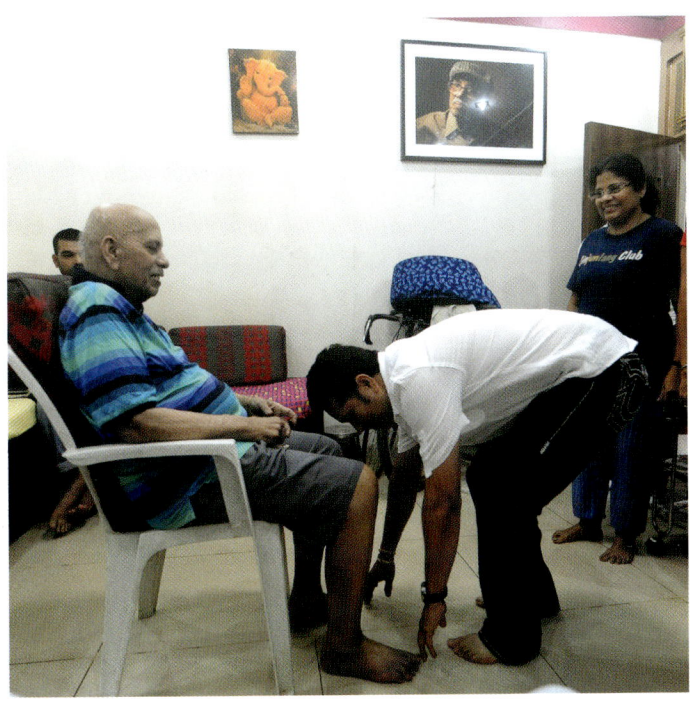
Guru Forever: The pupil seeks the blessings of Ramakant Achrekar.

Mentor: Sachin with Suryakumar Yadav (extreme left) and Shreyas Iyer, contemporary Mumbai cricketers.

2015: A return to the nets at the MCA's Sharad Pawar Indoor Cricket Academy, BKC, Mumbai (not very far from Sahitya Sahawas, where it all began in the early 1980s) to prepare for the All Stars Series.

The last dismissal: A standing and stirring ovation on his final return to the pavilion as a Test batsman.

Mentor: Sachin with young Arjun Tendulkar in the nets.

16 November 2013: The Tendulkars at the end of it all.

Jewel of India

see Sachin being quoted in an article that was critical of Mumbai cricket. I met him in Kolkata, during the Test against Pakistan, and told him that if he felt so strongly, then it would be great if he got involved in Mumbai cricket, in terms of talking to the age-group teams. He was happy to get involved. As far as I know, he never charged appearance money for the shoots which were organized by the sponsors of the Mumbai team. He had made it clear that he would honour all the commitments made to the sponsors. His commitment to Mumbai cricket could never be doubted.

—Prof. R.S. Shetty, personal interview

The two-month gap between the end of the Bangladesh series and the arrival of the Pakistani team in India gave Sachin and his colleagues the opportunity to assist their respective domestic sides. The Duleep Trophy encounter between South Zone and West Zone at the new cricket stadium in Hyderabad turned out to be the best game of the tournament. In charge were Dravid and Sachin respectively, and playing under them were the likes of Laxman and Kumble (South), and Zaheer Khan and Irfan Pathan (West). The bowlers outdid the batsmen, which wasn't something that happened regularly on the domestic circuit in India. Needing 222 to win, West Zone lost their first wicket at 76, when Wasim Jaffer was caught by Laxman off Kumble. The leg-spinner had taken four wickets in the first innings and a lot was expected from him in the second innings on a bowler-friendly strip. It was then that Sachin sprung a surprise by sending in Irfan at number three. Apart from showcasing his capabilities as a new-ball bowler in his brief international career till that stage, the left-hander from Vadodara had also done well as a batsman. He possessed a relatively orthodox technique, an impressive repertoire of strokes and an uncluttered mind. Irfan proceeded to take West Zone to a nine-wicket win, scoring 61 and adding an unbeaten 147 with Satyajit Parab, his Vadodara teammate.

On the eve of a clash against the old enemy at the end of what had been a below-par season, Team India needed all the positivity it could possibly muster. From being in a position wherein the selectors had to literally concoct an all-rounder by getting Dravid to keep wicket, the team now had in its ranks, one bowling all-rounder and two wicketkeeping ones. Dhoni had already made waves with his aggression in front of the wickets and Kartik was no mug with the bat either. It was certainly a happy note on which to begin a series against Pakistan.

The dosages of positivity did not quite work. The traditional weaknesses of the Indian team—an inability to deliver the knockout punch and playing under self-imposed pressure—that had been largely dormant from March 2001 to April 2004, re-asserted themselves with a vengeance. The Indian captain's poor form also did not help.

Sehwag's 173 and Sachin's 94 enabled India to take a first-innings lead of 204 in the first Test at Mohali. The ground went deathly silent when Sachin was caught by Asim Kamal off Naved-ul-Hasan, just six runs short of what would have been a record-breaking 35th Test century.

The hosts then had the opposition struggling at 10–3, before Inzamam-ul-Haq and Yousuf Youhana engineered a revival and inspired the lower order to drop anchor.

India did manage to finish the job in the second Test at Kolkata. In the first innings, Dravid scored 110 and Sachin 52, during which, he became the fifth batsman, second Indian and the fastest (in terms of innings) to complete 10,000 runs in Tests. He had taken 195 innings—the same as Brian Lara—to do so. India rode on these two knocks, along with Sehwag's 81, to reach 407. Day three was eventful. India gained a slim first-innings lead of 14 and lost two quick wickets in the second innings, including that of Sehwag. The innings was brought back on track by Dravid and Sachin. The crowd roared when Sachin, who was in ominous form from the Pakistani point of view, completed his second 50 of the game with the end of the third day's play not very far away. Then came a totally unexpected twist. He missed a delivery from Abdul Razzaq that swung away late. Akmal pouched the ball and the Pakistanis went up in appeal. To the dismay of the batsman and the nation, Steve Bucknor raised his index finger. The TV replays indicated that the ball had come nowhere close to the bat, but nothing could be done. Sachin had been dismissed for 52 for the second time in the game.

Not surprisingly, the media went into overdrive, going back in time to cite Bucknor's previous howlers against India in general and Sachin in particular. Of course, the rants were one-dimensional. No one brought up the famous final over in the Hero Cup semi-final in 1993, during which another umpire might well have stretched his arms after the wicketkeeper collected Sachin's fourth ball well outside the off-stump. However, the official who was standing at the bowler's end—a certain Steve Bucknor—had deemed it a legal delivery. The result: South Africa did not gain a run and an extra delivery, and India won by two runs.

> There have been a couple of times when I have given debatable decisions to Sachin, but it is important to remember that umpires are human and therefore can err. Whenever that has happened, I have been man enough to admit to my mistakes…. One of the things I would look forward to when I

officiated in India was the way the crowds reacted to Sachin.... Seeing this kind of reverence, it was understandable when fans would see any close decisions and conjure up suspicious theories where there were none.... It also helps that Sachin has always been superb in his on-field conduct. He never ever contested a decision and always took it and walked off. On the field, he never appealed unnecessarily, because he belongs to the old school that believes that the umpire's decision is final. These are important aspects of Sachin's persona that the new generation will do well to emulate.

—Steve Bucknor, CAB, 2013

The controversy was forgotten when India triumphed by 195 runs on the final day. After Dravid completed his second hundred of the game, Kumble took 7–63 to bowl Pakistan out for 226.

The visitors came back strongly in the third Test at Bengaluru. Younis Khan's 267 and Inzamam's 184 in his hundredth Test enabled them to reach 570. Sehwag scored a breathtaking 201 in response, but India conceded a first-innings deficit of 121. Still the pressure continued to be on Pakistan when Inzamam declared at 261–2 in the second innings to give his bowlers as much time as possible to take 10 wickets and square the series. But then, they were up against a redoubtable batting line-up. India had an entire day and a bit at their disposal to score 383 to win.

Sehwag (52) and Kumble (37*) apart, the Indian batsmen allowed themselves to get bogged down and the Pakistani bowlers kept it simple by sticking to the basics. Ganguly was booed as he returned to the pavilion after being bowled by Afridi. The match for all practical purposes ended after tea, when Kartik and Sachin, who had added 29, fell at the same score. Kartik was bowled by Sami. All of India heaved a sigh of relief when Sachin was put down by Asim Kamal at short-leg off the same bowler. However, Afridi induced Sachin to make another mistake and this time, Kamal made no mistake. Bowled out for 214, the Indians had only themselves to blame.

The six-match ODI series was no different from the Test series, in that India started well but lost steam. The hosts won the first game by 87 runs and the second by 58 runs, the highlight of which was an innings of 148 by the young man from Ranchi. Mahendra Singh Dhoni declared that he was here to stay with a knock that encompassed 123 deliveries and comprised 15 fours and four sixes.

Pakistan opened their account with a 106-run win in the third game. The next encounter, played at Ahmedabad, was the quintessential India–Pakistan clash; it had all the elements, from excellent batting and tight bowling and fielding in patches, to a last-ball finish. India's openers got their side off to a great start. Sehwag took the lead from the outset while Sachin took some time to play himself in. Once he had got through that initial phase, he was unstoppable. He punished the bowling on both sides of the wicket and inadvertently took down a TV cameraman who was hit by one of his two sixes. The only issue with his innings of 123 that helped India finish with 315–6 was that he had not been at his best against Abdul Razzaq, another 'non-frontline' bowler to have troubled him over the years. He and India might well have scored a lot more had the spell from the 15th over to the 25th yielded more than 41 runs. That 10-over spell came back to haunt the hosts when each of Pakistan's top five bats crossed 40.

With one over left, Pakistan needed only three, and Ganguly gambled. Sachin, who was only too happy to take on the challenge, conceded three runs off his first five balls. With one needed off the last ball and the field having been brought in to save the single, Inzamam-ul-Haq managed to pierce the tiniest of gaps and seal a win for his team. For the Indians, there was insult to injury when Ganguly was handed a six-match ban for his team's persistent failure to bowl its overs within the stipulated time. The visitors dominated the last two games and took the series 4–2, thus denying John Wright a happy farewell as India's coach after a stint that had lasted for four years. Followers of Indian cricket would always remain grateful to him for all that he had accomplished and indeed, changed.

On 25 May 2005, a little over a month after the end of the ODI series, Sachin went under the knife to sort his tennis elbow out for good. With the doctors advising at least four months' rest, his most arduous Test was about to begin. Since the age of 11, he had done virtually nothing other than play cricket. Not one who enjoyed sitting on the sidelines, he was restless.

In subsequent years, he refuted the charge that the tennis elbow was the consequence of his penchant for heavy bats.

> That was the wrong theory...[in fact], higher the weight, lesser is the impact on the hand.... I did not consider changing the weight...with a lighter bat, you will feel greater impact on the elbow.... I don't think it [tennis elbow] was because of a heavy bat...many others have had that injury, like Jacques Kallis and Nasser Hussain.... I spoke to Hussain before getting operated.... There is going to be a bit of wear and tear when you give it all.
>
> —Sachin Tendulkar, *Harsha Unplugged*, Star Cricket, 2007

Since the early 2000s, he had reduced the average weight of his bat to around

2.11 pounds, from the 3.2-pound willows that he had used at the turn of the millennium. The reduction in the weight apart, his stand on bats was what it had always been. If he picked up a bat and it felt right, then he would go ahead.

During his convalescence, he attempted to practise with a plastic bat used by toddlers. He hung a ball in a sock outside his residence and attempted to shadow-practise, but the pain was still there.

> I got operated on…and recovery took almost four to four-and-a-half months and in those months, a lot went through my mind. I thought I might not be able to hold a cricket bat again because I tried lifting a bat after three, three-and-a-half months and I hit a few balls and I had these ten-year-old boys stopping the ball at a 15 yard circle and I said, 'this doesn't look good' and I actually got worried after that. I thought that this is the end of my career. I've had sleepless nights because of that, so I think that time was the toughest of my life to deal with and my family had a huge role to play there, especially my wife. She showed me the positive side of life where in 2004–05 I had already completed 15 years and she told me that many guys don't last for 15 months and here you've been able to play for 15 years so you should be thankful to the Almighty for allowing you to play for 15 years without major injury and this is the first major injury you are dealing with so not everything is lost, you will recover. That made a huge difference, it just changed the way I thought.
>
> —Sachin Tendulkar, *Bradman Museum and International Cricket Hall of Fame Interview*, 2010

Tendulkar…is finding that there are a variety of subjects fighting for space in his head and he cannot clear mindspace for his cricket like he once could. I have no doubt that he wakes up some days and thinks, 'I hope I don't have to play cricket today.' In Tendulkar's case, I would put my money on the body leading the decline. He has struggled with tennis elbow for much of this year and that has made it hard for him to get his mind right…. I doubt that he is ready to retire, but if he is to return to his best, then he is going to have to recapture the thinking process that has allowed him to dominate bowlers from all over the world in both forms of the game. Because his focus is not clear he often finds himself looking for the cheap runs on the leg-side early in his innings. Early in his career, when his mind was clearer, he would walk in and meet the ball with the full face of the bat, and as often as not hit it back down the ground. This might explain why he was only out lbw 15 times in his first 91 Tests, but has been out lbw a further 12 times in the 25 Tests since then. If Sachin can recapture the thinking of his youth, he will return to his best, or near to it, and will be a valuable member of the team for years to come.

—Greg Chappell, *Wisden Asia Cricket,* November 2004

The man who penned these words was named India's new coach, five days before Sachin underwent the surgery. His first assignment was a tri-series in Sri Lanka, where India lost to the hosts in the final. Dravid was appointed captain and Ganguly joined the squad after serving his six-match ban, which had begun during the series against Pakistan.

It, therefore, came as a surprise when Ganguly, still woefully out of form, was reappointed captain for a short tour of Zimbabwe. The two-Test series was nothing short of farcical, with the home team badly depleted by the exits of quality cricketers who had either quit or had left the rapidly collapsing country for greener pastures. However, the action off the field more than made up for the lack of action on it. The tour witnessed a row between Ganguly and Chappell, which escalated when an email that Chappell had sent to the Board was leaked to the media.

What made the developments monumentally ironic were reports that while most of the players had wanted Chappell's compatriot Tom Moody as coach, Ganguly had insisted on Chappell, with whom he had a good equation and had even worked with prior to the tour of Australia in 2003–04. After losing out on the Indian coach's position, Moody was signed on by Sri Lanka.

'Ganguly vs Chappell' wasn't the only off-the-field drama in Indian cricket. At the Annual General Meeting of the BCCI in September 2005, Jagmohan Dalmiya's faction lost the elections to a group headed by Sharad Pawar, the president of MCA and a senior member of the Union Cabinet. With Dalmiya, Ganguly's fellow Kolkatan, no longer calling the shots at the Board, there were many who believed that the decks had been cleared for a change. And so it was; Rahul Dravid was formally appointed captain of India for successive ODI series against Sri Lanka and South Africa.

The Sri Lanka series was preceded by the triangular N.K.P. Salve Challenger Trophy, which witnessed Sachin's return to the field. He would have liked to represent the World XI against Australia in the much-hyped ICC Super Series that was played at the same time, but it was a pragmatic call to get the body moving and circulation going in a domestic set-up after such a long lay-off.

His delight at having returned all but evaporated when his right shoulder started throbbing and his 'unaffected' right elbow started acting up. Dr Andrew Wallace, who had performed the surgery earlier in the year, ruled that he had tried to compensate for the tennis-elbow affliction by putting excessive pressure on the other half of his body. Much to Sachin's relief, he did not have to take another break from the game.

India Seniors, for whom he turned out in the Challenger Trophy, won the title, but Sachin had a quiet time with scores of 12, 4 and 22. In each of the three games, he fell to bowlers who were just starting out on their respective careers. Laxmipathy Balaji, one of the heroes of the tour of Pakistan, had him caught behind in the first game. Shantakumaran Sreesanth, a speedster from Kerala who was knocking on the doors of international cricket, had him leg-before in the second encounter. Piyush Chawla, a teenaged leg-spinner from Uttar Pradesh, bowled the maestro all ends up, in the final.

> Biomechanically, he has a structure that is less likely to get injured, because he is more compact, has shorter levers, more muscle bulk around joints—things like that. So he's able to protect himself a lot better than perhaps someone who is a lot taller, and leaner and more flexible. He's also very powerful, so he has a great advantage there too. It has made him more durable as well, this ability to absorb loads better through his joints and his strength around them. I believe he is quite strong around the crucial areas, like lower back, knees, things like that.
>
> —John Gloster (former Physiotherapist, Indian cricket team), as quoted in *The Sachin Sunset*, Wisden India, November 2013

Sachin took the field for India in the opening game of the seven-match ODI series against Sri Lanka on 25 October 2005 at Nagpur, exactly five months after undergoing the tennis elbow surgery. He got off the blocks with a cover-drive and a flick to square-leg off paceman Farveez Maharoof, both of which went to the boundary. The capacity crowd could not stop cheering. He went on to score 98, adding 164 for the second wicket with Irfan Pathan, one of the many young Indian players who had impressed the new coach greatly. India won the first game by 152 runs and proceeded to dominate the series, winning 6–1. The five-match ODI series against South Africa that followed ended in a 2–2 draw.

Rahul Dravid, who scored a match-winning 78 in the last ODI against South Africa was was retained as captain for the upcoming Test series against Sri Lanka.

The first Test of the series against Sri Lanka nearly met with the same fate as the abandoned third ODI of the series against South Africa, which had been scheduled in the same city—Chennai. The north-east monsoon prevented play on the first three days and both teams indulged in batting practice on the last two. Mahendra Singh Dhoni was awarded with a first Test cap in the truncated game. It wasn't that Dinesh Kartik had kept badly in the Tests against Pakistan and Zimbabwe earlier in the season, but Dhoni's performances on both sides of the stumps in the ODIs were far too overwhelming to be overlooked.

In the second Test at Delhi, Sachin achieved the milestone that had eluded him at Mohali, earlier in the year. Arriving at the wicket with the score 56–2, he started watchfully and proceeded to frustrate the bowlers with his trademark cover drives. He also countered the bag of tricks unveiled by Muttiah Muralitharan, the spin wizard, with a few of his own. By the time he had entered the 90s, the shadows had lengthened. Marvan Atapattu, the Sri Lankan skipper, packed the off-side and asked his bowlers to bowl wide outside the off-stump. Being a batsman himself, Atapattu sensed Sachin's eagerness to get the century the same evening. Chaminda Vaas did bowl to his field, but Sachin outsmarted him with a deft waft through the vacant leg-side for four. Three singles took him to his 35th Test century. So exhilarated and relieved was he to have surpassed SMG that he permitted himself the indulgence of a roar of delight.

> It is to some extent a big mental relief. I know that people were more anxious than me. It was as if nothing mattered more than my 35th Test century. I can understand how they must have felt but I must confess that my wife Anjali played a huge role in ensuring that I remained focussed. She kept telling me not to think too much about the century and how it would happen....
>
> —Sachin Tendulkar, *The Sportstar*, 24 December 2005

Anil Kumble finished with match figures of 10–157 as India triumphed by a handsome 188 runs. However, Dravid's first win as India's full-time skipper was overshadowed by the decision of the selectors to drop Ganguly from the squad for the third Test at Ahmedabad. Strangely, he hadn't exactly flopped in the game, with scores of 40 and 39, but the 'five wise men' felt otherwise.

That Test was significant for three other reasons. A bout of gastroenteritis forced Dravid to miss a Test for the first time since his debut at Lord's in 1996; he was only six Tests short of playing a record hundred in a row since his baptism, at that stage. Secondly, it was Virender Sehwag's first Test as captain. Never could he have imagined at the start of his career that he would get to lead a side that would include his role model. Thirdly, India completed an emphatic win by 259 runs to take the series 2–0. This time, it was Harbhajan Singh who took 10 wickets, seven of them in the first innings.

The year 2006 began with a twist in the 'Sourav saga'. The former captain was recalled to the Indian team for its third series against Pakistan in three seasons. Like another Indian cricketer of the 1970s and 1980s who shared his initials, the ex-captain of India had always evoked extreme reactions, with one set of people swearing by him and the other swearing at him. Unlike Sachin and Dravid, who were perceived as the 'good boys', Ganguly was someone the average cricket fan found easier to relate to, probably because he was more human and fallible. He was as mercurial as he was marvellous and as excitable as he was exceptional.

While his supporters were jubilant at his recall, his detractors were apoplectic. They went so far as to allege that his inclusion had more to do with his connections than anything else. If anything, this sort of innuendo would have delighted the Prince of Kolkata. He would have viewed it as a lucky charm of sorts, considering what he had achieved after his controversial selection for the tour of England in 1996. Things got even better for him, with the team management picking him in the playing XI for the Lahore Test, ahead of specialist openers Gautam Gambhir and Wasim Jaffer. This meant that Sehwag would have a makeshift opening partner.

There was yet another twist on the morning of the game. With the start delayed due to rain, the TV cameras spotted the former captain and his successor in an animated conversation with the coach on the playing arena. The subject of the discussion was ostensibly Ganguly's spot in the batting order. The former captain had agreed to open, but it appeared that Dravid was having second thoughts. Much to the amusement of viewers in India, one news channel invited a lip-reader to its studio to watch the footage and decipher the conversation!

Eventually, the captain prevailed. Dravid accompanied Sehwag to the middle after the hosts had declared at 679–7. The makeshift pair almost created history. India lost their first wicket at a modest 410 when Sehwag nicked Naved-ul-Hasan into Akmal's gauntlets for a 247-ball 254. Four more runs, and the Indian vice-captain and captain would have broken the world record for the highest opening partnership in Tests. With inclement weather ensuring only an hour of play on the third day and just over two overs on the fifth, the match ended at that point.

Sachin's first outing of the series with the bat, on the third day of another 'batathon' at Faisalabad, was as dramatic as it was anti-climactic. His arrival at the wicket had an electrifying effect on Shoaib Akhtar. Bowling more like a Japanese bullet train than the Rawalpindi Express, Shoaib peppered Sachin with a succession of scorching deliveries. Watchers could not help but gasp when Shoaib made one delivery take off from a track that had been declared 'dead' at the start of the game and pinged Sachin on the helmet, even as the latter was not even halfway through his attempt to take evasive action. Sachin in fact committed the cardinal sin of taking his eyes off the ball. Fortunately, no damage was done. He had moved to 14 when he tried to flick a Shoaib delivery pitched on the leg-stump. It reared off the track a lot quicker than he had anticipated, and kissed his right glove on the way to Akmal. Sachin walked without waiting for the umpire to raise his index finger, convinced that he was out. Everything had happened so quickly that it did not strike him that his right hand had come off his bat before the ball had touched it. So technically, he was not out.

> The more I look back at his dismissal, the more convinced I get that the downhill journey for the little champion has started because it has been established that, according to the laws of the game, he was not out as the ball had made contact with the right glove that was not in play. What is even more mindblowing is that he did not look at the umpire and immediately started his long walk towards the pavilion. I am not willing to buy the theory that Sachin did not know the laws of the game. If Michael Kasprowicz knows them, then I am sure that after playing for 16 years at the highest level and having led his country for a couple of years, Sachin knows all the rules by heart. Then what prompted Sachin to leave the pitch on which six centuries and two 90s were scored? Hostile bowling by Shoaib Akhtar, or the tension-filled dressing room atmosphere that often gets on the nerves of the batsmen who start feeling suffocated? Whatever may be the real reason, the fact of the matter is that Shoaib Akhtar literally exposed Sachin's present-day ability against quality fast bowling during a spell that will certainly be remembered for long.
>
> —Moin Khan, www.rediff.com, 27 January 2006

The criticism of Sachin was drowned amidst the praise that some of his colleagues gathered. Dravid, opening the batting again, scored another ton, Laxman got 90 and Mahendra Singh Dhoni got his maiden Test century. Irfan Pathan's classy 90 vindicated the decision of the team management to play Dhoni and him at numbers six and seven respectively, thus enabling them to field five specialist bowlers. India scored 603 to Pakistan's 588 in another 'batathon'.

Sachin's detractors were back with a vengeance at the end of the third Test at Karachi, a game that witnessed another epic Houdini act by Pakistan. An

Indian defeat seemed inconceivable on the first morning of the game, shortly after Dravid won the toss and asked Pakistan to bat on the most bowler-friendly track of the series. Irfan Pathan took a hat-trick in the very first over to reduce Pakistan to 0–3. Soon, the hosts were 39–6 and Indian fans could not have been blamed for visualising a second successive series win on Pakistani soil. Enter Kamran Akmal and Abdul Razzaq, who had rescued Pakistan in the Mohali Test the previous year. They did an encore, and helped Pakistan reach 245. India managed to concede a first-innings lead of seven, and then the bowlers dished out some ordinary fare, allowing Inzamam the luxury of declaring at 599–7.

Sehwag and Dravid, the heroes of Lahore, were back in the pavilion with only eight on the board in the second innings. Sachin and Laxman tried to rally the innings before both were consumed by Mohammed Asif, who was making the ball talk, shout and scream. Sachin was fourth out at 74 for a counterattacking 26, which comprised five boundaries, to a delivery that kept low and crashed into off-stump. His ungainly squat on the pitch after hearing the death-rattle mirrored the plight of his team, which was thrashed and trashed for 265. Apart from demoralising millions of Indians the world over, the images of the squat succeeded in stimulating the creativity of someone who worked for a prominent Indian newspaper. The next day's edition carried a title that was self-explanatory—'END'ULKAR'.

Sachin was far too experienced to allow the fire to faze him. He responded with a statement at the same venue where he had made one 17 years previously—with his bat. In 1989–90, he had torn into a legend called Abdul Qadir; this time around, he was older and more circumspect. He was prepared to bide his time and offer the bowlers respect before forcing them to respect him.

A welcome interlude for the Indian team after the defeat at Karachi was a trip to the outskirts of the frontier city of Peshawar, venue of the first ODI. The cricketers made full use of the opportunity to get themselves photographed against the backdrop of the Khyber Pass, the entry point for invaders into India for centuries.

The visitors started shakily on the cricket field, with Sehwag falling for five. Sachin stabilized the innings with Irfan Pathan whom Chappell continued to be completely sold on, and for good reason. Sachin was lucky to be bowled off a Naved-ul-Hasan no-ball, and he made the most of that reprieve. With Pathan and then Dhoni going after the bowling, Sachin kept the scoreboard ticking at the other end and scored 100, during which, he passed the 14,000 run-mark in ODIs. Pakistan were 311–7 in response to India's 328 when play was called off due to poor light. The hosts were declared winners for being ahead as per the D/L calculations.

It was their last moment of joy in the series.

Never had India dominated an ODI series against Pakistan so comprehensively. The visitors' margins of victory in the next four games spoke for themselves: seven wickets in the second ODI, five wickets in the third and fourth, and eight wickets in the fifth. The visitors chased down 266 in the second game and 289 in the third with clinical efficiency.

The chase in the third game, a day-nighter at Lahore, was the best of the lot. India began disastrously, with Asif dismissing Sehwag and Irfan with only 12 runs on the board, on a pitch that was a lot livelier than the track that had been prepared for the Test. Sachin assessed the conditions and made up his mind to play a waiting game, especially against Asif. With Dravid struggling to get the ball off the square, Sachin kept the scoreboard operators busy by working the ball around for singles and twos and taking full toll of anything loose. Eventually, Asif was given a breather and the complexion of the game changed. As caution gave way to measured aggression, Sachin looked anything but a batsman whose career was supposedly at its end. He had scored 95 of India's 189-3 when he was caught at backward point. India at that stage needed exactly 100 from 96 deliveries. Mohammed Kaif fell for a duck, but the Indian dressing room was unflustered, as unlike the 1990s, they had the men to finish the job. Yuvraj Singh and M.S. Dhoni did the needful with more than two overs to spare. Rahul Dravid, the proud leader of a successful team, hailed Sachin's 95 as one of his best innings.

The 4-1 win over the old enemy gave the Indians enough momentum to have the better of the first two Tests of their home series against England; the first Test at Nagpur was drawn after solid batting performances by members of both sides, and the second Test at Mohali ended in an Indian victory with debutant Munaf Patel returning match figures of 7-97.

The captain of India completed a century of Test appearances in the third Test at Mumbai. He surprised one and all by electing to bowl on what looked like a batsman's dream. Five days later, England were celebrating a series-levelling win by 212 runs, after taking the last seven Indian wickets for only 25 runs. Among those who disappointed was Sachin, who batted well to score 34 before being caught at bat-pad off Shaun Udal, a veteran off-spinner on the English county circuit who had been ignored by his national selectors for years, for reasons best known to themselves. Udal, playing in only his fourth—and as it turned out, last—Test, took four wickets in the second innings.

The Mumbai spectators showed what they thought of the home team's performance by chanting pro-Ganguly slogans for the entire duration of the presentation ceremony. Andrew Flintoff, Dravid's opposite number, was the unanimous choice for the individual awards for both the game and series. When asked about Dravid's decision at the toss, the England captain quipped that he would have asked the opposition to take first strike only if the grass on the wicket had been 'knee-deep'.

India's capitulation on the final day was preceded by a shocker on the second day. In the closing stages, Sachin went in at 24–2, after Sehwag and Jaffer had fallen to the England quicks. In what was his 132nd Test, which made him India's most-capped Test cricketer ahead of Kapil Dev, he was expected to perform the all-too-familiar duty of bailing his team out of trouble.

For the next 33 minutes, the bowlers questioned, probed and interrogated him from both ends. Sachin did his best to negotiate the challenges, wait the period out, but the bowlers were not letting up. It was one of their good days and one of Sachin's pedestrian days. He had a solitary run against his name when he fished at an Anderson delivery and got an outside-edge. Geraint Jones, the keeper, did the rest. As Sachin made his way back to the pavilion, watched by a stunned audience, the unbelievable happened. On his home ground, he was booed.

The episode made national and international news. There were those who advocated that he ought to 'go', while others contended that he was a human being and was therefore bound to fail sometimes.

What the man himself felt mattered the most. Sachin was primed for the challenges that lay ahead. With the tour of the Caribbean three months away, he decided to skip the ODI series against England and went under the knife for the second time in three years, this time for his shoulder. During the surgery that was performed in London, the doctors discovered a ruptured tendon in his bicep, which they fixed along with the shoulder after obtaining his consent. His eagerness to return to cricket made him resume intensive practice a lot earlier than what the doctors had recommended, and that turned out to be a mistake, as his bicep gave way during a session. The doctors advised complete rest, thus ruling him out of the West Indies series.

> Tendulkar has been at the forefront of cricket and Indian life since he was a slip of a lad. He has survived the expectations of millions, has scored incomparably more hundreds in international cricket than anyone else, has played so many matches, and always with all eyes upon him. Is it not possible that he is worn out?.... To the dismay of some observers,

Tendulkar has responded to his travails by playing a more cautious game. What was he supposed to do? He is not a fool or an innocent but a seasoned campaigner, an professional sportsman, who knows full well the value of runs on the board.... His habit of leaving his back foot on leg stump widens his range but it means that the stumps are not fully covered.... Neither Lara nor Tendulkar can ever be quite the same again. Sportsmen fade away.... Although there can be no going back, Tendulkar, especially, has more runs in him. Revival is impossible but the master of Mumbai knows a thing or two, and might yet overcome the heaviness in his mind.

—Peter Roebuck, *Cricinfo Magazine*, May 2006

TRIAL BY FIRE

I had noticed a chink in his armour after he got out bowled on a few occasions. Believing that he was falling over to the off-side as the ball was released and in the process, losing his balance, I suggested that he should raise his bat back a bit earlier, flex his knees and keep his head steady—as Sunil Gavaskar did—so that he could get a clearer view of the ball and more time to decide on the appropriate shot. On another occasion, I observed that he was not happy with his off-drive and had asked one of the bowlers to help him practise the shot with throwdowns. Watching his front foot closely, I noticed that it was leading with the toes instead of the heel-toe action. This was upsetting his balance, with his head moving too far forward. As soon as I passed on this information to him, he practised this shot for over a hundred throwdowns and stopped only when he was satisfied.

—B.S. Sandhu, *Mid-Day*, 17 November 2013

Sachin took a pragmatic line on his return to the squad after the shoulder surgery. After discussions with his doctors and the team management, it was decided that he would shift back to the slips, where he had fielded for several years before his issues with his back had prompted him to move into the deep. However, slips were employed for only a few overs in ODIs, which meant that Sachin would have to field in the deep for the substantial part of an innings in the shorter version. Would his shoulder be able to take the load?

Damien Martyn certainly thought that it wouldn't, during an ODI against India in a tri-series at Kuala Lumpur, in August 2006. However, his attempt to steal a run right under Sachin's nose, who was at third-man, ended in a disaster. Sachin's throw from the deep was spot-on and Martyn had to depart. All the concerns regarding the status of the most famous right shoulder in India were laid to rest with that dismissal.

In the case of Sachin, he had a couple of well-documented injuries as we know: the elbow operation and the shoulder operation during my tenure with the cricket board, both of which he recovered from fantastically. But there were modifications that he had to make during a certain period of time to overcome that and ensure it didn't re-occur. It was a matter of limitations in things like throwing and fielding positions—things like that for a short period of time, in a match situation and in training.

—John Gloster, as quoted in *The Sachin Sunset*,
Wisden India, November 2013

Earlier in the year, Sachin confounded all those who had branded him a 'spent force', by signing a three-year marketing deal worth a mind-boggling ₹180 crore with Iconix, the marketing branch of Saatchi & Saatchi, the international advertising agency. This was shortly after the expiry of his five-year deal with WorldTel. Clearly, there were people out there who believed that the reports of Sachin's decline were grossly exaggerated.

His recuperation complete, Sachin flew to England to warm up for a return to international cricket by playing five matches for the Lashings World XI. The squad, whose primary purpose was to play junior and club teams across the UK to promote the sport of cricket, comprised some erstwhile opponents of Sachin's—Aravinda de Silva, Richie Richardson, Courtney Walsh and Chris Cairns, among others. Also in the squad was Clare Connor, the then captain of the England women's team.

Sachin returned to India with four centuries and a 98 from his five games for the club. He was subsequently declared fit to tour Sri Lanka for a tri-series with South Africa as the third team, which was to be followed by a three-match tussle against the Lankans. As it turned out, both series were washed out due to relentless rain. The only time the Indians got to take the field was in the first game of the bilateral series against Sri Lanka, and even there, the game was abandoned after 3.4 overs. Sachin, in his first international match after the Test series against England, was unbeaten on two when the heavens opened.

He was at his best in Team India's next engagement—a tri-series against the West Indies and Australia at Kuala Lumpur. On what was his first cricketing visit to Malaysia since the Commonwealth Games misadventure in 1998, he batted brilliantly to score 141 in India's first league game against the West Indies. His driving, straight and through the covers, was as majestic as ever, and his flicks on the leg-side as imperious as they had always been. He brought the crowd to its feet with his lofted strokes over the covers in the latter stages of the innings. Despite India scoring 309–5 in the game, the West Indies won after the D/L calculations were invoked. India won their next encounter against the West

Indies, with Sachin at the forefront once again. This time around, he scored 65 and his side defended a score of 162.

In his absence, India had registered their first Test series win in the Caribbean since 1971. But all was not well.

Ironically, a trait that Sourav Ganguly and his bête noire Greg Chappell had in common was their penchant for evoking extreme reactions. While the coach's backing of youngsters was initially welcomed, it was now increasingly being felt that he was needlessly rushing things through and in the process jeopardising the careers of some senior players who had a lot of cricket left in them. His handling of Ganguly, Zaheer Khan and Sehwag had not won him many admirers. The turbulence within the team ensured that spirits in the Indian camp were not very high on the eve of the fifth edition of the ICC Champions Trophy, which was being played in their own country. This was in stark contrast to the previous season, during which, the side had won ODI series against Sri Lanka, Pakistan and England and squared one against South Africa. The team had in fact created a world record of 17 consecutive victories while chasing. The sequence ended during the ODI series in the West Indies, which India lost.

The hosts fared poorly in the Champions Trophy, but there was a silver lining for their cricket board. It was during the tournament that the BCCI moved into its first-ever permanent headquarters in the Wankhede Stadium Complex in Mumbai, 77 years after its inception. The Board also took steps to admit professionals into its fold. At the helm of the cricket centre was Prof. Ratnakar Shetty, the chief administrative officer (CAO) of the Board. Assisting him was a group of dedicated managers, assistant managers and other support staff. This writer was among those who had the honour of being associated with the Board for seven-and-a-half years, as Manager—Media Relations and Corporate Affairs.

The Indian team's flop show continued in the ODI series in South Africa. The only consolation for the visitors was their victory in a one-off game that was played in a new format, in between the last two ODIs.

Twenty20 cricket had been devised in England in the new millennium for the same reason that limited-overs cricket had been invented in the early 1960s—to counter dwindling crowd attendances. The new format was a hit when first adopted by the counties in 2003. Among its features were a 20-overs-a-side game, played in coloured clothing and under lights (after office hours), with cheerleaders lining the boundary and doing their stuff whenever something significant happened on the field, in the form of a wicket, boundary or six. Critically, the entire game spanned just three hours, inclusive of a 20-minute break between innings. Australia and New Zealand played the first T20 international in 2005, but unlike its counterparts, the BCCI was reluctant to take the format seriously. Crowd attendances at 50-over games had never been an issue in India, and those representing the Board in ICC meetings had caustically wondered aloud whether 10-over or 5-over games would be introduced next.

The participation of the Indian team in the inaugural T20 World Cup, to be played in South Africa in 2007, was confirmed only through a barter deal of sorts. The subcontinental combine of India, Pakistan, Sri Lanka and Bangladesh missed the 1 April 2006 deadline to bid for the right to host the 50-over World Cup in 2011; when they requested the ICC to grant them extra time, the apex body said that 'it would help'—literally and figuratively—if the Indian team participated in the upcoming event. This was ironic in the light of what was to follow.

The Indian team excelled in its maiden T20 international, beating South Africa by six wickets in a tense penultimate-ball finish at Johannesburg. Television viewers were treated to innovations like Virender Sehwag, India's captain for the game, being 'wired up' and interacting with the commentators while setting his fields. Sachin, who opened with his skipper, fell for 10, but Sehwag, Dinesh Mongia and Dinesh Kartik took the Indians through.

The Indian XI for the first Test at Johannesburg comprised two stalwarts who were on a comeback trail. It was believed that Dilip Vengsarkar, who had taken over from Kiran More as chairman of selectors, had facilitated the return of Sourav Ganguly and Zaheer Khan to the team. Their talent was never in doubt, and they duly answered all the questions being asked of their respective temperaments when it mattered. Sourav Ganguly was India's only half-centurion in the first innings. Sachin contributed 44 and the visitors finished with 249. Zaheer Khan struck twice as South Africa were dismissed for a mere 84 in response. Shantakumaran Sreesanth was India's best bowler with figures of 5–40.

India scored 236 in the second innings and the bowlers then combined to bowl the hosts out for 278. It was India's first-ever Test win on South African soil, and one of their best ever. Not even their fans had expected them to perform the way they did after being outplayed in the ODI series.

At that point, the Test series was India's to lose. And lose it they did with some pedestrian cricket in the second and third Tests. South Africa won the second Test at Durban by 174 runs and the third at Cape Town by five wickets. Sachin scored 63 in the first innings at Durban and 64 in the first essay at Cape Town, but those knocks were forgotten in the wake of the disastrous second innings of the third Test.

Batting first, India scored 414 and restricted the hosts to 373. To try and build on the lead, the out-of-form Virender Sehwag, who had batted at number six in the first essay, was sent in with first-innings centurion Wasim Jaffer. However, the move backfired. Sehwag fell and he was followed by Jaffer. All eyes turned to the Indian dressing room, expecting Sachin to emerge, but there was a catch. He was not supposed to come in to bat for at least 18 minutes, having spent that amount of time outside the playing area, tending to an injury that he had sustained while fielding. The team management had forgotten about it until the fourth umpire had reminded them of the same. When Jaffer was dismissed, Sachin was padded up, but Laxman was in the shower and Ganguly was in his tracksuit. Nobody had expected two wickets to go down so quickly.

As the clock ticked and the South African players went from being amused to irritated, Daryl Harper, one of the field umpires, informed Graeme Smith, the home team skipper, that the delay was unintentional. Smith sportingly acceded to his request of not appealing for 'timed out', a law that he was technically entitled to invoke after the incoming batsman had taken more than three minutes to arrive at the wicket. Finally, a whole six minutes after Jaffer had returned to the pavilion, a fully ready Sourav Ganguly ran down the stairs to join his captain.

The captain and former captain added 84 before Ganguly was caught behind off Jacques Kallis for 47. What followed was nothing short of mystifying. Two of the greatest batsmen of all time got into a defensive rut and allowed the bowlers to dictate terms. There was no counterattack, no attempt to rotate the strike, and the South Africans were too professional a team to not capitalize. Dravid and Sachin batted together for 15 overs, from which they scored 24 runs. Nobody could quite understand what was happening and Ravi Shastri spoke for many people when he commented that 'Paul Harris [the South African left-arm spinner] was made to look like Lord Harris'.

When Ganguly fell, India were 90–3. It was just the ideal platform on which to build on their first-innings lead. But the overcautiousness of the middle-order cost them dear. Dravid fell at 114, Laxman was dismissed at 115, and then Sachin was leg-before to Shaun Pollock for a torturous 14 that lasted 62 deliveries. Dinesh Kartik, who had come in as a replacement for the injured Dhoni and had opened the batting in the first innings, tried to be assertive, but he kept losing partners and the innings ended at 169. South Africa needed only 211 to complete a memorable series win, which they achieved for the loss of five wickets.

The decision of the BCCI to reshuffle its annual domestic calendar and advance the Ranji Trophy enabled the Mumbai and Bengal players in the national team to turn out for their respective sides in the final, which was played in Mumbai in the first week of February. For Mumbai, its India stars could not have arrived too soon. The duo apart, only three batsmen entered double figures in the first innings, but the side still scored 320, thanks to Jaffer's 112 and Sachin's 105 in his first appearance in a Ranji final since 1999–00. Zaheer Khan, who had by then returned to Mumbai after a stint at Vadodara, took 5–40 to seal Bengal's capitulation for 143. The visitors batted brilliantly in their second innings in pursuit of a target of 472, but they simply had too many to chase and were all out for 339.

Sachin was happy to have contributed to a title triumph that had looked improbable at the league stage, when Mumbai had not even opened its account in terms of points, and was in fact confronting the possibility of being relegated to the lower tier for the next season. Finding themselves in much the same position as the Australians in the ICC Cricket World Cup 1999, Team Mumbai had gone on to do exactly what Steve Waugh's side had achieved back then.

The Ranji final was followed by back-to-back ODI series against the West Indies and Sri Lanka, in the lead-up to the eighth edition of the sport's premier quadrennial event, which was to be played in the Caribbean in March–April.

The Indian team management had taken note of the 'slow and low' pitches and the slow outfields in the Caribbean on their tour of the isles in mid-2006. Both Dravid and Chappell were of the view that in the World Cup, the team needed someone to bat in the middle order and muscle the ball around in the middle overs to give the innings an impetus. Virender Sehwag's reluctance to essay that role left the captain and coach with only one option. As had been the case in 2002, Sachin was not very happy about dropping down the order, but he agreed to do it for the side. He batted one-down in the first game of the ODI series against the West Indies and then moved to number four. The team management had reason to feel vindicated when he scored a half-century in the third game at Chennai and a century in the fourth at Vadodara.

Sachin came in at 148–2, after Brian Lara, in his second stint as West Indies captain, had put India in. He constructed a superb innings, getting more and more aggressive as the innings neared its end. Dhoni and he took 75 runs off the last 39 balls, and Sachin reached triple figures for the 41st time in the shorter format off the last delivery of the innings.

India won the game by 150 runs and the series 3–1. At the presentation ceremony, where he collected the individual awards for the match and series, Sachin provided an indication of the state of mind he was in when Arun Lal, the former India opener and now commentator, spoke about how it felt great to see 'Tendulkar bat like the Tendulkar we know'. Sachin's response was crisp: 'I have always played the way I wanted to play according to the situation. I have been playing for a long while now, so people should appreciate that.'

> Since he had come back in Malaysia [2006], Sachin's mental state was surprisingly fragile, and he came to me for help. He was just turning the corner into the later stage of his career, had had some injuries, and was starting to doubt himself. Fixing that became a priority for me.... For him, the challenge was to think like he had when he was a young player. 'If you can organise your mind the way it was, there is no reason you can't play like that again.' I noticed it, funnily enough, when he had a bowl. He always seemed light and happy when he bowled, a young player again. I said that if he could bat with the same spirit as he showed when he bowled, there was no reason he couldn't play into his forties. He said that was the best session talking about batting he had ever had, and we should have more.
>
> —Greg Chappell, *Fierce Focus*

None of these chats would have happened in early 2007, when the relationship between the coach and the senior players was at its lowest ebb.

> The first match of the series against the West Indies was played at Nagpur. After the game, Sachin requested me to meet a group of players who had something to discuss. They told us in no uncertain terms that if things continued to be the way they were, the team would not do well in the upcoming World Cup, as there was a genuine problem with the coach. The players wanted to talk to Mr Shashank Manohar, who was then the vice-president of the Board, and I suggested that they should. Sachin was also hurt after being told by Chappell that he ought to bat at number four 'in the interests of the team'. The point he made to me was that he had served Indian cricket to the best of his abilities for nearly 20 years and he did not need a Greg Chappell to tell him about 'team interest'; he understood and appreciated it better than most people.
>
> —Prof. R.S. Shetty, personal interview

Despite all the turbulence, the Indian team departed for the Caribbean with reasonably high hopes. John Wright, who was part of the World Cup TV commentary team, reckoned that the emergence of genuine all-rounders like Mahendra Singh Dhoni and Irfan Pathan had made India's team of 2007 more balanced than its predecessor of 2003, which he had coached.

The ICC Cricket World Cup 2007 was a veritable marathon. It was the first of eight World Cups to involve as many as 16 teams and four groups. Each group comprised two heavyweights and two teams who were supposedly there 'to make up the numbers'. As far as most cricket lovers were concerned, the 'real' World Cup would begin only at the Super Eights stage, which would involve the top two sides from each of the groups. The first round, wherein each team was to play the other three in its group, was perceived as a waste of time. But then, cricket had the last laugh.

Not one, but two heavyweights had a bad day at the office in the very first round. India had one at the start of their campaign, when they lost to Bangladesh. They were bowled out for a poor 195 that their eastern neighbours overhauled with plenty to spare. A win against Bermuda followed, and then came the must-win encounter against Sri Lanka. Needing 255 to win, India were bowled out for 185. Sachin, who was batting at number four as per the diktat of the management, inside-edged Dilhara Fernando onto his stumps before opening his account. Sehwag scored 48 and Dravid tried to rally the innings with a half-century, but it was all in vain. India's World Cup was over. An entire nation went into shock, and the effigy burners took over, with the support of sections of the media.

In another group, Pakistan went down against Ireland after losing to the West Indies; the following morning, Bob Woolmer, coach of the Pakistani team, was found dead in his hotel room. The local Police pronounced it an act of murder before examinations revealed that the former England opener had suffered a fatal heart attack.

The rabble-rousers left no stone unturned, literally and figuratively, to treat the Indian players like serial killers and paedophiles when they returned home. People expected Dravid to throw in the towel, but the captain of India was made of sterner stuff.

> Tell me, the world has gone on talking about all this [our defeat and exit] but has anybody spared a thought for us?.... Did they try to find out what we have been going through? I am shattered beyond words and I feel helpless. I've never felt so bad in my entire career.... No matter how many Tests or one-day series you win, nothing else even comes close to a World Cup triumph. The World Cup was our passion, our collective goal, our dream and that has been shattered. And we all are terribly disappointed over it.... Again, it's not that we are defending ourselves. We do realise that we played badly and, as a team, we take full responsibility for that. But what hurt us most is if the coach has questioned our attitude.
>
> —Sachin Tendulkar, *The Times of India*, 4 April 2007 (as posted on www.cricinfo.com on 4 April 2007)

These comments resulted in Sachin being slapped with a show-cause notice for the first time by his Board for violating the Players' Code of Conduct. The BCCI also took similar action on Yuvraj Singh, who had claimed on a TV channel that all the players supported Sachin. The players were given seven days in which to explain their comments. The *Hindustan Times* reported on 14 April 2007, 10 days after the outburst, that both players had apologized.

> From all accounts, Chappell's report, due to be submitted to the board before April 6, will be scathing in its criticism of the attitude of the senior players including Sourav Ganguly, Sachin Tendulkar, Virender Sehwag and Harbhajan Singh. It is learnt that Chappell, and some members of the board, believe that the return of Ganguly, and later on Tendulkar's captaincy aspirations, had a destabilising effect on the team, forming groups within the 11 and perhaps stifling the growth of some of the younger cricketers trying to make a mark.
>
> —Anand Vasu, www.cricinfo.com, 3 April 2007

Chappell put in his papers two days before he was to submit the report and on the same day on which Sachin's outburst appeared in the national daily. He has been quoted as saying that Sachin's statement had nothing to do with his decision to quit. In his 2011 autobiography, the former Australian captain has claimed that he had made up his mind to quit as coach of the Indian team regardless of what happened in the World Cup.

Sachin rebutted Chappell in his 2014 autobiography, in which he recalled Chappell meeting him prior to the 2007 World Cup and suggesting that he become captain of India. Sachin further wrote that Chappell had told him that 'together, they could control Indian cricket for years'. Sachin, shocked that the coach was talking about the removal of Dravid before a World Cup, turned him down.

The BCCI invited several former captains to their Working Committee meeting to seek their help in analysing what had gone wrong and what needed to be done to salvage the situation. Sharad Pawar, the BCCI president, declared that the time had come to take some 'harsh' decisions.

Would the representatives of the generation that had been inspired to play cricket after the 1983 World Cup win, get to play a World Cup again? All of them were on the wrong side of 30. The most experienced 'World-cupper' among them was 34. Would he still be around in 2011? No one knew.

I didn't communicate my plans well enough to the senior players. I should have let guys like Tendulkar, Laxman and Sehwag know that although I was an agent of change, they were still part of our Test cricket future. When I did communicate with them, I was sometimes too abrupt. Once in South Africa [2006–07], I called in Sachin and Sehwag to ask more of them, and I could tell by the look on their faces that they were affronted. Later, Dravid, who was in the room, said, 'Greg, they've never been spoken to like that before'.

—Greg Chappell, *Fierce Focus*

RESURGENCE

I never throw my bat; never—however disappointed I get. It is something I respect.

—Sachin Tendulkar, as quoted by Clayton Murzello, *Outlook Commemorative Issue*, 2010

You will never see Sachin blame the pitch after a bad performance. Never.

—Lalsuram Jaiswal, second-in-command groundsman at the Wankhede Stadium, as quoted in *Mid-Day*, 17 November 2013

The turmoil in Indian cricket showed no signs of letting up in the weeks that followed the team's exit from the World Cup. Zee Network, one of the country's premier media houses, announced the institution of the 'Indian Cricket League' (ICL), a Twenty20 tournament which for all practical purposes would run parallel to the official international and domestic commitments of the Indian cricketers. The ICL team signed up several domestic cricketers, some of whom had represented India at the senior and junior levels in the recent past, as well as some former stars as coaches/mentors. The signees were divided into different city-specific teams.

The BCCI and its member associations reacted sharply, banning the signees from all official cricket and denying the rebel league the use of the premier cricket venues.

The players picked for India's first official assignment after the World Cup—a tour of Bangladesh—were only too happy to stay in the background and do their stuff, even as the controversy raged on.

The crisis called for effective leadership. It was felt that an eminent former *Indian* cricketer, who was held in high esteem by the players and was closer to them in terms of age, could help them rediscover themselves. A request was accordingly made to Ravi Shastri to take a break from his commentating duties. Robin Singh and Venkatesh Prasad were brought on board as the fielding and bowling coaches respectively. Among those 'rested' for the ODI leg of the Bangladesh tour was Sachin himself. He joined the side for the two-Test series after India had won the limited-overs series and extracted some sort of revenge for their loss in the World Cup.

In more ways than one, it suited Indian cricket that the rebuilding process began against a team that was not among the most formidable in the world. Bangladesh had some exceptional talent in their ranks and were capable of the odd surprise, as they had shown in the World Cup with wins over India and South Africa, but they still had a long way to go in the traditional variety.

With Sehwag dropped from the Test side, the post of the vice-captain was offered to the seniormost member of the squad. Sachin accepted it.

He worked himself into form, as did Ganguly, with hundreds in the rain-hit first Test at Chittagong, which was drawn. The visitors then totally dominated the second Test at Dhaka, winning by an innings and 239 runs. Sachin scored his second consecutive hundred, and he had company. Wasim Jaffer bounced back from the ignominy of a king's pair in the previous Test to score a century. His opening partner Dinesh Kartik scored his maiden Test ton, and skipper Rahul Dravid also crossed triple figures, as India ran up a total of 610–3.

India's best bowler in the game was an individual who just 12 months previously had been deemed to have gone past his expiry date.

Zaheer Khan had not had the best of times since the tour of Australia in 2003–04, where he had pulled a hamstring after taking five wickets in the first Test. He had been in and out of the side for the next two seasons due to injuries. Advised by Sachin to make himself a more rounded bowler, Zaheer flew to England to represent Worcestershire in county cricket after being left out of the Indian team that toured the West Indies in mid-2006. His tally of 78 wickets meant that no one could begrudge the selectors' decision to recall him for the tour of South Africa. The Zaheer Khan who alighted at the Jan Smuts Airport in Johannesburg as a member of the Indian team was fitter and hungrier than ever before. He had a point to prove and prove it he did in the days and weeks to follow. He dismissed Graeme Smith, the South African captain, 6 times in 11 face-offs.

Zaheer's match figures of 7–88 at Dhaka were merely a prelude to his heroics in England.

Zaheer and Sreesanth continued their form in the first Test at Lord's, but they were outbowled by Rudra Pratap Singh, a left-arm paceman from Uttar Pradesh, who won a place on the honours' board in the Lord's dressing room with five wickets in the second innings. However, the Indian batting was a let-down. Sachin received a warm ovation from the capacity crowd, with even England supporters egging him on to score a hundred in what they believed would be his last Test appearance at 'Headquarters'. They did not expect Sachin to return to England with the Indian team in 2011, at which point, he would be 38.

In the middle, Sachin willed himself to forget the distractions and focus on the mission at hand. Having realized that there was a lot in the strip for the bowlers, he opted to allow them to assert themselves before opening out. Everything seemed to be going as per plan till he was trapped leg-before to James Anderson. He had scored 37, inclusive of six boundaries.

The highlight of England's second innings was Kevin Pietersen's 134. He was the only batsman who stood between the Indian bowlers—Zaheer and Singh in particular—and ensured a target of 380 for the visitors. With rain a persistent threat, India had no option but to play for a draw. The batsmen did try to dig their heels in, but when Laxman was sixth out at 231 for 79, the hosts went for the kill, and it was only Steve Bucknor who came between them and a 1–0 lead. India were 282–9 and looking down the barrel of the gun when Monty Panesar rapped Sreesanth, India's number 11, on the pads. Admittedly, the batsman looked plumb in front. However, Bucknor thought otherwise. At the other end was Mahendra Singh Dhoni, who had eschewed his natural belligerence and exhibited great resolve in an innings of 76. Barely five minutes later, the batsmen were offered the light and they were only too happy to take it.

What Bucknor did, or rather, did not do, on that final evening at Lord's was ironic in the light of what was to happen just six months later.

The second Test at Nottingham was when it all came together for the visitors. Zaheer Khan (4–59) and Anil Kumble (3–32) vindicated Dravid's decision to bowl after winning the toss, bowling England out for 198. The Indians then batted themselves into an invincible position, scoring 481. Five of the top six batsman scored 50s, with the captain the only one to miss out. He scored 37. Sachin got off to another tentative start, at one point not scoring a run for 28 deliveries and even being struck on the visor of the helmet by Anderson.

> It is not that I have intentionally cramped my style of play. I have never said, no, I will not play any shots. Yes, there are times you bat according to the needs of the situation. Also, it is a part of growing. You don't do at the age of 35 what you did at 16. The thinking changes.
>
> —Sachin Tendulkar, *Wisden Asia Cricket*, October 2004

Sachin tinkered with his bat and gloves more than once, and went back to the old stratagem of wearing the bowlers out. Eventually, things improved, as they had to. He opened out with a succession of drives and flicks, some of which rekindled memories of his 177 at the same venue, nearly a decade earlier. He was nine short of a hundred when umpire Simon Taufel upheld a leg-before shout by Paul Collingwood. Sachin, who was convinced that the ball would have missed the stumps, was far from happy, but he had to go. In the dressing room, he would have had an extra helping of ice cream; that was just about the most 'extreme' thing he was known to do, when really upset! Taufel, a three-time winner of the ICC's Umpire of the Year Award, realized his mistake and was brave enough to apologize to Sachin later.

England began their second innings in the shadow of what was termed as the 'jelly beans' controversy. Zaheer Khan was not thrilled to discover a cluster of jelly beans on the pitch when he came in to bat in the latter stages of India's innings, and he let his feelings be known. While the England fielders gave it back, none of them revealed who the culprit was. If the ploy was to upset Zaheer, then it backfired. He made the initial breakthrough in England's second innings, having Alastair Cook leg-before at 49. However, India's charge was halted by Michael Vaughan. The England captain lost Andrew Strauss and Kevin Pietersen, but Collingwood gave him splendid support. Vaughan batted quite delightfully, completing his 17th Test century and looking good for many more.

England were four runs ahead, with Vaughan well past a hundred, when Zaheer brought his team back into the game. Sachin's penchant for putting himself in the shoes of the opposition batsmen prompted him to advise Zaheer to switch to around the wicket. He had been watching Vaughan intently, and had a feeling that the England captain might not adjust to a change in the bowler's approach. Sure enough, Zaheer delivered. Vaughan attempted to guide a good-length delivery around the corner, but the ball kept low and struck him on his left pad as he shuffled across the crease. The England captain could only watch as the cherry lobbed off his pad and dislodged the bails. An ecstatic Zaheer celebrated the scalp by having Ian Bell leg-before for a duck; thereafter, it was only a matter of time.

Zaheer finished with figures of 5–75 in the second innings and India lost three wickets on the way to the target of 73. It was fitting that Dravid, who with his teammates had been through a lot since the World Cup debacle, was in the middle when the winning runs were scored.

The final Test at the Oval was a high-scoring draw, a memorable feature of which from the Indian point of view was Anil Kumble's maiden Test century. The hundred, the first by an Indian in the series, marked the culmination of another professional batting display by the visitors, wherein all the batsmen scored heavily and two of them missed centuries narrowly. Dhoni fell for 92 and Sachin essayed a splendid 82. India totalled 664 and then dismissed England for 345, but Dravid did not enforce the follow-on. The visitors then surprised one and all with some diffident batting in the second innings, which rekindled memories of their crawl at Cape Town earlier in the year. Their reluctance to force the issue enabled England to get back and achieve a draw. However, that did not take anything away from what the visitors had achieved. It was only their third series win on English soil, and first since 1986.

Two individuals who were probably more delighted than the winning side were Chandrakant Borde, who had replaced Ravi Shastri as the cricket manager for the tour, and was a contemporary of his. On the last day of the 2007 series, Borde and Mansoor Ali Khan Pataudi would have remembered their tour of England exactly four decades previously, on which they had been vice-captain and captain respectively. Despite some memorable individual performances, India had lost that series 0–3. India's charismatic leader of the 1960s and 1970s and a man who was not known to display his emotions in public, was beaming as he presented the newly instituted Pataudi Trophy to Rahul Dravid. Named after himself and his father, who had represented both England and India, the trophy would henceforth be awarded to the winners of all series between the two countries that would be played in England.

It had taken Sachin and Kumble four visits, and Ganguly and Dravid three each, to finish on the winning side in a Test series in England. The likes of V.V.S. Laxman and of course, Zaheer Khan, had played their parts as well, along with younger members of the side like Dhoni, Sreesanth, R.P. Singh and the new opening combination of Wasim Jaffer and Dinesh Kartik.

India drew the seven-match ODI series after trailing 1–3, before losing the final game with some marginal umpiring calls going against them. Sachin carried on from where he had left off in the Test series, not only in terms of scoring, but also in terms of missing hundreds. The jinx had in fact commenced in a three-match ODI series against South Africa in Ireland that had preceded the tour of England; Sachin had scored 99 and 93 in the first two games of a series that India won 2–1. He followed it with a 91 in the Nottingham Test and later, scores of 99 and 94 in the ODIs against England. More exasperated than him were his fans and family, particularly Arjun, his seven-year-old son, who asked him why he simply could not hit a six or four to reach triple figures.

> If you score a hundred, then you are accused of playing for a hundred…. If you get out in the 90s, then the question is: why is he not scoring a century?

What I want is smiles in the dressing room.... We play as a team.... If we win and I get out on 99, I am happy to do that....

—Sachin Tendulkar, *Harsha Unplugged*, Star Cricket, 2007

Sachin himself was not unduly concerned with his new-found proclivity to falter in the 90s. Far more important to him was the realization that his fitness concerns of 2004–06 were a thing of the past. He was batting beautifully, brilliantly and belligerently, like the Sachin of old. The 90s' 'jinx' would sort itself out sooner than later, he was convinced. Acting on a hunch, the official broadcaster of the England series had maxed the volume of the stump microphones when Sachin was on strike, during one of the matches in England. The crew was stunned to hear him utter the exact number of runs he expected to score from a delivery even before he played it! It appeared that Sachin knew what he could do with the ball as soon as it was released by the bowler. This was a genius at work.

Sometimes, when you don't play certain shots because the field-setting is different and you got to play accordingly, the bowlers are bowling a different line, you also have to take what surface you are playing on into consideration…your shot-selection becomes extremely important—that was the reason I wasn't doing certain things—when you connect the ball well and you hear that sound…that is how the confidence grows.... I think the connection and when you know you have got it right, that sound is something special—you want to hear it every now and then…it all boils down to the field-setting and surface.

—Sachin Tendulkar, *Harsha Unplugged*, Star Cricket, 2007

Sachin pulled out of the inaugural ICC World Twenty20, which was to be played in South Africa in September 2007. Like Ganguly, Dravid and Zaheer, he was of the view that he ought to step aside for what was a different brand of cricket. The reins of the team for what was perceived as a 'young man's format' were entrusted to Mahendra Singh Dhoni. India's first game of the tournament, against Scotland, was washed out. Their next encounter against Pakistan the following day, was preceded by an unexpected piece of news. Rahul Dravid had resigned as captain. On the eve of a season that was to feature series against Pakistan, Australia and South Africa, this development threw the BCCI into a quandary.

Sharad Pawar, the BCCI president, reacted to the development by doing what was expected of him; Sachin had been Dravid's deputy in England and in the captain's absence, had led from the front with an innings of 171 for the visitors against the England Lions in a three-day game at Chelmsford. He was the logical choice to take over from Dravid. His record as captain of India did not make for flattering reading, but the Indian team had changed by leaps and bounds since the early days of the new millennium.

Sachin was offered the captaincy. He declined it. After separate discussions with him and Rahul Dravid, the ex-captain, the Board president realized that both the legends thought highly of the wicketkeeper–batsman from Jharkhand, who was running operations in South Africa at the time. The reasons they offered were also similar, in that both reckoned Mahendra Singh Dhoni had the ability, the brains and the nous.

> It was a big compliment for me when I heard that he had recommended my name for the captaincy. People sometimes ask why and I guess it was the honest opinions I gave from behind the stumps. Or the times when we batted together and I used to express myself. I am not somebody who agrees just for the sake of it. Of course, Sachin was very professional when we used to have such interactions and I think that those were the ingredients that made paaji[*] think I would make a good captain.
>
> —Mahendra Singh Dhoni, as quoted in *Sports Illustrated*, May 2013

The Board then debated the matter, and concluded that the captaincy be split. Dhoni, under whom the team was impressing in South Africa, was assigned the leadership in the limited-overs scheme of things. For the traditional version, the Board approached Anil Kumble, one of India's greatest cricketers of all time.

In 2001, Sachin had been quoted as saying that while he was not thinking about the captaincy, he hadn't ruled it out either. Sourav Ganguly, the captain at the time, went on to lead India for four more years, after which Rahul Dravid assumed charge. So why then did Sachin not take up the job when it could have been his in 2007?

There is reason to believe that had Dravid quit as captain after the 2007 World Cup, Sachin may well have taken up the responsibility to resurrect Indian cricket. That hadn't happened of course, with Dravid not having taken the easier option of jumping ship after the debacle in the Caribbean. He abdicated only after helping the team rediscover its self-belief on the tour of England. The Indian team of mid-2007 wore a settled look. Sachin, therefore, had the option

---

[*] Punjabi term used for Sachin by his teammates in the latter stages of his career. It denotes an 'elder'.

to decide that he would continue to serve the team as its friend, philosopher and guide, instead of taking up an official responsibility.

Was Sachin really a 'poor' captain as is claimed by his detractors? His record as captain for Mumbai and indeed, his performance in the Titan Cup and home series against South Africa in his first stint, proved that he possessed the 'skill' to lead. However, subsequent months had proved that he had little or no 'luck'. In his first stint, he led India against South Africa in South Africa and the West Indies in the West Indies, daunting assignments both. India lost both series, but the team was by no means disgraced. In fact, India came very close to beating a strong West Indies side on their own turf. In his second stint, in which he had taken charge reluctantly, the Indian team had run into Steve Waugh's Invincibles at the peak of their powers. Hansie Cronje's South Africans, whom they played after that catastrophic tour of Australia, were no pushovers either.

A recurrent feature of Sachin's first stint was the Indian team's penchant for snatching defeat from the jaws of victory, which had more to do with some bizarre cricket by certain members of the Indian team than any last-minute heroics by the opposition. These individuals, who revelled in letting their team, nation and captain down, eventually got their just desserts in 2000.

Quite a few parallels can be drawn between Sachin's stints as captain and those of Kimberley Hughes, who led Australia on and off from 1979-80 to 1984-85. In what was a weird pattern, Hughes would lead overseas and Greg Chappell, who had by then more or less retired from touring, would be reinstated for the next home series, only for Hughes to be handed the job back for the next tour.

Just as Sachin as captain did not enjoy the support of some members of his team, Hughes also did not enjoy the respect of some of his big guns. These individuals went out of their way to be non-cooperative, hurling bouncers at him in the nets and challenging his authority during matches by openly questioning his field-placements. The Australian establishment ought to have taken a stern view of this, but it didn't, in much the same way as the one-man commission that the BCCI instituted in 1997 to ostensibly get to the bottom of the 'fixing' allegations, did not come up with anything substantial.

It was only after Chappell stepped down from the captaincy for good that Hughes got to lead in a full 'home' series against Pakistan in 1983-84. Australia won the series 2–0. Ideally, they ought to have played their next series against a not-very-formidable opponent, as that would have given Hughes breathing space and time to rebuild the side after the exits of some senior players. Instead, they flew to the Caribbean in early 1984, where they were hit by a cricketing tornado. After achieving two honourable draws, the visitors were blown away in the last three Tests. Barely six months later, the Australians ran into the West Indies again, this time at home. After being thrashed in the first two Tests of the 1984–85 series and his belief in his abilities as captain and batsman completely eroded, Hughes decided that enough was enough. He broke down as he announced his resignation after the second Test at Brisbane.

At the other end of the spectrum was England's Mike Brearley, a contemporary of Hughes. The jury is divided on whether Brearley was a great captain, but there is no doubt that he was lucky. His greatest triumphs as England captain were a 3–1 Ashes win against an Australian team badly crippled by the defections of its frontline cricketers to Kerry Packer's World Series Cricket in 1978–79, and another Ashes win by the same margin in 1981, in which a certain Ian Botham was, to put it as mildly as possible, in an 'inspired' mood with both bat and ball. Brearley never led England against the West Indies, the best team of the time, and the one time he led against a full-strength Australian side in 1979–80, his team was whipped 0–3.

It is also instructive to note how Australia's cricketing establishment treated Hughes' successor. Allan Border did not have a good time of it in his first three seasons in charge, but no effort was spared to help him along the way. Bob Simpson, the former Australian captain, was brought in as cricket manager to support him. Simpson's induction did not make much of a difference initially, as Australia lost to New Zealand and were outplayed in the 1986–87 Ashes. They turned a corner with their unexpected triumph in the 1987 World Cup, played on the Indian subcontinent. A few months after that victory, they were scheduled to tour the West Indies in early 1988 and then play the same team at home in the next season. This programme was eerily like the one of 1984 that had claimed Hughes. There is reason to believe that the Australian Cricket Board drew from its experience of 1984 and cancelled the tour of the Caribbean in 1988. Pakistan toured the West Indies instead and the two teams played a riveting series, which the hosts squared 1–1 by the skin of their teeth.

What Border and his team went on to achieve in the years to follow, starting with the Ashes win in England in 1989, is part of cricketing folklore. However, it cannot be denied that had it not been for the assistance, understanding and even patience that came his way during his early years at the helm, the history of Australian cricket and indeed, that of the game itself in the 1990s, might well have taken a different turn. Just as the Australian establishment learnt from what had gone wrong during Hughes' years at the helm and tried not to repeat those errors with Border, its Indian counterpart also went out of its way to support the man who succeeded Sachin after his second stint as captain.

The final word on Sachin's captaincy prowess—or the lack of it—should go to that individual who did not fare too badly as captain himself.

When I state that my favourite captain is Sachin Tendulkar, people always seem to have a questioning look, because if you look at the numbers, perhaps his stint as captain was not the most successful. But believe me, he was a very good captain indeed. He gave the freedom to newcomers which is required to blossom as a player. He had a young team when he became captain. Rahul Dravid, V.V.S. Laxman, myself, Javagal Srinath, Kumble, we were all in the maturing stage and so we couldn't deliver the way the captain wanted us to. But Sachin as a captain definitely defined my international career. He brought me up the order in the ODI format and gave me the opportunity to open the innings with him. It was the turning point of my life as a cricketer.

—Sourav Ganguly, *Sports Illustrated*, May 2013

THE GOLDEN AGE

During the series against India in 2007, I sat down with Sachin to ask him how he deals with the weight of expectation and the media scrutiny that has been constant for so much of his career, an area that I have struggled with at times. We spent an entire session chatting about how he handles that side of his life. He seemed genuinely excited to be able to help me out and give me advice. I was struck by how humble he was about all he has achieved, how happy he was to help a fellow cricketer and how generous he was with his time.

—Kevin Pietersen, *Sachin Forever*, MCA, 2013

An entire stadium and millions of TV viewers watched Joginder Sharma send down a length ball. As Pakistan's Misbah-ul-Haq made up his mind to play a 'cute' stroke instead of a definitive one and scooped the delivery in the direction of fine-leg, even the commentators went quiet. Like everybody else, they watched the ascent and then the descent of the ball, until Ravi Shastri found his voice: 'Fielder under it…Sreesanth…takes the catch…India win!'

That dismissal in the final over of the final of the inaugural ICC World T20 gave India the title. The World Cup win transformed not just lives and a lot more. For starters, it made an entire nation fall in love with the game's newest and shortest version. The BCCI, which had at no point hesitated from displaying its contempt for the new format, forgot the past and went the other way with a vengeance. India did not so much embrace Twenty20 as hijack it from England, the country that had devised the format.

Mahendra Singh Dhoni's team, which had beaten sides like Pakistan (bowl-out), England, South Africa, Australia and Pakistan again, on the way to the title, was accorded a ticker-tape welcome on their return to India from Johannesburg. The whole of Mumbai turned up on the streets to cheer the heroes as they travelled from the airport to the BCCI headquarters in an open-air double decker bus. The BCCI awarded the players handsome cash prizes, as did several state governments. The victory also sounded the death knell for the rebel Twenty20 league that had enticed many first-class cricketers from across the country.

Even before Dhoni and his team created history, the BCCI had announced its own inter-city league, which it christened the Indian Premier League (IPL), the first edition of which was to be played in April–May 2008. It got a fillip in the form of the victory in South Africa. With the best cricketers in the country and overseas evincing interest in the IPL, it seemed unlikely that the exodus of cricketers to the rebel league would continue.

The triumph marked the official restoration of cricket as the number one sport in the country, after the 50-over World Cup debacle earlier in the year.

The Twenty20 world champions were joined by the seniors who had skipped the tournament for a seven-match ODI series against the reigning 50-over world champions. Australia had the better of the games, but the cricket was overshadowed by some fractious face-offs between players of both sides. The visitors were eager to drive home the message that their loss to India in the semi-final in South Africa was nothing more than an aberration. They were the three-time 50-overs World Cup winners, after all. Having made up their mind to unleash their 'mental disintegration' tactics on the opposition, the Australians then came up against a group that was keen to return the verbals. Matters came to a head in the final ODI at Mumbai, where a spectator was evicted when he was caught on CCTV hurling racial jibes at Andrew Symonds, who had been targeted earlier on the tour as well. Although the camps tried to reach out to each other and mend fences, there was apprehension that something could go wrong during India's full tour of Australia, which was scheduled later in the season.

Sachin, who was among the millions who watched the ICC World Twenty20 final with family and friends and celebrated India's win, was his side's highest run-getter in the ODIs against Australia, with 278 runs from seven games. He carried on his good form in a five-match ODI series against Pakistan, finishing as India's second-highest scorer with 259 runs from five games. India won the series 3–2, but Sachin's fans were far from happy, with their hero still gripped by the 90s jinx. His dismissal for 99 in the second game of the series, played at Mohali on 8 November 2007 was his third at that score in an ODI, and his sixth dismissal in the 90s in an international game since 26 June of the same year.

Fittingly, Anil Kumble led India for the first time in a Test at Delhi's Ferozeshah Kotla. It was here that he had taken 13 wickets in an Irani Cup game to literally gatecrash into the Indian team that toured South Africa in 1992–93, after which he had never looked back, and it was here that he had claimed a Perfect Ten against Pakistan in 1998–99. Against the same team on his captaincy debut in November 2007, he returned match figures of 7–106 as India won an eventful game by six wickets. Sachin fell for just one in the first innings, but he made amends in the second. Arriving at the wicket at 81–2 with India needing 122 more to take a 1–0 lead in the series, Sachin batted with panache to remain unbeaten on 56. During his innings, he went past Allan Border's aggregate of 11,174 to become the second-highest scorer in Tests. Only Brian Lara was ahead of him.

Sachin had another productive outing in the second Test at Kolkata. He scored 82 and three of his teammates reached triple figures. Wasim Jaffer, who had impressed as opener ever since his recall to the Indian team for the series against England in 2005–06, was at his languid and elegant best in an innings of 202, his second double ton in Tests, as was Laxman, who extended his love affair with the Eden with a knock of 112. However, the maximum applause was reserved for Sourav Ganguly, who reached triple figures for the first time in a Test at his home ground. Since the tour of England, the former India captain had batted as if he had a point or two to prove, but like Sachin, he had not quite been able to convert his starts in both forms of the game into big scores. The series against Pakistan was when all came together for him. In the final Test at Bengaluru, which Sachin was forced to miss due to a knee injury, the left-hander batted excellently to score 239, his best in Tests. The series against Pakistan ended with India winning 1–0 and Ganguly's staunchest critics grudgingly acknowledging his resilience. The former India captain wasn't the only left-hander who made a statement of sorts in the Pakistan series. Irfan Pathan scored his maiden Test hundred at Bengaluru and Yuvraj Singh, who had replaced Sachin in the XI for the game, scored a spectacular 169 in the same game. It was a performance that convinced many people that he needed to be drafted into the XI in the Tests in Australia. The Indian middle order, 'born' in 1996, was not getting any younger and it was imperative that chances be given to every candidate who looked competent, to prove himself. Yuvraj had represented the ODI team for seven years, and had three Test centuries to his credit, all of them scored against Pakistan.

Although Yuvraj certainly had the credentials to be given another go in Tests even after Sachin returned to the XI, the fact of the matter was that the team management went overboard. Dravid, who had spent the better part of his career obliging his team's requests to adjust, was now asked to open the innings with Jaffer, so that Yuvraj could be accommodated in the side. The Indians, especially the likes of the new captain and the others who had been on the last two tours of Australia, ought to have known that it wasn't very smart to field a makeshift opening combination in a Test series 'down under', of all places. Not only did the new opening combination fail to deliver, but Yuvraj, batting in the middle order, fell for scores of zero and five. Australia capitalized on the chinks in the Indian armour and before the visitors realized it, the first Test at Melbourne was over in less than four days with the hosts winning by 337 runs. Not for the first time on a tour of Australia, the Indians had had inadequate preparatory time, having played just one four-day game prior to the first Test, but they did themselves no favours by tinkering with the balance of the side.

India's best performer with the bat in the Boxing Day Test was Sachin, who scored 62 in the first innings. The highlight of his innings was a calculated assault on Brad Hogg, the left-arm chinaman bowler; Sachin played him with the turn, taking the aerial route on the leg-side and forcing him to remove the close-in fielders. He was also fluent against the other bowlers, but he had little support. Scores of 196 and 161 hardly did the visitors any credit.

The New Year Test at Sydney witnessed some remarkable cricket and deplorable happenings. India put forth a spirited response to Australia's first-innings total of 463. Dravid, who opened the innings again, was more successful this time around, scoring 53, but the show was stolen by two batsmen who loved the Sydney Cricket Ground. Both Sachin and V.V.S. Laxman scored the third century of their respective Test careers at the venue.

Sachin did not impose as many restrictions on himself as he had during his unbeaten 241 at the venue, four years previously. He deployed all the strokes that were a part of his repertoire, including the cover-drive that he had put in cold storage four years previously, as well as the uppercut, which he essayed to splendid effect off Brett Lee, utilising the bowler's extra pace to help the ball along to the fence. The entire Indian team cheered from the balcony when he pushed Stuart Clark off the back foot between mid-off and cover for two, to break the 90s jinx. Far more relieved than him were his teammates and fans. He remained unbeaten on 154.

That evening, Sachin called up the man who had given him a pep talk nine months previously, at a time when he was contemplating retirement in the wake of all the jibes that were being hurled at him after India's first-round exit from the 2007 World Cup. He expressed his gratitude to Sir Vivian Richards for his encouragement during what had been a tough time.

For all his poise and panache, Sachin would have been stranded before completing his 38th Test century had Harbhajan Singh not matched him stroke-for-stroke in a stand of 129 for the eighth wicket. The off-spinner was positive and pugnacious, hitting the fast bowlers down the ground and belting them off his hips in front of square on the leg-side. It was during their stand that all hell broke loose. Harbhajan was in the middle of a repartee with Lee that was anything but unfriendly, when Andrew Symonds, with whom he had crossed swords in India, butted in and said something nasty. Harbhajan, never one to take a backward step, retorted with a comment that Symonds and his teammates construed as 'racist'. Ricky Ponting, the Australian captain, got involved, as did the umpires, to whom the comment was reported. Mark Benson, one of the umpires, then had a word with Harbhajan. The umpires subsequently reported the issue to Mike Procter, the match referee, who scheduled a hearing on the final day of the game.

The cornering of Harbhajan turned out to be just one of many frustrating episodes during the Test for the visitors. Both Symonds and Ponting had survived confident caught-behind shouts on the first day, with Symonds, who went on to score 162, adding insult to injury by admitting at the end-of-day media conference that he had nicked the ball. Four absorbing days of cricket later, Australia set India 333 to win in a minimum of 72 overs on the last day. The visitors decided to put down the shutters.

India lost their first three wickets with only 54 on the board. When Sachin played on to Stuart Clark, it was the first time he had been dismissed at the SCG in a Test since January 2000; his batting average at the venue came down to 249 from 326. The Australians sensed victory at this point, but in Rahul Dravid, India had just the man to take them through to the close. He batted resolutely to take the team past three figures, and was on 38 when he was handed a dubious caught-behind decision off Symonds, despite the ball having come off the knee-roll of his front pad, with his bat nowhere in the picture. Symonds then struck again at the same score, dismissing Yuvraj for his second duck of the series. Matters got progressively worse for the visitors when Ganguly, who completed his second 50 of the game, was deemed caught at slip despite the TV replays suggesting that the ball had touched the turf even as it was clasped by the fielder. Ricky Ponting, the Australian captain, checked with the fielder concerned and 'declared' the batsman out, at which point Mark Benson also raised his finger. When Ponting himself claimed a catch a little later, despite the TV pictures and replays indicating that the cherry had hit the turf after he got his right hand to it, there was bewilderment in the Indian ranks. Had catches taken on the half-volley suddenly become legitimate?

India still ought to have saved the game, but Michael Clarke snared three wickets in what was supposed to be the penultimate over. The Australians were besides themselves with joy after winning their 16th Test in a row, but the Indians were livid. At the post-match media briefing, Ponting reacted as self-righteously as he was expected to, when the Indian scribes posed uncomfortable questions. When Kumble got his turn to face the media, he elicited applause by declaring that only one team had played in the spirit of the game.

The mood in the Indian camp did not improve when Harbhajan was slapped with a three-Test ban for allegedly calling Symonds a 'monkey', a word that had racial overtones. The match referee heard the players' and umpires' versions of the on-field altercation after the end of the Test and implicated Harbhajan at the end of it all. The racism charge hurt the Indians deeply and the team stayed put in Sydney on the day after the Test, instead of proceeding to Canberra for its next game of the tour. Like the Mike Denness controversy of 2001, the issue hit the headlines back in India. The BCCI lodged an appeal against the sentence and requested V.R. Manohar, one of the most astute legal brains in India, to argue its side.

> The team and I spoke to both Sachin and Harbhajan.... We understood that Bhajji had been treated badly.... There was a feeling in the majority of the squad that we should go back home.... I felt that we should stay back and handle the issue. I spoke to Sachin and I knew that if he was convinced then it was easier to convince Bhajji. We had our discussions and stayed back.
>
> —Anil Kumble, *The Sportstar,* 26 October 2013

The Indian team proceeded to Perth, the venue of the third Test, after lodging the appeal. A second hearing, to be presided by Justice John Hansen, was scheduled after the fourth Test at Adelaide. Harbhajan was permitted to play the third Test, but he was left out of the playing XI on a track expected to favour the quicks. The Indian captain was to be his side's lone specialist spinner in the game.

There was a new face in the Indian dressing room in the West Australian city. Gary Kirsten, the former South African opening batsman, had joined the squad after being formally appointed coach a few weeks earlier.

After Kumble won the toss and elected to bat, two of the four former Test captains in the Indian XI batted superbly to enable their team to total a competitive 330. On the same piece of turf where he had scored a life-altering 114,16 years previously, Sachin batted with pluck to score 71. The teenager who had belted the likes of McDermott, Merv Hughes and Mike Whitney to the distant corners of the WACA in February 1992, successfully weathered a storm called Brett Lee in January 2008. The one stroke that stood out in the bout was an uppercut that Sachin directed over the wicketkeeper's head. He had initially aimed to guide the ball over the slips, but the cherry reared into him at tremendous pace. Most batsmen would have instinctively taken their eyes off the ball and tried to take evasive action, but Sachin was in the zone. He saw the cherry all the way and met it with his bat right in front of his face. Adam Gilchrist could only watch as the ball cleared him comfortably.

Dravid was livid at losing his wicket to an impetuous shot after batting classily to score 93. Ganguly missed out, falling for only nine, but Virender Sehwag, playing his first Test in 12 months, injected urgency at the top of the order with a quickfire 29. He owed his presence in the team to Kumble. Despite his not figuring in the probables for the tour, the Indian captain insisted on his inclusion, and the Dilip Vengsarkar-led panel obliged. After missing the first two Tests, Sehwag was picked ahead of Yuvraj for the third, with Dravid restored to his number three spot.

The Indian bowlers then did themselves proud by bowling the hosts out for 212. The Australian bowlers hit back in the second innings, dismissing half the Indian side with only 125 on the board, before V.V.S. Laxman combined with the lower order to produce another classic in a crisis. He was last out for 79. The Australians needed 413 to win. They were 65–2 at the end of day three.

Saturday, 19 January 2008, commenced with the teenage quick Ishant Sharma, who had got a chance to play only because Zaheer Khan had had to return home due to injury after the first Test, tying no less a batsman than Ricky Ponting in knots. The Australian captain came perilously close to getting out at least a couple of times, but he hung on. After grilling and interrogating Ponting for seven overs, Ishant was asked to take a break. However, Sehwag, his Delhi captain, suggested that the youngster not be taken off, as he was used to bowling long spells; Kumble agreed. Off the very first ball of his next over, he induced Ponting to nibble at one that pitched on the off-stump and climbed, and Dravid took a low catch at slip.

There was no stopping the visitors after that. Symonds, who had become Kumble's 600th Test victim in the first innings, fell to the same bowler again. Michael Hussey was leg-before to R.P. Singh and both Gilchrist and Lee fell to Sehwag, whose introduction into the attack seemed to have taken the Australians by surprise, in much the same way as Ganguly's move to bring on Sachin on the last day of the Kolkata Test in 2001. Michael Clarke scored 81 before Kumble beat him in the air and Dhoni did the rest. The tail-enders swung their bats around, but it was only a matter of time before the inevitable happened. When R.P. Singh breached the defence of Shaun Tait, it was all over. India had achieved what even their most diehard fans could not have imagined even a decade previously—a Test victory on one of the fastest wickets on the planet, at the WACA, Perth.

Sachin, who many people were convinced was playing his last series in Australia, capped another successful tour of the country with an immaculate century in the first innings of the final Test at Adelaide.

Sachin's approach was tailored to the situation at hand. Coming in at 82-2, he assessed the conditions and concluded that the ball was not coming onto the bat as it usually did at the Adelaide Oval. After being watchful for close to three overs, he got the circulation in his feet going with delectable drives off Brett Lee and Mitchell Johnson. The strokes were deliberately delayed until the ball had virtually passed the front pad and Sachin had figured out exactly how the cherry was behaving. After targeting the 'V' initially, he shifted his energies to behind square on both sides of the wicket, keeping the men behind the wicketkeeper busy with sweeps, paddle sweeps and off-glances. As he neared his second hundred of the series, he once again focussed on the area in front of the wicket. In what was the final segment of an innings in which he had literally toyed with the bowling and the field settings, he and Dhoni biffed 27 runs off 21 deliveries. Sachin was eventually dismissed by Lee for 153, a knock that comprised 13 boundaries and three sixes. He was aided by Laxman, Kumble, Harbhajan and Sehwag, all of whom scored 50s.

Australia replied to India's 526 with a total of 563. The Indian batsmen struggled in the second innings, with the notable exception of Sehwag, who completed his rehabilitation in Test cricket with an unbeaten 151, following up on his 63 in the first innings. The match was drawn and Australia retained the Border–Gavaskar Trophy.

A few hours after losing the series 1–2, the Indians registered a significant victory off the field, when their appeal against Harbhajan's ban was upheld and the sentence on the off-spinner reduced from a three-match ban to a fine of 50 per cent of his match fee for 'using offensive language not amounting to racism'. Sachin told Justice Hansen, who was presiding over the hearing, that he had overheard a heated exchange between Harbhajan and Symonds that was initiated by the Australian. He also said that he had heard Harbhajan using an Indian profanity that sounded like 'monkey'.

The Australians were far from happy at the turn of events. Ricky Ponting, in his 2013 autobiography, wondered why Sachin had not mentioned all this to Mike Procter during the first hearing.

However, Sachin in his autobiography has mentioned that he recounted the incident at length to the match referee during the hearing on the last day of the Sydney Test. There was little scope for the Australians to know what Sachin had or had not said to the referee during that hearing, as Procter had got the representatives of both sides to testify separately. The Indian take on the first hearing was that Procter had chosen to believe the Australian version of the events. The visitors were delighted to have their player exonerated of charges of racial abuse at the second hearing.

There was a queer footnote to the proceedings at Adelaide; Justice Hansen was quoted as saying that he had not been informed about Harbhajan's previous 'offences' by the ICC; the implication was that the sentence slapped on Harbhajan could well have been a lot harsher had he been briefed comprehensively.

Their resurgence in the Test series notwithstanding, India began the tri-series against Australia and Sri Lanka, winners and runners-up respectively in the ICC Cricket World Cup 2007, as the rank underdogs. The decision of the selectors to jettison the likes of Ganguly and Dravid from the limited-overs squad had not gone down too well with fans back home, and apprehensions were reinforced when Dhoni's side—minus Sachin—lost a one-off T20 International to Australia by nine wickets.

However, Mahendra Singh Dhoni had the last laugh. India's campaign got underway only in their third league game of the tournament, after their first two games were washed out. The pace triumvirate of Sreesanth, Irfan and Ishant packed the Australians off for 159, after Ponting opted to bat. The Indian supporters had an early scare when Sehwag fell off the last ball of the fourth over, but the events of the very next over relaxed them totally.

The second ball of Brett Lee's third over of the game was fuller in length and pitched outside off-stump. Sachin pounced on it and drilled it slightly uppishly between the fielders at point and cover. A couple of minutes later, the Indian supporters, who were still relishing their hero's square drive, were joined by their Australian counterparts in appreciating a stunner of a straight drive that rocketed past Lee on his follow-through; the bowler did not have the time to even consider sticking out a foot to try and stop it. Sachin, on his part, made no attempt to run after executing the stroke. He did not need to.

An impeccable back-foot defensive stroke later, the legend produced his pièce de résistance—another straight drive, this time between the umpire and the non-striker. As it turned out, those three strokes off four balls in the same Brett Lee over were the only boundaries that Sachin hit that evening. With wickets going down at regular intervals at the other end, he opted for a cautious approach and kept the scoreboard ticking along. He was on 44 when he was fourth out at 96, and the Australians sensed a chance, but the young Rohit Sharma closed out the game in the company of Dhoni.

India won only two more games at the league stage—both against Sri Lanka—but the team still qualified for the best-of-three finals, upping the ante in the must-win encounter against the Lankans at Hobart and gaining a precious bonus point, which enabled them to take a lead over their co-Asians in the points table. Sachin starred in the game, scoring 63 and helping India overhaul a target of 180 with more than 17 overs to spare.

The presence of Dhoni and Pathan had enabled the Indians to enjoy the luxury of playing as many as five specialist bowlers in most of the league matches. The best-of-three finals were no different. The bowlers did their job splendidly in the first final at Sydney, restricting the Australians to 239–8 in the first final at Sydney. The hosts then came up against the colossus. The innings that Sachin essayed on the evening of 2 March 2008 was not as thrilling as the one he had played against Pakistan at Centurion exactly five years previously, but it was every bit as decisive. He lost Robin Uthappa, his newest opening partner, at 50, Gautam Gambhir at 56 and Yuvraj at 87, but the blows made no difference. Neither did they provide any delight to the Australians, who sensed that the hero was in one of those moods. Rohit Sharma, who replaced Yuvraj in the middle, put his head down to provide the kind of support that Sachin had sought.

Sachin refused to be deterred by the pain in the groin area that he had been experiencing since his match-winning 44 at Melbourne. Investigations revealed that there was an issue with his adductor muscles. On the eve of the first final, he was barely able to move, but his determination won the day. He had pumped himself with painkillers and was fighting hard to focus on the task at hand. For the second time in that Australian summer, the Sydney crowd rose when he completed a century, his first in an ODI on Australian soil. Rohit Sharma contributed 66 to a fourth-wicket association of 123, and Dhoni came in to finish off the match in the company of his team's talisman.

The energy that had gone into his unbeaten 117 and the pain in his adductors ensured that Sachin was virtually immobile in the lead-up to the second final at Brisbane. He vetoed Dhoni's suggestion of skipping the game and playing the third final if needed. The pain wasn't going to stop him from trying to accomplish something that had eluded him on three previous visits to the land of the reigning world champions.

His teammates, all of whom had grown up idolising him, could only watch in awe as Sachin proceeded to defy his physical discomfiture with an innings of 91. His teammates batted around him and left Australia with 259 to get. The hosts started disastrously, with Gilchrist, Ponting and Clarke falling cheaply to Praveen Kumar, a seamer from Uttar Pradesh who had been a revelation in the latter half of the tournament. The way he bowled in the last league game against Sri Lanka and the two finals, it was as if he had tied the ball to a string and was making it dart around at will. The Australians never recovered from their poor beginning, although Hayden, Symonds, Hussey and James Hopes got off to starts. Poetic justice of sorts was achieved when Hayden, who had called Harbhajan Singh 'an obnoxious weed' earlier in the season, was run out and Symonds leg-before, with the Indian off-spinner being involved in both dismissals. Hopes brought his side to within 10 runs of the target before he was caught by Piyush Chawla off Irfan in the penultimate over. Never had an Indian team won a triangular series on Australian soil before. The last time they had won any series 'down under' was in 1985, when Sunil Gavaskar's team had triumphed in the World Championship of Cricket.

Sachin was thrilled to have struck a key item off his bucket list. Had Australia won the second final, he would have found it very difficult, if not impossible, to play the third final.

It took him a while to overcome the adductor affliction. He managed to play the first Test of the subsequent series against South Africa at Chennai, but was forced to pull out of the next two Tests. A high-scoring draw, the highlight of the Chennai Test was an innings of 319 by Virender Sehwag, his second triple hundred in Tests. It seemed unbelievable that he had missed nearly a year of Test cricket owing to poor form.

Sachin worked hard to bounce back in time for the start of the inaugural season of the Indian Premier League. He was the designated 'icon' player and captain of what was christened the 'Mumbai Indians'. Acquired by Reliance Industries Ltd for US$111.9, the Mumbai-based team was the most expensive of the eight city-based, franchise-owned squads that were to play each other in the first three seasons. Sachin had for company the likes of Sanath Jayasuriya, Shaun Pollock, Dwayne Bravo and Harbhajan Singh.

The first season of the IPL commenced on 18 April 2008, with Royal Challengers Bangalore playing a home game against the Kolkata Knight Riders. The inter-franchise tournament was a runaway success. India had come a long way since 1987, when prominent international cricketers like David Gower, Sir Richard Hadlee and Malcolm Marshall had skipped the World Cup that was played on the subcontinent. Thanks to the IPL and the riches it assured the cricketers, it was apparent that stars from across the world would give an arm and leg to figure in the event. So swiftly and overwhelmingly did the masses embrace the tournament and its format that the pundits and cricketers themselves were left flummoxed.

Unfortunately for the Mumbai Indians, they were deprived of the services of their captain for the first five games. In Sachin's absence, Harbhajan took over the captaincy. A post-game altercation with Sreesanth, who was representing the Mohali-based Kings XI Punjab, resulted in the off-spinner being suspended from the remainder of the season. Shaun Pollock then assumed charge.

Despite a late resurgence after a poor beginning, the Mumbai Indians failed to make it to the knockout stage. Jayasuriya, who scored an incredible hundred against the Chennai Super Kings in what was Sachin's first game of the tournament, became a friend. He would often have 20–30 kg of seafood flown in from Colombo for his captain during the tournament.

A foodie in the truest sense of the term, it was only the demands of international cricket and the emphasis on fitness that prevented Sachin from letting himself go when it came to indulging himself in gastronomical delights, during his playing days. He relished almost every variety—Indian as well as international—that he got the opportunity to sample, with Japanese delicacies like sushi and sashimi also figuring high on the list. Cooking was also a passion, with people swearing by the baingan ka bharta, fish curry and prawn masala prepared by him. His culinary guru was and is his mother Rajani Tendulkar, whose varan-bhaat stands head and shoulders above all his favourite dishes.

As much a music lover as he was one of food and automobiles, a memorable moment for Sachin was when he traded a bat for a guitar with Mark Knopfler, the co-founder, lead singer and guitarist of Dire Straits, one of his favourite bands.

The success of the IPL in its inaugural season helped obscure a drawback, which was likely to have an adverse effect in the long run. The tournament was far too long. In its first season, it featured 59 matches, played over seven weeks in eight cities in the heat and humidity of April–May; it was natural that a format in which each team was scheduled to play a minimum of 14 matches would tax the players, physically and mentally. From even the most diehard cricket lover's point of view, it was too much cricket. It was not very surprising that the Indian team failed to make it past the first round of the ICC World Twenty20 tournaments in 2009 and 2010, both of which were played immediately after the conclusion of the IPL; the players were exhausted.

Sachin missed a couple of limited-overs tournaments that followed the IPL, but he was back for the Test series in Sri Lanka after undergoing treatment for what was diagnosed as 'Gilmore's Groin', in Germany. Unlike the IPL, which most of the Indian cricketers lapped up despite the hectic schedule, they did not quite take a fancy to another innovation in the sport.

The India–Sri Lanka Test series was the first to feature the Umpire Decision Review System (UDRS), which gave teams the option of 'reviewing' a select number of decisions taken by the field umpire, by asking the latter to seek the feedback of the TV umpire. It was believed that the UDRS would help in terms of getting potentially controversial decisions right. However, the Indian players were not very happy with what they perceived as 'inconsistencies' within the system, and their arguments were endorsed by the BCCI. The Board consequently refused to adopt the system in its bilateral series, only changing its stance after eight years.

In the Emerald Isles, India lost the first and third Tests, but played some terrific cricket to win the second. Their star was Virender Sehwag, who carried his bat through the first innings to remain unbeaten on 201. He was the only Indian batsman to hold his own against the 'mystery spinner' Ajantha Mendis, who along with Muttiah Muralitharan won the series for Sri Lanka.

Sachin then skipped the ODI series in a bid to resolve his abdominal issues once and for all, and he underwent a Hernia surgery in Munich. The two operations were successful and he spent a frustrating time at home, unable to play with his children. Once the pain in his abdominal area abated and he was given the go-ahead to train, he went at it like a man possessed. For three weeks, he worked out at the National Cricket Academy in Bengaluru, doing a combination of cardio and strengthening exercises. His efforts, as also those put in by the staff who were working with him, paid off. He felt fit and confident on the eve of the 2008–09 edition of the Border–Gavaskar Trophy.

The series was to commence at Bengaluru. Two days before the first Test, the journalists who had congregated at the M. Chinnaswamy Stadium to cover the pre-match media briefings of both teams, were overjoyed when Sourav Ganguly, an all-time favourite of the Fourth Estate, made an appearance on behalf of his side. After receiving his replies on their questions pertaining to the preparations of the team for the Test and series, the journalists were in the process of packing up when the former India captain, almost as an after-thought, informed them that he was to retire at the end of the Australia series. The proceedings, which had been rather desultory till that stage even by Ganguly's standards, suddenly sprung to life. There was a scramble for quotes and some individuals even turned emotional.

If a cricketer's proficiency was to be evaluated in terms of the state of the team when he joined it and its standing in international cricket when he decided to move on, then Ganguly stood right at the top, both as batsman and as captain. He had been part of—and for several years had led—a group that had revolutionized Indian cricket.

Ganguly's fans rued his decision to retire, particularly as he had been in the form of his life in the previous season. However, the outgoing selection committee, which had ironically reinstated him in the side for the South Africa tour in 2006–07, had sent out mixed signals by not picking him in the Rest of India squad that played Delhi in the Irani Cup game at the start of the 2008–09 season. Virtually every member of the Indian team who was not a Delhite was part of the Rest squad, but not Ganguly. This sparked off speculation that he would miss the Tests against Australia, but the newly appointed selection committee, chaired by K. Srikkanth, retained him in the Test squad. The uncertainty and his omission from the limited-overs squad at the beginning of the year may well have contributed to Ganguly's decision to quit.

The first Test at Bengaluru was drawn, after Australia's old friend Harbhajan Singh and a rejuvenated Zaheer Khan bailed their team out with half-centuries from a potentially hazardous situation. Kumble missed the second Test at Mohali due to a shoulder injury, and M.S. Dhoni took over. The Indians totalled 469 in the first innings, with Ganguly scoring what would be his last Test hundred. Sachin got a flawless 88, during which, he surpassed Brian Lara's tally of 11,953 to become the highest scorer in Test cricket.* The icing on the cake was Sachin's completion of 12,000 Test runs during the same innings. The Indians then bowled splendidly, with Amit Mishra, the debutant leg-spinner, being the stand out performer with match figures of 7–106. The hosts won by 320 runs.

The next Test, played at Delhi, was drawn.

V.V.S. Laxman, in his 99th Test, scored the second double ton of his career. Sachin chipped in with 68. The game ended with Anil Kumble joining his former captain in the ranks of the 'retired'. India's greatest bowler drew the curtains on a glorious career at his favourite ground.

There was a significant happening in Nagpur, on the evening before the fourth Test got underway. The selectors had gathered at the hotel where the teams were staying to pick the Indian squad for the first half of the seven-match ODI series against England, whose team had already landed in India. Waiting outside their chamber, was this writer, in his capacity as Manager—Media Relations and Corporate Affairs of the Board, and a couple of officials. This writer's brief was to draft a media release mentioning the names that had made it to the squad.

---

*Gavaskar became the highest scorer in Tests against the West Indies at Ahmedabad in 1983–84.

Considering India's successes in their last ODI series in Sri Lanka, the meeting was not expected to last long, but it did. This writer and the officials who were with him were nonplussed when they started receiving frantic calls from the media, specifically asking them whether Sachin had been included in the team or not. It appeared that someone had tipped off the media that a significant development was in the offing. Even as they were negotiating the calls and advising the callers to wait for the media release to be issued, Sachin emerged from one of the lifts with a member of the support staff and made his way into the chamber; it seemed as if the selectors had called him downstairs for a discussion. After a while, it was officially announced that Sachin had sought the permission of the Board to skip the first three games, and the Board had agreed.

It subsequently came to light that Sachin had been diagnosed with golfer's elbow, a condition that was hearteningly not as serious as its tennis counterpart. However, it did necessitate a phase of rest. Sachin was understandably keener to be at his best in India's forthcoming tussles in the traditional version, as also the full tour of New Zealand in the new year. He wasn't getting younger, but his commitment had not diminished, and with both the Test and limited-overs squads in excellent shape, the Board indicated that he was most welcome to take a break whenever he wished. It was the least the BCCI could have done for someone who had served Indian cricket with diligence and distinction. There was of course, an understanding that Sachin would choose his hiatuses judiciously.

The Board officials, most of whom had watched and followed Sachin's career over the decades, also recognized the fact that the man who had taken over as captain in all three formats thought the world of Sachin; while his contemporaries had either retired or been excluded from the limited-overs side, Sachin was an integral part of the group that Dhoni had led to a famous victory in Australia, even more so than his junior Sehwag, who had been left out of the playing XI for the two finals. With the captain of the team valuing not only the veteran's proficiency but also his presence in the side, it was paramount to ensure his longevity and 'save' him for high-stake battles.

Sachin scored his 40th Test century on the first day of the Nagpur Test. The new cricket stadium in the 'Orange' city could not have asked for a more memorable baptism. His footwork was splendid and he did not hold himself back from playing his signature strokes. Fortune favoured him when he was put down once in the 1980s and then in the 1990s, off Jason Krejza, the off-spinner. The Australians did manage to keep him on 99 for a fair bit, till Krejza gave him some width, only to be cut imperiously for four.

Later in the day, Sachin was the recipient of a magnificent trophy, encrusted with 316 Belgian diamonds, for becoming the founder member of Test cricket's 'Class of 12,000'.

Ganguly scored 85 in his penultimate Test innings for India, and the hosts reached 441. Dhoni, who had enjoyed a great series with the bat, scored 56 in his first game after his official appointment as India's Test captain.

The Australians replied with 355. They could have scored a lot more after being 189–2 at stumps on day two, but they were outsmarted by India's new captain. Spurred on by Sachin, Dhoni pushed the fielders back and at one point, placed as many as eight of them in the outfield on the off-side. The bowlers were then instructed to bowl to the field, which they did very well, and the run-rate reduced substantially. The Indians were vindicated when the wickets started falling.

The Australians kept fighting, and they would have fancied their chances of squaring the series when they reduced India to 224–7 in the second innings. Dhoni then came to the rescue, along with Harbhajan Singh, who seemed to enjoy both batting and bowling against Australia. Earlier in the game, he had become the third Indian to take 300 Test wickets when he bowled Ricky Ponting. The Australian captain's thrust for a win was undone by an atrocious over-rate, which made it unavoidable for him to hold his pacemen back and try out his non-regular bowlers who had shorter run-ups, to try and catch up. India escaped and set the visitors a target of 382. Harbhajan and Mishra then shared seven wickets between them as India completed a win by 170 runs.

More than the batsmen, India owed their 2–0 triumph to their bowlers. Zaheer Khan and Ishant Sharma had been exceptional with both the new and old ball right through the series. The frontline spinners did not give the Australians any breathing space either, and when Harbhajan missed the Delhi Test, Kumble employed Sehwag's off-spin for 40 overs. The Delhi opener repaid his captain's faith with figures of 5–104.

India's new Test captain endeared himself to millions with two exemplary gestures in Nagpur. When Australia's last pair was at the crease, he requested Ganguly to 'take over', and the former India captain directed operations for a while. It was an extraordinary tribute to an extraordinary cricketer and captain. At the presentation ceremony, Dhoni insisted that Anil Kumble, who had flown to Nagpur at the insistence of the team, accompanied him to receive the Border-Gavaskar Trophy from the legends themselves, both of whom were in Nagpur as part of the TV commentary team.

The seven ODIs against England were to be followed by two Tests, the second of which was to be played at the Brabourne Stadium in Mumbai. The

Wankhede, which had been allotted the final of the 2011 World Cup, was practically being rebuilt from scratch and was hence not available. The BCCI had smartly scheduled the Test against England in such a way that it coincided with the dates of what had been the first-ever Test match on Indian soil—the four-day game between India and England at the Bombay Gymkhana Ground, which had been played from 15 December to 18 December in 1933, exactly 75 years previously. The Board had made elaborate plans to celebrate the Platinum Jubilee of Test cricket in India at the Bombay Gymkhana itself, on the eve of the Test. However, that was not to be.

Even as India were taking a 5–0 lead in the ODI series with a win at Cuttack, the city of Mumbai was attacked by Pakistani terrorists. Hundreds of innocents were massacred before the assailants could be neutralized. The immediate fallout of 26/11 was the cancellation of the last two ODIs and the Platinum Jubilee celebrations.

In what was a stinging slap to the proponents of terrorism, England agreed to play the Tests at alternate venues. Security was beefed up and the matches were shifted from Ahmedabad and Mumbai to Chennai and Mohali, respectively.

Cricket fans in India, all of whom could not thank the England team enough, did not grudge the visitors their fine showing on the first three-and-a-half days of the Chennai Test. The hosts took a first-innings lead of 75, and in their second innings, Andrew Strauss completed his second century of the game and Paul Collingwood also got a hundred, following which, Kevin Pietersen, the England captain, declared at 311–9. India had a minimum of 126 overs in which to score 387 to win. Pietersen was in fact criticized by some members of the TV Commentary team for not declaring 30–40 runs earlier. The highest target to have been chased successfully in a Test on Indian soil was 276.

On the fourth afternoon of the Chennai Test, the England bowlers did not quite know what hit them as India's only triple centurion in Tests pounded and pummelled them to every corner of the playing arena and occasionally beyond it. By the time Sehwag fell for 83, scored off only 68 deliveries, the match had turned on its head. He had literally stolen the psychological advantage from the other dressing room and implanted it in Indian heads. At the end-of-day media conference that evening, Gambhir left no one in any doubt that his team would be going for a win, the deteriorating pitch and the prowess of Graeme Swann and Monty Panesar, England's spin-twins, notwithstanding.

Exactly seven years previously, India had displayed neither the drive nor the desire to go for a target of 374 that England had set for them in a Test at Ahmedabad. But then, that team did not have Sehwag as opener, and it also did not have as impressive a record in Tests as its counterpart of 2008, which had excelled at home as well as overseas.

To press home the advantage, India needed to keep wickets intact till the last session-and-a-half of the game. But England struck early on the fifth day, with Dravid, who had not been in the best of form, nicking Flintoff to the keeper. The score was 141–2 when Sachin came in. He opened his account with an uppish flick that flew past the fielder at forward short-leg. By the time mid-on caught up with the cherry in the vacant mid-wicket region, the batsmen had completed a two. When Flintoff pitched one short and outside the off-stump, Sachin cut him ferociously for four to bring up the 150 of the innings. Against the off-spin of Graeme Swann, the talisman unveiled his deftness, paddling him around the corner with precise and unexaggerated movements and then sweeping him to the boundary. The running between wickets was excellent, with Gambhir responding to his senior's calls with alacrity. The opener was third out at 183, for a well-compiled 66, when Collingwood caught him brilliantly in the slips off Anderson.

Sachin's response to the wicket was a delightful uppercut over the slips' heads off the same bowler. He watched the ball, pitched short, till the very end and gave it the treatment. At lunch, India were 213–3.

The first hour of the second session would determine the outcome of the game. England started well, with Swann having Laxman caught in the close-in cordon. The score at that stage was 224–4. Yuvraj Singh, the next man in, watched his senior partner essay a reverse straight drive off Monty Panesar, dispatching a widish delivery down the leg-side right through the keeper's legs for four. A little later, Panesar overcompensated by pitching one short. Sachin pounced on it and pulled it handsomely over square-leg for four.

Even as Yuvraj got his feet moving, Sachin was lucky to survive a leg-before appeal by Steve Harmison. He was struck in line just over the knee-roll of his front pad, and some umpires might well have given a decision in the bowler's favour. However, umpire Daryl Harper stayed unmoved. Replays revealed that he had made an outstanding decision, as the ball would have most probably sailed over the bails. A back-foot tap to cover and a quick call enabled Sachin to complete his 52nd Test 50. The knock comprised as many as 25 singles, an indication of how well he had paced his innings and placed the ball around. The score was 261–4.

The batsmen concentrated on keeping the scoreboard ticking with ones and twos. They became more assertive when the target was reduced to less than a hundred. Sachin drilled Swann over the infield, the ball bouncing just before it crossed the long-on boundary.

The new ball was taken when the target was 77 runs away. England fought on, with Swann and Panesar doing their best to exploit the variable bounce in the fifth-day track. Sachin was beaten on more than one occasion, but that did not deter him from resorting to the paddle-sweep whenever the opportunity presented itself. As marvellous as his paddles was a defensive stroke that he offered to Swann, shortly after the 300 of the innings had been posted. The ball kept low after pitching, and Sachin, mindful of the close-in fielders breathing down his neck, played it with loose hands; Sunil Gavaskar, watching from the commentary box, would have approved.

The noise emanating from the stands got louder as the shadows across the M.A. Chidambaram Stadium got lengthier. A final flourish came in the form of back-to-back boundaries off Panesar; Sachin entered the 90s with a paddle-sweep, and he cover-drove the very next ball for four. He had moved to 96 and the target was only 11 runs away. By the time he had moved to 99, the target was five runs away. Nobody had noticed that Yuvraj Singh had batted quite brilliantly to score 84, his alleged susceptibility to spin conspicuous by its absence.

Sachin had another close shave when he got a glove to an attempted pull off Panesar and the ball not only missed the bails by very little, but also eluded the gloves of Matthew Prior, who had taken evasive action. A single by Yuvraj brought him back to strike. It was a scriptwriter's dream scenario—India needed four to win, and Sachin needed one run to complete his 41st Test century, and surely one that he would cherish for a long, long time. Would he achieve both with the same stroke?

He did. With a paddle-sweep that crossed the boundary and marked the end of the highest successful run-chase in a Test on the subcontinent. In what was an extraordinary coincidence, he had achieved the same individual score—103—against the same team in an innings of the Ahmedabad Test, in which India had preferred to play for a draw rather than try to reach a target that was 13 runs lesser than what they had achieved at Chennai in December 2008.

As the spectators went ballistic, Sachin permitted himself a whoop of delight and punched the air. Yuvraj, the unsung hero, ran across to his partner and picked him up. Sachin shook hands with the England players and then bent to touch the pitch, almost surreptitiously. It wasn't the last time he would express his reverence for a cricket pitch like this.

As he plucked out a stump to keep as a souvenir, Sachin was mobbed by members of the ground staff. In all the games he had played at Chennai, he had never seen them as excited. He had never heard the crowd cheer so animatedly. Probably it had something to do with what the country had been through recently, he thought.

> I think this is a very, very important hundred, because if the team wins, then the hundred becomes very, very special, and today, this hundred is right among the top ones.... What happened in Mumbai was extremely unfortunate.... These hundreds will give a certain amount of happiness to people, but it is very hard to recover from what happened in Mumbai.... I would like to take this opportunity to thank everybody who stood up and made sure that the terrorists were captured and killed.... I would like to salute the jawans, the hotel staff, the navy, the NSG [National Security Guard], firemen, everybody.... Coming to cricket, which is a lesser thing compared to what has happened, I feel whatever we can contribute in a small manner, we have been able to do that.... We are with the people who lost their dear ones.
>
> —Sachin Tendulkar, post-match TV interview

Like his unbeaten 117 in the second final of the tri-series in Australia earlier in the year, Sachin's unbeaten 103 against England at Chennai enabled him to tick off another item from his bucket list. The ghost of Chennai 1999 had been exorcised for good.

India took the series when the second Test at Mohali ended in a draw. Gambhir came very close to scoring a century in both innings, being dismissed for 97 in the second innings after getting 179 in the first, and Rahul Dravid ended a barren patch with a knock of 136. For England, Pietersen scored an outstanding 144. Unlike several England sides of preceding decades, the visitors did not grumble or whine. On the contrary, they had displayed exemplary professionalism, playing the Test series at a time when no Indian could have found fault with them had they decided to call off the series, citing safety concerns. The visitors also donated half their match fees from the first Test to the relief fund that had been set up for the victims of the attacks. So well did they imbibe the lessons that they learnt on the 2008–09 tour that they produced some exceptional cricket on their next visit in 2012–13.

The England series marked the end of an unforgettable and eventful year for Indian cricket. There was nothing the 12 months of 2008 had not witnessed—exceptional team and individual performances, controversies, retirements of all-time greats and the advent of a competition that took the cricketing world by storm.

Despite 19 years of international cricket, the hero was reluctant to look back. He had set his eyes on fresh targets. He was aware that he could no longer take his body for granted as he could, say 15 years previously. But he also knew that he still possessed the single-minded commitment to perform. There was still a lot of fuel left in the tank.

> There was a little dip for me, around 2005 and 2006. I had a lot of injuries—finger and elbow injuries and then a back injury. All these upper-body injuries may have altered my backswing a little. But that is behind me now and I have been able to put in the hours of practice I need.
>
> —Sachin Tendulkar, *Hindustan Times*, 31 October 2010

INTERNATIONAL CRICKETER OF THE YEAR

The daily drills, the emphasis on exercise, keeping one's eye on a diet—doing all this for a quarter of a century is well nigh unimaginable.... If his cricketing shots were textbook, his behaviour can also be termed as a manual for good behaviour. In a world where icons, particularly sporting ones, are found to have feet of clay, this diminutive bloke has been unimpeachable in his conduct. He rarely gets angry, never loses his cool when he is being mobbed and always accepts the bouquets and brickbats with humility. I do not think we must restrict the exemplary nature of Tendulkar's behaviour to cricket or to India; it should be a lesson to sportsmen the world over.

—Sir Viv Richards, *The Week*, 1 December 2013

Sachin was delighted to get the opportunity to represent Mumbai in the 2008–09 Ranji Trophy final against Uttar Pradesh at Hyderabad, before flying to Sri Lanka for a short limited-overs tour. He had always done well in Ranji Trophy finals, with as many as four centuries to his credit, plus a knock of 96 in the epic summit clash of 1990–91. At Hyderabad, Mumbai won the title for the 38th time, thrashing Uttar Pradesh by an innings and 243 runs, but the talisman had a forgettable time. In the first innings, he fell for a duck, being caught at short mid-wicket off Bhuvneshwar Kumar, a right-arm seamer who had not even been born when he made his international debut in November 1989. In the second essay, Sachin was dismissed by Piyush Chawla, the leg-spinner. For Mumbai, Rohit Sharma scored a century in both innings and speedsters Zaheer Khan and Dhawal Kulkarni excelled with the ball.

Team India got off to a flying start in 2009, winning an ODI series in Sri Lanka 4–1. Sachin did not get going in the three games that he played, but his colleagues more than made up for his below-par scores.

He compensated for his failures in Sri Lanka on the subsequent tour of New Zealand. In a five-match ODI series that India won 3–1, Sachin played in three games and scored 244 runs at an average of 122. He was at his best in the third ODI at Christchurch. Put in to bat, the Indians in general and Sachin made Brendon McCullum, the Kiwi skipper for the game, regret his decision. Sachin got going with placements down the leg-side. By the time he was firmly entrenched, Yuvraj Singh came in to launch an offensive, and it ceased to matter that the track was not very conducive for strokeplay, with the batsmen having to reach out for the ball rather than the ball coming onto the bat. Yuvraj scored 87 off only 60 balls, and his place was taken by Dhoni, who bludgeoned 68 off 58 deliveries. At the other end, Sachin maintained the momentum. He was on 163 when he had to retire hurt owing to a strained stomach muscle. In the dressing room, he received a reprimand of sorts from his disciple-turned-vice-captain. Sehwag was cross that his 'guru' hadn't converted his innings into a double hundred. Sachin assured him, in jest, that he would surely do so in the future.

A 1–0 victory in the Test series that followed—India's first in the Land of the Long White Cloud since 1967–68—helped those who were on the calamitous tour in 2002–03, obliterate their memories of that tour for good. The man who for the better part of the late 1990s and early 2000s had been vilified for 'not winning enough matches for India' did not quite infuse his detractors with delight with his performance in the first Test at Hamilton. After New Zealand had scored 279, Sachin batted for close to 400 minutes to compile 160. It was the quintessential match-winning Test innings.

When he went in, Sachin discovered that he wasn't anywhere close to being fluent. The ball was doing a bit and the bowlers were coming in hard at the batsmen. As he had done ever since his recovery from his various afflictions in the mid-2000s, he dropped anchor and confounded not only his opponents, but also Simon Taufel, the umpire, by adopting an open stance. He was living up to his old penchant for trying what made him feel good directly in the middle, instead of first trying things out in the nets. Inspired by him, the lower order also fired with the bat and India finished with 520. The innings was followed by a setback. Sachin jammed the index finger of his right hand between the ball and turf when he dived to catch Tim McIntosh, the New Zealand opener, in the second innings. It turned out to be a fracture. Harbhajan's 'six-for' ensured that India only had to get 39 to win.

Dhoni pulled out of the second Test at Napier due to injury. Sachin's participation was doubtful as well, but he would have none of it. He put three caps on the finger, along with a fibre plaster, and convinced himself and his colleagues that he would last the distance.

New Zealand dominated the early part of the game, enforcing the follow-on after bowling India out for 305, in response to their 619. For India, Dravid and

Laxman scored 50s and Sachin got 49 despite his fracture, but the others did not contribute much. The Indian side of 2002–03 might well have folded up meekly in the second innings as well, but then, the team of 2008–09 had learnt from its predecessors. Gautam Gambhir batted for nearly 11 hours to score 137 and those who followed him in the batting order took a cue from his tenacity. Sachin, Dravid and Yuvraj got 50s and Laxman scored an unbeaten hundred.

Gambhir did his team and country proud with another century, his second of the series and fifth of the season, in the third Test at Wellington. India held the upper hand for most of the game, and would have won had rain not put an end to the proceedings soon after lunch on the fifth day, when the hosts were 281-8 in pursuit of an impossible 617. Sachin took two wickets.

> He used to come over to me before bowling and ask, 'Leg-spin, off-spin, seam-up yaah phir mix daalun?' ['Should I bowl leg-spin or off-spin or a mixture of the two?'] And the very fact that he used to chat with me before bowling made me very comfortable from the very beginning. So, I was not overawed on the field and felt like I could give my inputs by saying sometimes that he should bowl off-spin instead of leg-spin.
>
> —M.S. Dhoni, as quoted in *Sports Illustrated*, May 2013

The hero had McCullum caught by Dravid, and James Franklin was out-thought by the talisman and his captain. With him struggling to pick Sachin's googly and trying to sweep everything, Sachin suggested to Dhoni that a gap be created at point and two men be placed on the leg-side. The ploy worked and Franklin, in trying for a cut, was trapped leg-before.

The Indians did not do themselves any favours by missing as many as three catches, and the rain then took over. Dravid came off the field as the most successful non-wicketkeeping 'catcher' in Tests. Of the three catches that he had pouched in the second innings, the first—that of Tim McIntosh, the opener—took him ahead of Mark Waugh's record tally of 181.

The series win in New Zealand was India's seventh on foreign soil in six seasons, starting from the triumph in Pakistan in 2003–04. The victory across the border apart, the wins in the Caribbean in 2006 and England in 2007 had been as memorable as the victory in Kiwiland. The team's consistency at home and overseas was reflected in the ICC rankings, where history beckoned. A victory in their next Test series, against Sri Lanka in November–December 2009, would enable India to top the ICC rankings for the first time ever. That series would also mark the completion of two decades in international cricket for the hero.

But there was a lot of cricket to be played before that series. With general election scheduled in India in April–May that year, the BCCI shifted the second season of the IPL to South Africa.

For the second year in succession, Sachin and the Mumbai Indians did not fare very well. The tournament maintained its proclivity to produce shock results, with the Hyderabad-based Deccan Chargers—one of the less-fancied sides—winning the title. A year before, not many had given even an outside chance to the Jaipur-based Rajasthan Royals, who had gone on to win under Shane Warne's inspirational leadership.

Sachin skipped a short limited-overs tour of the Caribbean before returning for a tri-series in Sri Lanka that had New Zealand as the third team. It was to be followed by the ICC Champions Trophy in South Africa. A surprise inclusion in the Indian team for both tournaments was Rahul Dravid, who had been ignored for ODIs since the series against Pakistan in 2007–08. He was recalled to ostensibly strengthen the batting, which had failed to fire in the second edition of the ICC World Twenty20. The defending champions had gone down in the very first round of the tournament, which was played just days after the end of a gruelling IPL.

There was a perverse tinge to Dravid's selection. While 'horses for courses' was a perfectly legitimate selection strategy, it was unfair that it was being applied to a cricketer of his stature. The team needed him and his technique in bowler-friendly conditions, but he was dispensable in matches that were to be played on batting tracks. That was exactly what happened, with the selectors leaving him out of the side for the seven-match ODI series against Australia at home that followed the Champions Trophy, despite his having done well in South Africa.

Sachin had a fabulous tournament in Sri Lanka, finishing as the highest scorer and the individual awards for the final and the series itself. In the summit clash against the hosts, he opened the innings with Dravid and proceeded to score one of his best ODI hundreds. The Sri Lankan bowlers went for runs on both sides of the wicket, and the fielders were kept on their toes with excellent running between the wickets. The statistics said it all—Sachin's first 50 comprised only six fours and his second, only two. Despite that, he took only 45 deliveries to move from 50 to hundred. Particularly satisfying for him was his assault on Ajantha Mendis, who looked a shadow of the 'mystery spinner' that he had been a year previously. Sachin handled him with aplomb, even reverse-sweeping him twice for four. He scored 138 and India finished with 319–5.

The Sri Lankans got off to a rollicking start, but lost too many wickets in the first 30 overs. The game swung decisively in India's favour with the freak dismissal of Kumara Sangakkara, the captain of the home team. He had batted fluently to score 33 and was looking good for many more when the bat slipped out of his sweat-drenched gloves and landed on the wickets. Harbhajan cleaned up the lower order, taking 5–56 as the hosts were dismissed for 273.

The trip to South Africa for the Champions Trophy wasn't as memorable. The Indians lost to Pakistan by 54 runs and their game against Australia was washed away. A three-wicket win over the West Indies was not enough to get them into the semi-finals.

India's 'home season' commenced with the ODI series against Australia. The hosts played some fine cricket to take a lead with victories in the second and third games after losing the first. Australia bounced back with a 24-run win in the fourth game at Mohali, and the series was thus interestingly poised on the eve of the fifth encounter at Hyderabad. The visitors won the toss and proceeded to rekindle memories of the 2003 World Cup final with a brutal assault on the Indian bowling. India needed at least two big partnerships, if they were to get anywhere close to their target of 351.

Sehwag and Sachin started well with a stand of 66 at more than a-run-a-ball, before the Delhite fell. Sachin took the initiative to keep the scoreboard ticking, but he kept losing partners at regular intervals. Gambhir, Yuvraj and Dhoni all fell to single-digit scores, but so brilliantly was Sachin batting by then that their dismissals went unnoticed. In his partnerships with the three individuals in question, Sachin contributed 18 out of 26, 24 out of 34 and 29 out of 36 respectively.

One of his strokes that stood out was a pull in front of square off Adam Voges; Sachin initially went for a conventional pull, but he realized that the delivery was too full for the stroke, so he adjusted his backlift and redirected his stroke past mid-on. That one stroke was proof that while his reflexes may not have been what they were when he was a teenager, they were not a concern either. His flicks were as impeccable as ever and his late-cutting in the latter stages, a joy to behold.

In Suresh Raina, who came in at 162–4, Sachin finally got the support he had been seeking. With Ponting, Sachin waged a war of wits, placing the ball just out of reach of the fielders and taking the aerial route every now and then, but only in the unmanned areas of the arena.

As India neared 300 with the duo going strong, the spectators sensed victory, but the world champions were not going to give up. They broke through when Raina top-edged Watson and Graham Manou, the keeper, ran yards to take the catch. The left-hander had scored 59. India now needed 52 to win off 45 balls, and Sachin was still in there and showing no sign of exhaustion. Harbhajan fell in the same over, but Ravindra Jadeja, a member of the under-19 team that had won the World Cup in 2008, kept the scoreboard ticking.

Only 19 were needed from 17 deliveries when Sachin tried to clear the fielder at short fine-leg. However, the delivery was a lot slower than he had anticipated. His timing went awry and the ball ballooned into the air for Nathan Hauritz, the fielder standing at the position, to take the catch. Sachin had scored 175 off 141 deliveries, inclusive of 19 boundaries and four sixes. Clint McKay, the bowler, could not have asked for a more critical wicket at a more critical juncture in what was his first international game. Three balls later, the pressure got to Jadeja who ran himself out. The tail-enders kept going; after all, it was a question of just one or two big shots. Praveen Kumar struck a six and brought the equation down to five off the last three deliveries, before he was last out, beaten by Hauritz's throw from the deep as he went for a second run. India had fallen a mere three runs short. Tragically, the innings that had reminded watchers of Sachin's heroics of the 1990s had met with the same fate as many of his knocks in that decade.

The next encounter at Guwahati was an anti-climax of sorts, with a dispirited Indian team surrendering the series with a six-wicket defeat. The final ODI, to be played at the D.Y. Patil Stadium on the outskirts of Mumbai, was abandoned due to rain and Australia took the series 4–2.

It was then time to discard the blues and don whites against the visitors from Sri Lanka. The first Test, played at Ahmedabad from 16 November to 20 November, marked the completion of 20 years in international cricket for Sachin. India scored 426, to which the Sri Lankans replied with a mammoth 760–7 declared. However, the visitors lacked the bowling firepower to bowl India out in the second innings, and the hosts drew the game with ease, helped by centuries from Gambhir and Sachin. The talisman's unbeaten 100 was his 43rd in Tests.

The second Test at Kanpur was where it all came together for the hosts. Sehwag, Gambhir and Dravid, the top three in the batting line-up, all scored hundreds as India totalled 642. Laxman and Yuvraj scored 50s and Sachin (40) in fact was the only one of the top six batsmen who did not cross 50. Dravid's 144 was his second successive century of the series, after his 177 in the first innings at Ahmedabad. Sri Lanka had no option but to hope for rain after being dismissed for 229 in their first innings. S. Sreesanth, playing a Test after a long time, took 5–75 in the first innings. India won by an innings and 144 runs.

The third Test was the first to be played at Mumbai's Brabourne Stadium since January 1973, with the Wankhede undergoing renovation for the 2011 World Cup. The game featured an incredible innings of 293 by Virender Sehwag, 284 of which were scored in a single day. Another commanding performance by the middle order saw India declare at 726–9, their highest Test total ever. Sachin scored 53 and Dhoni hammered a round ton. India completed a win by an innings and 24 runs on the final morning, thus winning the series 2–0 and in the process, topping the ICC Test rankings for the very first time. It was a good day on which to remember the likes of Ganguly, Kumble and Srinath, all of whom were no longer a part of the Indian team, but had inspired the side to commence its ascent to the top, in the early years of the new millennium.

> I think Test cricket will always be no. 1. That is where real challenges lie, the true test of one's character is tested there. Cricket to me is about learning to change the pace of the game and that can only be achieved in Test cricket and to a certain extent, maybe in one-day cricket.... T20 is also good, I mean it is exciting.
>
> —Sachin Tendulkar, *International Cricket Hall of Fame* interview, 2010

It was wonderfully appropriate that the team completed its ascent to the summit of Test cricket at an arena where Indian cricket's biggest names had distinguished themselves over the decades. From Col. C.K. Nayudu to Sachin himself, they had all excelled at the Brabourne Stadium in the years and decades gone by.

Raj Singh Dungarpur, Sachin's guardian angel in his formative years, would have approved. In what was a cruel quirk of fate, he had passed away just four months before the first Test to be played at his beloved Brabourne Stadium in nearly 40 years.

India outbatted the opposition in the ODI series that followed, winning 3–1. Sachin had a successful series with two 50s from four games, including an unbeaten 96 in the third encounter at Cuttack.

The tour of Bangladesh in early 2010 proceeded on expected lines, with the Indians winning both Tests comfortably. Sachin did what every seasoned batsman would have done in a similar situation, and made the most of his form to add to his tally of international hundreds. In the first Test at Chittagong, he saved India the blushes in the first innings, contributing 105 to a score of 243. The Indians regained their focus subsequently, gaining a first-innings lead of one and then declaring their second innings at 413–8, with Gautam Gambhir, winner of the BCCI's Polly Umrigar Award for being India's best cricketer of the 2008–09 season, scoring a hundred. The Indian bowlers then ensured victory by 113 runs.

In the second Test at Dhaka, Sachin and Dravid added 222 for the third wicket. Dravid was on 111 when he was rammed on the jaw by a Shahadat Hossein lifter and forced to retire hurt. Sachin fell for 143, his second straight ton of the series, and Dhoni, who replaced him in the middle, went on to score 89. India's first-innings lead of 311 was good enough for Zaheer Khan, who took 7–87 in addition to his 3–62 in the first innings, to set up a 10-wicket win for his team.

Indian cricket aficionados were hopeful that the 'Golden Age' continued in the 2010s as well. However, the joyride hit a roadblock of sorts in a Test against a formidable South African outfit at Nagpur. India were hurt by the absence of both Dravid and Laxman, who had not recovered from a finger injury that he had sustained in Bangladesh. Their woes were compounded when Rohit Sharma, who had been called in as Laxman's replacement, suffered a freak injury on the morning of the game, thereby forcing India to play Wriddhiman Saha, the designated reserve keeper, as a specialist batsman.

The visitors won the toss and batted India out of the game. Graeme Smith declared at 558–6 and then Dale Steyn, the fastest bowler in the world, blew the hosts away for 233; Sehwag (109) and debutant S. Badrinath (56) apart, there was only one other double-digit score in the innings. Asked to follow-on, India got off to another poor start, with both Gambhir and Sehwag back in the pavilion with only 24 on the board. With Dravid still out of action due to his jaw injury, the onus was on Sachin.

He essayed an outstanding innings. It was difficult to believe that the batsman standing between the South African bowlers and a comprehensive victory was someone who had been playing international cricket for over 20 years. Sachin may not have recalled his interactions with Greg Chappell fondly, but the fact was that he had worked extensively on one aspect that had come to the fore during those discussions; Chappell had told him that he could well play into his forties, if he managed to rediscover his boyish enthusiasm for the sport, which he exhibited every time he bowled. Sachin, who would turn 37 in a month's time, had achieved precisely that.

Steyn and his colleagues steamed in hard and gave it everything they had, but Sachin was equal to the challenge. He negotiated the good balls and took full toll of the slightest lapse by the bowlers. Steyn was getting the ball to reverse, the young Wayne Parnell was quick, and Paul Harris, the left-arm spinner, was making the cherry spit and rear from the 'rough' at the opposite end. Sachin batted like the champion he was, driving with the full face whenever the opportunity presented itself, and utilising the bowlers' pace to perfection by flicking deftly whenever the ball strayed onto his pads. He completed his 46th Test century and looked like getting many more when he fell *against the run of play* to Harris, when he missed a sweep and the ball lobbed off his pads to dislodge the bails. Taking heart from his innings, India's lower order delayed the inevitable as much as it could. When the curtains came down on the game, India were just six runs short of making South Africa bat again.

The hosts had everything to play for in the second and final Test at Kolkata. The number one ranking that they had recently acquired was on the line. That apart, they had not lost a series at home since 2004–05. Much to their delight, Laxman was declared fit to play at his favourite venue.

The South Africans were sailing smoothly at 218-1 on the first day when Zaheer Khan—initiated a collapse that saw the visitors decline to 296 all out. The Indian batsmen then got to work. As many as four of them scored hundreds as they ran up a total of 643-6. Among the centurions was Sachin. His 106 was his fourth hundred in four Tests. Both Sehwag and he batted as only they could. Indian fans feared the worst when both fell after a stand of 249, but the bowlers were thwarted by Amit Mishra, who went in as the night watchman in the closing stages of the second day and took India through to stumps in the company of Laxman. On day three, Laxman and Dhoni added an unfinished 259. The artiste and aggressor were unbeaten on 143 and 132 respectively when the declaration was made. The highest individual scorer in the innings was Sehwag, who scored 165.

India's quest to take 10 South African wickets was hampered by rain and poor light on day four, which robbed them of three-and-a-half hours of play. Still, they did well enough to dismiss the openers Graeme Smith and Alviro Peterson, as also the dangerous Kallis. Smith was bowled by Harbhajan, the man who was expected to win it for India, while the other two fell to Mishra. On the eve of the fifth day, the Indian team prayed for clear skies and the wicket of Hashim Amla. The South African batsman had already scored two centuries from two outings in the series, including one in the first innings of the Kolkata Test, and was looking good for another.

The final day produced some thrilling cricket. The Indians were relieved to be greeted by clear skies, but they were frustrated by Amla. They targeted the other end instead and worked their way through the middle and lower order.

Amla did his best to shield his partners from the strike, but the Indians proved to be one step ahead. When the ninth wicket fell with nearly 90 minutes of play left, all of India was gung-ho, but Morne Morkel, the last man, proved to be a tough nut to crack. Dhoni tried everything, shuffling his bowlers around and asking both Sachin and Sehwag to have a go, but to no avail.

With a minimum of 20 deliveries left in the game, Amla cut Sachin and ran a single to keep the strike, leaving Morkel with just one delivery to negotiate in the over. Sehwag ran *with* the cherry instead of chasing it, and willed it to reach the boundary. When it didn't, he briefly considered kicking it over the ropes, before prudence took over. A four would have increased the chances of Amla being off strike at the beginning of the next over.

Morkel lasted for 76 minutes before Harbhajan, with a minimum of nine deliveries and around 16 minutes of play left, trapped him plumb in front. As the crowd roared, the Turbanator broke into a sprint, which ended with him throwing himself into the arms of his teammates. India had won by an innings and 57 runs and retained their number one ranking. Amla was undefeated on 123, his third century of the series in three innings. India's four centurions were overshadowed by Harbhajan, who took eight wickets in the game, including 5-59 in the second innings.

The 2011 World Cup was exactly a year away, and that Sachin would lead India's charge at the top of the batting order in the tournament was a foregone conclusion after his performances in both forms of the game since mid-2007. He played a key role in India's victory in the ODI series against South Africa, first as a fielder and then by doing what he did best.

The first game at Jaipur went down to the wire, with the South African lower order staging a spectacular comeback after being reduced to 225-8 in pursuit of a target of 298. When Praveen Kumar was handed the ball for the final over, the visitors had their noses in front, with ten needed off six balls, a cakewalk in the 'Twenty20' age. Kumar conceded a single off the first ball, but bowled Steyn with his second. The next two deliveries yielded two runs. With seven needed off two balls, Charl Langeveldt, South Africa's number 11, picked Kumar's slower ball early, and pulled it with all his might. The ball had all but reached the boundary when Sachin, who had sprinted from his position at long-leg, made a desperate dive and was deemed to have saved one run inches from the rope, after the TV umpire scrutinized replays from different angles. That save made all the difference with the South Africans falling one run short.

On the eve of the second ODI, to be played at Gwalior, Sachin's body was acting up. It had been a long and eventful season. As had been the case during the tri-series in Australia two years previously, he was hoping that India would seal the series in the second game itself, so that he would be able to take the third game off. He proceeded to help himself.

From the time he pushed Parnell off the third ball of his first over and saw the ball rocketing past mid-off for four, he felt in good nick. The bowler then served a half-volley on Sachin's pads, which was duly flicked for another boundary. The strip was a batsman's paradise and the outfield was lightning quick, but you still had to put the ball away for runs. After those two fours, Sachin felt good and forgot about his aches of the previous day. He took on Steyn, flicking him on the up to the mid-wicket boundary and then square-driving him uppishly, but safely over the covers. Sehwag fell early, but so well was Sachin batting that it seemed that both batsmen were still in there; Sachin was batting like—and for—both. He brought up the 50 of the innings with a stunner of a drive off Parnell that bisected the two men patrolling the covers. He then improved upon the stroke with a magnificent 'tease' that got one of the fielders interested and prompted him to dive, but in vain. The fielder could only watch as the ball just beat him and sped to the fence.

After demoralising Parnell, Sachin turned his attention to the other bowlers. He completed his 50 with a leg-glance off Roelof van der Merwe, the left-arm spinner, which the short fine-leg fielder fell over and let run away for four; he had faced only 37 deliveries at that stage. He carried on, hitting the pacemen on the up whenever the opportunity presented itself and pulling the legs of the fielders posted behind square on both sides, literally and figuratively. His deft touches and nudges off the spinners were placed just wide of the fielders; they would give chase, even as the ball would go farther and farther away from them. Dinesh Kartik, who had come in at one-down, had the best view of a marvellous century; Sachin had taken only 90 deliveries to complete his 46th ODI hundred. As it turned out, he had only got started.

When he punched a short-pitched delivery by Kallis to the mid-wicket fence for four, Robin Jackman noted from the commentary box that he had a genuine chance of reaching a double century; there were over 20 overs left at that stage.

> Scoring a double hundred in a one-day match has not been a goal really....
> I would like to preserve my energy to score runs and not worry about getting a double century in a one-day match.
>
> —Sachin Tendulkar, *The Sportstar*, 21 April 2001

Jackman may well have felt that Sachin had heard what he had said, as he banged Kallis' next delivery over the bowler's head for another boundary. Shortly after India had crossed 200, Sachin came down the wicket to deposit J.P. Duminy over the long-on boundary. It was his first six of the afternoon. He followed it with an identical stroke, except that this one was flatter and faster, and it beat the bowler and went to the boundary. He was clearly seeing the white ball like a football.

Watchers could not help but beam when Sachin shuffled across the stumps to flick a Steyn full-toss to the leg-side for four. It was a stroke as disdainful as it was nonchalant. Just a couple of deliveries later, Sachin shuffled well beyond the stumps on the off-side to dispatch the paceman through mid-wicket for another boundary. It was 24 February 2010, exactly 22 years since two schoolboys had torn an opposition attack to pieces at Mumbai's Azad Maidan; one of them was still at it, more than two decades later.

The world's fastest bowler smiled wryly after the second boundary. It wasn't that he or his colleagues were bowling badly; it was just that for India's talisman, the bowlers had ceased to matter; Sachin, it appeared, was engaged in a contest with himself. He was egging himself on to better his strokes and the South Africans were decidedly unlucky to be at the receiving end.

Some more emphatic strokes later, Sachin picked up a Parnell delivery off his toes and found the long-on boundary to complete his 150. It had taken him only 118 deliveries. He then set out to spoil the figures of Langeveldt, who had been the pick of the bowlers till that point. The 300 of the innings was posted when Sachin pulled the seamer from outside the off-stump to over mid-wicket for six.

So enraptured were the watchers by Sachin's innings that the dismissals of Kartik and Yusuf Pathan had not registered. Sachin greeted Dhoni to the middle with two exceptional strokes off Van De Merwe; the first was a thump straight down the ground for four, and the second was a biff for six into the sightscreen. His trademark glance-flick off a Kallis full-toss in the 43rd over took Sachin to his highest score in ODIs, past his 186 against New Zealand at Hyderabad in 1999–00.

Sachin by this time was 'knackered', and justifiably so. He had batted for the entire duration of the innings, after all. It was then that his closest ally for more than 20 years—his willpower—took over. He had entered the 190s and history was only a couple of hits away. He continued to run with the same alacrity as at the start of the innings. A two off Parnell in the 46th over took him to 195, the highest individual score in ODIs, ahead of Pakistan's Saeed Anwar and Zimbabwe's Charles Coventry. Even as the crowd exploded and Mark Boucher, South Africa's keeper, shook his hand, Sachin was cramping in his feet.

Dhoni, sensing his partner's discomfiture and the number of deliveries that remained in the innings, then took charge. For the next three overs, he boomed and blazed away, bringing India closer to the 400-mark, even as Sachin crept closer to the 200-mark. Sachin did not face a single delivery in the penultimate over, bowled by Steyn, off which Dhoni took 17 runs and kept the strike. At the start of the final over, India were 385–3 and Sachin was on 199, but at the wrong end. Dhoni smashed the first ball for six and swung the second ball in the deep mid-wicket zone; the batsmen could have taken two, but then, nobody expected them to. The time had come. Langeveldt's third ball was a full delivery well outside off; Sachin lunged across the stumps to play it with a horizontal bat, turning the face at the point of impact. The ball beat the fielder at point and the batsmen crossed over for a single. Sachin had kept the promise he had made to Sehwag after retiring hurt at 163 in New Zealand the previous year.

It had taken him only 147 deliveries, inclusive of 25 boundaries and three sixes, to score the first double century in an ODI by a male cricketer; Australia's Belinda Clark had performed the feat in women's cricket more than a decade previously, coincidentally in a World Cup game against Denmark at the MIG Club in Bandra, Mumbai, where Sachin did most of his training.

Dhoni ended the innings with two more boundaries, the second of which took India past 400. The second half of the game was an anti-climax of sorts, with the South Africans being dismissed for 248.

Sachin's fine form rubbed off on the Mumbai Indians in the third season of the IPL. They played some fine all-round cricket to reach the final, where they went down to Chennai Super Kings. The defeat in the final was a disappointment, as the Mumbai Indians had clearly been the team of the tournament. They certainly did not help their cause with some strange alterations in the batting order in the summit clash. Chasing a stiff 169, the big-hitting Kieron Pollard was strangely held back and Harbhajan Singh promoted to number four. Even after he fell for just one, others were sent in, but not Pollard. When Sachin was fourth out at 99 in the 15th over, his team's only chance of scoring 70 in just over five overs was for Pollard to launch an offensive. By the time the Trinidadian came in at number eight with only three overs left, it was too late.

Dhoni could not replicate the IPL triumph with the Indian team in the ICC World 2010 edition of Twenty20, which was played in the Caribbean days after the end of the IPL, in what was an encore of the previous year. For the second year running, the Indians did not get past the first round.

Sachin skipped a couple of limited-overs tournaments, including the 2010 edition of the Asia Cup, with the blessings of the Board. He was not missed, as his younger colleagues overcame the World T20 disappointment with some fine performances to win the title.

The talisman returned to the fray for a three-Test series in Sri Lanka, the first Test of which belonged to Muttiah Muralitharan. The off-spinner had announced that the game, played at Galle, would be his last, and he and his team then set out to make it memorable. Sri Lanka won by ten wickets and the off-spinner took eight wickets to take his final tally to 800.

Asked to follow-on after being bowled out for 276 in response to Sri Lanka's 520, India's middle order battled hard. Sachin continued from where had left off at Gwalior, with an innings of 84 that enabled India to avoid an innings defeat.

He was in sparkling form in the next Test at the Sinhalese Sports Club at Colombo, a game in which the bowlers of both sides were treated with scant respect. India replied to Sri Lanka's 642-4 with their third 700-plus score in six years. Sehwag and Murali Vijay started well with a stand of 165, before the Delhi opener fell just one run short of what would have been his second hundred of the series. Vijay's dismissal just four runs later brought Sachin to the wicket.

Sachin proceeded to display his genius in an innings of 203, his fifth double ton in Tests. Suresh Raina could not have asked for a better initiation into Test cricket, with his childhood idol guiding them in a fifth-wicket stand of 256. The left-hander scored 120, becoming the 12th Indian—and first since Virender Sehwag in 2001–02—to score a century on his Test debut.

India ended the series on a happy note, with a series-levelling win in the final Test at the P. Saravanamuttu Stadium, also in Colombo. When Mohammed Azharuddin's side outplayed Arjuna Ranatunga's outfit 1–0 in mid-1993, no one in the Indian camp could have possibly envisaged that a key member of that side would play a prominent role in a series played in the same country, 17 seasons later.

India's five-wicket win was by no means a walk in the park; chasing 257 in the fourth innings—six less than what they had chased at Kandy in 2001—the visitors were struggling at 53–3 at stumps on the fourth day. The dismissal of Ishant Sharma, the night watchman, early on the fifth day, brought to the crease a player who revelled in crisis situations. V.V.S. Laxman did what came naturally to him, exhibiting his penchant for finding the gaps with unerring accuracy and regularity. Sachin played second fiddle in a stand of 109, before he fell for 54, his third substantial score of the series. Raina and Laxman then took India home, with the artiste remaining unbeaten on 103. It was India's fourth-highest successful chase in Tests, with three of those having been achieved in the new millennium (Kandy in 2001 and Chennai in 2008–09).

The series marked the end of Sachin's best-ever season since 1997–98. In mid-2010, he was looking as determined as he was during that phase when he had put the Australians to the sword, met the Don and pretty much walked on water. Even his staunchest detractors could not help but salute him for his tenacity.

The cricketing world rose to him on 6 October 2010, at the seventh annual ICC Awards Ceremony for 2009–10, which was held at Bengaluru. At 37, Sachin received the Sir Garfield Sobers Trophy for being ICC's Cricketer of the Year. The statistical details of his performances in the period under consideration made for astounding reading—1,064 runs at an average of 81.84 in 10 Tests and 914 runs in 17 ODIs at 65.28, inclusive of a historic double hundred at Gwalior. A panel that comprised the world's best cricketers and cricket writers could not think beyond Sachin for the award. He also received the People's Choice Award.

Life would be flat without dreams. It's really important to dream—and then to chase those dreams. I really believe it's this dreaming that makes me work so hard. I want to continue doing that because I have worked very hard the last couple of years on my batting. Gary Kirsten has been instrumental in this. He's given me the freedom to express myself, and to pace my innings as I see fit. Gary is more a friend than a coach.

—Sachin Tendulkar, *Hindustan Times*, 31 October 2010

A home season that was to culminate with the ICC Cricket World Cup 2011 commenced with a mini-series against Australia. There were many who were convinced that Sachin had spent the previous two seasons setting himself up, physically as well as mentally, to have a final crack at the biggest title of them all. The forthcoming World Cup would be his sixth.

Many people considered it a given that Sachin would call it a day after the tournament. As they viewed it, he had nothing else left to play for. If India did go the distance, his would be a fairytale farewell. If India fell short, it would still not take anything away from his achievements, although the regret would stay with him for the rest of his life.

The World Cup was temporarily forgotten when India and Australia produced yet another thriller. The first Test of the 2010–11 tussle for the Border–Gavaskar Trophy at Mohali went down to the wire. Sachin's 98 in the first innings helped the hosts keep the opposition's lead to a slim 21. Outstanding bowling by the Indians in Australia's second innings, kept the target down to 216. The Australian bowlers then reduced India to 76–5 before Sachin was joined by Laxman, who had been troubled by back spasms since the previous Test at Colombo. The duo added 43 before paceman Doug Bollinger had Sachin caught by Mike Hussey for 38. When Dhoni and Harbhajan also fell in quick succession, India were 124–8. What followed was something that only a batsman who felt invincible in a crisis could have accomplished. Laxman guided and goaded Ishant Sharma to stay in with him. The silken touch artiste tried to shield his partner from the strike, but when he saw Ishant putting a price on his wicket, he let him be. The duo added 81 before Ishant fell with 11 runs required. Ojha, the last man, held his nerve as the hosts crept across the finishing line by one wicket. An unsung hero was Suresh Raina who had run most of the artiste's runs.

The second Test commenced at Bengaluru a couple of days after Sachin received the ICC Cricketer of the Year Award. He celebrated the presentation with a performance that was nothing short of magnificent. After Australia had scored 478, Sachin came in at 38–2 and batted brilliantly to score his 49th Test century. A back-foot punch off Nathan Hauritz just before he reached triple figures took him past the 14,000-mark in Tests.

He then swung Hauritz for a six over long-on and repeated the stroke in the off-spinner's next over to become the first Indian to score six Test centuries in a calendar year. It was also his 11th Test hundred against the most formidable team of his era. The entertainment continued for the Bengaluru crowd, as Sachin was far from satiated. His nine-hour epic yielded 214 runs, his second double century in three Tests. India took a 17-run lead and the bowlers delivered again, dismissing Australia for 223. The hosts went on to win by seven wickets. Sachin's unbeaten 53 in the second innings gave him an aggregate of 403 runs in the two-Test series. India's highest individual scorer in the second innings was the debutant Cheteshwar Pujara, whom Dhoni sent in at number three, ahead of Dravid, who had not been in the best of form. Pujara lived up to the promise that he had displayed at the junior and domestic levels, with an innings of 72. With the likes of Pujara, Rohit Sharma, Suresh Raina and Virat Kohli making a mark at the highest level, and another talent in Ajinkya Rahane poised to break in; it appeared that the future of Indian batting was in good hands.

Fortunately for Sachin and the team, the law of averages caught up with him during the Test series against New Zealand and not later. Given his form since 2007–08, it seemed unreal that he finished a series of three Tests with only 126 runs. On the other hand, Dravid returned to form with two centuries, including a series-winning 191 in the final Test at Nagpur.

The Board acceded to Gary Kirsten's request to send some members of the Test side to South Africa, well in advance of their series in the Rainbow Nation. Kirsten, of all people, was mindful of the challenges that a tour of South Africa posed to visiting sides and he wanted the players to utilize the extra days to get used to the conditions and wickets. The players were to be based at Kirsten's Performance Zone Academy in Cape Town where the staff was instructed to prepare 'bouncy tracks with no lateral movement'.

Sachin was part of the 'advance party', along with the likes of Dravid and Laxman, both of whom were not in contention for selection for the ODI series against New Zealand anyway. Sehwag, Dhoni and Harbhajan Singh were also sent ahead. In their absence, Gautam Gambhir was entrusted the captaincy and he led India to a 5-0 win over the Kiwis.

Despite all the planning, India lost the first Test at Centurion. Steyn and Morkel flattened the visitors for 136 in the first innings. The hosts then amassed 620-4. The stage was set for a humiliating loss by an innings.

India did lose by an innings, but the visitors were not disgraced. Sehwag and Gambhir opened with a stand of 137. Both scored 50s and Dravid got 43. Ishant Sharma, who was sent in as the night watchman on the third evening, also resisted stoutly with a knock of 23.

Coming in at 214-3, Sachin responded to the demands of the situation and the bounce in the wicket by egging himself on to play as late as possible. His timing was spot-on, as was proved by a couple of 'firm pushes' through the covers that made it to the boundary. He played mostly off the back foot and used the pace of the bowlers to splendid effect. The wand in his hands that flicked, glided and nudged the ball through the gaps metamorphosed into a rapier whenever the bowlers pitched it short and gave him room on the off-side. Sachin employed the cut to perfection. A stunning cover drive 'on the up' off Steyn took him to his 60th Test 50.

He found an ally in his captain, who joined him at 277-6. Dhoni added 172 for the seventh wicket with Sachin before nicking Steyn to Boucher, when he was only 10 short of a hundred.

Sachin moved into the 90s with a six off Paul Harris. A little later, he pushed Steyn for a single to create history. His century was his 50th in Tests. The spectators and players rose from their seats to hail the titan. Back in Mumbai, Ramakant Achrekar would have permitted himself a smile as he watched the proceedings on the television. He had been forced to give up coaching due to an attack of paralysis in the mid-1990s, but he had not let that come in the way of his following cricket, especially the exploits of his most famous pupil.

Sachin stayed undefeated on 111 as the Indian innings ended at 459 on the fifth morning. South Africa won by an innings and 25 runs.

The visitors then produced an extraordinary display in the Boxing Day Test at Durban, winning by 87 runs. The triumph at a venue where India had been annihilated for 100 and 66, 14 seasons previously, was one of the team's finest overseas. Harbhajan had figures of 4-10 and Zaheer 3-36 as India bowled South Africa out for 131 after scoring 205. Leading by 74 on the first innings, India lost three quick wickets after the openers had put on 42. Sachin was the fourth to fall at 56. But then, V.V.S. Laxman was still in there. Even by his exceptional standards, his innings of 96 was a classic. He was last out at 228. Needing 303 to win, the hosts opened with a stand of 63 before the Indians took over. Sreesanth took three wickets in the second innings, each of which was worth its weight in gold; Smith and Amla were caught behind and Kallis received a brute of a ball that took off from just short of a length and forced the batsman to take evasive action. There was nothing Kallis could have done to avoid it, and the cherry flew off his glove to Sehwag at gully.

The series decider in the first week of the New Year at Cape Town was a spectacle that entered the 'what-might-have-been' echelons of Indian cricket. India scored 364 in response to South Africa's 362, primarily because of some magnificent batting by Gambhir and the talisman. A couple of weeks after completing a half-century of Test centuries, Sachin produced another exhilarating performance to score his 51st ton in Tests and eighth since January of the previous year.

Unlike his previous hundred at Centurion, this one was predominantly a 'front foot' innings, replete with deft flicks and elegant drives. He made one of those alterations that he often did in a game, standing outside the crease to negate the swing that the bowlers were extracting. After he had crossed 50, Sachin reminded watchers of his back-foot proficiency with a full-blooded pull and an exquisite uppercut off two consecutive short balls by the left-handed Lonwabo Tsotsobe. The interesting bit about the back-to-back strokes was that both deliveries had been pitched on a similar length from left-arm over the wicket and were angled across the right-handed batsman. Yet Sachin pulled the first one to the mid-wicket boundary on the leg-side and cut the second over point on the off-side.

Unbeaten on 94 at lunch on the third day, Sachin faced Morkel on the resumption. The paceman was armed with a new ball that was just a couple of overs old. Years of playing competitive cricket had honed Sachin's instincts to the point where he could put himself in the shoes of the individuals bowling to him. Something told him that Morkel would attempt a bouncer. Sachin accordingly abandoned his ploy of standing outside the popping crease. Sure enough, Morkel dug one in short. Sachin's withdrawal into the crease gave him an extra fraction of a second to watch the ball. He saw it all the way and went for the hook. The ball came onto him a little quicker than he had expected, and took the top-edge of his flashing blade to sail over the wicketkeeper's head, and over the ropes, for six.

The drives and cuts continued to flow from his blade until Morkel got one to go through his defences when he was on 146. Sachin returned to a standing ovation. He had scored eight centuries in 12 months, seven of them in the calendar year of 2010.

At Cape Town, the Indian team smelt an opportunity to perform a feat that would have been no less than winning the World Cup—a series win in South Africa. Harbhajan, bowling like a champion, had the hosts in all sorts of trouble in the second innings. They were 130-6 when Boucher joined Kallis for a match-saving stand. The Indians tried their hardest and gave it everything they had, but they were thwarted by the South African veterans and the lower order. The hosts escaped to 341 and India chose not to go for the target on the final day. The visitors were 166-3 at the close and the series ended in a 1-1 stalemate. It was the first time in five visits that India had not lost a Test series in South Africa, but it didn't quite come across as a sign of evolution as a 2-1 win would have.

India won the one-off T20 International that followed, but lost the ODI series 2-3. Sachin, who had not played a limited-overs series for a long time, was keen to get some invaluable match practice in the format before the World Cup. However, a hamstring injury forced him to pull out after the first two games, in which he got scores of 7 and 24.

The South African tour marked the culmination of a stupendous run. From the Chittagong Test against Bangladesh in January 2010 to the Cape Town Test against South Africa in January 2011, Sachin had scored 1,722 runs from 15 Tests at an average of 82, inclusive of eight hundreds, of which two were doubles. In the same period, he also played four ODIs and scored a double hundred in one of them. In the corresponding period from January 1998 to January 1999, the phase that is considered his 'annus mirabilis', he scored 850 runs from seven Tests at 77.7, inclusive of four centuries, which included two gems at Chennai—his match-winning 155* against Australia and his epic 136 against Pakistan. An integral part of India's limited-overs side at the point, he scored 1,967 runs from 38 ODIs at 59.6, inclusive of nine tons that included those back-to-back stunners at Sharjah, in the same period. In both phases, he had battled the best teams in the world—Australia and Pakistan in 1998–99 and Australia and South Africa in 2010–11. There was one key difference between 1998–99 and 2010–11—the Indian team was more successful in the latter phase as it was not overdependent on one player.

The transformation from a 'talented group of individuals who played like a team at home' to a 'team that played like one wherever it went' had taken at least 15 years longer than it should have. Had the cricketers of the 1980s capitalized on the gains made by the victories in the 1983 World Cup, the 1985 World Championship of Cricket and the 1986 tour of England, Sachin would have commenced his international career as part of a team that was rated highly not only at home, but also abroad. That did not happen, and Sachin along with Anil Kumble had to assume the lead role in rebuilding the side. The process was slow and, at times, frustrating. Support eventually came in the form of teammates, who came into their own as cricketers in the early years of the new millennium.

> Sachin did most of his training at the MCA's Academy at BKC [Bandra Kurla Complex] in the last phase of his career. I was based there at the time and so got to watch a lot of him. Two decades of international cricket hadn't satiated his passion for the sport. He hated getting out as much in the nets as he did in matches. Bowling to him in the indoor nets at the Academy would be the likes of Atul Ranade and Paras Mhambrey. Nilesh Kulkarni, another contemporary of his, would also join in sometimes. Sachin would bat for around two hours, with the last 15 minutes being devoted to a 'simulation' exercise. He and his friends would huddle and concoct a scenario, like say 50 needed to win from 25 balls. The bowlers would inform Sachin where they had 'placed the fielders'. They would also inform him about the 'changes' in their 'field' from time to time. The 'bout' would then begin, with one person keeping track of the equation. Invariably, a situation would arise wherein a bowler would claim that he had got Sachin out, mostly to a 'catch in the deep'. Sachin would of course refuse to take a backward step. He would come up with counter-arguments, like how no captain would place a fielder in the region in which he had hit the ball, or by simply claiming that the ball would have gone over the fielder's head. Like him, the bowler and the others would not budge, and they would end up debating heatedly like children over a make-believe situation! There were times when the arguments took place in front of Arjun, Sachin's son, who was practising in the adjoining net. He and his teammates would halt the proceedings and watch the adults in disbelief.
>
> —Anil Joshi, personal interview

If anything, Sachin's feats in 2010–11 were far more significant than those of 1998–99, considering what he had been through in previous seasons. From his toe to his shoulder, from a period wherein he struggled to complete a hundred after doing all the hard work to get into the 90s to even having his commitment to the team questioned, he had battled crisis after crisis and triumphed every single time.

> I do not play cricket to prove anything to anyone.... I play it because I love playing.... I need to just go out and play and enjoy.... I was made to feel part of the team and it becomes my responsibility to make a youngster feel comfortable.
>
> —Sachin Tendulkar, *Harsha Unplugged*, Star Cricket, 2007

THE PINNACLE

Every cricketer aspires to win the World Cup. It is the ultimate achievement. If affects not only the cricketers, but also their followers. Ask us, who witnessed the victory in the 1983 World Cup, as children! That win inspired my generation and I was no exception.

—Sachin Tendulkar, *World Champions*, BCCI, 2011

In 22 seasons of international cricket, Sachin had played with and against at least two generations of cricketers. Almost every batting record that mattered was his. His mere presence was a source of inspiration to all the cricketers who had entered the Indian team in the previous five seasons. These were individuals who as kids had pasted posters of his on their bedroom walls and whose batting as well as gestures they had tried their best to imitate whenever they took the cricket field. For the likes of Virat Kohli, Suresh Raina and Ravichandran Ashwin, to name just a few, the opportunity to share a dressing room and partnerships with their hero was their ultimate childhood fantasy coming true.

They did have one trait in common with their idol. Like them, he had something to play for. The World Cup was looming on the horizon, after all. Sachin on his part was extremely confident about his team's prospects. The Indian outfit was just as formidable as its counterparts of 2003 and 1996, which had made it to the final and semi-final of the event respectively. Limited-overs cricket had not changed much over the years, except for the fact that the gap between bat and ball had got wider. Totals in the range of 300–350 were no longer a novelty. As had been the case in 2003, India had a strong batting line-up. If only the bowlers could put up a good show on the batting-friendly wickets and restrict the opposition to gettable totals, there was no reason why the hosts could not go the distance.

The ninth Cricket World Cup and third to be played on the subcontinent got off to a dramatic start on 19 February 2011, with India playing co-host Bangladesh at the Sher-e-Bangla Stadium at Mirpur on the outskirts of Dhaka. The tournament was originally scheduled to be co-hosted by all four cricketing powers on the subcontinent, but Pakistan lost out because of security concerns. Their league matches were shifted to Sri Lanka.

Virender Sehwag smashed the first ball of the tournament, bowled by Shafiul Islam, through the covers for four; he would do likewise in five more games of the tournament. He brutalized the bowling on his way to 175, and Virat Kohli scored an unbeaten 100 on his 'senior' World Cup debut. India finished with 370–4. They won what sections of the media had built up as a 'grudge' game, after what had happened in the first round in 2007, by 87 runs.

India's box-office appeal ensured that most of their league games were scheduled on weekends, which gave them a lot of time in between matches to recharge their batteries and refocus. With Irfan Pathan losing form and consistency and slipping off the radar long ago, the Indians divided the fifth bowler's responsibilities between his brother Yusuf Pathan and Yuvraj Singh. The left-hander, whose brand of left-arm spin had broken many a stubborn partnership in the past, was assigned the prominent role of the two.

It had not been the best of times for Yuvraj Singh, on and off the field. He had been in and out of the limited-overs side in 2010, and the selectors had given up on him as a Test batsman long back. Three years after 'vice-captaining' the team that won the inaugural World Twenty20, he had been superseded by Gautam Gambhir. Off the field, things weren't great either. He was troubled by nausea and would throw up blood quite frequently. That he had continued to play despite his health issues spoke volumes about his character.

On the eve of the first game at Dhaka, Yuvraj was invited for dinner by an individual who meant everything to him. Sachin gave his junior colleague a pep talk and impressed upon him the value that he could add to the side with his batting, bowling and fielding. Even the most successful of players needed someone they admired to motivate them, and Yuvraj was no exception.

In the second league game, against England at Bengaluru, Yuvraj went in at a stage when India were scoring at exactly a-run-a-ball, and he took them ahead of that mark with a belligerent 58 off only 50 deliveries. His pyrotechnics were preceded by Sachin's, who brought the roof down with some brilliant strokeplay in an innings of 120 that took him only 115 deliveries. During the innings, he also brought the curtains down on one of his favourite bats, which he had used during the most successful 13 months of his career, getting it mended at regular intervals. Like many batsmen, he was loath to part ways with a piece of willow that had fetched him so many runs, but when he realized that the ball was not flying off the face as swiftly as it should have, he asked for a change in bat and picked one that he had been knocking into shape before the game.

The signature stroke of the knock was a cover drive off James Anderson that was so precisely timed and placed that it beat a cordon comprising a cover, mid-off and even a sweeper.

India should have scored over 350, but were 'restricted' to 338 after losing their last seven wickets for 33 runs. England responded with elan. Andrew Strauss, the skipper, and Ian Bell, put them in the driver's seat with a third-wicket stand of 170, before both fell at the same score. A thrilling finale ensued, and when the game ended the scores were level.

India then had the better of Ireland and Netherlands in their next two games before taking on South Africa at Nagpur. For the first 39.3 overs of their innings, the hosts did everything right; for the remaining 10.3 overs, they went the other way with a vengeance. After Dhoni won the toss and predictably elected to bat, Sachin and Sehwag blasted 142 runs in less than 18 overs. Sehwag fell for 73, but Gambhir, the next man in, maintained the scoring rate. Sachin took his time to get going, with Sehwag dominating the strike in the initial overs, but once he got off the blocks, there was no one stopping him. The Nagpur crowd was treated to some breathtaking strokes on both sides of the wicket, including a hooked six off Steyn. The capacity crowd at the Vidarbha Cricket Association Stadium went delirious when he completed his 48th ODI hundred.

India were 278–1 and Sachin was on 111 when he mishit Morkel to Duminy in the deep. He did not know it then, but his dismissal was the turning point of the game. India lost nine wickets for the addition of only 18 runs, thanks to a combination of tight bowling and spineless batting. When the final wicket fell, Dhoni was unbeaten on 12 and there were eight deliveries left in the innings. The collapse came back to haunt India when the South Africans, needing 13 runs to win off the final six balls, got home with two deliveries to spare. It was India's first defeat of the competition.

Yuvraj Singh's first World Cup hundred enabled India to end the league stage on a winning note with an 80-run win over the West Indies at Chennai. Batting first, India lost Sachin for only two, when he walked after nicking paceman Ravi Rampaul to the keeper, without waiting for the umpire's decision. Kohli scored 59 and Yuvraj followed up his 50s against England, Ireland and Netherlands earlier in the competition, with an innings of 113. His resolve to take his team to a winning score prevailed over his nausea, which made him throw up on the turf more than once. He would walk to the side, vomit and then return to the pitch and resume his innings. After India had scored 268, Yuvraj took 2–18 with his left-arm spin to win his third individual award of the competition in four games. As impressive as his batting had been his bowling, as figures of

5–31 and 2–43 against Ireland and Netherlands respectively, indicated. He was playing the all-rounder's role to perfection. His performances apart, a statement made by him about wanting to win the World Cup for 'someone special', also helped take the focus off his ill health. People were keener to know who he was referring to than trying to find out what exactly was ailing him.

India finished second in Group B with four wins, one tie and one defeat, and flew to Ahmedabad to play the team ranked third in Group A, in the quarter-final.

Australia may have been left behind by Pakistan and Sri Lanka in Group A, but they were the defending champions, and proficient at peaking at precisely the right time. The four-time World Cup winners won the toss and batted first. Ricky Ponting anchored the innings with a century and the holders totalled 260–6. Sachin and Sehwag put on 44 before the latter mishooked and was caught in the deep. The crowd went silent, but found its voice after a couple of boundaries by Sachin, who had been assertive from ball one. Mitchell Johnson, the left-arm paceman, was whipped contemptuously through mid-wicket for four in the twelfth over; off the very next delivery, the assassin transformed into an artiste. Sachin steered, or rather, helped along a short delivery outside the off-stump, to the thirdman boundary. A single off Brett Lee in the 14th over took him past 18,000 runs in ODIs. The Australians were running out of options when Sachin, after completing his 94th ODI 50, nicked a good delivery by Shaun Tait that left him after pitching, into the gloves of Brad Haddin, the keeper.

The Australians fancied their chances when Gambhir could not resolve his communication problems with Yuvraj and was run out. When Dhoni was fifth out at 187, India needed 74 more to win from 75 balls. However, Yuvraj was in imperial form. Suresh Raina, who had replaced Yusuf Pathan in the XI, complemented his senior's magnificence at the other end. The pair took India through in the 48th over. Yuvraj won his fourth individual award in five games for his unbeaten 57 and figures of 2–44 earlier in the day.

Six days after the Ahmedabad game, India came to a standstill all over again when Dhoni's side took on their traditional rivals at Mohali in the second semi-final of the competition. The PCA Stadium resembled a fortress as the spectators trickled in, among them industrialists, film stars and the prime ministers of the two countries.

Dhoni won the toss and elected to bat. India totalled 260–9 in a performance that swung from brilliant to pedestrian and back, in the truest traditions of India–Pakistan cricket. Sachin top-scored with 85, but it was by no means one of his best innings. He had a narrow escape at the start of his innings, when he tapped Abdul Razzaq to mid-on and called Sehwag for a run. He was halfway down the wicket when he realized that he had timed the ball a little too well, and it had reached Wahab Riaz at mid-on a lot earlier than he had expected. He did reach the non-striker's end safely, but it would have been a tight call had Riaz's shy hit the stumps.

That turned out to be the best fielding display of the afternoon by the Pakistanis. Sehwag got off to a rollicking start, opening his and India's account with a boundary in the first over and then taking five boundaries off the third. He played the dominant role in an opening stand of 48, which ended with his falling leg-before to Riaz for 38. Sehwag invoked the UDRS, which was in place for the event, but the TV umpire corroborated umpire Simon Taufel's decision. In the eighth over, Sachin struck two gorgeous fours off Riaz; a perfectly timed on-drive past mid-on was followed by a cover drive to cherish, as Sachin went down on one knee and gave a fuller delivery pitched outside the off-stump, the treatment.

He had moved to 23 when Saeed Ajmal, the off-spinner, who had been introduced into the attack earlier than expected, won a shout for leg-before; after a quick word with Gambhir, Sachin asked for a review. India had only one left, with Sehwag having used one unsuccessfully. A roar went up when the TV replays showed that the ball would have missed the leg-stump narrowly. Off the very next ball, Sachin got another reprieve when he missed a delivery that went straight on and almost lost his balance. Kamran Akmal, the wicketkeeper, dislodged the bails and appealed for a stumping. The square-leg umpire referred the decision, and Sachin was found to have grounded his back foot just in time.

The Pakistanis were in an extremely benevolent mood that afternoon, putting down as many as four regulation chances offered by Sachin, three of them off Afridi's bowling. Misbah-ul-Haq missed a catch at mid-wicket when he was 27 and Younis Khan spilt a sitter in the covers when he was 45. In a semi-final of the World Cup, it was imperative that he made the most of these reprieves. He was struggling with his timing, so he concentrated on rotating the strike. When the bowlers erred in line, length and concentration, he made sure to punish them. When he was on 70, he got an outside edge off Afridi, but Kamran Akmal failed to clasp the edge.

Somebody up there wants him to keep going.

—Sanjay Manjrekar, live commentary

Sachin had moved into the 80s when he mistimed a pull off Mohammed Hafeez, only for Umar Akmal to make a mess of what should have been a simple catch.

Ajmal and Afridi finally had their revenge when they combined to dismiss him in the 37th over of the innings. Sachin, 15 short of his hundredth international hundred, essayed a firm drive off Ajmal and Afridi took a good, low catch in the covers. With India 187–5, their opponents sensed an opportunity to bowl India out for a below-par score.

Earlier, the left-handed Wahab Riaz had brought his team back into the game by dismissing Virat Kohli and Yuvraj Singh at the same score. The bowlers then tightened the screws, and they were rewarded for their persistence when Sachin fell. More than eight overs were left when Dhoni was the sixth batsman to be dismissed, with 205 on the board. This sparked off concerns that India would not last for their full quota. Suresh Raina, the sole specialist batsman left in the middle, then rose to the occasion with a cameo that was replete with common sense. The lower order, comprising experienced heads like Harbhajan and Zaheer, complemented him. The Pakistanis would have been cross for letting India cross the 250-mark. Riaz finished with 5–46, thus vindicating his management's decision to play him ahead of Shoaib Akhtar.

The Indian bowlers then put up one of their best displays ever, striking at regular intervals and eventually dismissing Pakistan for 231. Dhoni used five bowlers, and all of them—Zaheer Khan, Ashish Nehra, Munaf Patel, Harbhajan Singh and 'fifth' bowler Yuvraj Singh—took two wickets each. Sachin had a hand in the dismissal of Wahab Riaz, catching him at mid-wicket off Nehra. India's opponents in the summit clash at the new Wankhede Stadium were co-hosts Sri Lanka, who had beaten New Zealand in the first semi-final.

The players of both sides had worked relentlessly and tirelessly to come within one step of the summit; all they needed was that one, final burst. Both camps knew what it felt like to stumble at the very end; Sri Lanka had lost the previous World Cup final to Australia, and five members of India's most likely playing XI—Sehwag, Yuvraj, Harbhajan, Zaheer and Sachin—had figured in the 2003 World Cup final, also against Australia. Ashish Nehra, who would have been the sixth, was ruled out of the final due to a hand injury.

The Wankhede Stadium was bursting at the seams by the time the captains emerged from their new dressing rooms. Dhoni tossed the coin and thought that he heard Kumara Sangakkara, his opposite number, say 'tails'. Ravi Shastri, the commentator covering the toss, said that the coin had fallen heads. Dhoni informed him that India would be batting, but then came a twist. Jeff Crowe, the match referee, said that he hadn't heard Sangakkara's call, and the Sri Lankan captain on his part claimed that he had called heads and not tails. The toss had to be redone and the coin fell the way Sangakkara wanted. He elected to bat,

always the pragmatic thing to do in a final.

Zaheer Khan, who had started the 2003 World Cup final with verbals and wayward deliveries, showed that he had learnt from the past. His first three overs in the 2011 World Cup final were maidens. He made the breakthrough in his fourth over, having Upul Tharanga brilliantly caught by Sehwag in the slips. The Indian bowlers had the better of the proceedings, striking just when the opposition looked to be putting together a partnership, before they ran into Mahela Jayawardene.

The former Sri Lankan captain essayed the sort of innings that forced even the most jingoistic Indian supporters to applaud. As he took the bowling apart with the most exquisite strokes and placements, paceman Nuwan Kulasekara and then Thisara Perera maintained the momentum at the other end. When Perera bashed the final ball of the innings, bowled by Zaheer Khan, over mid-wicket for six, the Sri Lankans had reason to be ecstatic. India needed 275 to win the World Cup final. Zaheer, who had conceded only six runs in his first five overs, had gone for 35 in his last two.

In the Indian dressing room, the usual positive things were said. The batsmen knew that they had to divide the target into chunks and play the bowling on merit. All they had to do was 'bat normally' and the match would be theirs. Of course, it was easier said than done.

All the victories, strategies, theories, injuries and comebacks the players had been through since the 2007 disappointment, everything that they had experienced and achieved in the last four years, all those talks delivered by Mike Horn, the celebrated explorer-turned-motivational speaker, especially in the last week of the tournament, would have made fleeting appearances in the minds of the players. The individuals who had helped them prepare physically, technically and mentally had done their bit; the players now had to execute everything that they had learnt and imbibed, out in the middle.

As they were getting ready for the chase, some members of the team stole a look at an individual who had seen it all since 1989. He was readying himself to open the innings, and so there was not much that he said, but his very presence was an inspiration.

The top priority for the openers was to see off the fiery Lasith Malinga and score off the other bowlers. Sri Lanka's bowling line-up, they knew, wore a diffident look. Muttiah Muralitharan was not at his fittest, Angelo Mathews, a genuine all-rounder, was not playing due to a thigh injury, and spinners Ajantha Mendis and Rangna Herath, both of whom had bowled well in the tournament, had been left out with off-spinner Suraj Randiv getting the nod ahead of them.

Malinga had played enough international cricket to have a fair inkling of India's gameplan; the second ball of his opening over was too quick for Sehwag. The Delhi batsman was hit on the pads plumb in front. He asked for a review, but it was all in vain. India were one down without a run on the board. Gautam Gambhir, the number three, got India off the mark with a flick for four.

In his second and last World Cup final, Sachin opened his account with a single to third man off Kulasekara. After Gambhir had taken another single, Sachin punched Kulasekara off the back foot through the covers. His timing wasn't quite spot-on and Tillakaratne Dilshan caught up with the ball well before it touched the ropes; the batsmen ran three. India, and Sachin, it appeared, were getting back on track, slowly and steadily.

In the fifth over, Sachin showed Kulasekara the full face of his bat, essaying a straight drive that rocketed between Gambhir and the umpire to the boundary. Just two balls later, he brought the spectators to their feet with a splendid square-cut that gave him his second boundary of the over.

The Indian cricket fan's fairytale climax—Sachin scoring the winning runs—was 244 runs away when Malinga commenced his fourth over of the evening. His first ball pitched on a length and moved away, Sachin went for the drive, but the ball deviated a little more than he had anticipated, and took the outside edge. Sangakkara dived to his right to come up with the catch. An ecstatic Malinga set off on a run of the infield, with his teammates chasing him. India were 31–2 and Sachin was gone. For the first time that evening, one could have heard a pin drop in the Wankhede.

Out in the middle, Gambhir and Virat Kohli pitted their respective temperaments against a team that had scented blood. The Delhi duo was equal to the task. Strangely and a little unfairly, their rebuilding operation went unnoticed by even their own supporters, who were reeling under the shock of Sachin's dismissal; by the time the spectators got their voice back, India had crossed 100 and the chase was well and truly on. The score had moved to 114, and Kohli was on 35, when he was brilliantly caught-and-bowled by Dilshan. The youngster left the field to a warm ovation. Thirty-five may not have been a big score, but in the context of the game in which it was made, it was priceless.

When Kohli fell, this writer was sitting in the media box of the Wankhede Stadium along with at least 200 mediapersons who had congregated in Mumbai from different parts of the country and planet to cover the summit clash. The Wankhede media box is situated above the sightscreen at the Tata End, bang opposite the dressing rooms that are located above the sightscreen at the Garware End. As Kohli made his way back to the pavilion, all eyes in the media box

always the pragmatic thing to do in a final.

Zaheer Khan, who had started the 2003 World Cup final with verbals and wayward deliveries, showed that he had learnt from the past. His first three overs in the 2011 World Cup final were maidens. He made the breakthrough in his fourth over, having Upul Tharanga brilliantly caught by Sehwag in the slips. The Indian bowlers had the better of the proceedings, striking just when the opposition looked to be putting together a partnership, before they ran into Mahela Jayawardene.

The former Sri Lankan captain essayed the sort of innings that forced even the most jingoistic Indian supporters to applaud. As he took the bowling apart with the most exquisite strokes and placements, paceman Nuwan Kulasekara and then Thisara Perera maintained the momentum at the other end. When Perera bashed the final ball of the innings, bowled by Zaheer Khan, over midwicket for six, the Sri Lankans had reason to be ecstatic. India needed 275 to win the World Cup final. Zaheer, who had conceded only six runs in his first five overs, had gone for 35 in his last two.

In the Indian dressing room, the usual positive things were said. The batsmen knew that they had to divide the target into chunks and play the bowling on merit. All they had to do was 'bat normally' and the match would be theirs. Of course, it was easier said than done.

All the victories, strategies, theories, injuries and comebacks the players had been through since the 2007 disappointment, everything that they had experienced and achieved in the last four years, all those talks delivered by Mike Horn, the celebrated explorer-turned-motivational speaker, especially in the last week of the tournament, would have made fleeting appearances in the minds of the players. The individuals who had helped them prepare physically, technically and mentally had done their bit; the players now had to execute everything that they had learnt and imbibed, out in the middle.

As they were getting ready for the chase, some members of the team stole a look at an individual who had seen it all since 1989. He was readying himself to open the innings, and so there was not much that he said, but his very presence was an inspiration.

The top priority for the openers was to see off the fiery Lasith Malinga and score off the other bowlers. Sri Lanka's bowling line-up, they knew, wore a diffident look. Muttiah Muralitharan was not at his fittest, Angelo Mathews, a genuine all-rounder, was not playing due to a thigh injury, and spinners Ajantha Mendis and Rangna Herath, both of whom had bowled well in the tournament, had been left out with off-spinner Suraj Randiv getting the nod ahead of them.

Malinga had played enough international cricket to have a fair inkling of India's gameplan; the second ball of his opening over was too quick for Sehwag. The Delhi batsman was hit on the pads plumb in front. He asked for a review, but it was all in vain. India were one down without a run on the board. Gautam Gambhir, the number three, got India off the mark with a flick for four.

In his second and last World Cup final, Sachin opened his account with a single to third man off Kulasekara. After Gambhir had taken another single, Sachin punched Kulasekara off the back foot through the covers. His timing wasn't quite spot-on and Tillakaratne Dilshan caught up with the ball well before it touched the ropes; the batsmen ran three. India, and Sachin, it appeared, were getting back on track, slowly and steadily.

In the fifth over, Sachin showed Kulasekara the full face of his bat, essaying a straight drive that rocketed between Gambhir and the umpire to the boundary. Just two balls later, he brought the spectators to their feet with a splendid square-cut that gave him his second boundary of the over.

The Indian cricket fan's fairytale climax—Sachin scoring the winning runs—was 244 runs away when Malinga commenced his fourth over of the evening. His first ball pitched on a length and moved away, Sachin went for the drive, but the ball deviated a little more than he had anticipated, and took the outside edge. Sangakkara dived to his right to come up with the catch. An ecstatic Malinga set off on a run of the infield, with his teammates chasing him. India were 31–2 and Sachin was gone. For the first time that evening, one could have heard a pin drop in the Wankhede.

Out in the middle, Gambhir and Virat Kohli pitted their respective temperaments against a team that had scented blood. The Delhi duo was equal to the task. Strangely and a little unfairly, their rebuilding operation went unnoticed by even their own supporters, who were reeling under the shock of Sachin's dismissal; by the time the spectators got their voice back, India had crossed 100 and the chase was well and truly on. The score had moved to 114, and Kohli was on 35, when he was brilliantly caught-and-bowled by Dilshan. The youngster left the field to a warm ovation. Thirty-five may not have been a big score, but in the context of the game in which it was made, it was priceless.

When Kohli fell, this writer was sitting in the media box of the Wankhede Stadium along with at least 200 mediapersons who had congregated in Mumbai from different parts of the country and planet to cover the summit clash. The Wankhede media box is situated above the sightscreen at the Tata End, bang opposite the dressing rooms that are located above the sightscreen at the Garware End. As Kohli made his way back to the pavilion, all eyes in the media box

always the pragmatic thing to do in a final.

Zaheer Khan, who had started the 2003 World Cup final with verbals and wayward deliveries, showed that he had learnt from the past. His first three overs in the 2011 World Cup final were maidens. He made the breakthrough in his fourth over, having Upul Tharanga brilliantly caught by Sehwag in the slips. The Indian bowlers had the better of the proceedings, striking just when the opposition looked to be putting together a partnership, before they ran into Mahela Jayawardene.

The former Sri Lankan captain essayed the sort of innings that forced even the most jingoistic Indian supporters to applaud. As he took the bowling apart with the most exquisite strokes and placements, paceman Nuwan Kulasekara and then Thisara Perera maintained the momentum at the other end. When Perera bashed the final ball of the innings, bowled by Zaheer Khan, over mid-wicket for six, the Sri Lankans had reason to be ecstatic. India needed 275 to win the World Cup final. Zaheer, who had conceded only six runs in his first five overs, had gone for 35 in his last two.

In the Indian dressing room, the usual positive things were said. The batsmen knew that they had to divide the target into chunks and play the bowling on merit. All they had to do was 'bat normally' and the match would be theirs. Of course, it was easier said than done.

All the victories, strategies, theories, injuries and comebacks the players had been through since the 2007 disappointment, everything that they had experienced and achieved in the last four years, all those talks delivered by Mike Horn, the celebrated explorer-turned-motivational speaker, especially in the last week of the tournament, would have made fleeting appearances in the minds of the players. The individuals who had helped them prepare physically, technically and mentally had done their bit; the players now had to execute everything that they had learnt and imbibed, out in the middle.

As they were getting ready for the chase, some members of the team stole a look at an individual who had seen it all since 1989. He was readying himself to open the innings, and so there was not much that he said, but his very presence was an inspiration.

The top priority for the openers was to see off the fiery Lasith Malinga and score off the other bowlers. Sri Lanka's bowling line-up, they knew, wore a diffident look. Muttiah Muralitharan was not at his fittest, Angelo Mathews, a genuine all-rounder, was not playing due to a thigh injury, and spinners Ajantha Mendis and Rangna Herath, both of whom had bowled well in the tournament, had been left out with off-spinner Suraj Randiv getting the nod ahead of them.

Malinga had played enough international cricket to have a fair inkling of India's gameplan; the second ball of his opening over was too quick for Sehwag. The Delhi batsman was hit on the pads plumb in front. He asked for a review, but it was all in vain. India were one down without a run on the board. Gautam Gambhir, the number three, got India off the mark with a flick for four.

In his second and last World Cup final, Sachin opened his account with a single to third man off Kulasekara. After Gambhir had taken another single, Sachin punched Kulasekara off the back foot through the covers. His timing wasn't quite spot-on and Tillakaratne Dilshan caught up with the ball well before it touched the ropes; the batsmen ran three. India, and Sachin, it appeared, were getting back on track, slowly and steadily.

In the fifth over, Sachin showed Kulasekara the full face of his bat, essaying a straight drive that rocketed between Gambhir and the umpire to the boundary. Just two balls later, he brought the spectators to their feet with a splendid square-cut that gave him his second boundary of the over.

The Indian cricket fan's fairytale climax—Sachin scoring the winning runs—was 244 runs away when Malinga commenced his fourth over of the evening. His first ball pitched on a length and moved away, Sachin went for the drive, but the ball deviated a little more than he had anticipated, and took the outside edge. Sangakkara dived to his right to come up with the catch. An ecstatic Malinga set off on a run of the infield, with his teammates chasing him. India were 31–2 and Sachin was gone. For the first time that evening, one could have heard a pin drop in the Wankhede.

Out in the middle, Gambhir and Virat Kohli pitted their respective temperaments against a team that had scented blood. The Delhi duo was equal to the task. Strangely and a little unfairly, their rebuilding operation went unnoticed by even their own supporters, who were reeling under the shock of Sachin's dismissal; by the time the spectators got their voice back, India had crossed 100 and the chase was well and truly on. The score had moved to 114, and Kohli was on 35, when he was brilliantly caught-and-bowled by Dilshan. The youngster left the field to a warm ovation. Thirty-five may not have been a big score, but in the context of the game in which it was made, it was priceless.

When Kohli fell, this writer was sitting in the media box of the Wankhede Stadium along with at least 200 mediapersons who had congregated in Mumbai from different parts of the country and planet to cover the summit clash. The Wankhede media box is situated above the sightscreen at the Tata End, bang opposite the dressing rooms that are located above the sightscreen at the Garware End. As Kohli made his way back to the pavilion, all eyes in the media box

were focussed on the 'home' dressing room. A batsman was seen descending the flight of stairs that led to the playing arena. This writer, along with many others, could not figure what was happening; the new batsman did not quite look like Yuvraj, the regular number five in the competition. It was only when the player stepped onto the arena that everybody realised who it was. Mahendra Singh Dhoni, who had had an average tournament with the bat, had promoted himself in the game that mattered the most.

There was something about Dhoni's walk and his body language which put Indian supporters at ease. At least this writer was convinced that India were going to win the World Cup. The rest is history.

Gambhir and Dhoni put together an incredible partnership. The opener was only three short of what would have been an epic hundred, when he stepped down the wicket to Perera, missed and was bowled. India at that stage needed 53 off 52 deliveries. With Dhoni entrenched in the middle and Yuvraj joining him, it was clear that India would have to do something incredibly daft to lose the game from that situation.

The batsmen opted for the dramatic instead. They pierced the gaps almost at will and ran between the wickets superbly. The celebrations started in the media box when the target was 15 runs or so away, when the ICC media manager announced that Yuvraj Singh had been selected as the player of the tournament for his all-round brilliance. The enormity of what Yuvraj had achieved for his team and country came to light a year later, when a malignant tumour was detected between his lungs, necessitating rounds of chemotherapy.

Four were needed from 11 balls when Kulasekara bowled a length ball to the Indian captain. Dhoni saw it early and flailed his arms. He met the ball on the up and swung with all his might. As the ball flew skywards and over the long-on boundary; the captain stayed rooted in his follow-through, watching its descent, before it was lost among the spectators. Within moments, he was hugged by Yuvraj. India had conquered the world.

The players in the middle were soon joined by their teammates. Yuvraj and Harbhajan broke down and so did many others, on the field, in the stands, in the media box and in front of TV screens, in homes and restaurants and theatres, across the country. Outside the Wankhede, fans halted their cars in the middle of Marine Drive, Mumbai's best-known thoroughfare. They alighted and clambered on the bonnets and roofs of their own vehicles, as well as those belonging to others, to dance away to glory; there were traffic jams there and elsewhere in the country, but no one cared.

On the turf of the Wankhede, the Indian players surrounded their preceptor.

A couple of them hoisted him on their shoulders and did a lap of the ground, surrounded by their teammates.

> Sachin Tendulkar has carried the burden of the nation for 21 years. It was time we carried him.
>
> —Virat Kohli (after the ICC Cricket World Cup 2011 Final)

As he acknowledged the deafening cheers of his home crowd, from atop the shoulders of his colleagues, Sachin may well have reflected on how and when it had all begun. It was only a few kilometres away, at the Shivaji Park, where his brother had introduced him to Achrekar in the summer of 1984; hardly a kilometre away from the Wankhede was the Azad Maidan, where he had been involved in that memorable partnership of 664; it was at the Brabourne Stadium, a five-minute walk from the Wankhede, where he had scored a triple hundred in an inter-school final and then excelled for the CCI in the Kanga League against men twice his age; it was at the Wankhede where a certain S.M. Gavaskar had first noticed him and earmarked him as a special talent. His aggregate of 482 from nine World Cup games was the second-highest in the tournament. Only Tillakaratne Dilshan was ahead of him with an aggregate of 500.

> We had an excellent outfit in 2011. We strategized, practised hard and most importantly, translated all that into performance on the field. Our performances kept getting better as the tournament progressed and peaked at precisely the right time. What we felt when the captain hit the winning six in the final was indescribable. I was touched when members of the team 'dedicated' the win to me. These are moments I will never ever forget.
>
> —Sachin Tendulkar, *World Champions*, BCCI, 2011

At the post-match media conference, Yuvraj disappointed the Page 3 gossip columnists by naming Sachin as the 'special person' for whom he wanted to win the World Cup.

> It was only natural to dedicate the triumph to Sachin Tendulkar. We wanted to win it for him. He has done so much for Indian cricket, and we all felt he deserved it more than we did. We were also very happy for Gary Kirsten. As our coach, he made us believe in ourselves. He fostered a 'family' environment in the dressing room, and kept us together. We will miss him.
>
> —Yuvraj Singh, *World Champions*, BCCI, 2011

For Sachin, as for the others, the World Cup win was the pinnacle of his career. It was a triumph he had set up, not only with his superlative batting in the league stage, but also with everything that he had accomplished since the 1990s. The likes of Ganguly, Dravid, Kumble, Laxman and Srinath had also motivated the 1990s' generation, but Sachin's impact was by far the greatest. He would have liked to have made a more substantial contribution to the victory in the summit clash, but then, what had happened was in a way, quite appropriate. His younger colleagues had completed what he had initiated several years previously.

A couple of days after the final, Gary Kirsten announced the end of his stint as coach of the Indian cricket team in a media conference at the BCCI headquarters. His stint, which began with the Test win at Perth in January 2008, had been eventful and memorable. In the days and weeks that followed, many people expected a similar announcement from another member of the team that had lifted the World Cup. In a career spanning 22 years, Sachin had achieved everything that had been expected of him when he had started out, and a lot more.

The history of sport is replete with instances of exponents whose dreams of bowing out in a blaze of glory were shattered by the vicissitudes of their chosen profession. This misfortune had befallen many of India's biggest cricketing names, who after bringing laurels to the team and country for years, had somehow failed to take cognizance of different factors, like advancing years and declining reflexes. Consequently, they had not 'timed' their exits as well as they would have wished.

After the World Cup win, Sachin had an opportunity to draw the curtains on an extraordinary cricketing career on as memorable a note as one could possibly imagine. He had scaled most of the peaks that every cricketer beheld and dreamt of conquering at the start of his career. His team had first scaled the summit in Tests by topping the ICC rankings and had now pocketed the biggest prize in limited-overs cricket. Coincidentally, both those peaks had been conquered in Mumbai, his birthplace and home, where he had seen his first cricketing dreams and begun his quest to realize them. It was a classic case of fact being grander than fiction. Even the most creative screenwriter could not have possibly done better than that.

Despite battling a succession of injuries and niggles, the frequency of which had increased of late, he had been in the form of his life in the previous four seasons. But then, sport was inherently fickle in nature. Combating a bad patch in one's late thirties was not quite the same as doing so in one's late twenties. Three weeks after the triumph, Sachin turned 38. This was the age at which Sunil Gavaskar had hung up his boots; Vivian Richards, Sachin's other he had quit at 39. Sachin had of course played a lot more international cricket than both his idols.

Batting-wise, both the legends had been in excellent nick when they chose to abdicate. Gavaskar had scored his maiden ODI hundred in just over 80 deliveries, in what was his penultimate game for India, and Richards had scored a 50 in each of his last five Tests against England in 1991. Their retirements did upset many people, but both believed that it was better to go when people would ask 'Why' rather than 'Why not'.

It seemed the right time for Sachin to go. Of course, the final decision would have to be his.

He chose to continue.

A nation that had long been used to lagging behind, whether in economics or sport, now boasted the world's best batsman and went on to become world champions again, 28 years after our first triumph. The No.1 ranking in both Tests and ODIs is no longer an impossible dream: we have held both, at different times. Television revenues from the growing and increasingly prosperous Indian audience have transformed India's place in world cricket too: today some 80% of the global game's resources are generated by India. As a result, in the cheerful words of a senior BCCI official, India is to the ICC what the USA is to the UN Security Council, the one country that all other members find indispensable–and impossible to ignore. Tendulkar's 24 years in top-flight cricket eerily mirror the transformation of India at the cusp of the 21st century. There is an Indian Dream, and in his own lifetime, Tendulkar is its Prophet.

—Shashi Tharoor, *The Sachin Sunset*, Wisden India, November 2013

JEWEL OF INDIA

> *As batsmen age, they lose the instinctiveness, impetuosity, and verve of their youth, when everything is an adventure, and settle into a pragmatism forged in the heat of experience.... Tendulkar looked vulnerable early on in an innings, as bowlers sought his outside edge or his pads, his movements no longer twinkling and just a fraction more ponderous now. He still played sublimely at times: the back foot punch through the covers; the flick through mid-wicket with nothing more than a turn of the wrist; the straight drive that was little more than a defensive stroke played with chronometric timing. But the air of invulnerability was no longer there. Respect for him never wavered but his aura had slipped.*
>
> —Peter Roebuck, *The Sachin Sunset*, Wisden India, November 2013

After the World Cup, Sachin led the Mumbai Indians in the fourth season of the IPL. He scored his first—and only—hundred of the competition, in a game against new entrants Kochi Tuskers Kerala, but the opposition chased down a target of 182 for the loss of only two wickets. The Mumbai Indians failed to replicate their form of the previous season and did not qualify for the playoffs.

The BCCI held its annual awards ceremony for the 2009–10 season on 31 May 2011, a few days after the conclusion of the IPL. Sachin was declared the winner of the Polly Umrigar Trophy for being India's most successful cricketer of the 2009–10 season. It was the second time he had won the trophy after 2006–07. In his acceptance speech, Sachin complimented his teammates and support staff for their achievements of the previous two years, the apogee of which was the World Cup triumph.

India's cricketers had exhibited pluck, character and above all, consistency in the first decade of the new millennium to win the inaugural ICC World T20, top the ICC Test rankings and then win the 50-over World Cup. However, they were found to be lacking the tenacity to *stay* at the top.

The players ought to have built on the gains made on their previous tours of England and Australia on their visits in mid-2011 and 2011–12, respectively, but that did not happen. They were soundly thrashed in both series and Indian cricket lovers were back to seeking solace in individual glory. The 38-year-old Rahul Dravid, who was among those who had sown the seeds of the 2011 World Cup triumph with his deeds in the 2000s, scored three splendid centuries in England. India's only Test centurion in Australia was the young Virat Kohli. His 116 in the final Test at Adelaide made critics wonder whether India had missed a trick by jettisoning some senior players who had not been among the runs and replacing them with Kohli's contemporaries like Ajinkya Rahane and Rohit Sharma, both of whom were part of the squad but did not get a single game.

Sachin did get runs, in the form of two 50s in both England and Australia, and two more in a home series against the West Indies, but not consistently enough.

He scored one international hundred during this phase, against Bangladesh at Dhaka on 16 March 2012 in a league encounter of the Asia Cup. It was his 49th ton in ODIs. He had already scored 51 hundreds in Tests. That made his innings of 114 his 'hundredth in international cricket', if one decided to add centimetres to inches. Putting centuries scored in different formats of the game in the same bracket made no sense, but then, sense was never going to be allowed to get in the way of good copy.

As 2011 gave way to 2012, the hype around the 'hundredth hundred' kept growing till an anti-climax seemed imminent, in keeping with the law of nature. That is exactly what happened. After Sachin had scored the hundred, Bangladesh chased down a target of 290 with five wickets in hand and four deliveries to spare.

A little over a week before the 'hundredth hundred' was scored, one of Sachin's long-time colleagues bid farewell to international cricket. Rahul Dravid had been in tremendous nick against England and the West Indies before the law of averages caught up with him in Australia. However, with India scheduled to play 10 Tests at home soil from August 2012 to March 2013, it appeared that it was only a matter of time before he would return to his scoring ways. This was precisely what a senior office-bearer of the BCCI tried to impress upon the former India captain.

The official was left speechless by the response. Dravid made the point that he was more comfortable with a youngster replacing him in the side in what was going to be a long home season in 2012–13, and thus attuning himself to the demands of Test cricket in familiar surroundings. This would give the youngster confidence and maturity, both of which would stand him in good stead when the team started touring in the 2013–14 season. The senior office-bearer could only marvel at Dravid's far-sightedness.

It was but natural for heads to start turning in Sachin's direction after Dravid's announcement. However, he was determined to carry on, convinced as he was that he still had a lot to offer to Indian cricket. Other challenges were also beckoning him.

On 4 June 2012, he took oath as a member of the Rajya Sabha, the Upper House of India's Parliament. He was the first active international sportsperson to be nominated for this honour. There were those who wondered whether he had it in him to measure up to the demands of being a Parliamentarian, while others hailed the move and expressed hope that he would provide a sportsperson's perspective in the Upper House at a time when the country was slowly but steadily moving away from its reputation as a one-sport nation.

Five years earlier, Sachin had been approached for an article on the 'India he dreamt of'. His response was to articulate a 'seven-point agenda', which comprised the eradication of hunger, universal access to clean drinking water, the right to shelter, an end to discrimination against women and female infanticide, access to proper healthcare, the end of terror and a more tolerant India, accepting of its diversity.

As a Parliamentarian, Sachin had the opportunity to contribute to the realisation of that agenda. He was responsible for the initiation of some fruitful ventures, like the adoption of Puttamraju Kandrika, a village in the state of Andhra Pradesh. He utilized the funds allotted to him to create infrastructure in the form of proper roads, storm water drains and even a playground. Measures were also taken to help some villagers resolve their addiction issues. He was also involved in Spreading Happiness, a project that sought to tap solar energy to provide electricity to far-flung areas. Thousands of people have benefited from the same already.

> I was never impressed with SRT's decision to take up a political position in RS as I felt in his entire career SRT never took a stand on issues which were more vital—match-fixing and chucking! His voice would have carried a lot of weight. So, I am a bit apprehensive about SRT rubbing shoulders with hardcore...you know what!
>
> —Bishan Singh Bedi, *The Sportstar*, 26 October 2013

The year 2012 also saw Sachin being conferred the membership of the Order of Australia. The country where he had achieved superstardom as an 18-year-old had never concealed its affection for India's talisman. He was only the fourth non-Australian cricketer to be accorded this honour, after the West Indian trio of Clive Lloyd, Sir Garfield Sobers and his contemporary Brian Lara.

A couple of months after Sachin was sworn in as MP, another colleague of his announced his retirement, just a few days before the start of a Test series against New Zealand. Like Dravid, V.V.S. Laxman would have also scored a lot of runs in familiar terrain in 2012–13, but he chose to step aside. Harbhajan Singh apart, Sachin was now the only member of the Test team to have played in the 1990s.

The absence of the two match-winners sunk in later in the year, during the home series against England. The visitors lost the first Test, but they came back strongly with comprehensive wins in the next two Tests, played at Mumbai and Kolkata respectively. The fourth Test, played at Nagpur, was drawn and Alastair Cook's team became the first from England to win a Test series in India since 1984–85.

> As long as I remember, it was December 12, 2012, Nagpur [during the Test match against England]. Sachin got out and the selectors decided to meet him and ask him about his wish. I was the one who staged the meet, being the chairman of selectors, and it was purely to understand what was running in his mind. It was a good thing to do. It did not happen in one day, one month or one year, it took two long years. Sachin retired in 2013. The meeting in Nagpur was just to ask his plans. Sachin wanted to concentrate more on Test cricket. So, it was decided that he would retire from one-day cricket. He called me and Sanjay Jagdale [then BCCI secretary]. Then it was collectively decided that he would retire from ODIs.
>
> —Sandeep Patil, as quoted in www.timesofindia.indiatimes.com
> 22 September 2016

This statement by Sachin's India, Mumbai, Sungrace-Mafatlal and Shivaji Park senior appeared on the website of a popular Marathi TV channel.

Sachin's call to leave the shorter forms of the game was anything but impulsive; in fact, he had started the process way back in 2007, when he had indicated his unavailability for T20 Internationals. A year later, he had started cutting down on his ODI appearances as well, with the blessings of the BCCI. In 2012, he had not played the shorter format since the Asia Cup. In India's next game of the Asia Cup after the loss to Bangladesh, Dhoni's side chased down a target of 330. Sachin got the innings off to a flying start, with a knock of 52 off 48 balls. Virat Kohli scored 183 and the target was overhauled with more than two overs to spare. That game turned out to be Sachin's last ODI.

That Sandeep Patil, one of Sachin's role models when he commenced formal cricket, was the chairman of India's National Selection Committee when the latter started 'winding up', was probably pre-ordained.

The announcement was made on the eve of India's T20 International and ODI series against Pakistan, which had been planned at the turn of 2012. Tributes were paid in print, on television and radio, and on social media, by fans from all over the world. Sachin's signature deeds were recalled—the final over in the Hero Cup semi-final, his 82 in his first ODI as opener, the 'Sandstorm' innings at Sharjah, his offensive against Henry Olonga, the 1996, 2003 and 2011 World Cups, and of course, the double hundred at Gwalior. While these memories did bring a smile to the faces of those who loved the sport, they did not quite inspire the Indian players themselves. The T20 International series against Pakistan was drawn 1–1, and the visitors won the ODI series 2–1.

Team India made a comeback in early 2013, in a home series against Australia. Dhoni's Indians avenged their 2011–12 humiliation by trouncing the visitors by the same margin—4–0. Ironically, but in a way appropriately, given that it was a time of transition, India's biggest series win ever was tinged with sadness; Virender Sehwag, one of the greatest entertainers the game has ever seen, was dropped after the second Test on grounds of poor form. He did not play for India again.

Sachin's best game of the series was the first Test at Chennai. He went in with his team wobbling at 12-2 and steadied the boat. He was fourth out at 196 for a well-compiled 81, and then skipper Mahendra Singh Dhoni and future skipper Virat Kohli took control. In the second innings, Sachin took guard in relatively comfortable circumstances, with India only 14 runs short of an emphatic win. He hit the first two balls he faced for six. Those two strokes off Nathan Lyon, the off-spinner, marked the end of a memorable association between him and the M.A. Chidambaram Stadium.

The Mumbai Indians were wearing a new look in the 2013 season of the IPL, with Ricky Ponting named captain and John Wright coming in as the coach. A few games into the competition, Ponting dropped himself on grounds of poor form and Rohit Sharma took over. Another legend withdrew from the squad in the days to follow. Sachin was batting well in a league game against Sunrisers Hyderabad when he started experiencing acute pain in his left hand after hitting a six. He was subsequently ruled out of action for three weeks and missed his team's last five games, including the final. It was during the summit clash, a memorable game for the Mumbai Indians, that Sachin announced his retirement from the annual competition. Still, a 'final' retirement was not on his mind.

He underwent a surgery on his left hand in London in July 2013 and then threw himself headlong into rehabilitation and training. However, something was wrong. Working out in the gymnasium no longer seemed as enjoyable as it had earlier. It wasn't a feeling he was used to.

The year 2013 witnessed a face-off between the BCCI and Cricket South Africa, over the scheduling of India's tour of the Rainbow Nation later that year. The BCCI then pulled off a surprise by scheduling a two-Test series against the West Indies at the start of the 2013–14 season. This meant that Sachin, whose tally of Tests stood at 198, now had an opportunity to become the first cricketer to complete a double century of Test appearances at home and not in South Africa.

This development got Sachin thinking. He had discussions with his near and dear ones, especially his wife and elder brother.

On the afternoon of 10 October 2013, this writer received a call from Sanjay Patel, the secretary of the BCCI. He was told by the secretary that he would be receiving a 'very important' email in the next couple of minutes. It needed to be forwarded to the media immediately, the secretary advised.

Sure enough, an email from the secretary's office popped up in this writer's inbox in less than a couple of minutes. It read as follows:

Sachin Tendulkar has contacted the President, BCCI, and has requested the BCCI to release the following statement to the Media, on his behalf:

All my life, I have had a dream of playing cricket for India. I have been living this dream every day for the last 24 years. It's hard for me to imagine a life without playing cricket because it's all I have ever done since I was 11 years old. It's been a huge honour to have represented my country and played all over the world. I look forward to playing my 200th Test Match on home soil, as I call it a day.

I thank the BCCI for everything over the years and for permitting me to move on when my heart feels it's time! I thank my family for their patience and understanding. Most of all, I thank my fans and well-wishers who through their prayers and wishes have given me the strength to go out and perform at my best.

—Sachin Tendulkar

This writer held his head in his hands as he read and re-read the mail a million times. He eventually gave up trying to regain his composure and forwarded the mail to the media.

For more than two years, those who had followed Sachin's career had expected him to make a certain announcement. His fans had convinced themselves that they had prepared themselves mentally for the inevitable, but they were mistaken. The news of his retirement left them numb. In letting go of Sachin Tendulkar, at least three generations of Indians were letting go of their respective childhoods.

Sachin's last bow at the international level was preceded by a final flourish for the city of his birth. It seemed as if the world had descended on the town of Lahli in the north Indian state of Haryana, which hosted a Ranji Trophy game against Mumbai at the start of the 2013–14 season. Sachin anchored his team's chase of a target of 240 on a wicket that was doing quite a bit, with an unbeaten 79. After Mumbai had completed a win by four wickets, Sachin was invited to the Haryana dressing room. The Haryana players hung on to every word that the master uttered, just like the members of Unmukt Chand's Indian team that had won the ICC under-19 World Cup in 2012, when Sachin addressed them in Mumbai before the tournament.

> I have never seen a man as patriotic as he is. He opens his bag and there is Ganpati and there is a flag of India. Underneath the Indian [BCCI] emblem [on his helmet], he has got a little flag.
>
> —Raj Singh Dungarpur, *Sachin Tendulkar—Mr. India*,
> PMG, 2002

Rajbhai would have liked the new rubber grip on Sachin's bats that he unveiled for his last Test series; it bore the colours of the Indian flag.

India walloped the West Indies in less than three days at both Kolkata, the venue of the first Test, and Mumbai, which hosted the second. However, the matches did not matter as much as the man did. The BCCI was only too happy to grant him his request of playing the two-hundredth and final Test of his career at his home ground.

On the eve of his 200th and last Test, Sachin posed for pictures with the media and ground staff. The final act of an extraordinary career commenced on 14 November 2013. Play was preceded by a felicitation and the unveiling of a postage stamp in Sachin's honour. He was only the fifth living Indian, after Maharshi Dhondo Keshav Karve, Dr Visvesvaraya, Mother Teresa and former Prime Minister Rajiv Gandhi,* to be accorded this distinction. Ministers of the Union Government and senior office-bearers of the BCCI and the MCA did

---

*Rajiv Gandhi was one of several leaders to feature on a stamp that was brought out to commemorate the centenary of the Indian National Congress in 1985.

the honours. In the stands and media box, it was the World Cup final all over again; the stands were packed to capacity and the media box was filled with journalists from across India and beyond. Some of them, like R. Mohan and Ayaz Memon, had also covered his first Test at Karachi in November 1989, and one of them—Debasish Datta—had covered Sachin's first, 50th, 100th, 150th and 200th Tests.

The capacity crowd went delirious on the evening of the first day, when the second Indian wicket went down. With Achrekar and Mrs Rajani Tendulkar, the latter on her first visit to a cricket ground, looking on from the President's Box, Sachin provided the world a final glimpse of his genius. The drives, flicks and, of course, intensity, were on show in a fine innings. He had moved to 74 when he went for a cut off Shane Shillingford, the left-arm spinner. The ball bounced a little more than he expected and the cherry flew to Darren Sammy, the West Indies captain, at slip. An age had passed.

As emotional as the spectators who gave him a standing ovation were members of the media, the Fourth Estate, who had praised and criticized him in equal measure in the years gone by, in line with their professional duties.

The Indian team accorded him a 'mobile' guard of honour after the final of the final West Indies wicket in the second innings, ensuring that the 'tunnel' formed by the players remained intact from the pitch till the stairs that led to the dressing room. And that was when the dam finally burst. Along with Sachin, a stadium and a nation wept. The childhood of at least three generations of cricket lovers officially ended on the afternoon of 16 November 2013, the designated third day of the Test, exactly 24 years and one day since Sachin's first day as an international cricket in another coastal city, Karachi.

The grand finale of the 'send-off' was a stirring speech, delivered by the man himself. He struggled to keep his emotions in check as he thanked his near and dear ones and family for their support. Fortunately for those hearing, they did not need to be inhibited. An officer in the Indian Army, who was in his late thirties and so would have been a schoolboy when Sachin made his international debut in November 1989, was driving on the streets of Delhi, listening to the post-match proceedings on the radio, when Sachin was handed the mike; after the first couple of minutes, the officer stopped the vehicle, turned off the engine and broke down. He was one of many.

Sachin was joined by his family as he undertook a lap of honour to thank the capacity crowd one last time, for making his final appearance memorable. The feeling was of course mutual. It was then that Virat Kohli, a player who had grown up idolising him, did what Sachin himself had assigned him to do.

He reminded his hero of something.

Right from the time the game had ended till he had walked around the ground, Sachin had been surrounded by his family, teammates, match officials, security officials, photographers and even some gatecrashers. But no one accompanied him as he made his way to the middle for one final time. He touched the Wankhede wicket with his right hand. He then held his right hand to his heart and looking at the strip, folded his hands. He could not have ended his career without paying obeisance to the 22-yeard plot of land that had given him everything.

Hours after the end of his last Test, the Government of India informed the nation that Sachin would receive the Bharat Ratna, the country's highest civilian honour. He was conferred the award by the President of India, His Excellency Shri Pranab Mukherjee, at a function at the Darbar Hall of the Rashtrapati Bhavan at Delhi on 4 February 2014. He was the first sports personality to receive the honour.

> I am humbled and honoured to be given the Bharat Ratna. This award is for my mother because of all the sacrifices she made for me right from my birth. As a child, it is difficult to understand life. You don't understand what your parents have to go through to make you happy. It is only when you grow up, you realise all these things.... I would like to go a step further. Not just my mother...but like my mother, there are millions and millions of mothers in India who sacrifice thousands of things for their children. So I would like to share my award with all the mothers for all the sacrifices they have made.
>
> —Sachin Tendulkar, *Mid-Day,* 18 November 2013

EPILOGUE

> *Sachin would come to the MCA Recreation Centre [Bandra-Kurla Complex] to play badminton in the days following his retirement. One day, when I went to the porch to see him off, he told me that he wanted me to see some 'magic.' He then opened the door of his car. What I saw inside was badminton racquets, shuttlecocks and shoes. The cricket equipment had disappeared. He did train before the Veterans' series that he had organized with Shane Warne [in 2015] but barring that, there have been only three or four occasions when I have seen him holding a cricket bat after his retirement. He had once come over to give tips to Arjun and there was another instance when he was requested by Virat Kohli, Suresh Raina and Yuvraj Singh to spend some time with them at the nets. Some of us were apprehensive about how he would react to retirement, but he has proved us wrong. He has moved on.*
>
> —Anil Joshi, personal interview

For all the emotions that Sachin stirred even within the most unsentimental individuals, on the afternoon of 16 November 2013, there were many who believed that he had overstayed his welcome. Some had even gone to the extent of drawing parallels between him and his former teammate Kapil Dev's final two years in international cricket.

From his Test debut on 15 November 1989 to the Cape Town Test against South Africa that concluded on 6 January 2011, Sachin played a record 177 Tests, in which he scored 14,692 runs at an average of 56.94, inclusive of 51 centuries. From his ODI debut at Gujranwala on 18 December 1989 to the World Cup final that was played on 2 April 2011, he played a record 453 ODIs, from which he amassed 18,111 runs at an average of 45.16, inclusive of 48 centuries. These were stupendous stats.

From mid-2011 till he called it a day in November 2013, Sachin played 23 more Tests, in which he scored 1,229 runs at an average of 32.34, inclusive of nine 50s that comprised two 90s. He did not score a single Test century during this phase. His Test batting average of 56.94 in January 2011 declined to 53.78 by the time he was done in November 2013. In the 10 ODIs that he played after the 2011 World Cup final, he scored 315 runs at the rate of 31.50, with a solitary century to his credit. His overall ODI average fell marginally, from 45.16 at the end of the 2011 World Cup to 44.83 by the time he quit the format for good.

A comparison with seven all-time greats, two of whom were Sachin's heroes and the other five his foremost contemporaries, is instructive.

Table: Batting Averages

Name of the player	Tests played	Batting average before the last 23 Tests of his career	Batting average in his last 23 Tests	Career batting average in Tests—overall
Sachin Tendulkar	200	56.94	32.34	53.78
Sunil Gavaskar	125	51.79	47.75	51.12
Vivian Richards	121	53.05	38.54	50.23
Brian Lara	131	53.71	49.37	52.88
Ricky Ponting	168	54.83	35.60	51.85
Jacques Kallis	166	56.82	46.82	55.37
Rahul Dravid	164	53.30	46.87	52.31
Kumara Sangakkara	134	56.73	60.19	57.40

Kumara Sangakkara apart, the 'legends mentioned in the table averaged less in their last 23 Tests than what they averaged for the better part of their respective careers. The difference was quite substantial in the cases of Vivian Richards and three modern greats—Jacques Kallis, Ricky Ponting and Sachin himself. It is, therefore, unfair to single Sachin out.

> He has left a legacy. Future generations should look to emulate cricketers like him. He was a fierce competitor on the field and was respectful of the game and its followers. I am not sure if he is interested in cricket administration, but he has got a lot to give Indian cricket. I was returning with him from Kolkata after the first meeting of the Cricket Advisory Committee, of which he was a member, along with Sourav Ganguly and V.V.S. Laxman, in June 2015. As we spoke, I could sense his keenness to do something. Indian cricket means everything to him and those who played with him, like

Sourav Ganguly, Rahul Dravid, V.V.S. Laxman and Anil Kumble, to name just a few. Some of them are already involved with Indian cricket. Sachin's proposal of allowing 14 players to participate in inter-school matches has recently been implemented by the MCA in its inter-school tournaments. Rahul Dravid also endorsed the suggestion recently. We can look forward to a long association between Sachin and Indian cricket, even after his retirement as a cricketer.

—Prof. R.S. Shetty, personal interview

The Virat Kohli of early 2017 is a far cry from the diffident young man who sought Sachin's advice after an unsuccessful tour of England in mid-2014. Apart from recommending some technical alterations, Sachin advised Kohli to stop 'looking up things that were written about him'. A few months after that England series, the Delhi batsman scored nearly 700 runs in four Tests in Australia. He hasn't looked back since. In February 2017, Kohli held the second, third and top spots in the ICC's batting rankings for Tests, ODIs and T20 internationals respectively. No other batsman in international cricket has been as dominant across formats. There was a lump in many a throat when the self-confessed 'devotee' of Sachin bowed to his hero seated in the stands at Eden Gardens, after completing a half-century against Pakistan in a league match of the 2016 ICC T20 World Cup.

Elevated to the captaincy of India's Test side after M.S. Dhoni announced his retirement from the traditional version, Kohli proceeded to lead India to series wins over Sri Lanka, South Africa, West Indies, New Zealand, England and Bangladesh.* There is every reason to believe that he and his band of conquerors will outdo their predecessors who did India proud in the first decade of the new millennium.

> This team reminds me of our times between 2000–11. They have a quality pace and spin attack. We believe that it is the best team in the world. Soon rest of the world will follow us.
>
> —Sachin Tendulkar, as quoted on www.firstpost.com, 3 December 2016

The cricketing legend has metamorphosed into an accomplished orator, entrepreneur, mentor and an inspiration for professionals aspiring to excel in different fields. Today, Sachin is, for all practical purposes, a life-coach.

---

*This epilogue was written in February 2017.

Apart from being a Parliamentarian, he is the United Nations International Children's Fund's (UNICEF) ambassador for hygiene and sanitation, and one of the faces of the Swachh Bharat (Clean India) campaign that was initiated by the National Democratic Alliance (NDA) government that came to power after the general election of 2014. Sachin's objective in this 'second innings', it appears, is no different from that of someone who in an incarnation went from being a 'prodigy' to a 'preceptor', and helped people help themselves, just like Sachin himself.

In 2016, Sachin commenced another second-innings venture in the form of SRT Sports, a sports management company. He also co-owns Kerala Blasters, one of the teams in the Indian Super League (Football) and Bengaluru Blasters, one of the sides in the Premier Badminton League.

> I can't see him too far away from sport and perhaps he can use his iconic status to give a leg-up to other sports that struggle to find place thanks to the overwhelming presence of cricket in India. I see Tendulkar playing a constructive role in his country's Olympics movement by travelling with the team to the games.
>
> —Steve Waugh, *The Week*, 1 December 2013

Cricket remains Sachin's first love, of course. His heart continues to beat for it and his brain continues to tick for it. The idea of fielding 14 players in inter-school cricket was by no means the only radical idea he has proposed. At the Hindustan Times Leadership Summit in December 2016, he suggested that first-class matches in India be played on two different pitches—a greentop and a turner—with balls of different makes. This, he felt, would give Indian batsmen the opportunity to hone their skills in different conditions in their formative years and thus enable them to evolve into better players.

Starting from the time his coach hurled challenge after challenge at him, Sachin Ramesh Tendulkar emerged from every 'test' that he faced as a cricketer with flying colours. However, it appears that his toughest cricketing challenge lies ahead of him, more than three years after his retirement as a player.

Cricket, or rather, international cricket, finds itself in a situation not too different from the one that Krishna encountered, 36 years after the end of the Mahabharata war. The curse of Gandhari, the mother of the Kauravs, manifested itself in the form of an internecine bloodbath, wherein Krishna's entire Yadav clan perished. Balaram, Krishna's elder brother, renounced his life and Krishna, left to himself, sat under a tree to reflect on the days gone by. His left foot was mistaken to be that of a deer's, by Jara, a hunter. The hunter's arrow found its mark, and Krishna gave up his mortal form. Seven days after his death, the city of Dwarka was swallowed up by the ocean from which it had originated. Arjun, Krishna's closest friend, had evacuated the women and other dependents from the city by then. The demise of Krishna marked the end of the Dwapar Yug and the start of the Kali Yug, the age of strife, degeneration, corruption and avarice, which continues to this day.

Difficult as it may seem to believe, cricket in the second decade of the new millennium finds itself confronting a crisis of sorts that could grow into an existential one if not tackled and resolved in time.

The sport is no longer the 'geographical' phenomenon that it exclusively was for decades. The country vs country and state vs state face-offs have been joined by inter-franchise duels. The IPL has been at the forefront of this change. While there is a lot to commend the IPL for, especially in terms of improving relationships between players from different countries who suddenly found themselves sharing a dressing room, and making it possible for players to make a comfortable living from the game without necessarily representing their respective countries or states on a regular basis, it has also unleashed a major concern.

Unless administrators in India and elsewhere pull up their socks, there is a genuine possibility of many cricketers redrawing their priorities in the years to come. Today, it is possible to earn substantially more from a seven-week inter-franchise tournament than by playing domestic cricket in a full season that stretches for five months or more. The lure of lucre can be overpowering enough to overrule the pride of representing one's country or state. Even in the contemporary era, there are cricketers who have refused to be bound to their respective Boards. They have opted to become 'freelancers' instead and play in the multiple Twenty20 leagues that have sprouted across the world. It is not that they do not feel proud to represent their country on the international platform; it is just that from their point of view, 'inter-franchise' cricket seems better run and gives them a greater sense of security.

The prospect of international and domestic cricket being superseded by inter-franchise Twenty20 leagues in the not-too-distant future cannot be ruled out. The game's administrators will need to ensure that this does not happen.

In India, everything seems hunky-dory, as of now. But that is because the members of the contemporary side have grown up idolizing the likes of Sachin, Rahul Dravid, Sourav Ganguly, Anil Kumble, V.V.S. Laxman, Zaheer Khan and Virender Sehwag, among others. For Virat Kohli, Ajinkya Rahane, Cheteshwar Pujara, Murali Vijay and R. Ashwin, to name just a few, international cricket is the apogee of the sport. It is what they aspired to play as children and teenagers.

However, what about those who have grown up in the era of the IPL? Once the current generation moves on, will those who succeed them feel as passionately about representing their country and state as the contemporary stars do?

In December 2010, by which time the IPL was three seasons old, this writer was witness to an incident that underscored the changing mindsets of the younger generation. A group of schoolboy cricketers was introduced to a former Test cricketer at a ground in Chandigarh. The boys were told by their coach to touch the former cricketer's feet and seek his blessings, which they did. The senior cricketer was flabbergasted when the boys proceeded to ask him what they ought to do to play in the IPL. He advised them to think about representing Punjab in domestic cricket first, but he did have a nagging suspicion that his sagacious suggestion had not gone down too well with the boys. That interaction between a stalwart and a group of youngsters has no doubt been replicated in other parts of the cricketing world.

For a connoisseur of the sport, the ultimate nightmare is the withering away of the longer forms of the game in the face of the Twenty20 storm. Some people may argue that Twenty20, which is a commercially viable proposition, is needed to sustain Test and first-class cricket, both of which have a niche audience and do not have the same box-office appeal as the game's shortest format. However, the fact is that Twenty20 will not be able to survive on its own in the long run, devoid of the systems and traditions that have been put in place by the longer forms of the game. Even if it does survive, it will 'not be cricket', pun very much intended.

There are many sports in which artistry has given way to brute force, and the same will happen in cricket, if Twenty20 is prioritized over its older and longer siblings. Already, it seems extremely unlikely that too many children across the cricketing world will be aspiring to become bowlers; the possibility of bowling machines replacing humans in a format loaded hopelessly in favour of the batsmen is anything but far-fetched.

There is of course no reason why cricket's three formats cannot coexist and thrive simultaneously, the way classical music and its 'lighter' variations like film music have coexisted with pop and rap for decades. But for that to happen, they will need to be managed properly.

This is where Sachin Ramesh Tendulkar can play a critical role. Those who run the game of cricket will do well to utilize his experience, expertise and enterprise to emphasize the importance of international and domestic cricket to future generations.

In that sense, the legend who was a bridge between generations in his 24 years as an international cricketer is luckier than Krishna. Sachin has options at hand to salvage the situation and with it, the sport itself, unlike Krishna, who knew that the destruction of his clan was inevitable.

As Sunil Gavaskar, one of his heroes, had written several years ago in the context of Sachin's reluctance to 'express himself' on a tour of Australia: 'When Tendulkar speaks, the world will stop and listen.'

Given the hero's passion for the sport, there is reason to believe that this will happen sooner than later.

To paraphrase what his better half had said on his last day as an international cricketer, 'We can imagine cricket without Sachin Tendulkar, but we cannot imagine Sachin Tendulkar without cricket.'

APPENDIX 1

THE SACHIN TENDULKAR FACTFILE

Compiled by Sudhir Vaidya and Devendra Prabhudesai
Full name: Sachin Ramesh Tendulkar
Born: 24 April 1973, Bombay (now Mumbai), Maharashtra
Prominent teams: India, Mumbai, West Zone, Rest of India, Yorkshire, Mumbai Indians
Nicknames/Appellations: Tendlya, Little Champion, God of Cricket, Sachu, Master
Batting style: Right-hand bat
Bowling style: Right-arm off-break, Leg-break googly, Medium Pace

Prominent Awards and Distinctions

1. Bharat Ratna: India's highest civilian honour: 2014
2. Padma Vibhushan: India's second-highest civilian honour: 2008
3. Padma Shri: India's fourth-highest civilian honour: 1998
4. Rajiv Gandhi Khel Ratna Award in Sports and Games (the highest sporting honour of the Republic of India): 1998
5. Honorary Group Captain: Indian Air Force: 2010 (the first individual from a non-aviation background to be accorded this distinction)
6. Arjuna Award for Sporting Excellence by the Government of India: 1994
7. The ICC's Sir Garfield Sobers Award for being the International Player of the Year: 2009–10
8. The BCCI's Polly Umrigar Award for being the Indian Cricketer of the Year in 2006–07 and 2009–10
9. Maharashtra Bhushan: The highest civilian award given by the Government of the State of Maharashtra: 2001
10. Membership of the Order of Australia: 2012
11. Listed among the '100 Most Influential People in the World' by *TIME* magazine in May 2010

Sachin Tendulkar in International Cricket

Table: Batting and Fielding

	Matches	Inns	NO	Runs	HS	Avg.	100s	50s	Cts
Tests	200	329	33	15,921	248*	53.78	51	68	115
ODIs	463	452	41	18,426	200*	44.83	49	96	140
T20Is	1	1	0	10	10	10.00	0	0	1

Notes: NO: Not out; HS: Highest score; Cts: Catches held

Table: Bowling

	Matches	Inns	Balls	Runs	Wkts	BBI	BBM	Avg.	4w	5w
Tests	200	145	4,240	2,492	46	3/10	3/14	54.17	0	0
ODIs	463	270	8,054	6,850	154	5/32	5/32	44.48	4	2
T20Is	1	1	15	12	1	1/12	1/12	12.00	0	0

Notes: BBI: Best bowling figures in an innings; BBM: Best bowling figures in a match; 4W: Four wickets in an innings; 5W: Five wickets in an innings

Sachin Tendulkar in First-Class Cricket

Sunil Gavaskar scored 25,785 runs from 349 first-class matches, the highest by an Indian. Tendulkar is a close second with 25,239 runs from 304 first-class matches.

Table: Batting and Fielding

Matches	Inns	NO	Runs	HS	Avg.	100s	50s	Cts
304	483	51	25,239	248*	58.42	81	116	173

Notes: NO: Not out; HS: Highest score; Cts: Catches held

Table: Bowling

Balls	Runs	Wkts	BBI	Avg.	4w	5w
7,561	4,357	70	3/10	62.24	0	0

Notes: BBI: Best bowling figures in an innings; 4W: Four wickets in an innings; 5W: Five wickets in an innings

APPENDIX 2

SACHIN TENDULKAR'S LONGEVITY IN TEST CRICKET

Country	Total number of Test cricketers from 15 March 1877 to 16 November 2013 in the 2,102 Tests played in this 137-year period	Number of Test cricketers (team-wise) before Tendulkar commenced his Test career on 15 November 1989	The number of Test cricketers to have debuted between 15 November 1989 and 16 November 2013
Australia	435	347	88
England	657	541	116
South Africa*	316	236	80
South Africa returned to Test cricket in 1991–92			
West Indies	297	194	103
New Zealand	262	168	94
India	280	185	95
Pakistan	215	109	106
Sri Lanka	124	42	82
Zimbabwe*	87	All*	97
Zimbabwe started playing Tests in 1992–93			
Bangladesh*	69	All*	69
Bangladesh started playing Tests in 2000–01			
	2,742	1,822	920

Of the 2,742 individuals who played Test cricket from 15 March 1877 to 16 November 2013, as many as 920 (nearly one-third) made their respective debuts from 15 November 1989 (Sachin's first day as a Test cricketer) to 16 November 2013 (Sachin's last day as a Test cricketer).

England's Wilfred Rhodes had a Test career that lasted nearly 30 years. He made his Test debut against Australia at Nottingham in 1899 and bid farewell to Test cricket after playing the West Indies at Kingston in 1928–29. Three of his teammates in his last Test—Bob Wyatt, Leslie Ames and Bill Voce—were not even born when he made his Test debut in 1899. Wyatt was born in 1901, Ames in 1905 and Voce in 1909.

Likewise, two of Sachin Tendulkar's teammates in the final Test of a career that spanned 24 years and 1 day were not born when he made his Test debut against Pakistan at Karachi in 1989–90. Both Bhuvneshwar Kumar and Mohammed Shami were born in 1990.

Sachin Tendulkar is one of the few cricketers to have played Tests against a father–son combination:		
His Tests against Geoff Marsh (Father)	1st Test at Brisbane	1991–92
	2nd Test at Melbourne	1991–92
	3rd Test at Sydney	1991–92
	4th Test at Adelaide	1991–92
His Tests against Shaun Marsh (Son)	1st Test at Melbourne	2011–12
	2nd Test at Sydney	2011–12
	3rd Test at Perth	2011–12
	4th Test at Adelaide	2011–12

APPENDIX 3

SACHIN TENDULKAR'S FIRST-CLASS CENTURIES

Sachin Tendulkar shares the Indian record for the highest number of first-class hundreds (81) with Sunil Gavaskar.

Sr. No.	Runs	Match/ Tournament	Team for which played	Opponent	Venue	Country	Season
1	100*	Ranji Trophy (On debut)	Mumbai	Gujarat	Mumbai (Wankhede)	India	1988–89
2	103	Irani Cup (On debut)	Rest of India	Delhi	Mumbai (Wankhede)	India	1989–90
3	**119***	**Test**	**India**	**England**	**Manchester**	**England**	**1990**
4	108	On the tour of England	Indians	Parkinson's World XI	Scarborough	England	1990
5	125	Ranji Trophy	Mumbai	Delhi	Delhi (Kotla)	India	1990–91
6	159	Duleep Trophy (On debut)	West Zone	East Zone	Guwahati	India	1990–91
7	131	Duleep Trophy	West Zone	South Zone	Rourkela	India	1990–91
8	**148***	**Test**	**India**	**Australia**	**Sydney**	**Australia**	**1991–92**
9	**114**	**Test**	**India**	**Australia**	**Perth**	**Australia**	**1991–92**
10	100	County Cricket Championship In England	Yorkshire	Durham	Durham	England	1992
11	131	On the tour of South Africa	Indians	South African Students XI	East London	South Africa	1992–93
12	**111**	**Test**	**India**	**South Africa**	**Johannesburg**	**South Africa**	**1992–93**
13	**165**	**Test**	**India**	**England**	**Chennai**	**India**	**1992–93**
14	**104***	**Test**	**India**	**Sri Lanka**	**Colombo (SSC)**	**Sri Lanka**	**1993**
15	138	Ranji Trophy	Mumbai	Maharashtra	Thane	India	1993–94

Sr. No.	Runs	Match/ Tournament	Team for which played	Opponent	Venue	Country	Season
16	142	Test	India	Sri Lanka	Lucknow	India	1993–94
17	179	Test	India	West Indies	Nagpur (VCA)	India	1994–95
18	175	Ranji Trophy	Mumbai	Vadodara	Mumbai (Wankhede)	India	1994–95
19	166	Ranji Trophy	Mumbai	Tamil Nadu	Mumbai (Wankhede)	India	1994–95
20	109	Ranji Trophy	Mumbai	Uttar Pradesh	Mumbai (Wankhede)	India	1994–95
21**	140	Ranji Trophy	Mumbai	Punjab	Mumbai (Wankhede)	India	1994–95
22**	139	As above	As above	As above	As above	As above	As above
23	151	Ranji Trophy	Mumbai	Maharashtra	Thane	India	1995–96
24	122	Test	India	England	Birmingham	England	1996
25	177	Test	India	England	Nottingham	England	1996
26	169	Test	India	South Africa	Cape Town	South Africa	1996–97
27	143	Test	India	Sri Lanka	Colombo (RPS)	Sri Lanka	1997–98
28	139	Test	India	Sri Lanka	Colombo (SSC)	Sri Lanka	1997–98
29	177	Ranji Trophy	Mumbai	Gujarat	Valsad	India	1997–98
30	135	Ranji Trophy	Mumbai	Orissa	Mumbai (Wankhede)	India	1997–98
31	148	Test	India	Sri Lanka	Mumbai (Wankhede)	India	1997–98
32	204*	Australians	Mumbai	Australia	Mumbai (Brabourne)	India	1997–98
33	155*	Test	India	Australia	Chennai	India	1997–98
34	177	Test	India	Australia	Bengaluru	India	1997–98
35	113	Test	India	New Zealand	Wellington	New Zealand	1998–99
36	154	On the tour of New Zealand	Indians	Central Districts	Napier	New Zealand	1998–99
37	136	Test	India	Pakistan	Chennai	India	1998–99
38	124*	Test	India	Sri Lanka	Colombo (SSC)	Sri Lanka	1998–99

SACHIN TENDULKAR'S FIRST-CLASS CENTURIES • 467

Sr. No.	Runs	Match/ Tournament	Team for which played	Opponent	Venue	Country	Season
39	126*	Test	India	New Zealand	Mohali	India	1999–2000
40	217	Test	India	New Zealand	Ahmedabad (Motera)	India	1999–2000
41	233	Ranji Trophy	Mumbai	Tamil Nadu	Mumbai (Wankhede)	India	1999–2000
42	128	Ranji Trophy	Mumbai	Hyderabad	Mumbai (Wankhede)	India	1999–2000
43	116	Test	India	Australia	Melbourne	Australia	1999–2000
44	108	Ranji Trophy	Mumbai	Vadodara	Mumbai (Wankhede)	India	2000–01
45	122	Test	India	Zimbabwe	Delhi	India	2000–01
46	201*	Test	India	Zimbabwe	Nagpur (VCA)	India	2000–01
47	126	Test	India	Australia	Chennai	India	2000–01
48	199	Duleep Trophy	West Zone	East Zone	Pune	India	2000–01
49	155	Test	India	South Africa	Bloemfontein	South Africa	2001–02
50	103	Test	India	England	Ahmedabad (Motera)	India	2001–02
51	176	Test	India	Zimbabwe	Nagpur	India	2001–02
52	117	Test	India	West Indies	Port of Spain	West Indies	2001–02
53	193	Test	India	England	Leeds	England	2002
54	169	On the tour of England	Indians	Worcestershire	Worcester	England	2002
55	176	Test	India	West Indies	Kolkata	India	2002–03
56	241*	Test	India	Australia	Sydney	Australia	2003–04
57	194*	Test	India	Pakistan	Multan	Pakistan	2003–04
58	248*	Test	India	Bangladesh	Dhaka	Bangladesh	2004–05
59	109	Test	India	Sri Lanka	Delhi	India	2005–06
60	101	Test	India	Bangladesh	Chittagong	Bangladesh	2006–07
61	122*	Test	India	Bangladesh	Mirpur	Bangladesh	2006–07
62	105	Ranji Trophy	Mumbai	Bengal	Mumbai (Wankhede)	India	2006–07
63	171	On the tour of England	Indians	England Lions	Chelmsford	England	2007

Sr. No.	Runs	Match/ Tournament	Team for which played	Opponent	Venue	Country	Season
64	154*	Test	India	Australia	Sydney	Australia	2007–08
65	153	Test	India	Australia	Adelaide	Australia	2007–08
66	109	Test	India	Australia	Nagpur (Jamtha)	India	2008–09
67	122*	Ranji Trophy	Mumbai	Saurashtra	Chennai	India	2008–09
68	103*	Test	India	England	Chennai	India	2008–09
68	160	Test	India	New Zealand	Hamilton	New Zealand	2008–09
70	100*	Test	India	Sri Lanka	Ahmedabad (Motera)	India	2009–10
71	105*	Test	India	Bangladesh	Chittagong	Bangladesh	2009–10
72	143	Test	India	Bangladesh	Mirpur	Bangladesh	2009–10
73	100	Test	India	South Africa	Nagpur (Jamtha)	India	2009–10
74	106	Test	India	South Africa	Kolkata	India	2009–10
75	203	Test	India	Sri Lanka	Colombo (SSC)	Sri Lanka	2010
76	214	Test	India	Australia	Bengaluru	India	2010–11
77	111*	Test	India	South Africa	Centurion	South Africa	2010–11
78	146	Test	India	South Africa	Cape Town	South Africa	2010–11
79	140*	Irani Cup	Mumbai	Rest of India	Mumbai (Wankhede)	India	2012–13
80	137	Ranji Trophy	Mumbai	Railways	Delhi (Karnail)	India	2012–13
81	108	Ranji Trophy	Mumbai	Vadodara	Mumbai (Wankhede)	India	2012–13

Notes:
Sachin's Test centuries have been marked in bold.
*denotes 'not out'.
**denotes centuries in the same match.
Sachin's 81 first-class centuries comprise eight double hundreds, six of them in Tests. He scored two double hundreds for Mumbai—one against Tamil Nadu in the 1999–2000 Ranji Trophy semi-final and another against the Australians in 1997–98.

APPENDIX 4

SACHIN TENDULKAR'S HUNDREDS IN LIST 'A' MATCHES

Sr. No.	Runs	Match/ Tournament	Team for which he played	Opponent	Venue	Date
1	105*	Tour match	Indians	Derbyshire	Chesterfield	7-16-1990
2	107	County Cricket Championship of England	Yorkshire	Lancashire	Leeds	8-2-1992
3	107	Ranji One-Dayer	Mumbai	Vadodara	Vadodara (GSFC)	12-5-1993
4	110	One-Day International	India	Australia	Colombo (RPS)	09-09-1994
5	115	One-Day International	India	New Zealand	Vadodara (IPCL)	28-10-1994
6	116	Ranji One-Dayer	Mumbai	Haryana		11-8-1994
7	105	One-Day International	India	West Indies	Jaipur	11-11-1994
8	120	Ranji One-Dayer	Mumbai	Gujarat	Mumbai (Wankhede)	01-25-1995
9	139	Tour match	Indians	Central Districts		02-14-1995
10	112*	One-Day International	India	Sri Lanka	Sharjah	09-04-1995
11	122	Wills Trophy	Wills XI	Hyderabad	Rajkot	11-1-1995
12	112	Wills Trophy	Wills XI	Madhya Pradesh	Ahmedabad (Motera)	11-3-1995
13	127*	One-Day International	India	Kenya	Cuttack	18-02-1996
14	137	One-Day International	India	Sri Lanka	Delhi	02-03-1996

Sr. No.	Runs	Match/Tournament	Team for which he played	Opponent	Venue	Date
15	100	One-Day International	India	Pakistan	Singapore	05-04-1996
16	118	One-Day International	India	Pakistan	Sharjah	15-04-1996
17	110	One-Day International	India	Sri Lanka	Colombo (RPS)	28-08-1996
18	114	One-Day International	India	South Africa	Mumbai (Wankhede)	14-12-1996
19	104	One-Day International	India	Zimbabwe	Benoni	09-02-1997
20	104	Challenger Trophy	India Seniors	India 'B'	Chandigarh	09-29-1996
21	113	Challenger Trophy	India Seniors	India 'B'	Chandigarh	10-1-1996
22	117	One-Day International	India	New Zealand	Bengaluru	14-05-1997
23	100	One-Day International	India	Australia	Kanpur	07-04-1998
24	143	One-Day International	India	Australia	Sharjah	22-04-1998
25	134	One-Day International	India	Australia	Sharjah	23-04-1998
26	100*	One-Day International	India	Kenya	Kolkata	31-05-1998
27	128	One-Day International	India	Sri Lanka	Colombo (RPS)	07-07-1998
28	127*	One-Day International	India	Zimbabwe	Bulawayo	26-09-1998
29	141	One-Day International	India	Australia	Dhaka	28-10-1998
30	118	One-Day International	India	Zimbabwe	Sharjah	08-11-1998
31	124*	One-Day International	India	Zimbabwe	Sharjah	12-11-1998
32	140*	One-Day International	India	Kenya	Bristol	23-05-1999
33	120	One-Day International	India	Sri Lanka	Colombo (SSC)	29-08-1999

SACHIN TENDULKAR'S HUNDREDS IN LIST 'A' MATCHES • 471

Sr. No.	Runs	Match/ Tournament	Team for which he played	Opponent	Venue	Date
34	186*	One-Day International	India	New Zealand	Hyderabad (LBS Stadium)	08-11-1999
35	122	One-Day International	India	South Africa	Vadodara (IPCL)	17-03-2000
36	101	One-Day International	India	Sri Lanka	Sharjah	20-10-2000
37	146	One-Day International	India	Zimbabwe	Jodhpur	08-12-2000
38	139	One-Day International	India	Australia	Indore	31-03-2001
39	122*	One-Day International	India	West Indies	Harare	04-07-2001
40	101	One-Day International	India	South Africa	Johannesburg	05-10-2001
41	146	One-Day International	India	Kenya	Paarl	24-10-2001
42	105*	One-Day International	India	England	Chester-le-Street	04-07-2002
43	113	One-Day International	India	Sri Lanka	Bristol	11-07-2002
44	152	One-Day International	India	Namibia	Pietermaritzburg	23-02-2003
45	100	One-Day International	India	Australia	Gwalior	26-10-2003
46	102	One-Day International	India	New Zealand	Hyderabad (LBS Stadium)	15-11-2003
47	141	One-Day International	India	Pakistan	Rawalpindi	16-03-2004
48	123	One-Day International	India	Pakistan	Ahmedabad (Motera)	12-04-2005
49	100	One-Day International	India	Pakistan	Peshawar	06-02-2006
50	141*	One-Day International	India	West Indies	Kuala Lumpur	14-09-2006
51	139	Challenger Trophy	India Blue	India Green	Chennai	10-2-2006
52	100*	One-Day International	India	West Indies	Vadodara (IPCL)	31-01-2007

Sr. No.	Runs	Match/ Tournament	Team for which he played	Opponent	Venue	Date
53	117*	One-Day International	India	Australia	Sydney	02-03-2008
54	163*	One-Day International	India	New Zealand	Christchurch	08-03-2009
55	138	One-Day International	India	Sri Lanka	Colombo (RPS)	14-09-2009
56	175	One-Day International	India	Australia	Hyderabad (RGIS)	05-11-2009
57	200*	One-Day International	India	South Africa	Gwalior	24-02-2010
58	120	One-Day International	India	England	Bengaluru	27-02-2011
59	111	One-Day International	India	South Africa	Nagpur (Jamtha)	12-03-2011
60	114	One-Day International	India	Bangladesh	Mirpur	16-03-2012

Notes:
The ODI 100s have been marked in bold.
*denotes 'not out'.

BIBLIOGRAPHY

Primary Sources

Ansari, Khalid. 1985. *Wills Tribute to Excellence—Champions of One-Day Cricket*. Delhi: Orient Longman Ltd.
Atherton, Mike. 2002. *Opening Up: My Autobiography*. London: Hodder & Stoughton.
BCCI. 2008. *From Learners to Leaders—Commemorative Volume*. Mumbai: BCCI.
———. 2011. *World Champions—2011 World Cup Commemorative Volume*. Mumbai: BCCI.
Bhattacharya, Gautam. 2011. *Sach*. New Delhi: Vikas Publishing.
Bhogle, Harsha. 1994. *Azhar: The Authorised Biography of Mohammad Azharuddin*. New Delhi: Penguin Books.
Bose, Mihir. 2002. *A History of Indian Cricket*. UK: Andre Deutsch.
CBI. 2000. 'Report on Cricket Match-fixing and Related Malpractises'. New Delhi: CBI.
Chappell, Greg. 2011. *Fierce Focus*. Australia: Hardie Grant Books.
ESPNcricinfo. 2015. *Sachin Tendulkar—The Man Cricket Loved Back*. New Delhi: Penguin Books.
Ezekiel, Gulu. 2002. *Sachin—The Story of the World's Greatest Batsman*. New Delhi: Penguin Books.
Greig, Tony. 1985. *Wills Tribute to Excellence, Champions of One-Day Cricket*. New Delhi: Orient Longman Ltd.
Hopps, David. 2014. *Sachin Tendulkar: The Man Cricket Loved Back*. New Delhi: Penguin Books.
John Wisden & Co. (Various Years). *Wisden Cricket Almanacks*. UK: John Wisden & Co.
John Wisden & Co. 2016. *Tendulkar in Wisden, An Anthology*. UK: John Wisden & Co.
Magazine, Pradeep. 1999. *Not Quite Cricket—The Explosive Story of How Bookmakers Influence the Game Today*. New Delhi: Penguin Books.
Majumdar, Boria and J.A. Mangan (eds). 2004. *Cricketing Cultures in Conflict—World Cup*. New Delhi: Routledge.
MCA. 2013. Sachin Forever (Anthology). Mumbai: MCA.
Patherya, Mudar. 1987. *Wills Book of Excellence—Cricket*. New Delhi: Orient Longman, 1987.
Ponting, Ricky. 2013. *Ponting: At Close of Play*. New Delhi: Harper Sports.
Prabhudesai, Devendra. 2009. *SMG—A Biography of Sunil Manohar Gavaskar*. New Delhi: Rupa Publications.
Purandare, Kunal. 2016. *Ramakant Achrekar—Master Blaster's Master*. New Delhi: Roli Books.
Samiuddin, Osman. 2014. *The Unquiet Ones—A History of Pakistan Cricket*. New Delhi: Harper Sports.

Tendulkar, Ajit. 1996. *The Making of A Cricketer—Formative Years of Sachin Tendulkar in Cricket*. Mumbai: Sachin Tendulkar Promotions Pvt Ltd.
Tendulkar, Sachin. 2014. *Sachin Tendulkar: Playing It My Way*. London: Hodder & Staughton.
Wisden India. (Various Years). *Wisden India Almanacks*. Bangalore: Wisden India.
———. 2013. The Sachin Sunset (Anthology). Bangalore: Wisden India.
Wright, John, Sharda Ugra and Paul Thomas. 2006. *John Wright's Indian Summers*. New Delhi: Penguin Books.

Newspapers and Periodicals (Inclusive of Commemorative/Special Issues):

Ashtapailu (Marathi)
Cricinfo Magazine
Cricket Talk
Daily News & Analysis (DNA)
Hindustan Times
India Today
Live Mint and the Wall Street Journal
Mid-Day
Mumbai Mirror
Open
Outlook
Sportsweek
Sportsworld
The Hindu
The Indian Express
The Sportstar
The Times of India
The Week
Wisden Asia Cricket
Wisden Cricket Monthly

News Agencies

Press Trust of India

Websites:

www.cricinfo.com
www.youtube.com
www.icc-cricket.com
www.rediff.com

www.wikipedia.com
www.timesofindia.com
www.thatscricket.com
www.cricketcountry.com
www.cricketarchive.com
www.cricketforindia.com
www.cricketnext.com
www.tribuneindia.com
www.facebook.com
www.linkedin.com
www.aumamen.com

ACKNOWLEDGEMENTS

I extend my thanks to those who helped bring this book to life.

My mentors, whom I can never thank enough—Sumedh Shah, Sunil Gavaskar and Prof. R.S. Shetty.

Anil Joshi, for sharing stories of the 'hero' that I had never heard before.

Prakash Parsekar, Clayton Murzello and Mark Ray for the images that have appeared in the book.

Ritika Hiranandani, Raju Mehta, Ricky Couto, Marcus Couto and Stuti Sharma.

Kindergarten friends: Nachiket Joshi and Shishir Mankad.

Shailaja Mudhale, Urvashi Howal and the 'Everard' group—Shashank Patkar, Mayuresh Patkar, Devendra Parulekar, Yogita Parulekar, Prakash Bhavnani, Gareth Saldanha, Jules Goudinho, Faisal Zardi and Mangish Kenkre.

The Class of 1996 (Arts) at D.G. Ruparel College, especially Vidyanand Joshi, Praneel Jadhav and Abhijit Kotak for all the birdwatching and nonsense talk.

The Class of 1998 (SW), Tata Institute of Social Sciences, for 'facilitating many a different perspective'.

Ex-colleagues—the BCCI staff and the PMG staff.

The Brat Pack—Samindara Sawant, Teju Pathare and Smitha Patankar.

The Barista Group.

The Rupa team—Mr R.K. Mehra and Mr Kapish Mehra for their encouragement and support; Ms Elina Majumdar and Ms Shreya Chakraborti for their assistance and infinite patience.

And last but not the least, the family, which never lets you down—Medha Prabhudesai, Anuradha Prabhudesai, Chinmay Prabhudesai, Sonal Prabhudesai, P.V. Satyanarayana, Neela Satyanarayana and Chaitanya Satyanarayana.

INDEX

Abbas, Zaheer, 74, 245
Abdomen guard, 329
Abysmal record, 132
Achrekar, Kalpana, 40
Achrekar, Ramakant, 15, 15–16, 18–22,
    25–33, 35, 39–43, 46–47, 52–54, 73,
    94–95, 101–103, 108, 121, 126, 129,
    141, 156, 218, 251, 313, 426, 440, 450
Action Shoes, 226
Adams, Jimmy, 156, 241
Adams, Paul, 185
Adams, Solly, 118
Adaptability, 92
Adelaide, 110, 167, 225, 255–256, 258, 339,
    341, 394, 396–397, 444
Adhatrao, Mangesh, 31
Adidas, 102, 161
Advertisements, 301
Advertising campaigns, 246
Aerial strokes, 115, 146
Afridi Shahid, 198, 209, 235, 237, 242,
    346, 357, 435–436
Agarkar, Ajit, 218, 257, 259, 264, 268, 276,
    309, 311, 314, 337, 339
Ahmed, Ijaz, 202, 209, 242, 245
Ahmed, Mushtaq, 78, 101, 114
Ahmed, Shabbir, 346
Ajmal, Saeed, 435
Akhtar, Shoaib, 243, 330, 333, 363–364,
    436
Akmal, Kamran, 365, 435
Akmal, Umar, 435
Akram, Wasim, 70, 73, 75, 100, 115, 149,
    151, 169, 180, 201, 235, 244–245,
    258–259, 330
All-too-familiar duties, 367
Almanack, Wisden, 42

Alridge, Brian, 147
Alter, Tom, 58–59
Amarnath, Lala, 174
Amarnath, Mohinder, 25, 60, 64–65, 68,
    186
Ambrose, Curtly, 59–60, 104, 109,
    153–154, 165, 195–196, 303
Amla, Hashim, 418
Amre, Pravin, 102, 110, 121
Anand Vasu, 377
Anand, Vishwanathan, 164
Anderson, James, 381, 433
Anjali, 159–160, 246–247, 261, 350
Anjuman-E-Islam, 44, 48, 62
Ankle injury, 323
Ankola, Salil, 55, 65, 69, 74, 76, 95, 140,
    146, 186, 192, 194, 319
Anticipatory skills, 28
Anti-cricket brigade, 228
Anwar, Saeed, 169, 198, 209, 235, 254, 329,
    332, 421
Apprenticeship, 37
Apte, Madhav, 47–48
Arch-rivals, 225, 234
Armstrong, Lance, 78
Arm-wrestling bouts, 27
Arthurton, Keith, 105
Asher, Kiran, 45
Ashes, 210–211, 245, 344, 387
Ashwin, Ravichandran, 431
Asia Cup, 21, 56, 93, 158–159, 200–202,
    276, 350, 353, 422, 444, 446
  1988 edition, 56
  1995 edition, 158
Asian Cricket Council, 234
Asian Games, 227
Asian Test Championship, 243, 249

Asif, Mohammed, 365
Association of Cricket Statisticians and Scorers of India (ACSSI), 42
Association of Indian Cricketers (AIC), 64, 68–69, 79
Astle, Nathan, 231
Atapattu, Marvan, 200, 203, 362
Ata-ur-Rehman, 169
Atherton, Michael, 128, 224
Atherton, Mike, 88, 175
Athleticism, 190
Atlanta Olympics, 164
Austral-Asia Cup, 84, 99, 148, 151
last-ball six in the final, 99
Australian Cricket Academy, 251
Australian spinners, 216
Autograph-seekers, 62
Ayub, Arshad, 57
Azad Maidan, 29, 39, 421, 440
Azad, Kirti, 13, 15, 66, 141
Azharuddin, Mohammed, 25, 36, 63, 71, 74, 74, 79–80, 84–89, 92–93, 99–102, 105–106, 108, 110–114, 122, 124–128, 130–133, 135, 138–139, 142, 145, 147, 151, 153, 155, 158, 165–169, 173, 177–179, 182–183, 185–186, 189–190, 193, 199–200, 202, 208–210, 216–217, 219, 221–222, 224, 226, 229, 237, 240, 246, 249, 252, 254, 262, 264, 268, 270, 423

Back-and-across shuffle, 190
Back-foot strokes, 54, 123, 406, 427
Badani, Hemang, 265, 284
Bahutule, Sairaj, 42, 52, 140, 148, 212, 287, 337
Balaji, Laxmipathy, 346, 361
Ball-boys, 36
Ball-tampering, 133
Balmohan Vidyamandir School, 3, 13–15
Bandra-Kurla Complex, 4, 429, 453
Banerjee, Sambaran, 173
Banerjee, Subroto, 104, 106, 108
Bangabandhu Stadium, 229

Bangar drilling, 303
Bangar, Sanjay, 303, 305
Bangladesh Liberation War, 4, 78
Banned diuretic, 334
Banning of senior players, 63
Baptism, 51, 295, 354, 362, 403
Barker, Lloyd, 180
Barlow, Eddie, 123
Barnes, Peter, 251
Batting
abilities, 205, 258, 325
capabilities, 238
techniques, 204, 277
BCCI, 9–10, 56, 63, 68, 70, 77, 79, 93–94, 101, 118, 124, 136–138, 148, 164, 173, 186, 199, 223, 226–228, 234, 240, 247, 250, 258, 260, 268–269, 276, 279–280, 290, 292, 296, 310, 318, 325, 344, 353, 360, 371–373, 377, 379, 384, 386, 389–390, 394, 401, 403, 405, 413, 416, 431, 440–444, 446, 448–449
Becker, Boris, 68
Bedade, Atul, 149
Bedi, Bishan Singh, 80, 87, 142, 225, 261, 445
Bee-invasions, 219
Behavioural patterns, 68
Bell, Ian, 382, 433
Belligerence, 17, 54, 205, 294, 352
innate, 33, 189
natural, 381
Belligerent strokes, 115
Benaud, Richie, 90, 219, 223, 313–314
Bengaluru crowd, 170, 425
Benjamin, Kenneth, 154
Benjamin, Winston, 60
Benson, Mark, 393
Best Junior Cricketer Award, 34
Betting syndicates, 269
Bevan, Michael, 151, 288
Bewilderment, 393
Bhandari, Yogendra, 96
Bharadwaj, Vijay, 252
Bharat Ratna, 451

Bharati, Dharamvir, 4
Bhogle, Harsha, 47, 91, 112, 201, 223, 251, 296, 306, 312
Biased ticket-distribution, 148
Bichel, Andy, 334
Big match temperament, 116
Bindra, 136, 268
Bishop, Ian, 60, 64, 86, 165, 195
Bizarre reasoning, 246
Black comedy, 271
Black, Bill, 230
Blind spot, 211
Blofeld, Henry, 137
Board of Control for Cricket in Pakistan (BCCP), 70
Body language, 72, 111, 303, 330, 439
Boje, Nicky, 263, 295
Bollinger, Doug, 424
Bolt, Usain, 78
Bomb scares, 219
Bombay Gymkhana, 29, 405
Bond, Shane, 323
Bookies, 198, 223, 268–271
Boon, David, 106–107, 111
Borde, Chandrakant (Chandu), 70, 260, 383
Border, Allan, 104, 106, 108, 110, 113, 131, 210, 221, 387, 391
Border-Gavaskar Trophy, 181, 210, 255, 258, 287, 344, 351, 396, 401, 404, 424
Borg, Bjorn, 7
Botham, Ian, 93, 113, 153, 233, 387
Boucher, Mark, 264, 421
Bouchier, Anthony, 233
Bowlers
  bogey, 264
  chinaman, 342
  demon, 341
  frontline, 237, 255, 315
  frustration, 165
  hammered, 57
  legendary, 78
  non-frontline, 358
  non-regular, 404
  pace, 50
  regular, 133
Bowling
  lynchpin, 210
  machines, 62, 205, 458
  muscles, 187
  opponent, 53
  shoulder, 194
  skills, 258
Box-office appeal, 458
Boycott, Geoffrey, 9, 117, 131, 137, 201–202, 212, 241, 294
Boyishness, 53
Brabourne Stadium, 5, 44–45, 47–48, 212, 260, 281, 404, 415–416, 440
Bracken, Nathan, 342
Bradman, Don, 9, 15, 126, 161, 175, 225, 230, 250, 254, 299, 306, 313–314, 316, 336, 343
Brandes, Eddo, 193
Bravo, Dwayne, 399
Brearley, Mike, 387
Breathing space, 24, 260, 290, 404
Brijnath, Rohit, 22, 51, 157, 162, 220, 229
British Broadcasting Corporation (BBC), 87, 91, 137
Broken finger, 176, 192
Browne, Courtney, 165, 195
Bryson, Rudi, 193
Bucknor, Steve, 121, 338, 356–357, 381
Bunch of jokers, 60
Burge, Peter, 133
Burman, Sachin Dev, 4

Caddick, Andrew, 316–317, 319, 328
Cairns, Chris, 231, 252, 278, 370
Captaincy, 181–205
Captaincy debut, 56, 180, 391
Carefree child, 23
Carpet strokes, 189, 331
Cash prizes, 389
Castrol Indian Cricketer Year Award, 231
Catching positions, 119, 197
CBI report, 280

CCI, 44, 47–49, 92–93, 117, 218, 260, 440
CCI Golden Jubilee game, 92
CCTV hurling, 390
Celebrity management, 301
Challenger Trophy, 361
Champions Trophy, 318, 320, 351, 354, 371, 413–414
Chanderpaul, Shivnarine, 204, 321
Chandrachud, Justice, 223
Channel Nine network, 25
Chappell, Greg, 219, 276, 339, 360, 371, 375, 378, 386, 417
Chappell, Ian, 110, 166
Charter of demands, 68–69
Chauhan, Rajesh, 118, 126, 200, 202–203, 345
Chavan, Laxman, 41
Chawla, Piyush, 361, 399, 410
Chennai Super Kings, 400, 422
Chidambaram Stadium, 129, 218, 235, 286, 407, 447
Chidambaram Trophy, 102
Chinnaswamy Stadium, 169, 276, 288, 298, 401
Chopra, Akash, 338, 348, 352
Christchurch, 83, 148, 323, 411
Chronometric timing, 443
Chucking, 28, 260, 445
Clark, Belinda, 422
Clark, Stuart, 392–393
Clarke, Michael, 352, 393, 395
Clinical precision, 291
Close-in fielders, 175, 392
Club-level cricket, 10
CNN, 137
Cock-a-hoop, 287
Code of Conduct, 127–128, 260, 377
Collingwood, Paul, 382, 405–406
Collins, Pedro, 307
Colville, Charles, 137
Comăneci, Nadia, 45
Comeback trail, 337, 372
Comfort zone, 24
Commentary box, 90, 150, 170, 353, 407, 420

Commitments for Mumbai, 47
Commonwealth Games, 227–228, 370
Communal riots, 124, 234
Compactness, 225
Competitive temperament, 175
Compton, Denis, 91, 175
Confident run-out appeal, 129
Conflict resolution, 6
Connor, Clare, 370
Conservatism, 65, 163
Consistency, 102, 117, 165, 183, 194, 231, 246, 432, 443
Consternation, 199
Cooch Behar Trophy, 61
Cook, Alastair, 382, 446
Cook, Jimmy, 120
Cork, Dominic, 175, 177
Corridor of uncertainty, 72, 123, 165, 174, 195, 281
Cosmopolitan hub, 124
Couto, Marcus, 36, 42, 44
Couto, Ricky, 28, 39, 46
Coventry, Charles, 421
Cowboys, 14
Cowdrey, Colin, 68
Craig, Ian, 64
Credit card company, 172
Cricinfo Magazine, 368
Cricket Advisory Committee, 454
Cricket Club of India (CCI), 44, 47
Cricket lovers, 8, 13, 60, 78, 87, 98, 116, 140, 177, 195, 213, 232, 236, 331, 450
Cricket quizmaster, 42
Cricket World Cup, 431
Cricketing ambitions, 5, 17, 40
Cricketing die-hards, 146
Cricketing greatness, 187
Cricketing skills, 245
Crisp strokes, 26
Critical innings, 165
Cronje, Hansie, 123–124, 181, 183, 185, 188, 191, 231, 268, 271, 386
Cross-batted swipe, 167
Crowd attendances, 372

Crowe, Jeff, 436
Crowe, Martin, 322
Cuffy, Cameron, 306, 321
Cullinan, Daryll, 192, 335
Cummins, Anderson, 104
Curtly Ambrose, 60, 104, 109, 153, 195, 241
Customary optimism, 231
Cynicism, 271

Dadar Parsee Zoroastrian club, 33
Dadar Union, 13–14, 35, 56, 60, 86
Dadkar, Ramesh, 12
Dahiya, Vijay, 288
Dalmiya, Jagmohan, 136, 173, 226–228, 296, 301, 309–310, 360
Das, Shiv Sunder, 282, 284, 295, 305
Dasgupta, Deep, 295–297, 305
Datta, Debasish, 327, 450
David, Noel, 194
Dayanand Balak Vidyalaya, 15
De'Silva, Aravinda, 132, 170, 203, 224, 370
Debut game, 52, 58, 279, 321
Deccan Chargers, 413
Defensive field-setting, 175
DeFreitas, Philip, 87
Dehydration, 242
Demoralized bowlers, 17
Denness, Mike, 295, 394
Deodhar, D.B., 93
Derbyshire bowlers, 86
Desai, Ramakant, 199, 249
Deshpande, P.L., 3
Dev, Kapil, 8, 14–15, 25, 36, 47, 52, 56, 63–64, 69–71, 73, 75, 79–80, 84–89, 92–93, 95–96, 101, 103–104, 106, 113–114, 119–120, 123, 125, 130, 132–133, 139, 141–142, 145, 149, 152, 153, 155, 219, 233, 248, 259, 268, 270, 276, 309, 314, 316, 319, 367, 453
Dharmani, Pankaj, 186
Dharmasena, Kumara, 170
Dhoni, Mahendra Singh, 354, 357, 362, 364, 375, 381, 384, 385, 389, 397, 439, 447

Diamond jubilee of the CAB, 136
Dickie Bird, 176
Dighe, Sameer, 158, 259, 265, 287, 297
Diktats, 204, 354, 376
Dillon, Mervin, 195
Dilshan, Tillakaratne, 438, 440
Discipline and ethics, 40
Discomfiture, physical, 221, 398
Domestic
 circuit, 171, 355
 commitment, 379
 cricket structure, 176
Don Bosco High School, 26, 31
Donald, Allan, 102, 121–122, 124, 183, 188, 193, 224, 262
Doongursee, Kirti M., 13
Doordarshan, 5, 87, 91, 116, 136–137
Double-wicket tournament, 84, 96
Dravid, Rahul, 81, 154, 171, 173, 176, 180, 185, 188, 190, 198, 204, 215, 227–228, 232, 246, 252, 255, 276, 279–280, 292–293, 297, 300, 305, 309, 311, 316, 319, 321, 323, 327, 332, 338–339, 345, 348, 350, 353, 360–361, 366, 380, 383–385, 388, 393, 408, 413, 444, 454–455, 457
Dronacharya Award, 141
Drought relief game, 103
Duckworth-Lewis method, 172, 197, 366, 370
Duleep Trophy, 79, 93–94, 118, 135, 355
Dungarpur, Raj Singh, 44, 48, 51, 53, 64, 66, 79–80, 240, 250, 276, 292, 416, 449
Dunne, Steve, 237–238
Dutta, B., 79

Eating competition, 74–75
Eden Gardens, 102, 126–127, 136, 138, 163, 283, 353, 455
Eden Park, 145
Elbow injuries, 409
Elworthy, Steve, 264
Emirates Cricket Board, 148

Emotional insecurity, 4
Endorsement, 160, 260, 301, 318
Exceptional players, 223
Exhibition game, 92, 224, 230, 246
Extraordinary 'bat-speed' and reflexes, 129
Extraordinary bowling attack, 75

Fairytale climax, 438
Fairytale farewell, 424
Farhat, Imran, 347
Fast-bowling aspirations, 172
Fatal mistake, 193
Federer, Roger, 78
Felicitation, 46, 449
Ferozeshah Kotla, 168, 234
Festival of Colours, 146
Field placements, 183, 231, 386
Field umpires, 373, 401
Fielding
  practice, 17
  restrictions, 145
First 'night' game, 138
First Test century, 90, 92, 130, 303, 321
Fleming, Damien, 165, 220–221, 257, 281
Fleming, Matthew, 203
Fleming, Stephen, 231, 253
Fletcher, Keith, 123
Flintoff, Andrew, 298, 313, 328, 367, 406
Flower, Grant, 230
Fondness for Western music, 33
Food poisoning, 128
Foot movement, 76, 112
Foot punch, 443
Foresightedness, 310
Foster, James, 298
Foul play, 148
400-wickets' club, 83
Franklin, James, 412
Fraser, Angus, 88
Friday clash, 149
Friday pressure, 158
Front foot innings, 427
Full-blooded pull, 190, 427

Gadgil, Gangadhar, 4
Gaekwad, Anshuman, 208, 215, 237, 276
Gambhir, Gautam, 352, 363, 398, 405–406, 408, 412, 414–417, 426–427, 432–435, 438–439
Gandhe, Pradeep, 118
Gandhi, Devang, 252, 255
Gandhi, Rajiv, 25–26, 225, 449
Ganesh, Dodda, 186, 189, 194
Ganguly, Sourav, 38, 63, 81, 81, 107, 173, 173, 176–178, 180–182, 189–193, 201, 223–224, 246, 251, 253–255, 263–265, 276–280, 282–284, 291–293, 295, 302–303, 306–311, 313, 315–316, 318–321, 333–334, 337–345, 349, 360, 371–373, 377, 385, 388, 391, 401, 454–455, 457
Gattani, Kailash, 49, 62
Gatting, Mike, 127, 210
Gavaskar, Meenal, 67
Gavaskar, Sunil, 8–9, 14, 17, 20–21, 23, 25, 33–36, 38, 42, 47, 52–53, 55–58, 67–68, 82, 83, 88, 92, 116–118, 125, 137, 149, 152, 155, 163, 180–181, 190, 201, 210, 213, 219, 237, 255, 258–260, 287, 306, 314, 316, 316, 319, 322, 336, 343–344, 351, 353, 369, 396, 399, 401–402, 404, 407, 424, 440–442, 454, 459
Gayle, Christopher, 7
Gibbs, Herschelle, 264, 295, 320
Gilchrist, Adam, 219, 281–284, 286, 352, 395, 399
Giles, Ashley, 297–298, 303–304
Gillespie, Jason, 277, 285, 334, 342
Gloster, John, 361, 370
Godbole, Kedar, 52
Golden Jubilee of India, 198
Gooch, Graham, 87–88, 113, 127–128
Gordon, Sandy, 325
Gowariker, Avinash, 6, 10, 21, 76
Gower, David, 92, 128, 137, 399
Greatbatch, Mark, 115
Green and White Revolutions, 4
Green-topped pitch, 37

Greig, Tony, 219, 286
Groundkeepers, 21
Groundstaff, 32
Guinness Book of World Records, 42
Gully cricketers, 147
Gunn and Moore bat, 38
Gupta, Amit, 31
Gupta, Ram Babu, 238

Haddin, Brad, 434
Hadlee, Richard, 83–84, 125, 141, 152, 174, 248, 399
Hafeez, Mohammed, 435
Hair-standing-on-end moments, 247
Hall, Andrew, 278
Hampshire, John, 65, 80, 86
Hands-on approach, 184
Hansen, Justice John, 394, 396–397
Harbhajan, Singh, 280–281, 283–285, 287, 290, 293, 295, 297, 304–305, 352, 393–394, 396–397, 404, 414–415, 418–419, 436
Harmison, Steve, 315, 406
Harper, Daryl, 373, 406
Harper, Roger, 88
Harris, Chris, 115
Harris, Paul, 373, 417, 426
Harshe, Sunil, 6
Hart, Matthew, 147
Hassell, Chris, 117
Hattangadi, Shishir, 38, 54, 95, 140
Hauritz, Nathan, 352, 415, 425
Hayden, Matthew, 109, 282, 285, 334, 339–340
Haynes, Desmond, 40, 104, 223, 228
Haywards Heath Cricket Club, 62
Hazare, Vijay, 20, 38, 51
Healy, Ian, 108, 167, 216
Heaviest Test defeat, 216
Hemmings, Eddie, 87–88
Henry, Omar, 121
Hernia surgery in Munich, 401
Hero Cup, 136–140, 142, 153, 164, 183, 340, 356, 447

Hick, Graeme, 128–130
Hind Sewak, 30–31
Hind Sports Club, 15
Hirwani, Narendra, 56, 88, 108, 127
Hogg, Brad, 392
Hoggard, Matthew, 298
Holder, John, 65, 80
Home ground, 186, 203, 316, 321, 367, 391, 449
Hooliganism, 148
Hooper, Carl, 109, 139, 155, 204, 307
Hopes, James, 399
Hopps, David, 118
Horizontal-bat strokes, 140, 211–212
Horn, Mike, 437
Horrific injury, 217
Hossein, Shahadat, 417
Houghton, Dave, 248
Hudson, Andrew, 120, 123, 184–185, 187
Hughes, Kimberley, 386
Hughes, Merv, 105–106, 108, 394
Humid conditions, 242
Hussain, Nasser, 297–298, 311, 358
Hussey, Michael, 395
Hussey, Mike, 424

ICC Champions Trophy, 228, 319, 351, 371, 413
ICC Cricket World Cup, 290, 304, 374–375, 397, 424, 440
ICC T20 World Cup, 455
ICC under-19 World Cup, 277, 449
Income-tax authorities, 276
Independence Cup, 198–199, 204, 332
Index finger, 289, 356, 364, 411
Indian Cricket League, 379
Indian Premier League (IPL), 390, 399–400, 422, 443, 447, 457–458
Indian Super League, 456
Indian Telegraph Act, 138
Indoor facilities, 205
Injury, 35, 106, 117, 122, 126, 158, 180, 189, 192–193, 291–292, 347–348, 350–351, 358–359, 409, 436–437

arm, 126
complex, 350
finger, 106, 194, 282, 417
freak, 417
hamstring, 428
heel, 142
jaw, 417
knee, 391
shoulder, 254, 304–305, 307, 311, 315, 402
thigh, 437
upper-body, 409
wrist, 139
Intensive practice, 367
Inter-club matches, 13
International Cricket Conference (ICC), 9
Inter-net matches, 19
Inter-school cricket, 22, 26–27, 33, 45, 129, 140, 212, 456
Inter-school game, 40
Inter-school tournaments, 15, 31, 33, 455
Inzamam-ul-Haq, 114, 150, 170, 198, 235, 245, 345, 356, 358
Irani Cup, 64–67, 93, 119, 337–338, 354, 390, 402
Irani, Ronnie, 175
Irregular bowlers, 191
Islam Gymkhana, 58
Islam, Shafiul, 432
Ismail, Abdul, 32
Issues with his home state's educational authorities, 92

Jackman, Robin, 420
Jade Stadium, 323
Jadeja, Ajay, 96, 113, 119, 126, 139, 141, 169, 192, 247, 251, 254, 270
Jadeja, Ravindra, 415
Jaffer, Wasim, 262, 315, 355, 363, 373, 380, 383, 391
Jagdale, Sanjay, 446
Jain, Pradeep, 96
Jaiswal, Lalsuram, 379
Jaitley, Arun, 345

Jardine, Douglas, 299
Jarvis, Paul, 129–130
Javed, Aaqib, 101, 114, 149, 158, 201, 209
Jawaharlal Nehru Stadium, 103
Jayasuriya, Sanath, 168, 170–171, 180, 200, 203, 279, 399–400
Jayawardene, Mahela, 244, 437
Jinnah Stadium, 75
John Bright Cricket Club, 32
Johnson, David, 186–187
Johnson, Mitchell, 396, 434
Jolly, Prabhu, 31
Jones, Andrew, 115
Jones, Dean, 104, 107–108
Joseph, Manu, 11
Joshi, Anil, 43, 62, 94–95, 134, 160, 429, 453
Joshi, Sunil, 173, 176, 192, 235, 239
Jubilation and acknowledgement of his proficiency, 108
Junior College Cricket Tournament, 79

Kadrekar, Mayur, 29
Kaif, Mohammed, 262, 305, 309, 312–313, 319, 326–327, 331, 345–346, 350, 366
Kailash Gattani's Star Cricket Club, 62
Kale, V.P., 4
Kallis, Jacques, 262, 294, 358, 373, 454
Kaluwitharana, Romesh, 168, 170, 180
Kamal, Asim, 356–357
Kamat Memorial Club, 16, 20
Kamath, P.K., 57
Kambli, Vinod, 39–40, 45, 58, 62, 81, 95, 100–101, 113, 118–119, 126, 130–132, 135–136, 147, 150, 154, 156, 158, 169, 171, 173, 180, 198, 217, 223, 246, 277, 337
Kaneria, Danish, 349
Kanga League, 30, 32, 47–49, 218, 440
Kanitkar, Hrishikesh, 209, 254
Kapoor, Aashish, 265
Karandikar, Vinda, 4
Kargil battle, 252
Karim, Saba, 186, 199, 202, 265

Kartik, Dinesh, 362, 372–373, 380, 420
Kartik, Murali, 262, 264, 345–346, 352, 354–355, 357, 421
Kasliwal, Pradeep, 37
Kasprowicz, Michael, 216, 218–219, 221–222, 229, 285–286, 364
Katich, Simon, 342
Kenkre, Hemant, 36, 47–48
Kerry Packer's World Series Cricket, 387
Khan, Imran, 48, 65, 69, 75, 77–78, 92, 116, 150, 170, 242, 245
Khan, Moin, 115, 235, 237–238, 243, 345, 347–348, 364
Khan, Nadeem, 237, 243
Khan, Younis, 332, 357, 435
Khan, Zaheer, 276, 278, 307, 311–312, 315, 323, 333, 339, 345, 348, 352, 355, 371–372, 374, 380–383, 395, 402, 404, 410, 417–418, 436–437, 457
Khar Gymkhana, 31
Khettarama Stadium, 150
Khurasiya, Amay, 246
Khurram Darbar, 45
King George School, 13
King, Chris, 147
Kiran Mokashi, 38, 57
Kirmani, Syed, 186
Kirsten, Gary, 185, 192, 264, 278, 293, 295, 394, 424–425, 440–441
Kirsten's Performance Zone Academy, 425
Kirti College, 3, 28, 63, 79, 92
Klusener, Lance, 186, 192, 263, 294
Knockout game, 157, 169
Knopfler, Mark, 400
Kohli, Virat, 425, 431–432, 436, 438, 440, 444, 446–447, 450, 453, 455, 457
Kolkata Knight Riders, 399
Krejza, Jason, 403
Kulkarni, Dhawal, 410
Kulkarni, Nilesh, 200, 212, 337, 429
Kulkarni, Raju, 37–38, 58–59, 90, 95, 140, 233
Kumar, Bhuvneshwar, 410
Kumar, Praveen, 399, 415, 419

Kumaran, Thiru, 265
Kumble, Anil, 91, 119, 123, 126, 131–132, 155, 180, 185, 196, 224, 242–243, 245, 257, 270, 280, 292, 300, 303, 307–318, 334, 344, 348, 351, 362, 381–382, 385, 390, 394, 402, 404, 429, 455, 457
Kuruvilla, Abey, 95, 97, 140, 186, 194, 266

Lacklustre performances, 259, 350
Ladha, Amar Singh, 85
Lady luck, 165, 218, 306
Lal Bahadur Shastri, 4
Lal, Akash, 64
Lal, Arun, 63–64, 374
Lamb, Allan, 87
Lamba, Raman, 74, 94
Langer, Justin, 258, 282
Langeveldt, Charl, 419
Lara, Brian, 92, 99, 139, 142, 150, 157, 183, 195, 200, 226, 240, 307–308, 320, 356, 374, 391, 402, 446, 454
Larsen, Gavin, 115, 146
Larwood, Harold, 299
Last-minute injury to Raman Lamba, 74
Latif, Rashid, 199, 208, 272
Law, Stuart, 166, 183
Le Roux, Adrian, 310, 325
League Cricket Conference, 86
Lee, Brett, 256, 277, 340, 342, 392, 395–397, 434
Left-arm paceman, 244, 276, 307, 328, 380, 434
Leg-breaks, 210, 214–215, 229, 284, 348
Leg-guards, 17, 35–36, 103
  ultra-light, 35
Leg-spin, 217, 412
Leg-spinner, 56, 114, 129, 140, 149, 211–212, 214, 216, 250, 256, 285, 339, 344, 355, 410
Leipus, Andrew, 284, 292
Lele, Jaywant, 250, 276
Lele, Rajendra, 37
Lewis, Chris, 87, 89, 130, 174–175, 177
Lewis, Rawl, 204

Lewis, Tony, 175
Liberalization era, 140
Life Insurance Corporation of India, 3
Like-minded democracies, 181
Lillee, Dennis, 65, 75, 129
Limited-overs cricket, 14, 48, 103, 136, 152, 157, 161, 180, 253, 312, 314, 371, 431, 441
  career, 145
  innings, 167
  plethora of, 136
  popularity of, 136
  tournament, 25, 30, 64, 93, 136, 251, 400, 422
  tri-series, 84
Lindsay, Denis, 297
Lloyd, Clive, 171, 446
Lokapally, Vijay, 168, 226, 322, 341
Lyon, Nathan, 447

M.A. Chidambaram Stadium, 129, 235, 286, 407, 447
M.A. Chidambaram Trophy, 102
Maalis (groundkeepers), 21
MacGill, Stuart, 339, 342
MacMillan, Brian, 121
Madan Lal, 61, 66, 181, 208, 250
Madhya Pradesh Cricket Association, 94
Madras Rubber Factory (MRF), 161, 176
Mafatlal, Atulya, 43
Magic formula, 293
Mahale, Dushyant, 16
Mahanama, Roshan, 133, 200
Maharoof, Farveez, 361
Mahmood, Azhar, 180, 209
Maidan cricketer, 108
Malayala Manorama, 265
Malcolm, Devon, 89–90, 130
Malik, Salim, 100, 115, 235, 243
Malik, Shoaib, 345–346, 350
Mandatory fielding position, 183
Mandela, Nelson, 101
Manjrekar, Sanjay, 14, 38, 41, 60–61, 63, 73–75, 83, 85, 87–89, 93–95, 100–103, 105–106, 109–111, 113–114, 119–120, 122, 124–127, 131, 135, 140–141, 153–155, 158, 167, 169–170, 174, 175–176, 178–179, 184–185, 188, 212–214, 216–217, 275, 328, 435
Manjrekar, Vijay, 14, 20, 60
Mankad, Ashok, 231, 266
Manohar, Shashank, 375
Manou, Graham, 414
Mantri, Madhav, 14, 86, 92, 95
Maradona, Diego, 78
Marqusee, Mike, 249
Marshall, Malcolm, 59–60, 109, 399
Martyn, Damien, 220, 277, 288, 334, 339, 369
Mascarenhas, Mark, 160–162, 172, 219, 301
Match-fixing, 223, 245, 268–272, 275, 445
Match-practice, 19
Match referee, 171, 193, 209, 238, 292, 295, 393–394, 397, 436
Match-saving effort, 82
Match-winning
  abilities, 241
  cameo, 165
  century, 117, 198, 214, 223, 278–279
  contributions, 241
Matthews, Craig, 121–122
Matunga Gujarati Seva Mandal Shield, 33
Matunga Maidan, 12–14, 19, 33, 61
MCA's annual award, 34
McDermott, Craig, 105–108, 110–111, 113, 117, 151, 394
McEnroe, John, 7–8, 25
McEnroe, Sachu, 8
McGrath, Glenn, 151, 165–166, 224, 248, 255–256, 277, 281, 285, 334
McIntosh, Tim, 411–412
McKay, Clint, 415
McMillan, Brian, 185, 224
McMillan, Craig, 231
Media attention, 58
Media box, 438–439, 450
Melbourne Cricket Ground, 109

Memon, Ayaz, 58, 450
Mendis, Ajantha, 401, 413
Merchant Trophy, under-15, 38, 54
Merchant, Vijay, 9, 14, 20, 32, 38, 54, 79, 85
Mhambrey, Paras, 140, 176, 266, 429
Miandad, Javed, 99, 101, 114–155, 169–170, 233, 240, 245, 252, 332–333
   last-ball six of 1986, 101
Microphones, 137
Middle-class cricketer, 5
Middle-stump guard, 329
Mid-wicket rope, 166
MIG Club, 422
Miller, Colin, 286, 298
Misbah-ul-Haq, 389, 435
Mishra, Amit, 402, 418
Mistry, Bharat, 54, 81
Mitchley, Cyril, 120
Mohammed, Hanif, 64
Mohammed, Mushtaq, 83
Mohan, R., 107, 174, 179, 184, 450
Moist wickets, 174
Mokashi, Kiran, 38, 41, 57
Mongia, Dinesh, 309, 372
Mongia, Nayan, 125, 141, 154, 174, 181, 194, 215, 237, 252, 262, 281
Montreal Olympics, 45
Moody, Tom, 110, 113, 222, 360
Moral victory, 196
More, Kiran, 63, 73, 80, 86, 108, 113–114, 119, 121, 125, 132, 372
Morrison, Danny, 83, 142
MRF Pace Academy, 65
MRF Pace Foundation, 129, 187
Mukherjee, Pranab, 451
Mullally, Alan, 175
Multi-sporting events, 227
Mulye, Rupak, 39
Mumbai Cricket Association (MCA), 27
Mumbai School of Batting, 36, 48
Mumbai Schools Sports Association, 32
Murali Vijay, 423
Muralitharan, Muttiah, 276, 291–292, 362, 401, 422, 437

Murzello, Clayton, 379
Mushtaq, Saqlain, 172, 180, 202, 235–236, 258, 345
Muzumdar, Amol, 22, 32, 40, 45, 148, 266

Naik, Sudhir, 53
Nairobi Gymkhana, 277
Narang, Sanjay, 337
Nash, Dion, 148, 231
Nataraja stroke, 316
Natarajan, H., 68
National Cricket Academy, 401
National Democratic Alliance (NDA), 345, 456
National Security Guard, 408
National Selection Committee, 44, 51, 53, 64–65, 79, 447
Natural game, 197
Naved-ul-Hasan, 356, 363, 365
Nayudu, C.K., 47, 416
Nayyar, Manu, 66
Neck spasms, 235
Nehra, Ashish, 244, 315, 323, 328, 333, 345, 349, 436
Nehru Cup, 64, 68, 136
Net practice, 16, 19
Neutral official, 121
Neutral umpires, 65
New ball, 113, 154, 184, 194, 238, 276–277, 297, 407, 427
New generation of cricketers, 15
New Hind Sports Club, 15, 49
New phase in life, 24
New-ball
   bowlers, 48, 146, 155, 176, 195, 209, 235, 355
   duo, 170, 189
   duties, 218
   pair, 149, 151, 187
   partner, 66
Non-vegetarian delicacies, 6
Non-violent battle, 120

O' Neill, Norman, 112

Observation skills, 53, 127
Octogenarian, 167
Off-spinning
  legends, 216
  rivals, 251
Olonga, Henry, 230, 447
Olympics, 227
One-man commission, 223, 386
On-field
  altercation, 394
  conduct, 357
  misdemeanours, 292
Operation Desert Storm, 223
Oram, Jacob, 323
Overs
  eight-ball, 322
  fifty, 328
  maiden, 165
  mandatory, 90–91, 192
  slog, 173

P. Saravanamutthu Stadium, 133
Pace academy, 172
Pace Age, 9, 141
Paddle-sweep, 212, 237, 288, 407
Pagnis, Amit, 212
Pain-barrier, 239
Pakistan Cricket Board (PCB), 70
Palton, T., 42
Pandit, Chandrakant, 38, 61, 95, 108, 140
Paranjape, Jatin, 118, 265
Paranjape, Vasu, 14, 35, 37, 52–53, 67, 118, 139
Pardhe, Laxman, 7
Parnell, Wayne, 417
Parsi Gymkhana, 79
Pataudi, Mansoor Ali Khan, 155, 233, 383
Patel, Ashok, 54–55
Patel, Munaf, 366, 436
Patel, Nisarg, 53
Patel, Parthiv, 315, 318, 342, 354
Patel, Rashid, 94, 119, 244
Pathan, Irfan, 348, 350, 355, 361, 364–365, 375, 391, 432

Pathan, Yusuf, 421–432, 434
Patil, Sandeep, 14–15, 18, 33, 37, 48, 94, 134, 181, 415, 446–447
Patil, Sanjay, 95
Patterson, Patrick, 105, 109
Pawar, Satish, 37
Pawar, Sharad, 360, 377, 384
Payyoli Express, 265
Pedestrian days, 367
People's Choice Award, 424
Persuasive skills, 16
Peterson, Alviro, 418
Phadke, Y.D., 4
Pietersen, Kevin, 311, 381–382, 389, 405
Pivotal spot, 189
Platinum Jubilee celebrations, 405
Players' Code of Conduct, 377
Playing Conditions, 101
Poetic justice, 203
Political protests, 234
Pollock, Shaun, 193, 263–264, 294–296, 373, 399–400
Polly Umrigar Award, 416
Polly Umrigar Trophy, 443
Ponting, Ricky, 106, 229, 255, 282, 333–334, 339–340, 393–396, 399, 404, 414, 434, 447, 454
Popping crease, 127, 195, 243–244, 427
Port Elizabeth, 123–124, 153, 292, 295
Post-game/match
  altercation, 400
  presser, 142
  proceedings, 450
Post-net sessions, 179
Powar, Ramesh, 346–347
Powell, Darren, 321
Prabhakar, Manoj, 71, 75, 80, 89–90, 101, 103–104, 106, 108, 111, 115, 123–126, 130, 132–133, 139, 142, 145, 149, 151, 154–158, 167, 171, 180, 268–269, 309,
Practice session, 24, 58, 211, 326
Pradhan, Kunal, 24
Prasad, Venkatesh, 169, 176–177, 188–189, 192, 195, 235, 276, 278, 280, 379

Prasanna, Erapalli, 216
Premadasa Stadium, 151–152
Premier Badminton League, 456
Premier clubs, 13
Presentation ceremony, 138, 222, 240, 332, 367, 374, 404
Press Trust of India, 60, 292
Prime Sports, 116, 137, 146
Princess Diana Memorial Fund, 224
Pringle, Chris, 146
Pringle, Meryick, 121
Procter, Mike, 393, 396–397
Professional Management Group, 172
Professionalism, 100, 109, 117, 216, 285, 301
Psychological damage, 316
Pujara, Cheteshwar, 425, 457
Purohit, Shrirang, 6

Qadir, Abdul, 72, 77–78, 245, 365
Quality spinners, 119, 127, 354
Quick bowlers, 218
Quick-bowling skills, 129

R. Premadasa Stadium, 150
R.A. Podar College of Commerce and Economics, 13
Racial
  abuse, 397
  jibes, 390
Radcliffe Line, 346
Radical batting strategy, 168
Radical innovations, 322
Rahane, Ajinkya, 425, 444, 457
Raina, Suresh, 414, 423, 425, 431, 434, 436, 453
Rainbow Nation, 181, 425, 448
Raja, Rameez, 70, 77
Rajiv Gandhi Khel Ratna, 225
Rajput, Lalchand, 52, 95, 140
Raju, Venkatapathy, 57, 66, 93, 113, 126, 157
Raman, W.V., 86, 131, 187, 189
Ramesh, Sadagoppan, 235, 282

Ramnarain Ruia College of Arts and Science, 13
Rampaul, Ravi, 433
Ranade, Atul, 6, 39, 202, 246, 429
Ranatunga, Arjuna, 168, 202, 244, 259
Ranji Trophy, 6, 16, 36–37, 44, 46–48, 50–52, 54, 57, 60–61, 80–81, 93–95, 119, 140, 148, 158, 173, 183, 186, 200, 246, 262, 265–268, 302, 337, 354, 373, 410, 449
Rao, Narsimha, 98
Rathour, Vikram, 176, 187
Ratra, Ajay, 305, 307, 315
Raut, Pratap, 26
Rawalpindi Express, 330, 363
Razdan, Vivek, 65–66, 75, 77
Razzaq, Abdul, 331, 346, 356, 358, 365
Reckless batting, 199
Rege, Milind, 27, 47–48, 52, 55, 57
Reid, Bruce, 105–106
Reiffel, Paul, 111
Responses to challenges, 29
Reverse-sweep, 299
Reverse-swing, 185, 235, 285
Rhodes, Jonty, 121, 185
Riaz, Wahab, 435–436
Rice, Clive, 102
Richards, Barry, 224, 313
Richards, Vivian, 21, 17, 33, 56, 88, 207, 219, 221, 230, 298, 317, 336, 392, 410, 441, 454
Richardson, Richie, 99, 104, 153, 370
Rigorous cricket schedule, 27
Rippon, N., 42
Robertson, Gavin, 215–216
Roebuck, Peter, 368, 443
Roller-coaster ride, 245
Romanticism, 343
Rose, Franklyn, 195–196
Rotator cuff injury, 194
Round-robin format, 112
Royal Challengers Bangalore, 399
Rubber balls, 30, 156, 212
  cricket, 20, 96

Ruparel, D.G., 13
Rutherford, Ken, 146

Saha, Wriddhiman, 417
Sahitya Sahawas, 3–8, 10, 20, 22, 28, 30–31, 53–54, 94, 160, 167, 247
Salgaonkar, Pandurang, 233
Salisbury, Ian, 129–130
Salve Challenger Trophy, 360
Sami, Mohammed, 350
Sammy, Darren, 450
Sampras, Pete, 78
Samuels, Marlon, 321
Sandhu, Balwinder Singh, 85
Sandstorm innings, 447
Sanford, Adam, 306
Sanghi, Rajesh, 32
Sanghvi, Rahul, 282
Sanspareils Greenlands (SG), 235
Sanzgiri, Dwarkanath, 67
Saqlain Mushtaq, and, 258
Saraiya, Suresh, 120
Saravanamutthu Stadium, 133, 423
Sardar Patel Stadium, 184
Sardesai, Dilip, 20
Sassanian Club, 29, 39–40
Savita, 3, 5, 7
Sawai Man Singh Stadium, 126
Saxena, Ramesh, 64
Schoolboy cricketers, 4, 42, 458
Schultz, Brett, 121
Schumacher, Michael, 78
Scindia, Madhavrao, 94
Scoreboard pressure, 105
Seam-and-swing, 232
Second successive triple hundred, 45
Sehwag, Virender, 288, 290–291, 293–295, 298–300, 303–304, 309–311, 314–317, 319–321, 323, 327–328, 330–331, 338–339, 347, 351–352, 356–358, 362–363, 372–374, 377, 395–397, 399, 401, 416–420, 423, 426–427, 432–438, 447, 457
Sekhar, T.A., 233

Selectors as a 'bunch of jokers', 60
Self-belief, 258, 385
Semi-defensive field, 175
Senior management, 176
Series-winning performance, 287
Shadow-practising, 107
Shah, Sumedh, 173
Shaheed Smriti tournament, 133
Shardashram, 16, 22, 24, 26, 29, 32–33, 39–41, 43–45, 47, 54, 62, 87, 94, 102, 114, 126–127, 129–133, 139, 148, 151, 156, 202, 218, 265–266, 314
Sharjah, 26, 56, 64, 66, 84, 98–99, 101–102, 104–105, 113, 119, 148–149, 151, 157–158, 173, 203–205, 209, 217–218, 221, 229–230, 245, 265, 301, 332, 337, 340, 428, 447
Sharma, Ajay, 131
Sharma, Chetan, 95–96, 119, 332
Sharma, Gopal, 61
Sharma, Ishant, 395, 397, 404, 423–426
Sharma, Joginder, 389
Sharma, Rohit, 398, 410, 417, 425, 444, 447
Sharma, Sanjeev, 66
Sharma, Yashpal, 15
Shastri, Lal Bahadur, 4
Shastri, Ravi, 15, 25, 38, 56, 63, 72–73, 75, 80, 85, 87, 92–94, 100–103, 105, 107–110, 113, 118, 121, 125, 131, 135, 140, 148, 150, 160, 210, 219, 230, 313, 343, 373, 379, 383, 389, 436
Shastri, Suresh, 15
Shaw, Tim, 102
Shepherd, David, 121, 124, 330
Sher-e-Bangla Stadium, 431
Shetty, R.S., 45, 79, 201, 347–348, 355, 375, 455
Shield, Giles, 15, 26, 31, 33, 41, 45
Shield, Gordhandas, 30
Shield, Harris, 15, 31–33, 39, 41, 44–45, 48, 62
Shield, Purshottam, 47
Shillingford, Shane, 450

Shin fracture, 242
Shine-removers, 155
Shiv Chhatrapati Awards, 141
Shiv Sena, 12
Shivaji Park, 3, 12–19, 24, 27–30, 32–33, 39, 45, 47–48, 60, 62, 65, 84, 122, 156, 160, 202, 440, 446
Shortcomings, 204
Shoulder surgery, 280, 369
Show-stealer, 314
Siddiqui, Iqbal, 297
Sidhu, Navjot, 63, 73–77, 86, 100, 102, 106, 111, 126, 128–133, 145, 148–149, 151, 155, 158–159, 165, 169–170, 173–174, 176, 176, 180, 194, 194, 197, 203, 215–216
Simmons, Phil, 139
Simpson, 80, 131, 387
Simpson, Bob, 80, 131, 387
Singapore trip, 173
Singer Cup, 150, 159, 268
Singh, Bhupinder, 135
Singh, Gurcharan, 141
Singh, Gursharan, 66
Singh, Harbhajan, 217, 280, 286–287, 290, 295, 339, 344, 351, 363, 377, 392, 399, 402, 404, 422, 426, 436, 446
Singh, Kanwaljeet, 268
Singh, Maninder, 61, 64, 66, 131, 141, 233
Singh, Manmohan, 78
Singh, Robin, 183, 192–193, 202, 209, 247–248, 265–267, 379
Singh, Rudra Pratap, 380
Singh, Sarandeep, 280, 305
Singh, Yuvraj, 278, 305, 309, 311–312, 319–320, 332, 347–348, 354, 366, 377, 391–393, 398, 406–407, 411–412, 414–415, 432–434, 436, 439–440, 453
Single-minded commitment, 409
Sinhalese Sports Club, 132, 152, 423
Sippy, Alan, 38
Sir Garfield Sobers Trophy, 334, 424
Sivaramakrishnan, Laxman, 25, 211–212, 233

664-run partnership, 42
Slater, Michael, 282, 286
Slip-catching practice, 106
Slow bowlers, 204, 212, 344
Smith, Robin, 87
Snell, Richard, 102
Sobers, Garfield, 187, 446
Sohail, Aamir, 100, 114, 169
Solkar, Eknath, 53
Solly Adams, 118
Somasunder, Sujith, 182
South Africa, re-induction of, 101
South African Broadcasting Corporation (SABC), 137
South African links, 57
South Asia' Cup, 93
Special net session at the Matunga Maidan, 122
Specialist openers, 86, 363
Specialist wicketkeeper, 174, 345
Spectator-invasions, 219
Spinners, 57, 118–119, 128, 130, 141, 153, 155, 168, 171, 185, 215, 222, 315, 373, 420
  extraordinary, 126
  frontline, 404
  leftarm, 45
  legendary, 233
  mystery, 413
  orthodox, 212
Sponsorship contract, 160
Sports Journalists Association of Mumbai, 42
Sports management company, 456
Square-leg boundary, 222
Sreesanth, S., 415
Srikkanth, K., 15, 28, 64, 69–71, 73, 75, 78–80, 85, 105, 109–110, 113–115, 344, 402
Srinath, Javagal, 104, 113, 121, 124, 142, 155, 157, 171, 182, 184, 194, 202, 205, 210, 233, 235, 240, 253, 280, 282, 306, 311, 321, 323, 325, 388
SSC exams, 61, 63

St Xavier's cricket team, 41
Stand-in coach, 221
Standing ovation, 244, 247, 332, 428, 450
Star Cricket Club, 49, 62, 81
Star's Prime Sports Channel, 137
State Bank of India, 5, 15–16
Stewart, Alec, 128
Steyn, Dale, 417
Stopgap measure, 189
Straight bat, 198, 230, 236, 308, 317, 321
Strauss, Andrew, 382, 405, 433
Streak, Heath, 169, 193, 302
Street delicacies, 28
Street-smart cricket, 203
Strokes
  audacious, 220, 316
  back-to-back, 427
  best, 328
  breathtaking, 433
  emphatic, 421
  exceptional, 421
  identical, 420
  incredible, 299
  stupendous, 316
Structured cricket, 19
Study tour, 50
Suji, Martin, 164
Summer vacation camps, 20
Sunday League, 117
Sungrace-Mafatlal, 42–43, 62, 94–95, 133, 160, 446
Swachh Bharat (Clean India), 456
Swann, Graeme, 405–406
Symonds, Andrew, 288, 390, 393

T20, 219, 371–372, 446–447
Tagore, Rabindranath, 3
Tagore, Vijay, 343
Tail-enders, 176, 283, 415
Tait, Shaun, 396, 434
Talent-spotters, 13
Talyarkhan, A.F.S., 80
Tamhane, Naren, 52–53, 64
Taufel, Simon, 382, 411, 435

Taylor, Mark, 110, 151, 166, 182, 210, 216
Taylor, Peter, 106
Technical alterations, 455
Technique and temperament, 8, 89, 204, 312
Telegraph Act of 1885, 138
Television advertisements, 226
Tendulkar, Ajit, 10, 13, 15–16, 18, 44, 76, 103, 107, 139
Tendulkar, Rajani, 3, 400, 450
Tendulkar, Ramesh, 3, 5, 7, 21–23, 28, 31, 61, 65, 116, 247, 456, 458
Tennis elbow, 351, 354, 358–359, 361
Tennis-ball circuit, 15
Test
  baptism, 108
  batting average, 454
  career, 71, 82, 123, 237
  century, 9, 90, 92, 130, 176, 216, 238, 253, 257, 286, 290, 362, 382, 391–392, 425
  debut, 80, 119, 121, 141, 176, 184, 217, 280, 294–295, 319, 423, 453
  fiftieth, 176
  first century, 303, 321
  hundredth, 71, 357
  innings, 177, 257, 259, 317, 320
  maiden, 157, 191, 258, 391
  playing nation, 9, 25, 353
Thackeray, Balasaheb, 12
Thakur, Shraddhanand, 3
Tharoor, Shashi, 442
Third umpire, 121
Thomas, Paul, 290
300-barrier, 173
Thumb injury, 262
Ticket-distribution, biased, 148
Tillakaratne, Hashan, 141, 168
Time-and-tested technique, 53
Titan Cup, 217, 386
Tongue-in-cheek reference, 226
Tooth-and-nail, 199
Toronto Cricket, 251
Track

bouncy, 329, 425
dry, 104
fifth-day, 407
racing, 103
slow, 197
turning, 141
Tradition of losing the first Test, 88
Traditional rivals, 55, 99, 101, 113, 180, 209, 235, 237, 245, 434
Traditions of Mumbai cricket, 48
Traicos, John, 120
Training camp, 179
Trans World International (TWI), 137–138
Trans-Sahyadri clash, 55
Trescothick, Marcus, 300
Trial game, 262
Tri-series at Sharjah, 64, 98, 245, 279
Trivedi, Suresh, 42
Tsotsobe, Lonwabo, 427
Tudor, Alex, 316
Tuffey, Daryl, 323
Tulsidas Tejpal Chawl, 3
Tumult in Indian cricket, 63
TV Commentary team, 219, 404–405
TV rights, 137–138, 301
TV umpire, 121, 129, 401, 419, 435
Twain, Mark, 11

Udal, Shaun, 366
Ugra, Sharda, 82, 290
Ultra-light leg-guards, 35
Umpire Decision Review System (UDRS), 401, 435
Umpire's decision was as questionable, 111
Umrigar, Polly, 124, 416, 443
Under-15 and under-17 levels, performances at the, 39
Under-arm cricket, 27
Underprepared
 horror, 154
 pitch, 57
Unique tributes, 175
United Cricket Board of South Africa (UCBSA), 120

United Nations International Children's Fund's (UNICEF), 456
Unruly behaviour, 171
Unsavoury practices, 224, 269
Unseasonal rain, 203
Unstructured cricket, 41
Uthappa, Robin, 398

Vaas, Chaminda, 170, 362
Vaidya, Anna, 15, 32, 37
Valson, Sunil, 134
Vaughan, Michael, 315, 319, 382
Vengsarkar, Dilip, 14–15, 25, 29, 33, 37–38, 44, 51–53, 55–58, 60–61, 63–65, 73, 80–81, 85–89, 95–97, 105–106, 111, 186, 186, 319, 372, 395
Venkataraghvan, 251, 263
Verbal compliment, 173
Verbal duels, 170
Vettori, Daniel, 231
Vijay Hazare Trophy, 38, 51
Vijay Merchant Trophy, 32, 38, 54
Vijay, Murali, 423, 457
Viswanath, Gundappa, 20, 64, 125, 173, 186
Viswanath, Sadanand, 25
Voges, Adam, 414

Wadekar, Ajit, 5, 15, 120, 126, 131, 171, 249, 261
Waingankar, Hemant, 34, 42
Walsh, Courtney, 56, 60, 153, 155–157, 165, 195, 370
Wankhede Stadium, 17, 36–37, 40, 53, 61, 64–66, 84, 94–96, 97, 101, 148, 154–155, 158, 165, 167, 183, 186, 260, 281, 290, 320, 371, 379, 405, 416, 436, 438–440, 451
Warne, Shane, 106–108, 149, 151–152, 157, 166–167, 181, 210–217, 222, 225, 255–258, 282–288, 334, 348, 413, 453
Warrier, Sunil, 33
Wassan, Atul, 65–66
Waugh, Mark, 106, 151, 165, 167, 183,

216, 222, 282, 286–287, 412
Waugh, Steve, 98, 110, 113, 167, 220–222, 229, 234, 255, 259, 275, 277, 280–281, 283, 289, 298, 339, 341–342, 374, 386, 456
Wedding festivities, 160
Wessels, Kepler, 103, 120
West–North rivalry, 66
White-hot situation, 89
Whitney, Mike, 110–111, 394
Wickremansinghe, Pramodya, 132
Williams, Brad, 340
Willis, Bob, 14
Wills Trophy, 153
Wimbledon, 7–8, 68
World Championship of Cricket, 25–26, 70, 399, 429
World Cup
debut, 113, 432
in 1983, 9–10, 25, 70, 85, 88, 125, 181, 248, 284, 377, 429, 431
in 1987, 36, 56, 112, 137, 387
in 1992, 116, 136, 150, 153, 170
in 1996, 136, 138, 153, 163–164, 172, 173, 211, 217, 227
preparations for the, 161
WorldTel, 138, 160–161, 301, 370
Wright, John, 83–84, 276, 279, 290, 300, 333, 341, 346, 358, 375, 447

Yadav, Shivlal, 250
Yadav, Vijay, 119, 125, 139, 154
Yohannan, Tinu, 297
Young Cricketers' Organization, 49
Younis, Waqar, 70–71, 75–77, 89, 99, 169, 180, 201, 236, 243, 258, 330